BACKGROUNDS OF EARLY CHRISTIANITY

Backgrounds of Early Christianity

Third Edition

EVERETT FERGUSON

WILLIAM B. EERDMANS PUBLISHING COMPANY
GRAND RAPIDS, MICHIGAN

First edition 1987
Second edition 1993
Third edition 2003

Published by
Wm. B. Eerdmans Publishing Co.
2140 Oak Industrial Drive N.E., Grand Rapids, Michigan 49505 /
P.O. Box 163, Cambridge CB3 9PU U.K.

Printed in the United States of America

19 18 17 16 15 14   14 13 12 11 10

Library of Congress Cataloging-in-Publication Data

Ferguson, Everett, 1933–
    Backgrounds of early Christianity / Everett Ferguson. — Third ed.
       p.   cm.
    Includes bibliographical references and index.
    ISBN 978-0-8028-2221-5 (paper)
    1. Christianity — Origin.   2. Rome — History — Republic, 510-30 B.C.
   3. Philosophy, Ancient.   4. Judaism — History — Post-exilic period,
   586 B.C.–210 A.D.   I. Title.
   BR129.F47   1993
   270.1 — dc20   93-1584
                                        CIP

www.eerdmans.com

To My Wife Nancy,

    with whom I have shared all things,

        including the studies and travel

            that have entered into the writing of this book

CONTENTS

PREFACE

THIS book has grown over a long period of time: from the first introduction to the material during student days at Abilene Christian University, through an association as student and graduate assistant at Harvard University under A. D. Nock (whose influence is felt through his lecture notes, writings, and personal observations), through many years of teaching a graduate course in Backgrounds of the New Testament and Early Christianity, to the process of trying to produce the manuscript. As I release it now for publication, I am keenly aware of my limitations. No person can be the master of such a huge body of primary material, much less the enormous secondary literature. A book that touches on so many areas of specialized scholarship is certain to contain many mistakes, and even where it reflects the current consensus, later scholarship will often make revisions. Yet a comprehensive guide will help the student to attain a grasp of the field more quickly than would be possible without an introduction. The introductory nature of the presentation often calls for generalizations to be made: it is hoped that these will aid students; specialists can make the necessary adjustments.

This volume is intended as a textbook, not as a history of the ancient world nor an interpretive synthesis of culture, philosophy, and religion. The reader should not confuse the analytical approach in the presentation with the reality of the time. The approach adopted may give a false sense of compartmentalization — for example, between Hellenism and Judaism — when in fact there was much interaction between the influences discussed separately in this book. Perhaps enough is said in various places in the book to avoid a wrong impression, and books cited in the bibliographies written with other approaches will redress imbalances in this presentation.

This book aims to introduce as many of the primary sources as possible, but is not a substitute for them. To paraphrase the apostle Paul, "Five words in an original source are worth a thousand words in a secondary source." By frequent reference to New Testament texts, I hope to make evident the relevance of the material introduced here, but the emphasis throughout will be on the wider body of material and not Christian literature itself. The student will be in a stronger position by coming to the New Testament and other early Christian literature from a broad acquaintance with its surrounding world than by simply making excursions into the non-Christian sources in search of parallels to Scripture.

Since I consider Judaism the principal context of early Christianity, the chapter on Judaism is the longest. But first-century Judaism was heavily Hellenized, and most students come to this study less well informed on the larger Greco-Roman environment; moreover, my intention is to provide the background for Christianity not only in the New Testament but also in its early centuries when it moved farther from its Jewish roots into the wider Greco-Roman world. Hence, there is what may appear a disproportionate attention to some matters (e.g., philosophy) not so directly relevant to the New Testament texts.

The bibliographies move from the more general works listed at the beginning of each chapter to the more specialized works at the end of each subsection. In an effort to avoid repetition, I have made some arbitrary classifications. The specialized bibliographies are often only supplementary to more basic treatments in the general works; therefore, on particular topics the general bibliographies should not be neglected. The order of listing is chronological, with ancient sources first. Since this is a textbook for students, the bibliographies are largely limited to English works. Foreign language works are included when they are standard reference works, when I am particularly indebted to a given work, or when they include information usable by someone with little or no knowledge of the language. The specialized bibliographies are placed at the end of the respective sections so that the student can add later works.

Harold Attridge, Randall Chesnutt, Carl Holladay, William Lane, A. J. Malherbe, Richard Oster, and David Scholer read various parts of the manuscript; but they are not to be held responsible for the obtuseness of the author.

ACKNOWLEDGMENTS

THE publisher gratefully acknowledges permission to quote from copyright material granted by the following:

A. R. Allenson, for J. T. Milik, *Ten Years of Discovery in the Judaean Wilderness* (1958).

Columbia University Press, New York, for M. P. Nilsson, *Greek Folk Religion* (1961).

Doubleday Publishing Co., New York, for F. M. Cross, *The Ancient Library of Qumran* (1958).

Farrar, Straus & Giroux, New York, for R. Graves's translation of Apuleius, *The Golden Ass* (1951).

Harvard University Press, Cambridge, Mass., for the Loeb Classical Library: Isocrates, *Panegyricus*; Polybius, *Histories*; Augustus, *Res Gestae*; Philo, *Works*; Josephus, *Works*; Virgil, *Eclogues*; Cicero, *On the Nature of the Gods*; Plato, *Phaedrus*; Diogenes Laertius, *Lives of the Philosophers*; Lucian, *Death of Peregrinus*.

Liberal Arts Press for T. W. Higginson's and A. Salomon's translation of Epictetus, *Enchiridion* (1948), and for F. C. Grant, *Hellenistic Religions* (1949).

Oxford University Press, Oxford, for A. D. Nock, *Conversion* (1933); H. Danby, *The Mishnah* (1933); C. H. Dugmore, *The Influence of the Synagogue upon the Divine Office* (1944); R. Walzer, *Galen on Jews and Christians* (1949).

Putnam Publishing Group, New York, for G. Gianelli, ed., *The World of Classical Athens* (1970).

Scholars Press, Decatur, Ga., for A. J. Malherbe, *The Cynic Epistles* (1977), and J. Fitzgerald and L. M. White, *The Tabula of Cebes* (1983).

SPCK, London, for J. Stephenson, *A New Eusebius* (1957).

Unless otherwise noted in the credit line, the photographs are those of the author taken in the institutions or at the locations noted in the captions. We express our gratitude to those institutions and organizations that granted us permission to reproduce photographs from their collections.

ABBREVIATIONS

AJA	*American Journal of Archaeology*
ANRW	*Aufstieg und Niedergang der römischen Welt.* Edited by H. Temporini and W. Haase.
Ant.	Josephus, *Antiquities of the Jews*
BA	*Biblical Archaeologist*
BJRL	*Bulletin of the John Rylands Library*
CBQ	*Catholic Biblical Quarterly*
Essays	A. D. Nock, *Essays on Religion and the Ancient World.* Edited by Zeph Stuart. 2 vols. Oxford, 1972.
HTR	*Harvard Theological Review*
IGB	Iconography of Religions
JBL	*Journal of Biblical Literature*
JJS	*Journal of Jewish Studies*
JQR	*Jewish Quarterly Review*
JRS	*Journal of Roman Studies*
JSJ	*Journal for the Study of Judaism*
JSS	*Journal of Semitic Studies*
JTS	*Journal of Theological Studies*
NTS	*New Testament Studies*
RQ	*Revue de Qumran*
War	Josephus, *The Jewish War*

GENERAL BIBLIOGRAPHY

Collections of Sources

Kee, Howard Clark. *The New Testament in Context: Sources and Documents.* Englewood Cliffs, N.J., 1984.

Barrett, C. K. *The New Testament Background: Selected Documents.* Rev. ed. San Francisco, 1987.

Cartlidge, David R., and David L. Dungan. *Documents for the Study of the Gospels.* Rev. ed. Minneapolis, 1993.

Boring, M. Eugene, Klaus Berger, and Carsten Colpe. *Hellenistic Commentary to the New Testament.* Nashville, 1995.

Strecker, Georg, and U. Schnelle. *Neuer Wettstein: Texte zum Neuen Testament aus Griechentum und Hellenismus.* Berlin, 1966-. II.1 and 2: *Texte zume Brief-literatur und zur Johannesapolkalypse* (1996). I.2: *Texte zum Johannes-evangelium,* ed. U. Schnelle (2001).

Elwell, Walter A., and Robert W. Yarbrough, eds. *Readings from the First-Century World: Primary Sources for New Testament Study.* Grand Rapids, 1998.

Harding, Mark. *Early Christian Life and Thought in Social Context: A Reader.* Shef-field, 2003.

Secondary Works

Halliday, W. R. *The Pagan Background of Early Christianity.* Liverpool, 1925.

Tarn, W. W. *Hellenistic Civilization.* 3d ed. London, 1952.

Hadas, Moses. *Hellenistic Culture.* New York, 1959.

Bomar, Th. *Hebrew Thought Compared with Greek.* London, 1960.

Toynbee, A., ed. *The Crucible of Christianity.* New York, 1969.

Nock, A. D. *Essays on Religion and the Ancient World.* Edited by Zeph Stewart. 2 vols. Cambridge, Mass., 1972.

Leipolt, J., and W. Grundmann. *Umwelt des Urchristentums.* 3 vols. Berlin, 1986–1988.

Grant, M., and R. Kitzinger, eds. *Civilization of the Ancient Mediterranean: Greece and Rome.* 3 vols. New York, 1988.

Newsome, James D. *Greeks, Romans, Jews: Currents of Culture and Belief in the New Testament World.* Philadelphia, 1992.

Bell, Albert A. Jr. *A Guide to the New Testament World.* Scottdale, Pa., 1994.

Koester, Helmut. *Introduction to the New Testament.* Vol. 1, *History, Culture, and Religion of the Hellenistic Age.* Rev. ed. Berlin and New York, 1995.

Wallace, Richard, and Wynne Williams. *The Three Worlds of Paul of Tarsus.* London, 1998.

Jeffers, James S. *The Greco-Roman World of the New Testament Era: Exploring the Background of Early Christianity.* Downers Grove, Ill., 1999.

Reference Works

Dictionnaire des antiquités grecques et romaines. Ch. Daremberg and E. Saglio. Paris, 1877–1919.

Realencyklopädie der Classischen Altertumswissenschaft. A. Pauly, G. Wissowa, W. Kroll, et al. Stuttgart, 1893–.

The Jewish Encyclopedia. Cyrus Adler, et al. New York, 1901–1910.

Reallexikon für Antike und Christentum. Th. Klauser. Leipzig, 1941–.

Interpreter's Dictionary of the Bible. G. Buttrick. 4 vols. New York, 1962. Supplementary vol., 1976.

Lexikon der alten Welt. Carl Andresen, et al. Zurich and Stuttgart, 1965.

Aufstieg und Niedergang der römischen Welt. H. Temporini and W. Haase. Berlin, 1972–.

International Standard Bible Encyclopedia. Rev. ed. G. W. Bromiley, et al. 4 vols. Grand Rapids, 1979–1988.

Cambridge Ancient History. J. B. Bury, et al. 2d ed. Vols. 7-11. Cambridge, 1984-2000.

Anchor Bible Dictionary. D. N. Freedman, et al. 6 vols. New York, 1992.

Oxford Classical Dictionary. Simon Hornblower and Anthony Spawforth. 3d ed. Oxford, 1996. Revised, 2003.

The World of Rome: An Introduction to Roman Culture. Peter Jones and Keith Sidwell. Cambridge, 1997.

The Cambridge Illustrated History of Ancient Greece. Paul Cartledge. Cambridge, 1998.

Ancient Greece and Rome: An Encyclopedia for Students. Carroll Moulton. 4 vols. New York, 1998.

Ancient Greece: A Political, Social, and Cultural History. Sarah Pomeroy, et al. Oxford, 1999.

Dictionary of New Testament Background. Craig A. Evans and Stanley E. Porter. Downers Grove, Ill., 2000.

Encyclopedia of the Ancient World. Thomas J. Sienkewicz. 3 vols. Pasadena, 2002.

Chronology and Atlases

Bickerman, E. J. *Chronology of the Ancient World.* Ithaca, N.Y., 1968.

Van der Heyden, A. A., and H. H. Scullard, eds. *Atlas of the Classical World.* New York, 1959.

Grant, Michael. *Ancient History Atlas, 1700 B.C. to A.D. 565.* London, 1976.

Aharoni, Yohanan, and Michael Avi-Yonah. *The Macmillan Bible Atlas.* New York, 1977.

Tsafrir, Y., L. DiSegni, and J. Green. *Tabular Imperii Romani: Iudaea-Palestina. Eretz Israel in the Hellenistic, Roman and Byzantine Periods: Maps and Gazeteer.* Jerusalem, 1994.

Talbert, Richard J. A. *Barrington Atlas of the Greek and Roman World.* 1 vol. of maps and 2 vols. of directory. Princeton, 2000.

INTRODUCTION:
PERSPECTIVES ON PARALLELS

THE historical setting for the New Testament and early Christianity may be described as a series of concentric circles. The Roman world provided the outer circle — the governmental, legal, and economic context. The Greek world provided the cultural, educational, and philosophical context. The Jewish world was the matrix of early Christianity, providing the immediate religious context. Palestine, itself already Hellenized, was the home of Jesus and his first disciples and the setting of Jesus' ministry. The diaspora synagogues provided the most important points of entry for early Christianity into the wider Greco-Roman world.

This illustration from geometry, however, may be misleading. Many readers have observed that the title *Backgrounds* . . . is ill-chosen, for the word "backgrounds" has connotations of distance and disengagement not intended by the title. I suppose that I am stuck with the word and can only disavow the intention that the material surveyed here should be left in the "background," whether distant or near. Others prefer the words "environment," "milieu," or better "context." A friend facetiously suggested "cultural ecology." Early Christians lived in a world that had many components and cultural influences and seldom, if ever, thought of sorting out where each came from. The analyses given in this book are meant to serve pedagogic purposes and, as said in the preface, should not be confused with reality, which for most people was more unified than my presentation.

Another image from geometry that has been used to describe the relation of Christianity to its context is "parallels," and these have caused various concerns to modern readers. This volume will call attention to a number of similarities between Christianity and various aspects of its environment. Many more could have been included, and probably many more than are currently recognized will become known as a result of further study and future discoveries. What is to be made of these parallels? Do they explain away Christianity as a natural product of its environment? Must they be explained away in order to defend the truth or validity of Christianity? Neither position is necessary.

Perhaps the first thing to observe is that there are only a limited number of options in any given historical setting. Only a certain number of ideas are possible and only a certain number of ways of doing things are available. We need not wonder at similarities, which need not be necessarily a sign of borrowing, in one direction or the other. Many things in a given historical and cultural setting will be arrived at independently by more than one group, simply because there is not an unlimited number of options available about how to do something. For example, how many ways are there to select leaders in a community? We could list inheritance, election, appointment by one or a few in authority, or chance (e.g., casting lots). Any additions made to the list will not greatly extend the range of possibilities. That two groups use the same method does not necessarily mean that one is copying the other.

Even where there is a direct dependence, one must determine its kind and significance. Early Christianity obviously had a great dependence on the Old Testament and its Jewish background. It did not deny this, but even exaggerated the relationship in order to claim fulfillment of the biblical message. This dependence was greater than the dependence on Greek sources, yet it does not affect the central features of Christianity.

The kind and significance of the parallels may be further clarified by commenting on the cultural parallels. That Christians observed the same customs and used words in the same way as their contemporaries is hardly noteworthy in itself. Those things belonged to the place and time when Christianity began. The situation could not have been otherwise for Christianity to have been a real historical phenomenon, open now to historical study. To expect the situation to have been otherwise would require Christianity to be something other than it is, a historical religion. Indeed, if Christianity did not have these linguistic and cultural contacts with the first-century Mediterranean world the presumption would be that it was a fiction originating in another time and place.

What about parallels in doctrine and practice? It is possible to emphasize the similarities of Christianity to elements in its environment, and one may stress these items either to argue for the providential preparation for Christianity or to give a naturalistic explanation of Christianity as another syncretistic religion of the time. Conversely, it is possible to deny significant similarities in an effort either to defend Christianity's uniqueness or to make it out as a fraud. Either approach, from whatever motivation, seems to me to be misguided. My own studies have led me to be more impressed with the differences. Where major similarities are found, the present state of knowledge more often than not fails to document the similarity to the non-Christian environment as early as the item is attested in Christianity. On the other hand, it should not disturb the believer if the situation were reversed. Christian faith does not depend on uniqueness (see comments on pp. 619-20). Questions of parallels are historical questions, not faith questions. Where there has been major discussion of contact between Christianity and elements of its environment — mystery religions, Stoicism, Gnosticism, Pharisees, the Dead Sea Scrolls — I have given more attention to detailing differences, but without the intention of denying similarities. As an illustration of the standpoint from which I would view the material, one may consider the presentation of Jesus as Redeemer in relation to Gnostic thought (pp. 308-9). Either way the priority is decided, we are dealing with a historical question that no more affects the faith-claims for the significance of Jesus than does the recognition that Messiah was a pre-Christian Jewish category. Even as Christians used the already existing title of messiah to interpret the significance of Jesus, and in the process filled the concept with a new content because of the experience of Jesus, so they might have used imagery from Gnostic thought in order to interpret him, and again in the process modified the concept according to what was proclaimed about Jesus. The origin of the Gnostic idea of a Revealer/Redeemer is still not decided to everyone's satisfaction; the point is that the answer should be decided on historical grounds and not because of theological commitments. Christian missionaries approaching persons influenced by Gnostic thinking may very well have employed a Revealer/Redeemer concept congenial to that milieu in explaining the significance of Jesus, even as the category of Messiah (pp. 551-54) was useful in presenting Jesus to Jews. What is important is to determine what the categories meant to different persons so that we know more precisely what was being said in assigning Jesus to a given category. If the Gnostic category of Redeemer was employed, then we know more about the content of this image; if Christian preaching was itself a significant ingredient in the development of Gnosticism, then we know something else about the religious history of the ancient world.

Where genuine dependence and significant parallels are determined, these must then be placed in the whole context of thought and practice in the systems where the contacts are discovered. Although Christianity had points of contact with Stoicism, the mysteries, the Qumran community, and so on, the total worldview was often quite different, or the context in which the items were placed was different. Originality may be found in the way things are put together and not in the invention of a completely new idea or practice. So far as we can tell, Christianity certainly represented a new combination for its time.[1]

I have no special quarrel with those who see the historical situation differently from the way I do, either in whole or in specific parts. I hope that the facts are here presented objectively enough for the work to be useful to all stu-

---

1. For a succinct statement of some of the parallels and differences between Christianity and classical culture see A. D. Nock's review of T. Klauser, ed., *Reallexikon für antike and Christentum* in *JBL* 67 (1948):251-60 (*Essays,* 676-81).

dents at the introductory level and to all teachers, whatever interpretive frame-work they choose to adopt. The purpose of this textbook on the backgrounds of early Christianity is to illumine the historical setting in as many of its ramifications as feasible so as better to understand the real world in which people lived. The student then can use the available materials to determine what Christianity was in its early days. The better one sees and knows the background, the more clearly that person can see the cutting edge of Christianity.

BIBLIOGRAPHY

Kim, Seyoon. *The Origin of Paul's Gospel.* Grand Rapids, 1982.
Nash, Ronald. *Christianity and the Hellenistic World.* Grand Rapids, 1984.

1. POLITICAL HISTORY

BIBLIOGRAPHY

Barker, Ernest. *From Alexander to Constantine.* Oxford, 1956.

Peters, F. E. *The Harvest of Hellenism: A History of the Near East from Alexander the Great to the Triumph of Christianity.* London, 1972.

Boardman, John, ed. *The Oxford History of the Classical World.* Oxford, 1986.

INTRODUCTION

The time span for the study of the Hellenistic-Roman backgrounds of early Christianity is broadly from 330 B.C. to A.D. 330, from Alexander to Constantine. The Greek element predominated in political influence from 330 to 30 B.C., from Alexander to Augustus; hence it is known as the Hellenistic Age. Rome ruled the Mediterranean world from 30 B.C. onward, the interest here being from Augustus to Constantine. Each of these two major periods can be subdivided culturally into two parts, with breaks, in a round date, at 200 B.C. and A.D. 200. For the first century and a half of the Greek period, the Greek culture was creative and expansive, penetrating the eastern Mediterranean as the dominant influence. After about 200 B.C. the native cultures of Egypt, Palestine, Syria, and Asia began to reassert themselves and the Greek element began to retreat. The Roman influence was expansive for the first two centuries of the Roman empire, preserving Hellenistic culture in the Near East. The climax of Roman administration came in the second century A.D. Thereafter the Roman world was plagued with internal economic problems and external pressure from barbarian peoples on the frontiers, bringing on a severe crisis in the

5

third century. The empire was saved by the soldier emperors from Illyria and received a new lease on life after the reform under Diocletian and reconstruction under Constantine.

The sources we will draw from are not, however, limited to this time span. The starting points for Greek religion and philosophy fall earlier than 330 B.C. There is a cultural continuity within Greco-Roman times that justifies drawing upon information over so many centuries. Nevertheless, one must be careful about chronology and not assume, unless with good reasons, that an idea or practice only attested at a later date did exist at an earlier time. The focus of this book will be the first century B.C. and the first two centuries A.D. In order to achieve a proper focus on those centuries surrounding the beginning of the Christian era, we must consider a wider background, both before and after this period.

NEAR EAST BEFORE ALEXANDER

Persian Empire

The connection between Old Testament history and Hellenistic history is provided by the Persian empire.

Cyrus (538–529) was king of Anshan and vassal of Media from about 550. After a successful rebellion he gained control of the Median empire and founded the Achaemenid dynasty. In 539 he took Babylon and from 538 dated his years as "king of Babylon and king of the countries." Reversing the policy of earlier conquerors in the Near East, the Persians permitted conquered peoples to maintain their cultures in their homelands. Accordingly, Cyrus allowed the Jews in Babylon to return to Judea and rebuild the temple (Ezra 1:1-4; 2 Chron. 36:22-23; see p. 400). The Persian empire was the first in the Near East with a great degree of tolerance and decentralization of government.

Cambyses (529–522) enlarged the empire in 525 by doing what few have accomplished, conquering Egypt.

Darius (522–486) was the real organizer and consolidator of the Achaemenid empire. He ruled long enough to give stability and a consistent administrative policy to the extensive domains that by the time of his successor stretched "from India to Ethiopia" (Esth. 1:1), the largest empire in the Middle East up to his time.

Xerxes (485–465) was the Ahasuerus of the Book of Esther. He had to subjugate Egypt again and invaded Greece in 480–479 (about which more below).

Artaxerxes (464–424) was the king under whom Nehemiah served as cupbearer. His long reign foreshadowed the future in being filled with struggles against Greeks, Syrians, and Egyptians.

The *last five rulers* saw a progressive disintegration of the Persian empire. We may recall one event of this last century of the Achaemenid empire — the expedition of the eleven thousand Greeks whose exploits in 401–399 were told by Xenophon in the *Anabasis*. The Greeks were hired as mercenaries by Cyrus the Younger to overthrow Artaxerxes II (404–358). Cyrus's army won the battle but lost its leader. With Cyrus dead the Greek mercenaries had no more reason to be in Persia and through many hardships marched back home. Xenophon, a journalist who was elected general by the troops, told their story in such a memorable way that the Greeks became aware of the internal weaknesses of the power they had feared for so long. Hopes began to be aroused that Persia could be conquered. That story, however, must follow a look at fifth-century Greece.

Greece

Although the Persian empire combined a minimum use of force with a maximum of respect for local customs, the universal law "thou shalt pay taxes" was still in force. The Greek cities of Ionia revolted against Persia, and Athens sent ships to help. The Greeks burned Sardis. Meanwhile the Persians under Darius took Thrace and undertook a punitive expedition to Marathon. The Athenian victory at Marathon under Miltiades in 490 B.C. led the Persians to plan a major expedition. The big Persian invasion under the great king Xerxes came in 480. Themistocles, with the help of his interpretation of the oracle from Delphi that "Zeus would give a wooden wall" for the protection of the Athenians, persuaded the Athenians to put their confidence in a navy.[1] The Persian advance was slowed by the valiant Spartan resistance under their king Leonidas at the pass of Thermopylae, but the Persians swept on, confirming the views of those Greeks who had argued for accepting the inevitable and yielding to Persia. The Athenian Acropolis was burned, as most of the Greek troops waited on ships in the bay of Salamis. The Athenian navy won the decisive battle in the narrow straits between the island of Salamis and the mainland. The Persian defeat was made complete in the land battle at Plataea in 479. The victory was accomplished by the Greek alliance pulling together for one and one-half years — no mean accomplishment for any alliance among the independent-minded Greek city-states. Herodotus, "the father of history," tells the story; in general he is reliable except for his numbers.

The defeat of Persia had far-reaching implications. There was pious gratitude to the gods. There was a tremendous increase of energy and the opportunities to release it in the rebuilding that the destruction of the war necessitated. Greek monumental sculpture in the fifth century was dominated by the theme

1. Herodotus 7.141ff.

of the Persian wars, interpreted symbolically as the victory of civilization over barbarism.

Athens took the decisive lead among the Greek cities. Although Sparta was strong with a disciplined army, the need to keep watch on a large number of serfs (helots) limited her involvement in foreign affairs. Athens with her navy began the "liberation" of the Greek cities held by Persia. The Athenian alliance became in fact the Athenian empire, and great wealth and power came to Athens. The fifth century thus became a strange, new time. It is remembered as the classical period of the Athenian democracy. The middle of the century is sometimes called the Age of Pericles, because he was the leading political figure and the embodiment of the new activity. Seldom has so much genius in so many areas of human activity been concentrated in one place in such a short period of time. This period marked the beginning of the Greek culture capable both of becoming a vehicle of thought and of being exported to other peoples. Especially notable was the educational revolution, which took place unseen, and is associated with the rise of the Sophists (see pp. 326ff.).

A new view of humanity appeared among Greek thinkers of the fifth century — they became conscious of human beings as human. The Sophist Protagoras best expressed this thought as "The measure of all things is man."[2] If we may generalize this statement outside its context, it expresses what we may regard as the distinguishing characteristic of Greek culture. In Homer human beings had appeared as individuals, as victims of fate and facing death. In classical thought human beings overcame fate. The heritage of Greece, therefore, was essentially secular. Yet it was a religious secularism, for one cannot draw a line between the sacred and profane in ancient Greece as sharply as moderns do. There were few public buildings and events in Athens that were not religious. Yet, in keeping with the emphasis on man, the ideals of life were health, beauty (the Greeks had an uncommonly high regard for the male physique), respectable wealth, and enjoyment of youth with friends.

Social organization in Greece was according to the family, tribe, and city. The *polis* (city) was an independent state comprising a town and its surrounding country. The individual took turns ruling and being ruled (if the government was an oligarchy, the turns were within a more limited number). By the fourth century the city-state was not working so well, but the Greeks did not want to be united, preferring to fight each other "every baseball season." They were especially fond of competition — in athletics, in literature and music, even among doctors in their diagnoses of patients.

The democrats looked to Athens for leadership, the oligarchs to Sparta. The Athenian alliance, however, amounted to an empire ruled by a city. Theoretically, a city could withdraw from the alliance, but attempts to do so were met with retaliation from Athens. A showdown between Athens and Sparta

2. Plato, *Cratylus* 386a; *Theaetetus* 152a.

came in the ruthless civil wars known as the Peloponnesian wars. Sparta's defeat of Athens was sealed in 404. Democracy continued after 403, but there were no more allies to rob from, and Athens settled down to live in greater poverty and misery. Thucydides has left us the story of the Peloponnesian wars. He has less sense of the supernatural than most ancient writers, and his search for historical causation has made him a model historian.

By the time Alexander the Great appeared on the Greek scene in the fourth century two changes had taken place that were to make his conquests significant. One was the intellectual change. No longer were poetry, athletics, and cameolike beauty the leading ideals. Such would have had little appeal to Jews and Egyptians; but now as a result of the Sophists (teachers of public speaking — see pp. 326-27) there was a concern with natural law and the practical sciences of mathematics, medicine, and astronomy. Along with this went another change: an increase in individualism. Aeschylus' epitaph speaks of his part in the Persian wars: "Marathon may tell of his well-proved valor." If he had died one hundred years later, his dramas would have been mentioned, not his civic life.

These changes may be epitomized in Isocrates (436–338 B.C.), an overly clever and long-winded but perceptive Athenian orator. He was a genuine descendant of the Sophists. Being a publicist as well as a teacher, he used the speech form as the vehicle for communicating his ideas; after his time the public lecture had decisive importance in Hellenistic culture and thus in education. He taught a way of life — moral, good, and useful — a humanistic education as opposed to the abstract discipline of philosophy. His school taught not metaphysics but letters and history. The basis for Hellenism was laid in his dictum that education and not birth is what makes the true Greek:

> And so far has our city [Athens] distanced the rest of mankind in thought and speech that her pupils have become the teachers of the rest of the world; and she has brought it about that the name "Hellenes" suggests no longer a race but an intelligence, and the title "Hellenes" is applied rather to those who share our culture than to those who share a common blood. (*Panegyricus* 50, trans. George Norlin in Loeb Classical Library)

Isocrates' own horizons may have been somewhat limited, but his words were an unconscious prophecy that was soon put into practice. In the Hellenistic age the citizen bodies of Greek cities of the Near East were more and more composed not so much of persons of Greek birth as persons of Greek culture (education, lifestyle, and often name). As a result, in Roman times the apostle Paul in writing to the church at Rome could consider the cultural division in humankind to be "Jews and Greeks" or, more comprehensively, Jews, Greeks, and barbarians (Rom. 1:16, 14; cf. Gal. 3:28; Col. 3:11), and the Hellenized population of Phoenicia could be called "Greek" (Mark 7:26 — culturally, not racially).

This situation was the result of a broader diffusion of Greek culture, and before that occurred any religious or philosophical movement would have been regionally or racially limited.

Isocrates made several attempts to get the Greeks to fight Persia and not one another. His last appeal to Philip II of Macedon to unite the Greeks pointed the way by which his observation quoted above was to receive broader realization.

Bibliography

Frye, Richard N. *The Heritage of Persia.* New York, 1963.

Briant, Pierre. *From Cyrus to Alexander: A History of the Persian Empire.* 2 vols. Winona Lake, Ind., 1998.

Fornara, C. W. *Archaic Times to the End of the Peloponnesian War.* Translated Documents of Greece and Rome, vol. 1. Baltimore, 1977.

Bengston, Hermann. *The Greeks and the Persians from the Sixth to the Fourth Centuries.* London, 1965.

Botsford, G. W., and C. A. Robinson. *Hellenic History.* 5th ed. Revised by Donald Kagan. New York, 1969.

Green, Peter. *A Concise History of Ancient Greece.* London, 1973.

Hammond, N. G. L. *The Classical Age of Greece.* London, 1975.

Green, Peter. *The Greco-Persian Wars.* Berkeley, 1996.

ALEXANDER THE GREAT

Macedonia

Macedonia had a kingship of the Homeric type. A rural, aristocratic way of life with conservative traditions continued there longer than in Greece. Demosthenes, in his efforts to rouse the Greeks against Philip of Macedon, called the Macedonians "wild beasts" and the country "a place where one could not even buy good slaves in the old days" (*Third Philippic* 31). The Macedonians were extravagant in their joys, fights, drinking, and sorrows. But their monarchs began to introduce Greek culture, and Philip II brought Aristotle to educate his son Alexander.

Philip II (359–336 B.C.) made war less amateurish. He fought year-round, winter as well as spring (cf. 2 Sam. 11:1 for the older practice), which was something like using chemical weapons now. He became ruler of all Greece after the battle of Chaeronea in 338 B.C. He did not change the internal organization of the Greek cities, and his legal position was that of a general at the head of a

ALEXANDER THE GREAT AS DIVINE HERO
The conquests of Alexander spread Greek culture throughout the
eastern Mediterranean world. (© Erich Lessing/Art Resource, NY)

league to fight the weakened Persian empire. The kind of ruler liable to be assassinated, he suffered that fate in 336 B.C.

Life of Alexander III (356–323)

Alexander inherited his father's monarchy (although the Greek cities were theoretically allies) and his plans to invade Persia. When Thebes revolted, Alexander demolished the city with such fierceness that no other "ally" attempted the same. He crossed the Hellespont in 334 and after the battle of the Granicus he quickly accomplished the "liberation" of the Greek cities of Asia Minor. The next major battle at Issus left the western part of the Persian empire open to him. He proceeded to take Phoenicia, Palestine, and Egypt — the city of Tyre offering the most stubborn resistance on the way. At the battle of Gaugamela (331) in Mesopotamia Alexander dealt the final blow to Darius III and then proceeded to occupy the Persian capitals and claim their treasures. With the death of Darius III he took the title of "Great King." Alexander pushed his conquests to the Indus River before his army's restlessness forced him to turn back. He died of a fever in Babylonia.

In his conquests Alexander recognized and accepted what he found. He came to preserve and not to destroy, so he retained the governmental systems he found. He had a notable interest in reconciling native worship with the fact of conquest, but he showed his Greek feeling by founding Greek cities. These became centers for the diffusion of Greek culture, even though there was no systematic effort at Hellenization. They were somewhat like the later Roman colonies in being founded for strategic and economic purposes, especially to provide a manpower pool. Alexander determined the temples to be built and the Greek deities to be worshiped along with the native deity.

Alexander had a passion for Homer. The invasion of Asia Minor was recounted as another Trojan War, and the first thing Alexander did at Troy was to pay an act of homage to Achilles, who was initially his heroic prototype. Later, Heracles, a hero who became a god in virtue of his achievements, filled this role. Alexander was also connected with Dionysus, whom the Greeks believed came from Asia and who became "the god" of the Greek expansion into the Middle East, receiving the greatest amount of personal devotion in the Hellenistic kingdoms. Alexander held a Dionysiac celebration at Nysa where, according to the tradition, Dionysus was born. This religious emphasis was characteristic of Alexander. He gave his own adhesion to Zeus, and religious acts (e.g., seeking omens) were not antiquarian features for him. The recognition of Alexander himself as a deity will be considered in the section on ruler cult (pp. 204-5).

Alexander, moreover, had a romantic flair for the striking gesture. He often acted on impulse: as the ancient accounts say, "a desire seized him." Such acts, plus his personal courage and ability as a strategist, account for much of the personal devotion his troops gave to him.

One striking gesture that attracted later attention (down to modern times) was a banquet at Opis where different races sat at one table, made joint libations to the deities, and prayed for the unity of the empire. W. W. Tarn has advanced the thesis that Alexander, dreaming of a world-state, believed in a universal brotherhood of man, being perhaps the first to do so. It seems, however, that only Persians, Greeks, and Macedonians were included, as no Babylonian priest was present although the banquet was in Babylonia. Political motivations were probably uppermost in his mind. At any rate, unity for Alexander was to be practical as well as ideal, but often actions have greater significance than one anticipates, and some Stoics later were to generalize from Alexander's actions.[3] Alexander did treat Greeks and Persians on an equal level, a policy that brought a severe strain on the loyalty of his soldiers. He had the Macedonian officers marry Persian wives; but the effort to fuse the Persian and Macedonian military classes failed, for after his death only one general kept his Persian wife. Alexander himself stepped into the role of the Persian monarch and so introduced the eastern idea of an absolute monarchy into the Hellenistic world, an idea uncongenial to the Greeks, who looked upon themselves as those who had made him their leader.

Alexander's Influence

Concerning the old debate whether the great person or the circumstances of the time are more important in historical causation, we may say that both are necessary. Things are done by a great person, not by abstract trends. But the circumstances have to be right. Alexander would not have done anything a hundred years earlier; on the other hand, if he had died in childhood, the world would have been quite different. The great person serves as a catalyst of the age. Alexander ushered in the Hellenistic Age, but the ingredients of that age were already there. He accelerated the pace of change.

The Greek superiority that first made itself felt through military conquest and civil administration soon brought more important cultural changes. Salient features that followed the conquests of Alexander were these: (1) The movement of Greeks abroad. Greek colonies had been planted all around the Mediterranean world since the eighth century B.C., as Greece always had a surplus population; but the number of Greeks abroad now significantly increased, and they were in positions of influence. There were too few Macedonians, and

3. Plutarch, *On the Fortune of Alexander* 1.6 (*Moralia* 329B-D) relates the one-world idea of Zeno's *Republic* to what Alexander accomplished, but this probably represents a later idea than Alexander himself.

Greece provided the reserve manpower. (2) The accelerated speed of the conquest by Greek culture. Greek culture was already penetrating the eastern Mediterranean before Alexander's time, but his conquests carried it farther inland and hastened its acceptance in more areas and by more people. The closer contact between Greeks and others produced significant impacts on the peoples of the Near East, not least the Jews, which we will see in later topics. This may be described, at the beginning, as a transplanting rather than the transformation of cultures, but in time the real differentiation became a way of life, culture not descent. To see Greeks and non-Greeks as remaining isolated or to see them as harmoniously mixed would both be distortions of Hellenistic civilization. (3) The emergence of one world economically. Alexander established one currency, silver coins based on the Attic standard. Instead of hoarding the Persian wealth he took its silver, coined it, and paid his soldiers. Extraordinary prosperity ensued. (4) The further spread of the Greek language. Herodotus in the fifth century already assumed everyone could understand Greek, if it was spoken loudly enough and sternly enough. The form of Greek that emerged is called *koinē* (common) Greek, and is largely based on the Attic dialect. In the third century B.C. Berossus, a Babylonian priest, and Manetho, an Egyptian priest, wrote histories of their respective countries in Greek. (5) A body of ideas accepted by all. A far larger proportion of the non-Greek population acquired a modicum of Greek ideas. (6) A higher level of education. Literacy became more general, and education spread. Both abstract thought and practical intelligence were enhanced in a greater proportion of the population. This change coincided with the spread of Greek language and ideas, so that the level and extent of communication and intelligibility became significant. (7) The spread of Greek deities and cultus. This too had already begun but now occurred in a more thorough sense than before. Greek deities were identified with native deities and vice versa (e.g., the old Semitic deities of Palestine were given Greek names). (8) The emergence of philosophy as representing a way of life. This was prepared for in the influence of the Sophists and Socrates and will be considered in the chapter on philosophy (pp. 320-26). (9) The framework of society around the *polis*. City life was civilized life to the Greeks. Cities — rather than temple-states, villages, or the countryside — became the bases of society. The Greek gymnasia emphasized public life, and such institutions spread with the founding of Greek cities in the east. The city remained the basis of social and economic life through the Roman empire. Alongside this social development was the decline in the political importance of the city-states. The human horizon was expanded from the city-state to the *oikoumenē* (the inhabited, civilized world). Yet there was no diminution in local pride. The new thing, however, was an *oikoumenē* speaking the *koinē*. (10) Increase of individualism. Individualism may seem a paradox alongside universalism, but the two are corollaries. The breaking of traditional patterns of inherited conduct in the enlarged world of the Hellenistic age threw people back upon themselves and gave opportunity for individual expression. Chosen things became more important than inherited things. As one example, personal religion stems from the philosophical individualism of Socrates (see pp. 325, 327-30).

It is hard to imagine Christianity succeeding in any other environment than that which resulted from the conquests of Alexander the Great.

BIBLIOGRAPHY

Heisserer, A. J. *Alexander the Great and the Greeks: The Epigraphic Evidence.* Norman, Okla., 1980.

Quintus Curtius Rufus. *History of Alexander.*

Hamilton, J. R. *Plutarch, Alexander: A Commentary.* Oxford, 1969.

Arrian. *Anabasis.* A. B. Bosworth, *A Historical Commentary on Arrian's History of Alexander,* Oxford, 1980–.

Hammond, N. G. L. *Sources for Alexander the Great: An Analysis of Plutarch's* Life *and Arrian's* Anabasis Alexandrou. Cambridge, 1992.

Burch, Nancy J. *Alexander the Great: A Bibliography.* Kent State University Press, 1970.

Tarn, W. W. *Alexander the Great.* 2 vols. Cambridge, 1948. Reprint. Boston, 1956.

Griffith, G. T., ed. *Alexander the Great: The Main Problems.* Cambridge, 1966.

Lane Fox, Robin. *Alexander the Great.* London, 1973.

Bosworth, A. B. *Conquest and Empire: The Reign of Alexander the Great.* Cambridge, 1990.

Green, Peter. *Alexander of Macedon, 356-323 B.C.* Berkeley, 1991.

Roisman, J. *Alexander the Great: Ancient and Modern Perspectives.* Lexington, Ky., 1995.

Carlsen, J. et al. *Alexander the Great: Reality and Myth.* Analecta Romana Instituti Danici, Suppl. XX. Rome, 1997.

Stoneman, Richard. *Alexander the Great.* London, 1997.

Bosworth, A. B. and E. J. Baynham, eds. *Alexander the Great in Fact and Fiction.* Oxford, 2000.

THE HELLENISTIC KINGDOMS

The Diadochi

Alexander's generals at first attempted to maintain a regency for Alexander's half-wit brother and the son of his wife Roxanne, still unborn at the time of his death. But by the year 305 the fiction of unity was over. The Hellenistic age began in a complicated series of alliances, intrigues, perfidy, and wars, and such remained characteristic of it.

The more important of Alexander's successors were Antipater and his son Cassander, who gained control of Macedonia; Lysimachus, who ruled in Thrace; Ptolemy I, who secured Egypt; and Antigonus I, whose base of operations was Asia. The battle of Ipsus in 301 put an end to the efforts of the most powerful of these, Antigonus I, to gain the whole domain for himself. By 280 three dynasties descended from Alexander's generals were well established: the Ptolemaic in Egypt, the Seleucid from Persia across Syria to Asia, and the Antigonid now controlling Macedonia. A fourth dynasty, unconnected with Alexander, the Attalids of Pergamum, grew up in Asia at the expense of the Seleucids. The breakup of Alexander's empire delayed the universalizing tendency he anticipated until the Romans fulfilled it.

The position of king (a title the successors took) — what it meant to be a king — in the Hellenistic kingdoms is important for the development of the ruler cult and will be considered in that connection (pp. 199ff.).

By the end of the third century B.C. the shadow of Rome was falling across the eastern Mediterranean. Rome fought its First Macedonian War in 215 as incidental to the Second Punic War and in 212 entered into alliance with Pergamum. The last of the Hellenistic kingdoms to be absorbed by Rome was Egypt in 30 B.C., at which time the Hellenistic Age passed into the Roman. Before telling the story of Roman expansion we need to say something of two of the kingdoms that, because of their contacts with Jews and Palestine, are of special importance for the backgrounds of early Christianity.

Ptolemies — Egypt

Each Egyptian king in the Hellenistic age wore the name of the dynasty's founder, Ptolemy, son of Lagus, a Macedonian noble.

Ptolemy I Soter (367–283) became satrap (governor) of Egypt in 323 and took the title of king in 304.[4] Besides establishing the political basis (legal, military, and administrative) for his kingdom, he began its cultural development by founding the library in Alexandria. Ptolemy II Philadelphus (308–246) succeeded to effective rule in 285. He carried forward the financial and cultural enterprises begun by his father, completing the laying out of the city of Alexandria and the library, and building the museum (a scholarly academy dedicated to the Muses). By 200 Alexandria was the greatest city of the Mediterranean world and was surpassed later only by Rome. The Ptolemies made Alexandria the intellectual and spiritual center of the Greek world, and this became their greatest contribution to later history. Through its impact on Jewish and Christian intellectual life, Alexandria significantly influenced religious history.

The Ptolemies founded or developed only three Greek cities — Alexan-

---

4. Walter M. Ellis, *Ptolemy of Egypt* (London, 1994).

Ptolemy I (Soter I)	304-283/282
Ptolemy II (Philadelphus)	285-246
Ptolemy III (Euergetes I)	246-221
Ptolemy IV (Philopator)	221-205
Ptolemy V (Epiphanes)	205-180
Ptolemy VI (Philometor)	180-145
Ptolemy VII (Neos Philopator)	145-144
Ptolemy VIII (Euergetes II)	144-116
Ptolemy IX (Soter II)	116-108/107, 89/88-81
Ptolemy X (Alexander I)	108-89/88
Ptolemy XI (Alexander II), the last fully legitimate Ptolemaic king	80
Ptolemy XII (Auletes)	80/79-51
Ptolemy XIII and Cleopatra VII	51-47
Ptolemy XIV and Cleopatra VII	47-44
Ptolemy XV (Caesar) and Cleopatra VII	44-30

Because of the rival claimants to the throne, there is not full agreement among scholars on the numbering and dates after Ptolemy VI.

dria, Naucratis, and Ptolemais. Outside of the Greeks and the Egyptian priestly class (its power broken), a few privileged Macedonians stood on one end of the social scale and the mass of the Egyptians on the other. The Ptolemies adhered to a strong central government with a tightly organized system of administration. The dynasty accumulated great wealth, so much as to be both famous and envied for it. Herondas (third century B.C.) said:

> For all that is and will be, can be found in Egypt:
> Riches, stadiums, power, fine weather,
> Reputation, theatres, philosophers, gold, young men,
> The sanctuary of the kindred gods, the king,
> A just one, the museum, wine, every good thing,
> Whatever you want, and women.   (*Mime* 1.26-32)

(For the sources of Ptolemaic wealth see p. 85.)

At times the Ptolemies controlled Palestine, Cyprus, some Aegean islands, and parts of Asia Minor. Despite their wealth, however, they did not maintain a strong military base at home. Once the immigration of Greeks ceased, the military power of the Ptolemies soon decayed. For a century, the Greeks in Egypt did not mix with the Egyptians. During the second century B.C., however, there was a native revival, paralleled by a policy on the part of the kings of promoting Egyptian culture. Internal revolts and invasions from Syria brought such a crisis that only Roman intervention in 168 B.C. in order to preserve the balance of power in the east saved the dynasty. The Greeks were thereafter on the defensive. The coming of Roman rule under Augustus in the next century prevented Hellenism from being absorbed. Indeed, all the Hellenistic governments were not so much well run bureaucracies as they were instruments for securing as much revenue as possible from their subjects, but the Ptolemies were more efficient than the others.

Seleucids — Syria

Seleucus I Nicator (c. 358–280 B.C.) was the son of the Macedonian Antiochus. The names Seleucus and Antiochus alternate through the Seleucid dynasty. Seleucus obtained the satrapy (territory) of Babylonia after Alexander's death, but was not able to gain secure control until 312, from which year the Seleucid era of dating begins. He had conquered the lands to the east but lost India before 303. This was more than compensated for by gains to the west: northern Syria and Mesopotamia in 301, Cilicia in 296, and Asia Minor except for the native kingdoms and some cities by 281. Between 250 and 227, with the gradual establishment of the Greco-Bactrian and Parthian kingdoms, everything east of Media was lost to the Seleucids. Antiochus III the Great (223–187) began a revival and expansion. He defeated the Ptolemaic forces at Paneion (modern

Seleucus I (Nicator)	312-281
Antiochus I (Soter)	281-261
Antiochus II (Theos)	261-246
Seleucus II (Callinicus)	246-225
Seleucus III (Soter)	225-223
Antiochus III (the Great)	223-187
Seleucus IV (Philopator)	187-175
Antiochus IV (Epiphanes)	175-163
Antiochus V (Eupator)	163-162
Demetrius I (Soter)	162-150
Alexander Balas	150-145
Demetrius II (Nicator)	145-139, 129-125
Antiochus VI (Epiphanes)	145-138
Antiochus VII (Euergetes, also Sidetes)	139/138-129
Antiochus VIII (Grypus)	125-96
Antiochus IX (Cyzikenus)	115-95

Banias) near the source of the Jordan in 200, and by 198 occupied the Egyptian province of Phoenicia and Syria; but he was defeated by the Romans at Magnesia in Asia in 190, and the peace of Apamea in 188 excluded Seleucid power from western Asia Minor. Antiochus IV Epiphanes (175–163) almost conquered Egypt, but was checked by Roman intervention. Decline set in, and the death of Antiochus VII Sidetes in 129 entailed the final loss of Babylonia and Judea, reducing the Seleucids to a local dynasty in north Syria. The Seleucid empire had three nerve centers — Ionia (Sardis), Syria (Antioch), and Babylonia (Seleucia) — but was finally reduced to the middle region.

The Seleucid territory included many ancient temple-states of Syria and Asia. These were territories centered in a temple, some possessing large amounts of land, where the priest held a dominant position in political and economic affairs. They dated back to a pre-Aryan social system; originally they probably all worshiped the great fertility goddess and the companion god who was sometimes her son and sometimes her consort. The feature that so struck the Greeks was the crowd of temple slaves and sacred prostitutes who ministered for part of their lives to the fertility worship of the goddess. Artemis of Ephesus, for example, was originally the fertility goddess whose temple had been annexed to a Greek city and who was superficially Hellenized through identification with the Greek nature goddess Artemis. To external observers Judea, despite differences more obvious to Jews and Christians than to third-century Greeks, would have appeared (politically and sociologically) as simply another one of these temple-states so common in Asia and Syria.

The Seleucids promoted Hellenism in parts of their territories through Greek cities and settlements. That Zeus and Apollo were the two chief deities of the Seleucids shows their cultural identification with Hellenism. In contrast to the Ptolemies, they built large numbers of new cities and refounded old ones. In Greek theory a collection of houses, no matter how numerous, was a *polis* only if it possessed municipal self-government and certain organs of corporate life (citizens divided into tribes, a council chosen from those tribes, responsible magistrates, its own laws and finances, a primary assembly of the citizens, and local subdivisions of the city land). Founding a city often meant giving these forms of corporate life to an existing village. For early Christian history the greatest of these Seleucid foundations was Antioch on the Orontes. Unlike Alexandria, it was not a center of learning in Hellenistic times; it was a great trade center with a reputation as a pleasure city.

Another type of Seleucid foundation was the *catoecia* ("settlement"), especially for military veterans but also including free peasants with hereditary rights.

The Attalid kingdom of Pergamum replaced Seleucid power in Asia north of the Taurus mountains during the third and second centuries B.C. The Attalids, consistent friends of Rome, shielded the Greek cities of Asia from the nomadic Galatians (a Celtic people) and copied the Ptolemies' cultural policy in maintaining the Pergamum library. The native kingdoms of Asia Minor (Cappadocia, Pontus, and Armenia) were only superficially Hellenized during the Hellenistic age. Deeper in Bithynia the warlike Galatians remained largely untouched by Hellenism until the Roman period.

BIBLIOGRAPHY

Austin, M. M. *The Hellenistic World from Alexander to the Roman Conquest: A Selection of Ancient Sources in Translation.* Cambridge, 1981.

Bagnall, Roger S., and Peter S. Derow. *Greek Historical Documents: The Hellenistic Period.* Chico, Calif., 1981.

Burstein, S. M. *The Hellenistic Age from the Battle of Ipsos to the Death of Kleopatra VII.* Translated Documents of Greece and Rome 3. Cambridge, 1985.

Hansen, Esther V. *The Attalids of Pergamon.* Ithaca, N.Y., 1947.

Downey, G. *A History of Antioch in Syria.* Princeton, 1961.

Welles, C. B. *Alexander and the Hellenistic World.* Toronto, 1970.

Fraser, P. M. *Ptolemaic Alexandria.* 3 vols. Oxford, 1972.

Grant, M. *From Alexander to Cleopatra: The Hellenistic World.* New York, 1982.

Gruen, E. S. *The Hellenistic World and the Coming of Rome.* 2 vols. Berkeley, 1984.

Lewis, N. *Greeks in Ptolemaic Egypt.* Oxford, 1986.

Bilde, Per et al., eds. *Religion and Religious Practice in the Seleucid Kingdom.* Aarhus, 1990.

Green, Peter. *Alexander to Actium: The Historical Evolution of the Hellenistic Age.* Berkeley, 1990.

Hammond, N. G. L. *Miracle of Macedonia.* New York, 1991.

Wallbank, F. W. *The Hellenistic World.* Rev. ed. Cambridge, Mass., 1993.

Ginouves, Rene et al. *Macedonia: From Philip II to the Roman Conquest.* Princeton, 1994.

ROME

The Roman Genius

Polybius, the second-century-B.C. Greek historian, devoted a book to the source of Roman strength. He decided that the reason for Rome's achievement was internal. Her constitutional system was a perfect balance of the monarchic (consul), oligarchic (senate), and democratic (assemblies) elements. And the cement that held it together was the fear of the gods expressed in due performance of the traditional rites.

> The quality in which the Roman commonwealth is most distinctly superior is in my opinion the nature of their religious convictions. I believe that

it is the very thing which among other peoples is an object of reproach, I mean superstition *(deisidaimonia)*, which maintains the cohesion of the Roman state. (*Histories* 6.56)

In other words, Roman power was due to Roman piety.[5] This balance and this cement were in time to crumble, but Rome had a remarkable power of endurance.

Rome was originally a city-state, but different from the Greek city. Citizenship in Rome was infinitely expansible. For example, freed slaves became citizens, unlike in Greece. Greek cities only extended citizenship in cases of emergency, and for it to become effective one had to take up residence in the city. Rome more readily extended citizenship to those in other cities, such as in the region of Latium (the Latin league). It had a great ability to absorb alien populations — human and divine. The Persians too had sought to absorb conquered peoples; they allowed a freedom of development but did not create a unity. The Romans could take borrowed things and make them their own as the Persians did not. Rome was a borrower — culturally and religiously — but it could put its own stamp on things. The Latin phrase is significant: when one became a citizen, he was "made a Roman." Rome could do this with cultures too — first the Etruscan and later the Greek. We can see this in Rome's absorption of foreign cults. Through its ceremony of *evocatio,* Rome called upon the gods of an enemy city to change sides, promising that the Romans would give more dutiful service to the deities than the people from whom they had been accustomed to receive homage. The appeal must have been effective: Rome always seemed to win. Peoples from all over the Mediterranean world eventually flowed into Rome. It was the great melting pot of the ancient world, yet in the end nothing was melting but the pot. Before that happened, however, the city of Rome became the basis of an empire with great elasticity, infused with Rome's own spirit and political wisdom.

For all of Rome's ability to absorb, the traditional ways of doing things remained the standard. There was a prominent feeling that what Rome did was rooted in the eternal order of right.

Rome's political genius exceeded its deficiencies in imagination, a quality in which the Greeks excelled. Legal formulation or definition was Rome's great strength. Everything in Rome depended on right or jurisdiction. The magistrates had *imperium,* or complete power. *Ius* (the ordinary Latin word for force, "civil law") and *fas* ("religious law," what had divine sanction apart from the state) were combined in the ruling bodies. Rome might look like a theocracy, but it was not, for all was legal. If for Greece the measure of all things was man,

---

5. Cicero, *Concerning the Response of the Soothsayers* 9.19: "We have excelled neither Spain in population, nor Gaul in vigor, nor Carthage in versatility, nor Greece in art, nor, indeed Italy and Latium itself in the innate sensibility characteristic of this land and its peoples, but in piety, in devotion to religion, . . . we have excelled every race and every nation."

for Rome the measure of all things was law. For the east the measure of all things was the king, and it will be seen that for the Jews the measure of all things was God.[6]

Rome had a reasonably continuous policy. Long generations of rulers set themselves to one task — the growth of Rome. Their ideal was great statesmanship, not the search for the good, the true, and the beautiful, as in Greece. True, the Romans were great builders and knew road building as a device for strategy (Rome built on the earlier road systems of the Persians and the Macedonians in the Near East and perfected roads for strategic purposes), but the real greatness of Roman policy lay in the government's interest in people. Moral authority of a high standard was preserved for a long time in the senate, until demoralization came in the first century.

Conquest brought new problems. Rome, like Sparta at the end of the Peloponnesian War, found it difficult to maintain discipline away from home. A permanent court had to be created in Rome in 149 B.C. to deal with charges by provincials against Roman officials for extortion. Governors enriched themselves. This was not true of all governors by any means, but it was said that a governor must make three fortunes while in office: one to pay the debts incurred in obtaining the office, one to buy acquittal from the charges that would be brought for his administration, and one to finance retirement.

Rome and the West

By the end of the fourth century B.C. Rome had consolidated its hold south of the Po River. Carthage was Rome's chief rival in the western Mediterranean. A sea power, Carthage used mercenaries on land; Rome's strength was in its citizen soldiers. Rome fought three major wars with Carthage, known as the Punic Wars ("Punic" from the Phoenician settlers of Carthage). As a result of the First Punic War (262–241 B.C.) Rome acquired Sardinia, Corsica, and Sicily. During the Second Punic War (218–201 B.C.) Hannibal launched an invasion of Italy from Spain by crossing the Alps. His invasion brought great suffering and anxiety. Rome, however, found its own great general in Scipio Africanus, who finally defeated Hannibal in Africa. Rome now came to control northern Italy, southern Gaul, and Spain. The Third Punic War (149–146 B.C.) brought the final defeat of Carthage, and all of the western Mediterranean was now in Roman hands.

Although not brought about by deliberate policy, the Latin language and culture were planted in Spain, Gaul, Britain, the Rhineland, and North Africa.

---

6. Cf. A. D. Nock, "Religious Attitudes of the Ancient Greeks," *Proceedings of the American Philosophical Society* 85 (1942):480 (*Essays*, 547).

Rome and the East

The Etruscans appear to have had connections with Asia Minor, so Rome in effect had her Near East right at home in central Italy. Rome's contacts with (and eventual conquest of) the Etruscans gave it an early experience in taking over Near Eastern institutions and infusing them with its own natural temper.

The campaigns in southern Italy from 280–275 B.C. by Pyrrhus, king of Epirus in Greece, on behalf of the Greek colony of Tarentum engaged Rome in military conflict with Greece. The fall of Tarentum in 272 B.C. brought Greek slaves to Rome. Thereafter Rome would be significant in the Greek world, and Greek ideas were to penetrate Rome.

At the conclusion of Rome's four Macedonian Wars (214–205, 200–196, 171–167, 150–148 B.C.), Macedonia was made a Roman province (148 B.C.). In 146 B.C. the Greek leagues were dissolved into their component city-states and the city of Corinth was destroyed.

Rome was already involved farther to the east. In 188 B.C. the Seleucid king Antiochus III was driven from Asia, with Rome's friend Eumenes of Pergamum the chief benefactor. In 168 Rome ordered Syria to withdraw from Egypt. The envoy of the senate, C. Popilius Laenas, drew a circle on the ground and told Antiochus IV not to step out of it until he had given his pledge to withdraw from Egypt.[7] By enforcing his will on Hellenistic monarchs, the Roman envoy made a profound impression. A few days before this the consul L. Aemilius Paullus had dealt Macedonia a decisive defeat in the battle of Pydna. Thus within a week Rome had defeated Macedonia, taken Egypt under its protection, and forced Syria to submit to its wishes. A new power now overshadowed the three chief segments of Alexander's empire.

Attalus III bequeathed the kingdom of Pergamum to Rome in 133 B.C., and in 129 Rome organized the province of Asia, leaving the rest of Asia Minor under native client kings (about whom more later). Syria was made a province in 63 B.C. and Egypt in 31 B.C. (see below).

Rōmē is the Greek word for strength. Roman power was respected in the east, if not always admired, and from the second century (in keeping with the practice of worshiping power) the personified city of Rome was honored as a goddess there.

Rome thus took over the political and cultural heritage of Alexander west of the Euphrates and became his real successor. It accomplished politically his vision of one unified world. Rome brought security and roads to the Near East. It did not bring a new culture. It made no effort to Latinize, and Greek remained the effective language. The Greek culture prevailed in the eastern Mediterranean, whereas culture in the west owed and still owes its stamp to the Ro-

---

7. Polybius, *Histories* 29.27; Appian, *Roman History* 11.11.66; Livy 45.12; Plutarch, *Moralia* 202F.

man conquest. The educated man from the second century B.C. spoke Greek and Latin. As Roman military might and political administration moved east, Greek culture flowed west and came to prevail even in Rome. Horace stated the situation epigrammatically: "Captured Greece took captive her savage conqueror and brought civilization to rustic Latium" (*Ep.* 2.1.156).

The Later Republic: Civil Wars

The Roman Republic knew social upheaval and civil war for a century from 133 B.C. The turmoil began with the land reform measures of Tiberius Gracchus, which were extended to a broader program of social and political reform by his brother Caius Gracchus. Both brothers lost their lives as a result of violence stirred up by senatorial reaction against their proposals, the former in 132 and the latter a decade later. The Gracchi's proposals were not extreme according to later developments, but this opening conflict in a century of strife showed that reformers needed more secure support than the fickle urban proletariat could provide in the Popular Assembly, and the physical force by which extremists among the aristocracy put them down revealed what the decisive weapon would be.

The wars against Jugurtha in Numidia and the Teutons invading from the north at the end of the second century B.C. brought Marius to leadership. He was placed in command by the people, an encroachment on the senate's right of military control. Marius opened the army to voluntary enlistment apart from a property qualification and so introduced a professional standing army. Now the poorer people served, and their loyalty was to the commander, upon whom they were dependent for pay and promises of land on retirement, rather than to the state. The intervention of Marius's army in civil strife in Rome in 100 B.C. showed the potential for military solutions to political problems. As the next century progressed, Rome's internal and external difficulties increased. Large numbers of troops were required for extended campaigns, and long campaigns abroad weakened the economic system. When men were away from Rome for a long time together, they acquired new ideas.

The Civil Wars began in 90 B.C. with a rebellion by a confederacy of Italian peoples. L. Cornelius Sulla's part in putting down the rebellion made him the champion of the senate. His troops seized Rome in order to suppress opposing political elements. When Sulla retired from Rome to prepare for war in the east, Marius led an army into the city, but he died early in 86.

Meanwhile Mithridates VI, king of Pontus, had been expanding his control in Asia and posed a serious challenge to Roman authority in the eastern Mediterranean. His invasion of Greece in 87 precipitated the First Mithridatic War. Mithridates had made the most of dissatisfactions with Rome in the east, but Sulla was able to win a decisive military victory, forcing the king to evacuate his conquered territory in Asia Minor and the Greek cities that supported him to pay a heavy tribute.

Sulla returned to Italy in 83 and by 80 had put an end to the civil war by disposing of the armies that had supported Marius. Sulla exacted bloody vengeance on supporters of the Marian party and imposed heavy financial exactions. He had himself appointed dictator in order to put the republican constitution back in working order. He laid down the office in 79 and retired from Rome to allow the restored government of the senate to function. No one else was to do that.

The old Roman constitution had its checks and balances, but the new government was not able to cope with the altered political forces. In the ensuing period Pompey established himself as a military leader and statesman by sweeping the Mediterranean of pirates, ending the threat of Mithridates VI, and bringing the remaining Seleucid territories within Roman control and settling their administration. The so-called First Triumvirate came into the open with the first consulship of C. Julius Caesar in 59.[8] Pompey and Crassus had been rivals, but the alliance of Pompey with Caesar's rising star brought Crassus into the partnership to safeguard his own interests. Pompey held command in Spain and was in charge in Rome. Crassus held the Syrian command, but his death in 53 removed an important balancing factor within the coalition. Caesar's conquest of Gaul brought him prestige but also hatred from those who feared his power. The senate maneuvered Pompey into a position of opposition to Caesar. Civil war returned to Rome when Caesar crossed the Rubicon River and invaded Italy in 49 B.C. Pompey's troops were not ready for battle, and he removed them across the Adriatic to Greece. The decisive battle at Pharsalus in Thessaly in 48 left Caesar master of the Roman world, though he had to fight battles against pockets of resistance until 45. His assumption of a perpetual dictatorship in February 44 convinced the champions of the Republic, who resented Caesar intensely, that they must act quickly. C. Cassius and M. Brutus planned the assassination that occurred on the Ides (15th) of March, 44 B.C., but some of Caesar's own staff officers as well as some whom he had aided were in on the plot.

Cicero could hope that Caesar's death meant the restoration of the old Republic, but such was not to be. "The tyrannicides had planned the murder of Caesar well, but they had planned nothing more."[9] Octavian, nephew of Caesar and adopted by the latter in his will, Mark Antony, Caesar's chief lieutenant, and Lepidus, former consul and governor of Gaul and Spain, formed a "Second Triumvirate." The triumvirs gained control of Rome and began a massive proscription of the senatorial and equestrian classes. Brutus and Cassius had gath-

---

8. Michael Grant, *Julius Caesar* (London, 1969); Erik Wistrand, *Caesar and Contemporary Roman Society* (Göteborg, 1979) interprets Caesar's success in terms of Roman social practices and attitudes.

9. Max Cary, *A History of Rome* (2d ed.; London, 1954), 422.

ered armies in the Balkans and Syria, but Antony and Octavian disposed of them in the battle of Philippi in 42 B.C.

Conflict was inevitable between Octavian and Antony. The latter's affair with Cleopatra VII, the last of the Ptolemaic rulers, in Egypt gave Octavian all the propaganda he needed to stir up national sentiment in Rome against Antony. The clash was treated as a war against Egypt, and so it was, although much more. The defeat of Antony and Cleopatra at Actium in 31 B.C. caused both to commit suicide in Egypt (30 B.C.). The Ptolemaic dynasty was extinguished and the last of the Hellenistic kingdoms was now in Roman hands. The Roman civil wars were finally at an end, but so too was the Republic. Rome had been an imperial republic for some time; now only the empire remained. It was for Octavian to establish a new constitution.

BIBLIOGRAPHY

Jones, A. H. M., ed. *A History of Rome Through the Fifth Century.* 2 vols. New York, 1968, 1970.

Errington, R. M. *The Dawn of Empire: Rome's Rise to World Power.* London, 1971.
Cary, M., and H. H. Scullard. *A History of Rome down to the Age of Constantine.* 3d ed. London, 1975.
Grant, Michael. *History of Rome.* London, 1978.
Balsdon, J. P. V. D. *Romans and Aliens.* London, 1979.
Christ, K. *The Romans: An Introduction to Their History and Civilization.* Berkeley, 1984.
Ridley, R. T. *History of Rome: A Documented Analysis.* Rome, 1987.
Crawford, Michael. *The Roman Republic.* 2nd ed. Cambridge, Mass., 1993.
Dupont, Florence. *Daily Life in Ancient Rome.* Oxford, 1994. (Under the Republic)
Shotter, D. *The Fall of the Roman Republic.* London, 1994.

Augustus (31 B.C.–A.D. 14)

Octavian (later called Augustus) had absolute power. He secured election as consul every year, but this was not the basis of his power. He was a despot by universal consent, yet he realized that this was not a satisfactory position. He understood the new situation and its needs: there had to be a strong hand (Rome had to have a central policy for the frontiers and could not continue just to meet emergencies); there could be no overt absolutism, which would alienate the conservative forces in Rome; there had to be a rebuilding of morale and the support of the governing class had to be gained (the support of the governed is a luxury, but an empire cannot be governed by a democracy or by one man alone); and there was a need for order and stability (people were tired of change and the years of war and uncertainty).

The new ruler's official version of the constitutional settlement reached in 27 B.C., his *res gestae* (the acts or things of note), is a combination of political testament and propaganda. It tells the truth, with some exaggeration, but not the whole truth. The *res gestae* says that Octavian's position rested on his exceeding everyone in *auctoritas* — a word that means a combination of innate power and prestige and refers to one whom the people naturally followed. Concerning the new arrangements, it continues:

> When I had extinguished the flames of civil war, after receiving by universal consent the absolute control of affairs, I transferred the republic from my own control to the will of the senate and the Roman people. For this service on my part I was given the title of Augustus by decree of the senate.[10]

"Augustus" was an ancient word suggesting the numinous and something more than human, but no precise category. By this epithet Octavian has continued to be known. A Roman name had three parts: praenomen (personal name of which there were very few and so usually abbreviated), nomen (the gens or family name), and the cognomen (nickname) — as M(arcus) Tullius Cicero. In a full designation the name of the father would be inserted between the nomen and cognomen. Thus the ruler's name had been C(aius) Julius C f [*filius*, son, of C(aesar)] Octavianus. After 27 his official name was Imp(erator) Caesar divi f(ilius) ["son of a god," in this case the now deified Julius Caesar] Augustus. In every respect this was not a normal Roman name and was indicative of the unique position he held.

What were the reasons for ostensibly restoring an outmoded and ineffective Republic? There was the problem of how one with superior power legalizes his position. Augustus had to provide for a transmission of power. With a legal arrangement he could channel patronage and answer his critics. Moreover, he had to consider the sentiments of the people. But there was no doubt who was in control. In 27 B.C. Augustus was voted a very large military command, comprising about three-fourths of the legions, to be held for ten years. And he continued to be elected consul until 23 B.C. It was not very republican to hold office this long; and by doing so he was squeezing out other men from gaining administrative experience and was extending the power of the office beyond its content.

The final legal definition of the new constitutional arrangement was made in 23 B.C. Augustus was allowed to have proconsular power over the

---

10. The text of the *res gestae* is most completely preserved in an inscription in the Temple to Rome and Augustus in Ancyra; Eng. trans. in the Loeb Classical Library in the volume with Velleius Paterculus, *History of Rome*; commentaries by E. G. Hardy, *The Monumentum Ancyranum* (Oxford, 1923) and P. A. Brunt and J. M. Moore, *Res Gestae Divi Augusti* (London, 1967); E. S. Ramage, *The Nature and Purpose of Augustus' "Res gestae"* (Stuttgart, 1987).

EMPEROR AUGUSTUS, from Prima Porta
Augustus as a general gives an address. The Eros at his feet alludes to the
claim that the Julian family was descended from Venus. *(Philip Gendreau)*

provinces without living there and without the title of proconsul. This was
known as the *imperium maius* of the provincial army. Further, he received the
right of interference in any province. Augustus gave up the office of consul and
was invested with the *tribunicia potestas,* the power of the tribunate. To protect
the power of the people, the Republic had elected ten tribunes — a troublesome office to the aristocracy, for a tribune held veto power and could initiate
legislation, and an offense against a tribune was considered an offense against
the gods. The office had been kept under control until the time of the Gracchi.
Augustus was now given the power of the board of tribunes. Since the power

(in distinction from the privileges) of the office had never been clearly defined, it was elastic enough to be extended as far as Augustus desired, while keeping the republican forms. Augustus's legal position now rested on the tribunate and the imperium of the provincial army.

A habit developed of calling Augustus the *princeps,* the chief citizen, and the government the principate. This is descriptive terminology; it occurs on no monument as an official title of the emperor. It had harmless and benevolent connotations, but as *princeps senatus* (from 28 B.C.) he had the right of speaking first in debate. A new system was developing. Several efforts have been made to define it, but it changed with the passing of time and with the viewpoint (in the provinces it was monarchy and they liked it, and at Rome it was a continuation of what was flexible in the old constitution). In a sense the new government was a delegated absolutism. There is much to be said for the view that Augustus introduced a revolutionary tyranny. On the other side, his achievements were great and he well answered the needs of the time.

Without any delegated authority, Augustus would still have been master of the world: he exceeded all in *auctoritas,* extraconstitutional power; all the clientele of the opposing families were swept into his allegiance after Actium; he had the army and the money; and he had the resources of Egypt. So clear was the new reality as a permanent fact that all took an oath of allegiance to Tiberius in A.D. 14, as they had to Augustus, without another word about a successor.

Augustus was careful to act in the right ways as a citizen, but he accepted the halos of artists and writers (who did an important service in promoting the new reign), and in the east he stepped into the place of earlier monarchs. There was a great emphasis on peace: his rule ushered in the *pax romana.* After the wars of the preceding period a genuine sense of gratitude was expressed toward Augustus for the restoration of peace. He promoted this virtue of his reign, given monumental expression in the *ara pacis* (altar of peace) in Rome, whose reliefs are a noble expression of the ideals of the principate (pp. 137-39). Security and safety made possible travel, trade, and renewed economic development and prosperity. Augustus took the office of *pontifex maximus* in 12 B.C. as part of his program of restoring the religion of the Republic. Some historians have considered this as merely keeping up appearances, but there was a very real accomplishment by Augustus in this regard. The Roman gods were not yet dead, and Roman religious emotions were still strong. Further, Augustus initiated significant building activity, boasting that he found Rome a city of brick and left it a city of marble.[11]

Philo of Alexandria was special pleading in contrasting Augustus with Caligula, but his words represent the contemporary provincial estimate of Augustus:

11. Suetonius, *Augustus* 28.3.

This is he who exterminated wars both of the open kind and the covert which are brought about by the raids of brigands. This is he who cleared the sea of pirate ships and filled it with merchant vessels. This is he who reclaimed every state to liberty, who led disorder into order and brought gentle manners and harmony to all unsociable and brutish nations, who enlarged Hellas by many a new Hellas and hellenized the outside world in its most important regions, the guardian of the peace, who dispensed their dues to each and all, who did not hoard his favors but gave them to be common property, who kept nothing good and excellent hidden throughout his life. . . . He was also the first and the greatest and the common benefactor in that he displaced the rule of many and committed the ship of the commonwealth to be steered by a single pilot, that is himself, a marvellous master of the science of government. . . . The whole habitable world voted him no less than celestial honors. These are so well attested by temples, gateways, vestibules, porticoes. . . . They knew his carefulness and that he showed it in maintaining firmly the native customs of each particular nation no less than of the Romans, and that he received his honours not for destroying the institutions of some nations in vain self-exaltation but in accordance with the magnitude of so mighty a sovereignty whose prestige was bound to be enhanced by such tributes. That he was never elated or puffed up by the vast honours given to him is clearly shown by the fact that he never wished anyone to address him as a god.[12]

As the rule of Alexander marks one turning point for our period, so the rule of Augustus marks another. He did not look at himself as the first of a series of emperors. He was a man undertaking a constitutional experiment that depended on a delicate balance. Although he refused the discredited office of dictator, he could still act arbitrarily. He was repeatedly frustrated in his plans to transmit power to his sons, but the new order endured for a remarkably long time. Concerning Alexander's supposed despondency after his conquests over what to do with the rest of his life, Augustus was quoted as saying he was surprised "that Alexander did not regard the right ordering of the empire he had won a greater task than winning it" (Plutarch, *Moralia* 207D). The saying, even if unhistorical, well states their respective achievements.

The contributions of Augustus of significance for early Christianity include peace, economic prosperity, improved communications, stable government, and a sense of renewal. The literature of the Augustan age celebrates the birth of a new age (pp. 114-15). There was a strong sense of a new beginning, an old era of upheaval and warfare ended and a new era of peace and prosperity beginning. Christian authors later concurred in the sentiment, but saw in it an even deeper meaning, for Jesus had been born under Augustus's reign (Luke 2:1).

---

12. *Embassy to Gaius* 145-54, trans. F. H. Colson in Loeb Classical Library, *Philo* 10.75ff. For a comparable adulation of the reign of Augustus by a Roman, see Velleius Paterculus 2.89.

BIBLIOGRAPHY

Ehrenberg, Victor, and A. H. M. Jones. *Documents Illustrating the Reigns of Augustus and Tiberius.* Oxford, 1949.

Chisholm, K., and J. Ferguson. *Rome: The Augustan Age: A Source Book.* Oxford, 1981.

Braund, D. *Augustus to Nero: A Sourcebook of Roman History. 31 B.C. – A.D. 68.* London, 1985.

Sherk, R. K., ed. and trans. *The Roman Empire: Augustus to Hadrian.* Translated Documents of Greece and Rome 6. Cambridge, 1988.

Syme, Ronald. *The Roman Revolution.* Oxford, 1939.

Bowersock, G. W. *Augustus and the Greek World.* Oxford, 1965.

Jones, A. H. M. *Augustus.* London, 1970; New York, 1971.

Reinhold, Meyer. *The Golden Age of Augustus.* Toronto, 1978.

Earl, Donald. *The Age of Augustus.* London, 1980.

Millar, F., and E. Segal. *Caesar Augustus: Seven Aspects.* Oxford, 1984.

Raaflaub, K. A. and M. Toher, eds. *Between Republic and Empire: Interpretations of Augustus and His Principate.* Berkeley, 1990.

Shotter, D. *Augustus Caesar.* London, 1991.

MacMullen, Ramsay. *Romanization in the Time of Augustus.* New Haven, 2000.

The Early Empire

Tiberius (A.D. 14–37).[13] Tiberius was the son of Augustus's second wife Livia by a previous marriage. He seems not to have been considered for the succession until all other possibilities had been exhausted. Augustus's manipulation of the private lives of those near him is seen in his requiring Tiberius to marry his daughter Julia, the talk of Rome for her infidelities. As stepson, son-in-law, and then adopted son of Augustus, he came to power at fifty-five years of age. Although a brilliant military commander, Tiberius had grown bitter and melancholy by the time he became emperor. He did not approve of the cult of the ruler (pp. 207-11), but he took an interest in astrology (pp. 237-43).

Tiberius disliked the trappings of power, and although he professed a desire for the senate to have freedom, its own debasement under the long rule of Augustus and Tiberius's isolation from it (from A.D. 26 he lived on Capri and did not attend another meeting of the senate) strained relations between them. This isolation plus the oppressive practices of Sejanus, the prefect of the praetorian guard (pp. 54-55, 57), gave to the senatorial class the black picture of Tiberius that is reflected in Tacitus. Tiberius allowed Sejanus to exercise effective power, but Sejanus finally overreached himself and Tiberius in a counterplot had him executed in A.D. 31.

13. Robin Seager, *Tiberius* (London, 1972); Barbara Levick, *Tiberius the Politician* (London, 1986); D. Shotter, *Tiberius Caesar* (London, 1992).

Sejanus was anti-Jewish; Pontius Pilate, governor of Judea at the time of Jesus' crucifixion, was one of his appointees. Pilate's dealings with the Jews may reflect the varying fortunes of his sponsor in Rome (see pp. 416-18). During this time the Jews were expelled from Rome, with four thousand Jewish youth sent to Sardinia to fight brigands (Tacitus, *Annals* 2.85).

Although Tiberius alienated the senate at home, he was vigilant in foreign affairs. His reign brought stability to the frontiers, and he brought better order to the provinces by leaving men in office longer (the practice in the Republic was to change provincial governors annually). Pilate's ten years in Judea exemplifies this policy.

Gaius Caligula (A.D. 37–41).[14] Gaius was the grandson of Tiberius's brother Drusus. He acquired the nickname Caligula ("little boots") from the soldiers among whom he grew up while his father Germanicus was on campaign in Germany.

Gaius began with the favor of the senate, but he had grown up in an atmosphere of family tragedy and suspicion and this perhaps had something to do with the signs of mental derangement that appeared before his assassination. He foolishly depleted the treasury and became convinced of his divinity, demanding divine honors.

His reign was marked by conflict with the Jews. When his friend Agrippa I was returning from Rome to take possession of the kingdom assigned to him in northeast Palestine, he stopped in Alexandria. This became the occasion of an anti-Jewish riot in the city: an idiot was paraded through the city in royal robes to mock Agrippa, statues of Gaius were set up in the synagogues, and there was burning and pillaging in the Jewish sections of the city.[15] The prefect of the city, Flaccus, was arrested and later executed for the outrage, but a Jewish embassy to Rome under Philo did not receive a friendly welcome. Gaius was a personal friend of Agrippa's, but he had no appreciation for Jewish religion and customs. When the Jews in Jamnia tore down an altar erected to him in A.D. 40, he ordered a statue of himself set up in the temple in Jerusalem. Petronius, the legate in Syria, knew what this would mean to Jewish sensibilities and successfully stalled on the order (see pp. 418-19 for a fuller account). Jews were not the only people relieved when in A.D. 41 Caligula learned he was not a god.

Claudius (A.D. 41–54).[16] Claudius was Gaius's uncle. The praetorian guards who killed Gaius found Claudius hiding in some curtains in the palace and took him as their candidate for *princeps*. The negotiator between the

14. E. Mary Smallwood, *Documents Illustrating the Principates of Gaius, Claudius, and Nero* (London, 1967); A. A. Barrett, *Caligula: The Corruption of Power* (New Haven, 1989).

15. Philo, *Against Flaccus*. See p. 479.

16. M. P. Charlesworth, *Documents Illustrating the Reigns of Claudius and Nero* (Cambridge, 1939); A. Momigliano, *Claudius, the Emperor and his Achievement* (Oxford, 1934; repr. Cambridge, 1961); B. Levick, *Claudius* (New Haven, 1990).

praetorians and the senate was none other than Agrippa I, whom Claudius rewarded with an enlarged kingdom throughout Palestine. Involvement with the military was a fateful precedent for the future: Claudius himself knew the value of keeping the army behind him. An early injury had left him with an ungainly limp, and he drooled saliva: such gave his contemporaries the idea that he was a half-wit. He had spent the years during which he had been overlooked in the imperial family (he was fifty at the time of his accession) reading and studying. Modern scholars are now making a case for him as a statesman and more than the figurehead that earlier generations considered him.

The Jewish question still had to be dealt with. Claudius confirmed the privileges of the Jews in Alexandria, warning the Greeks there to maintain the peace and the Jews to be content with what they had and not to seek more privileges (quotation from the papyrus copy of the letter on pp. 587-88). Because of disturbances "at the instigation of one Chrestus [Christ?]," he expelled Jews from Rome (Suetonius, *Claudius* 25.4; cf. Acts 18:2).[17]

Claudius's major venture in foreign affairs was the addition of Britain to the empire. In domestic affairs he set higher standards for Roman citizenship yet also opened it up to worthy men in the provinces. He sought to make the business of the senate more efficient, but his own activities in public projects in Italy further eroded the distinction between areas administered by the senate and those by the *princeps*. The growth of an imperial bureaucracy run by freedmen centralized administration. The senate resented the power of these men but had only themselves to blame because they considered such tasks demeaning for men of their social rank. The three most powerful freedmen were the secretaries Palas, who handled imperial financial accounts, Narcissus, who had charge of official correspondence, and Callistus, who dealt with petitions. Besides these men, Claudius's fourth wife, his niece Agrippina (marriage to a niece was supposed to be illegal in Rome, but customs change, especially for a ruler), had great influence over affairs.

Nero (A.D. 54–68).[18] According to the ancient rumors, Agrippina had Claudius poisoned when he was of no further use to her in order to secure the throne for her son Nero. The accession was without difficulty: he was proclaimed by the praetorian guard and presented to the senate for its approval. Nero's rule began with the *quinquennium* (the five good years), when af-

17. F. F. Bruce, "Christianity under Claudius," *BJRL* 44 (1962):309-26. Helga Botermann, *Das Judendikt des Kaisers Claudius: Römischer Staat und Christiani im 1. Jahrhundert* Stuttgart, 1996) argues that the edict was due to unrest caused by the Christian mission among Jews; H. Dixon Slingerland, *Claudian Policymaking and the Early Imperial Repression of Judaism at Rome* (Atlanta, 1997) argues against the interpretation of Chrestus as Christ.

18. B. H. Warmington, *Nero: Reality and Legend* (London, 1969); Michael Grant, *Nero* (London, 1970); M. Griffin, *Nero: The End of a Dynasty* (New Haven, 1985); Jás Elsner and Jamie Masters, eds., *Reflections of Nero: Culture, History, and Representation* (Chapel Hill, N.C., 1994).

fairs were under the control of Seneca, whose brother Gallio had been governor of Greece (Acts 18:12), and Burrus, the prefect of the praetorian guards, advisors of the sixteen-year-old Nero. Paul's description of the Roman state in Romans 13 was written during this period. Agrippina was removed from influence and finally murdered, on Nero's orders, in A.D. 59. Nero increasingly took the direction of affairs into his own hands. Burrus died in 62 (there were suspicions of poisoning), and Seneca retired, finally receiving a command to take his life in 65. Their influence was replaced by that of the new praetorian prefect, Tigellinus, who brought out Nero's worst disposition and instituted a despotism.

Nero also had his wife Octavia killed in 62 so he could marry Poppaea, described by Josephus as a "worshipper of God," perhaps a proselyte. His other associations with things Jewish and Christian were not so pleasurable. The

EMPEROR VESPASIAN, from Ostia
Vespasian was conducting the siege of Jerusalem in A.D. 69 when the legions in the east proclaimed him emperor. (© Erich Lessing/ Art Resource, NY)

great fire of Rome in 64 was blamed on the Christians, now recognized as distinct from the Jews and marked for disfavor (pp. 593-94). Tradition puts the martyrdom of Peter and Paul in Rome in the aftermath. The great Jewish revolt in Palestine broke out in 66 (pp. 420ff.), and Vespasian was placed in charge of suppressing it.

The unpopularity of Nero's love of things Greek and his dilettante participation in athletic and artistic competitions (he was touring Greece during the first year of the Jewish revolt) were nothing compared to the response to the reign of terror he instituted. Revolts broke out among the legions in the west, and when the praetorian guards rebelled in Rome, Nero fled the city and finally committed suicide, still only thirty. With his death ended the Julio-Claudian dynasty: all of the emperors from Augustus to Nero were in one way or another related to the Julian and Claudian senatorial families, with other families of equal rank having been steadily eliminated.

Civil War: 68/69.[19] The confusion following Nero's flight brought on civil

19. P. Greenhalgh, *The Year of the Four Emperors* (New York, 1975); Charles L. Murison, *Galba, Otho and Vitellius: Careers and Controversies* (New York, 1993).

EMPEROR TITUS
The toga emphasizes
Titus's posture as "first
among equals" in rela-
tion to the senate.
*(© Alinari/
Art Resource, NY)*

war. The legions and generals discovered the "secret of empire," that "the
princeps could be made elsewhere than at Rome" (Tacitus, *Histories* 1.4). Four
different men in succession came to the purple within the space of one year:
Galba, governor in Spain; Otho, former governor of Lusitania; Vitellius, commander of the legions in Germany; and Vespasian. Vespasian gained the support of the east, and leaving his son Titus to continue the Jewish War, made his
march on Rome in late 69, arriving in the city himself in 70. One of the first to
declare for Vespasian was the governor of Egypt, Tiberius Alexander, an apostate Jew and nephew of Philo.

EMPEROR DOMITIAN, from his temple at Ephesus The colossal statue corresponds to Domitian's claims to divine honors. According to Christian tradition the Book of Revelation was written during his reign. (© *Erich Lessing/ Art Resource*)

Vespasian (A.D. 69–79).[20] Vespasian inaugurated the Flavian dynasty. He came from a small town in the Sabine hills of Italy. His grandfather had been a centurion in the army, so he represents the rise of the governing class of the Italian towns to the highest influence in Rome. Vespasian changed the character of the senate by drawing new members from the municipal aristocracy of Italy and the west. His chief order of business was the restoration of order — financial stability, confidence in the central government, tidying up the provinces. From his time emperors were known by and knew their armies. He and Titus celebrated a triumph in Rome in 71 for the successful suppression of the revolt in Judea. Vespasian's frugal and old-fashioned virtues were a needed respite in Rome. He treated the cult of the emperor lightly and, when he was dying, joked about the practice of declaring a dead emperor divine: "I think that I am becoming a god" (Suetonius, *Vespasian* 23).

Titus (A.D. 79–81).[21] A fever cut short the life of the popular Titus. His

20. M. McCrum and A. G. Woodhead, *Select Documents of the Principates of the Flavian Emperors* (Cambridge, 1961); B. W. Henderson, *Five Roman Emperors: Vespasian, Titus, Domitian, Nerva, Trajan, A.D. 69–117* (1927; repr. New York, 1969); B. Levick, *Vespasian* (London, 1999).

21. B. W. Jones, *The Emperor Titus* (New York, 1984).

reign was remembered for two events: first, the eruption of Vesuvius, which destroyed Pompeii and Herculaneum in 79 and gave him the opportunity to demonstrate his generosity; second, the extravagant opening of the Colosseum, begun by his father and completed by his brother Domitian, and his further expenditures on games and shows, another feature of his reign and a reason for the favor in which the populace held him.

Domitian (A.D. 81–96).[22] Domitian's reign was characterized by the exile and execution of quite a number from senatorial families, so his memory was formally condemned by the senate after his assassination. Domitian insisted on the title *dominus et deus* ("lord and god"), and Christian tradition remembered him as a persecutor and the emperor under whom the Book of Revelation was written.

"Five Good Emperors." Nerva (A.D. 96–98)[23] was a transitional figure. The senate liked him, but the army, which resented the murder of Domitian, did not. Nerva, childless and in his sixties, adopted the commander of the army of Upper Germany, Trajan. What was probably an emergency measure to give military support to the new ruler became the method of settling the succession followed by the next three rulers.

This practice of adopting one's successor gave Rome a series of good emperors under whom the empire reached its highest development. The provinces were prosperous and generally well governed, the empire itself enjoyed internal peace, and a flourishing cultural development left imposing monumental remains throughout the Mediterranean countries.

Trajan (A.D. 98–117)[24] came from Spain, and with him the provinces became full partners in the rule of the empire. He gave the empire its largest territorial extent through his successful campaigns, which pushed the frontiers in the north and east to the Danube and the Euphrates.

Hadrian (A.D. 117–138)[25] introduced a policy of stabilization on the frontier and at home. He was a lover of things Greek. He spent much time traveling in the eastern provinces, and many material remains testify to his interest in the Greek east. Under Hadrian occurred the second major Jewish revolt in Palestine (pp. 424ff.).

Antoninus Pius (A.D. 138–161)[26] enjoyed a peaceful and largely uneventful reign. The empire was prosperous. There was no discordant note. The emperor

22. B. W. Jones, *The Emperor Domitian* (London, 1992); Pat Southern, *Domitian: Tragic Tyrant* (Bloomington, 1997).

23. E. Mary Smallwood, *Documents Illustrating the Principates of Nerva, Trajan, and Hadrian* (Cambridge, 1966).

24. Julian Bennett, *Trajan: Optimus Princeps,* 2d edition (Bloomington, 2001).

25. Stewart Perowne, *Hadrian* (London, 1960); A. R. Birley, *Hadrian: The Restless Emperor* (London, 1997).

26. M. Grant, *The Antonines: The Roman Empire in Transition* (London, 1994). Covers Antoninus, Marcus Aurelius, and Commodus.

gathered around himself men of letters and philosophers. His character, represented by the epithet Pius, conferred on him by the senate and suggesting an amiable personality, made a great impression on the age.

Marcus Aurelius (A.D. 161–180)[27] had to face the problems that were to bring disasters to the Roman world in the next century. Soldiers returning from Mesopotamia brought with them the plague, which had lasting consequences for the political and economic development of the empire. It was still going when Germans and Sarmatians invaded the empire. Marcus was devoted to duty and principle; much of his time was occupied with wars on the northern frontier, fought with inadequate reserves of troops.

Although later Christian authors joined the general chorus of praise for the Antonine age, Jews and Christians both had good reasons for reservations about the second century as an age of peace and justice. Jewish disturbances in Egypt, Cyrene, and Cyprus in 115 during Trajan's rule destroyed much property and took many lives and had to be ruthlessly suppressed. Hadrian's plan to rebuild Jerusalem as a Roman colony, Aelia Capitolina, with a temple to Jupiter and himself on the site of the Jewish temple perhaps contributed to the Bar Kokhba revolt in 132, not put down until 135 (p. 425). There were sporadic persecutions of the Christians under the second-century emperors, with more martyrs made under Marcus Aurelius than under any emperor before the Decian persecution of the third century (see p. 606).

BIBLIOGRAPHY

Tacitus. *Annals. Histories.* See R. Syme, *Tacitus.* 2 vols. Oxford, 1958.

Suetonius. *Lives of the Caesars.*

Aelius Aristides, *Orations* 26 ("Regarding Rome") and 35 ("Regarding the Emperor") in C. A. Behr, *P. Aelius Aristides: The Complete Works,* Vol. 2. Leiden, 1981. Saul Levin, *Eis Rōmēn, To Rome, By Aelius Aristides.* Glencoe, Ill., 1950; J. Oliver, *The Ruling Power.* Philadelphia, 1953; from *Transactions of the American Philosophical Society* 43 (1953):871-1003.

Augustan History. See R. Syme, *Ammianus and the Historia Augusta.* Oxford, 1968; R. Syme, *Emperors and Biography.* Oxford, 1971.

Lewis, Naphtali. *The Roman Principate.* Greek Historical Documents Series. Sarasota, Fla., 1974.

Novak, R. P. *Christians and the Roman Empire: Background Texts.* Harrisburg, 2001.

MacMullen, Ramsay. *Enemies of the Roman Order: Treason, Unrest, and Alienation in the Empire.* Cambridge, Mass., 1966.

Grant, Michael. *The Twelve Caesars: From Julius Caesar to Domitian.* New York, 1975.

Petit, Paul. *Pax Romana.* London and Berkeley, 1976.

Millar, Fergus. *The Emperor in the Roman World.* Ithaca, N.Y., 1977.

---

27. A. S. L. Farquharson, *Marcus Aurelius: His Life and his World* (Oxford, 1952); Anthony Birley, *Marcus Aurelius: A Biography* (New Haven, 1987).

Cunliffe, Barry. *Rome and Her Empire.* London, 1978.

Grant, Michael. *The Roman Emperors: A Biographical Guide to the Rulers of Imperial Rome.* New York, 1985.

Wells, Colin. *The Roman Empire.* 2d ed. Cambridge, Mass., 1995.

Goodman, Martin. *The Roman World 44 BC-AD 180.* London, 1997.

Alston, Richard. *Aspects of Roman History AD 14-117.* London, 1998.

The Later Empire

The return to hereditary succession with Marcus's son Commodus (A.D. 180–
192) turned out badly. War followed his assassination. Septimius Severus finally
won out and inaugurated the Severan dynasty, under which Syrian influence
became prevalent in Rome.

The second century, which had brought the high-water mark in the material culture of the empire, also saw its share of emergencies, with pressure
from enemies on the frontier, strains on the economy, and religious conflict
within the empire; but these problems became a flood during the third century. The movement of peoples from central Asia exerted ever more pressure
on the northern frontiers, and Parthia (where the Sassanid dynasty had replaced the Arsacid in 230) gave trouble on the east. A drop in purchasing power
of money and the debasement of the currency ruined the middle class. The
third century was a bad time for the Roman world. Nevertheless, the empire
showed astounding powers of recovery. It is extraordinary that the system survived some of the strains that it did.

Decius and the Illyrian soldier-emperors began to stabilize the situation.
With Diocletian and Constantine the constitutional realities changed the
principate into the dominate: all pretense of partnership with the senate was
gone, and the emperor ruled as supreme lord in name as well as in reality. The
remarkable thing is that the empire held together as long as it did. Constantine's rejuvenation gave the empire a century and a half lease on life in the west
and laid the basis for the Byzantine state, which remained an important power
in the eastern Mediterranean for the next millennium.

ADMINISTRATION OF THE EMPIRE

Cities

The Roman empire, as far as power and government were concerned, was a
collection of cities.[28] The cities were what counted for something, and most

---

28. For the appearance of cities and a descriptive catalogue, see P. Grimal, *Roman Cities*

people wanted to have a home in the city (even though many of the nobility, who could afford to be snobbish, often expressed strong preference for the peacefulness of their country estates in contrast to the noise and confusion of the city). The city was where things happened, where the opportunities were. The civilization of the Roman empire was an urban civilization to a greater extent than any time in the west up to the modern age.

We may classify the cities of the empire according to the privileges they possessed. At the top of the scale were the *coloniae civium romanorum* (colonies of Roman citizens). These were mostly towns in which military veterans were settled. They were sometimes granted partial or complete immunity from taxation. Each was a little Rome, Rome away from home. Some of the Roman colonies mentioned in the New Testament are Philippi, Corinth, Antioch of Pisidia, Iconium, Lystra, and Troas. Next in importance were the other towns that possessed the Roman franchise, the *municipia* or *oppida civium romanorum* (towns of Roman citizens). The "Latin" towns came next, where the Roman franchise could be obtained by holding a magistracy in the town government. Other cities possessed no official privileges, but among them were a few that still called themselves "free" (Ephesus, Smyrna, Tarsus, and Antioch of Syria), meaning their internal affairs were governed by their own laws, or "federate" (Athens, Tyre, and Rhodes), although this was anachronistic under the empire.

The form of municipal government in the cities of the west tended to copy that at Rome. Under the Republic the major political offices were consul, praetor, and quaestor. The highest officials were the two consuls elected annually. Their ordinary one-year term of office was often abridged under the empire by the choice of supplementary consuls *(suffecti)* for part of a term in order to advance more men favored by the emperor. Under the empire the chief post in the city of Rome, filled by former consuls, was city prefect *(praefectus urbi)*. Next in rank to the consuls were the praetors, normally twelve chosen each year. The praetors were judges, but after their term of office they filled other administrative posts. Quaestor was the lowest office that gave entry to the senate. Twenty quaestors were chosen each year; they had financial functions. All of the above offices were filled by men from the senatorial class (p. 56). Of the lesser offices filled by those who were not senators, we may mention the six *aediles,* who had charge of various public works and public services.

Roman towns in the west normally had two chief magistrates, *duovirs,* on the pattern of the two consuls in Rome. Inferior to them were two *aediles,* who superintended buildings and public works. One such *aedile,* named Erastus and mentioned on an inscription at Corinth, has been identified as possibly the same as Erastus, the "city treasurer," mentioned in Romans 16:23 (written

---

(Madison, Wis., 1983); J. E. Stambaugh, *The Ancient Roman City* (Baltimore, 1988); E. J. Owens, *The City in the Greek and Roman World* (London, 1991).

from Corinth).[29] Financial administration might be in the hands of quaestors. There was also a local council (curia) of former magistrates (called decuriones) like the senate in Rome. In the west there was a zealous imitation of Roman constitutional forms; in the east loyalty to Rome was expressed by extending divine honors to the emperor (see pp. 207ff.).

In contrast to cities of the west, those in the eastern Mediterranean show much more variety in their local government, because they could keep older forms of municipal organization rather than imitate Rome.[30] The best-known city in this regard is Athens, which may be taken as a sample of the Greek cities. Its constitution was assembled by Aristotle's students as a basis for his study of politics.[31] The assembly (ekklēsia, the usual term for the political assemblies of citizens in Greek cities; see Acts 19:39, 41) of citizens in Athens provided a kind of direct democracy for many legislative and judicial decisions. The senate or council (boulē) contained five hundred members. The elaborate and complicated arrangement involved a large number of different officials. Athenian democracy presumed an equal right to govern as well as an equal right to choose, hence there was frequent use of the lot in choosing men for functions that did not require technical skills (those who did exercise such functions, like generals, were elected). Each of the ten tribes into which the citizens were divided selected ten candidates by lot. One from the ten candidates of each of nine tribes was chosen by lot, and these nine served as archons, the principal magistrates. The tenth tribe supplied the clerk. The court of the Areopagus at one time was limited to jurisdiction in capital crimes, at other times it was the principal governing body in Athens; during the first century it appears to have regulated educational and religious affairs.[32] Originally it met on the hill northwest of the Acropolis ("Mars Hill"), but in Hellenistic times it met in the Agora below (Paul in Acts 17:19, 22 appeared before the court, not on Ares' hill).

Greek cities in the east (notably Alexandria) were often subdivided into politeumata (corporations; cf. the Greek of Phil. 3:20). The politeuma was a self-governing division of the city based on nationality. The Greek politeuma had a religious center, a council and magistrates, division of citizens into tribes, and other features of a Greek polis. The Jews in Alexandria, it seems, also formed a politeuma.[33] This method of organization supplied a means of

---

29. ERASTUS PRO AEDILITATE S. P. STRAVIT. "Erastus in return for the aedileship paved it [the pavement adjoining the theatre] at his own expense." For a survey of opinions and literature, see David W. J. Gill, "Erastus the Aedile," Tyndale Bulletin 40 (1989):293-301.

30. Victor Ehrenberg, The Greek State (2d ed.; London, 1969), describes the typical features.

31. J. E. Sandys, Aristotle's Constitution of Athens (2d ed.; London, 1912); A. H. M. Jones, Athenian Democracy (Oxford, 1957).

32. That the Areopagus held the real power in Roman times is stated by M. Nilsson, Geschichte der griechischen Religion (Munich, 1950), 2:296. For the early history, see R. W. Wallace, The Areopagos Council, to 307 B.C. (Baltimore, 1988).

33. This is the correct explanation for the privileges of Jews in Alexandria and not full citi-

incorporating a large body of aliens into the city without making them full citizens.

Provinces

The Augustan settlement in 27 B.C. involved cooperation between the emperor and the senate in the administration of the provinces.[34] The peaceful and civilized provinces where no legions had to be quartered — about ten in number — were administered by the senate. A provincial governor had the title of proconsul (Acts 19:38), that is, "in the place of consul" or functioning with the power of a consul in that *provincia* (which was originally a sphere of authority and later a geographical term). The proconsuls were chosen by lot out of the former magistrates at Rome. The emperor could manipulate this process in various ways, for of course he could not be indifferent to the persons who qualified for such important positions. Former consuls were assigned to Asia and Africa, and the other senatorial provinces were governed by former praetors. There was normally an interval of five years for praetors and ten years for consuls between their magistracy in Rome and receiving a provincial governorship. The summit of a senatorial career was to serve, after becoming a consul in Rome, as proconsul of Asia or Africa. As we have seen, Augustus's *maius imperium* gave him the right after 23 B.C. to intervene anywhere. As new provinces were created, none went to the senate.

The imperial provinces were the military provinces (e.g., Syria), where by reason of the lack of progress toward internal civilization or danger on the frontier legions were stationed. Augustus stepped into the position of proconsul but did not so call himself. He was assisted in the more important provinces by a senator as his legate *(legatus)*, drawn from the ex-consuls and ex-praetors, who functioned as governor. In senatorial provinces a quaestor was appointed over financial affairs; in the military provinces an official of equestrian rank (see p. 57), called a procurator, did this work.

The smaller, troublesome provinces (such as Judea) that were under imperial control received for governor a member of the equestrian order who had a command of auxiliary troops, but not ordinarily legions. Following the terminology employed after Claudius these men have been called procurators, for they were primarily finance officers. In the period before Claudius, however, their title was *prefect,* and the Greek term *(hēgemōn)* in the New Testament represents the Latin *praefectus.* The Pontius Pilate inscription from Caesarea now confirms that the official Latin title of Pilate as governor of Judea was

---

zenship as indicated by Josephus — see V. Tcherikover, *Hellenistic Civilization and the Jews* (Philadelphia, 1961), 296-332.

34. Suetonius, *Augustus* 47; Strabo, *Geography* 17.3.25 (840); Dio, *Roman History* 53.12.

praefectus.[35] Although *prefect* emphasizes military command and *procurator* financial responsibility, the office combined military, financial, and judicial authority. In ordinary circumstances the governor of Judea was not subject to the legate in Syria, but in special circumstances the latter (as a higher-ranking official) could intervene.

Standing outside the usual provincial organization was Egypt, which was a special representative of the class of imperial provinces governed by an equestrian with the title of prefect. It was treated as the personal property of the emperor (who in this respect as in other things stepped into the position of the Ptolemaic kings, as they had into the position of the Pharaohs). The governor was the only equestrian with a legionary force; other governors of this rank had only auxiliary troops. Egypt was so important that Augustus forbade any senator to set foot in the country without his permission. With its strategic defensibility, wealth, and importance for the food supply of Rome it would have been an ideal place from which to challenge the emperor's authority.

An intermediate organization outside the usual administrative machinery of the provinces was the *concilium* (Gk. *koinon*). Consisting of representatives of the cities or tribes in a province who met regularly (annually in most cases) in the capital of the province or other chief city, it became a channel to Rome for expressing the views of the local ruling classes. An important function of these provincial assemblies came to be the promotion of the imperial cult (pp. 209-12). Although not a part of the recognized chain of authority, the *concilia* came in practice to exercise a great deal of influence. They became an instrument of empire, not by imperial action, but by what the provincials made of them. The Asiarchs of Acts 19:31 were members of the *koinon* of Asia. It is notable that these men are described as friendly to Paul, but the Asiarchs personally did not necessarily have priestly duties in the imperial cult. The regular meetings of provincial leaders in the capital of a province are thought to have provided a pattern for the church councils that we know began meeting in Asia Minor in the second century.

Roman rule was unpopular in the eastern Mediterranean in the half century before the establishment of the principate. Rapacity of tax collectors and immunities of Roman citizens from accountability to local authorities were factors in this dissatisfaction. But a definite change of attitude is evident by the second century. Good government and peace were a large part of the explanation.

35.   TIBERIEUM
[— PO]NTIUS PILATUS
[PRAEF]ECTUS IUDA[EA]E
[FECIT D]E[DICAVIT]

"Pontius Pilate, prefect of Judaea, built and dedicated the Tiberieum [a building in honor of Tiberius]." Jerry Vardaman, "A New Inscription Which Mentions Pilate as 'Prefect,'" *JBL* 81 (1962):70-71; Jack Finegan, *The Archaeology of the New Testament* (Princeton, 1969), 80. Josephus, *War* 2.9.2 [169] and Tacitus, *Annals* 15.44 use "procurator" for Pilate.

Client Kingdoms[36]

Rome preferred to leave the government of areas in the east where Hellenization had not advanced very far in the hands of native rulers, who could rule their own people best and by reason of their dependency could serve Rome's interests without Rome assuming responsibility. The modern term for these rulers is client kings because they stood in the relation of clients (see p. 67) to the Roman emperor and held the title of king only with Rome's sanction, but the Romans called them "friends" and "allies." Herod (Matt. 2:1) and his descendants (Acts 12:1; 25:13) who ruled in Palestine occupied this status. Galatia was ruled this way until it became an imperial province in 25 B.C. The client kings were left free in internal administration, levied taxes for their own use, and maintained armies under their own control. They could not pursue their own foreign policy and were limited in their right to mint coins. Their duties were to supply auxiliaries and military aid on demand for the Roman army, maintain order and security on the frontiers, and pay taxes to Rome. These kingdoms also served to protect trade routes, as buffers between barbarians and the empire proper, and in general to advance Rome's purposes.

In the course of time the client kingdoms disappeared and were incorporated into the provincial structure. The uniformity of the status of towns became more general, and the provinces drew closer in status to Italy.

BIBLIOGRAPHY

Levick, B. *The Government of the Roman Empire: A Source Book.* Totowa, N.J., 1985.

Abbott, F. F., and A. C. Johnson. *Municipal Administration in the Roman Empire.* Princeton, 1926. Reprint. New York, 1968.

Jones, A. H. M. *The Greek City from Alexander to Justinian.* Oxford, 1940.

Magie, David. *Roman Rule in Asia Minor to the End of the Third Century.* Princeton, 1950.

Levick, B. M. *Roman Colonies in Southern Asia Minor.* Oxford, 1967.

Jones, A. H. M. *The Cities of the Eastern Roman Provinces.* 2d ed. Oxford, 1971.

Ward-Perkins, J. B. *Cities of Ancient Greece and Italy: Planning in Classical Antiquity.* New York, 1974.

Richardson, J. *Roman Provincial Administration 227 B.C. to A.D. 117.* London, 1976; repr. Bristol, 1984.

Talbert, R. J. A. *The Senate of Imperial Rome,* Princeton, 1987.

Lintott, Andrew. *Imperium Romanum: Politics and Administration.* London, 1993.

Millar, Fergus. *The Roman Near East 31 B.C.–A.D. 337.* Cambridge, Mass., 1993.

---

36. P. C. Sands, *The Client Princes of the Roman Empire* (Cambridge, 1908); David C. Braund, *Rome and the Friendly King: the Character of Client Kingship* (London, 1984).

POLITICAL CONNECTIONS OF THE NEW TESTAMENT

Political history is more than an external frame of reference for early Christianity. The New Testament contains many points of contact with the political ideology of the Roman empire (for which see the full treatment of Ruler Cult [pp. 199ff.]). On several matters it presents implicitly, and sometimes explicitly (book of Revelation), an alternative viewpoint. A few observations will be suggestive of what an attentive reading may bring out.[37]

The beginning and end of the story of Jesus relate to the political context in which the Christian movement began. The star followed by the Magi to Bethlehem (Matt. 2:1-12) had religio-political connotations (for the religious, see on Astral Religion pp. 238-43). The appearance of a comet signalled the apotheosis of Julius Caesar after his assassination in 44 B.C. (p. 208), and another appearance in 17 B.C. in connection with the Secular Games celebrated by Augustus in that year proclaimed the new era Augustus initiated. Coins depicted Caesar and Augustus with a star or a flame of fire on the head, with allusion to their heavenly status. The star of Bethlehem heralded that Jesus was born "king of the Jews" (Matt. 2:2). His title "king" *(basileus)* was the same word used for Herod (Matt. 2:1, 3) and for the emperor.

The word "gospel" *(euangelion)* used for the story of Jesus (Mark 1:1) had a contemporary usage for the blessings brought by Augustus and celebrated on his birthday. A particularly striking combination of terms used by early Christians occurs in an inscription from Priene, dated 9 B.C.

> Since the Providence [*Pronoia*] which has ordered all things and is deeply interested in our life has set in most perfect order by giving to us Augustus, whom she filled with virtue [divine power] that he might benefit mankind, sending him as a Saviour [*Sōtēr*], both for us and for our descendants, that he might end war and arrange all things, and since he, Caesar, by his appearance [*phaneis*] [excelled even our anticipations], surpassing all previous benefactors [*euergetai*], and not even leaving to posterity any hope of surpassing what he had done, and since the birthday of the god Augustus was the beginning for the world of the good tidings [*euangelion*] that came by reason of him . . .[38]

This inscription shows how many words in early Christian vocabulary could be read with political overtones. Indeed, the very term for "church," *ekklēsia,*

---

37. Richard Oster, "Numismatic Windows into the Social World of Early Christianity: A Methodological Inquiry," *JBL* 101 (1982):195-223; Helmut Koester, "The Memory of Jesus' Death and the Worship of the Risen Lord," *HTR* (1996):335-50.

38. W. Dittenberger, *Orientis Graeci inscriptiones selectae* (2 vols.; repr. Hildesheim, 1960) number 458. Trans. A. D. Nock in *Early Gentile Christianity and its Hellenistic Background* (repr. New York, 1964), 37 (*Essays, 79*).

was a political term in secular Greek — the citizen assembly of a Greek city (Acts 19:39), over against which Christians defined their own community (1 Thess. 1:1).

The charge against Jesus for which he was crucified was a political charge. The whole passion narrative is highly charged with political overtones, climaxed with the inscription on the cross, "King of the Jews." All four Gospels, despite minor variations of other words, agree (Matt. 27:37; Mark 15:26; Luke 23:38; John 19:19) on this designation. So, Jesus ended his life with the same title announced at his birth. John's Gospel was careful to explain that Jesus' kingdom was "not of this world" (John 18:36), but this was accompanied by a declaration that earthly political authority is derived from a higher Power (John 19:11).

2. SOCIETY AND CULTURE

BIBLIOGRAPHY

Collections of Sources

Lewis, N., and M. Reinhold. *Roman Civilization: Sourcebook.* Vol. 2. New York, 1955.
Shelton, Jo-Ann. *As the Romans Did: A Sourcebook in Roman Social History.* Oxford, 1988.
Cherry, David. *The Roman World: A Sourcebook.* Oxford, 2001.

Basic Secondary Works

Dill, S. *Roman Society from Nero to Marcus Aurelius.* New York, 1905.
Friedlander, L. *Roman Life and Manners under the Early Empire.* 4 vols. London, 1908–1913.
Jaeger, W. *Paideia.* 3 vols. Oxford, 1939–1944. Reprint, 1957–1965.
Carcopino, J. *Daily Life in Ancient Rome.* New Haven, 1940; new edition, 2003.
Stambaugh, John E., and David L. Balch. *The New Testament in Its Social Environment.* Philadelphia, 1986.
Hornblower, S., and A. Spawforth, eds. *Oxford Companion to Classical Civilization.* Oxford, 1998.

Supplementary Works

Cochrane, C. N. *Christianity and Classical Culture.* Oxford, 1957.
Judge, E. A. *Social Pattern of Christian Groups in the First Century.* London, 1960.
Ehrenberg, Victor. *Society and Civilization in Greece and Rome.* Cambridge, Mass., 1964.
Malherbe, Abraham J. *Social Aspects of Early Christianity.* Philadelphia, 1983.
Jenkins, Ian. *Greek and Roman Life.* Cambridge, Mass., 1986.
Grant, Michael, and Rachel Kitzinger, eds. *Civilization of the Ancient Mediterranean: Greece and Rome.* New York, 1988.

Winter, Bruce W., ed. *The Book of Acts in Its First Century Setting.* Vol. 2. David W. J. Gill and Conrad Gempf, eds. *The Book of Acts in Its Graeco-Roman Setting.* Grand Rapids, 1994.

Brunschwig, Jacques, and G. E. R. Lloyd, eds. *Greek Thought: A Guide to Classical Knowledge.* Cambridge, Mass., 2000.

Sampley, J. Paul, ed. *Paul in the Greco-Roman World.* Harrisburg, 2003.

INTRODUCTION

This chapter will focus on the first century. Where direct evidence is absent or meager, we will employ the evidence of closest proximity. Nevertheless, our concern will be with the general circumstances rather than with chronological exactitude.

THE ROMAN MILITARY

Military power had brought the various provinces under Roman rule. Not only did the Roman army create the empire but it was also one of the most important cultural factors. The army made possible social advancement, was an influence for Romanization, and provided an economic stimulus. The military safeguarded Roman peace and so made possible social and cultural developments, and provided mobility both geographically and socially for its members. The army was important in the spread of various eastern religions and observed its own official religious ceremonies.[1] Although most military personnel were on the frontier, knowledge of them provided an ever present frame of reference from which writers could draw illustrations (e.g., 2 Tim. 2:3-4).

The Legions

The legions were composed of citizen soldiers. With the extension of the citizenship the provinces came to provide many of the legionaries, and by the time of Tiberius the main strength of the army lay in its non-Italian element. Probably many recruits obtained citizenship on induction. From the end of the second century B.C. the army became a largely volunteer force of professional soldiers.

---

1. A. D. Nock, "The Roman Army and the Roman Religious Year," *HTR* 45 (Oct. 1952):187-252 (*Essays,* 2:736-90); John Helgeland, "Roman Army Religion," *ANRW* II, *Principat,* 16.2 (Berlin and New York, 1978), 1470-1505; Eric Birley, "The Religion of the Roman Army: 1895–1977," ibid., 1506-41.

TOMBSTONE OF A CENTURION Marcus Favonius Facilis was stationed in Britain in the mid–first century. Centurions, indicated by the stick and sword, were the backbone of the Roman army. *(Courtesy Colchester and Essex Museum)*

The nominal strength of a legion was 6,000 men, about 5,300 infantry and 700 cavalry and technical specialists, but for various reasons the legions were normally of smaller size. Under Tiberius there were twenty-five legions. The distribution at his time (according to Tacitus, *Annals* 4.5) placed eight on the Rhine, three in Spain, two in Egypt, four in Syria, two in Africa, and six in the Danube provinces. Seven commands were held by men of consular rank who constituted the greatest men next to the ruling family, the elite in peace and men to be reckoned with in civil war: two commands on the Rhine, one in Spain, one in Syria, and three in the Balkans (Pannonia, Dalmatia, and Moesia).

A legion was divided into ten cohorts of six centuries (one hundred men) each. It was commanded by a legate (normally of senatorial rank), with six tribunes serving as staff officers. The most important tactical officers in the legion were the sixty centurions (six in each of the cohorts), each of whom commanded a century. These were the professionals in the army, commonly promoted from the ranks. A centurion entered the equestrian order (see p. 57) on his retirement. Centurions, as the most important professionals stationed in an area for a long time, meet the reader frequently in the Gospels and Acts (e.g., Matt. 8:5; Mark 15:39; Acts 10:1; 21:32; 27:1, etc.).

Augustus set the term of service in the legions at twenty years, but this was raised to twenty-five under the Flavians. He set the pay for ordinary soldiers at 225 denarii a year (Tacitus, *Annals* 1.17); Domitian raised it to 300 (Suetonius, *Domitian* 7.3). Part of the pay was held in deposit to be received on honorable discharge. In addition there were special donatives from the emperor and a substantial separation allowance. Before his enrollment the new recruit swore an oath *(sacramentum)* of loyalty that was renewed annually. Augustus's reforms were directed toward having the soldiers look to the central government and not their generals for rewards of service.

When not engaged in war, the legionaries performed many civil service functions, notably in construction and maintenance, including the Roman roads, which had the strategic function of permitting the rapid movement of troops. As in a modern army, there were many specialists, so not all of the legionaries were fighting men. A nonliteral use of the word *legions* occurs in Mark 5:9 and Matthew 26:53.

Emblems, Weapons, and Dress

The eagle *(aquila)* was the principal legionary emblem and the object of special veneration. It was silver or gold, mounted on a pole, and carried by one man. The standards, rectangular ensigns on staffs, carried the name or special emblem of the legion. A "chapel" in each camp housed the eagle and standards and statues of gods and of the emperor.

COPIES OF ROMAN STANDARDS
The emblems of the Roman legions and their use in religious
ceremonies were offensive to Jewish sensibilities about idolatry.
(© Scala/Art Resource, NY)

The main weapons of the foot soldier were the short sword and the lance
(*pilum*; John 19:34). The lance was about three and one-half feet long with an
iron point on a long stem joined to a shaft of light wood. The neck where the
tip was fastened to the shaft was left soft so as to bend easily on striking a
shield, thus preventing its being pulled out and used against the Romans and
making the shield in which it lodged unmanageable. The wooden shield was

MODEL OF ROMAN SOLDIER
A soldier's equipment included a crested helmet, breastplate,
belt with short sword, shield, and lance. *(Worms Museum)*

usually oval, covered with leather. After throwing the *pilum,* a soldier drew his sword. The long broad sword *(spatha)* was the characteristic weapon of the cavalry; it was worn on the right side, suspended from the left shoulder by a sword belt.

The tunic was girt with a military girdle with the sword attached (cf. Eph. 6:10ff.). When soldiers were in dress uniform they wore no breastplate or helmet. The breastplate or cuirass was made of bands of metal over a kilt of leather or metal-plated strips, and the helmet was of metal.

Auxiliaries

The legions were supported by *auxilia* of about equal number. The *auxilia* originated in specialized troops, such as cavalry,[2] slingers, and archers. They were normally recruited from native populations, but some units were employed in other areas. Auxiliaries served for twenty-five years and on discharge received Roman citizenship for themselves and family. This practice plus the transfer of troops did much to spread Roman culture and to mix races.

A regiment (cohort) of auxiliary troops was either five hundred or one thousand men strong and was commanded by a prefect of equestrian rank (p. 57) who was a professional soldier. The cavalry regiment was known as an *ala* and a foot regiment as a *cohors.* Auxiliaries might be attached to legions or assigned to the governor in areas of trouble where legions were not stationed. One *ala* of cavalry and five cohorts of infantry were stationed in Judea. Since legions would not normally be stationed in a province like Judea, the *cohors italica* of Acts 10:1 presumably was an auxiliary unit in spite of being associated with Italy. Where auxiliary units bore an ethnic or geographical name, this records where it was first raised but no attempt was made to preserve the original ethnic nature. In this case the name may have nothing to do with the unit's origin. Acts 21:31 and the following narrative mentions the *chiliarch* (lit. "commander of a thousand" but signifying the tribune) of the *speira* (cohort), and Acts 23:23ff. mentions some of the auxiliary troops in Judea.

Praetorian Guard

Nine or twelve cohorts of five hundred or one thousand men (at different times in the first century) formed the bodyguard of the *princeps.* Each was commanded by an equestrian with the title of tribune, and together they were commanded by the prefects of the guard, normally two in number *(praefecti praetorio).* The office of praetorian prefect was among the most important

2. Karen R. Dixon, *The Roman Cavalry* (London, 1997).

posts in Rome. The praetorian guard (Phil. 1:13) held a higher status and received higher pay than other soldiers.

Other Units

Three urban cohorts, commanded by tribunes and responsible to the city prefect *(praefectus urbi),* provided a police force and military garrison for the city of Rome. The *vigiles* were a paramilitary fire brigade and police force for Rome. Drawn from freedmen, they were organized in seven cohorts of one thousand men under tribunes and commanded by an officer of equestrian rank *(praefectus vigilum).*

Service in the navy ranked lower than legionary service and no class of naval officers was created. Augustus ordered two Italian naval bases — Misenum and Ravenna.

Bibliography

Campbell, J. B. *The Roman Army, 31 BC–AD 337: A Sourcebook.* London, 1994.

MacMullen, R. *Soldier and Civilian in the Later Roman Empire.* Cambridge, Mass., 1967.

Watson, G. R. *The Roman Soldier.* Ithaca, N.Y., 1969.

Webster, G. *The Roman Imperial Army of the First and Second Centuries A.D.* London, 1969.

Fink, Robert O. *Roman Military Records on Papyrus.* Philological Monographs of the American Philological Association, vol. 26. Cleveland, 1971.

Grant, Michael. *The Army of the Caesars.* New York, 1974.

Holder, P. A. *The Auxilia from Augustus to Trajan.* Oxford, 1980.

Saddington, D. B. *The Development of the Roman Auxiliary Forces from Caesar to Vespasian.* Harare, 1982.

Campbell, J. B. *The Emperor and the Roman Army.* Oxford, 1984.

Keppie, L. *The Making of the Roman Army, from Republic to Empire.* Totowa, N.J., 1984.

SOCIAL CLASSES

Roman society was stratified but not closed. Military service, among other things, made possible a certain upward social mobility, and the favor or disfavor of the emperor affected the standing of many families. Class or rank consciousness is very evident in the snobbery of the upper classes and in the fawning deference shown by the lower orders. The aristocracy was composed of the senatorial and equestrian orders. Ownership of land was the principal source of wealth and social standing. Nevertheless, social class was not always the same as social status. Wealth, education, and ability could confer status and influence apart from social class.

The Senatorial Order

Augustus set the roll of senatorial families at six hundred. There was a minimum property qualification of 250,000 denarii (see p. 93 for the value of a denarius) for admission to the senate. Membership in the senate was actually obtained by filling one of the principal magistracies of Rome (quaestor, praetor, consul). The sign of senatorial standing was a broad purple stripe *(latus clavus)* on the toga. It is possible to classify the senators in other ways than by the offices attained, however. In terms of birth and prestige the patricians represented the oldest nobility of Rome, ostensibly going back to the time of the kings. In addition to these were the *nobilis,* descendants of anyone who held the consulship; at the end of the Republic there were only about twelve such families. The monarchy came from two of these patrician consular families, the Julian and Claudian. Besides prestige and birth, another classification is that of wealth and education. Many noble families were impoverished, and their sons took wives from wealthy townspeople. Under the empire one could go a long way with a combination of wealth and education. And as new members of the senatorial and equestrian orders were recruited from Italy and then the provinces, proximity to Rome became another basis of pride.

Although the senate itself played little part in the government of the empire, the senatorial class was important for providing the chief civilian and military administrators. A young man of a senatorial family proceeded through a *cursus honorum* (order or sequence of positions). He started his official career, following completion of his education at about the age of twenty, with a minor post in Rome. Then followed military service as one of the six tribunes of a legion, usually spent as a staff officer to acquire military experience rather than in the field. The office of quaestor and a seat in the senate came next. Since the quaestor was a finance officer, he might be assigned to a province rather than serve in Rome itself. After a time out of office, ornamental offices might be held until the age of thirty. For some then came the office of praetor, involving judicial work. Ex-praetors became provincial governors, legionary commanders, or judges, depending on their interests and talents. A few men were rewarded with a consulship followed by governorship of a major province. Such would be the climax of a full senatorial career.

Under the empire there was a steady change in the composition of the senate as the emperors raised wealthy equestrians and plebeians, members of the Italian and provincial bourgeoisie, and finally the military aristocracy into the highest positions.

The Equestrian Order

The knights *(equites)* were a much larger group, with a property qualification of only 100,000 denarii. Their name is derived from earlier times when a man who could outfit his own horse for war was so named. The political distinction from senators was not always social or even economic. The knights were often wealthy, educated, and related to senatorial families. A few sons of knights in each generation went into the senate, and those sons of senators who chose not to follow a political career became knights.

Besides being born into the order, one could advance to the equestrian rank (signified by being placed on the roll of *equites*) through acquiring wealth or through promotion in the army. Since business and trade were considered beneath the dignity of senators, many knights amassed great wealth in these pursuits. If one had the right talents, he could become more important than if he were in the senate, and besides the senate could be expensive, boring, and dangerous if the emperor was suspicious. Among the posts open to equestrians were the following: military — as legionary tribune or commander of auxiliary detachments, of fleets at Ravenna and Misenum, or of a cavalry detachment; financial (procurators) — in management of mines or other imperial or state properties, or as finance officials in the provinces; bureaucratic and administrative (prefectures) — as secretariats of state in Rome, in command of the fire and police brigade in Rome, in charge of the food supply in Rome, in command of the praetorian guard, as governors of smaller provinces, or as governor of Egypt. The equestrian order flourished because it was less exposed to an emperor's jealousy and faced no barrier in pursuing commercial enterprises. Equestrian rank was granted rather freely in the second half of the first century. Within the order there were considerable gradations in wealth, birth, and rank according to offices held.

Municipal Aristocracies

At the top of the municipal aristocracies around the empire were the decurions, the members of the municipal senates. There were usually one hundred in the towns of the west and in the colonies or towns that copied Rome in the east. The municipal councils in the east varied in size from thirty to five hundred. Decurions had to be rich. They paid heavily for the prestige of civic magistracy and a leading role in the affairs of their community. Their benefactions included financing public buildings that would commemorate their name (temples, fountains, baths, theatres, etc.), providing food in times of emergency, and providing public entertainments. They had an economic and social reason for maintaining public order and supporting the ruling power.

Plebeians and Other Free Persons

Roman citizens who did not belong to the senatorial or equestrian orders, or in other cities those citizens who did not belong to the order of decurions, were called plebeians. When Tiberius transferred all elections to the senate, the political importance of plebeians vanished. The state policy of subsidized idleness to keep the people of Rome contented debased their position.

Besides the aristocracy at the top, free persons might be classified as citizens, residents, transients, and rural folk. *Peregrini,* citizens of any city other than Rome, to whom Rome gave special recognition, and metics, resident aliens in Greek cities who were given a recognized status distinct from other foreigners, were not properly called social classes, but occur frequently in the sources as significant in the population of larger cities and commercial centers.

Freedmen[3]

An important role in all phases of life was played by freedmen. As former slaves, they remained in a relationship with their previous owners in which there were mutual responsibilities. Circumstances determined whether the freedman remained in the household of his former owner with responsibility for part of its work or went into the world to conduct a business under a financial arrangement with his previous master. In Rome the freed slave of a citizen had citizenship. Typical Roman magistracies and priesthoods were closed to freedmen, but their sons could reach equestrian rank. Some freedmen by skill and hard work became wealthy and advanced to important positions. The vulgarities of a newly rich freedman are exaggerated in Petronius's *Satyricon.* Claudius used freedmen of his household to handle the highest bureaucratic functions of the empire. Felix, governor of Judea (Acts 23:26), was a freedman of the imperial household and brother of Palas, one of Claudius's secretaries (p. 420).

BIBLIOGRAPHY

Gagé, J. *Les classes sociales dans l'empire romain.* Paris, 1964.
MacMullen, R. *Roman Social Relations, 50 B.C. to A.D. 284.* New Haven, 1974.
Judge, E. A. *Rank and Status in the World of the Caesars and St. Paul.* Canterbury, 1982.

---

3. A. M. Duff, *Freedmen in the Early Roman Empire* (Cambridge, 1958); S. Treggiari, *Roman Freedmen during the Late Republic* (Oxford, 1969).

SLAVERY

Slavery was a basic element in ancient society. Much of the initiative as well as the work done belonged to this class. Slavery was very extensive in both the Hellenistic and Roman periods, as the large number of prisoners of war made slaves cheap in Hellenistic Greece and republican Rome. However, the stable conditions of the early empire made home-bred slaves the main source of supply, an expensive procedure. Nonetheless it is estimated that one in five of the residents in Rome was a slave. A proposal in the senate that slaves be required to wear a distinctive dress was defeated lest the slaves learn how numerous they were (Seneca, *De clementia* 1.24.1).

The condition of slavery might result from war, piracy and brigandage, exposure of a child, sale of a child or self to pay debts, condemnation in the law courts, or birth to a slave mother. An individual acquired slaves by purchase from slave dealers, by inheritance, or by home breeding (a child took the status of the mother). Most slaves seem to have come from the eastern part of the empire, but Germans, Gauls, and Britons were important new sources in the early empire. By and large the slaves were denationalized and simply became a part of Greco-Roman civilization.

The legal status of a slave was that of a "thing." Aristotle defined a slave as "living property" (*Politics* 1.2.4-5, 1253b); "the slave is a living tool and the tool a lifeless slave" (*Nicomachean Ethics* 8.11). Varro's description is similar: slaves are "articulate instruments" (*On Agriculture* 1.17.1). The slave had no legal rights and was subject to the absolute power of the master. Slaves had no right to marry and their children belonged to the owner of the slave mother, yet slaves did form *de facto* marriages *(contubernia),* and inscriptions indicate some slaves were able to maintain family life. The Greeks defined four characteristics of freedom, which were denied to the slave: the right to be his own representative in legal matters, to protection from illegal seizure, to work where he pleased, and to freedom of movement. Of course, everything depended on the kind of master, and daily life was often better than the legal theory, especially for household slaves. There was some effort under the early empire to mitigate a master's absolute control over slaves. The increasing recognition of the slave as both property and a person brought legal ambiguities in Hellenistic and Roman times.

The work of slaves covered the entire gamut of activities in the ancient world, with few exceptions. Their circumstances varied all the way from the privileged imperial slaves *(familia Caesaris* or *Caesariani)* to the convicts sentenced to the mines. Slaves of the state, of townships, and of the emperor did the work that now falls to the civil service, including some of the highest administrative functions in the bureaucracy. Their inscriptions show that the imperial slaves were proud of their status, and rightly so for the many necessary functions they discharged. The administrative machinery of the empire developed in part from institutions of the Republic and in part from the household of the emperor. At the other end of the slave social scale were the mine workers, who had incredibly bad working conditions and long hours (Diodorus of Sicily 5.38). They were not expected to live long. In between the extremes were a multitude of varied functions: temple slaves who took care of the sacred precincts and assisted in the ceremonials of religion; agricultural slaves on the great estates of wealthy Italians; domestic slaves who tended to household affairs and cared for the children; pedagogues and teachers (see pp. 110-11); industrial slaves who were skilled craftsmen; agents of their masters in widespread business and commercial transactions (for slaves could be managers in agriculture, business, and trade as well as workmen). The practice of using slaves in responsible positions was due to the preference of free men to hire out rather than be accountable to another man and the preference of the wealthy to use a trusted slave instead of a person not accustomed to obeying orders.

Slavery seems not to have had the adverse economic consequences on free labor sometimes attributed to it. It became expensive enough that it did not replace free peasant labor on farms or depress wage rates of craftsmen. Incentives in the form of wages or commissions were given to skilled slave laborers, and owners of slaves often hired them out at the going rate for free workers in order to make a larger profit rather than undercut the free laborers.

The reference to "wages" paid to slaves introduces a curious feature of ancient slavery that was an important means by which a slave could secure freedom. The *peculium* was money or property that legally remained in the possession of the owner but was available to the slaves for their own use. Slaves could, and did, save funds allotted to their use and purchase their own freedom. The expectation of manumission was an effective incentive for good service.

A popular form of manumission was sacral manumission. The slave's freedom was purchased in a pagan temple in the name of the deity and with funds furnished to the deity by the slave (the Jewish synagogue served the same function). The deity served as an intermediary, negotiating the purchase in the place of the slave, who could not enter into a legal contract. The slave became free and the fact was recorded in the temple's records (see p. 216). Some have thought this to provide the background to the redemption language for the atonement in the New Testament, but the pertinent passages (e.g., 1 Cor. 6:19; 7:22-23; Gal. 3:13; 4:5) employ different terminology (the general words for any kind of purchase) from that employed in the inscriptions for sacral manumission.[4] It was not a "fictitious sale," and the slave did not become a slave of the deity. The same function of intermediary was served by a friend or free relative, an association, or an infor-

---

4. A. Deissmann, *Light from the Ancient East* (London, 1927), 320-34; W. L. Westermann, "The Freedman and the Slaves of God," *Proceedings of the American Philosophical Society* 92 (1948):55-64; S. Bartchy, *First-Century Slavery and 1 Corinthians 7:21* (Missoula, Mont., 1973), 121-25; K. Hopkins, *Conquerors and Slaves* (Cambridge, 1978), 149-54.

mal dinner club. Freedom for a slave could be purchased out of a common fund by a synagogue, a pagan association, and later by the church.

The most frequent form of manumission was by the master, especially in his will. It might also be done formally before a magistrate or informally before friends. Manumission was often conditional, entailing continuing responsibilities to the former owner, who remained the patron of the freedman. The freedman owed the former master reverence and gratitude, work for a specified number of days a year, and a portion of his estate at death (see below on Patron-Client Relationship).

Slaves *(douloi)* and slavery *(douleia)* are frequently mentioned in the New Testament. Most famous is the runaway slave of Philemon who is known by the common name for a slave, Onesimus ("beneficial"). Christianity gave instructions for the existing social structure (see Philem. 5-9; Col. 3:22–4:1; 1 Tim. 6:1-2; 1 Pet. 3:18ff.) but directed attention to higher concerns (1 Cor. 7:21-24). The language of a "slave of God" was unique to Jews and Christians, and Paul's use of "slave of Jesus Christ" reflected the Hebrew idea of "servant of God" more than the Greco-Roman chattel slave.

BIBLIOGRAPHY

Seneca. *On Benefits* 3.18-28. *Epistle 47*.
Dio Chrysostom. *Discourses* 10, 14, 15.
Wiedemann, T. *Greek and Roman Slavery: A Sourcebook*. Baltimore, 1981.

Coleman-Norton, P. R. "Paul and the Roman Law of Slavery." In *Studies in Roman Economic and Social History in Honor of A. C. Johnson*. Princeton, 1951. Pp. 155-77.
Westermann, W. L. *The Slave Systems of Greek and Roman Antiquity*. Philadelphia, 1955.
Weaver, P. R. C. *Familia Caesaris: A Social Study of the Emperor's Freedmen and Slaves*. Cambridge, 1972.
Bartchy, Scott. *First-Century Slavery and 1 Corinthians 7:21*. SBL Dissertation Series, vol. 11. Missoula, Mont., 1973.
Vogt, Joseph. *Ancient Slavery and the Ideal of Man*. Cambridge, Mass., 1975.
Finley, M. I. *Slavery in Classical Antiquity: Views and Controversies*. New York, 1980.
Bradley, K. R. *Slaves and Masters in the Roman Empire: A Study in Social Control*. Oxford, 1987.
Watson, Alan. *Roman Slave Law*. Baltimore, 1987.
Garlan, Yvon. *Slavery in Ancient Greece*. Ithaca, 1988.
De Ste. Croix, G. E. M. *The Class Struggle in the Ancient Greek World*. Ithaca, 1989.
Martin, D. B. *Slavery as Salvation: The Metaphor of Slavery in Pauline Christianity*. New Haven, 1990.
Llewelyn, S. R. *New Documents Illustrating Early Christianity*. Vol. 6. Macquarie, 1992. Pp. 48-81. Vol. 7. Macquarie, 1994. Pp. 163-196.
Bradley, K. R. *Slavery and Society at Rome*. Cambridge, 1994.

Harrill, J. A. *The Manumission of Slaves in Early Christianity.* Tübingen, 1995.

Garnsey, Peter. *Ideas of Slavery from Aristotle to Augustine.* Cambridge, 1996.

Callahan, Allen Dwight, Richard A. Horsley, and Abraham Smith, eds. *Slavery in Text and Interpretation, Semeia* 83/84 (1998).

Glancy, J. A. *Slavery in Early Christianity.* Oxford, 2002.

Byron, John. *Slavery Metaphors in Early Judaism and Pauline Christianity.* Tübingen, 2003.

Vogt, Joseph. *Bibliographie zur antiken Sklaverei.* Bochum: Buchhandlung Brockmeyer, n.d. [titles through 1967].

ROMAN CITIZENSHIP

The Romans through their experience of alliances in Italy gradually discovered the notion of dual citizenship and applied it to the provinces of their overseas empire. An infinitely expansible concept of citizenship became an instrument of promoting loyalty to Rome and the sign of unification of the empire within one system of law. Under the empire it became normal for provincials to make use of the citizen status without surrendering their connections with their original homes and so to break down the principle that no one could be a citizen of two cities (so Paul was a citizen of Tarsus — Acts 21:39 — and a citizen of Rome — Acts 22:26-27). Beginning with the *pax Augusta* the connection of citizenship with Italian birth and later with Latin culture was gradually loosened. Concurrently it became a "passive citizenship" in the sense that it was sought as an honor and not for its political significance.

Claudius greatly extended Roman citizenship, but probably not as indiscriminately as some of the ancient authors charged (Seneca, *Apocolocyntosis* 3); rather, he continued the steady advance of the policy begun under Caesar and Augustus. Claudius revoked the citizenship of a man who did not know Latin (Dio Cassius, *Roman History* 60.17.4), and he regarded the two languages of Greek and Latin as "our tongues" (Suetonius, *Claudius* 42.1). The requirement of a knowledge of Latin would have been hard to enforce, but the report does suggest that Claudius tied extension of citizenship to a preparation for receiving it. However, this official policy is not necessarily contradictory to Dio's further information that Claudius granted citizenship indiscriminately. He adds that subordinates allowed it to be bought, accepting bribes to include names on the list of candidates for citizenship (*Roman History* 60.17.6-8). This provides the setting in which the tribune Claudius Lysias secured his citizenship (Acts 22:25-28). It was normal on becoming a citizen to take as one's *nomen* (see p. 27) the name of one's patron or the emperor under whom one received it.

Citizenship could be obtained in the following ways: (1) birth to citizen parents — a "birth certificate" was issued certifying the citizen status; (2) manumission of slaves of citizens at Rome; (3) as a favor for special service to the empire — probably in this way Paul's family obtained it so that he was a born citizen (Acts 22:28); (4) on discharge from service in the auxiliaries or on enlistment in the legions in cases of emergency recruitment, special classes of the preceding.

The privileges and advantages of citizenship included the following: (1) voting — but one had to be in Rome to exercise this right, and there was a grant of citizenship "without the franchise"; (2) freedom from degrading forms of punishment, such as scourging (Acts 16:22ff.; 22:25ff.; cf. Cicero, *Against Verres* 2.5.161-70) — the traditions of the different kinds of death experienced by Peter and Paul reflect their different status, the former by crucifixion upside down and the latter by beheading[5] (a swifter and therefore considered a more merciful form of execution suitable for citizens); (3) right of appeal to Rome and thus exemption from ultimate jurisdiction of the local authorities and the Roman governor (which privilege Paul exercised; Acts 25:10-12).[6] Under the Republic citizenship had carried certain duties, especially the possibility of military service, but under the principate such duties were increasingly severed from citizenship.

The Flavians and Antonines continued the policy of extending citizenship. Whereas in the first century the initiative was normally with the emperor, in the second century cities and not individuals petitioned for citizenship. By the second century, too, the content of citizenship had been reduced as concerns public duties and honors. The status of a Roman citizen was more a matter of honor and titular distinction, carrying no special privileges and leaving a man in daily life and with local duties where he was, although it still brought men directly into the sphere of Roman law with the right of appeal. The *Constitutio Antoniana* of Caracalla (212) climaxed the development by giving citizenship to all the free inhabitants of the empire. The dominant motive was the majesty of Rome, but its effect was to strip citizenship of any specific content.

BIBLIOGRAPHY

Sherwin-White, A. N. *The Roman Citizenship.* Oxford, 1939.
Cadbury, H. J. *The Book of Acts in History.* New York, 1955. Pp. 65-82.
Sherwin-White, A. N. *Roman Society and Roman Law in the New Testament.* Oxford, 1963. Lecture 7.

ROMAN LAW

The Roman law is a subject of such magnitude and technicality that we cannot adequately introduce it here; we will mention only some aspects of its working that are relevant for early Christian history.

5. Eusebius, *Church History* 2.25.5.
6. A. H. M. Jones, "I Appeal to Caesar," in *Studies in Roman Government and Law* (Oxford, 1960), 53-65.

The sources of Roman law were the following:[7] laws and statutes enacted by vote of assembly of the people (the last one in A.D. 97); resolutions of the senate (*senatus consulta* — under the Republic they lacked the force of law but from Augustus onward became a means of development of law); edicts of magistrates (governors and praetors); constitutions of emperors (*edicta* — saying what must be done, *decreta* — judicial decisions in lawsuits, *rescripta* — responses to requests or an embassy, and *mandata* — instructions issued to officials); and replies of jurists when consulted. Of course, usage or custom provided an unwritten source of law. Imperial decisions may have died with the emperor who issued them, especially those emanating from emperors whose memory was condemned by the senate *(damnatio memoriae)*, such as Nero and Domitian, unless they were explicitly renewed by his successor. Since law, however, is built up by precedents, such decisions often served as guides to later judges. During the second century and later, jurists began to collect and organize the laws, judicial decisions, and other components of the legal system in a way to guide future officials. Some of these important jurists were Salvius Julianus (second century), Gaius (second century),[8] and Ulpian (early third century). This activity reached its climax in the great codes of Theodosius[9] and Justinian[10] in the fifth and sixth centuries.

The Roman provincial governors (of all ranks) held the *imperium*, which gave them almost unlimited power of life and death over provincials, restricted only by the laws against extortion and treason. Only the holder of the *imperium* could impose the death sentence, and the governor could not delegate this power (John 18:31 agrees with this, but cf. p. 569). The governor was accountable only to the emperor and senate. The administration of justice was highly personal, and cases were heard wherever the governor was.

Major offenses were defined in a number of detailed statutes that prescribed procedures and punishments. These laws together constituted the *ordo judiciorum publicorum*, which was binding in Rome. The many crimes not covered in the *ordo*, those *extra ordinem*, were left to the jurisdiction of magistrates in the exercise of their *imperium*. Public law in Rome and Italy did not apply automatically in the provinces, where Roman officials were not bound to follow the *ordo*, even in crimes it covered. For these and other crimes they might

7. See Cicero, *Topica* 28, and Gaius, *Institutes* 1.2.

8. W. M. Gordon and O. F. Robinson, tr. and int., *The Institutes of Gaius* (Ithaca, 1988).

9. C. Pharr, *The Theodosian Code and Novels, and the Sirmondian Constitutions* (Princeton, 1952); J. Harries and I. Wood, eds., *The Theodosian Code* (Ithaca, N.Y., 1995); John F. Matthews, *Laying Down the Law: A Study of the Theodosian Code* (New Haven, 2000).

10. Th. Mommsen, P. Krueger, and A. Wilson, *The Digest of Justinian*, 4 vols. (Philadelphia, 1985); R. W. Lee, *The Elements of Roman Law with a Translation of the Institutes of Justinian* (4th ed.; London, 1956); J. A. C. Thomas, *The Institutes of Justinian: Text, Translation, and Commentary* (Amsterdam, 1975); Peter Berks and Grant McLeod, tr. and int., *Justinian's Institutes* (Ithaca, 1987); Alan Watson, ed. of English translation, *The Digest of Justinian*, rev. ed. (Philadelphia, 1998).

(or might not) follow the precedents of their predecessors or local customs. This personal dispensing of justice was known as *cognitio* (judicial examination or inquiry). Many areas of minor jurisdiction were left to local courts; Roman officials became involved mainly in matters affecting public order (e.g., Acts 18:12-16; 19:40; 21:31ff.). A Roman governor by virtue of his *imperium* could enforce public order at his own discretion without reference to specific legislation (the power of *coercitio*). Otherwise, the laws and legal customs of local peoples remained in force.

According to the normal working of things, the judicial process was initiated by the drawing up of charges and penalties and the formal act of accusation *(delatio)* by an interested party. The Roman system had no public prosecutor or inquisitorial initiative. Apart from manifest offenders, enforcement of the law depended on private initiative, hence the place for a *delator,* a private prosecutor. An illustration would be the role of Jewish officials in the trial of Jesus; their deliberations (the Jewish "trial") would have been to determine what charges could be sustained before the Roman governor. The accuser could proceed with the prosecution, or the magistrate could conduct an inquisitorial examination. The case would be heard by the responsible magistrate in person seated on his tribunal (Gk. *bēma;* cf. John 19:13; Acts 18:12), perhaps assisted by his council *(consilium)* of friends and officials. The principle of the accused meeting the accusers face to face (Acts 25:16) is confirmed in Appian, *Civil War* 3.54 and *Digest* 48.17.1. The magistrate took whatever action he deemed just and proper. As a safeguard against abuse of the system of *delatio,* the law provided for *calumnia,* by which a person bringing a false charge was subject to the same punishment he sought against the accused.

Neither the praetor nor governor was necessarily a legal expert, hence the importance of those "learned in the law" *(iuris prudentes)* for consultation. Nor were there professional lawyers; those who pleaded a case were rhetoricians (as was Tertullus in Acts 24:1-8, a *rhētōr*).

One practice recognized by Roman law and common in Roman society was used by Paul to express an important theological principle — adoption (Gal. 4:5; Rom. 8:15, 23; 9:4; Eph. 1:5).[11] Adoption was far more frequent and important in Roman society than it is today. The person adopted (at any age) was taken out of his previous condition, all old debts were cancelled, and he started a new life in the relation of sonship to the new *paterfamilias,* whose family name he took and to whose inheritance he was entitled. The new father now owned the adoptee's property, controlled his personal relationships, and

---

11. Francis Lyall, "Roman Law in the Writings of Paul — Adoption," *JBL* 88 (1969):458-66; A. Watson, *The Law of Succession in the Late Roman Republic* (Oxford, 1971); James M. Scott, *Adoption as Sons of God: An Exegetical Investigation into the Background of* ΥΙΟΘΕΣΙΑ *in the Pauline Corpus* (Tübingen, 1992) (review in *JTS,* n.s. 44[1993]:288ff.).

had the right of discipline, while assuming responsibility for his support and liability for his actions — all just as with natural children born into the home. Adoption was a legal act, attested by witnesses.

BIBLIOGRAPHY

Lawson, F. H. *The Roman Law Reader*. Dobbs Ferry, N.Y., 1969.

Wolff, H. J. *Roman Law: An Historical Introduction*. Norman, Okla., 1951.

Berger, A. *Encyclopedic Dictionary of Roman Law*. Transactions of the American Philosophical Society 43. Philadelphia, 1953. Pp. 333-808.

Jolowicz, H. F. *Historical Introduction to the Study of Roman Law*. 2d ed. Cambridge, 1954.

Sherwin-White, A. N. *Roman Society and Roman Law in the New Testament*. Oxford, 1963.

Buckland, W. W. *A Textbook of Roman Law*. 3d ed. Cambridge, 1963.

Kunkel, W. *An Introduction to Roman Legal and Constitutional History*. Oxford, 1966.

Crook, John. *Law and Life of Rome*. Ithaca, N.Y., 1967.

Daube, D. *Roman Law: Linguistic, Social, and Philosophical Aspects*. Edinburgh, 1969.

Watson, Alan. *The Law of the Ancient Romans*. Dallas, 1970.

Sampley, J. Paul. *Pauline Partnership in Christ: Christian Community and Commitment in the Light of Roman Law*. Philadelphia, 1980.

Lyall, Francis. *Slaves, Citizens, Sons: Legal Metaphors in the Epistles*. Grand Rapids, 1984.

Watson, Alan. *The State, Law, and Religion: Pagan Rome*. Athens, Ga., 1992.

Tellegen-Couperus, Olga. *A Short History of Roman Law*. London, 1993.

Robinson, O. G. *The Sources of Roman Law: Problems and Methods for Ancient Historians*. London, 1997.

SOCIAL RELATIONSHIPS

Much current study of the New Testament focusses on insights sociology and anthropology bring to the study of ancient texts. A few of these topics are presented here. Family relationships receive separate treatment below.

BIBLIOGRAPHY

Malina, B. J. *The New Testament World: Insights from Cultural Anthropology*. Rev. ed. Louisville, 1993.

Elliott, J. H. *Social-Scientific Criticism of the New Testament*. London, 1995.

Stegemann, Ekkehard W. and Wolfgang Stegemann. *The Jesus Movement: A Social History of Its First Century*. Minneapolis, 1999.

deSilva, David A. *Honor, Patronage, Kinship and Purity: Unlocking New Testament Culture.* Downers Grove, Ill., 2000.

Patron-Client Relationship

Recent studies have emphasized the importance of patronage in Roman society.[12] Patronage was a reciprocal relationship, in which both patron and client had duties to each other, was a personal and not a business or commercial relationship, existed between parties of different status, and was a voluntary (not a legal) relationship that could be initiated by either party, but the social conventions were stronger than any regulations of law. A regular code of etiquette governed the duty *(obsequium)* of a client to the patron. The client appeared daily at early morning at the house of the patron to offer salutations and requests. The client was responsible for assisting the patron in political and private life and for showing respect by walking in the funeral procession. The patron's importance was gauged by the number who attended the morning audience. Since a status symbol was the number of clients attending a person, there was an incentive to free slaves who as freedmen became one's clients. The patron's role was to give a small dole of gifts or money. The patron rendered assistance in need, welcomed the client from time to time to his house and table, and offered legal protection as needed. The relationship operated on all levels and in various groupings: between former masters and freedmen, rich and poor, generals and conquered peoples, aristocrats and *collegia* or clubs. Everyone from slave to aristocrat felt bound to display respect to someone more powerful than himself, up to the emperor.

In addition to social relations, there was literary patronage (support of an author by a wealthy person), political patronage ("client" kings — p. 45), and economic patronage (of the rural poor).

Phoebe, the servant of the church at Cenchreae, is described as a patroness (Rom. 16:2), one who gives aid and who had the resources to do so.[13]

Friendship

The interactions between patrons and clients and between members of a household (pp. 72-76) represented the principal vertical relationships in soci-

---

12. R. P. Saller, *Personal Patronage under the Early Empire* (Cambridge, 1982); F. W. Danker, *Benefactor: Epigraphic Study of a Graeco-Roman and New Testament Semantic Field* (St. Louis, 1982); A. Wallace-Hadrill, ed., *Patronage in Ancient Society* (London, 1989); B. W. Winter, *Seek the Welfare of the City: Christians as Benefactors and Citizens* (Grand Rapids, 1994). Relevant ancient literary sources include Cicero, *On Duties* and Seneca, *On Benefits.*

13. R. A. Kearsley, "Women in Public Life in the Roman East: Iunia Theodora, Claudia Metrodora, and Phoebe, Benefactress of Paul," *Tyndale Bulletin* 50 (1999):189-211.

ety; friendship was the ideal horizontal relationship.[14] Many philosophers and others wrote treatises on friendship: for example, Aristotle (*Nicomachean Ethics* 8 and 9), Cicero *(Laelius: On Friendship)*, Plutarch (*How to Tell a Flatterer from a Friend* and *On Having Many Friends* [*Moralia* 48E-74E; 93A-97B]), and Lucian *(Toxaris)*. Friendship was the glue for Epicurean communities (p. 377).

Friendship was the ideal for social relationships. The ideal called for considering all things as common property and sharing one mind or one soul. Friends held mutual love and kindly affection for each other. Such a relationship allowed for mutual exhortation and frankness of speech. Signs of true friendship were a willingness to share the other's troubles and to sacrifice self for the other's benefit. Such ethical ideals were readily adapted to mutual relations in the Christian communities.[15]

Friendship applied to those who were basically social equals, but after Aristotle's time friendship language was also used by patrons for their clients and benefactors for their beneficiaries.

Social Networks[16]

Identity groups in the ancient world were formed by neighborhoods, ethnic groups, cities of origin when away from home, associations, occupations, and religious cults. It helped for these groups to have well-connected patrons (sponsors). Social networks developed from kinship, intermarriage, membership in the same clubs, common social status such as holding high offices, and neighborhood and regional connections. The Roman equivalent of "God and country" was "gods, state, and family."

Conversion to Christianity often depended not on ideological appeal alone but also on social ties between individuals. Kinship, friendship, and patronage provided important social contacts for the expansion by Christianity and other religions.[17]

---

14. John T. Fitzgerald, ed., *Friendship, Flattery, and Frankness of Speech: Studies on Friendship in the New Testament World* (Leiden, 1996); idem, ed., *Greco-Roman Perspectives on Friendship* (Atlanta, 1997).

15. L. M. White, "Morality Between Two Worlds: A Paradigm of Friendship in Philippians," in David L. Balch et al., eds., *Greeks, Romans, and Christians: Essays in Honor of Abraham J. Malherbe* (Minneapolis, 1990), 201-15.

16. L. Michael White, ed., *Social Networks in the Early Christian Environment: Issues and Methods for Social History, Semeia* 56 (1992).

17. This section depends on L. Michael White, "Prolegomena: Social Networks and Social History" and "Social Networks: Theoretical Orientation and Historical Applications," *Semeia* 56 (1992):3-22, 23-36.

Honor and Shame

Classical culture was a shame culture as distinct from a guilt culture. In general the standard was public opinion. This continued to be the situation in the first-century Mediterranean world, although the presence of many different cultures within the Roman empire broke down the uniformity of standards of conduct that had once prevailed within smaller cultural units. Seneca expressed the fundamental viewpoint: "The one firm conviction from which we move to the proof of other points is this: that which is honorable is held dear for no other reason than because it is honorable" (*On Benefits* 4.16.2). It is typical for the moral teachers to judge conduct with the words honorable and dishonorable more often than as right and wrong[18]

Honor and shame were group categories. An individual's behavior was judged according to what brought honor or shame on the social group (family, city, cult, or association). The virtues that preserved the order and stability of the society were rewarded with honor, but actions that threatened the values of the community brought reproach, insult, or punishment, depending on their seriousness.

Honor came to a person because of birth (family or ancestry), adoption by a person of high status, or wealth. It might be achieved by such things as acts of courage, benevolence, or just dealings with others — whatever was deemed honorable in the culture. Shame came from conduct that "was not done" in the society.

In those matters where Jews and Christians did not share the values of the dominant Greco-Roman culture, they might emphasize their own group values as the standard of reference for their members (including the favor of God as the reason for their conduct) and provide their own means of honoring or shaming individuals.

SOCIAL MORALITY

Several features of the social organization contributed to the debasing of morality. Slavery gave occasion for cruelty and sexual license. The punishment of criminals, notably through sentencing to the mines and execution by crucifixion, showed the brutality of the times. The gladiatorial contests and wild beast fights, discussed below, reflect a brutal and cruel outlook. The Roman policy of "bread and games" to keep the populace content prevented initiative and emphasized sensual satisfactions.

18. For this section, see David A. deSilva, *Honor, Patronage, Kinship, and Purity: Unlocking New Testament Culture* (Downers Grove, Ill., 2000), 23-93.

Paul's judgment on Gentile morality in Romans 1:18-32 finds considerable confirmation in other sources of the time. Both Jewish and Christian writers agreed that the Greco-Roman world was characterized by moral corruption. The Jewish apologists said that the low morality sprang from idolatry.[19] Sex sins were prevalent, and nearly all of the catalogs of sins in the New Testament have many synonyms for licentiousness (e.g., 1 Cor. 6:9; Gal. 5:19; Col. 3:5). The numerous words in the Greek language for sexual relations suggest a preoccupation with this aspect of life.[20] Homosexuality was a common result in Greek society, which considered the noblest form of love to be friendship between men. Some of the greatest names in Greek philosophy regarded it as not inferior to heterosexual love, but it was practiced primarily among males between their early teens and early twenties.[21] All kinds of immoralities were associated with the gods. Not only was prostitution a recognized institution, but through the influence of the fertility cults of Asia Minor, Syria, and Phoenicia it became a part of the religious rites at certain temples. Thus there were one thousand "sacred prostitutes" at the temple of Aphrodite at Corinth.[22] Dio Chrysostom (*Discourse* 7.133-37) is the only Gentile author known to have attacked brothels on moral grounds.

Much of the confirmation for the dismal picture of Roman morality comes from the writings of Martial and Juvenal in the late first and early second century A.D. They undoubtedly found elements in society doing those things they talked about, and Martial's salaciousness appealed to his readers. On the other hand, they were satirists, especially Juvenal, who expected to find readers who appreciated the caricature. So their evidence points both ways. Paul himself corrects a one-sided understanding of his condemnation by pointing to the moral sense and ethical theories of the Gentiles in Romans 2:12-16. Some of the philosophers did attain high levels in their moral and ethical teaching, and we will consider this in the chapter on philosophy.

Inscriptions on grave monuments have been an important source for giving a just estimate of moral virtue in the ancient world. Whereas Martial and Juvenal reflect a particular upper-class viewpoint, the grave inscriptions provide a broader perspective. The praises of the kindness and faithfulness of husbands and wives in these records are a reminder that many people lived lives of quiet virtue. Not all were given to the sexual sins that appear to have been so prominent in the society.

19. Wisdom of Solomon 13–15.

20. On sexual morality see Epictetus, *Enchiridion* 33.8.

21. J. Kenneth Dover, *Greek Homosexuality* (London, 1989); Craig A. Williams, *Roman Homosexuality: Ideologies of Masculinity in Classical Antiquity* (Oxford, 1999).

22. Strabo 8.6.20, referring to classical times; 8.6.21 on Roman times only mentions a "small temple of Aphrodite." It is possible that the statement about classical times is incorrect, arising from Strabo's misunderstanding information about the dedication of figurines to Aphrodite as a reference to women who served at her temple.

Rhetoric and popular philosophy inculcated public duties according to one's responsibilities to different groups in society. [Ps.] Plutarch, in *The Education of Children* 10 (*Moralia* 7E), for instance, outlines "how a man must bear himself in his relations with the gods, with his parents, with his elders, with the laws, with foreigners, with rulers, with friends, with women, with children, with slaves."[23] Quite frequent was the grouping of duties in three pairs: husbands-wives, parents-children, and masters-slaves.[24] One may compare the pattern of instruction in the household codes of the New Testament (Eph. 5:21–6:9; Col. 3:18–4:1; Titus 2:2-10; 3:1; 1 Pet. 2:16–3:7) and early Christian literature (Polycarp, *Philippians* 4-6).[25]

That moral instruction came from philosophers and teachers is a reflection of the separation of religion and ethics in Greco-Roman paganism. Cultus had little to do with morality except in cases of grave offense, and priests did not function as moral guides. This distinction between religion and morality, strange to those of the Judeo-Christian heritage, will be seen further in the chapter on Hellenistic religions (p. 177).

BIBLIOGRAPHY

Plutarch. *Dialogue on Love*. Expresses various viewpoints among the Greeks on sexual love, both hetero- and homosexual, ending with praise of marital love.

Pleket, G. W. *Epigraphica*. Part 2. Textus Minores 41. Texts on the Social History of the Greek World. Leiden, 1969.

Malherbe, A. J. *Moral Exhortation: A Greco-Roman Sourcebook*. Philadelphia, 1986.

Ferguson, John. *Moral Values in the Ancient World*. London, 1958.

Flaceliere, Robert. *Love in Ancient Greece*. London, 1962.

Pearson, L. *Popular Ethics in Ancient Greece*. Stanford, 1962.

Lindsay, Jack. *The Ancient World: Manners and Morals*. New York, 1968.

Den Boer, W. *Private Morality in Greece and Rome*. Leiden, 1979.

Meeks, Wayne. *The Moral World of the First Christians*. Philadelphia, 1986.

Edwards, Catharine. *The Politics of Immorality in Ancient Rome*. Cambridge, 1990.

McGinn, Thomas A. J. *Prostitution, Sexuality, and the Law in Ancient Rome*. Oxford, 1998.

---

23. Cf. Hierocles (second century A.D.), *On Duties*, treated with relation to gods, country, parents, brothers, kinsfolk, and wives (household and marriage). English translation in A. J. Malherbe, *Moral Exhortation: A Greco-Roman Sourcebook* (Philadelphia, 1986), 85-104.

24. Aristotle, *Politics* 1.2.1-2, 1253b; 1.5.1-2, 1259a-b; *Nicomachean Ethics* 8.10.1161b; Seneca, *Epistle* 94.1; Dionysius of Halicarnassus, *Roman Antiquities* 2.25.4-5; 26.1-3; 27.1-2; Arius Didymus, *Epitome*, in Stobaeus 2.148, 16-19; 149, 5-8 (Wachsmuth).

25. James E. Crouch, *The Origin and Intention of the Colossian Haustafel* (Göttingen, 1972); David L. Balch, *Let Wives Be Submissive: The Domestic Code in 1 Peter* (Chico, Calif., 1981). A survey of scholarship on the household codes by David Balch is found in David Aune, ed., *Greco-Roman Literature and the New Testament* (Atlanta, 1988), pp. 25-50.

Marriage and Family

The family unit could take various forms but might include in addition to husband, wife, and children (and their spouses if married), other relatives, slaves, and sometimes freedmen and other clients. The family was the basic unit of society in all of the cultures that provide the background for early Christianity. The family was united by common religious observances (see Chap. 3, esp. pp. 178ff.) as well as by economic interdependence. In Rome the father as head of the family convened a family *consilium,* which might include close family advisers, to deliberate and decide important cases.

Greek law required that marriage be preceded by a betrothal agreement. A father's pledge of his daughter to a prospective bridegroom was formal with witnesses on both sides and her dowry agreed upon. In Rome by the end of the

VASE DEPICTING GREEK WEDDING, 5th c. B.C.
The lower register shows the departure of the couple for the groom's house, the central element in the ceremony, while a man above throws away a sandal as a good omen. *(National Archaeological Museum, Athens)*

FRAGMENT OF SARCOPHAGUS WITH SCENE OF
ROMAN BETROTHAL OR WEDDING, 2d c. A.D.
The couple join hands, the man holds a scroll (the marriage contract),
and the goddess Juno (between the couple) unites them. *(British Museum)*

Republic this betrothal became a looser system — an informal business arrangement in writing before witnesses, which was easily renounced by either
party and did not necessarily lead to marriage. The dowry was considered the
daughter's share of the parental estate.

Under the Roman Republic three forms of marriage brought a woman
under the power (*manus,* hand) of her husband: *confarreatio* (a religious

ceremony and the most solemn and elaborate form), *coemptio* (a sale of the woman to her husband), and *usus* (living together uninterruptedly in the man's house for one year). There was also marriage without *manus,* based on mutual consent. In this case the woman remained a part of her father's family instead of entering the husband's. This became practically the only type of marriage under the empire. The *Digest* of Justinian attributes to the third-century jurist Modestus the following definition: "Marriage is the union of a man and a woman, a partnership for life involving divine as well as human law."

The bride was prepared for the wedding by a bath and clad with special garments (cf. Eph. 5:26-27; Rev. 21:2). The ceremony included the placing of crowns (wreaths) on the heads of both bride and groom. Essentially, the wedding in Greece and Rome was the conducting of the bride in a torchlight procession to the bridegroom's house. This scene is the way a marriage is depicted on classical Greek vases. In the formal Roman marriage ceremony the couple clasped hands, formulas of marriage were pronounced, and the marriage contract was read before witnesses and signed by them. This scene, in which the goddess Juno appears between the couple to unite them, appears in Roman representations of a wedding. After this and the wedding meal the bride was formally removed from the arms of her mother, escorted to the new home, and carried over the threshold. As is typical, Greek art focuses on the dramatic and Roman art on the legal aspect of the wedding.

Jewish marriages according to rabbinic sources show many formal similarities to the Greek and Roman practices. The marriage was a contract between families. It was effected in two stages: the betrothal (or "acquisition" of the bride) and the wedding proper (taking the bride into the husband's home). The betrothal had the legal force of marriage and could be broken only by divorce (cf. Matt. 1:18-19). It was accomplished by the bridegroom paying the bride-price (or a part of it) or delivering a deed. The customary written contract *(ketubah)* included the husband's duties to his wife and the sum due her in the event of a divorce or his death. The bridegroom moving into his father-in-law's house to live with the bride without further ceremony was also recognized but discouraged in rabbinic writings. The wedding ceremony was held under a canopy *(huppah)*. The bride was prepared by bathing, anointing, and clothing with special adornments. She was then escorted from her father's house to the accompaniment of song, dance, musical instruments, and (since usually in the evening) torchlight. The essential element of the wedding was the introduction of the bride into the groom's house, where the *huppah* was set up. Seven blessings were pronounced on the couple and the marriage contract was read, followed by seven days of festivity.

Consent to live together constituted marriage in all societies, and the procreation of children was its explicit object. Marriages were registered in order to make the children legitimate.[26] Girls were normally married young, in their early teens;[27] men much later, Greek men in particular about thirty.[28] Jewish men, however, were expected to marry at eighteen (Aboth 5.21, quoted on p. 112).[29] Jewish religious teachers praised marriage, and it was considered the normal state of human life. Frequent was the saying, "He who has no wife lives without joy, blessing, or good."[30]

The prevailing type of marriage in Jewish, Greek, and Roman society was monogamous. Extramarital sexual relations, however, were readily available (at least in Greek and Roman circles), with prostitution and adultery common. Moreover, since consent was necessary for the marriage, the withdrawal of consent made divorce easy. We know more about the practice of the upper classes, but the indication is that the privilege of divorce was often exercised. Divorce required little formality. A simple oral or written notice was sufficient, by one or both parties. In Rome and Greece, by the first century, the marriage could be terminated by the woman as well as by the man, unlike the situation in Jewish law where the right of divorce belonged only to the husband (cf. Mark 10:11-12 with Matt. 5:32). (See p. 518 for the dispute in Judaism over justifiable causes for divorce.) Marriage contracts from Egypt allowed the wife to divorce her husband for his sexual misconduct. Under Augustus the divorce was witnessed and brought within recognition of the law. The dowry could be a deterrent to divorce, for it returned to the woman in case of a divorce. In all societies of the ancient world, in case of divorce any children went with the father, for they belonged to the father (except for slaves — see above).

Augustus in 19/18 B.C. had legislation passed bringing the family under the laws of the state. His aim, directed at the upper classes, was not to regulate public morals but to increase the birthrate through encouraging marriage and stable family life. Men between twenty-five and sixty and women between twenty and fifty were given every encouragement to be married, and special benefits were offered to the fathers and mothers of three or more children. Bachelors were limited in the inheritances they could receive; penalties were placed on the childless; and widowed and divorced women were required to remarry within stipulated times. Jurisdiction in cases of adultery was taken from the family and became the responsibility of a public court. The wronged hus-

26. The third-century Roman jurist Ulpian declared, "It is not consummation but consent which makes marriages" (Justinian, *Digest* 35.1.15).

27. Roman girls typically were married at 12–15; see M. K. Hopkins, "The Age of Roman Girls at Marriage," *Population Studies* 18 (1964/1965):309-27 argues Roman girls typically were married at 12-15; but Brent D. Shaw, "The Age of Roman Girls at Marriage: A Reconsideration," *JRS* 77 (1987):30-46 revises his arguments.

28. Hesiod, *Works and Days* 696-98; this remains the Greek custom.

29. 1QSa i.10 puts the age at 20.

30. *Genesis Rabbah* 17.2; b. Yebamoth 63a; *Midrash Psalms* 59; quoted in H. Montefiore and R. Loewe, eds., *A Rabbinic Anthology* (repr.; Cleveland, 1963), nos. 1430, 1432, 1437.

band had to divorce his wife before witnesses and then bring a prosecution against her within sixty days. If he did not divorce her, she was immune from prosecution, but a member of the public could prosecute the husband. If he failed to prosecute the woman after the divorce, a member of the public could prosecute her. If adultery was proved, the wife and her lover were banished to different islands for life. The law did not allow the woman to prosecute her husband for his infidelities; adultery was (in the eyes of the law) possible only for a man with a married woman. A man could be prosecuted by another man, however, for a liaison with an unmarried girl (unless she was a registered prostitute or a recognized concubine) or a widow and for homosexuality. The law probably did not improve morals, although it did increase blackmail. The grant of imperial exemptions minimized the effect on the birthrate.

BIBLIOGRAPHY

Plutarch. *Advice to Bride and Groom* (*Moralia* 138Bff.). Sarah Pomeroy, ed., *Plutarch's Advice to the Bride and Groom and A Consolation to His Wife: English Translations, Commentary, Interpretive Essays, and a Bibliography.* Oxford, 1999.

Plutarch. *On Brotherly Love* (*Moralia* 478-492) and *On Affection for Offspring* (*Moralia* 493-497).

Mishnah tractate Kiddushin.

Gardner, Jane, and Thomas Wiedemann. *The Roman Household: A Sourcebook.* London, 1991.

Rawson, B. "Family Life among the Lower Classes at Rome in the First Two Centuries of the Empire." *Classical Philology* 61 (1966):71-83.

Lacey, W. K. *The Family in Classical Greece.* Ithaca, N.Y., 1968.

Rawson, B., ed. *The Family in Ancient Rome: New Perspectives.* Ithaca, N.Y., 1986.

Dixon, Suzanne. *The Roman Mother.* Norman, Okla., 1988.

Wiedemann, Thomas. *Adults and Children in the Roman Empire.* New Haven, 1989.

Bradley, K. R. *Discovering the Roman Family: Studies in Roman Social History.* Oxford, 1991.

Keener, Craig. *And Marries Another: Divorce and Remarriage in the Teaching of the New Testament.* Peabody, Mass., 1991.

Rawson, B., ed. *Marriage, Divorce, and Children in Ancient Rome.* Oxford, 1991.

Treggiari, Susan. *Roman Marriage: Iusti Coniuges from the Time of Cicero to the Time of Ulpian.* Oxford, 1991.

Dixon, Suzanne. *The Roman Family.* Baltimore, 1992.

Llewelyn, S. R. *New Documents Illustrating Early Christianity.* Vol. 6. Macquarie, 1992. Pp. 1-47.

Barton, Stephen C. *Discipleship and Family Ties in Mark and Matthew.* Cambridge, 1994.

Deming, Will. *Paul on Marriage and Celibacy: The Hellenistic Background of 1 Corinthians 7.* Cambridge, 1995.

Rawson, B., and Paul Weaver, eds. *The Roman Family in Italy: Status, Sentiment, Space.* Oxford, 1997.

Osiek, Carolyn, and David Balch. *Families in the New Testament World: Households and House Churches.* Louisville, 1997.

Pomeroy, Sarah B. *Families in Classical and Hellenistic Greece: Representations and Realities.* Oxford, 1997.

Gardner, Jane. *Family and Familia in Roman Law and Life.* Oxford, 1998.

Patterson, Cynthia B. *The Family in Greek History.* Cambridge, Mass., 1998.

Balch, David, and Carolyn Osiek, eds. *Early Christian Families in Context: An Interdisciplinary Approach.* Grand Rapids, 2003.

Epstein, L. M. *The Jewish Marriage Contract.* New York, 1927.

Epstein, L. M. *Marriage Laws in the Bible and Talmud.* Cambridge, Mass., 1942.

Epstein, L. M. *Sex Laws and Customs in Judaism.* New York, 1948. Reprint, 1967.

Kahana, K. *The Theory of Marriage in Jewish Law.* Leiden, 1966.

Feldman, D. M. *Marital Relations . . . in Jewish Law.* New York, 1968.

Friedman, M. A. *Jewish Marriage in Palestine.* New York, 1980.

Cohen, Shaye J. D., ed. *The Jewish Family in Antiquity.* Atlanta, 1993.

Place of Women

Although the picture of classical Greek women kept in seclusion has been overdrawn, their sphere was definitely the home. The degree of their confinement resulted from the importance of not allowing any suspicion to fall on young girls or wives in order to protect the legitimacy of children. A separate part of the house was designated the "women's quarters" and was off-limits to others. Women managed the household, and in that sphere they were supreme. The description of the place of women in the Pastoral Epistles matches very closely the Greek conception (note esp. 1 Tim. 5:14; Titus 2:3-5).

In an oft-quoted statement, Apollodorus (mid–fourth century B.C.) describes the situation: "We have courtesans *[hetairai]* for pleasure, handmaidens for the day-to-day care of the body, wives to bear legitimate children and to be a trusted guardian of things in the house" ([Ps.] Demosthenes 59.122). The *hetairai* (lit., female companions) were not simply prostitutes, but many were.[31] They provided companionship and entertainment for men at dinner parties, which wives did not attend. Their entertainment might be musical, acrobatic, conversational (some were well educated and cultured), as well as sexual. Slave girls were kept in well-to-do homes for various household functions. The wife was to bear legitimate children, but she was also trusted with the

---

31. A male satirist's view of their life and attitudes is found in Lucian's *Dialogues of the Courtesans.*

management of affairs in the husband's absence and in this capacity often carried great influence.

Macedonian women had greater independence and importance in public affairs. This coincides with the greater prominence that women held in the Macedonian churches (notice esp. the women associated with the Philippian church — Acts 16:14-15; Phil. 4:2-3). Under the influence of the Macedonian princesses women came to have greater freedom in the Hellenistic age.

The old Roman ideal was for women to pass from subjection of father to husband. "Never, while their men survive, is feminine subjection shaken off; and they themselves abhor the freedom which the loss of husbands and fathers produces" (Livy 34.1.12). Nevertheless, the Roman woman from the first enjoyed a higher status than the Athenian woman. "Roman history supplies a picture of women attaining gradually more and more liberty, higher legal status, and greater power and influence."[32] Women from noble families in the first century came to excel in vice and immorality as well.

Jewish women were not as restricted in public appearance as Greek women but did not have the freedom of first-century Roman women. The Jewish woman was the mistress of the home, but was not qualified to appear as a witness in court and was exempt from fulfilling religious duties that had to be performed at stated times (because her first duties were to her children and the home and she might not be in the required state of ritual purity). The prayer from the Jewish prayer book often cited as evidence of Jewish misogyny, "Blessed art thou, O Lord our God, who has not made me a woman," must be understood in this context as referring to woman's inability to fulfill all the commands of the law, which was the highest privilege recognized by rabbinic Judaism. It must be balanced by many statements in rabbinic literature giving a positive estimate of women.[33] Household duties of the Jewish woman included grinding flour, cooking, laundry, making beds, and spinning wool. She was supposed to maintain an attractive appearance for her husband. The husband was required to provide her with food and clothing, maintain regular sexual relations (cf. 1 Cor. 7:5), provide for the children, and was forbidden to strike her. The woman's influence in the family was considered greater than the man's.

The modern interest in women's studies has brought to the surface much information, directed attention to women's concerns, and has begun to tell history from women's perspectives. The life of women was often difficult because of unequal treatment. The exposure of female babies, malnutrition due to inadequate diet, and childbearing at an immature age meant women's life expectancy was shorter than men's with the result that there were smaller numbers of women in the society. This in turn, by the first century, led some to be more considerate of women.

32. C. T. Seltman, *Women in Antiquity* (New York, 1956), 174.
33. See, for example, the references in note 22.

Women in the early Roman empire in practice were more prominent than some ancient texts would indicate. Wealth and social position made some women patrons and gave them considerable power and influence apart from the social theory of the time. Many others as well acted with great independence. Women frequently held civic offices. Especially in religion were women prominent, often serving as priestesses and doing so not only in cults of female deities. Women, moreover, were found in a wide variety of occupations. In addition to expected roles — wives, mothers, prostitutes, midwives, wet nurses — they are found as physicians, musicians, artists, winners of athletic events, selling groceries, and in all sorts of manufacturing and commercial activities. Virtues of women commended in inscriptions and literature included being chaste, loyal to the husband, hardworking, able to manage the household, and training the children. A son eulogized his mother as follows:

> My dearest mother deserved greater praise than all others, since in modesty, propriety, chastity, obedience, woolworking, industry, and honor she was on an equal level with other good women, nor did she take second place to any woman in virtue, work, and wisdom in times of danger.[34]

BIBLIOGRAPHY

Lefkowitz, M. R., and M. Fant. *Women's Life in Greece and Rome.* Baltimore, 1983; 2d ed., 1992.

Rowlandson, Jane, ed. *Women and Society in Greek and Roman Egypt: A Sourcebook.* Cambridge, 1998.

Kraemer, Ross S. *Women's Religions in the Greco-Roman World: A Sourcebook.* Oxford, 2003.

Epstein, L. M. *Sex Laws and Customs in Judaism.* New York, 1948.

Loewe, Raphael. *The Position of Women in Judaism.* London, 1966.

Meiselman, Moshe. *Jewish Woman in Jewish Law.* Library of Jewish Law and Ethics, vol. 6. New York, 1978.

Wegner, R. R. *Chattel or Person? The Status of Women in the Mishnah.* Oxford, 1988.

Archer, L. J. *Her Price is Beyond Rubies: The Jewish Woman in Graeco-Roman Palestine.* Sheffield, 1990.

Levine, A.-J., ed. *"Women Like This": New Perspectives on Jewish Women in the Greco-Roman World.* Atlanta, 1991.

Ilan, Tal. *Jewish Women in Greco-Roman Palestine.* Peabody, 1996.

Ilan, Tal. *Integrating Women into Second Temple History.* Peabody, 2001.

Baldson, J. V. D. *Roman Women.* Rev. ed. London, 1974.

Pomeroy, Sarah B. *Goddesses, Wives, Whores, and Slaves: Women in Classical Antiquity.* New York, 1975.

34. *Corpus Inscriptionum Latinarum* 6.10230, Augustan period. Trans. in M. R. Lefkowitz and M. B. Fant, *Women's Life in Greece and Rome* (Baltimore, 1983), 136.

Balch, David L. *Let Wives Be Submissive: The Domestic Code in 1 Peter.* Chico, Calif., 1981.

Cameron, A., and A. Kuhrt, eds. *Images of Women in Antiquity.* Detroit, 1983.

Pomeroy, Sarah B. *Women in Hellenistic Egypt.* New York, 1984.

Gardner, Jane F. *Women in Roman Law and Society.* Bloomington, Ind., 1986.

Cantarella, E. *Pandora's Daughters: The Role and Status of Women in Greek and Roman Antiquity.* Baltimore, 1987.

Waithe, M. E. *A History of Women Philosophers.* Vol. 1: *Ancient Women Philosophers, 600 B.C.–500 A.D.* Dordrecht, 1987.

Dixon, Suzanne. *The Roman Mother.* Norman, Okla., 1988.

Pantel, P. S., ed. *From Ancient Goddesses to Christian Saints.* Vol. I of *A History of Women in the West,* ed. G. Duby and M. Perrot. Cambridge, Mass., 1992.

Kraemer, Ross S. *Her Share of the Blessings: Women's Religions among Pagans, Jews, and Christians in the Greco-Roman World.* Oxford, 1992.

Osburn, Carroll D., ed. *Essays on Women in Earliest Christianity,* Vol. 1. Joplin, Mo., 1993. Chap. 3 — Gregory E. Sterling, "Women in the Hellenistic and Roman Worlds (323 BCE–138 CE)," pp. 41-92, and Chap. 4 — Randall D. Chesnutt, "Jewish Women in the Greco-Roman Era," pp. 93-130.

Demand, Nancy. *Birth, Death, and Motherhood in Classical Greece.* Baltimore, 1994.

Fantham, Elaine, et al. *Women in the Classical World: Image and Text.* Oxford, 1994.

Blundell, Sue. *Women in Ancient Greece.* Cambridge, Mass., 1995. (Classical times)

Goodwater, Leanna. *Women in Antiquity: An Annotated Bibliography.* Metuchen, N.J., 1975.

Children

The dominant fact about children in the ancient world was their high mortality rate. They were regarded as important for the security of the community and of their parents. The Romans viewed children as particularly vulnerable, physically and mentally weak. Puberty was commonly regarded as bringing not only physical changes but also the ability to reason; modern parents tend to draw the opposite conclusion about adolescence. The decisive dividing line between childhood and adulthood (and the most important social event) was marriage for a girl and being registered as a citizen (at seventeen) for a boy. Little attention is given in the literature to the separate personality of children, even as in much of the art they are treated as little adults. When under the empire the formal distinction between child and adult lessened, educational attainments became the criterion for distinguishing the child and the adult. Childhood (including play activities) was viewed primarily as a preparation and training for adult life.

The Hellenistic world lived under the shadow of too many mouths to feed. This fact meant that many children were abandoned, exposed to die.[35] W. W. Tarn has presented evidence that from 230 B.C. onward the one-child family was commonest in Greece.[36] Families of four or five children were very rare. There was a certain desire for two sons, in case one should die or be killed, but seldom did families raise more than one daughter. A daughter was an economic liability, because a dowry had to be supplied at her marriage. The first child of a marriage, if healthy, was almost never exposed.

The answer to overpopulation was infanticide. Abortions were often attempted, but not infrequently were fatal to the mother; they were made illegal under Septimius Severus. More frequent was the exposure of the newborn child. The unwanted child was simply left to die on the trash heap or in some isolated place. Sometimes slave traders would take the child to be reared in slavery. Girl babies might be taken to be reared for a life of prostitution (see Justin, *Apology* 1.27). Infanticide was not viewed in the same moral light by Greeks and Romans as it was by Jews and Christians. The modern debate on abortion has raised anew the question of when human life is a person entitled to the protection of the law: at conception (the traditional Judeo-Christian view), with the ability to live outside the womb (the view sanctioned by the U.S. Supreme Court), or at birth (the view of many people). The Greeks and Romans put that moment even later. The newborn was not considered a part of the family until acknowledged by the father as his child and received into the family in a religious ceremony.[37] Thus, they did not consider exposure murder but the refusal to admit to society. Jewish law, on the other hand, prohibited abortion and exposure,[38] a position adopted also by Christians.[39] Otherwise no moral voice was raised against infanticide until Musonius Rufus and Epictetus. In the second century the city of Thebes made the practice illegal, perhaps the only people except the Jews to do so until Christianity intervened.

A papyrus from Egypt, notable for its date (1 B.C.) as well as for its contents, illustrates the pagan attitude. Hilarion writes from Alexandria to his wife Alis at home in the interior:

> I beg and entreat you, take care of the little one, and as soon as we receive our pay I will send it up to you. If by chance you bear a child, if it is a boy, let it be, if it is a girl, expose it.[40] (*P. Oxy.* 744)

---

35. H. Bennett, "Exposure of Infants in Ancient Rome," *Classical Journal* 18 (1923):341; A. Cameron, "The Exposure of Children and Greek Ethics," *Classical Review* 46 (1932):105-14.

36. W. W. Tarn, *Hellenistic Civilization* (repr.; Cleveland, 1961), 100-103.

37. H. J. Rose, *Religion in Greece and Rome* (New York, 1959), 30-31, 189-90.

38. On abortion, see Josephus, *Against Apion* 2.202; b. Sanhedrin 57b. On exposure, see Philo, *Special Laws* 3.110-19; *Virtues* 131-32; *Sibylline Oracles* 3.765; Tacitus, *Histories* 5.5.

39. *Didache* 2:2; Justin, *Apology* 1.27; *Epistle to Diognetus* 5; Athenagoras, *Plea* 35; Minucius Felix, *Octavius* 30-31.

40. For the word cf. also Acts 7:19, 21.

Even apart from such practices, miscarriages were common and infant mortality was extremely common. If a newborn survived infancy, there was a good prospect of a long life, but life expectancy in the ancient world was much lower than in modern times largely because of the high infant mortality rate.

ECONOMIC LIFE

The subject of economic conditions in the Roman world is too large and complex for an adequate sketch here. Even the standard syntheses given in the bibliography are in need of correction and supplementation, so that only specialists have a command of the subject. Fortunately, this subject does not enter directly into the understanding of early Christianity (although obviously providing an important part of the larger background), so we will attempt only a few generalizations, along with a characterization of Palestine and the lands adjacent to it. We will then treat in some detail three aspects of economic life significant for our purposes: one for its influence on the development and spread of Christianity — travel — and two for their bearing on the interpretation of certain passages — coinage and taxation.

The olive, the vine, grain, and sheep were the basis of the agricultural economy of the Mediterranean world. The food supply of Rome under the early empire increasingly came from Egypt and Africa.

There was no large industry in the ancient world, and the major limitation on its economic development was the absence of a technology for mass production. The traditional industries continued — notably ceramics (which

ROMAN GLASS
Blown glass was developed commercially about the beginning of the
Christian era and provided an alternative to pottery for many household vessels.
(© Erich Lessing/Art Resource, NY)

AGORA, Ephesus
Commercial and political life of Greek and Roman cities
centered around the marketplace of the forum.

in the mid–first century saw the rise of *terra sigillata* from Gaul as a rival to the more expensive Aventine ware), mining (esp. lead, silver, and iron), textiles (wool and silk), and small handicrafts. One new industry emerged near the beginning of New Testament times — blown glass. Glass had been in use for centuries, but the technique of glass-blowing was not invented until the first century B.C., probably in Phoenicia. It provided cheap glass products in abundance, and soon Italian manufacturers took the lead in producing glass products, fragments of which show up in archaeological finds with regularity.

Those with money could invest in commercial enterprises, although interest rates were high by modern standards. Invested funds made possible the extensive trade noted in the next section.

Mediterranean cities were built around a marketplace (Gk. *agora*, Lat. *forum*). In those cities influenced by Hellenistic town-planning the marketplace was a large open area, rectangular in shape, given over to public monuments and statues. It was surrounded by a covered porch *(stoa)*, which had shops and offices behind. Life then, as now, in Mediterranean countries was lived mostly outdoors, and the town marketplace was the center of life — a marketplace of conversation and ideas as well as of economic activities (cf. Acts 17:17).

RECONSTRUCTED STOA OF ATTALUS, Agora, Athens
Attalus II, king of Pergamum (159–138 B.C.), built this stoa as a gift to Athens on
the east side of the Agora. Reconstructed by the American School of Classical
Studies, it houses the Agora Museum.

Pausanias identified the attributes of a city *(polis)* as offices for magistrates, gymnasium, theater, public fountain, and agora (10.4.1); contrast the Jewish requirements (p. 571).

The Hellenistic and Roman periods present a startling contrast between the low wages paid the poor and the great liberality of the rich. The wealthy would give to public works and respond to needs in time of crisis, but they would not pay adequate wages. Public benefactions memorialized the name of the giver in a way that high wages did not. The general indications are of prosperity after Augustus, reaching a climax in the early second century. But not all regions shared equally in this prosperity: the provinces of Asia and Africa flourished more than others. The cities of Asia particularly seem to have prospered under the Roman peace, and in their gratitude they were foremost in promoting the imperial cult.

The land of Egypt under the Ptolemies was divided into two categories: king's land in the narrower sense of land in hand, and king's land in grant. The latter fell into four classes: temple lands — the king cultivated and allotted what produce was required to the temple; cleruch land — assigned to military settlers, originally mercenaries with Greeks predominating; gift land — extensive estates conferred on officials; and "private land" — house and garden cultivated by peasants. Every parcel of land in Egypt contributed a fixed amount to the king as a first charge. In the event of a poor crop the loss fell on the cultivator alone, the allotted amount of tax having to be paid regardless. Many staples were royal monopolies — olive oil, papyrus, mines, and quarries; those businesses that were not, paid for licenses or rendered a part of their product to the king. It is no wonder that the dynasty acquired great wealth. Ptolemaic Egypt was a thoroughgoing system of state nationalization. The registration and supervision were thorough, requiring a whole army of administrative and financial officials. In regard to the native population, the basis of the system was that each man had his "own place," which he could not leave except by official permission.

The land within the Seleucid empire fell into three categories: king's land, temple land, and city land. The Seleucids fought the temporal power of the priest-kings in the temple states. They adhered to a percentage system of taxation and never amassed the wealth the Ptolemies did. On the whole the Seleucid territories were better governed from the standpoint of the people than was Egypt.

Palestine in the first century was less prosperous than some other regions, but Josephus tries to present the country as quite productive. He accurately depicts the Jewish population there as primarily engaged in agriculture:

> Ours is not a maritime country; neither commerce nor the intercourse with the outside world has any attraction for us. Our cities are built inland, remote from the sea; and we devote ourselves to the cultivation of the productive country with which we are blessed. (*Against Apion* 1.60, trans. from Loeb Classical Library)

The chief products of Palestine were the staples of olives, wine, and cereals (wheat and barley). The Jordan valley was noted for its groves of date palms and balsam trees. Sheep and goats, but few cattle, were raised, and fishing was common where it was possible. The parables and teaching of Jesus give an accurate portrayal of the life of the common people in Palestine.

Bibliography

Grant, F. C. *The Economic Background of the Gospels.* Oxford, 1926.
Frank, Tenney, ed. *Economic Survey of Ancient Rome.* 6 vols. Baltimore, 1933–1940.
Rostovtzeff, M. I. *Social and Economic History of the Roman Empire.* 2 vols. Oxford, 1957.
Rostovtzeff, M. I. *Social and Economic History of the Hellenistic World.* 3 vols. 7th ed. Oxford, 1986.
Giardina, Andrea, ed. *The Romans.* Chicago, 1993. (Includes article on occupations.)

Trade and Travel

Epictetus exclaimed, "Caesar has obtained for us a profound peace. There are neither wars nor battles, nor great robberies nor piracies, but we may travel at all hours, and sail from east to west" (*Discourses* 3.13.9).

Trade flourished under the empire. Roman ships and overland traders reached India, Ceylon, and China. The quantity and extent of trade is staggering to those who do not realize the highly developed commercial activity of ancient times. Revelation 18:11-13 provides a thorough list of the goods transported over the Roman trade routes.

During the Hellenistic age the island of Delos in the Aegean, sacred to Apollo and Artemis (who were born there), was the principal port between Rome and the east, with (among other things) a flourishing slave market. After the destruction of Delos by Mithridates in 88 B.C. commercial activity centered at Puteoli, Italy (cf. Acts 28:13). After Trajan deepened and enlarged the harbor of the Claudian port at Ostia, it began to replace Puteoli as the principal port for Rome. Excavations at Ostia, a site in some ways more informative than the more popularly known Pompeii, have greatly enlarged the knowledge of commercial activity under the empire.

The principal trade routes of the Roman world may best be studied from a map.[41] There were four main lines of communication between Rome and the eastern Mediterranean, the first two primarily by sea and the other two pri-

---

41. E.g., *Westminster Historical Atlas to the Bible,* ed. G. E. Wright and F. V. Filson (rev. ed.; Philadelphia, 1956), Plate XIII; W. M. Ramsay, "Roads and Travel (in N.T.)," *A Dictionary of the Bible,* ed. James Hastings, Extra Volume (New York, 1909), between pp. 384 and 385.

marily by land: (1) the sea route from Ostia or Puteoli to Alexandria, which was used by the merchant ships taking advantage of the prevailing westerly winds on the Mediterranean as they went to Egypt to pick up grain; (2) by land on the Appian Way to Brundisium and then by ship to Corinth and beyond; (3) the same as (2) to Corinth and then to Ephesus and from there by land to the interior; (4) by land to Brundisium, across the Adriatic to Dyrrachium, and then by the Egnatian Way across Macedonia, crossing to Asia at the Hellespont or Bosporus and continuing by land. Each of these routes could be reversed except the first; the prevailing westerly winds forced ships going from east to west to take a more circuitous route, staying close to shore, as represented by the route described in Acts 27:1-8. The route most frequented by travelers and most important in the early history of Christianity was (3), the great central route that made Ephesus and Corinth such significant transit points and so places from which Christianity radiated to other areas. Antioch and Alexandria were the great commercial centers of the east, the point of contact for Syria and Egypt respectively with the Roman world.

Travel followed the trade routes. Sea travel was dangerous but frequent. There was a literary convention among classical authors to speak against travel, especially by sea, but there is an abundance of evidence of contrary practice. Merchants obviously traveled: an inscription from the second century A.D. records that a man from Hierapolis in Phrygia sailed around the southern coast of Greece seventy-two times on journeys to Italy.[42] So also did the military, government officials, and all sorts of other people. Sea transportation was mainly on the commercial cargo vessels, but travelers were always able to find a ship to carry them in any direction along the coasts of the Mediterranean, as we can see from Paul's experience. Most of the ships stayed close to land and coasted from port to port (cf. Paul's travels in Acts 20:13-15; 21:1-8; 27:2ff.), although large grain ships did take to the open sea, especially when they could catch the winds in the direction of their destination. Since Egypt was the principal granary for Rome in the first century, Alexandrian grain ships often were on the seas between Egypt and Italy (Acts 27:6; 28:11). Sea travel was fairly cheap: from Alexandria to Athens was only two drachmae for a family. But there was no life or accident insurance, and the fare did not include meals. Any cabin accommodations were exclusively for the crew. On the local routes the ships did not normally sail at night, and passengers would sleep in port or on the beach. Sailing was normally suspended during the winter (Acts 27:9-12; cf. 2 Tim. 4:13), from about November 10 to March 10, and the only really "safe" season was between May 26 and September 14. In order to maintain the grain supply in Rome the emperor Claudius guaranteed a profit and insurance against loss by storm for traders bringing grain to Rome in winter, and that may account for the willingness of the captain and shipowner in Acts 27:11-12

---

42. *Inscriptiones Graecae* 4.841 (CIG 3920).

to take the risk involved in reaching a better harbor for the winter. The narrative in Acts 27–28 and Lucian, *The Ship or the Wishes* 1-15 are principal sources on sea travel in the early empire.[43] The Roman peace and suppression of piracy gave greater safety to sea travel.

The Roman contribution to land travel was a more positive one. The estimated fifty-three thousand miles of Roman roads from Scotland to the Euphrates had a strategic and communications value for Rome and her army, but commerce and travel over these roads had an incalculable cultural impact of far greater significance. The remains of the Roman roads testify to the permanence of their construction. The bridges on these roads were great achievements as well, and some of them still bear traffic. Although the people preferred land travel to sea travel, it was not free from its own dangers — bad weather in winter and robbers in the more remote districts (2 Cor. 11:26)[44] — but it was more reliable.

Of the many Roman roads two well-known ones are definitely connected with New Testament narratives. The Via Appia ran south from Rome to Capua and angled across Italy to Tarentum and Brundisium on the Adriatic coast. Begun in 312 B.C., it was considered by Rome's historians as the city's oldest road. Although in rough condition, stretches of the Appian Way are still in use. It was the route on which Paul's party made their approach to Rome from Puteoli (Acts 28:15-16). The Via Egnatia was begun c. 145 B.C., soon after Macedonia was conquered. It ran from Dyrrachium on the west coast of Greece (modern Albania) to Neapolis on the northeast coast and eventually to Byzantium. Roman armies moved across it in the struggles between Caesar and Pompey and between Octavian and the forces of Brutus and Cassius. Roman roads were named for their builders or their destination, and an inscription confirms that this road takes its name from the proconsul of Macedonia. It would have been the route taken by Paul from Neapolis to Philippi, Amphipolis, Apollonia, and Thessalonica (Acts 16:12; 17:1). He left the road when he was smuggled off to Beroea (Acts 17:10) rather than follow it on to Pella and the west.

Paul's mission activity at Derbe, Iconium, and Pisidian Antioch was on the main Roman road that led from Antioch of Syria and Tarsus to Apamea, Laodicea, and Ephesus (Acts 13:14, 51; 14:20-21; 15:41–16:2). Troas (Acts 20:5-6; 16:11; 2 Cor. 2:12; Ignatius, *Polycarp* 8) was important to sea traffic through the Dardanelles between the Aegean and Black Seas and to land traffic between Asia and Macedonia (usually shortened by sea between Troas and Neapolis; Acts 16:11).

The traveler was not so fortunate in the accommodations for the night

---

43. See James Smith, *The Voyage and Shipwreck of St. Paul* (4th ed., repr.; Grand Rapids, 1978).

44. On the difficulties of travel cf. Apuleius, *Florida* 21.

EGNATIAN WAY, Philippi
The Egnatian Way was the main Roman road across Macedonia.
It runs alongside the forum at Philippi and is paralleled by a modern highway.
Note the chariot ruts in the stone.

as he was in the quality of the roads on which he traveled by day. Not that inns were lacking, but their reputation (in quality and morals) was notorious. The wine was often adulterated (or after the patron was drunk on good wine, bad was substituted), sleeping quarters were filthy and insect and rodent infested, innkeepers were extortionate, thieves were in wait, government spies were listening, and many were nothing more than brothels. The literary complaints are supplemented by the graffiti from taverns in Pompeii (kissing, gambling, and fighting). There were some excellent inns in Italy, but they seem to have been the exception. The upper classes avoided the public accommodations and stayed with friends when they traveled. The moral dangers at the inns made hospitality an important virtue in early Christianity. Hospitality occupies a prominent place in Christian literature (Rom. 16:23; 1 Pet. 4:9; 2 John 10; 3 John 5-8; Heb. 13:2; 1 Clement 10–12; *Didache* 11–13) because of the needs of missionaries and messengers of the churches and other Christians who happened to be traveling. The churches provided an extended family, giving lodging and assistance for the journey. Christians here followed and expanded a Jewish practice of caring for their own away from home (cf. Mark 6:10). Many synagogues had guest rooms attached for the use of Jews on a journey.[45]

All in all, there was more frequent and easier travel during the Roman empire than at any other period of human history before the nineteenth century.

BIBLIOGRAPHY

Charlesworth, M. P. *Trade-Routes and Commerce of the Roman Empire.* 2d rev. ed., 1926. Reprint. New York, 1970.

Von Hagen, V. W. *The Roads that Led to Rome.* London, 1967.

Chevallier, Raymond. *Roman Roads.* Berkeley, 1976.

Casson, L. *Ancient Trade and Society.* Detroit, 1984.

Casson, L. *Ships and Seamanship in the Ancient World.* Princeton, 1986.

Casson, Lionel. *Travel in the Ancient World.* Rev. ed. Baltimore, 1994.

Coinage

Herodotus (1.94) attributed the invention of gold and silver coinage to the Lydians. Archaeological evidence shows that coinage made its appearance in western Asia Minor in the seventh century B.C. — lumps of metal stamped to guarantee weight and quality. The first coins that can be localized with greater accuracy were issued by the Lydian kings from Sardis around 600 B.C. They were staters (the most common surviving denomination is one-third of a stater) of electrum, which was found in Lydia as a natural alloy. Croesus replaced electrum with gold and silver staters and made changes in the animals stamped on the coin. After 516 Persian coins were issued: the gold stater is the daric (Ezra 8:27, etc.); silver is the siglos.

The first Athenian coins were struck in silver about 580 B.C. Athens doubled the old stater, creating a new standard coin, the tetradrachm. About 525 the silver Athenian "owls" were introduced: a helmeted head of Athena on the obverse and her owl on the reverse with the first three letters of the city's name. During Athens' fifth-century hegemony the Athenian "owls" became the most popular coins of the Aegean, still impressive prizes of numismatic collections at major museums. Mythological scenes of gods and heroes were the most common representations and for a long time the only motif on Greek coins.

Alexander the Great had an extensive coinage. The obverse of his stater has a helmeted Athena and the reverse a Victory. His tetradrachm used the head of a young Heracles (from whom the Macedonian kings traced their descent) on the obverse and a seated Zeus on the reverse. In literature Alexander was presented as

---

45. As mentioned in the inscription of Theodotus quoted on p. 575 and found in excavated synagogues at Ostia, Stobi, Khirbet Shema, Hamat Tiberias, etc.

a new Heracles, and in legend he was the son of Zeus by his mother Olympias. At least an allusion to Alexander in person evidently was intended by the appearance of Heracles, even though this hero was common on Greek coins before this time. Alexander's successors at first kept his types but added their own names. Then they put idealized heads of the deified Alexander with the ram's horns, the emblem of the Egyptian god Ammon (see p. 205), on the obverse of their coins. After taking the title *basileus* ("king"), some of Alexander's successors began to put their own heads on their coins. Whereas images of human beings cannot be found on Greek coins before Alexander, they are not uncommon outside of the Greek world. Persian coins had an image symbolizing the idea of kingship, and the fifth-century satraps put their own portraits on coins. The prancing horseman on the coins of Alexander's father, Philip II, is a symbolic portrait of the king. Since previously only deities and heroes had appeared on the obverse of Greek coins, the individual portrait introduced into the Hellenistic world by Alexander's successors is evidence of the developing ruler cult of the Hellenistic monarchs, which will be considered more fully in the next chapter.

Nearly as popular as gods and heroes were sacred animals — the "bee" and "stag" of Artemis on the coins of Ephesus, the winged Pegasus at Corinth, the eagle of Zeus, etc. Sometimes the coins give us the appearance of temples and other data useful in historical reconstruction.

If there was any coinage in use in early Rome, it was rough lumps of bronze of irregular weight and without any mark of value. By the beginning of the third century B.C. appeared a series of bronze bars with roughly regulated weight and devices on both sides. Then came bronze pieces in circular form with a mark of value. The earliest coinage proper begins in 269 B.C., silver didrachms in imitation of Greek coins. About 211 B.C. Rome introduced a new silver coinage, the denarius (equal to ten bronze asses) and the sestertius (two and a half asses), which were to remain standard coins for Roman currency.

A special issue of gold coins struck in Greece in honor of Flamininus, who defeated Philip V of Macedon in 197 B.C., are the first coins to carry a portrait of a living Roman. Julius Caesar was the first politician in his lifetime to be portrayed in Rome. The troubles of the late Republic provided a setting for regularly portraying and honoring living men and current events. Under the Second Triumvirate the tendency for the obverse to have a portrait and a title became almost a rule whereas types for the reverse achieved even greater variety.

Rulers used coins for propaganda purposes, making known the government policies and ideology or commemorating significant events. In the absence of modern means of communication this was the most effective way of reaching the largest number of people with the messages the government wanted to convey. From the time of Caligula the emperor's titles as well as portrait appear on the obverse of principal coins. From Claudius the reverses not only proclaim achievements of the emperor but make members of his family known and emphasize the emperor's qualities and policies by the personification of virtues.

Since the titles provide a closely dated sequence for the coins and because of the events commemorated on the various issues, Roman coins have become an exceedingly valuable historical source. Numismatics provides important information about the culture and official ideology of the Roman world.

The currency needs of Palestine were supplied in the fifth and fourth centuries B.C. by Persian coinage and after Alexander by that of its Hellenistic rulers. The shekel of the Old Testament was a designation of weight, only later a coin. It is unresolved whether Jewish coinage began with John Hyrcanus I (134–104 B.C.), Aristobulus (104–103 B.C.), or Alexander Jannaeus (103–76 B.C.), probably not earlier. (Coins previously attributed to Simon, Hyrcanus's predecessor, are now recognized as belonging to the Jewish revolt against Rome.) Alexander Jannaeus put his name and title in Greek on the reverse with a Hebrew inscription on the obverse. The Hasmoneans avoided images and pagan symbols and used the cornucopia, anchor, and pomegranate on their coins. The Herodian kings used Greek inscriptions, and Agrippa I and Agrippa II even put their own likenesses on some coins intended for their non-Jewish areas. Local mints in Palestine issued only bronze coins; the imperial mints issued gold and silver coins. The "thirty pieces of silver" from the temple treasury (Matt. 26:15) would have been tetradrachms from Antioch or Tyre, accepted as equivalent to the shekel. The Phoenician mint did not follow the Athenian standard, as did other mints in the Hellenistic Age; their heavier staters were accepted as equivalent to "holy shekels" by the Jews. The silver shekels issued during the Jewish revolt have a chalice on them, bronze coins the lulab and ethrog; other symbols are pomegranates, amphora, vine, or palm tree, the emphasis being on the temple and the annual festivals. Rome commemorated the suppresion of the revolt by issuing coins inscribed "Judaea capta." A tetradrachm of the second revolt has the Tabernacle and Ark of the Covenant. A cluster of grapes was a prominent symbol on coins of Bar Kokhbah, as were musical instruments, in addition to types known from the first revolt. Legends on the coins of both revolts proclaimed "freedom" and "redemption."

Matthew 10:9 lists the metals used in coins in the order of their value in New Testament times — gold, silver, and copper (bronze). A comparative chart of the value of Roman and Greek coins with the New Testament references to them will permit the reader to see the force of certain passages. The fluctuating value of currencies and changes in purchasing power make it unprofitable to give equivalents in modern currency (but see n. 47 below).

The "tribute money" of Matthew 22:19 would have been the silver denarius, many of which have been found. The obverse has the head of the emperor wearing a wreath and the inscription "Augustus Tiberius Caesar, son of the deified Augustus." The reverse depicts a seated female (Livia, Tiberius's mother, as pax or Roma?) with the inscription "Pontifex Maximus." Such coins were a daily reminder to subject peoples that in return for Roman peace and prosperity they owed taxes.

Roman Currency		Greek Currency		Jewish
quadrans	[bronze]	= 2 lepta (Mark 12:42)[46]		
4 quadrans =	1 as (assarion — Matt. 10:29; Luke 12:6)			
2 semis	= 1 as			
2 asses	= 1 dupondius			
4 asses	= 1 sestertius [silver; bronze under empire]			
16 asses	= 1 denarius [silver] (Matt. 20:2; 22:19; Rev. 6:6)[47]	6 obols	= 1 drachma (Luke 15:8)	
		= 4 drachmae (tetra-drachm)	= 1 stater (Matt. 17:24-27; 26:15; Exod. 30:13)[48]	= 1 shekel
25 denarii	= 1 aureus [gold]	100 drachmae	= 1 mna (Luke 19:13)	
240 aurei	= 1 talent	6,000 drachmae =	1 talent (Matt. 25:14ff.;[49] 18:23-35)[50]	

46. Note the exceedingly small amount of the gift. The lepton was the smallest coin in value in circulation. Two lepta together did not equal the value of a sparrow (Matt. 10:29).

47. The denarius represented an average pay for a day laborer according to the parable of Matt. 20:1-15. Cf. Tobit 5:14 for a drachma a day and Tacitus, *Annals* 1.17, for a soldier's pay as less than a denarius a day. The denarius and the drachma, the basic silver coins of the Romans and Greeks respectively, were roughly equivalent in value.

48. The didrachm is equivalent to the half-shekel, but note that the Septuagint took the didrachm as equal to the shekel; Exod. 30:13. See p. 530.

49. The mna and talent were sums of money and not coins. Note that the talent in Matt. 25 is a sum of money, not one's abilities.

50. Realizing the value of the sums of money involved makes this parable a powerful teaching on the "debt" to God in relation to "debts" of others to us and on the value of forgiveness. Cf. Josephus, *Ant.* 17.11.4 (318-30), on the value of the talent.

DENARIUS OF TIBERIUS

Tiberius was emperor during the ministry of Jesus, and such a coin as this would have been the "tribute money" of Matt. 22:19. *(British Museum)*

Bibliography

Carson, R. A. G. *Coins — Ancient, Medieval, and Modern.* Vol. 1, *Coins of Greece and Rome.* 2d ed. London, 1970.

Oster, Richard E. "Numismatic Windows into the Social World of Early Christianity: A Methodological Inquiry." *JBL* 101 (1982): 195-223.

Casey, P. J. *Understanding Ancient Coins: An Introduction for Archaeologists and Historians.* Norman, Okla., 1986.

Kreitzer, Larry J. *Striking New Images: Roman Imperial Coinage and the New Testament World.* Journal for the Study of the New Testament, Supplement 134. Sheffield, 1996.

Hill, G. F. *Catalogue of the Greek Coins of Palestine in the British Museum.* London, 1914. Reprint. Bologna, 1965.

Kraay, C. M., and Max Hirmer. *Greek Coins.* London, 1966.

Jenkins, G. K. *Ancient Greek Coins.* The World of Numismatics. London, 1972.

Davis, N., and C. M. Kraay. *The Hellenistic Kingdoms: Portrait Coins and History.* London, 1973.

Mattingly, H., and E. A. Sydenham. *Roman Imperial Coinage.* Vol. II. *Vespasian to Hadrian.* London, 1926.

Sutherland, C. H. V. *Coinage in Roman Imperial Policy. 31 b.c.–a.d. 68.* London, 1951.

Breglia, L., and R. B. Bandinelli. *Roman Imperial Coins.* London, 1968.

Crawford, M. *Roman Republican Coinage.* 2 vols. Cambridge, 1974.

Sutherland, C. H. V. *Roman Coins.* The World of Numismatics. London, 1974.

Sutherland, C. H. V. *The Emperor and the Coinage: Julio Claudian Studies.* London, 1976.

Sears, D. R. *Greek Imperial Coins and Their Values: The Local Coinages of the Roman Empire.* London, 1982.

Sutherland, C. H. V. *Roman History and Coinage, 44 B.C. – A.D. 69.* Oxford, 1987.

Sutherland, C. H. V. *Roman Imperial Coinage.* Vol. I. *31 B.C.-A.D. 69.* London, 1984.

Burnett, Andrew. *Coinage in the Roman World.* London, 1987.

Reifenberg, R. *Israel's History in Coins from the Maccabees to the Roman Conquest.* London, 1953.

Kadman, L. *Corpus numorum Palaestinensium.* Jerusalem, 1956–.

Mayer, L. A. *A Bibliography of Jewish Numismatics.* Jerusalem, 1966.

Meshorer, Y. *Jewish Coins of the Second Temple Period.* Tel Aviv, 1967.

Rosenberg, M. *City-Coins of Palestine and the Coinage of Eastern Palestine.* 4 vols. Jerusalem, 1972–1978.

Meshorer, Y. *Ancient Jewish Coinage.* 2 vols. Dix Hills, N.Y., 1982.

Taxation

Augustus undertook to acquire an exact knowledge of the resources of the empire through a periodic census (cf. Luke 2:1) similar to but distinct from that of Roman citizens under the Republic. He also did excellent work in supervising tax collection and trying to make taxation equitable.

Direct taxes, *tributa*, were collected by the governor of a province and his staff. The main tax in every province was the *tributum soli*, a tax on agricultural produce paid by those who occupied the land; owners of other forms of property were liable to a *tributum capitis* (a head tax; cf. *kensos* or *census* in Matt. 17:25; 22:19). Of indirect taxes, *vectigalia* (cf. *telos* in Matt. 17:25), the frontier dues *(portoria)* were the most important. They were collected solely for revenue, not to control production or trade. The *publicani*, contractors employed to collect indirect taxes, agreed to furnish a certain sum to the government; amounts collected above this sum were the profit of the tax-raisers. This system of collecting taxes — paying Rome for the privilege of collecting — encouraged corruption under the Republic.[51]

The translation of the *telōnai* ("tax collectors") in the Gospels as "publicans" has confused them with the Roman tax-raisers.[52] Augustus began the gradual suppression of the tax-raisers by taking direct taxes out of their hands. The Roman *publicani* came from the class of knights and had been financial masters of the empire. The *telōnai* in the east, in contrast, were local men of wealth and influence who contracted with their city or district to

---

51. E. Badian, *Publicans and Sinners: Private Enterprise in the Service of the Roman Republic* (Oxford, 1972).

52. Fritz Herrenbrück, *Jesus und die Zöllner: Historische und neutestamentlichexegetische Untersuchungen* (Tübingen, 1990).

gather the taxes it paid to Rome. It seems that, as in Egypt, the Palestinian *telōnai* were not the actual collectors and had no authority to compel payment but took the matter up with officials. Zacchaeus's words in Luke 19:8, "bring false charges," suggests he could be an informer to the officials but could not on his own authority imprison or confiscate property. These men may have been paid on a percentage basis. The *telōnai's* morals were neither better nor worse than other businessmen's. The contemptuous references to them is due more to their equivocal position between their fellow-Jews and the Romans and nationalistic feeling than to any general estimate of them as dishonest. The *telōnai* met by name in the Gospels, Zacchaeus and Matthew, were at Jericho and Galilee respectively, and so probably were involved in assessing taxes on the trade routes that crossed the country. Matthew certainly, and probably Zacchaeus, was in the employ of Herod Antipas and not directly of the Romans.

Rabban Gamaliel II said, "By four things does the empire exist: by its tolls, bathhouses, theatres, and crop taxes,"[53] that is, taxation and entertainment. That was a subject's version of the Roman "bread and circuses."

CLOTHING AND APPEARANCE

The Greek *chitōn* (Latin *tunica*) was the undergarment but was also worn by workers in their jobs. The *himation* (Latin *pallium* or *palla*) was the outer garment. In Matthew 5:40 the *chitōn* is mentioned first because the context is a lawsuit in which one is sued for his garment ("to go to court"); in Luke 6:29 the *himation* is mentioned first because the context is a robbery ("one strikes you") in which the assailant seizes the outer garment. In the Hellenistic age Greek women also began to wear the *himation* instead of the traditional garment (the *peplos*).[54]

The distinguishing Roman garment was the toga, worn by the freeborn male. Those of high rank were entitled to have a purple border along the toga's upper edge (p. 56).

In which cultures in the first century women wore veils in public, in what numbers, and with what significance are not perfectly clear now. Jewish sources rather uniformly call for women to be veiled in public, but Greek and Roman sources are mixed in their evidence. In classical Greece the veil was worn outside the house by women who had reached sexual maturity — married women and

---

53. *The Fathers According to Rabbi Nathan* 28.

54. L. M. Wilson, *The Clothing of the Ancient Romans* (Baltimore, 1938); D. M. Johnson, E. B. Abrahams, and M M. L. Evans, *Ancient Greek Dress* (Chicago, 1964); L. Llewellyn-Jones and Sue Blundell, *Women's Dress in the Ancient Greek World* (London, 2002).

young women of marriageable age,[55] and Jewish sources may be read the same way. In depictions of a Greek wedding, the bride lifts her veil to her husband. A Roman woman on her wedding day was given a red veil. Statuary makes clear that the Greco-Roman veil was the top of the garment pulled over the head; one should not think of the modern Arabic and Islamic veil that covers most of the face as well as the head. In Roman religion the men as well as women were veiled when offering a sacrifice.[56] The Jewish custom for men to cover their heads when praying and studying the law is later than New Testament times.

Portrait sculpture of the Flavian period gives specificity to the type of hairstyles and jewelry forbidden in 1 Timothy 2:9 and 1 Peter 3:3. The braiding of the hair was very elaborate and ostentatious, quite unlike the simple braid of modern times. The items mentioned in the biblical texts were characteristic of the wealthy upper classes and those who imitated them.

Mirrors were made of polished metal, usually bronze but sometimes silver. Hence, unlike modern glass mirrors, ancient mirrors gave only a "dim reflection" (1 Cor. 13:12).

ENTERTAINMENT

Early Christian moralists and apologists criticized three types of "spectacles" in the pagan world: those of the theatre, the arena (amphitheatre), and the circus. Tertullian is typical in his reference to "the customary pleasures of the maddening circus, the bloodthirsty arena, and the lascivious theatre."[57] We will discuss the entertainments at these places and then turn to other social settings — gymnasia, baths, and banquets.

Theatres

Greek drama, according to the usually accepted theory, began in the festivals of Dionysus. The theatre of Dionysus in Athens set the pattern in that a temple of

---

55. Caroline Galt, "Veiled Ladies," *American Journal of Archaeology* 35 (1931):373-393.

56. Richard Oster, "When Men Wore Veils to Worship: The Historical Context of 1 Corinthians 11:4," *NTS* 34 (1988):481-505; Cynthia Thompson, "Hairstyles, Head-coverings, and St. Paul: Portraits from Roman Corinth," *BA* 51(1988):99-115; David W. J. Gill, "The Importance of Roman Portraiture for Head Coverings in 1 Cor. 11:2-16," *Tyndale Bulletin* 41 (1990):245-60.

57. *Against Marcion* 1.27; cf. *Apparel of Women* 1.8. Tertullian and Novatian wrote treatises *On the Spectacles,* and Chrysostom preached a sermon "Against the Circus, Games, and Theatre" (MG 56.263-70). Cf. Clement of Alexandria, *Instructor* 3.11, 5, and 9 and 2.1, 2, 4, and 7; Lactantius, *Divine Institutes* 6.20. For entertainment in general, see J. P. Toner, *Leisure and Ancient Rome* (Cambridge, 1995); games, the theater, funerals, and triumphs between 80 B.C. and A.D. 63 are discussed by Richard C. Beacham, *Spectacle Entertainments of Early Imperial Rome* (New Haven, 1999).

GREEK THEATRE, Epidaurus

The largest and one of the most nearly perfect of the Greek theatres, Epidaurus well preserves its fourth-century plan and is still used for theatrical productions.

GREEK THEATRE, Ephesus

The crowd in Ephesus gathered here to protest Paul's preaching (Acts 19)

Dionysus frequently adjoins the theatres of the Greek world, and an altar of Dionysus customarily occupies the center of the orchestra. The Greek theatre was essentially a round area *(orchestra)* for the chorus and actors with tiers of seats built against a hillside extending around as much as two-thirds of the orchestra. The stage building came later as a retiring room for the actors (Gk. *skēnē,* from which we get *scene,* means tent) and yet later formed the background or "stage-setting" for the performance. The Roman theatre differed from the Greek in that it was an enclosed structure with the *skēnē* rising to the full height of the auditorium and joined to it at the side. The orchestra was a half-circle added to the seating with the acting taking place on the stage. The back of the *skēnē* in Roman theatres was often richly decorated with tiers of colonnaded niches filled with statuary.

The theatres were often the largest place for a public gathering inside a city, and so were important centers of public life (cf. Acts 19:29ff.). The dramas themselves were popular and well attended.

The Greeks loved competition in all areas, and at the great festivals the playwrights competed among themselves. In these contests were produced the great tragedies and comedies of Sophocles (496–406), Euripides (c. 485–406), and Aristophanes (c. 450–385). The "new comedy" of the Hellenistic age represented the masses of the Greco-Roman world with their interests in self and family, rather than as citizens of the classical city-state. Its leading figure was Menander (342–291), quoted by Paul in 1 Corinthians 15:33; his presence in the educational curriculum made him a readily recognized source of quotation. Audiences continued to prefer the old tragedies of Aeschylus, Sophocles, and Euripides, so few new tragedies were written, but comedy flourished in the Hellenistic age. Tragedy more easily communicates to new historical situations than does comedy, which is more dependent on immediate circumstances.

By the time of Christianity the great age of Greek drama was long past. The most popular theatrical performances were the farces and mimes, parodies of everyday life. Herondas in the third century B.C. achieved some skill in character portrayal, but much of the popular amusement acting descended to the vulgar and sexual to get its laughs. The immoralities exhibited on the stage became a common subject of criticism. Under the empire the pantomime — in which a dramatic plot was enacted by a masked and costumed dancer supported by an actor, chorus, and various instruments — became popular.[58] Apuleius in the second century A.D. said that the theater "is sometimes the scene for the foolery of the mime, the dialogue of comedy, the sonorous rant of tragedy, the perilous antics of the rope-walker, the juggler's sleight of hand, the gesticulation of the dancer" (*Florida* 18).

From the Hellenistic age forward traveling groups of Dionysiac artists went from city to city to produce plays. These professional actors, sacred to the

58. Lucian, *The Dance.*

god Dionysus, enjoyed international protection from the rulers. A few actors would take all of the parts; hence the word for actor *(hypokritēs)* has given us our word *hypocrite,* one who acts a part (Matt. 6:5). The masks worn by actors for their different roles became the symbol for the stage, often decorating theatres and Dionysiac altars and identifying actors in statuary and inscriptions.

The plays performed in the theater became a metaphor for life employed by philosophers and others (e.g., pp. 324, 367).

Although Latin authors (e.g., Plautus [251–184] and Terence [195–159]) successfully adapted Greek models, the Romans preferred other types of entertainment, and many surviving Greek theatres show the architectural modifications made to permit gladiatorial and wild animal contests, principally the addition of a low wall around the orchestra in front of the first row of seats. Josephus (*Ant.* 19.8.2 [344-51]) places the onset of Herod Agrippa's fatal illness (Acts 12:19ff.) in the theatre at Caesarea where he was celebrating spectacles in honor of the emperor.

BIBLIOGRAPHY

Arnott, Peter. *An Introduction to the Greek Theatre.* London, 1959.
Bieber, M. *The History of the Greek and Roman Theatre.* Princeton, 1971.
Adrados, F. R. *Festival, Comedy, and Tragedy: The Greek Origins of Theatre.* Leiden, 1975.
Gentili, B. *Theatrical Performance in the Ancient World: Hellenistic and Early Roman Theatre.* London, 1979.
Beacham, R. C. *The Roman Theatre and Its Audience.* Cambridge, Mass., 1992

Athletics

The Greeks always prized male good looks and much admired the physically perfect male specimen — especially evident in the athlete. Athletic contests accompanied Greek religious festivals; in fact, these games often occurred in contexts that seem startling today: in Homeric times they were held as part of the funeral commemoration in honor of a fallen hero. The games at the great sanctuary of Zeus in Olympia are well known from the ancient Greek custom of dating events by the olympiads and from their modern revival. But athletic competition was a feature of other important festivals in the Greek world — the Nemaean games to Zeus, the Isthmian games near Corinth in honor of Poseidon, the Pythian at Delphi to Apollo, and the Panathenaic to Athena in Athens. The religious games began with sacrifice and prayer, and the contestants made vows to the deity (such as prayer before football or the national anthem before baseball). During Hellenistic and Roman times a favorite form of benefaction by rulers and wealthy men was the institution of games for entertainment (including the contests in the arena and circus; see pp. 102-4), and conversely cities flattered rulers by instituting games in their honor. Professional athletes in Hellenistic and Roman times came to receive the financial reward and adulation that they do today.

Physical training was an important part of Greek education and centered in the gymnasium (see below). Foot races were held in the stadium (Gk. *stadion,* a distance of 192 meters or a little over two hundred yards). Several of these stadia still survive with their starting and finish lines (cf. the mark or goal in Phil. 3:14). The Greek stadia accommodated spectators on the grassy slopes on each side of the flat running surfaces.

The major sports were running, boxing, the *pankration* (an all-out combination of boxing, wrestling, and kicking in which no holds were barred except for biting and gouging), and the pentathlon (which included running, long-jumping, throwing the discus, throwing the javelin, and wrestling).

The Greeks exercised and competed in the nude. They oiled their bodies before the competition and afterward scraped the dirt and sweat off with the oil by means of a curved metal instrument called a strigil. The nudity shocked Jewish sensibilities (this was part of the objection to the building of a gymnasium in Jerusalem; 2 Macc. 4:7-17), and the Romans too were slow to accept Greek athletics.

The proximity of the Isthmian games to his readers may account for Paul's extensive use of athletic terminology (foot race and boxing) in 1 Corinthians 9:24-27. But Paul and other New Testament writers frequently employ athletic metaphors (e.g., the foot race in Heb. 12:1; 2 Tim. 4:7; the crown in 2 Tim. 2:5). Such metaphorical language was part of the stock-in-trade of pop-

GREEK STADIUM, Aphrodisias
The stadium for foot races illustrates Heb. 12:1,
"Surrounded by witnesses, . . . run the race."

ular philosophers and moralists and need not indicate any extensive firsthand acquaintance by Paul or others with the games.

BIBLIOGRAPHY

Lucian. *Anacharsis* or *On Athletics.*
Robinson, Rachel. *Sources for the History of Greek Athletics.* Chicago, 1979.
Sweet, W. E. *Sport and Recreation in Ancient Greece: A Sourcebook in Translation.* Oxford, 1987.

Pfitzner, V. C. *Paul and the Agon Motif.* Leiden, 1966.
Harris, H. A. *Sport in Greece and Rome.* Aspects of Greek and Roman Life. Ithaca, N.Y., 1972.
Pleket, H. W. "Games, Prizes, and Ideology: Some Aspects of the History of Sport in the Greco-Roman World." *Stadion* 1 (1975):49-89.
Finley, M. I., and H. W. Pleket. *The Olympic Games: The First Thousand Years.* London, 1976.
Harris, H. A. *Greek Athletics and the Jews.* Cardiff, 1976.
Gardiner, E. N. *Athletics of the Ancient World.* Chicago, 1978.
Poliakoff, M. *Studies in the Terminology of the Greek Combat Sports.* Frankfurt, 1986.
Kyle, Donald G. *Athletics in Ancient Athens.* Leiden, 1987.
Sansone, D. *Greek Athletics and the Genesis of Sport.* Berkeley, 1988.

Scanlon, Thomas F. *Greek and Roman Athletics: A Bibliography.* Chicago, 1984.

Arenas[59]

Whereas Greeks preferred the exercises of the gymnasium and stadium, Roman interest in sport went to the events at the amphitheatre and circus. In the Roman west are found the remains of many oval amphitheatres (the Greek word means a double theater with seating all round) or arenas. The earliest known is that at Pompeii from the first century B.C. Best known is the Colosseum (the Flavian Amphitheatre) at Rome begun by Vespasian and enlarged by Titus. The three tiers of seats would hold an estimated fifty thousand spectators. The floored arena covered dens for beasts. The Colosseum was a multipurpose structure that could be used for plays, gladiatorial combats, or wild animal shows; it could even be flooded for mock sea battles. The amphitheatres of the west testify to the lust for blood under the empire. The spectacles of gladiatorial combat — man against man, man against animal, and animal against animal — drew huge crowds and replaced Greek drama and athletics in

59. Roland Auguet, *Cruelty and Civilization: The Roman Games* (London, 1994); Alison Futrell, *Blood in the Arena: The Spectacle of Roman Power* (Austin, 1997); D. M. Bomgardner, *The Story of the Roman Amphitheatre* (New York, 2000).

COLOSSEUM, Rome

The Flavian Amphitheatre, dedicated under Titus in A.D. 80, was 188 meters by 156 meters with a height of 57 meters. Note the facilities, now exposed, that were beneath the floor of the amphitheatre. *(Courtesy Philip Gendreau)*

popularity.[60] Schools trained professional gladiators, and enormous numbers of criminals and wild animals were required to satisfy the bloodthirsty populace. The cruelty of the games had a debasing effect on moral sensibility. The Christian emperors enacted legislation to regulate these cruelties. Gladiatorial fights were first banned in 325, but this was not fully applied until the 430s.

Circuses[61]

The circus, or hippodrome as it was called in the Greek east, was an enclosure for chariot racing. An important sport among aristocratic Greeks, it became the

60. A. Cameron, *Bread and Circuses: The Emperor, and the Roman People* (London, 1974); T. Wiedmann, *Emperors and Gladiators* (London, 1992); M. Wistrand, *Entertainment and Violence in Ancient Rome: The Attitudes of Roman Writers of the First Century A.D.* (Gothenburg, 1992).

61. J. Humphrey, *Roman Circuses and Chariot Racing* (Batsford, England, 1984); idem, *Roman Circuses: Arenas for Chariot Racing* (Berkeley, 1986).

RESTORATION OF CIRCUS MAXIMUS, Rome
The racing of chariots drawn by four horses was a major form of
professional entertainment. *(© Alinari/Art Resource, NY)*

major professional entertainment in Roman times. The earliest example is the
Circus Maximus in Rome, estimated to have held 255,000 persons. Business
firms supplied the horses, chariots, and drivers. Charioteers were able to acquire
huge sums of money and became popular heroes. Public officials or wealthy citizens would finance the races for the entertainment of the people and enhance-
ment of their own prestige.[62] The chariot races and the games became important political functions where the emperors granted favors and the populace of a
city demonstrated on behalf of their demands. Professional teams were identified by their color (Reds, Whites, Blues, Greens) and became the focus for political factions on into Byzantine times.[63] Four horses pulled a light two-wheeled
chariot *(quadriga);* as many as twelve teams could participate in a race.

Gymnasia and Baths

With these structures we turn from spectator to participatory entertainment.
The gymnasium was characteristic of the Greek world and the baths of the Roman world, but under the empire hybrid or combination structures developed
(as in the Harbor Bath Gymnasium at Ephesus built under Domitian) so that

62. P. Veyne, *Bread and Circuses* (London, 1990) on acts of philanthropy by the wealthy.
63. A. Cameron, *Circus Factions* (Oxford, 1976).

the gymnasia had swimming pools and the baths had exercise facilities. Both were general cultural and social institutions and did not have only athletic or recreational functions. Both were primarily for citizens or the at least moderately well-to-do.

Some gymnasia included an extensive complex. The main feature was a running ground with accompanying facilities. Usually there was also a courtyard covered with sand and surrounded by porticos and rooms; this was the palaestra (sports ground) for wrestling. The rooms in a gymnasium complex included bathing rooms, dressing rooms, and storage rooms. There could also be a lecture hall, for the gymnasium was the center of activities for the ephebes (p. 111). Since athletics were under the patronage of Hermes and Heracles especially, statues, altars, and cult emblems to them were regularly present.

Baths ranged from small private establishments to the huge public complexes built by Caracalla and Diocletian in the third century A.D. in Rome.[64] Every town seems to have had one or more bathing establishment, the erection of which was a favorite form of public benefaction. Essential were the pools for bathing, usually several for different temperatures of water. The usual order was a warm water pool, hot bath, warm again, and finally a cold plunge. The Romans were skilled at constructing furnaces and hypocausts (underground ducts) with hot air flues for controlling the heat in the warm and hot rooms. Some baths were able to take advantage of natural hot mineral springs as at Bath in England and Hierapolis in Asia Minor (perhaps the tepid waters alluded to in the letter to neighboring Laodicea, from which they are visible, in Rev. 3:16). The larger establishments had large halls, smaller game or conversation rooms, gardens, swimming pools, dressing rooms, and palaestrae.

The atmosphere was somewhat that of a country club combined with a community center. Here one came to meet with friends, converse, and have a snack of food and drink. Here one could read, exercise, get a massage, listen to philosophers or poets, as well as bathe.

Some baths had special hours reserved for women, and a few cities had a women's bath. However, mixed bathing began sometime in the first century A.D. and became widespread by the end of the century, so that double baths gave way to a single set of facilities.[65] Public nudity was not always a matter of concern. The baths were very popular, had an equalizing effect, and drew mixed moral judgments because they were sometimes associated with immorality and some philosophers thought they had a weakening effect on the body. A Latin inscription expresses one attitude: "Baths, wine, and women corrupt our bodies, but they make life worth living" (*CIL* 6.15258).

---

64. See Lucian (?), *Hippias or The Bath,* for a description of a luxurious one; I. Nielsen, *Thermae et Balnea: The Architecture and History of Roman Public Baths* (Aarhus, 1990); F. Yegül, *Baths and Bathing in Classical Antiquity* (Cambridge, Mass., 1992).

65. Roy Bowen Ward, "Women in Roman Baths," *HTR* 85 (1992):125-47.

Banquets[66]

Turning to the home or small group entertainment, we find the banquet or dinner party one of the most important and widespread social occasions. Greek and Roman banquets had established conventions. At the Greek dinner the guests elected a president, who determined the mixture of wine and water and presided over the evening's entertainment. Table wine in the ancient world was always taken diluted with water. Average mixtures would have been from two to four parts of water to one part of wine. If a stronger mixture was desired, the beverage may have been taken half and half; the wine was taken straight only if early drunkenness was desired.[67] The Roman banquet's established rules about rank and honor determined one's place in the dining room. There were three couches (hence the name for the dining room, *triclinium*), and one ate reclining (the general custom of the ancient world). Food was served from a table in the middle of the room. Slaves brought in the food and attended to everyone's needs.

Two atypical banquets from classical literature illustrate the wide range of entertainment possible: Plato's *Symposium* with its high philosophical discourses and Petronius's *Banquet of Trimalchio* (mid–first century A.D.) with its broad satire on the efforts of the "new rich" to put on a show and succeeding only at being vulgar. Banquets were made the literary setting for writings detailing an author's antiquarian learning: Plutarch's *Table Talk* and *Dinner of the Seven Wise Men* and Athenaeus's *Learned Banquet* are especially valuable for the information from earlier writers that the participants quote.[68] The popularity of the banquet setting for literary works is further exemplified in the pseudepigraphal *Epistle of Aristeas* (pp. 450-51).

Wine was served after dinner; if the evening was to be spent primarily in conversation — political, philosophical, or just social — the wine would be weak. The guests might play games, or be entertained by dancers (cf. Mark 6:21-22), acrobats, or jugglers. An author might recite a recent composition, or musicians might play (see further below). Female companionship might be provided by *hetairai*. Again, the percentage of the wine had something to do with the intimacy of the entertainment.

---

66. Dennis E. Smith and Hal E. Taussig, *Many Tables: The Eucharist in the New Testament and Liturgy Today* (London, 1990), 21-35 has a useful summary of meal practices in Greco-Roman society; O. Murray, ed., *Sympotica: A Symposium on the Symposion* (Oxford, 1990), includes ritual dining at sanctuaries; W. J. Slater, ed., *Dining in a Classical Context* (Ann Arbor, Mich., 1991); Dennis E. Smith, *From Symposium to Eucharist: The Banquet in the Early Christian World* (Minneapolis, 2003).

67. Everett Ferguson, "Wine as a Table-Drink in the Ancient Word," *Restoration Quarterly* 13, no. 3 (1970):141-53.

68. J. Martin, *Symposion: Die Geschichte einer literarischen Form* (Paderborn, 1931); E. S. Steele, "Luke 11:27-54 — A Modified Hellenistic Symposium?" *JBL* 103 (1984):379-94; Dennis Smith, "Table Fellowship as a Literary Motif in the Gospel of Luke," *JBL* 106 (1987):613-38.

BANQUET, wall painting from Pompeii
Diners recline around a *triclinium*. A slave removes a guest's shoes while
another offers a cup of wine. Another guest has overindulged and is led away.
(Courtesy National Archaeological Museum, Naples)

Music

Music was found at banquets and other entertainments, at weddings and funerals, at official occasions, and as an accompaniment to sacrifice and other ritual acts in cultic practice. These uses in the Greek and Roman cultures were also present in the Jewish (Sir. 32:3-6; 50:16; Matt. 11:17; 9:23; Luke 15:25).

First Corinthians 14:7-8 (see also Rev. 18:22) lists the three principal instruments of the day: *aulos* (pipe, often but not very accurately translated flute), *kithara* (the harp or zither), and trumpet. The last was mainly used in war and to herald public announcements, so in everyday life the *aulos* and the *kithara* were the main instruments. The *aulos* was a wind instrument, giving an oboelike sound. A common form was the double *aulos,* with two pipes coming from the mouthpiece. It was associated with orgies, sacrifices, frenzy, and exciting the emotions. A smaller instrument, the *syrinx,* had different lengths of pipes and was popular with shepherds and rural folk. The *kithara* was a stringed instrument often used to accompany singing. The philosophers associated it with harmony, gaiety, and artistic sensitivity. It was invented, according to legend, by Hermes, but became Apollo's attribute. Athena invented the *aulos,* but she threw it away because it distorted her face to play it. According to this story Marsyas (a satyr) picked it up and invented a form of music on it. He challenged Apollo with his *kithara* to a musical contest. Apollo defeated him and took advantage of the agreement that the winner could do as he liked with the loser in order to flay Marsyas. The story reflects the higher evaluation given to stringed music, but there is no evidence that in popular estimation or in general use the pipe was inferior. Stringed instruments were played either with the fingers *(psallō)* or with a plectrum. There were, moreover, various kinds of percussion instruments.

Many ancient cities had in addition to a large theatre a small music thea-

CONTEST OF APOLLO AND MARSYAS, marble relief, 330 B.C.
The judges decided the music of Apollo on the lyre to be superior to the music of Marsyas (a satyr) on the pipe. (© *Alinari/Art Resource, NY*)

tre known as the *ōdeion*. It had the same general features as the drama theatres, but being smaller it was normally enclosed.

Athletics and music played an important part in classical Greek education, but by the Christian era both were in decline in the ordinary curriculum.

BIBLIOGRAPHY

Barker, Andrew. *Greek Musical Writings.* 2 vols. Cambridge, 1984, 1989.

Mathiesen, T. J. *A Bibliography of Sources for the Study of Ancient Greek Music.* Hackensack, N.J., 1974.

Wellesz, E. *Ancient and Oriental Music.* New Oxford History of Music. London, 1957.
Smith, W. S. *Musical Aspects of the New Testament.* Amsterdam, 1962.
Mountford, J. "Music and the Romans." *BJRL* 47 (1964):198-211.
Anderson, Warren D. *Ethos and Education in Greek Music.* Cambridge, Mass., 1966.
Wille, G. *Musica Romana.* Amsterdam, 1967.
Michaelides, S. *The Music of Ancient Greece: An Encyclopedia.* London, 1978.
Quasten, J. *Music and Worship in Pagan and Christian Antiquity.* Washington, 1983.
Comotti, G. *Music in Greek and Roman Culture.* Baltimore, 1988.
Anderson, Warren D. *Music and Musicians in Ancient Greece.* Ithaca, N.Y., 1995.

EDUCATION

The Greek word for education was *paideia*, which meant "training, discipline." It was translated into Latin as *humanitas*, which expressed the ideal of Hellenistic education — the formation of the human person.

Most schools were small and private, the work of a single teacher who received a fee from his pupils, except in some of the cities where rulers or wealthy citizens endowed educational institutions. The teaching profession in classical antiquity was a humble, even despised occupation, because it meant running after customers asking for money and working long hours. The school year was basically what it has remained in Europe, from October to June. The classroom was usually a shop near the town center.

Both Greco-Roman and Jewish education may be classified according to a three-stage system — primary, secondary, and advanced.[69] Children normally began school at the age of seven. Primary education was mainly in reading and writing, but might include some simple arithmetic. Teaching methods

---

69. Cf. Apuleius, *Florida* 20: "In the feasts of the Muses the first cup is poured by the literator, who teaches us to read. Then comes the grammaticus, who adorns us with different sorts of knowledge. Finally the rhetor places in our hands the weapons of eloquence."

SCHOOL SCENE, grave relief, A.D. 185
The heavy clothes and shoes mark this scene as from the northern borders
of the Roman world, but the stern teacher and tardy student evoke universal
memories of school days. *(Rhineland Museum, Trier)*

emphasized memorization and copying. People are capable of enormous feats
of memorization when this skill is cultivated. The ancients highly valued memory as an indication of intelligence and even morality, and had more confidence in memory than in writing, perhaps a survival of earlier times when this
was the only or principal means of preserving and transmitting information.
By the time of the early empire, writing was assuming a greater importance.
Discipline in the schools was stern. Children were accompanied to and from
school by a pedagogue ("custodian"), who was usually a slave charged with
looking after his charge's morals and general welfare (cf. Gal. 3:23-25). The pedagogues generally had a reputation for treating the children harshly.

Children from the upper classes (by the age of eleven or twelve) received
"secondary" education in the classics under a *grammaticus* ("grammarian").
Cicero and Quintilian advocated a well-rounded education in the liberal arts
(by the first century B.C. already established as the seven that medieval education inherited — grammar, rhetoric, dialectic, geometry, arithmetic, astronomy,
and music), but the student was fortunate who acquired much more than mathematics and music in addition to literature. The method of instruction was for
the teacher to read aloud a passage and then explain it in detail (textual criticism, meaning of words and idioms, references to mythology and history, points
of grammar, figures of speech, and moral lessons to be learned). The students
then read the passage aloud and were questioned on it. Recitations and exercises
taught spelling, grammar, correct usage, and rules of composition.

The prominence of physical education in classical education at all levels was not just a matter of sport but of moral training and was related to the ideal of the perfect physical specimen and the characteristic competitiveness in Greek life.

Advanced education involved a parting of the ways, although the different options were not mutually exclusive. The Greek citizen-aristocrats entered the *ephebeia,* the only educational institution of the ancient world that was always publicly supported. Associated with the city gymnasium, it was a kind of finishing school for young men. In addition to its emphasis on physical education, some attention was given to rhetoric and philosophy and there was access to the library of the gymnasium. At the age of eighteen, one year (generally) was spent as an ephebe. This institution originally had been for military training, but during the Hellenistic age this aspect fell into the background and it became a training ground for public life. The members participated in festivals and processions, became aware of their cultural and political heritage, and gained experience in public life, inasmuch as the *ephebeia* was organized like a miniature city. The *ephebeia* had greater social than intellectual significance, for graduation from it was essential for full acceptance into the social and political life of the Greek cities.[70]

Whether or not he had finished the *ephebeia,* a young man could choose a profession — philosophy, medicine, or law. This involved placing oneself under a philosopher, doctor, or lawyer, and learning the field from him.

The most common form of advanced education, also available to one who entered a "profession," was in rhetoric. It was something of the ancient equivalent of the college arts degree. We can hardly exaggerate the influence of rhetorical education on ancient culture and literature. Isocrates (p. 9) had championed the oratorical tradition against the philosophical type of education advocated by Plato. Quintilian provides an attractive summary in Latin of the rhetorical educational ideal at the end of the first century. Since reading was done aloud, the spoken word had a great influence on literature. Speech was the queen of studies. (See further under Rhetoric in the next section.) Since one might have to speak on any subject and could find useful illustrative material from a wide range of subjects, rhetorical education included some philosophy, astronomy, history, and so forth. The teaching of both rhetoric and philosophy was usually accomplished in one of three ways: by wandering popular lecturers, by private teachers established in the cities, or in institutions of learning in educational centers such as Athens and Alexandria.

Education was voluntary, but elementary schools at least were widespread. The indications, especially on the evidence of the papyri, are that the literacy rate of Hellenistic and early Roman times was rather high, probably

---

70. For the efforts of Alexandrian Jews to gain acceptance for their children into the *ephebeia* see Tcherikover and Fuks, *Corpus Papyrorum Judaicarum* (Cambridge, 1957), 1:38-39, 59, 61, 64, 75-76.

higher than at any period prior to modern times (see further on pp. 132-33). Girls as well as boys were often included in the elementary schools, and although education for girls was rarer than for boys, it could be obtained. The key for everyone was to get what you could on your own. Thus, most boys learned a trade through an apprenticeship or continued their father's work, and most girls learned household tasks at home.

Jewish education superficially followed the same stages as Greco-Roman education, but with a significantly different content. The aim of Jewish education was a religious one, the knowledge and practice of the Torah. Instead of studying Homer and the dramatists, students learned the Scriptures and the oral traditions of the scribes.[71] The third-century rabbi Judah b. Tema summarized the stages of education in Pirke Aboth 5:21: "At five years of age [one is ready] for Scripture; at ten, for Mishnah; at thirteen for [keeping] the commandments; at fifteen for Talmud; at eighteen for marriage; at twenty for pursuing [a trade]."

The home was the center for Jews of religious education and an elementary education in reading and writing. Jewish primary schools seem not to have been widespread outside Jerusalem until the second century A.D. The primary school was known as the *beth sepher* (or *sopher*) — "house of reading" or "of the scribe." It was taught by a *sopher*, or scribe, or in poorer communities by the *ḥazzan*, the synagogue attendant (p. 581), whose salary was paid by the synagogue. Classes often met inside the synagogue or in an adjoining room. The Jewish child was expected to be able to read the Hebrew Scriptures, to memorize a standard translation in his own language if not Hebrew (called a Targum), and to recite certain parts of the liturgy. There was a great emphasis on memorizing Scripture.

Secondary schools are thought to have existed from the second century B.C. They were known as *beth midrash* ("house of instruction") or *beth talmud* ("house of learning [oral law]") and were concerned with the study of the oral law. This might take the form of commentary on Scripture (midrash) or of a topical arrangement of the legal requirements (mishnah). Thirteen was probably the more common age for beginning this study. Few would undertake it, but it too was supported by the synagogue in an adjoining building.

Advanced study required that one attach himself to a great scholar (Acts 22:3) or, after the destruction of Jerusalem, to go to one of the academies, such as the one at Jamnia. At this level the student learned advanced scriptural interpretation and rabbinic legal opinions (talmud). This study would prepare one for ordination as a rabbi or religious scholar (post 70), one entitled to make legal decisions within the Jewish community.

Greco-Roman rhetorical education is evident in the methods of Jewish

---

71. Josephus, *Against Apion* 2.178, emphasizes the thorough knowledge of their law by all Jews.

instruction. Memorization was quite important in both systems of education. Quite un-Roman was the Jewish requirement that every boy, rich or poor, scholar or unlearned, acquire a trade (so Paul, Acts 18:3).[72] Jewish women were discouraged from engaging in legal studies, but most Jewish boys would have studied until age thirteen so that there was probably a higher degree of learning among a larger number of Jews than among any other people of the ancient world.

BIBLIOGRAPHY

Pseudo-Plutarch. *The Education of Children* (*Moralia* 1-14).
Dio Chrysostom. *Discourse* 18.
Quintilian. *On Teaching Rhetoric.*
Philo. *On the Preliminary Studies.*

Drazin, N. H. *History of Jewish Education from 515 B.C.E. to 220 C.E.* Baltimore, 1940.
Laistner, M. L. W. *Christianity and Pagan Culture in the Later Roman Empire.* Ithaca, N.Y., 1951.
Nilsson, M. P. *Die Hellenistische Schule.* Munich, 1955.
Marrou, H. I. *A History of Education in Antiquity.* New York, 1956.
Clark, D. L. *Rhetoric in Greco-Roman Education.* New York, 1957.
Jaeger, W. *Paideia: The Ideals of Greek Culture.* 3 vols. Reprint. Oxford, 1957–1965.
Barclay, William. *Educational Ideals in the Ancient World.* London, 1959.
Gerhardsson, B. *Memory and Manuscript.* Lund, 1961.
Van Unnik, W. C. *Tarsus or Jerusalem: The City of Paul's Youth.* London, 1962.
Clarke, M. L. *Higher Education in the Ancient World.* London, 1971.
Bonner, S. F. *Education in Ancient Rome: From the Elder Cato to the Younger Pliny.* London, 1977.
Too, Yun Lee, ed. *Education in Greek and Roman Antiquity.* Leiden, 2001.

LITERATURE AND LANGUAGE

Authors

This section is a discussion of the principal Latin and Greek authors and writings of the period from Augustus to Marcus Aurelius. Other authors are discussed in connection with religion or philosophy, and some of those listed below are discussed more fully in these sections. Jewish literature is introduced in Chapter 5 on Judaism.

The period at the close of the Republic and beginning of the Principate

---

72. In Tos. Kiddushin 1:11 the obligations of a father to a son include "to teach him the Torah and to teach him a craft."

formed the "Golden Age" of Latin literature. The model of Latin prose ever since has been the orator Marcus Tullius *Cicero* (106–43 B.C.). Known for his orations, his letters are an important source for Roman social customs. However, Cicero falls properly outside the limits intended for this section and we will treat him more fully in Chapter 4 (pp. 357ff.).

Augustus's minister Maecenas saw that it was a good idea to mobilize some of the better emerging poets as propagandists for the Augustan establishment among the educated classes. Maecenas patronized the arts on behalf of the new order. These literary men were not insincere or hirelings, but neither were they writing innocently.

Virgil (Publius Vergilius Maro, 70–19 B.C.) gave classic expression to the values and destiny of Rome. The *Eclogues* and *Georgics* reflect rural life and literary conventions. His great national epic, the *Aeneid*, recounts the legend of the settlement of Rome by Aeneas and his Trojan companions, taking its point of departure from Homer's *Iliad*. Book 6 contains the "future prophecy" of Rome put into the mouth of Anchises. Whereas Greek cities thought of themselves as founded once for all by one man who was their lawgiver, Rome looked upon itself as the product of the ages and the labors of many men. The heroes of the republican years are given, and the account climaxes with Augustus. Anchises proudly granted that Greece had taught arts and sciences to the Romans, but Rome was appointed to rule the world and impose the habit of peace. Virgil's *Eclogue* 4, written in 40 B.C., shows the almost "messianic" aura that surrounded the expectations of people in the Augustan age.

> Now is come the last age of the song of Cumae; the great line of the centuries begins anew. Now the Virgin [Justice] returns, the reign of Saturn returns [a new golden age]; now a new generation descends from heaven on high. Only do thou, pure Lucina, smile on the birth of the child, under whom the iron brood shall first cease, and a golden race spring up throughout the world! Thine own Apollo now is king!
>
> And in thy consulship, Pollio, yea in thine, shall this glorious age begin, and the mighty months commence their march; under thy sway, any lingering traces of our guilt shall become void, and release the earth from its continual dread. He shall have the gift of divine life, shall see heroes mingled with gods, and shall himself be seen of them, and shall sway a world to which his father's virtues have brought peace.
>
> But for thee, child, shall the earth untilled pour forth. . . . [There follows a description of prosperity and abundance.]
>
> Enter on thy high honors — the hour will soon be here — O thou dear offspring of the gods, mighty seed of a Jupiter to be! Behold the world bowing with its massive dome — earth and expanse of sea and heaven's depth! Behold, how all things exult in the age that is at hand! (*Ecl.* 4.4-52, trans. H. R. Fairclough in Loeb Classical Library)

Christian writers were later to see in the reference to a "child" a pagan prophecy of Christ.[73] If Virgil had a specific child in mind, it was probably the child of Pollio the consul, but the words may have been applied later to some child in the imperial family.

Horace (Quintus Horatius Flaccus, 65–8 B.C.)[74] lacks the elevated tone of Virgil. He was alert, liked comfort, and was mildly skeptical, but his sympathies were won for the ideals of the Augustan regime. In a period of disturbance people had begun to take religion more seriously, and Horace seems to be an example of this. Yet religiosity and precise belief are quite different. Horace's poetry includes *Satires, Epistles,* and the *carmen saeculare* (p. 194). His *Odes (Carmina)* established him as the leading Latin lyric poet. The first six odes of Book 3 are the best commentary we have on the social and political policies of Augustus.

Livy (Titus Livius, 59 B.C.–A.D. 17) belongs with Virgil and Horace in sympathies and influence. Livy was a prose writer whose *History of Rome* from its founding to 9 B.C., large parts of which are lost, is a principal source for Roman history. Livy was lacking in critical skill and political penetration; his main interest was the ethical aspect of history. He stresses the continuity between the past and his own time, and in the preface praises the Republic and its virtues. Livy is important for what he has preserved and for showing the interpretation and outlook given in the Augustan Age.

An author outside the mainstream of ideas that Augustus wanted propagated was *Ovid* (Publius Ovidius Naso, 43 B.C.–A.D. 18). Ovid said that though his verse was licentious, his conduct was orderly. He was married three times. His *Ars Amatoria* is a parody of a didactic poem. It was partially responsible for his being banished from Rome, but also involved was some association with a scandal in the imperial family that touched high politics as well as morals. Ovid's *Metamorphoses*[75] is a storehouse of mythology, and his *Fasti* is a calendar of Roman religious festivals. Also belonging to the Augustan Age was *Vitruvius,* our principal source for architecture.[76]

The literary quality of works of the Julio-Claudian Age is not so high. We should mention *Gaius Velleius Paterculus* (c. 19 B.C. to after A.D. 31), whose *Roman History* is an important source for information on Augustus and especially Tiberius, whom he holds in admiration, and *Lucan* (Marcus Annaeus Lucanus, A.D. 39–65), whose *Civil War* treats the struggle between Pompey and

73. S. Benko, "Vergil's Fourth Eclogue in Christian Interpretation," *ANRW* II, *Principat,* 31.1 (Berlin, 1980), 646-705.

74. *Horace, the Complete Odes and Epodes,* Translated with Introduction and Notes by David West (Oxford, 1997); P. Levi, *Horace: A Life* (London, 1998).

75. Allen Mandelbaum, tr., *The Metamorphoses of Ovid* (New York, 1993).

76. Of less significance for Christian origins is Albius *Tibullus* (48–19 B.C.), friend of Horace and perfecter of Latin elegiac poetry, who wrote mostly of love and longing for country life. Another writer, like Ovid, outside the mainstream was Sextus *Propertius* (last half of the first century B.C.). He and Ovid were also writing about love, but not married love.

Caesar in epic poetry. Of value for understanding this period of time is *Valerius Maximus,* who during Tiberius's reign compiled a handbook of illustrations for rhetoricians.[77] *Seneca* is of major significance and will be treated in Chapter 4 (pp. 363-65).[78]

The greatest authors of the "Silver Age" flourished under the Flavians and Trajan. *Pliny the Elder* (Gaius Plinius Secundus) died at the eruption of Mount Vesuvius in A.D. 79 when his interest in scientific knowledge brought him too close to the noxious fumes and he died of asphyxiation. His thirty-seven-volume *Natural History* is an encyclopedia of the lore of ancient times. His nephew *Pliny the Younger* (A.D. 61–114) became governor of Bithynia under Trajan. His ten books of letters, written with a view to publication, are an important source for social history.[79] The tenth book contains letters exchanged with Trajan, including the important account of his dealings with Christians (10.96, 97). Those letters and his *Panegyric* are major sources of information for the reign of Trajan.

Other writers include *Martial* (Marcus Valerius Martialis, c. A.D. 40–104), who wrote *Epigrams,* a realistic reflection of life in his society (his language is often obscene), and *Juvenal* (Decimus Iunius Iuvenalis, c. A.D. 50–130), author of *Satires,* the greatest in the Latin language. He speaks as a moralist.[80]

The greatest of the Roman teachers and writers on rhetoric was *Quintilian* (Marcus Fabius Quintilianus, c. A.D. 35–100). His work is important not only for ancient techniques of constructing and delivering a speech but for Quintilian's own good sense and educational philosophy.

The Silver Age produced two outstanding historians. Cornelius *Tacitus* (c. A.D. 55–120), through his *Histories* and the *Annals,* is the major source for the history of the empire in the first century.[81] Other works are the *Agricola,* an

77. R. Hodgson, "Valerius Maximus and the Social World of the New Testament," *CBQ* 51 (1989):683-93; W. Martin Bloomer, *Valerius Maximus and the Rhetoric of the New Nobility* (Chapel Hill, NC, 1992); C. J. Skidmore, *Practical Ethics for Roman Gentlemen* (Exeter, 1996); there is a translation of Book I by D. Wardle, *Valerius Maximus: Memorable Deeds and Sayings* (Oxford, 1998); H.-F. Mueller, *Roman Religion in Valerius Maximus* (New York, 2002).

78. Others writing during this time were *Columella,* a principal source for agriculture; *Phaedrus,* a writer of fables; Aulus *Persius* Flaccus (A.D. 34–62), whose satires show Stoic influence from his friend the philosopher Cornutus; *Petronius* (consul and adviser to Nero but finally forced by him to commit suicide), whose *Banquet of Trimalchio* satirizes Neronian society and provides an unexampled store of "vulgar Latin"; and Quintus Curtius *Rufus,* rhetorician and historian writing under Claudius.

79. A. N. Sherwin-White, *The Letters of Pliny: A Historical and Social Commentary* (Oxford, 1966); W. Williams, *Pliny the Younger: Correspondence from Bithynia (Epistles X)* (Warminster, 1990).

80. Of less significance are the poets *Valerius Flaccus* (d. c. 93 A.D.), author of *Argonautica; Silius Italicus* (d. about 101) whose *Punica* about the Second Punic War is the longest Latin poem; and Publius Papinius *Statius* (c. 45–96), whose *Silvae* celebrate events in the personal lives of his friends. Sextus Julius *Frontinus* (c. 30–104) wrote on Greek and Roman military science.

81. Ronald Mellor, *Tacitus* (London, 1993).

encomium on his father-in-law, and *Germania,* a description of Germany. Tacitus wrote from the standpoint of the senatorial aristocracy, which had suffered the most under the emperors, but in general we may rely on his factual accuracy. Gaius *Suetonius* Tranquillus (c. A.D. 69–140) was a friend of Pliny the Younger and government official under Hadrian.[82] Parts of his *Lives of Illustrious Men* have survived. More significant was his *Lives of the Caesars,* from Julius to Domitian. The work had great influence on biographical writing and is important to historians for the anecdotes, details of personal life, and official documents he drew on. He indiscriminately used material from enemies and friends of the emperors.

Authors of the Antonine period of interest to this study are *Aulus Gellius* (c. 123–165), whose twenty-volume *Attic Nights* is a miscellaneous collection of material on a wide variety of subjects; Marcus Cornelius *Fronto* (c. 100–166), a rhetorician from North Africa (honored by Gellius) whose correspondence with Marcus Aurelius has survived; and *Apuleius* (born c. A.D. 123 in North Africa), whose *Metamorphoses* ("The Golden Ass"),[83] a tale of sex, violence, magic, and religion, is one of the best introductions to the culture of the second century. Latin cultural leadership was moving from Rome to the provinces, especially North Africa.

Greek writers of the early empire did not attain the literary excellence of Latin authors; the golden age of Greek literature had come in the fifth century B.C. Some of the important Greek sources for this period — Dio Chrysostom, Epictetus, Plutarch, and Marcus Aurelius — can be better treated in the chapter on philosophy. However, some important historical sources come from other Greek authors. Between 60 and 30 B.C. *Diodorus Siculus* wrote a world history from earliest times to Caesar's Gallic wars, compiling his information from various sources.[84] *Dionysius Halicarnassus,* who taught in Rome from 30 to 8 B.C., covered Roman history from the founding of Rome to the First Punic War in *Roman Antiquities,* but his ignorance of early Roman conditions mitigates the value of his work. *Arrian* (Flavius Arrianus), who wrote the history of Alexander the Great *(Anabasis),* flourished in the second century A.D. He was a pupil of Epictetus, whose teachings he preserved in the *Discourses. Appian* of Alexandria, a second-century historian with ethnographic interests, treated the Roman conquests according to races and regions in his *Roman Things.* Stretching the chronological limits of this section, we include the *Roman His-*

82. Barry Baldwin, *Suetonius* (Amsterdam, 1983); A. Wallace-Hadrill, *Suetonius: The Scholar and his Caesars* (New Haven, 1983).

83. P. G. Walsh, *Apuleius, "The Golden Ass"* (Oxford, 1994) (trans., int., and notes); on Apuleius in general, S. J. Harrison, *Apuleius: A Latin Sophist* (Oxford, 2000); G. Luck, "Magic, Miracle, and Salvation: The Spiritual Journey of Apuleius," *Ancient Pathways and Hidden Pursuits* (Ann Arbor, Mich., 2000), 223-38; on the *Golden Ass,* J. Tatum, *Apuleius and the Golden Ass* (Ithaca, N.Y., 1979); F. Millar, "The World of the Golden Ass," *JRS* 71 (1981):63-75.

84. K. S. Sacks, *Diodorus Siculus and the First Century* (Princeton, 1990).

tory of Dio Cassius,[85] which covered events from the beginnings to A.D. 229. Most is missing, but part of what is missing is known from later epitomizers.

Strabo of Amaseia in Pontus (64 B.C.–A.D. 21) wrote a *Geography* in seventeen books that describes the countries and peoples of the Roman world. He gives useful information on the cities of New Testament times. *Pausanias* (c. A.D. 150), in his *Description of Greece*,[86] sketches the history and topography of important sites, describes their monuments, and includes information on mythology, customs, superstitions, and cult practices. His is the ancient version of a travelers' guidebook, valuable to the archaeologist and historian of religion.

Lucian of Samosata (c. A.D. 120 to after 180),[87] though raised in an Aramaic-speaking environment, made himself a master of Attic Greek. He was a rhetorician who set himself to entertain society. He combined comedy and the dialogue form and was proud of this new literary creation.[88] These satirical dialogues provide such insights into the common assumptions and customs of ancient society that his writings frequently appear in the bibliographies of this book. Since many of his satires deal with the philosophical schools or philosophical themes, more on Lucian will be found in Chapter 4 (pp. 352-53).

The Pseudo-Longinus treatise *On the Sublime* is a work on style from the first century A.D. and is one of the greatest works in antiquity on literary criticism. *Aelius Aristides* (117 or 129–189)[89] was a practicing rhetorician, enthusiastic for Rome and the blessings of the Antonine Age. Fifty-five of his speeches survive; they represent the Atticizing style of the second century. One group of these speeches are the "Sacred Discourses," or "Sacred Tales" (delivered 170/ 171), important for religious ideas in the early empire. Aristides was a leading representative of the "Second Sophistic" of the second and third century, Greek rhetoricians who spoke on historical themes. They received the name from Flavius Philostratus, whose *Lives of the Sophists* tells about them.[90]

Artemidorus in the late second century wrote *On the Interpretation of Dreams* (see pp. 220-21), a treatise containing rich information on ancient superstition, folklore, and symbolism. Another kind of learned work is that of

85. P. M. Swan and J. W. Humphreys, eds., *An Historical Commentary on Cassius Dio's "Roman History,"* American Philological Association Monograph Series, 11 vols. (Atlanta, 1988–).

86. P. Levi, *Guide to Greece*, 2 vols. (New York, 1971, 1979); C. Habicht, *Pausanias' Guide to Ancient Greece* (Berkeley, 1999); K. W. Arafat, *Pausanias' Greece: Ancient Artists and Roman Rulers* (Cambridge, 1996).

87. Barry Baldwin, *Studies in Lucian* (Toronto, 1973); J. Hall, *Lucian's Satire* (New York, 1981); C. P. Jones, *Culture and Society in Lucian* (Cambridge, Mass., 1986); R. B. Branham, *Unruly Eloquence: Lucian and the Comedy of Traditions* (Cambridge, 1989). See also pp. 352-53n.55.

88. See *Double Indictment* and "*You're a Prometheus in Words.*"

89. C. A. Behr, *Aelius Aristides and the Sacred Tales* (Amsterdam, 1968); P. W. van der Horst, *Aelius Aristides and the New Testament* (Leiden, 1980); C. A. Behr, *P. Aelius Aristides: The Complete Works Translated into English*, 2 vols. (Leiden, 1981, 1986).

90. For the social setting of the "Second Sophistic," see G. W. Bowersock, *Greek Sophists in the Roman Empire* (Oxford, 1969).

Ptolemy (Claudius Ptolemaeus) of Alexandria on astronomy in the mid–second century. It provided the mathematical calculations on which the geocentric theory of the universe was established throughout the Middle Ages. His *Geography* too was the standard work on the subject before modern times.

BIBLIOGRAPHY

Loeb Classical Library for texts and translations.

Harvey, Paul. *The Oxford Companion to Classical Literature.* Oxford, 1951.
Bowra, C. M. *Landmarks in Greek Literature.* Cleveland, 1966.
Lesky, A. *A History of Greek Literature.* New York, 1966.
Williams, G. *Change and Decline: Roman Literature in the Early Empire.* Berkeley, 1978.
Kenney, E. J., and W. V. Clausen. *The Cambridge History of Classical Literature.* Vol. 2: *Latin Literature.* Cambridge, 1982.
Easterling, P., and B. Knox. *The Cambridge History of Classical Literature.* Vol. 1: *Greek Literature.* Cambridge, 1985.
Dihle, A. *History of Greek Literature from Homer to the Hellenistic Period.* London, 1994.
Dihle, A. *Greek and Latin Literature of the Roman Empire: From Augustus to Justinian.* London, 1994.
Fantham, Elaine. *Roman Literary Culture from Cicero to Apuleius.* Baltimore, 1999. (Social setting)
Conte, Gian Biaggio. *Latin Literature: A History.* Baltimore, 1999.

Rhetoric

The handbooks produced by the Greek and Latin rhetoricians enlarge significantly our knowledge of the forms and composition of Christian literature. Greek rhetorical theory was a development from Aristotle's *Rhetoric.* Not much of the theoretical work of Hellenistic rhetors survives, but Dionysius of Halicarnassus (age of Augustus), *On Literary Composition,* and the textbooks by Hermogenes (second century A.D.) are significant. Greek rhetorical theory is best preserved by Latin authors: from the first century B.C. the anonymous *Rhetorica ad Herennium* and Cicero's many works (e.g., *De Inventione, Partitiones Oratoriae, Topica,* and *De Oratore*), and from the late first century A.D. Quintilian, *Institutio.* These give a good understanding of rhetoric as taught at the beginning of the Christian era.

The steps taught in speech preparation were: invention of ideas, arrangement, diction, style, memorization, and delivery. From Aristotle oratory was divided into three types: judicial or forensic, with its setting in the law courts, where accusations and defenses were designed to convince the judges; deliberative, with its setting in the citizen assemblies, where persuasion and dissuasion were applied to political decisions; and epideictic or demonstrative, with its setting in ceremonial occasions, where praise and blame were employed to celebrate common values. These types were employed in other settings, and it was recognized that the categories were flexible and were not exhaustive. The parts of a speech could be outlined as four (proem or exordium, *narratio* [statement of the facts], proof [*probatio*], and peroration), five (exordium, statement of the facts, proof, refutation [*refutatio*], and peroration), or six (introduction, statement of facts, division [*divisio*], proof, refutation, and conclusion). Cicero described the duties of the orator as to inform, to delight, and to motivate. Since Aristotle three kinds of arguments were recognized: an appeal to *ethos* or character, to *pathos* or the emotions, and to *logos* or the reason.

In rhetorical education use was made of the declamation. The student was assigned a *thesis*, an abstract general theme, or a *hypothesis*, a particular person or situation, on which to develop a speech. The initial stage of instruction in rhetoric involved the study of preliminary exercises, the *progymnasmata*. Collections of these exercises survive, notably the one of Theon of Alexandria (second century) and the one ascribed to Hermogenes. They dealt with such literary forms as *mythos* (fable), *diēgēma* (narrative), *chreia* (moral anecdote), *gnōmē* (maxim), *anaskeuē* and *kataskeuē* (refutation and confirmation), *enkōmion* (encomium), *synkrisis* (comparison), and *ekphrasis* (description). These school exercises had a greater effect on literature than did the theoretical works on oratory.

BIBLIOGRAPHY

See the Bibliography to Education.

Kennedy, G. A., trans. *Progymnasmata: Greek Textbooks of Prose Composition and Rhetoric.* Atlanta, 2003.

Clarke, M. L. *Rhetoric at Rome.* London, 1953.
Kennedy, G. A. *The Art of Persuasion in Greece.* Princeton, 1963.
Kennedy, G. A. *The Art of Rhetoric in the Roman World.* Princeton, 1972.
Kennedy, G. A. *Greek Rhetoric Under Christian Emperors.* Princeton, 1983.
Russell, D. A. *Greek Declamation.* Cambridge, 1983.
Kennedy, G. A. *New Testament Interpretation Through Rhetorical Criticism.* Chapel Hill, 1984.
Porter, Stanley E., ed. *Handbook of Classical Rhetoric in the Hellenistic Period, 330 B.C.–A.D. 400.* Leiden, 1997.
Anderson, R. Dean Jr. *Ancient Rhetorical Theory and Paul.* Rev. ed. Leuven, 1999.

Literary Forms and Genres

The literary forms mentioned in the preceding paragraph, and others, could be employed in constructing larger works of literature. The New Testament Gospels, for example, contain *chreiai*, pronouncement stories, miracle stories, parables, and other literary units; New Testament letters sometimes incorporate hymns, prayers, confessions, and other liturgical materials. Literary forms are such smaller units with common features that provide a recurring pattern. A literary genre is a broader category, referring to a group of texts that exhibit common features of structure, style, content, and function. There were many such forms and genres in the ancient world, and literary critics often differ on their classifications.

The New Testament contains four principal genres of literature: Gospels, Acts, Epistles, and Apocalypse. The following subsections will deal with the comparable literary genres in the Greco-Roman world to the first three of these. Apocalypses will be discussed in the next to last chapter as part of Jewish literature.

BIBLIOGRAPHY

Berger, Klaus. "Hellenistische Gattungen im Neuen Testament," *ANRW* II, *Principat*, 25.2. Berlin and New York, 1984. Pp. 1031-1432.

Aune, David E. *The New Testament in Its Literary Environment*. Philadelphia, 1987.

Aune, David E., ed. *Greco-Roman Literature and the New Testament*. Atlanta, 1988.

Bailey, James L., and Lyle D. Vander Broek, *Literary Forms in the New Testament: A Handbook*. Louisville, 1992.

Biographies

Greco-Roman biographical writings are grouped into the following main categories: (1) The encomium type, praising an individual (e.g., Tacitus, *Agricola*); (2) the Peripatetic biographies (featuring prose narratives), aiming at literary unity, broadly chronological, and allowing character to be revealed through a person's actions (Plutarch's *Lives* were a new achievement in this tradition by their interest in personality); (3) the "Alexandrian" biographies (sometimes taking dialogue form), which made an attempt to weigh conflicting evidence and accumulated material topically within a broad chronological framework marked by notices of birth and death (Suetonius's *Lives of the Caesars* represents a development of the literary form); and (4) the popular or romantic life (e.g., *Life of Aesop*), which may include collections of sayings.

Greco-Roman biographies were mainly concerned with ideal types as a means of moral instruction and so do not meet modern standards of historical realism. Personality was considered fixed at birth, so any attention to chronology was not for the purpose of tracing individual development. The subjects of biography were generally men prominent in public life. Philosophers used biographies to teach about the founder of their school and its beliefs and to make a defense of their positions.

There has been much discussion of the extent to which the Gospels may be treated as biographies. In terms of literary classification, the Gospels as overall works must be considered biographies, because they are concerned with the "life of Jesus" and only Hellenistic culture offers a comparable type of literature, but the label must be applied in such a broad sense as hardly to be helpful for interpretation. The pericopes in the Gospels bear closer stylistic resemblance to rabbinic stories than to any other body of literature, with the difference that rabbinic stories were not told primarily to portray the person involved but in order to make an edifying or legal point. A fair characterization would be that the Gospels are Hellenistic biographies in form and Jewish in content. The distinctive purpose of the Gospels — to deepen faith (Luke 1:1-4; John 20:30-31), what has been called "explanatory evangelism" — makes them different from Greco-Roman biographies. Even in Christianity, in spite of the large number of apocryphal "Gospels," few if any works were produced that are fully comparable to the canonical Gospels.[91]

BIBLIOGRAPHY

Martin, Francis, ed. *Narrative Parallels to the New Testament.* Atlanta, 1988.

Momigliano, A. *The Development of Greek Biography.* Cambridge, Mass., 1971, 1993.
Talbert, C. H. *What Is a Gospel? The Genre of the Canonical Gospels.* Philadelphia, 1977.
Talbert, C. H. "Biographies of Philosophers and Rulers as Instruments of Religious Propaganda in Mediterranean Antiquity," *ANRW* II, *Principat*, 16.2. Berlin and New York, 1978. Pp. 1619-51.
Shuler, Philip L. *A Genre for the Gospels: The Biographical Character of Matthew.* Philadelphia, 1982.
Burridge, R. A. *What Are the Gospels? A Comparison with Graeco-Roman Biography.* Cambridge, 1992. (Rev. in *JBL* 112[1993]:714-715.) 2nd ed., Grand Rapids, 2005.

Histories and Novels

The Greek word *historia* meant "inquiry" but came to be restricted to research on the past, whether distant or immediate. It covered reporting not only about events but also about the world and its peoples, including works of genealogy, travel descriptions, local history, and chronography. Works that more nearly correspond to what is today called "history" may be classified as historical monographs on a particular period, general histories of a nation, and antiquarian accounts from the distant past to more recent times. Ancient authors distinguished history (*historia* — the narrative of actual events), fiction (*plasma* — the invention of what did not happen but could happen), and myth

---

91. K. L. Schmidt, *The Place of the Gospels in the General History of Literature* (Columbia, S.C., 2001) argues that the Gospels represent a unique literary genre.

or legend (*mythos* or *fabula* — a story that could not happen but might reveal a truth or serve another useful purpose), but in practice did not always observe the distinctions.

History was the most important prose genre of the Hellenistic age; we know of more than 800 now lost Greek historians who wrote in this time. Of the historical writings produced from the second century B.C. to the second century A.D., most took some period of Rome's history as a subject. In addition to the historians noted in the section on authors above, mention should be made of Polybius (c. 200–after 118 B.C.), whose *Histories* tell of Rome's rise to preeminence, Sallust (c. 86-35),[92] who wrote of Rome's recent wars, and Josephus, whose works on Jewish history are discussed in Chapter 5. An important work on historiographical theory was Lucian of Samosata's *How to Write History.*

There was a wide diversity in historiographical practice in the Greco-Roman world. There were those who advocated a rigorous theory of historical accuracy and criticized works where it was absent. Stress was laid on eyewitness participation, interviewing eyewitnesses, access to sources of guaranteed reliability, travel to the scene of events, and checking details with contemporary documents.

Historians often included speeches by participants in their narrative in order to dramatize events, allow expression of the viewpoints of the participants, and give opportunity for interpretation of the events. Practice again seems to have been diverse, some historians using speeches for their own rhetorical compositions (Dionysius of Halicarnassus), some editing or epitomizing actual speeches (Thucydides, Polybius), and others taking a middle path by allowing rhetorical embellishment of what was appropriate to the occasion (Lucian).[93]

Literary parallels to the Book of Acts have been sought also in the Greek novels.[94] Complete surviving representatives of this genre include Chariton, *Chaereas and Callirhoë* (first century A.D.); from the second century A.D., Xenophon, *Ephesian Tale;* Achilles Tatius, *Leucippe and Cleitophon;* and Longus, *Daphnis and Chloe;* and from the fourth century Heliodorus, *Ethiopian Tale.* Latin novels include Petronius, *Satyricon* (first century A.D.) and Apuleius, *Metamorphoses* (second century A.D.). These fictional prose narratives did not constitute a rigid genre but had common themes. They fall into two broad categories: the ideal type presenting a positive model of life

92. Ronald Syme, *Sallust* (Berkeley, 1964).

93. For contrasting views on the speeches in Acts see M. Dibelius, *Studies in the Acts of the Apostles* (London, 1956), 138-85; F. F. Bruce, *The Speeches in the Acts of the Apostles* (London, 1944) and idem, "The Speeches in Acts — Thirty Years After," *Reconciliation and Hope,* ed. R. Banks (Grand Rapids, 1974), 53-68.

94. Richard I. Pervo, *Profit with Delight: The Literary Genre of the Acts of the Apostles* (Philadelphia, 1987).

(Chariton, Xenophon, and Heliodorus) and the satirical that shocked conventional notions (Petronius and Apuleius; milder in approach — Longus and Achilles Tatius). The Greek novels are tales of travel and adventure, usually set in the plot of two lovers from the upper class who are separated, suffer many hardships, and are finally reunited. Speeches are particularly prominent. The apocryphal acts of apostles, produced in the second century when the novels were most popular, and the Pseudo-Clementine *Recognitions* offer closer parallels to the Hellenistic novels than do the canonical Acts.

Bibliography

History

Grant, Michael. *The Ancient Historians.* London, 1970.

Crawford, Michael, ed. *Sources for Ancient History.* Cambridge, 1983.

Fornara, C. W. *The Nature of History in Ancient Greece and Rome.* Berkeley, 1983.

Hemer, Colin J. *The Book of Acts in the Setting of Hellenistic History.* Tübingen, 1989. Pp. 63-100, 415-27.

Momigliano, Arnauld. *The Classical Foundations of Modern Historiography.* Berkeley, 1990.

Sterling, Gregory E. *Josephos, Luke-Acts and Apologetic Historiography.* Leiden, 1992.

Winter, Bruce W. *The Book of Acts in Its First Century Setting.* Vol. 1. Bruce W. Winter and Andrew D. Clarke, eds. *The Book of Acts in Its Ancient Literary Setting.* Grand Rapids, 1993.

Novels

Reardon, B. P., ed. *Collected Ancient Greek Novels.* Berkeley, 1989.

Perry, B. E. *The Ancient Romances: A Literary-Historical Account of Their Origins.* Berkeley, 1967.

Anderson, G. *Eros Sophistes: Ancient Novelists at Play.* Chico, Calif., 1982.

Hägg, Thomas, *The Novel in Antiquity.* Berkeley, 1983.

Anderson, G. *Ancient Fiction: The Novel in the Graeco-Roman World.* Totowa, N.J., 1984.

Morgan, J. R. and Richard Stoneman, eds., *Greek Fiction: The Greek Novel in Context.* London, 1994.

Holzberg, Niklas. *The Ancient Novel: An Introduction.* London, 1995.

Schmeling, G. *The Novel in the Ancient World.* Leiden, 1996; rev. ed., 2003.

Hock, Ronald F., J. Bradley Chance, and Judith Perkins, eds. *Ancient Fiction and Early Christian Narrative.* Atlanta, 1998.

Letters

Much study has been given in recent years to the relationships between New Testament letters and ancient practices in writing letters. In addition to the large number of literary letters published by ancient authors (e.g., Cicero, Seneca, Pliny the Younger, Philostratus, and Libanius) and of private and official letters found among the papyri of Egypt, there exist a few rhetorical handbooks on letter writing. The most important of these works on epistolary theory are Pseudo-Demetrius of Phalerum, *On Style* (between the third century B.C. and the first century A.D.); Pseudo-Demetrius, *Epistolary Types* (between 200 B.C. and A.D. 300 in its present form); and Pseudo-Libanius, *Epistolary Styles* (fourth to sixth century A.D.). From these theorists and the comments of other authors we learn that the ideals for letter writing were brevity, clarity, suitability to the circumstances and mood of their addressees, and style appropriate to the subject matter.

Letters functioned to convey information, to make requests or give commands and instructions, and to maintain personal contact. Some of the most important types of ancient letters for early Christianity, according to recent study, are the following: letters of friendship, family letters, letters of praise and blame, letters of exhortation and advice (subdivided as letters of paraenesis, advice, protrepsis, admonition, rebuke, reproach, or consolation), letters of mediation (or recommendation), and finally accusing, apologetic, and accounting letters. The types of letters were influenced by social relationships — whether between friends (equals), between patron and client (superior and subordinate), or between members of a household (combining elements of both). In early Christianity most letters reflect a familial relationship, an indication of the understanding of the church as a household. At the same time, the position of Paul as a founding apostle of his churches and later the position of bishops of churches gave to their letters some of the characteristics of official letters. Jewish authorities were accustomed to send authoritative instructions to Jewish communities, especially in the diaspora, and Paul adopted this practice to instruct Christian communities.

The form of Greek and Latin letters in general was as follows:

(1) Opening or Prescript. This was composed of three parts: the sender, the addressee, and an expression of greeting (often expanded by a wish for good health). Various qualifications might expand on the identification of the sender and addressee. The simplest and most common greeting was "Hail" *(chairein)*.

(2) Body. The letter might begin with an expression of thanksgiving or of prayer to the gods. Or there might be a mention of a favorable remembrance of the addressees, prayer for them, or disclosure of the sender's circumstances. Such transitional statements provided the basis of the relationship between the sender and the recipient or the occasion for writing. Such preliminary remarks were optional and often the author went directly to the body proper. The message of the letter might be long or short and serve many different purposes — making a request, introduction of a friend, consolation, exhortation (paraenesis), advice, congratulations, or personal apologetic, to name a few of the principal types. Style varied with the nature and contents of the letter. The body

of the letter might be rounded out with a summary statement, a summons to act, request for further communication, or notification of a coming visit.

(3) Closing. The conclusion might consist of a final greeting, a repeated wish for the health or welfare of the recipient, wishes for persons other than the addressee, or a prayer sentence. The word *farewell (errōsthe)* normally stood at the end. Sometimes a date was given.

Acts 15:23-29 and 23:26-30 are typical Hellenistic letters in form. Second and Third John too are typical in structure and motifs.

Paul modified the conventional vocabulary of the opening and closing of Greek letters, and of course the content of his letters was distinctive. Some elements in the Pauline letters, such as doxologies and benedictions, and the wordings of his greetings (peace) derive from Jewish letters. The emphasis on grace in the opening and closing is characteristic of Paul. The distinction between epistles (written for publication or stylistic effect) and letters (informal communications in a specific situation) is not adequate for understanding Paul's letters, for they partake of both public, authoritative features and immediate, personal communication. The Pauline letters developed into distinctive features two elements that might or might not be present in a Hellenistic letter:

(1) Thanksgiving. The transition between the opening and body of a Greek letter, which might take the form of a thanksgiving or prayer, was expanded by Paul into a main section. In his statement of thanksgiving for the addressees Paul summarized and announced the principal concerns of the letter.

(2) Paraenesis. Some Greek letters made requests or gave exhortations to the recipient. An extended section of some Pauline letters is the practical or ethical instruction that followed the doctrinal exposition in the body of the letter and preceded the closing. The arrangement of material into a doctrinal argument followed by a practical application, although unparalleled in private letters, is paralleled in philosophical/moral literature. Paul sometimes wove paraenesis into his entire letter (1 Thessalonians). For the paraenetic style, see p. 322. He particularly liked the verb *parakalō* ("beseech"), an intimate word for exhortation and encouragement.

Where Paul breaks open or departs from his typical letter form indicates his special concerns: for instance, the absence of a thanksgiving at the beginning of Galatians, and the expression of confidence in his readers (e.g., Philem. 21; Rom. 15:14-15), not typical of Greek letters of the time. A special function of the letter, especially as Paul employed it, was as a substitute for the writer's presence.[95] The comments on amanuenses below apply especially to letters.

Aspects of letters could be appended to a written speech (Hebrews) or woven into a treatise (1 John).

---

95. Robert Funk, "The Apostolic Parousia: Form and Function," in W. R. Farmer, C. F. D. Moule, and R. R. Niebuhr, eds., *Studies in Christian History and Interpretation: Studies Presented to John Knox* (Cambridge, 1967), 249-68.

The government maintained a postal service for administrative, military, and diplomatic communications, but private citizens had to depend on slaves, employees, or friends to serve as couriers. Paul sent letters through his associates, who supplemented the written message with oral information (Eph. 6:21-22; Phil. 2:25-30).

BIBLIOGRAPHY

Hercher, Rudolph. *Epistolographi Graeci*. Paris, n.d.

Stowers, Stanley K. *Letter Writing in Greco-Roman Antiquity*. Philadelphia, 1986.

White, John L. *Light from Ancient Letters*. Philadelphia, 1986.

Malherbe, Abraham J. *Ancient Epistolary Theorists*. Atlanta, 1988.

Schubert, Paul. *Form and Function of the Pauline Thanksgivings*. Beihefte zur Zeitschrift für die neutestamentliche Wissenschaft, vol. 20. Berlin, 1939.

Sanders, Jack T. "The Transition from Opening Epistolary Thanksgiving to Body in the Letters of the Pauline Corpus." *JBL* 81 (1962):348-62.

Funk, Robert. "The Letter: Form and Style." In *Language, Hermeneutic, and Word of God*. New York, 1966. Pp. 250-74.

Bahr, Gordon J. "Paul and Letter Writing in the First Century." *CBQ* 28 (1966):465-77.

Funk, Robert. "The Form and Structure of II and III John." *JBL* 86 (1967):424-30.

Bahr, Gordon J. "The Subscriptions in the Pauline Letters." *JBL* 87 (1968):27-41.

Mullins, Terence Y. "Greeting as a New Testament Form." *JBL* 87 (Dec. 1968):418-26.

Mullins, Terence Y. "Formulas in New Testament Epistles." *JBL* 91 (1972):380-90.

White, John L. *The Form and Function of the Body of the Greek Letter*. Missoula, Mont., 1972.

Doty, W. *Letters in Primitive Christianity*. Philadelphia, 1973.

O'Brien, Peter T. *Introductory Thanksgivings in the Letters of Paul*. Novum Testamentum Supplements, vol. 49. Leiden, 1977.

White, John L., ed. *Studies in Ancient Letter Writing*. Semeia 22 (1981).

White, John L. "New Testament Epistolary Literature in the Framework of Ancient Epistolography." *ANRW* II, *Principat*, 25.2. Berlin and New York, 1984. Pp. 1730-56.

Francis, Fred O., and J. Paul Sampley. *Pauline Parallels*. Philadelphia, 1984.

Schnider, F., and W. Stenger. *Studien zum neutestamentlichen Briefformular*. Leiden, 1987.

Taatz, Irene. *Frühjüdische Briefe: Die Paulinischen Briefe im Rahmen der offiziellen religösen briefe des Frühjudentums*. Göttingen, 1991.

Stirewalt, M. Luther. *Studies in Ancient Greek Epistolography*. Atlanta, 1994.

Weima, Jeffrey A. D. *Neglected Endings: The Significance of the Pauline Letter Closings*. Sheffield, 1994.

Weima, Jeffrey A. D. "The Pauline Letter Closings: Analysis and Hermeneutical Significance." *Bulletin for Biblical Research* 5 (1995):177-98.

Making of Books

Literature in the pre-Christian centuries employed the papyrus scroll; from the fourth century A.D. it was commonly preserved on the parchment codex. The New Testament writings were produced near the time of the beginning of this change in book production.

The preparation and use of the Egyptian papyrus plant for a writing material is described by Pliny the Elder in *Natural History* 13.68-83. The use of papyrus for writing in Egypt was two millennia older than Alexander's time, to which Pliny attributes it, but its widespread use dates from his time.

Parchment was made from skins of sheep or goats, and vellum from the skins of calves. (Present usage does not make a distinction between these terms, using *parchment* primarily but sometimes reserving *vellum* for a higher grade of writing material.) The skins were washed, scraped to remove hairs, rubbed with pumice stone to make them smooth, and dressed with chalk. Pliny tells the story of the rivalry of the Pergamene and Alexandrian kings over their libraries. Eumenes II, king of Pergamum in the third century B.C., tried to kidnap the librarian of Ptolemy from Alexandria. Whereupon Ptolemy put the librarian in prison and placed an embargo on the export of papyrus. This led Eumenes to develop an alternative writing material, parchment (the name is derived from Pergamum). Discoveries of parchment from an earlier period indicate that if there is any truth in this story it was only that parchment was first put to general use for literary purposes in Eumenes' time.

The universal form of a book in ancient times was the roll (Lat. *volumen*). Papyrus rolls were made by gluing sheets of papyrus together. A sheet rarely exceeded thirteen inches by nine inches, but ten by seven and one-half inches was more common. Pliny says twenty would be glued together for a normal roll. The extreme limit for a normal Greek literary roll would be thirty-five feet (or about eleven meters), but we know of rolls much longer. The columns of writing were independent of the sheets: two to three inches wide (giving eighteen to twenty-five letters) with one inch of space between. A column would normally hold twenty-five to forty-five lines. Writing was on one side only (Rev. 5:1 indicates either lack of paper or fullness of the message by being written on both sides). The scroll was unrolled with the right hand and rolled up with the left; the beginning of the work was on the outer part of the roll and the conclusion on the inner part.

The Jews wrote the Old Testament Scriptures to be kept in their synagogues on leather scrolls. These would unroll from right to left (since Hebrew is written that way) and for long scrolls would be wound on two rollers.

Third John 13 refers to the writing implements of reed pen and ink made from carbon soot, and 2 John 12 to paper (*chartēs* or papyrus) and ink.

The codex or book form *(liber, libellus)* originated with binding wax-covered wood tablets together with rings or leather cords. The word *codex* is from

WRITING MATERIALS, wall painting from Pompeii
The woman holds a stylus and wax tablet for household accounts and the man a
scroll for literature. *(Courtesy National Archaeological Museum, Naples)*

caudex, a trunk of a tree, and then a block of wood. Household and small business accounts and records would be kept on such wax tablets, inscribed with a stylus. Children also used them for school exercises. Parchment replaced the wax tablet for some uses, including the first draft of literary works. Second Timothy 4:13 refers to "books" (rolls, which might be Scriptures) and "parchments" (*membranai,* which might be Paul's notebooks or perhaps Christian writings).[96]

96. The meanings suggested are often reversed, but I judge that, if any distinction is intended, the usage of the words favors the interpretation in the text.

Martial notes in his *Epigrams* the first certain appearance of the parchment codex in the book trade about A.D. 84. He seems to celebrate a new departure. Every indication is that the codex originated in Italy and spread from there. Its use for books would seem to be an adaptation from its use by businessmen and lawyers.

A half-century after Martial Christians were publishing their works in Egypt on papyrus codices. All of the great papyri finds of New Testament manuscripts of this century (Chester-Beatty, John Rylands, Bodmer) are from codices. In Egypt the papyrus was the most convenient writing material. The codex proved its usefulness to Christians — it was more compact because it permitted writing on both sides; it gave easier reference; and it was better suited to a collection of volumes. Papyrus 46 contains Paul's letters in one handy volume, whereas his letters would have filled two cumbersome rolls. The Gospels or the Gospels and Acts occur together in other codices. Whatever may have been the original reasons for the adoption of the codex, this form proved providential for a "library of sacred books," a canon, and Christians seem to have been mainly responsible for making it the standard in the book business. In contrast to the great predominance of codices in Christian literature of the early centuries, in the second and third centuries most pagan literature continued to appear on scrolls.

The one-chapter epistles in the New Testament would have fit a single sheet of papyrus. The longest New Testament books — Matthew, Luke, and Acts — would reach the maximum scroll length, thirty-two or thirty-five feet.

Professional scribes were available for literary works in the ancient world. Paul and other New Testament writers employed such amanuenses (e.g., Rom. 16:22; 1 Pet. 5:12), who in some cases may have been given a certain freedom in drafting a letter within the instructions given by the author concerning subject matter and approach. This practice may account for some stylistic and other differences between letters in the Pauline corpus. The author wrote a final greeting and signed the letter in his own hand (cf. Gal. 6:11). Manuscripts survive written in a careful book hand with an author's scrawled conclusion at the end; a Pauline letter may have looked something like that.[97]

What constituted publication in an age without printing presses? What constituted the difference between a work intended for the public (of which there might be only one copy, although scribes were available to make multiple copies of works intended for sale) and an author's worksheets or private productions (of which there might be more than one copy)? One distinguishing feature was prefixing a formal dedication. Authors even kept several standard

97. Gordon J. Bahr, "Paul and Letter Writing in the First Century," *CBQ* 28 (1966):465-77; Richard N. Longenecker, "Ancient Amanuenses and the Pauline Epistles," in *New Dimensions in New Testament Study* (Grand Rapids, 1974), 281-97; E. R. Richards, *The Secretary in the Letters of Paul* (Tübingen, 1991).

PAPYRUS LETTER,
dated August 24, A.D. 66
A Pauline letter probably looked like this,
with the book hand of the amanuensis and
the author's cursive additions (Gal. 6:11).
(Courtesy University Library, Cambridge)

types of dedications on hand for use when needed. The formal dedications to Theophilus in Luke and Acts mark these works for the book trade and are one indication of the author's familiarity with the literary conventions of the Hellenistic world; they are the only books in the New Testament with this feature, which shows that they were intended for a wider audience than that of the Christian communities and reflect a higher level of culture. Another way of making a work "public" was by recitation. The reading of literature to a circle of one's friends was a type of entertainment in the ancient world. By this means the Gospels and letters (including Revelation) of the New Testament became "public" — although only within the circles of the churches and of course by reading in the context of Christian assemblies and not in the formal way of Hellenistic recitations.

BIBLIOGRAPHY

Hussein, M. A. *Origins of the Book: Egypt's Contribution to the Development of the Book from Papyrus to Codex.* Greenwich, Conn., 1972.

Reynolds, L. D., and N. G. Wilson. *Scribes and Scholars.* 2d ed. London, 1974.

Lewis, Naphtali. *Papyrus in Classical Antiquity.* Oxford, 1974.

Idem. *Papyrus in Classical Antiquity: A Supplement.* Brussels, 1989.

Turner, E. G. *The Typology of the Early Codex.* Philadelphia, 1977.

Roberts, C. H., and T. C. Skeat. *The Birth of the Codex.* Oxford, 1983.

Blanck, H. *Das Buch in der Antike.* Munich, 1992.

Llewelyn, S. R. "The Development of the Codex." *New Documents Illustrating Early Christianity.* Vol. 7. Macquarie, 1994. Pp. 249-256.

Murphy-O'Conner, Jerome. *Paul the Letter-Writer: His World, His Options, His Skills.* Collegeville, Minn., 1995.

Gamble, Harry Y. *Books and Readers in the Early Church.* New Haven, 1995.

Haines-Eitzen, Kim. *Guardians of Letters: Literacy, Power, and the Transmitters of Early Christian Literature.* Oxford, 2000.

Millard, Alan. *Reading and Writing in the Time of Jesus.* Sheffield, 2000.

Reading and Studying of Books

A significant minority of the population was literate.[98] A distinction must be made between the top layer of society that was learned and capable of producing their own literature and a much larger number (but still definitely a minority) who had a minimal but functional literacy. Professional scribes were available to assist in drawing up and reading legal documents.

The availability of papyrus and slaves made it possible for books to be produced in the Hellenistic age on a scale previously unknown. Learning was

98. W. V. Harris, *Ancient Literacy* (Cambridge, Mass., 1989).

prized, and there were publishers and booksellers in the major cities to satisfy the desire for reading. Silent reading was virtually unknown; even in private one read aloud (cf. Acts 8:30). Authors catered not only to the learned in the artificial and archaizing "Alexandrian Poetry" (the *Hymns* of Callimachus are a notable example) but to the popular audience in satiric and moralizing poetry and amusement literature (e.g., the mimes and diatribes; see pp. 322-23). This period also saw the development of the Hellenistic romance or adventure novel.

Kings established libraries, the greatest being at Alexandria, the center of scholarly study in the ancient world. By the first century B.C. the library at Alexandria had perhaps seven hundred thousand rolls in its collection when it was partially destroyed during the time Caesar was besieged there. Its final destruction apparently belongs to the Arab conquests. Most of the cities of the Greek world had libraries.[99]

Zenodotus of Ephesus, one of the librarians at Alexandria, invented textual criticism by comparing manuscripts. The Alexandrian scholars handed down the texts of the Greek classics and introduced accentuation. They laid the foundation of philology.

To the first century A.D. belongs the earliest work of Hellenistic allegory to survive, Heraclitus's *Homeric Questions*. It is a collection of the opinions of grammarians in which embarrassing passages of Homer were allegorized into either psychological or scientific statements. The allegorizing of Homer and Hesiod was much older, flourishing already in the fifth century B.C. It was practiced both by grammarians like Theagenes of Rhegium (to defend morally offensive passages in Homer) and by philosophers who sought to find their teachings in the hallowed tradition of ancient literature. The Stoics (Chrysippus and Cornutus) especially developed allegory for this purpose (see p. 357).

Inscriptions and Papyri

The inscriptions and papyri are specialized areas of study in themselves. They have become independent disciplines more recently than the study of the authors of the classical and Hellenistic periods, the knowledge of whom was never completely forgotton, as a result of the archaeological discoveries of the last two centuries. We highlight their importance for the study of early Christianity by this separate section but do not attempt to do more than make the student aware of their existence and of the works to consult in pursuing their study further. The inscriptions and papyri have a twofold importance for the student of early Christianity: (1) they provide much of the source material for

---

99. Jenö Platthy, *Sources on the Earliest Greek Libraries with the Testimonia* (Amsterdam, 1968); Lionel Casson, *Libraries in the Ancient World* (New Haven, 2001).

the history, customs, and daily life of the times, and (2) they provide primary data for the meaning and usage of words in early Christian literature.

The inscriptions have the advantage over literary texts of bringing the observer into direct contact with the original and making the reader contemporary with the writing: there is no intermediate period of transmission and the possibility of scribal errors introduced later into the texts (any errors are those of the stonecutter himself). Two major classes of inscriptions are epitaphs (grave monuments) and official decrees (by governments or associations). The former are a rich source of religious attitudes as well as often providing data for sociological study. The latter provide basic constitutional, legal, and economic information. The inscriptions have the disadvantage that they presented what individuals or officials wanted to be known and not necessarily what really was. (The bibliography includes the older standard collections and some of the works that report new finds.)

Most of the papyri finds have come from Egypt, where the dry climate has been conducive to the preservation of this writing material (see pp. 128-30). The papyri have often preserved earlier copies of the text of literary works than were otherwise known. Of special interest at this point, however, are the nonliterary or documentary papyri. These have been classified as official or private. The official documents preserved on papyri include government edicts, public announcements, reports of meetings, judicial proceedings, petitions and applications, contracts, receipts, accounts, and official correspondence. The private documents also include business contracts, receipts, and accounts; but in addition they include wills, marriage contracts, divorce agreements, invitations, school exercises, and private correspondence. The nonliterary papyri thus provide primary data for the study of governmental administration, economic affairs, family life, and many other topics. The large number of private letters provide the form of the typical letter (pp. 125-26) and the vocabulary and syntax of ordinary people. Indeed, a special value of the papyri is that they often put us in contact with the common people, not the intellectuals and upper classes represented in literature.

The papyri are dispersed in so many libraries and even private collections that the bibliography is not an attempt to list published collections; rather, reference works to the Greek language, such as Liddell and Scott's *Greek Lexicon*, will provide a more complete listing.

BIBLIOGRAPHY

Inscriptions

Corpus Inscriptionum Graecarum. 4 vols. Berlin, 1828–1877.
Inscriptiones Graecae. 14 vols. Berlin, 1873–1890.
Dittenberger, W. *Orientis Graeci Inscriptiones Selectae.* 2 vols. Leipzig, 1903–1905.
    Reprint. Hildesheim, 1970.

Dittenberger, W. *Sylloge Inscriptionum Graecarum.* 3d ed. 4 vols. Leipzig, 1915–1924.
Supplementum Epigraphicum Graecum. Leiden, 1923–.

Corpus Inscriptionum Latinarum. Berlin, 1863–.
Dessau, H. *Inscriptiones Latinae Selectae.* 3 vols. Berlin, 1892–1916.

Woodhead, A. G. *Study of Greek Inscriptions.* Cambridge, 1967.
Giancarlo, Susini. *The Roman Stonecutter: An Introduction to Latin Epigraphy.* Oxford, 1972.
Gordon, A. E. *Illustrated Introduction to Latin Epigraphy.* Berkeley, 1983.
Keppie, Lawrence. *Understanding Roman Inscriptions.* Baltimore, 1991.

L'année épigraphique. 1885–.

Papyri

Kenyon, F. G., et al. *Greek Papyri in the British Museum.* 5 vols. London, 1893–1917.
Grenfell, B. P., A. S. Hunt, et al. *The Oxyrhynchus Papyri.* London, 1898–.
Hunt, A. S., and C. C. Edgar. *Select Papyri: Non-Literary.* 2 vols. Cambridge, Mass., 1932–1934.

Turner, E. G. *Greek Papyri: An Introduction.* 2d ed. Oxford, 1980.
Pestman, P. W. *The New Papyrological Primer.* 2d ed. Leiden, 1994.
Oates, John F., Roger S. Bagnell, and William H. Willis. *Checklist of Editions of Greek Papyri and Ostraca.* Chico, 1985.
Pestman, P. W., and H. A. Pupprecht. *Berichtigungsliste der Griechischen Papyrusurkunden aus Aegypten.* Leiden, 1992.

Bulletin of the American Society of Papyrologists. 1963–.
Zeitschrift für Papyrologie und Epigraphik. 1967–.
Horsley, H. R., ed. *New Documents Illustrating Early Christianity.* 1981–.

Language

The only way to understand the thinking of persons in ancient times is inductively through their language. Language, in turn, had a impact on cultural and religious developments.

Although the first century was a more important period in the history of the Latin language than of the Greek, Greek remained the dominant language in the eastern Mediterranean and the principal language of commerce throughout the Roman world. Following the conquests of Alexander the Great, throughout the east Greek was the official language, the language of communication between those of different races, and the language of settlers in the Greek cities. Although Palestine was multilingual in the first century — Greek, various Aramaic dialects, Hebrew, and some Latin — Greek was clearly the language of choice in order to disseminate a message as widely as possible.[100] Therefore, all the New Testament was written entirely in Greek. Attic Greek had developed into the so-called *koinē* (common or everyday) Greek of the Hellenistic age. This in turn became the Byzantine, and finally modern Greek.

When the knowledge of Greek was confined primarily to that of the classics, the New Testament seemed to represent a peculiar Greek that was accounted for as "Holy Spirit Greek," a form of the language specially inspired by the Holy Spirit for purposes of revelation. When Greek contemporary with New Testament times became available through the inscriptions and papyri, this attitude changed. Scholars such as Deissmann stressed that the language of the New Testament was essentially that of the times. A reaction set in, as many argued for the distinctiveness of New Testament Greek as a manifestation of "Jewish Greek." The New Testament has been much influenced by the Septuagint, the Greek translation of the Old Testament. This plus the fact that all but perhaps one of the New Testament authors was a Jew has given a certain Semitic cast to parts of the New Testament, at least to the extent of a preference for certain constructions even when these are paralleled in other Hellenistic sources. These distinctive features to the grammar and vocabulary in the New Testament, however, may often be the result of bilingualism and not constitute evidence of a distinct Jewish Greek dialect. The extent to which the New Testament belongs to a special category of *koinē* Greek remains under debate, but on linguistic grounds it may be said that it fits well into the non-literary language known from other sources in the first and second centuries. The New Testament avoids much of the ordinary language of Hellenistic religion and did not appropriate pagan religious terms.[101]

The Attic Greek of fifth-century-B.C. Athens was being recognized already in the second century B.C. as the standard for the language. This attitude gave rise to Atticism (the imitation of earlier Attic forms), which flourished in the second and again in the fourth century A.D.

BIBLIOGRAPHY

Moulton, J. H., W. F. Howard, and Nigel Turner. *A Grammar of New Testament Greek.* 4 vols. Edinburgh, 1908–1976.

Deissmann, G. A. *Light from the Ancient East.* New York, 1927.

Moulton, J. H., and George Milligan. *The Vocabulary of the Greek Testament.* London, 1952. Reprint. Grand Rapids, 1974.

Voelz, James W. "The Language of the New Testament." *ANRW* II, *Principat*, 25.2. Berlin, 1984. Pp. 893-977.

100. G. Mussies, "Greek as the Vehicle for Early Christianity," *New Testament Studies* 29 (1983):356-69.

101. A. D. Nock, "The Vocabulary of the New Testament," *JBL* 52 (1933):134 (*Essays*, 343), cites examples.

Horsley, G. H. R. "The Fiction of 'Jewish Greek.'" *New Documents Illustrating Early Christianity* 5 (1989):5-40.

Porter, Stanley E., *The Language of the New Testament: Classic Essays.* Sheffield, 1991.

Porter, Stanley E. "The Greek Language of the New Testament." In idem, *Handbook to Exegesis of the New Testament.* Leiden, 1997. Pp. 99-130.

ART AND ARCHITECTURE

With the Hellenistic age the classical restraint in art was abandoned. It has been said that all the tendencies of the age were in its sculpture: lack of repose, self-consciousness, romanticism, realism even to ugliness, and individualism (much portrait statuary).[102] But it was not an age of decadence in sculpture: the winged Victory of Samothrace alighting on the prow of a ship (c. 200 B.C.), the Aphrodite from Melos (Venus d'Milo) from the second century B.C., and the frieze depicting the war of the gods and the giants from the altar of Zeus at Pergamum (second century B.C.) influenced in composition and details by the pediment sculptures of the Parthenon and the largest monumental sculpture of Greek art to survive, belie any such idea.[103] This was the golden age of portraiture, but Hellenistic sculptors never wholly abandoned the idealization of their subjects, a feature distinguishing their work from the real-life work of Roman artists. Much of Greek sculpture is known today only from inferior, later Roman copies. Roman skill in portraiture was not matched by technical excellence in other aspects of statuary, such as balance.

Very little of Hellenistic painting survives. For this the art student must turn to the Roman period. Much decorative wall painting of houses was preserved in Pompeii,[104] and much of this goes back to Hellenistic models. One of the great pieces from Pompeii is the mosaic from the House of the Faun representing the confrontation of Alexander the Great and Darius in battle.[105] The work appears to be true to an original painting composed not long after Alexander's death. Mosaic may have been an invention of Alexandria, but that city's great contributions were in the smaller arts.

Rome imposed a certain restraint on the exuberance of Hellenistic art. One may compare the noble dignity of the figures of Augustus's *Ara Pacis* (Al-

---

102. W. W. Tarn, *Hellenistic Civilization* (Cleveland, 1953), 316.

103. A. Adriani, "Hellenistic Art," and O. Vessberg, "Hellenistic-Roman Art," in *Encyclopedia of World Art* (New York, 1963), 7:283-411 and accompanying plates; see index of same for pictures of art works referred to in this unit.

104. All the pictures from Pompeii are available in the encyclopedia edited by G. P. Carratelli and I. Baldassarre, *Pompei: Pitture e Mosaici* (Rome, 1990–1999), 9 vols.

105. Ada Cohen, *The Alexander Mosaic: Stories of Victory and Defeat* (Cambridge, 1997).

FRIEZE FROM ALTAR OF ZEUS, Pergamum, 180–159 B.C.
The goddess Athena conquers the giant Alkyoneus as part of the depiction of
the struggle of Greek civilization against barbarism. Ge, the earth mother, is
subjected under Athena's feet, while Nike flies to crown the victorious Athena.
(© Bildarchiv Preussicher Kulturbesitz/Art Resource, NY)

tar of Peace, dedicated in 9 B.C.)[106] with the confusion of figures in the Altar of
Zeus from Pergamum. Part of the Roman interest in portraiture stems from
the practice of preserving images of deceased ancestors in the home and of
placing portraits of the head of the family in the house that was under his control. The former were first waxen masks, but later marble or stone busts became popular. One of the most remarkable sculptural creations of the early
empire, and a valuable historical source besides, is Trajan's column in the Forum of his name on which a continuous spiral relief depicts the emperor's two
Dacian wars. The finds at Pompeii and Herculaneum have shown the extent to
which paintings were used as room decoration in private houses, often covering complete rooms as wallpaper might today.

In architecture the Doric and Ionic forms had reached perfection in the

---

106. Paul Zanker, *The Power of Images in the Age of Augustus* (Ann Arbor, 1988) for the visual representations of the Augustan Age, of which the *Ara Pacis* is an outstanding example, celebrating victory and order so as to restore the people's morale and optimism; David Castriota, *The
Ara Pacis Augustae and the Imagery of Abundance in Later Greek and Early Roman Imperial Art*
(Princeton, 1995).

Parthenon and Erechtheum respectively on the Acropolis of Athens (fifth century B.C.). From the fourth century B.C. and after preference was for the Ionic (e.g., the temple of Artemis at Ephesus) and its offshoot the Corinthian (Tholos at Epidaurus and the temple of Zeus in Athens).

The Greeks knew how to erect columns and the Romans knew how to bridge space. Thus may we briefly characterize the major architectural glories still to be seen at classical sites: columns around Greek temples, marketplaces, and public buildings; arches supporting Roman aqueducts, bridges, theatres, triumphal monuments, and at city gates. The Roman success with the arch was extended to vault structures such as the Pantheon and the Colosseum (Flavian Amphitheatre). Classical sites around the Mediterranean show what were the important public buildings: every city had its temples, marketplaces, theatre, town hall, and gymnasium or baths (see pp. 83, 85). The architectural achievements of the early empire in particular were considerable.

Private houses in the eastern provinces were one-family dwellings up to four stories high. The dining room on the top floor was the only large room and often opened on a terrace. This is the "upper room" of Acts 1:13; 9:37, 39;

FRIEZE FROM ALTAR OF PEACE, Rome, built by Augustus
The calm and order of the figures in this procession represent the
ideals of the Augustan Age and the contrast of Roman art with
the restless energy of Hellenistic art.

ROMAN AQUEDUCT, Segovia, built under Augustus
The most spectacular of the aqueducts, the Segovia aqueduct rises
to a maximum height of 28.29 meters. *(© Art Resource, NY)*

20:8; Mark 14:15. Dining rooms, especially those under Roman influence, had a table in the center for food and three surrounding couches for the diners to recline, from which the room takes its name — *triclinium*. The main couch was opposite the entrance.

The house *(domus)* of the wealthy most often followed the plan of the Hellenistic and Italian peristyle house, that is, the rooms were built around a central garden court with a colonnade around the court (some attractively restored at Pompeii). The houses at Pompeii have an atrium, an entrance area open to the sky with an impluvium to catch rainwater, but this feature is thought to have been obsolete by the mid–first century except in similar small country towns. The entrance area and receiving rooms were public space open to visitors and often used for conducting business, but the interior rooms (e.g., bedrooms) were private space. The country villas were enlarged versions of the same plan, with farm buildings as well as the living quarters built in a rectangle around a large open central area. The masses lived in tenement houses of five or six stories (tall tenement buildings are mainly after Nero), either towerlike with apartments on top of each other as in Alexandria (or modern-day Athens) or forming large blocks *(insulae)* as in Rome and Ostia with shops or warehouses at street level and numerous apartments on each of the upper floors.

CLAY LAMP

Clay lamps such as this one, which features a menorah on either side of the wick, burned olive oil to light houses. *(© Erich Lessing/Art Resource, NY)*

The earliest known Christian meeting places were private houses adapted for church use (as Dura Europus, mid–third century) or assembly halls modeled on domestic or commercial (warehouses) architecture and modified for the needs of worship (such were the earliest churches in Rome). With the Constantinian peace, church buildings became public monuments, and the basilica type predominated. The basilica style (a long rectangular open assembly area with a semicircular extension [apse] as a focus of attention) was widely used in Hellenistic and imperial times for both private and public purposes: as audience halls in homes of the wealthy and of imperial officials, as law courts and exchange buildings on the forums, and as gathering places in the larger baths. Because of this variety of function and design, considerable debate continues as to the specific origins of the basilica style in church architecture. The Christian basilica was one variant among many within this general type of structure.[107]

---

107. R. Krautheimer, "The Beginning of Early Christian Architecture," *Review of Religion* (1939):127-48 (*Studies in Early Christian, Medieval, and Renaissance Art* [London, 1971], 1-20); J. G. Davies, *Origin and Development of Early Christian Church Architecture* (New York, 1953); J. B. Ward Perkins, "Constantine and the Origins of the Christian Basilica," *Papers of the British School at Rome* 22 (1954):69-90; R. Krautheimer, "The Constantinian Basilica," *Dumbarton Oaks Papers* 21 (1967):117-40; idem, *Early Christian and Byzantine Architecture* (Baltimore, 1965); L. M. White, *Building God's House in the Roman World: Architectural Adaptation among Pagans, Jews, and Christians* (Baltimore, 1990); idem, *The Social Origins of Christian Architecture*, Vol. II: *Texts and Monuments for the Christian Domus Ecclesiae in its Environment*, Harvard Theological Studies (Valley Forge, Penn., 1997).

BIBLIOGRAPHY

Bieber, M. *The Sculpture of the Hellenistic Age.* Rev. ed. New York, 1961. Reprint, 1980.

Hanfman, G. M. *Hellenistic Art.* Washington, 1963.

Boardman, John, et al. *The Art and Architecture of Ancient Greece.* London, 1967.

Pollitt, J. J. *Art in the Hellenistic Age.* Cambridge, 1986.

Lawrence, A. W. *Greek Architecture.* 5th ed. New Haven, 1996.

Higgins, R. A. *Greek and Roman Jewelry.* London, 1961.

Kähler, Heinz. *The Art of Rome and Her Empire.* Art of the World. New York, 1963.

Toynbee, J. M. C. *The Art of the Romans.* London, 1965.

Becatti, G. *The Art of Ancient Greece and Rome.* London, 1968.

Bieber, M. *Ancient Copies: Contributions to the History of Greek and Roman Art.* New York, 1977.

Andreae, Bernard. *The Art of Rome.* London, 1978.

MacDonald, Wm. L. *The Architecture of the Roman Empire.* 2 vols. New Haven, 1982, 1988.

Pollitt, J. J. *The Art of Rome c. 753 B.C.–A.D. 337: Sources and Documents.* Cambridge, 1983.

Kleiner, Diana E. E. *Roman Sculpture.* New Haven, 1992.

McKay, A. G. *Houses, Villas, and Palaces in the Roman World.* Ithaca, N.Y., 1975; Baltimore, 1998.

Bebe, H. Keith. "Domestic Architecture and the New Testament." *BA* 38 (1975):89-104.

Clarke, John R. *The Houses of Roman Italy, 100 B.C.–A.D. 250: Ritual, Space, and Decoration.* Berkeley, 1991.

CLUBS AND ASSOCIATIONS

Greek Clubs

Club life was as highly developed among the Greeks as it is in modern American society. Voluntary associations had been recognized in law by Solon.[108] The earliest societies for which epigraphical records survive (fifth century B.C.) were groups of *orgeones* ("sacrificing associates").[109] They were essentially religious in character, existing for the cult of some deity or hero, and at first limited to citizens (with membership often hereditary). Next in the records comes the kind of society named a *thiasos* (some of which can be traced back to the fourth century). They too were primarily religious but with a far more developed social

---

108. The jurist Gaius cited the law of Athens that any deme, brotherhood, cult association, dining club, social club, or body organized for commerce is lawful so long as a specific law does not forbid it; Justinian, *Digest* 47.22.4.

109. W. S. Ferguson, "The Attic Orgeones," *HTR* 37 (April 1944):61-140.

side. The members *(thiasotai)* were largely foreigners, and *thiasoi* seem sometimes to be almost national clubs. The next stage in the development of Greek associations is represented by the societies of *eranistai* (from *eranos,* a dinner), which flourished from the mid–third century B.C. to imperial times. The religious element was not absent, but more and more the social and economic basis replaced the religious. The number of clubs grew tremendously after 300 B.C., and freedom of association was deeply ingrained in Hellenistic life.

Often the societies were composed of those with a common interest (as the athletic guilds) or common occupation. The latter are sometimes called trade guilds, but should not be thought of in terms of medieval guilds or modern labor unions. They were local groups, primarily or even exclusively religious and social, and did not set economic policies. Women sometimes formed clubs of their own; at other times they were found in the same club with men. Children too were sometimes admitted. Slaves and freedmen frequently formed their own associations.

Some societies limited the number of members; others had no restrictions. Few seem to have contained less than ten members or more than one hundred, the average membership being thirty to thirty-five. Admission to a club was gained by the vote of the members. The new member paid an entrance fee and swore to observe the society's regulations.

In contrast to the practice in Roman colleges (see below), only one leading person was in the rule in Greek clubs. There is almost invariably a priest or priestess among the officials. Greek associations were characterized by the very large number of officials and the wide variety of titles employed for them, almost as if the intention was to give everyone a special position.

BIBLIOGRAPHY

Poland, Franz. *Geschichte des Griechischen Vereinswesens.* Preisschriften von der Fürstlich Jablonowskischen Gesellschaft zu Leipzig, vol. 38 (1909). Reprint, 1967.

Tod, Marcus N. *Sidelights on Greek History.* Oxford, 1932.

Roman Colleges

We may distinguish three periods in the history of Roman private associations: (1) to the middle of the last century of the Republic the right to form private associations of all kinds was not limited by any special law; (2) until the end of the third century A.D. the right of association was regulated by strict laws, and the trade and professional *collegia* gradually assumed a certain official character; (3) under the despotism inaugurated by Diocletian the trade and professional associations became public institutions with enforced membership, while associations with a primarily religious character gradually disappeared.

The most common general term in Latin for associations was *collegia.*
Foreigners in particular initially formed associations in Rome. The purposes
of these associations with their characteristic terms were economic *(stationes),* religious *(cultores),* or social *(tenuiorum,* "of the poor"). Religion was
characteristic of all of them, because even the economic *stationes* were groups
of foreign merchants who maintained their national identity in part by preserving their adherence to the native deity of their city or country. Funerary
obligations were assumed by all associations except the purely commercial
organizations.

Since private associations were often a source of political groupings and
intrigue, the late Republic and early empire saw several laws aimed at outlaw-
ing or keeping a firm control on all nonofficial groups. An association had to
be licensed, and an unlicensed one was properly illegal. An exception to this
were the funerary associations, which were not strictly speaking *collegia* but
were cooperative burial societies. These societies were tacitly permitted by the
Julio-Claudian emperors without a license and were recognized by law as
collegia no later than 133 and probably under the Flavians. Their full title was
collegia tenuiorum religionis causa (associations of the poor with a religious basis). Membership provided a kind of poor man's burial insurance and a certain
social life (a monthly meeting was permitted) in return for the payment of the
(monthly) dues. The college was under the patronage of a deity (often the emperor), whose name it took. The association either owned its own burial plot
or contracted for the expenses of burial. It has been conjectured that it was as
such a *collegium* that the church at Rome came to own burial property in the
catacombs from the end of the second century (most of the catacombs were
private property, but it seems that San Callisto was in the hands of the church;
Hippolytus, *Refutation of All Heresies* 9.7). This fact cannot be established, but
a private religious association did provide one category of sociological understanding by which the church could be interpreted to the pagan world, and
Tertullian (*Apology* 39) accommodates his presentation of Christian assemblies
to what was recognizable from the burial clubs.

The Roman associations followed the pattern of civil organization more
closely than did the Greek. There was a statute *(lex collegii),* the titles of officials
were those of magistrates, usually two men held the leading position, and there
was an *ordo* (a kind of senate) of former chief officers alongside an assembly of
the members who elected the officers.

BIBLIOGRAPHY

Liebenam, Wilhelm. *Zur Geschichte und Organisation des Römischen Vereinswesens.*
    Leipzig, 1890.
LaPiana, George. "Foreign Groups in Rome During the First Centuries of the Em-
    pire." *HTR* 20, no. 4 (1927):183-403.

Egyptian Associations

Texts containing the "constitution and by-laws" of certain Egyptian associations of Hellenistic and Roman times reveal some organizational differences between Egyptian and Greco-Roman associations. A Greek or Roman association was commonly formed with the idea that it was to last indefinitely, but these Egyptian statutes are limited to one year's duration, although they were capable of renewal. The idea of a corporate body was not developed in Egypt, and associations possessed no rights or duties beyond those of individual members. The meeting place was a public temple, not a private shrine or other building belonging to the association or a member as would have been common in Greece. The only officials were a president and his assistant, both of whom were empowered to enforce the regulations of the society. The laws of the society were of the nature of a contract to which the members bound themselves. In this last feature and in many of the other provisions the Egyptian clubs were like their Greek counterparts: dues and contributions for special occasions, monthly banquets, assistance to fellow members, assuming burial responsibilities, and fines for violating the rules of conduct.

BIBLIOGRAPHY

Roberts, Colin, T. C. Skeat, and A. D. Nock. "The Gild of Zeus Hypsistos." *HTR* 29 (1936):39-88.

Boak, A. E. R. "The Organization of Gilds in Greco-Roman Egypt." *Transactions and Proceedings of the American Philological Association* 68 (1937):212-20.

The Statutes of an Association

The Greek pattern of club life was widely influential. The following statute gives a vivid picture of club life during the early empire. Excerpts are quoted here from *Inscriptiones Graecae* II² 1368, dated shortly before A.D. 178, which contains the minutes of a meeting of the Society of Iobacchi in Attica and a complete copy of its revised statutes.[110]

> No one may be an Iobacchus unless he first lodge with the priest the usual notice of candidature and be approved by a vote of the Iobacchi as being clearly a worthy and suitable member of the Bacchic society. The entrance fee shall be fifty denarii. . . . The Iobacchi shall meet on the ninth of each month and on the anniversary of its foundation and on the festivals of Bacchus and on any extraordinary feast of the god, and each member shall take part in word or act or honorable deed, paying the fixed monthly contri-

110. Translation by Marcus N. Tod, *Sidelights on Greek History* (Oxford, 1932), 86-91.

bution for the wine. If he fail to pay, he shall be excluded from the gathering. . . . When anyone has lodged his application and has been approved by vote, the priest shall hand him a letter stating that he is an Iobacchus, but not until he has first paid to the priest his entrance fee, and in the letter the priest shall cause to be entered the sums paid under one head or another. No one may either sing or create a disturbance or applaud at the gatherings, but each shall say and act his allotted part with all good order and quietness under the direction of the priest or the arch-bacchus. No Iobacchus who has not paid his contributions for the monthly and anniversary meetings shall enter the gathering until the priests have decided either that he must pay or that he may be admitted. If anyone start a fight or be found acting disorderly or occupying the seat of any other member or using insulting or abusive language to anyone, the person so abused or insulted shall produce two of the Iobacchi to state upon oath that they heard him insulted or abused, and he who was guilty of the insult or abuse shall pay to the Society twenty-five light drachmas. . . . And if anyone come to blows, he who has been struck shall lodge a written statement with the priest or the vice-priest, and he shall without fail convene a general meeting, and the Iobacchi shall decide the question by vote under the presidency of the priest, and the penalty shall be exclusion for a period to be determined and a fine not exceeding twenty-five silver denarii. And the same punishment shall be imposed also on one who, having been struck, fails to seek redress with the priest or the arch-bacchus but has brought a charge before the public courts. And the same punishment shall be imposed upon the orderly officer if he failed to eject those who were fighting. . . . And no one shall deliver a speech without the leave of the priest or the vice-priest on pain of being liable to a fine of thirty light drachmas to the Society. The priest shall perform the customary services at the meeting and the anniversary in proper style, and shall set before the meeting the drink-offering for the return of Bacchus and pronounce the sermon. . . . And the arch-bacchus shall offer the sacrifice to the god and shall set forth the drink-offering on each tenth day of the month Elaphebolion. And when portions are distributed, let them be taken by the priest, vice-priest, archbacchus, treasurer, bucolicus, Dionysus, Core, Palaemon, Aphrodite, Preteurythmus; and let these names be apportioned by lot among all the members. And if any Iobacchus receive any legacy or honor or appointment, he shall set before the Iobacchi a drink-offering corresponding to the appointment. . . . The orderly officer shall be chosen by lot or appointed by the priest, and he shall bear the thyrsus of the god to him who is disorderly or creates a disturbance. And anyone beside whom the thyrsus is laid shall, with the approval of the priest or of the arch-bacchus, leave the banqueting-hall; but if he disobey, the "horses" who shall be appointed by the priests shall take him up and put him outside the front door and he shall be liable to the punishment inflicted upon those who fight. The Iobacchi shall elect a treasurer by ballot for a term of two years, and he shall take over all the property of the Bacchic Society in accordance with an inventory, and he shall likewise hand it over to his successor as treasurer. And he shall provide out of his own pocket the oil for the lights on each ninth day of the month and on the anniversary and at the assembly and on the customary days of the god. . . . And he shall be allowed the treasurer's drink-offering and shall be free from the payment of subscriptions for the two years. And if any Iobacchus die, a wreath shall be provided in his honor not exceeding five denarii in value, and a single jar of wine shall be set before those who have attended the funeral.

This description seems to provide the background for the disturbances in the church at Corinth. The Greek converts were still being Greeks and treating their Christian assembly as they did their meetings in honor of pagan deities.

Conclusion

Clubs and associations afforded opportunities of common worship, enjoyment of social intercourse, and in some cases the satisfaction of holding office. These societies further promoted a spirit of comradeship and mutual aid in time of difficulty. Most of them tended to funerary responsibilities and provided tombstones. Associations formed the natural organization for foreigners and foreign worship entering a city. Clubs were associated with a deity, often met in a temple, offered libations and sacrifices, and ate meat from idol temples. The religious element in these social gatherings thrusts again to the forefront the problem Jews and Christians faced in ancient society. First Corinthians 8–10 is but the major surviving literary witness to the problems of social intercourse in an idolatrous society. Political, economic, and family life and public entertainment were organized around the pagan deities; so also were the ordinary social groupings. Early Christian churches would have appeared to pagans very much like the religious associations of worshipers of various foreign deities in their midst, even without their priestly and sacrificial aspect.[111]

BIBLIOGRAPHY

Kloppenborg, John S., and Stephen G. Wilson, eds. *Voluntary Associations in the Graeco-Roman World*. London, 1996.
Harland, Philip A. *Associations, Synagogues, and Congregations: Claiming a Place in Ancient Mediterranean Society*. Minneapolis, 2003.

111. Robert L. Wilken, "Toward a Social Interpretation of Early Christian Apologetics," *Church History* 39 (1970):449-56; revised as "Collegia, Philosophical Schools, and Theology," in *The Catacombs and the Colosseum*, ed. Stephen Benko and John J. O'Rourke (Valley Forge, 1971), 279-86; idem, *The Christians as the Romans Saw Them* (New Haven, 1984), 31-47.

3. HELLENISTIC-ROMAN RELIGIONS

BIBLIOGRAPHY

Sources

Aelius Aristides. *Orations* 40 ("Heracles"), 41 ("Dionysus"), 43 ("Regarding Zeus"), 45 ("Regarding Sarapis"), and 46 ("The Isthmian Oration: Regarding Poseidon"). Behr, C. A. P. *Aelius Aristides: The Complete Works.* 2 vols. Leiden, 1981, 1986.

Grant, F. C. *Hellenistic Religions.* Library of Religion. New York, 1953.

Grant, F. C. *Ancient Roman Religion.* Library of Religion. New York, 1957.

Ferguson, J. *Greek and Roman Religion: A Sourcebook.* Park Ridge, N.J., 1980.

Valantasis, Richard, ed. *Religions of Late Antiquity in Practice.* Princeton, 2000.

Basic Secondary Works

Nock, A. D. "Early Gentile Christianity and its Hellenistic Background." In *Essays on the Trinity and the Incarnation,* edited by A. J. Rawlinson. London, 1928. Reprinted as *Early Gentile Christianity.* New York, 1964. Reprinted in *Essays.* 1:49-133.

Nock, A. D. "Religious Development from the Close of the Republic to the Reign of Nero" and "The Development of Paganism in the Roman Empire." Vol. 10, Chapter XV and Vol. 12, Chapter XII in *Cambridge Ancient History,* edited by S. A. Cook et al. Cambridge, 1934 and 1939.

Nilsson, M. P. *Greek Piety.* Oxford, 1948.

Nilsson, M. P. *Geschichte der Griechischen Religion.* Vol. 2, *Die Hellenistische und Römische Zeit.* 3d ed. Munich, 1974.

MacMullen, Ramsay. *Paganism in the Roman Empire.* New Haven, 1981.

Klauck, Hans-Joseph. *The Religious Context of Early Christianity: A Guide to Graeco-Roman Religions.* Edinburgh, 2000.

Supplementary Works

Cook, A. B. *Zeus.* 3 vols. Cambridge, 1914–1940.

Nock, A. D. "Religious Attitudes of the Ancient Greeks." *Proceedings of the American Philosophical Society* 85 (1942):472-82. Reprinted in *Essays* 2:534-50.

Nilsson, M. P. "Problems of the History of Greek Religion in the Hellenistic and Roman Age." *HTR* 36 (1943):251-75.

Dodds, E. R. *The Greeks and the Irrational.* Boston, 1951.

Guthrie, W. K. C. *The Greeks and their Gods.* Boston, 1951.

Grant, F. C. *Roman Hellenism and the New Testament.* New York, 1962.

Ferguson, J. *The Religions of the Roman Empire.* London, 1970.

Versnel, H. S., ed. *Faith, Hope, and Worship: Aspects of Religious Mentality in the Ancient World.* Leiden, 1981.

Meyer, Ben F., and E. P. Sanders, eds. *Jewish and Christian Self-Definition.* Vol. 3, *Self-Definition in the Greco-Roman World.* Philadelphia, 1982.

Martin, Luther. *Hellenistic Religions: An Introduction.* Oxford, 1987.

Hägg, R., ed. *Ancient Greek Cult Practice from the Epigraphical Evidence.* Stockholm, 1994.

Cohn-Sherbok, Dan, and John M. Court, eds. *Religious Diversity in the Graeco-Roman World: A Survey of Recent Scholarship,* Sheffield, 2001.

Tripolitis, Antonia. *Religions of the Hellenistic-Roman Age.* Grand Rapids, 2002.

Klauck, H.-J. *Magic and Paganism in Early Christianity: The World of the Acts of the Apostles.* Minneapolis, 2003.

ANCIENT GREEK RELIGION

I do not intend to provide a complete survey of early Greek religion here.[1] Criteria for inclusion are (1) what forms the common background of the later development and (2) what remained important in the Hellenistic age. The main features of Greek religion took shape well before the time of Alexander the Great. We will survey these in this section, but first some quotations of a general nature. "The religion of ancient Greece had no creed and, although certain actions were irreligious and therefore generally condemned as displeasing to the supernatural powers, there was nothing like a code or system of morality which must be accepted by everyone who worshipped Athena or Zeus."[2] "Greek religion was decidedly a thing of every day" life;[3] otherworldliness did not form the main trunk of the tree. The deities that were worshiped were those presiding over the affairs of life, and there was a very material view of gifts to the deity. Moreover, religion was essentially a corporate or community matter.

---

1. My indebtedness to A. D. Nock goes beyond his lectures on Greek and Roman religion and his writings on the subject.

2. H. J. Rose, *Religion in Greece and Rome* (New York, 1959), 9.

3. Ibid., 12.

To the ancients the essence of religion was the rite, which was thought of as a process for securing and maintaining correct relations with the world of uncharted forces around man, and the myth, which gave the traditional reason for the rite and the traditional (but changing) view of those forces.[4]

For these things we must begin with Homer.

BIBLIOGRAPHY

Aldrich, K., ed. *Apollodorus: The Library of Greek Mythology.* Lawrence, Kans., 1975.
Farnell, Lewis. *The Cults of the Greek States.* 5 vols. Oxford, 1896–1909. Reprint. Chicago, 1971.
Rice, David G., and John E. Stambaugh. *Sources for the Study of Greek Religion.* Missoula, Mont., 1979.

Nilsson, M. P. *A History of Greek Religion.* Oxford, 1925.
Burkert, Walter. *Greek Religion.* Cambridge, Mass., 1985.
Bremmer, Jan N. *Greek Religion.* Oxford, 1994.

The Epic Age: Homer[5]

The study of Greek religion in the Hellenistic age need not begin with the earliest evidence, that of the Minoan-Mycenaean civilization, but it must go back to the Homeric epics. Homer lies at the foundation of the Greek tradition, and his prominence in the educational curriculum until the end of antiquity means that he is fundamental for Greek religious thought in the Hellenistic and Roman periods. Homer exerted such a pervasive influence on literary culture that Homeric religious thought had a place in the Greek development not unlike that of the Scriptures in Jewish and Christian education. Nevertheless, Homer was no Moses and his poems were not inspired Scripture, so the cultural background was primarily secular.

The *Iliad* and the *Odyssey* originated in the traditional ballad literature of the heroic age recited for entertainment. The *Iliad* is the story of the Trojan war: between the Greeks (under Agamemnon, king of Mycenae) and the city of Troy; the *Odyssey* relates the adventures of one of the heroes on his return from the war. Differences between the *Iliad* and *Odyssey* suggest different authors, but not necessarily so. The *Odyssey* is a few years later than the *Iliad*. "Homer" (whether one, two, or more) based his epics on a stock of ballads transmitted orally about the gods and wars, and assumed that most of the divine stories

---

4. A. D. Nock, *Conversion* (Oxford, 1933), 161.
5. C. A. Trypanis, *The Homeric Epics* (Warminster, England, 1977). English translations: M. Hammond, *The Iliad* (London, 1987); E. V. Rieu and D. C. H. Rieu, *The Odyssey* (London, 1991).

BUST OF THE BLIND HOMER
The epics of Homer lay at the foundation of Greek education,
culture, and religion. *(© SEF/Art Resource, NY)*

ZEUS
Zeus, the ruler and the sky god, is identified by his scepter and thunderbolt.
(© Art Resource, NY)

were known. The Homeric poems are a deliberate attempt to reproduce conditions of about 1200 B.C. at the final stage of Mycenaean civilization just before the Dorian invasions brought the interruption of a "dark age" in the Greek cultural development. The compilation of the Homeric epics may be dated to perhaps the latter half of the eighth century. They mark the new intellectual beginnings that led into classical Greece.

The Gods. The Greek gods were the most anthropomorphic of the gods of any people with the exception of those in Scandinavian mythology. The gods, of course, did have some important differences from human beings: they were ageless and deathless; they were not limited by physical restrictions and so could take any shape and go anywhere quickly and invisibly; and they could do things (morally speaking) that humans should not do (their mode of operation was amoral). Yet in Greece the "measure of all things" was man: it has been said that the difference between Greek and Israelite religion was that the Greeks worshiped "the holiness of beauty" whereas the Jews worshiped "the beauty of holiness."

The deities were already thought of as belonging to all people (cf. *Odyssey* 9.552, 286-96), although others call them by different names. Generally each of the deities has his or her own special function. However much they may have human characteristics, they remain superior to humankind. They give gifts, and one must remember that he or she is human and they are the gods.

The gods formed something of a divine society living around Zeus on Mount Olympus. Theirs was the highest layer in the social system; their society was a reflection of the organization of society in the heroic age, which formed an earthly counterpart of the divine community. Olympus was a generic term for a high mountain, but it was associated with a large range in north Thessaly around which clouds are gathered most of the year. The gods were thought of as dwelling either on top of the mountain or in the sky.

The deities in Homer are the same as those met later in Greek history, except that Demeter and Dionysus come in only seldom and do not have the prominence they have later. It is somewhat arbitrary to list "The Twelve Olympians" at any given period, but a "classical" listing would be those in the chart on page 154.[6] To these may be added Hades (Pluto), another brother of Zeus, who as god of death and the powers of the underworld was obviously not an Olympian but ranks with them in importance. Deities whose abode was the earth or underworld are called chthonian (note 1 Cor. 8:5 for a possible allusion to the Olympian deities, "gods in heaven," and to chthonian deities, "gods on earth," unless the latter refer to or include deified rulers; see pp. 198ff.).

---

6. The Homeric Hymns (not by Homer) include other deities and heroes but are a good place to begin for the traditional views of the deities: see Susan Shelmerdine, tr., *The Homeric Hymns* (Newburyport, Mass., 1995); A. Stassinopoulos and R. Beny, *The Gods of Greece* (London, 1983); and C. R. Long, *The Twelve Gods of Greece and Rome* (Leiden, 1987); H. Newman and J. O. Newman, *A Genealogical Chart of Greek Mythology* (Chapel Hill, 2003).

Greek Name	Roman Name	Description
Zeus	Jupiter	Father of gods and men in a patriarchal sense (the center of family life, authority, and discipline). The sky and weather god represented by the thunderbolt. (Acts 14:12)
Hera	Juno	Wife of Zeus, associated with marriage and women.
Poseidon	Neptune	God of sea, water, and earthquakes (viewed as caused by underground rivers). Subduer of horses and brother of Zeus. Symbol the trident.
Apollo[7]	—	The "all-Greek boy" who was the ideal type of young manly beauty, associated with music, archery, prophecy, medicine, flocks and herds, law, civilization, and later the sun. Lyre and bow his attributes.
Artemis	Diana	Twin sister of Apollo, chaste goddess of the countryside and wild animals, who also presided over childbirth.[8]
Athena	Minerva	Virgin goddess of wisdom, fine and skilled arts, protectress of Athens. She sprang forth fully armed from the head of Zeus.
Hermes	Mercury	Messenger of the gods who presided over roadways and all who used them (robbers as well as travelers) and so honored by stone piles (herms). God of herdsmen, conductor of souls to Hades, divine rogue and trickster who embodied the Greek respect for cleverness. (Acts 14:12)
Ares	Mars	God of war.
Aphrodite	Venus	Goddess of love, beauty, and fertility — the personification of the sexual instinct and mother of *erōs*.
Demeter	Ceres	Grain goddess.
Dionysus	Bacchus	Wine god.
Hephaestus	Vulcan	God of fire and so of crafts.

7. Andrew M. Miller, *From Delos to Delphi: A Literary Study of the Homeric Hymn to Apollo* (Leiden, 1986).

8. These features account for the identification of the Ephesian goddess (originally a goddess of fertility according to traditional interpretation) with Artemis (Acts 19:24-35); neither, however, was associated with sexual promiscuity, as was Aphrodite. For Artemis of the Ephesians, see pp. 198-99.

APOLLO
This statue shows Apollo, god of order and culture, with his characteristic attribute, the lyre.
(© Scala/Art Resource, NY)

The gods can do things for you if you know how to address them, but some things have to be as they are. The gods were active in Homer, but there was a power to which even they were subject — fate *(moira)*. The Homeric fate was not determinism, but that portion which comes to you, one's "lot" in life. One's fate included evil, but one could bring even more on himself. Life deals certain circumstances, but in the classical Greek understanding there were always alternatives.

Morality. The gods were protectors of the moral order when particularly needed. Here the *Odyssey* generally represents a later stage of thought than the *Iliad.* Some things just were not done: perjury, incest, violation of hospitality. Perjury was an insult to the god, for his name was taken in vain. The sexual affairs of Zeus were a matter of genealogy, not lust, in order to bring some system into the divine society. These affairs became a point of sharp criticism by later pagan philosophers as well as Christian apologists and were a frequent subject for allegorical interpretation. Zeus was the protector of strangers and suppliants (cf. *Odyssey* 9.269-78). An order of justice *(nemesis)* stands behind human beings. On the human level Homer represents a shame culture (what was "not done") as distinct from a guilt culture (the sense of sin in a Jewish or Christian sense). In general the standard was public opinion and not a code of conduct (p. 69).

Religious Observances. Although Homer describes the heroic age when one would fight with anyone, he expresses the belief that all people have need of the gods (*Odyssey* 3.48). The ritual of sacrifice and the animals employed are in general what one finds in the later period. The sacrifices were offered to make wished-for things happen or unwanted things to go away; a bargaining spirit long pervaded the Greek relations with the divine. There was no priestly class; the ordinary individual performed the sacrifice. One specialized functionary was the *mantis,* a diviner or soothsayer, who told the inquirer what was expedient. His word was not so much foretelling the future, because it was conditional. Favorable signs were important in propaganda.

It is important to note the distinction between cultus (or worship) and tendance (services performed or homage offered). In cultus one gave offerings either to receive favors in return or to make the bad go away. In tendance, such as the observances honoring the dead (pp. 243-44), giving was a matter of benefiting the dead by providing for their needs without fear of evil or hope of blessings. It became a matter of kindness and respect so that food offerings to the deceased at the grave site may be compared to the placing of flowers on a grave today.

The Soul and the Afterlife. Proper burial was considered very important, because without it the soul of the deceased would wander around as a permanent "displaced person" and always be at unrest. This concern was based on an aspect of fear, but what was done for the dead thereafter primarily sprang from kindness.

What seems to have been a common view was that the dead continue engaging in the same activities as on earth. So in the Homeric poems the persons involved were unable to avoid the associations of this life. Thus, as Nilsson has observed, it is better to think in terms of associations than of concrete concepts. One thought of the afterlife, therefore, in terms of the life with which one was familiar, keeping in mind that these terms should not be taken too literally or too specifically.

In Homer the important people in this life continued to be so in the next. His heroes had a great desire to be remembered. *Aretē* (later, virtue) was the excellence of a man, and *timē* (honor) was the reward for this excellence. Remembrance conferred a kind of immortality on the hero.

The *Iliad* opens with a reference to "souls *[psychai]* hurled down to Hades." For Homer the soul was not one's personality or real self; nor was it the organ of will, intelligence, and desires. Rather, it had some association with the breath, making one inactive when it leaves; it is what is left apart from the physical shell. He describes souls as having the same height, build, etc. of the person, so that one is recognizable, but there was nothing to embrace (*Iliad* 23.62-107).[9] Death meant passing into a mere shadow of existence in which the soul could do no more than engage in a kind of pale reflection of its earthly activities.

Nearly all persons go to Hades — a dreary place where, although "life" continues, what makes life worth living is gone. There is no future reward or punishment. There was the idea of an Elysium where the temperature remains the same year round and the weather is always good, but only a few — the very good — go there; and they are translated directly and do not die. Similarly, very few are punished in the afterlife. In the *Odyssey* (11.489-91) Achilles expresses the view that he would rather be a slave on earth than lord of the underworld. The fear of the unknown was strong.

Hesiod

Hesiod (about 700 B.C.) is next to Homer in time and in importance for the Greek tradition, but his writings are in many ways the antithesis of the Homeric poems. Homer describes the monarchy of late Mycenaean times; Hesiod describes the oligarchy of his own time. Homer's stage is the whole Greek world; Hesiod's scene is local (his native Boeotia). In the Homeric poems the author is in the background; Hesiod is personal and writes in his own name. Homer narrates myths (epic poetry); Hesiod writes didactic poetry. Morality is incidental in Homer; it is stressed in a strong way in Hesiod.

Justice. Hesiod had two passions: justice and work. Justice is human

---

9. This old conception may be relevant to Acts 12:13-16, although phrased in Jewish terms as an "angel."

moral duty. The word refers to retributive justice, that which counters wrong-doing. Justice is presented as the hallmark of Zeus, and Hesiod is almost like an Old Testament prophet in presenting social justice as the will of god. He had a sense of personal vocation: the Muses had called him to the task and breathed on him a kind of inspiration. Hesiod spoke on behalf of the small farmers in relation to the ruling class. His principal writing, *The Works and Days,* lays down various agricultural precepts and discusses auspicious and inauspicious days for many events. These are set in the framework of a universal order of justice and include many moral counsels. Prosperity or misfortunes would be the result of righteousness or unrighteousness.

Origins. Hesiod was also concerned with guilt, impurity, and the causes or reasons for things. His *Theogony* is the earliest explicitly religious poem produced by the Greeks. Here he shows an interest in cosmogony (origin of the world) and attempts to systematize the account of the gods and arrange them in a family tree. The gods of popular worship were still not thought of as identical with the creators of the world.

Heroes.[10] The cult of the heroes appears in literature for the first time in Hesiod. *Hēroēs* was a courtesy title that referred to someone who was supposed to have existed but after death remained powerful enough to protect those on earth and thus was someone worthy of homage. The hero cult was originally the cult of a deceased person who belonged not to a single family but to a people generally. The word was used in a wider sense to include lesser or local gods. Heroes were worshiped in particular localities; their power was associated with their remains and the place of their burial. They belonged to the chthonian (underworld) deities.

The Delphic maxim "Know thyself" originally meant to recognize that you were a human and not a god and by its admonition shows the ambition was present to become more than human. Some of the Greek heroes attained the status of the great gods, winning entrance to Olympus (e.g., Heracles [Greek], Hercules [Latin])[11] and becoming widely worshiped (e.g., Asclepius; see pp. 221ff.). The Dioscuri ("sons of Zeus"), Castor and Pollux, were perhaps originally heroes who gained more than usual celebrity; they were especially popular with seamen as protective deities (cf. Acts 28:11) and saviors from danger and disaster. Some features of the cult of heroes continued in the cult of saints under Christianity (p. 182).

10. L. R. Farnell, *Greek Hero-Cults and Ideas of Immortality* (Oxford, 1921); A. D. Nock, "The Cult of Heroes," *HTR* 37 (1944):141-74 (*Essays,* 2:575-602).

11. The twelve labors of Heracles were interpreted by Hellenistic philosophers to refer to winning immortality through suffering and overcoming the passions — see the Hercules tragedies of Seneca, *Hercules Furens* and (authorship questioned) *Hercules Oetaeus.*

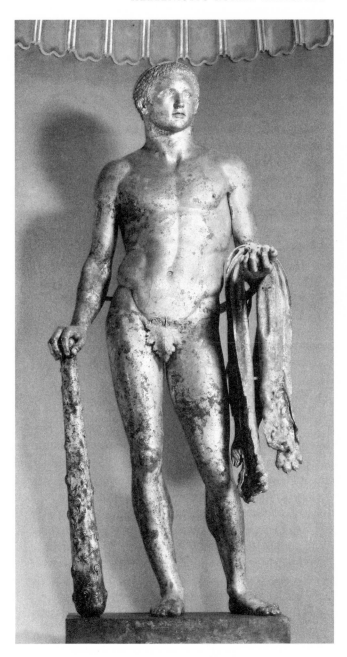

HERACLES/ HERCULES

Heracles was most often represented with a club and lion skin, referring to his killing of the lion — one of his twelve labors, which were allegorized as a victory of good over evil. *(© Scala/Art Resource, NY)*

ONE OF THE DIOSCURI, 3d c. A.D.
The divine twins were popular as guardians of sailors (Acts 28:11).
(© Timothy McCarthy/Art Resource, NY)

The Archaic Period

Sanctuaries.[12] The first Greek temples appeared in the archaic period. They were not large and were used on special occasions only. Although Greek deities were universal, their cult was attached to definite places. Shrines were located at places that were already "holy" and were not necessarily located for the convenience of worshipers. Temples were set within a *temenos,* a sacred precinct set aside for a deity, frequently with a spring (for purifications) and a grove of trees. The altar was placed in front of the temple; it was the one indispensable item at a shrine, since it was necessary for sacrifice, the central act of worship.[13] The Greeks attached no special sanctity to an altar; usually a new one was better for a special sacrifice. The Greek temple *(naos;* Lat. *cella)* housed the de-

12. Evi Melas, *Temples and Sanctuaries of Ancient Greece* (London, 1973); R. A. Tomlinson, *Greek Sanctuaries* (New York, 1976); Vincent Scully, *The Earth, the Temple, and the Gods: Greek Sacred Architecture* (New Haven, 1979); N. Marinatos and R. Hägg, eds., *Greek Sanctuaries: New Approaches* (London, 1993); S. E. Alcock and R. Osborne, eds., *Placing the Gods: Sanctuaries and Sacred Space in Ancient Greece* (Oxford, 1994).

13. C. G. Yaris, *Greek Altars: Origins and Typology* (St. Louis, 1949).

ity's image and possessions; it was not a place of assembly for worshipers but the home of the deity (cf. Matt. 23:21; 1 Cor. 6:19; Eph. 2:20-21). One went to the temple for votive offerings (gifts made in fulfillment of a vow; see pp. 192-93), not usually for private prayer. The cult images were life-size or larger. In the seventh century larger temples and cult images emerged. Many small shrines still existed but were seldom opened, usually only for special observances.

Religious Observances. A large percentage of the population was committed to taking an active part in religious observances (in contrast to Rome). If one did participate in the corporate ceremonies, the gods would not let him down. Every house had its own small shrines, regular prayers, and sacrifice, in addition to the observances of the clan and city. Priesthood did not involve separate status or character (see pp. 185ff. for activities of priests).

The principal acts of individual piety were votive offerings (pp. 192-93) and purifications (pp. 185-88). It was not proper to make a petition to the deity without bringing a sacrifice, and the granting of a petition called for a gift, so many of the great temples had treasury rooms to hold the gifts to the deity. In order to present an offering one had to be ritually pure. In addition, purifications might be required for a trespass, certain diseases, birth, or contact with death.

Greek religion essentially was based on the agrarian cycle. The great majority of the festivals were related to agriculture. They grew up gradually in honor of the deities who gave fertility to the crops and herds. Although Apollo at Delphi regulated the calendar of festivals, they were geared to the rhythm of nature. It was a matter of daily bread. Among the religious festivals of Athens were the *hekatombaion* or Great Sacrifice in the month of the same name in mid-summer to Apollo, the Panathenaia to Athena in the same month, the Eleusinian Mysteries in early fall instituted by Demeter, the Thesmophoria (a fertility festival celebrated by women alone) later in the fall and also in honor of Demeter, Poseidon in the month and to the god of that name in mid-winter, Anthesterion in the month of that name in early spring (not only a feast of flowers but also a ceremony to pacify the dead), the great feast of Dionysus later in the spring important for the development of drama, and the feast of Dipolieia in honor of Zeus in the last month of the year (approximately June). This is only a partial listing[14] — the deities most frequently represented in the calendar were Apollo, Demeter, Dionysus, Athena, and Zeus.

For most Greeks true human life meant the life of the individual in community. Civic life was more important than it is now. Social organization was according to family, tribe, and city; and the same applied to the organization of worship. A good illustration of the strong civic basis of religion in Greece is the hero cults. When a person founded a city or colony, he was often honored as its hero, and the official cult of the founder was a unifying factor in civic life. The

---

14. See H. J. Rose, *Religion in Greece and Rome* (New York, 1959), 67-89.

city festivals were patriotic and religious; there was no distinction between the sacred and profane such as is made today. Every public meeting of the people was preceded by purifications, sacrifice, and prayer.

Trends in Regard to Deities. The oracle of Apollo at Delphi (pp. 213ff.) greatly influenced colonization, the development of sacred law, and ritual purifications. Codes of law were put in writing during this period, and worship by the state was a part of their legal enactments. Apollo brought an emphasis on law, order, and morality and exemplified the Greek ideals of life (cf. p. 8).

Another trend that developed was not to bother Zeus about details. Rather, it was much better to have a local hero specializing in such things. This seems to be more the situation than a case of the heroes finally "making the club," as it were. Besides, they also had the appeal of being something new.

Dionysus. The cult of Dionysus became firmly established in the Greek world in the seventh century B.C. Dionysus became especially associated with wine, but he was the god not of the vine alone but of vegetation and fertility in general (though not of grain, which was the preserve of Demeter). The phallus was his symbol and was nowhere so conspicuous as in the Dionysiac processions. Comedy and tragedy both had their origin in the cult of Dionysus. Ritual patterns have not been found as the background of drama, but the plays were performed in the setting of festivals of Dionysus and were supposed to give him pleasure. The worship of Dionysus was characterized by ecstatic frenzy (see pp. 259ff.). The influence of Delphi toned down the Dionysiac excesses and made a place for the cult in regular Greek life. Thus Apollo and Dionysus have been seen as representing the two sides of Greek (and human) experience — the rational and the emotional.

Orphism.[15] Orphism began in the sixth century B.C., and its ideas are reflected in Pindar's *Odes.* It does not represent a single entity or systematic doctrine but a movement characterized by common concerns and a likemindedness. Orphic literature consisted of poems given in the names of Orpheus and Musaeus, mythical singers. Early Orphic texts survive mostly in fragmentary form through later quotations. A new source is a papyrus from 340-320 B.C. discovered at Derveni containing a commentary on an Orphic hymn.[16] Ancient authors associated Orpheus with founding mysteries and Musaeus with

---

15. O. Kern, *Orphicorum Fragmenta* (1922); M. P. Nilsson, "Early Orphism and Kindred Religious Movements," *HTR* 28 (July 1935):181-230; Ivan Linforth, *The Arts of Orpheus* (Berkeley, 1941); W. K. C. Guthrie, *Orpheus and Greek Religion* (London, 1952; repr. with new foreword by Larry Alderink, Princeton, 1993); Walter Burkert, "Orphism and Bacchic Mysteries: New Evidence and Old Problems of Interpretation," *Center for Hermeneutical Studies Colloquy* 28 (Berkeley, 1977); Larry J. Alderink, *Creation and Salvation in Ancient Orphism* (Chico, Calif., 1981); M. L. West, *The Orphic Poems* (Oxford, 1984).

16. Jeffrey S. Rusten, "Interim Notes on the Papyrus from Derveni," *Harvard Studies in Classical Philology* 88 (1985):121-140; Andrée Laks and Glenn W. Most, *Studies on the Derveni Papyrus* (Oxford, 1997), include a translation of the papyrus.

oracles. This literature dealt with cosmogony and prescriptions for ritual and conduct. Orphism is primarily a literature associated with a legendary character who was described as a teacher and founder of a religious life. Orphism was a "reform" movement of Dionysiac worship, whose central rite, the dismembering and eating of an animal representing Dionysus (p. 261), was transformed into the crime of the wicked Titans. According to Orphic mythology a child of Zeus, Dionysus Zagreus, was dismembered and eaten by the Titans. Athena saved the infant's heart and Zeus swallowed it; of him a new Dionysus was born by Semele. Zeus killed the Titans with his thunderbolt and from their ashes came human beings. The earliest philosophical interpretation of the story seems to have been that persons could imitate either the Titans (evil) or Dionysus (divine). A later interpretation assigned to human nature a Titanic element within itself, something innately evil. However, the ancient texts do not contain the inference that there is something of Dionysus in us because the Titans had eaten him. The world itself was morally neutral.

A revival (or survival) of Orphism in the early Christian centuries is witnessed to by the *Orphic Hymns,* but these provide no cultic details, although they frequently refer to initiates.[17] Other possible sources of information are questionable. Verses to be recited by the deceased on arrival in the underworld written on gold leaves during the Hellenistic Age and found in tombs in south Italy and Crete may not be specifically Orphic but from a kindred movement.[18]

Several features in the genuine or early Orphic literature are at variance with the general Greek tradition. Whereas in Homer the soul is a vague and shadowy concept, in the context of this literature *psychē* does denote a personality existing before and after the present bodily life: the soul is distinct from and enters into the body. We in our suffering now are working out the guilt of the Titans. The body *(sōma)* was regarded as the tomb *(sēma)* of the soul (Plato, *Cratylus* 400C). The dualism of body and soul gave to Orphism a certain ascetic streak that had not characterized Greek life. Asceticism served to liberate the soul from the impurity of the body. This seems to be the basis for Orphism's prohibition of killing animals and eating their flesh. Whereas in Homer the living body was the person and the soul had no prehistory and only a shadowy repetition in the afterlife, in this literature the soul is the real "you" liable to a reincarnation and in the afterlife paying for sins or being rewarded for virtues. There are two worlds — this world and the other world. One pays the penalty in one for sins in the other. Rewards and punishments were not new in Greek thought, but that the underworld (Hades) is a place of punishment was. After three good lives one goes to the tower of Cronus in the Isles of the Blest.[19] There is no suggestion of a change

17. Apostolos Athanassakis, *The Orphic Hymns* (Missoula, Mont., 1977).

18. G. Zuntz, *Persephone: Three Essays on Religion and Thought in Magna Graecia* (Oxford, 1971).

19. Pindar, *Olympian Ode* 2.70.

into animal shape. According to the literature, however, persons could escape the cycle of rebirth by rituals of purification for self and for one's dead relatives. An initiation could secure for one a happy afterlife. The sense of cyclical time remained nothing more than a theory, and the idea of transmigration never became axiomatic.[20] The idea of rewards and punishment in another life and the conception of the soul as personality apart from the body very nearly did. A concern for another world entered Greek thought. Here for the first time in Greece the next life was geared in a significant way to each person's action in this life.

Orphism was an attempt to explain the human situation. It reflected a sense of guilt that was related to human existence as such. An increasing tragic sense developed in Greece, colored by the tragic poets of the fifth century (Sophocles, Aeschylus). This pessimism, although not consistently followed in Greece, agreed with the proverb that it was best never to be born and next best to die young.[21] Orphic ideas and mysteries continued through the Hellenistic age, often, it seems, in connection with Pythagoreanism (pp. 382-84).

Signs of Dissolution in the Classical Age

The fifth and early fourth century B.C. was the time of greatest outward splendor in Greek religion. The greatest monuments of classical religion were created, highlighted by the Parthenon on the Acropolis of Athens, designed by the architect Ictinus and decorated under the supervision of the sculptor Phidias. But this was only one of the great achievements in a period that saw many splendid temples and statues dedicated to the national deities.

The classical age, however, saw trends that were to undermine the traditional Greek religion. (The discussion of these developments will find their place, for various organizational reasons, in other places in this book and will only be mentioned here.) The individualism noted in connection with the influence of Alexander the Great had its roots in the late fifth century. The trend to look to the lesser gods and heroes rather than to the great deities of the state increased. New cults were introduced: most spectacular in its spread was the cult of the healing hero Asclepius. These developments in themselves did not necessarily challenge the position of the traditional religion; but the criticism from the Sophists and poets (Aristophanes and Euripides) was quite otherwise. The Sophists by offering rationalistic explanations of belief in the gods relativized them (pp. 326-27), and the poets challenged their immoral conduct. As Euripides said, "If the gods do anything shameful, they are no gods"

20. Transmigration occurs at about this time in India, but it is unlikely to have been borrowed from there directly. Ideas do not travel as easily as do stories and art objects. The idea had different destinies in the two cultures: it became axiomatic in India, but it remained a fringe idea in Greece.

21. See p. 247 and n. 177.

TEMPLE OF HEPHAESTUS, Athens
The temple of Hephaestus (5th c. B.C.) on the Agora in Athens is the best
preserved of the Greek temples. *(Corel)*

(*Bellerophon* Frg. 17[19].4). The new philosophical schools that grew up became the real religion of the educated. By the Hellenistic age the outward forms of religion were being applied to new loyalties — ruler worship and the personification of abstractions like *Tychē* (luck). But very few would have attempted to dismantle the old religion, and the traditional gods and the civic religion showed a remarkable staying power, as the later record shows. Paul's experience at Lystra (Acts 14:8ff.) illustrates the continuation of the old polytheistic religious practices.

ANCIENT ROMAN RELIGION

The Tiber River valley was settled by the Latin group of Indo-Europeans. Unlike the settlers of Greece, the Latins did not take over a local religion, had no heroic age, and had few native myths and poetic background of their own. The Romans were a hard people with little imagination and little of what is now considered a Mediterranean temperament. The traditional religion was ascribed to Numa, lawgiver and king.

The principal early cultural contact of the Romans was with the Etruscans, who ruled at Rome for a time. Our knowledge of them comes from what the Romans said about them and from archaeological finds. Typically the

Romans on encountering native institutions infused them with their own national temper. Thus, temples, cult images, and methods of divination were taken over from the Etruscans, as was the practice of combining deities in a triad.

BIBLIOGRAPHY

Latte, K. *Römische Religionsgeschichte*. Munich, 1960.

Ogilvie, R. M. *The Romans and Their Gods in the Age of Augustus*. New York, 1969.

Stambaugh, J. E. "The Functions of Roman Temples." *ANRW* II, *Principat*, 16.1. Berlin, 1978. Pp. 554-608.

Liebeschuetz, J. H. W. G. *Continuity and Change in Roman Religion*. Oxford, 1979.

Lyttleton, M., and W. Forman. *The Romans: Their Gods and Their Beliefs*. London, 1984.

Turcan, R. *Religion romaine*. Leiden, 1988.

Beard, Mary, John North, and Simon Price. *Religions of Rome*. Vol. 1: *A History*. Vol. 2: *A Sourcebook*. Cambridge, 1998.

Feeney, Denis. *Literature and Religion at Rome: Cultures, Contexts, and Beliefs*. Cambridge, 1998.

Scheid, John. *An Introduction to Roman Religion*. Bloomington, Ind., 2003.

TEMPLE OF CONCORD, Agrigento
Some of the best-preserved Greek temples are in southern Italy and Sicily.
The temple was the house of the deity, where was kept the cult statue.

Deities

Most of the early Roman deities had no personality and are best characterized by the word *numen* (divine power or influence with no sense of personality; plural, *numina*). Another Latin word for them was *genius,* the spirit of a place. There were countless small deities who were strictly departmental and functional, with no clear-cut sex distinctions. New circumstances frequently led to the recognition of new divine powers to be pacified or to be channeled for the benefit of the people.

What early mythology the Romans had was largely subsumed under Greek mythology. From the late third century B.C. there was a thoroughgoing identification of Roman with Greek deities. It was not a case of Zeus is *also* Ammon, as in Egypt, but Zeus *is* Jupiter. Earlier contacts had a continuing effect, and the identification was hastened by the popularity of the legend of Trojan origins for the Romans (told in epic form in Virgil's *Aeneid*). However, except for Jupiter with Zeus ("Jupiter" is Latin for Zeus and for father) and Vesta with Hestia (goddess of the hearth), the fit was not so good. The identification of Mars (who was a general protective deity concerned with youth and some of the interests of the Greek Apollo) with the supernatural cutthroat Ares has given him his rough and crude reputation. Venus and Aphrodite also were a bad match: Venus was an innocent power connected with agriculture before Aphrodite gave her sexual charms and functions. Since the sexual rhythm of women tends to fall into periods about equal in length to a lunar month, Juno took on an association with the moon. Janus, the two-headed god of the doorway, was a distinctive Roman deity for which there was no Greek equivalent.

On the Capitoline hill a temple was dedicated around 500 B.C. to Jupiter, Minerva, and Juno. The original Capitoline triad had been Jupiter, Mars, and Quirinus (an early god similar to Mars), the gods who from early times had some degree of personality. The Capitoline deities were the principal gods of Rome, and temples in other cities to Jupiter Capitolinus (i.e., he who is worshiped on the Capitol) were frequently called the Capitol. A favorite epithet for Jupiter was Optimus Maximus (best and greatest).

These deities were placated in various ways. The Romans were more concerned with their actions than with them; hence the distinctive features of Roman thought about the deities were careful *definition* of their function and relations (this was always the Roman genius and not imagination) and the sense of *obligation* (see further p. 172 on *religio*) toward them.

Religious Personnel

The state corresponded to the family. Affairs were handled by small groups, known as *collegia,* which had responsibility for the different religious activities.

**APHRODITE/
VENUS**
The Eros and
dolphin are
Roman additions
to this copy of a
classical repre-
sentation of the
goddess of love.
*(© Réunion des
Musées Nationaux/
Art Resource, NY)*

During the Republic there were five major colleges of priests: the pontiffs, the augurs, the "Board of Ten" (later 15), who kept the Sibylline Books, the Haruspices, and the Fetiales.

Flamen was an old word for priest. Particularly important was the *flamen dialis,* the priest of Jupiter. He was a full-time functionary and so holy that he could hardly do anything. He had to observe an elaborate system of taboos to preserve purity, because he was in a strategic position. Except for him there was no sacerdotal class set apart as sacred.

Pontifex (pl. *pontifices*) was a more common word for priest. These priests presided at ceremonies on certain days but were not professional and did not form a separate class. The college or board of priests *(collegium pontificum)* was a self-perpetuating body of priests of the principal cults. They numbered fifteen after the constitution established by Sulla in the first century B.C. Their head was the *pontifex maximus,* probably at first the oldest member of the college but later elected.

The college of augurs (again numbering fifteen after Sulla) did not themselves routinely take the auspices (i.e., observing the flight of birds or examining entrails of animals to obtain omens) to determine the attitude of the gods toward some action. The magistrates did this or commanded this to be done. However, one could call upon the augurs to decide if there was any flaw in the procedure or interpretation. They were to give answers, to speak when spoken to by the magistrate in authority.

The six Vestal Virgins were chosen by lot out of a list of twenty compiled by the *pontifex maximus.* Their job was rather literally to "keep the home fires burning." Where fire is hard to get, people do not let it go out, and the Vestals were probably successors to the king's daughters who originally had the duty to tend his fire, which was a supply for all the people. The Vestals lived together in a separate house near the temple of Vesta; they served for thirty years.

The priests were primarily professional experts in matters relating to the gods. Although they performed certain routine duties without special instructions, when unusual circumstances arose it was only at the command of the civil authorities that they became active. Religion was largely a function of the state at Rome; this is particularly evident in the religious observances.

Religious Observances[22]

From the early first century comes a summary of Roman religious ceremonies that relates them to the religious functionaries and shows the Roman concern for proper legal order and respect for tradition:

---

22. H. H. Scullard, *Festivals and Ceremonies of the Roman Republic* (Ithaca, N.Y., 1981).

> Our ancestors wanted fixed and customary ceremonies to be regulated by the knowledge of the pontiffs, authorizations for the successful conduct of affairs by the observations of the augurs, the prophecies of Apollo by the books of the seers, and the averting of omens by the Etruscan discipline. Also by ancient practice attention is paid to the divine: through prayer when anything requires entrusting to the gods; through a vow when a favor is requested; through a ceremony of thanksgiving when a vow is to be paid; through receipt of a favorable omen when it is necessary to consult either entrails or oracles; through sacrifice (by which also the warnings or prodigies and lightening strikes are averted) when a customary rite is to be performed.[23]

There was a common idea in the ancient world that the deities needed the food and drink sacrificed to them. This was especially so in Rome. Sacrifice was thought of as increasing their supply of *numen,* which would be used up in helping people. A good illustration was the sacrificing of a cow with calf to Tellus Mater (Earth Mother) during the growing season. Strictly speaking a human being could not originate *numen* but through proper ceremonies could direct it.

The sacrificial ceremony typically involved a procession of the victims to the altar, prayer of the officiant with offerings of wine, incense, and other foods, pouring of the wine over the animal's head by the officiant, killing of the animal by slaves, examination of the entrails for omens, burning of parts of the animal on the altar, followed by a banquet on the rest of the meat.

Rome had both domestic worship and state calendar observances. The latter were the adaptation of the former on a larger scale. (We will discuss domestic worship later.) The calendar ceremonies were performed by the state. The people's responsibility was passive, to abstain from prohibited acts. These days *(dies nefasti)* belonged to the gods and not to men; other days *(dies fasti)* belonged to men for civil use.

The connection of the state with the official religion may also be seen in the *pomerium,* the sacred boundary of Rome. Only authorized cults could be practiced within it, and only there could the civil auspices *(auspicium,* certain types of divination) be taken. The essential features of a Roman sanctuary, as of a Greek, were an enclosure and an altar. The building *(aedes)* was the house of the deity. Roman temple buildings were characteristically placed on a podium approached by a flight of steps.[24]

Special days of entreaty or thanksgiving might be proclaimed in which the average individual did take part. These "extraliturgical" occasions were a

---

23. Valerius Maximus 1.1.1 (tr. D. Wardle, *Valerius Maximus: Memorable Deeds and Sayings Book I* (London, 1998), 30.

24. On vows to build new temples and their dedications see Eric M. Orlin, *Temples, Religion, and Politics in the Roman Republic* (Leiden, 1997).

supplicatio (lit. "bowing down") when all the people were expected to come before the gods with special requests.

A peculiarity quite characteristic of the legal nature of Roman religion was the requirement that certain ceremonies be done just right, with exact, minute prescriptions. If a mistake was made, the ceremony had to be done over from the beginning; when the ritual had to be repeated, it was called *instauratio*. Hence, these ceremonies were recited from a book.

The Greeks made their sacrifices with uncovered heads, but the Romans covered theirs (cf. 1 Cor. 11:4-5; see p. 97). There was a practical, legal reason for this: to the Roman mind omens portended nothing if unseen, so the priest was veiled from seeing anything inauspicious out of the side of his eye and looked directly at what he or she was doing.

Soul and the Dead

One was not much of an individual in life in early Roman society, so a person was not in death either. The dead belonged to the impersonal *manes,* a polite name for the dead, which hovered between the dead collectively and the forces of the underworld. Many Roman tombstones carry a dedication to the *diis manibus* (the divine dead or the spirits of the underworld), often simply abbreviated D.M. After the first century B.C. the Romans acquired from the Greeks a more definite belief in individual survival.

The word for clan, *gens,* referred to all free-born persons with the same family name. The term *genius* referred to the life principle (a kind of *numen*) of the family, especially as embodied in its head. The *genius* was the procreative force of a person (*Juno* is more frequently used for women). In later times *genius* was identified with the Greek *daimōn,* in the sense of "guardian spirit" or supernatural power accompanying an individual (pp. 236-37). The word could be private and personal (*genius* of an individual) or public and corporate (*genius* of the Roman people or some smaller group). The only *genius* revered by the Roman family was that of the living male head of the family (*pater familias*). The cult of the *genius* of a *pater familias* became a state religion when the worship of the *genius* of Augustus was linked with the public cult of the *lares* (pp. 180-82). The *genius* was depicted either as a mature, bearded man in a toga (*genius* of the senate) or as a seminude youth most often holding cornucopia and patera (*genius* of Roman people and most private *genii*).

Characteristics of Roman Religion

Roman religion was corporate (group solidarity) and legal (a contract relationship). Whereas in the Greek city the individual participated in a whole cycle of religious activities, in Rome the concentration of control was in the *collegia*, with limited personal participation. Religion, like law in our day, was a matter for the experts. Hence, in order to satisfy religious needs of the populace new cults were often introduced in times of crisis (as the *Magna Mater* from Pessinus in Phrygia in the Second Punic War, 205 B.C.; see pp. 281-82). Such new cults had to be admitted in proper form: by formal action of the magistrates and *collegia*. They not only provided an extra outlet for religious emotions but brought the further psychological lift of additional supernatural assistance. In addition, the populace had a tendency to take up new cults from the outside.

The distinctive Roman religious feeling may be seen in the words *pietas* and *religio*. *Pietas* meant doing one's obligations. A "pious" person was one who observed all the rites most scrupulously. *Religio* meant scruple or awe in the presence of the divine, the feeling of uneasiness if anything in the sphere of *pietas* was not performed. A person was under obligation.

The Latin terminology for vows is a prime illustration of the legal character of Roman religion (pp. 21-22, 167, 169, 171; cf. 192-93). When a person made a vow, he was a *voti reus*, "one accused of a vow," obliged to do something for the god. The obligation was in suspense, however, until the condition was accomplished; then the person had to fulfill his vow. Until he did so, he was *voti damnatus*, "one under condemnation for his vow." There was nothing like these terms in Greece.

The customs of the ancestors *(mos maiorum)* were even more binding in Rome than in Greece. A major difference between the modern world and the ancient world is in the attitude toward the "modern." For us the newest is the truest and the best, but in ancient times what was older was truer and better. The principle "it is not done" was deeply rooted in the ethos of Rome, only partially modified under the impact of Hellenism. Things had a "staying power" in Rome.

The traditional and external nature of Roman religion is summarized in words attributed to a person otherwise of skeptical leanings:

> This no doubt meant that I ought to uphold the beliefs about the immortal gods which have come down to us from our ancestors, and the rites and ceremonies and duties of religion. For my part I always shall uphold them . . . , and no eloquence . . . shall ever dislodge me from the belief as to the worship of the immortal gods which I have inherited from our forefathers. . . . The religion of the Roman people comprises ritual, auspices, and the third additional division consisting of all such prophetic warnings as the interpreters of the Sibyl or the soothsayers have derived from portents and prodigies. Well, I have always thought that none of these departments of religion was to be despised, and I have held the conviction that Romulus by his auspices and Numa by his establishment of our ritual laid the foundations of our state, which assuredly could never have been as

great as it is had not the fullest measure of divine favor been obtained for it. (Cotta in Cicero, *On the Nature of the Gods* 3.2.5.)

Features of ancient Roman and Greek religion may be discerned in the respective development of Catholic and Orthodox Christianity: in the former the legal and juridical precision, organizational development, priestly monopoly, and emphasis on rites and correct formulas; in the latter a larger place for vows and voluntary piety by the populace and speculative interest in doctrines.

RELIGION IN HELLENISTIC-ROMAN TIMES: GENERAL CHARACTERISTICS

Although religion was not all of one piece in Hellenistic and early Roman times, we may make certain generalizations. Some of these characteristics were continuations from earlier times that attained a greater prominence during these periods. Even during the empire the essential spirit of religion was Greek. Rome's greatest contribution was creating security and uniting the people in one state. Rome, with little of its own to give in religion, filled its skeleton of religion with a Greek content; the old native forms continued in the various countries, but the spirit was Greek.[25] Listed here are some of the prevailing features; several will receive more detailed treatment in the following sections.

(1) Greco-Roman paganism was *nonexclusive*. Worship, even the giving of one's own exclusive devotion to a deity, did not preclude the acknowledgment of other deities. The exclusive demands made by Jews and Christians for their God were part of the scandal of these faiths to pagans. This nonexclusive nature of polytheism remained in spite of the tendencies to monotheism noted below.

(2) The *identification of deities* tended to reduce their number and contributed to the monotheistic trend of thought. Female deities tended to be identified with one another, and the chief god of each people was thought of as the same. This blending together of the deities of different peoples depended on the transplanting of peoples, the Greek opinion that the name of a god is translatable like any other word, and the attraction of things foreign to the Greeks. This combination of deities was a principal expression of the syncretism of the times in which there was considerable borrowing from one cult to another, transfer of ideas, and reinterpretation of older concepts into Greek modes of thought, although not to the extent that distinctive features were lost.

(3) The anthropomorphism of classical Greek religion was weakened in the *worship of power*. People became more interested in divine deeds and power

---

25. M. P. Nilsson, *Geschichte der Griechischen Religion* (Munich, 1974), 2:301. In the following section I have drawn heavily on Nilsson, *Greek Piety* (Oxford, 1948), chap. III.

ARTEMIS/DIANA
The classical Artemis, the huntress and lover of nature, was also the goddess of childbirth. *(© Réunion des Musées Nationaux/ Art Resource, NY)*

than in divine personalities, which climaxed in the concern with the occult at the end of paganism. This worship of power lies behind the phenomena noted by Nock and separately treated below: "Astrology, magic, and the expression of devotion to the Emperor were the universal phenomena of paganism in Roman times."[26] Power was undefined, wonderful, and marvelous, and its manifestations were deserving of worship and worth trying to explain and control.

26. Review of Gunkel, *Neue astrologische Texte des Hermes Trismegistos*, in *Gnomon* 15 (1939):368 (*Essays*, 502).

ARTEMIS OF
THE EPHESIANS

The Ephesian goddess was one of the mother goddesses of Asia. The eggs (or breasts) were a fertility emblem, but promiscuity was not associated with her. The mural crown marks her as protectress of the city. The Greeks identified her with Artemis. *(© Erich Lessing/Art Resource, NY)*

(4) On the other hand, there was a *deification of virtues or benefits* (with a corresponding personification of these abstract ideas).[27] The Greek spirit did not leave things indefinite, so there was a tendency (much increased in Roman times) to name a benefit after the god from which it came (as grain was called Ceres) or to designate the deity by the specific type of power manifested — as Salus (salvation), Libertas (liberty), and especially Victoria (victory). Since whatever benefits people must be the product of the working of divine benevolence, certain qualities were treated as divine. For example, concord (Concordia) and peace (Pax) were honored as deities with sanctuaries dedicated to them. The cult of *Tychē* ("luck," or simply the course of events) was the most widespread and popular expression of this development.

(5) The tendency to *monotheism* influenced the terminology of pagan authors but was seldom carried through consistently. The several influences contributing to the spread of a monotheistic view (pp. 297-98) left room for lesser deities under the highest god and so in reality the popular religion was able to continue.

(6) Since lesser gods and intermediary powers were identified with demons, there was a *demonizing of religion* (pp. 236-38). The word *demons* did not have the negative connotations it does today, but as unlucky happenings were attributed to intermediary beings or forces it began to acquire even in pagan thought something of a pejorative sense. The demons filled the gap between the gods and human beings and between the superlunary world and the earth. Demons had their starting point in abstract powers, ghosts, and the unexplained in human nature. They came to be identified with beings under the one God. Peoples of the Roman empire, if not "demon possessed" or rather demon influenced (as the Christian apologists suggested), were certainly demon conscious.

(7) The power of *fate* was very strongly felt in the early empire (pp. 241-43). It found philosophical justification in Stoicism and was even worshiped as a deity. On the other hand, it is characteristic of the deities that gained prominence in the Hellenistic-Roman world (Asclepius, Isis, Sarapis) that, unlike the older Greek deities, they claimed power over fate.

(8) The belief in fate was often linked with belief in the influence of the stars, so *astrology* came to prominence (pp. 238-42). Astrology applied the law of causality strictly. It was a complicated and technical operation, at once mathematical and astronomical.

(9) *Magic* was another popular expression of human relations with the powers of the universe (pp. 227-35). Although moderns distinguish magic from the spirit of religion, the ancients did not do so. Superstition, sorcery, use of amulets, the magical power of statues, formulas for healing and cursing, and private divination were all on the increase in late antiquity.

---

27. Cicero, *On the Nature of the Gods* 2.60-62. See J. Rufus Fears, "The Cult of Virtues and Roman Imperial Ideology," *ANRW* II, *Principat*, 17.2 (Berlin, 1981), 827-948.

(10) The *corporate nature* or social side of religion was not lost in the Hellenistic-Roman periods. That religion is a private matter of one's own belief and practice would not have been advocated in antiquity. The meaning of the traditional civic religion in Hellenistic times has been undervalued. Religion without cult was still practically unthinkable, except in certain philosophical circles, and cult required an organized expression.

(11) There was, however, a new prominence to *chosen relationships*. Cult associations flourished in Hellenistic times; associations of artisans, athletes, actors, etc. were prominent under the empire, and even these had a religious aspect (pp. 142-47). So new groupings in addition to those based on family, state, or nationality added a new dimension to the social aspect of religion and made easier an acceptance of new cults.

(12) *Morality* was not closely associated with religion. Rules of ritual purity were normally ceremonial and seldom ethical or moral. There are notable exceptions to this generalization: Apuleius in *Metamorphoses* 11 (pp. 273ff.) was in his predicament because of sin, and his conversion to Isis included moral change; and moral rules are included in the prescriptions for entrance into a religious association at Philadelphia (p. 187; cf. pp. 285-87). For the most part, codes of conduct were derived from one's national customs or from the ethical teachings of the philosophical schools. Cicero (pp. 380ff.) provides a good example of the typical distinction between religion and ethics. He believed in the existence of God and the immortality of the soul, but when he wrote his treatises on ethics, *De officiis* (On Moral Duties) and *De finibus* (On the Ends of Goods and Evils), he did not regulate the precepts he gave by those beliefs. The wedding of ethics and religious belief, based on divine revelation, was one of the important strengths of Judaism and Christianity in the ancient world.

For the remainder of this chapter we will take a topical approach, grouping the topics according to domestic religion, civic or state cults, and personal religion. These are not firm categories, for there is much overlapping. Appropriate chronological notes will be made, but the effort will be to present a cross-section of religious life during the centuries surrounding the beginning of the Christian era.

DOMESTIC AND RURAL RELIGION

The religion of the home and countryside shows the greatest continuity with the earlier, formative periods of Greek and Roman religion. Not a great deal has been preserved about this side of religious life in the Hellenistic-Roman period. We will take note of some features that are attested and seem to have been constant.

Greek[28]

Excavations at Delos supplement literary evidence in confirming a continuation of features of the domestic cult for the Hellenistic Age. Near the door or in the midst of the court of a Greek home was an altar to *Zeus Herkeios* (Zeus of the Enclosure, from *herkos,* fence), who watched over the dwelling. (The city of Athens, too, as a collection of the families, had an altar to *Zeus Herkeios.*) A stone pillar erected near the door was dedicated to *Apollo Patroos* or *Phratrios* (Apollo as the protector of all the relatives). The citizen was recognized by his possession of these emblems and practice of the associated cult.[29] Zeus was worshiped inside the house, in association with Hestia (the goddess of the hearth) under the designation *Zeus Ktesios* (Zeus of the pantry). Here Zeus was represented as a snake. This indicates that the sky god in becoming the house god had replaced the old *daimones* or spirits who watched over the court, provisions, and family.

Also represented as a snake was the *Agathos Daimōn* (the Good Demon or Spirit). The name is frequently inscribed on household altars. The *Agathos Daimōn* was a protective household spirit. Greek houses were built with an earth floor, and small, nonpoisonous snakes often nested in the pantry. They ate the offerings left out for the deity, and were helpful in keeping the house free of rodents. Thus the snake came to be considered a friendly, if somewhat remote, member of the household and the embodiment of the guardian spirit of the household.[30]

The hearth was the center of the Greek domestic cult. The meal began and ended with a religious act: before a meal Greeks offered a few pieces of food on the hearth; after the meal they poured out a libation of unmixed wine to the *Agathos Daimōn.*

From birth the child was surrounded by domestic piety. His earliest recollections were of the father sacrificing on the family altar and all the household assembled for sacred meals. Birth, puberty, marriage, and funerals were accompanied by ceremonial acts.

The Greeks thought the countryside was filled with supernatural powers, with demons or spirits inhabiting mountains, forests, trees, stones, rivers, and fountains. Hellenistic art often pictured river gods as animals or persons, and even the breezes were personified. The most frequently occurring of the nature spirits were the female nymphs, always shown in human shape.[31] They dwelled

---

28. M. P. Nilsson, *Greek Popular Religion* (New York, 1940); repr. as *Greek Folk Religion* (New York, 1961).

29. The scrutiny of a prospective archon in Athens included the question whether he possessed an ancestral Apollo and a household Zeus and where their sanctuaries were. These questions plus the identification of his father and mother and their deme and the possession of a family tomb established the candidate's citizenship. Aristotle, *Constitution of Athens* 55.

30. Cf. Theophrastus, *Characters* 16 and Virgil, *Aeneid* 5.84ff.

31. Jennifer Larson, *Greek Nymphs: Myth, Cult, Lore* (Oxford, 2001).

in trees, mountain caves, the sea, and springs or rivers. The wilder stretches of the countryside were inhabited by male demons thought of as half-human, half-animal in appearance — centaurs, sileni, and satyrs. The most popular of these was Pan, son of Hermes, who had the legs and face of a goat.[32] He was associated with the life of shepherds, and is often shown holding the syrinx, a pipe played by shepherds in times of rest, but he could cause a panic when animals were frightened. He is remembered on a higher level as the addressee of the prayer of Socrates:

> O beloved Pan and all ye other gods of this place, grant to me that I be made beautiful in my soul within, and that all external possessions be in harmony with my inner man. May I consider the wise man rich; and may I have such wealth as only the self-restrained man can bear or endure. (Plato, *Phaedrus* 279B-C)[33]

But this is exceptional, both for Pan and for the nature of Greek prayers.

To placate these nature spirits, the Greeks marked their roadways by stone heaps. A traveler would add another stone to the heap or perhaps place a bit of food on it as an offering. Hermes derived his name from the stone heap *(herma)* in which he lived.

Many of the nature deities, such as the centaurs, did not receive a cult. Some, such as Artemis — the leader of the nymphs — and Hermes became important deities. All contributed to the sense of wonder about nature and to Greek folklore. Nilsson summarizes their importance in this way:

> Nature was peopled with spirits, daemons, and gods. They haunted the mountains and the forests. They dwelt in trees and stone, in rivers and wells. Some of them were rough and dreadful, as the wilderness is, while others were gentle and benevolent. Some of them promoted the life of nature and also protected mankind. . . . This aspect of Greek religion was certainly not the highest, but it was the most enduring. It was close to the earth, which is the source of all religion and from which even the great gods sprang. The great gods were overthrown and soon forgotten by the people. The nature daemons were not so easily dealt with. The nature spirits have lived on in the mind of the people to this day.[34]

The towns as well as the countryside were filled with these sacred spots: "One could hardly have taken a step out of doors without meeting a little shrine, a sacred enclosure, an image, a sacred stone, or a sacred tree."[35]

---

32. Philippe Bourgeaud, *The Cult of Pan in Ancient Greece* (Chicago, 1988).
33. Translation by Harold North Taylor in Loeb Classical Library.
34. M. P. Nilsson, *Greek Folk Religion* (New York, 1961), 20-21.
35. Ibid., p. 18.

Roman[36]

Since the household and not the individual was the unit of society, in all aspects of domestic life — including religion — responsibility fell primarily on the head of the family *(pater familias)*, who acted on behalf of the household. Certain observances, *sacra privata*, were binding on him. An inheritance without these was a rose without a thorn. A principal such duty was the burial of the dead. Offerings accompanied meals and the ceremonies at birth, marriage, and death.

Pompeii offers some concrete evidence for the continuation of the Roman domestic cult in the first century.[37] Near the entrance to a Roman house was a niche that served as a shrine to the *lares*, who were watchful, protective spirits of the family and household. The *lararium* (household shrine) was a wooden cupboard or a stone or masonry niche or aedicula for images or paintings of the household deities. The paintings often depict a gay, dancing *lar* or two holding a drinking cup *(rhyton)*, a man in a toga usually holding a libation dish to personify the *genius* of the family, and a snake representing the spirit (or *genius*) of the family or of the place. Snakes were associated with the *lares*. Bronze statuettes of the *lares* corresponding in appearance to the pictures were found in some houses. Several types of altars are found in association with the household shrines. At every meal a small portion of food was placed before the *lararium*. Three times each month an offering of flowers was made as well. The wealthier households had elegant statues of the *lares*, which would be brought to the table if the meal was not in the room containing the *lararium*. The *penates* were the guardians of the pantry; they were closely associated with the *lares* and *Vesta* (goddess of the hearth). The *lares* and *penates*, with *Janus* (god of the doorway) and *Vesta*, protected the home. The *lares* were offered fire, the family *genius* (p. 171) wine, and the *penates* incense.

Another popular deity, especially in the second and third centuries, for the domestic religion of the lower classes was Silvanus, god of agriculture and forests.[38] He had no public cult, but private individuals dedicated many inscriptions to him.

The *lares* were also worshiped at crossroads as protectors of travelers, corresponding in this respect to the Greek Hermes. When Augustus undertook the restoration of Roman religion, he reorganized the cult of the *lares compitales*. Rome was divided into districts, and at the principal crossroads were erected shrines dedicated to Augustus and the *genius* of the place. This practice was extended to the provinces: the spirits of the road would protect

36. David G. Orr, "Roman Domestic Religion: The Evidence of the Household Shrines," *ANRW* II, *Principat*, 16.2 (Berlin and New York, 1978), 1557-91; Daniel P. Harmon, "The Family Festivals of Rome," ibid., 1592-1603.

37. G. K. Boyce, *Corpus of the Lararia of Pompeii*, Memoirs of the American Academy in Rome, vol. 14 (Rome, 1937).

38. P. F. Dorcey, *The Cult of Silvanus: A Study in Roman Folk Religion* (Leiden, 1992).

the transplanted Romans. In the provinces these spirits were called the *lares augustales*. These cults were intended to answer the religious needs of slaves and freedmen, who had no part in the civic cult. Priesthoods, awarded to freedmen and knights, were an official extension of what had been domestic and rural religious practices in earlier days.

LARARIUM, from Pompeii
The shrine for the Lares, protective deities of the household, were the center of the domestic cult in Roman religion. *(© Werner Forman/Art Resource, NY)*

The powers of the home, road, and field gained more favor with the masses than the great Capitoline gods, and as in Greece they survived longer. For travelers and people in the country and small towns the real protectors were the *penates* and *lares*. They have been described as "benevolent, familiar, and gay — simple as those who honored them."[39]

In the Latin west and in the Greek east the church won only by detouring the traditional piety to other objects. The martyrs and the saints received the homage once given to the heroes and nature and household spirits. The similarity between the cult of heroes and spirits in ancient Greece and Rome and the cult of the saints in medieval Christendom (Roman and Greek) has often been observed.[40] The old hung on: a sacred spring in antiquity kept on being a sacred spring. When Christianity replaced paganism, the saints took over the functions of the specialized local deities. The situation may be described as "the old firm doing the same business at the same place under a new name and a new management." But this perhaps says too much. It was not the ancient religion itself that survived but the mentality that was part of it.

CIVIC CULTS

We have already stated the civic basis of Greek and Roman religion; yet more needs to be said. Modern Western ideas that put religion in a separate category from government, society, and culture can seriously mislead us. Religion was closely interwoven with society in the Greco-Roman world. It was official and a part of the civil order. Each city had its patron deity or deities. Sacrifice and prayer accompanied meetings of the assembly and council, and priests of the public cults were selected in the same ways as the magistrates. Temples were built out of public funds, and taxes were levied for the support of certain cults.[41] The state decided expenditures for the cult and derived income from it. Much of our information about religious practices comes from the "Sacred Laws" enacted by the cities to regulate official cults. These regulations touch personnel, perquisites, the festival and sacrificial calendar, and provisions for additional ceremonies — just such details as were regulated in connection with purely secular offices — but seldom the details of ritual, which remained the preserve of priests. Human life was thoroughly permeated with religion, and numerous ceremonies punctuated the course of life. In Chapter 2 we saw

---

39. A. J. Festugière, *Le monde gréco-romain au temps de notre-Seigneur* (Paris, 1935), 2:40.

40. For survivals in general see Gordon J. Laing, *Survivals of Roman Religion* (London, 1931), and J. C. Lawson, *Modern Greek Folklore and Ancient Greek Religion* (New Hyde Park, N.Y., 1964).

41. Robert Schlaifer, "Notes on Athenian Public Cults," *Harvard Studies in Classical Philology* 51 (1940):233ff.

how idolatry permeated all phases of life — political, social, economic, and military.

Each city had a patron deity who protected it. If the city was powerful, the deity became pan-Hellenic, e.g., Athena. Other cults, not properly civic, had an international character based on a legend (e.g., Delos — the birthplace of Apollo and Artemis), an oracle (Delphi — Apollo), or ancient games (Olympia — Zeus).

The citizen or sojourner who respected and practiced the civic cult and the priest who discharged his tasks faithfully were called "pious" *(eusebeia)*. In the inscriptions this word designated above all the manner in which one accomplished the external rites.

The civic cult in its forms remained essentially unchanged from the past into the period surrounding the birth of Christianity. The old Greek religion drew its life from the literature that was the basis of education in the schools and from its association with civic life. The Hellenistic age often has been seen as a time of decline for the traditional religion. The decline of the old city-states certainly brought on a crisis. The conquests of Alexander produced a universalizing and personalizing of religion as of so much else. Abundant archaeological evidence, however, shows that the decline of autonomy for the cities of the Greek east was accompanied by an awakening of the civic cult. The traditional civic cults remained vital in the Hellenistic age. The glory of the cities was concentrated in the memory of the past. A great body of literature attests to the antiquarian interests of the Hellenistic age (cf. the *Hymns* of Callimachus and the sources Plutarch used in his *Greek Questions*). The local sanctuary with its temple, treasures, priesthood, and festivals attracted visitors and was visible testimony to the grandeur of former times and the principal tangible source of pride for the present. The reconstruction of temples, the dedications to deities, and the pomp of the festivals were if anything even greater than before. This is true to the experience of towns and small cities today: as their importance in the larger field of affairs seems less, civic pride finds expression in activities of local interest.

The importance of the local civic cults is seen in the way Rome identified herself with them. Rather than combat the patriotic cults, the imperial religion was associated with them. Rome furthered the custom of exchanging ambassadors for games, temple dedications, etc. between cities. Images of the emperor and sanctuaries for the imperial cult were set up in the sacred precincts of the civic cult. This imperial favor and alliance profited the civic religion in imperial times. The important cults were those joined to the emperor and national god; the other old cults declined.

Augustus's program for restoring order to Roman government and society included regulation of religious affairs. He revived old cults, filled vacant priesthoods, and rebuilt eighty-two temples. He identified himself and his rule with old cults and instituted new ones (e.g., *lares compitales* were made public and official; p. 180) for elements of the population left out of the old republican religion. By the celebration of the Secular Games in 17 B.C. he sought to link the piety of his age with the traditions of the past. The Augustan restoration was another demonstration of the close ties between civic life and religious observances.[42]

The extent of the information provided about the civic cults makes this the appropriate place to consider the formal aspects of religion that apply even to those cults which were not official — priesthood, ritual prescriptions, sacrifice — as well as the festivals and ceremonies that characterized the worship of the civic deities (for temples see pp. 160-61).

BIBLIOGRAPHY

Ziehen, L., and I. de Prott. *Leges Graecorum Sacrae.* Leipzig, 1906.
Ryberg, Inez Scott. *Rites of the State Religion in Roman Art.* Memoirs of the American Academy in Rome, vol. 22. New Haven, 1956.
Zaidman, L. B., and P. S. Pantel. *Religion in the Ancient Greek City.* Cambridge, 1992.
Parker, Robert. *Athenian Religion: A History.* Oxford, 1996.
Mikalson, Jon D. *Religion in Hellenistic Athens.* Berkeley, 1998.

Priesthood[43]

Aeschines, the orator, spoke of priests as "persons who receive perquisites . . . and whose occupation is to pray to heaven for you" (3.18). Even more pertinent is Plato's definition:

> There is also the priestly class, who, as the law declares, know how to give the gods gifts from men in the form of sacrifices which are acceptable to them, and to ask on our behalf blessings in return from them. (*Laws* 290)[44]

Greek religion was not fostered by a professional class. The priesthood was not centralized and seldom was full-time. Theoretically anyone might perform priestly functions, allowing for the restrictions in particular cults.[45] Nevertheless, in the major civic cults a specialization of function was necessary.

---

42. A. D. Nock, "The Augustan Restoration," *Classical Review* 39 (1925):50-67 (*Essays,* 1:16-25).

43. M. Beard and J. North, eds., *Pagan Priests: Religion and Power in the Ancient World* (London, 1990).

44. Another ancient description is that the priest is one "skilled in the rules of sacrifice, prayer, and purification" (Stobaeus, *Ecl. Apoph.* [or *Florilegium*] 2.122 [Wachsmuth and Hense, vol. 2, p. 67]).

45. Isocrates 2.6 says the office of priest is one which any man can fill.

The essential qualification as indicated by the above descriptions was that one "know how" to approach the deity. But the regulations of particular cults specify other requirements. The most commonly expressed requirement is freedom from physical defects or infirmity. In the civic cults it was also necessary that one be a citizen. The conditions relative to age were quite variable. There are several cases on record of priesthoods held by children. This may be related to a fairly frequent demand for celibacy during the term of office. The requirement was not a matter of morality, but of ritual purity, and the assigning of priesthoods to the elderly or the very young conforms to the ancient view that sexual functions were ceremonially defiling (cf. Lev. 22:4-6). The normal tendency, however, was probably to put the civic priesthoods into the hands of men of leisure and substance, as was the case with civic magistracies.

The methods of filling the priesthoods fall into three categories: inheritance, election, or purchase. Hereditary priesthoods occur in cults closely connected with a given family, either because the family was regarded as descended from the deity worshiped or had introduced the cult, which then in time became public. The ordinary civic priesthoods were chosen by vote or by drawing of lots or by some combination of the two. Lots was most common, and could be interpreted as permitting the deity to choose his own minister,[46] but this was also the common method of filling many magistracies in Greek cities. The Hellenistic period saw a strong development of the practice of selling priesthoods. The vendor was always the state. The purchase of a priesthood was one method of making an investment for a livelihood or provisions for one's family, with a sound title. Priesthoods acquired by inheritance or purchase were normally for life. When officers were elected or chosen by lot their term was normally one year, as with the magistracies. Where longer terms are known the tenure most likely coincided with the frequency of major periodic festivals.

The priest was the officiant appointed to a sanctuary. He was always the servant of a particular deity at a particular sanctuary, although this did not preclude (at least in late Hellenistic times) one individual serving more than one deity or at more than one shrine. His duties may be grouped in two categories: administrative and ritual. The priest was personally responsible for the care of the temple, the cult image, the contents of the shrine, and the sacred precinct about the sanctuary (which contained above all a fountain, necessary for purifications). At a small sanctuary this was no large task. At a large temple, however, there were subordinate functionaries or employees and sacred slaves to assist in these matters under the priest's supervision. The priest's chief administrative assistant was known as the *neokoros* (temple-keeper, a kind of sacristan) and in Asia Minor had great importance.[47] Financial administration,

---

46. Plato, *Laws* 759C; *Inscriptiones Graecae* 12.3, 178.

47. Cf. the city of Ephesus calling itself the temple-keeper *(neokoros)* of Artemis in Acts 19:35.

except in the smaller temples, belonged to state officials. The ritual duties, included in the definitions above, distinguished the priest from other sacred functionaries. The stated public sacrifices in the civic cult might be monthly or yearly or at other stated times. Beyond these occasions the priest had to assist those who came to sacrifice in fulfillment of a vow. The presence of the priest was not required in order to make the sacrifice ritually effective. A temple attendant, or anyone who knew how, could perform the actual slaughter, but the priest was normally involved. His principal function was to sacrifice according to the rules; he was the one who knew the proper ritual. Furthermore, he pronounced the prayer or invocation. The liturgical functions of the priest also included presiding at the festivals of the deity.

Certain benefits went with the office of priest. The most substantial and nearly universal was the perquisite of a portion of the sacrificial animal — a leg was most common — or if not an animal a portion of whatever was offered. Sometimes a salary was paid or goods furnished to the priest. Exemptions from taxes and from public duties were sometimes conferred. On the other hand, certain priesthoods involved considerable expense, since the priest had to defray the costs of the celebration of great festivals, which included public entertainment. Among the honors that went with the office were a special place in religious processions, chief seats at the theatre and contests, and the privilege of wearing a garland wreath or gold crown. The close tie with civic life is shown in that for many cities the eponymous official (the magistrate who gave his name to the year, as one of the archons did in Athens and the consuls did in Rome) was the priest of the patron deity of the city. Under the empire priests took on more and more the character of civil officers.

This description of priesthood in the civic cults is fairly representative for private religious associations, allowing for the difference in circumstances, for a priest was a priest. Priesthood in the Near Eastern cults, however, was far more often lifelong and professional. When these cults entered the Greek world, they, like Greek private religious associations, lacked a connection with the local governing bodies. Their priests, however, were increasingly assimilated to Greek priests, since their qualifications and functions were similar.

Ritual Prescriptions[48]

"For it cannot be that the impure attain the pure."[49] Not everyone was authorized to enter a sanctuary. Generally an inscription at the entrance indicated

---

48. For this and the following sections I am greatly dependent on A. J. Festugière, *Le monde gréco-romain au temps de notre-Seigneur* (Paris, 1935), 2:83-109.

49. Plato, *Phaedo* 67B. Although spoken in a different context, this may be taken as an axiom of ancient religion.

who was excluded and what were the conditions of purity. In most civic cults a woman was not admitted, nor was a noncitizen or slave. But another could sacrifice for you, so one was not totally excluded from participation. Other cults often lacked these limitations on sex, citizenship, and social condition.

The ritual precepts had in no way, in their origin, a moral character. The rules of purity for visitors to the temple of Athena at Pergamum illustrate this:

> Whoever wishes to visit the temple of the goddess, whether a resident of the city or anyone else, must refrain from intercourse with his wife (or husband) that day, from intercourse with another than his wife (or husband) for the preceding two days, and must complete the required lustrations. The same prohibition applies to contact with the dead and with the delivery of a woman in childbirth.[50]

The motifs of impurity that excluded a person from entrance were numerous, each resulting in a certain number of days of impurity. In some cases the clothing was regulated — for example, a woman's hair was to be loose and a man's head had to be uncovered.[51] Sometimes the regulations included what animals could enter the sacred enclosure.

Under the influence of poets and philosophers some elements of moral purity were introduced into the ritual precepts. Epictetus reflects the elements involved in an approach to deity along with the added concern of proper attitudes: One "ought to come with sacrifice and with prayers, and after a preliminary purification, and with his mind disposed to the idea that he will be approaching holy rites" (*Discourses* 3.21.14). The code of a household cult in Philadelphia from the first century B.C.[52] is notable on several counts. The shrine was under the protection of Agdistis but was dedicated to other deities as well. The rules included purifications and sacrifices but also prohibited entrance to robbers, murderers, users of drugs, adulterers, or those who induced abortion. The regulations are presented as the commands of god (Zeus) to the owner of the house. Such moral commandments among the ritual regulations are exceptional in the surviving inscriptions, but they concern such matters as were important for preserving the integrity of an extended household.

Sacrifices, ablutions, and other ceremonies could remove impurities. The purifications implied a sense of "sin," although not in the full Christian sense

---

50. W. Dittenberger, *Sylloge Inscriptionum Graecarum* (3d ed.; Leipzig, 1920), vol. 3, no. 982; translation from F. C. Grant, *Hellenistic Religions* (New York, 1953), 6.

51. Dittenberger, *Sylloge*³ 999 (Grant, pp. 26-27). Is this relevant to 1 Cor. 11:1ff.?

52. Ibid., 985 (Grant, pp. 28-30). S. C. Barton and G. H. R. Horsley, "A Hellenistic Cult Group and the New Testament Churches," *Jahrbuch für Antike und Christentum* 24 (1981):7-41 offer a maximum interpretation of its parallels to the church; important corrections to their interpretation are made by Stanley K. Stowers, "A Cult from Philadelphia: Oikos Religion or Cultic Association," in A. J. Malherbe, et al., *The Early Church in Its Context: Essays in Honor of Everett Ferguson* (Leiden, 1998), 287-301.

of that word. The underlying feeling was that impurities contracted in ordinary life require a period of quarantine in which to wear off, during which time the impure person was excluded from ceremonies. Fasting, purification, and offering were preliminary exercises in healing cults (preparatory to incubation), to receiving visions, and even to engaging in a magical ritual. Purification most often involved some form of washing.

Regulations of matters of worship were the least subject to change of any aspect of religion, and the ritual precepts kept their force throughout antiquity.

Sacrifice[53]

Herondas, in *Mime* 4, shows united the three principal acts of worship in the ancient world — sacrifice, votive offering, and prayer.[54] The scene is set in the temple of Asclepius on Cos about the year 250 B.C. Two women accompanied by a slave-woman had come to offer a cock and set up a tablet as a gift for a healing granted by Asclepius. They explained that they were poor and so offered a cock instead of an ox or a fat sow. While the women admired the works of art set up in the temple, the *neokoros* immolated the victim on the altar before the temple. He returned to announce that the offering was acceptable to the god. The formula was no doubt stereotyped:

> Your meat offerings are simply perfect, and they certainly guarantee good fortune for both of you. No one ever found more favor in the god's eyes than you have. . . . Be thou propitious on account of these fine offerings, and likewise to their husbands and children!

Of the sacrificed animal, a part belonged to the god, a leg went to the *neokoros*, and the rest was taken by the women to be eaten at home along with some bread provided by the *neokoros*. One of the women dropped a coin in the treasury.[55]

The Aristotelian philosopher Theophrastus gave three reasons for sacrifice: to give honor, to make a return for benefits, or to avert evil or receive benefits. Sacrifice might be private or public, to gods or heroes, at regular public festivals or spontaneously on special occasions, and for praise, thanksgiving, or supplica-

53. Homer, *Odyssey* 3.430-463; Lucian, *De sacrificiis*. Note G. S. Kirk, "Some Methodological Pitfalls in the Study of Ancient Greek Sacrifice," *Le Sacrifice dans l'antiquité, Entretiens sur l'Antiquité Classique* 17 (Geneva, 1980); M. Detienne and J. P. Vernant, eds., *The Cuisine of Sacrifice among the Greeks* (Chicago, 1989); F. T. van Straten, *Hierà Kalá: Images of Animal Sacrifice in Archaic and Classical Greece* (Leiden, 1995).

54. W. Headlam, ed., *Herondas: The Mimes and Fragments* (Cambridge, 1922, 1966).

55. For this interpretation see M. P. Nilsson, "The Dragon on the Treasure," *American Journal of Philology* 68 (1947):302ff., in preference to Grant's translation (*Hellenistic Religions*, p. 6) of a wafer placed in the den for the live snakes kept at the sanctuary.

For the practice of taking home blessed bread cf. the *eulogia* or blessed bread the Greek Orthodox worshiper takes home from the service.

SACRIFICIAL SCENE, relief
A bull is brought to sacrifice, while the priest (veiled, as was characteristic for
Roman sacrifice) burns incense on the altar. *(Hall of Statues, Vatican)*

tion. Both animals and vegetables were offered. The offering might be eaten,
burned, or poured out. Animal sacrifice normally came in festivals celebrated annually or at a home sacrifice. The old Greek religion knew only yearly or (especially in domestic cult) monthly observances. Less costly rites could be observed
more frequently. Apart from the Egyptian cult's daily observances, a daily cult is
found among the Greeks only in Asclepius's temples and then in ruler cult.

Bloody sacrifices were of two kinds. A sacrifice to a heavenly deity involved generally burning only a part of the animal for the deity while the rest
was distributed among the temple staff and the worshipers. Sacrifice to
chthonic powers (heroes or the dead) included burning the entire animal. Yet
the distinction must allow for considerable exceptions.[56] The priest had the
right to sell to the markets the sanctuary's share of the offerings (cf. 1 Cor. 8:10
for eating sacrificial food in a cult meal; 9:13 for the priests receiving their food
from the offerings; and 10:25 for eating what had been sold in the markets). In
the civic cults at the festivals the offerers' portion went to the magistrates to be
distributed to the people. Animals considered appropriate for sacrifice were
naturally those nourishing to human beings. Some cults, however, prohibited
certain animals for reasons of which we are now ignorant. The animal had to
be without defect. The skins of sacrificed animals were sold for profit, usually
by the temple or priest, but in Athens by the state. Meat was not the common

56. A. D. Nock, "The Cult of Heroes," *HTR* 37 (1944):141ff. (*Essays,* 575ff.).

part of the diet in the ancient world that it has been in modern Western countries. One of the principal occasions for eating meat was at a sacrifice, particularly the state festivals.

Other food items offered as sacrifice included bread, meal, oil, and wine. Libations accompanied many sacrifices (cf. Phil. 2:17; 2 Tim. 4:6). Such drink offerings before or after a sacrifice or a meal were a way of reserving a part for the divinity, as was burning meat on the altar.

Altars of various sizes and shapes have been recovered from excavations. The most common are small round altars, with a garland and bulls' heads sculptured around the side, and larger rectangular altars. Reliefs and paintings testify to the practice of placing a garland wreath around the bull led to sacrifice (Acts 14:13). Roman practices appear to have been similar. A common sacrificial scene represented on Roman monuments is the *suovetaurilia,* in which were sacrificed a pig, ram, and bull. Larger animals were not killed on the small altars but near them; some of the blood, the god's portion, and some barley might be burned on such altars.

The god's presence was symbolized by his statue. That deities were invited to be present and were thought of as present has led to the modern theory that giving food to them made them table companions, but this lacks support in the ancient texts. The purpose was not to establish fellowship (1 Cor. 10:20 is an interpretation from the Christian standpoint of the meaning of eating a sacrificial meal) but was a matter of a gift or tribute and of effective action by reason of the offering (i.e., in thanks for a favor received or in order to obtain a favor). The Latin equivalent for the concept of the presence of the deity was *lectisternium* when one received a god in whose honor a banquet was given, and *sellisternium* when one received a goddess.

A. D. Nock distinguishes three types of ancient religious meals: (1) eating together by a cult society that thereby gives expression to its fellowship or commemorates a founder or benefactor; (2) eating together when a deity was thought to preside; and (3) the enthusiastic rending of animals and eating their raw flesh, as done by votaries of Dionysus.[57] Many temples had adjoining dining rooms for cultic meals. Archaeological evidence indicates these were common in the area of Corinth, a fact that provides the background for the problems addressed in 1 Corinthians 8–11.

The dominant sentiment in the sacrifice was that "I give in order that you may give to me." Plato's dialogue *Euthyphro* examines this attitude. Socrates says, "Sacrificing is making gifts to the gods and praying is asking from them,"

---

57. *Early Gentile Christianity and its Hellenistic Background* (New York, 1964), 72-74 (*Essays,* 107-9). H.-J. Klauck, *Herrenmahl und hellenistischer Kult* (Münster, 1982), 31-40, offers a more elaborate "phenomenology of holy meals": meals eaten by the gods, gods eating what humans provide, meals at a sacrifice, communion sacrifices, eating the deity, treaty meals guaranteed by a deity, club meals, meals for the dead, daily meals, meals in the mystery religions, and sacramental eating.

MARCUS AURELIUS SACRIFICING, relief

In front of the Capitoline temple of Jupiter, Juno, and Minerva are shown
the typical components of a Roman sacrifice — the covered head, burning
incense, a pipe player, and an ox. (© Nimatallah/Art Resource, NY)

ALTAR
The altar was the essential
item for sacrifice. Many
were decorated with
bull's head and garland
(cf. Acts 14:13).
(© Erich Lessing/Art Resource, NY)

and concludes from Euthyphro's comments that "holiness would be an art of
barter between gods and men."[58] The sacrifice was an exchange. The more
abundant and better the offering, the more acceptable it would be.[59] The philosophers combatted this material view of sacrifice common with the masses
and said it was the quality of the heart that counted.[60]

Votive Offerings[61]

A vow in the formal sense was a conditional promise to make a certain sacrifice
if a request was granted. The procedure was as follows. A person made a vow to
the deity: if he was healed of a disease, or given safety on a journey, or success
in some undertaking, he would perform some service or give some gift to the
deity. The offering in fulfillment of a vow when the blessing was received was in
some sense obligatory.[62] Offerings were also made in thanksgiving without a

58. Plato, *Euthyphro* 14C and E.
59. Cf. Theopompus in Porphyry, *De abstinentia* 2.16; see p. 215.
60. So Theophrastus in ibid., 2.15.
61. W. H. D. Rouse, *Greek Votive Offerings* (Cambridge, 1902; repr. New York, 1976).
62. See p. 172 for the strong attitude taken in Roman religion.

formal vow having been expressed and on certain occasions were viewed as required. One of the principal occasions of sacrifice was to fulfill a vow, but votive offerings were not limited to sacrifices. The votive offering showed a constant sense of dependence on the gods.

The women in Herondas, *Mime* 4, offered a cock and set up a commemo-
rative tablet in thanksgiving for a healing. The sanctuaries of the healing gods
— such as Cos and Epidaurus dedicated to Asclepius (on whom see pp. 221ff.)
— have left to archaeologists a rich harvest of objects offered to the deity in fulfillment of a vow.[63] Such an object is called an *ex-voto*. Votive offerings were
not limited to the cult of the savior gods; all the major temples had storerooms
to receive the offerings of the worshipers, and the religious centers (such as
Delphi and Olympia) had many treasure houses built by various cities to receive and advertise the generosity of their contributions to the particular deity.

To make a gift to the divinity was as old as religion itself. Our oldest inscriptions (seventh century) are written on some offerings. The votive offering
remained the "touchstone of piety" throughout the ancient world. The usual
designation for gifts to the deity was *anathema* ("set up" — i.e., in the temple,
and so dedicated to the god), but sometimes *dōron* (gift). Often the offering
was made in virtue of an order of the divinity (expressed in a dream or through
an oracle). The firstfruits were called *aparchē* or *dekatē* (a tithe). The local god
had certain rights; thus, regardless of one's occupation, it was good to treat him
right and give a product of one's labor or art. When certain places of worship
became pan-Hellenic (e.g., Delphi, Delos), the firstfruits (official or private)
flowed in from all parts of the world. A tenth of the booty won from an enemy
in war was given to the deity, for victory would not be won without the help of
the national god. Victors in the games left offerings in appreciation for their
success. To become a civil magistrate or a priest was a manifestation of the divine choice and called for an offering. Quite interesting for the religious psychology of the ancient world are the presents offered on the occasion of an
event in private life — birth, puberty, and marriage. A charming practice was
the consecration of the hair from a first haircut.[64]

Prayers and Hymns

Mime 4 of Herondas begins with the prayer of the offerer addressed to
Asclepius, which includes the petition, "Come, receive graciously this cock, this
herald on the walls about our house, which I am sacrificing." Prayer regularly
preceded and followed a sacrifice.

All of the fragments of Greek prayers that survive are organized on the

63. See pp. 224-26 for the variety of objects offered.
64. Charles Michel, *Recueil d'inscriptions grecques* (Brussels, 1900), no. 1170.

same plan as the prayer in Herondas. They open with an invocation to the god of the sanctuary. Then follows (under the form of a direct address or a brief recital) the parentage and family of the deity or identifying epithets and attributes. Finally, the deity is invited to come to the sacrifice or festival, to receive it, and to be gracious (as in the sentence quoted above). As usually summarized, these three parts were invocation, praise, and petition; sometimes a reminder of the piety of the worshiper preceded the requests. Roman prayers were similar, always including a narrative statement establishing the right of the person praying to make the requests (e.g., recalling earlier sacrifices, etc.). When the sacrifice or festival was ended, the god was asked to return his favors to those who honored him. Sometimes the requests were quite specific. The attitude was that of self-interest. Only the prayers of the philosophers were more disinterested.[65]

On the occasion of the great public festivals a chorus, often made up of children, chanted the prayers. This was properly called the hymn or paean. A hymn was any metrical address to a god; although originally sung, it came to be applied to prose compositions as well. The word *paean* occurs especially in the cult of Apollo and his son Asclepius as a praise for healing, but it too had a wider use. The *carmen saeculare* of Horace was a paean or hymn to Apollo and Diana composed for the celebration of the Secular Games in 17 B.C. ordered by Augustus to commemorate the end of one age and the beginning of another.[66] Hymns were sung in all periods and in all cults, but the choirs appear more organized in the imperial period. For example, an inscription from Stratonikeia in Caria treating the cult of Zeus Panamaros and Hecate, the gods of the city, provides that thirty young men of good birth be chosen, clothed in white, crowned with twigs in hand, accompanied by a *kithara* player and a herald, in order to sing a hymn daily at the morning rites.[67] Hellenistic hymns generally have four parts: (1) invocation identifying the deity by names, nature, cult sites, genealogy, and relation to other gods; (2) general powers and accomplishments of the deity; (3) specific works, miracles, and inventions of the deity; (4) personal requests.

Musical instruments were frequently played at the sacrifices.[68] Sculptured scenes depicting Roman and Greek sacrifices normally show a musician

---

65. See Socrates' prayer to Pan, quoted on p. 179, and Cleanthes' *Hymn to Zeus,* referred to on p. 355.

66. Translated in F. C. Grant, *Ancient Roman Religion* (New York, 1957), 182-84; see Michael C. J. Putnam, *Horace's "Carmen Saeculare": Ritual Magic and the Poet's Art* (New Haven, 2001).

67. *Corpus Inscriptionum Graecarum,* vol. 2 (Berlin, 1843), no. 2715a. Cf. Lucian, *Alexander the False Prophet* 41.

68. J. Quasten, *Music and Worship in Pagan and Christian Antiquity* (Washington, 1983), 3ff.; G. Wille, *Musica Romana: Die Bedeutung der Musik im Leben der Römer* (Amsterdam, 1967), 26-74.

playing the *aulos*. The loud wailing of the pipe may have served the practical function of drowning out the squeals of the dying animal, as the incense did of sweetening the odor at the sacrifice. In origin, however, the practice is usually understood as apotropaic magic, to frighten evil spirits away. Another suggestion is that the music soothed the gods and made them more favorably disposed toward the worshiper.[69] Regardless of its purpose, instrumental music normally accompanied animal sacrifice in the ancient world.

Prose hymns may be called sermons. Speeches in honor of the deities became a feature of pagan worship in late antiquity.[70] Originally, the *theologos* ("theologian") was the composer of praises or narrations about a deity. The prose hymns of the rhetorician Aelius Aristides in the second century A.D. are examples of this form.[71] Some aretalogies (see pp. 275-76) may be included in this category.

BIBLIOGRAPHY

Fairbanks, A. *A Study of the Greek Paean*. Cornell Studies in Classical Philology, vol. 12. Ithaca, N.Y., 1900.

Fritz, Kurt Von. "Greek Prayers." *Review of Religion* 10 (1945):5-39.

Bakker, W. F. *The Greek Imperative*. Amsterdam, 1966.

Wille, G. *Musica Romana*. Amsterdam, 1967. Chap. II.

Quasten, J. *Music and Worship in Pagan and Christian Antiquity*. Washington, 1983.

Pulleyn, S. *Prayer in Greek Religion*. Oxford, 1997.

Chapot, F., and B. Laurot, eds. *Corpus de prières grecques et romaines*. Turnhout, 2001.

Furley, William D. and Jan Maarten Bremer. *Greek Hymns I/II: Selected Cult Songs from the Archaic to the Hellenistic Period*. Tübingen, 2001.

Festivals

The stated occasions of sacrifice were normally annual and geared to the natural cycle of the seasons. These public or official occasions of worship were accompanied by public banquets, entertainment, and processions.

Especially important were the great festivals of the major deities at sanctuaries that attained a greater than local significance. These meetings, which the Greeks called *panegyreis* ("gatherings of all"), were a combination of religion, art, trade, athletics, and amusement, and normally occurred at intervals of two, three, or four years. The Panathenaic festival in Athens was annual, but every

---

69. J. A. Haldane, "Musical Instruments in Greek Worship," *Greece and Rome* 13 (1966):98-107.

70. M. P. Nilsson, "Pagan Divine Service in Late Antiquity," *HTR* 98 (1945):67.

71. Text and translation in C. A. Behr, *P. Aelius Aristides: The Complete Works*, 2 vols. (Leiden, 1981, 1986).

fourth year was the great Panathenaia, to which special importance was attached. Colonies sent embassies and offerings to their founding city at its major cult celebration. Other cities even from great distances often did the same.

Each of the *panegyreis* had its own meaning and character, but some elements were common to all: sacrifice, contests (athletic and artistic), and a procession. There was a secular side to the *panegyreis,* and they might not even seem to us to have been religious at all. The market that went along with the gathering (cf. the medieval "fairs") was a major attraction. So was the athletic competition, so much so that some *panegyreis* are chiefly remembered for their games (as at Olympia). Yet the competition was a religious celebration and had the element of the worship of beauty and strength. Originally there must have been a religious motive behind the athletic contests, even as the dramatic productions may have had a ritual character in the Dionysiac festivals. Yet even the more obviously religious acts of sacrifice and procession had other appeals. The major sacrifices provided the opportunity for a banquet at public expense and was accompanied by instrumental and choral music. Nevertheless, the *panegyreis* were religious in foundation, dedicated to a deity, and centered in a sacred precinct. They often had the performance of some mystery rite as part of the proceedings. The festivals are dramatic testimony of the mutual interpenetration of religion and all phases of life in pagan antiquity.

The procession *(pompē)* was a central feature of religious festivals. Although the baptismal ceremony of the ancient church included a renunciation of Satan and all his pomp and all his works,[72] processions continued in a Christianized version in the commemorations of the saints. The sculptures of the Parthenon give an impressive testimony to the grandeur of the procession in the great Panathenaic festival in Athens.[73] The chief element of this procession was the bearing of a new robe, woven by the maidens of Athens during the preceding year, to clothe the wooden statue of Athena on the Acropolis. The order of the procession was as follows: maidens carrying baskets, cups, jars, and incense burners; the victims — oxen, rams, and heifers — accompanied by the marshals; the tray bearers with offerings of sweets and honey; the water carriers; the musicians; the robe for Athena, hung on the mast of a cart made to look like a ship; the priests and magistrates; and finally the citizens escorted by the ephebes on horseback. Such pageantry in the carrying of sacred images or sacred emblems of the various cults offered considerable eye-appeal and was a part of the ritual in most Hellenistic-Roman cults.[74]

72. Hippolytus, *Apostolic Tradition* 21.9; Tertullian, *On the Shows* 4; *On the Crown* 3; Cyril, *Catechetical Lectures* 19.2-8.

73. H. W. Parke, *Festivals of the Athenians* (Ithaca, N.Y., 1977); Jenifer Neils et al., *Goddess and Polis: The Panathenaic Festival in Ancient Athens* (Princeton, 1992).

74. See A. D. Nock, "Diatribe Form in the Hermetica," *Journal of Egyptian Archaeology* 11 (1925):130 (*Essays,* 1:28-29), for a footnote with a long list of cults where sacred processions are attested.

ATHENA
This Roman copy
shows the appearance
of the cult statue of
Athena for the
Parthenon made
by Phidias of gold
and ivory.
*(© Alinari/
Art Resource, NY)*

Other Features

The civic cults often had mysteries, oracles, healing, etc., attached to them, but
we will treat these elements separately below. The reader should remember that
the classification followed here is arbitrary and exists only as an aid to study;
the components of ancient religious life and practices were not neatly com-
partmentalized in the minds of the participants.

A Sample of a Civic Cult: Ephesus and Artemis

Although other deities are attested at Ephesus, the religious, economic, and social aspects of life were dominated by the cult of Artemis of the Ephesians.[75] She was a pre-Hellenic divinity, who was presumably a symbol of the fecundity of nature — sea and land — but during imperial times there is no evidence of her connection with fertility. According to the common practice of identifying native deities with Greek deities, the Ephesian goddess was identified by the Greeks and the native population with the Greek goddess Artemis (pp. 154, 174-75). The abundant statuary that has been found sometimes emphasizes her role as tutelary deity of the city (by the mural — city wall — crown), sometimes claims for her power over astrology and fate (by the necklace with the signs of the zodiac). No explanation of the multiple oval protuberances on the upper body of her statues has won general consent — eggs, breasts, imitations of the shape of a meteor that had fallen in the vicinity (see p. 175)? In the first century A.D. Artemis of the Ephesians was "The Ephesian," the sovereign and protectress of the city. Her cult spread to other cities; a variety of evidence — sculpture, coins, and inscriptions — supports the claim that "all Asia and the world worships" the Ephesian Artemis (Acts 19:27).

The temple of Artemis (the Artemisium) at Ephesus was one of the seven wonders of the ancient world for its size and beauty. The right of asylum for the temple was recognized by Augustus in 6 B.C. A temple of Rome and Julius Caesar, founded in 29, was united to the Artemisium in 5 B.C. Other cults were attached to the worship of Artemis, and in the second century A.D. a small sanctuary of Isis appeared in the Artemisium. Moreover, the temple was the banking and financial center for the province of Asia.

Prior to the empire, the supreme priest of the Ephesian Artemis appears to have been a eunuch, who adopted his successor. The Romans were little disposed to ritual castration and transferred the lead function to a grand priestess, a virgin assisted by a college of virgins, chosen from the noble families. Her charge lasted for one year, after which she could marry. Other functionaries included the "dressers of Artemis," who adorned the cult statue for processions.

---

75. A. J. Festugière, *Le Monde Gréco-Roman au temps de notre-Seigneur,* Vol. 2, *Le Milieu Spirituel* (Paris, 1935), II.B.2.a; Robert Fleischer, *Artemis von Ephesos und verwandte Kultstatuen aus Anatolien und Syrien* (Leiden, 1973); R. E. Oster, "The Ephesian Artemis as an Opponent of Early Cchristianity," *Jahrbuch für Antike und Christentum* 19 (1976): 27-44; R. E. Oster, "Ephesus as a Religious Center under the Principate, I. Paganism before Constantine," *ANRW* II, *Principat* 18.3 (Berlin and New York, 1990), 1661-1726; Guy M. Rogers, *The Sacred Identity of Ephesos: Foundation Myths of a Roman City* (London, 1991) (studies an inscription of A.D. 104 setting up an endowment to commemorate the founding of Ephesus); Lynn R. LiDonnici, "The Images of Artemis Ephesia and Greco-Roman Worship: A Reconsideration," *HTR* 85 (1992):389-415; Helmut Koester, ed., *Ephesos Metropolis of Asia: An Interdisciplinary Approach to its Archeology, Religion, and Culture* (Valley Forge, Pa., 1995).

Among the male personnel was a confraternity in charge of sacrifice. Known as Essenes, during their one-year of service they guarded ritual chastity, lived apart from the world, and held their meals in common. A number of acolytes provided chants and music. As these requirements indicate, the worship of the Ephesian Artemis did not involve promiscuity. An army of servants, sacred and public, lived under the patronage of the goddess.

The Ephesian goddess presided over the festivals celebrated in her honor, the principal one of which was Artemisia, the annual procession in the month Artemision (March–April). Few if any cities in the ancient world had a closer identity with their patron deity than Ephesus did with Artemis.

RULER CULT

The climax of the civic religion was reached in the ruler cult of Hellenistic-Roman times. The offering of divine honors to kings is the aspect of Hellenistic-Roman religion that perhaps seems most remote to moderns and therefore requires a somewhat more thorough and careful exposition. The ruler cult started as an expression of gratitude to benefactors and became an expression of homage and loyalty. It was a matter of giving to the ruler, not getting from him (except indirectly); that is, supernatural assistance was not expected from him in the same way it was sought from the gods. The religious meaning of the ruler cult was not as great as its social and political importance wherein it served to testify to loyalty and to satisfy the ambition of leading families. Nevertheless, material and political well-being could arouse genuine religious emotions. Ruler cults were expressions of religious belief, not because the rulers were thought divine, but the Hellenistic monarchs and especially the Roman emperors had a power that could only be compared to that of the gods and the people received from them what only the gods could give. The subject of the ruler cult has special importance for the study of early Christianity because it formed the focal point of the early church's conflict with paganism. Moreover, the phenomenon of Hellenistic-Roman ruler cult had a lasting importance for the political theory that invested even Christian monarchs with a divine aura through medieval to modern times.

BIBLIOGRAPHY

Nock, A. D. "Notes on Ruler Cult, I–IV." *Journal of Hellenic Studies* 48 (1928):21-43. Reprinted in *Essays,* pp. 134-59.

Nock, A. D. "Sunnaos Theos." *Harvard Studies in Classical Philology* 41 (1930):1-62. Reprinted in *Essays,* pp. 202-51.

Taylor, L. R. *The Divinity of the Roman Emperor.* Philological Monographs, vol. 1. Middletown, Conn., 1931. See review by A. D. Nock in *Gnomon* 8 (1932):513-18.

Charlesworth, M. P. "Some Observations on Ruler-Cult, Especially in Rome." *HTR* 28 (1935):5-44.

Cerfaux, L., and J. Tondriau. *Le Culte des souverains dans la civilisation greco-romains.* Tournai, 1957.

Den Boer, W., ed. *Le Culte des souverains dans l'Empire romain.* Geneva, 1973.

Cuss, Dominique. *Imperial Cult and Honorary Terms in the New Testament.* Fribourg, 1974.

Fears, J. R. *Princeps a Diis Electus: The Divine Election of the Emperor as a Political Concept at Rome.* Rome, 1977.

Herz, Peter. "Bibliographie zum römischen Kaiserkult (1955–1975)." In *ANRW* II, *Principat,* 16.2. Berlin, 1978. Pp. 833-910.

Hesberg, Henner von. "Archäologische Denkmäler zum römischen Kaiserkult." In *ANRW* II, *Principat,* 16.2. Berlin, 1978. Pp. 911-95.

Price, S. R. F. *Rituals and Power: The Roman Imperial Cult in Asia Minor.* Cambridge, 1984.

Fishwick, Duncan. *The Imperial Cult in the Latin West.* 2 vols., 4 parts. Leiden, 1987–1993.

Schowalter, D. N. *The Emperor and the Gods: Images from the Time of Trajan.* Minneapolis, 1993.

Friesen, Steven J. *Twice Neokoros: Ephesus, Asia and the Cult of the Flavian Emperors.* Leiden, 1993.

Small, A., ed. *Subject and Ruler: The Cult of the Ruling Power in Classical Antiquity.* Journal of Roman Archaeology, Supplementary Series 17. Ann Arbor, Mich., 1996.

Antecedents and Presuppositions

The cult of the Roman emperors had its proximate cause in the peace, prosperity, and flourishing of the eastern provinces during the first two centuries of the Christian era — but its background was much older. The Greek east had had a long preparation. Although the Latins had honored the *manes* of ancestors and the *genii* of great men, they kept the distinction between divine and human. The Greeks blurred this distinction, however, and the expressions of the ruler cult under the empire show the influence of Greek ideas. The ruler cult found its climax and strength in the cult of the Roman emperors. The origins of the phenomenon are diverse, but three main ones have been noted.[76]

Eastern Influences.[77] The pharaoh in Egypt was king because he was divine, the son of a god — the god incarnate as it were. His coronation was the transfer of power from certain sacred objects to the king. This divine character

---

76. A. J. Festugière, *Le monde gréco-romain au temps de notre-Seigneur* (Paris, 1935), 2:7-23.

77. See Henri Frankfort, *Kingship and the Gods* (Chicago, 1948), esp. pp. 337-43 for the distinction between Israel's ideas of kingship and those of her neighbors.

DEA ROMA
Minerva provided the
pattern for depicting
the personification
of Rome as a deity,
Dea Roma.
(© Timothy McCarthy/
Art Resource, NY)

of the Egyptian pharaoh passed to the Ptolemies and certainly accounts for their position in relation to their Egyptian subjects. Egypt provided the most important single eastern source to the development of the ruler cult in the Greek world (see further pp. 206-7).

The divinity of the Assyro-Babylonian monarchs and of their Persian successors is no less certain. Here, however, the king was more an official deity, a divinity by reason of office. He was the chosen servant of the gods for the exercise of certain divine functions. The political order was divinely ordained, and the king was a necessary bond between the people and the divine powers. The insignia of office were charged with the powers of kingship and made the recipient fit to rule. The king held the place of deity in relation to the people. Various features of Persian ceremonial passed to the Hellenistic and then to the Byzantine royal courts. The Seleucids followed the usages of the countries over which they ruled; they were the "sons of Apollo." The Attalids in Asia Minor traced their descent from Dionysus.

Notably, the first testimonies of the imperial religion come from the Greek cities of Asia Minor. Thus, the concept of royal divinity was derived from the countries of the ancient Near East combined with Greek ideas.

Greek Influences. The honors paid by Greeks to their Hellenistic rulers had Greek antecedents. A current of Greek thought divinized certain outstanding men. The earlier discussion of heroes (p. 158) shows that the line between human beings and the gods (conceived anthropomorphically) was not sharply drawn. Greek heroes were men who had become gods because of benefits conferred on others or because of significant achievements. Benefits given to human beings were the surest proof of divinity, and cults of rulers and other mortals were acts of homage for benefits received. This attitude introduced the possibility of treating outstanding people *in this life* as already worthy of receiving divine honors (although it was the first century b.c. before a living man was designated a "hero"). The gods were regarded by the Greeks as the supreme type of human excellence, as a higher aristocracy rather than another order of beings; and they could beget human children. Moreover, there was no clear distinction between honor and homage on one hand and worship on the other. Aeschylus suggested that sacrifices might be given to men for acts of deliverance.[78] Giving divine honors was not too much for great benefactors; they should be treated like gods. Isocrates told Philip of Macedon that if he defeated Persia, there was nothing left but to become a god (a matter of status or rank).[79] When his son Alexander accomplished this, deification seemed the only appropriate honor. Aristotle noted the common opinion that by an excess

---

78. "We should pray and offer sacrifice and libations to the Argives, just as to the Olympians, for they are undoubtedly our deliverers." *Supp.* 980. Later Pliny the Elder would say, "To enroll such men among the deities is the most ancient method of paying them gratitude for their benefactions" (*Natural History* 2.5.19).

79. *Ep. ad Phil.* 5.

of *aretē* (excellence, virtue, glorious deeds) men could become gods.[80] Related to this was Euhemerus's theory that all the gods had once been men who received divine honors for their deeds (see p. 327). Statements like "seek not to be a god" were not in point unless there was some desire to become like a demigod. From another direction was the thought that there was something divine in humans (cf. the "soul" according to Plato; pp. 334-35) or at least in outstanding persons.

The first case in which a man was offered honors "as to a god" was Lysander, a Spartan general, by Samos in 404 B.C. Philip of Macedon was not divinized but received honors that brought him near the gods. The above considerations made it easy for Alexander and his successors to accept divine honors, especially in conjunction with eastern ideas of divine kingship. Roman rulers in the east and then the emperors stepped into this same position. Thus, deification in Rome came from Greek antecedents.

Traditional Civic Basis of Religion.[81] The most deeply ingrained religious beliefs and practices in both Greece and Rome, as seen above, were associated with the traditional civic cult. In each case the symbol of the city was its patron deity. In Hellenistic times the cities came to be personified, and cult was offered to the personified people of the state. In combination with the above influences it was easy to identify the city with its ruler — and under Rome the city *(urbs)* became the world *(orbis)*.

Alexander had perhaps envisioned a world community. A religious idea would have been at its base, for religion and patriotism could not be separated in the ancient world. Augustus, who perceived that a universal monarchy called for a universal religion, was prepared to restore the old faith of Rome. When he accepted divine honors in the east he insisted that his name be associated with Rome *(Roma et Augustus).* Thus the notions of the traditional civic cult and traditional civic patriotism were directed toward Rome, the universal city symbolized by a living ruler instead of an older god; and these notions contributed to the new imperial cult. The imperial religion was almost the inevitable result of the extension of the *polis* to the *oikoumenē* and the extension of the civic divinity to the imperial divinity. The result was a kind of universal civic cult in which one showed loyalty by participation.

The cult of the emperor thus became something more than another phenomenon of idolatry. It was attached to the most solidly established religious traditions of the ancient world. In this context a conflict between Caesar and Christ (both called Lord and Savior), between church and empire, was inevitable.

---

80. *Nicomachean Ethics* 1145A; *Rhetoric* 1.5.9 (1361a28-39) for honors to benefactors. Cf. his *Politics* 3.8.1 (1284a10f) that a true king "seems to be accounted as a god among human beings."

81. R. Mellor, *THEA ROMA. The Worship of the Goddess Roma in the Greek World* (Göttingen, 1975).

Historical Developments

Alexander the Great. The brief sketch in Chapter 1 of Alexander's career noted
that he was himself a religious man, interested in the deities of different peoples, scrupulous in his respect for the religion of conquered peoples, and regular in the performance of sacrifice and divination. It remains now to discuss his
significance in the development of the Hellenistic ruler cult.

When Alexander arrived in Egypt, he was welcomed as a deliverer, for the
Egyptians had turned against Persian rule in a revival of nationalism and had
frequently rebelled against Persia. Thus Alexander was acclaimed as pharaoh,
and he accepted this standing — no doubt gladly, for it meant that he was there
not as a robber baron or temple marauder but as the lawful king. As noted
above, the pharaoh was deemed by Egyptians as having a certain divine character. One of his titles was "son of Ammon" (a deity accepted by the Greeks as
identical with Zeus). A "desire seized" Alexander to go to the oracle of Ammon
at Siwah, deep in the desert of Cyrene. When he arrived, the priest greeted him
as "son of Ammon" and promised him rule over the world. All of this was conventional to the priest as the traditional salutation of a pharaoh. But it was not
a common form to Alexander and the Greeks and appears to have made a profound impression on Alexander.

The statement is ascribed to Alexander that "Zeus is father of all, but he
makes especially his those who are worthy."[82] Alexander thought of himself as
especially adopted by Zeus. Later, Alexander's sonship to Zeus was made more
explicit in a legend that developed concerning his birth: on the night before his
mother Olympias's marriage to Philip II was consummated she received a divine thunderbolt that sent shocks throughout her womb. Other accounts reported that a serpent was seen lying with her.

The people in Persia bowed before Alexander. This act of obeisance was
normal in Persia, but for the Greeks it was shameful for a free man to bow before another although it might be done before something considered holy.
Thus, once more, the reception of Alexander by conquered peoples suggested
that he was something more than an ordinary human being.

Alexander probably did think of himself as something more than a man
and there is evidence that he was recognized as a deity in his lifetime.[83] He requested that the Greek cities send to him *theōroi* (delegates to a god, the name
for ambassadors of a city sent to the sanctuary of a god in another locality for a
festival or to receive an answer from an oracle). This has been interpreted as a
political move. There were a great many exiles at the time whose chief interest
was in getting back home, and Alexander tried to get the cities to take exiles

---

82. Plutarch, *Life of Alexander* 27 (680F); cf. *Moralia* 180D.
83. C. A. Robinson, "Alexander's Deification," *American Journal of Philology* 64 (1943):286-
301; J. P. V. D. Balsdon, "The 'Divinity' of Alexander the Great," *Historia* 1 (1950):383-88.

back. Yet he had no constitutional right to interfere in the internal affairs of Greek cities. In theory he was the general of the armies of an alliance into which the cities had voluntarily entered, but a god was not bound by treaties. This explanation is weak, however, for the Greeks ignored their gods when they wanted to, and if this was the purpose it failed. Rather, it was the drama of the demand that was important, another expression of Alexander's flair for the striking gesture. We should think of this purely as a matter of status — a titular matter. To honor someone as a god was not so unusual in a highly stratified society where the gods held the highest rank but were not essentially different in nature. Notice that he did not request a temple or sacrifice; he did not seek cultus. Even this could be paid; it was proper and was evidently rendered to him at some places. Distinctions should be made between the divine honors Alexander claimed as a matter of status, those he received from Alexandria as its founder (it was traditional in the Greek world for a city to honor its founder as a hero), and those he received voluntarily from the official cult in various cities.

After Alexander's death divine honors came more readily, as shown, for example, in the placing of his portrait on coins by his successors. The cult given after his death was the beginning of divine monarchy in the Western world.

The Hellenistic Kings. What did it mean to be a king *(basileus)*? It was not monarchy in the modern sense of a ruler over a clearly defined territory. A kingdom was rather a sphere of power. Where we say "state," or "Seleucid kingdom," the ancients said "subjects of king (so and so)." The title of king was a claim to be a legitimate ruler. The king was various things to various persons. The situation was such that the Hellenistic monarchs were always in the midst of multiple, complicated relationships. This was especially so in Asia Minor and Syria, where in addition to the cities and temples there were many different racial groups to deal with. In order to enhance a king's claim to legitimacy a little faking of genealogy was in order, especially to provide a divine ancestry, and a miracle accompanying the birth or the founding of a new capital did not hurt any. In all the Hellenistic kingdoms except Macedonia some form of ruler cult evolved to hold together the diverse elements.

A popular thought, as reflected in a child's exercise book, was this: "What is a god? That which is strong. What is a king? He who is equal to the divine."[84] This is very revealing about the Hellenistic conception of deity, kingship, and the presuppositions behind the cult of rulers. The deities provided the only point of comparison for the power wielded by Hellenistic kings, and divine honors the only adequate expression of homage to such power.

After Alexander his titles were attributed to the Ptolemies and Seleucids. They were treated like gods, but there was not the least illusion that they could act supernaturally. Miracle stories did not circulate about kings as they did

84. A. D. Nock, *Conversion* (Oxford, 1933), 91.

about philosophers. It was important to have the right ancestors — heroic or divine. Miracle stories, therefore, were manufactured to authenticate a king's rule, but there was no tendency to ascribe miraculous works to the king himself.

The granting of "honors equal to the gods" was largely an expression of gratitude — the language of Aeschylus translated into action — and acknowledgment of power. Some of the seemingly extravagant terminology was the courtly language of compliment (cf. Acts 12:22 for flattery of a king). The kings were the principal patrons of writers, who found a little metaphor all right in comparing the ruler to the gods. Some of the language in those cases should not be taken too seriously. It is not easy to draw the line between comparison and identification, especially when the god was thought to be an ancestor. The principal epithets applied to rulers were "benefactor" (*euergetēs;* Luke 22:25, where the point is not benefactions as such, but the title given to rulers because of their likeness to the gods), "manifest" (*epiphanēs,* a religious term for divine revelation that also means simply "distinguished" or "brilliant"), and "savior" (*sōtēr,* a term that had been of old applied to the gods, but in *koinē* Greek referred to deliverances in the secular realm of everyday life).[85] The Athenians greeted Demetrius Poliorcetes, son of Antigonus, in 307 B.C. with particularly extravagant language, declaring him a "savior god" for "liberating" the city. A hymn to him declared, "The other gods are either far away or have no ears, or are not, or pay no slightest heed to us; but thee we see face to face."[86] Manifest power and benefaction were the starting points for such honors.

Sacrifices offered for or in honor of a person could easily become sacrifices to him. The inscription of King Antiochus I of Commagene set up in the first century B.C. gives him the titles "The Great King Antiochus, the God, the Righteous One, the Manifest Deity," provides for the setting up of his image alongside that of "the great gods," and establishes sacrifices "in honor of the gods and in my honor."[87]

Quite decisive for showing that the line between the kings and the gods was observed is that votive offerings were not made to the kings. Ruler cult remained a matter of homage and not worship in the full sense. It was a matter of status, loyalty, and unity.

The worship of the Ptolemies by the native Egyptians was entirely different from anything known by the Greek-speaking world before. This is the most

85. A. D. Nock, "*Soter* and *Euergetes,*" in *The Joy of Study,* ed. S. E. Johnson (New York, 1951), 127-48 (*Essays,* 2:720-35).

86. Quoted in Athenaeus, *Deipnosophists* 6.63.253. See K. Scott, "The Deification of Demetrius Poliorcetes," *American Journal of Philology* 49 (1928):137-66, 217-39.

87. Dittenberger, *OGIS* 383; Grant, *Hellenistic Religions* (New York, 1953), 20-25. H. Dörrie, "Die Königskult des Antiochos von Kommagene in Lichte neuer Inschriften-Funde," *Abhandlungen der Akademie der Wissenschaften in Göttingen,* Philol.-Hist. Kl., III Folge, Nr. 60 (Göttingen, 1964).

likely eastern origin of the Hellenistic ruler cult. The four phases of the development of the ruler cult in Hellenistic Egypt offer a good demonstration of four types of homage. The first phase was the giving of divine honors out of gratitude. This was a matter of homage and loyalty, and the initiative came from the beneficiaries. It was simply the highest form of compliment and a recognition of a superior status. The next phase was the deification of the first generation by their successors.[88] This was an official deification inaugurated by the ruler (by the Ptolemies and Seleucids alike). Its precedent was in the treatment of Alexander. The cult of the founder of the dynasty became a composite thing by which succeeding rulers and members of the royal family were included. New priesthoods were established, which were largely decorative. The kings began to put their own face on coins — previously only deities and objects of reverence had been so shown in the Greek world. The cult provided a cement of loyalty. The third phase was peculiar to Egypt, where the worship of the ruler was offered in established temples devoted to the native gods. Concomitantly, Ptolemy II Philadelphus and his consort Arsinoe were deified in Alexandria during their lifetime (272/271). The language of compliment and the divine honors (temples, priesthoods) to the living ruler became routine. All of this was still quite official, however. Finally, there are a few isolated instances of individuals putting up shrines to the ruler as a deity, often in what seems to be an attempt to gain favors.

Roman Emperors.[89] After an age of wars and catastrophes Augustus brought peace. He was a "savior." There was no way to explain a power so prodigious without appeal to a divine ("demonic" in the Greek sense; pp. 336-37) nature residing in the soul of Augustus.[90] According to the customs of the time the feelings of his subjects had to find expression in divine honors. Thus the same reasoning that inclined to divinize Alexander and the Hellenistic kings worked to deify Augustus. The emperor did not step into a vacuum in these matters. Already the Roman proconsuls and triumvirs had been honored spontaneously by the Greek and Asiatic cities as the Hellenistic monarchs before them had been.

The situation in Rome, however, was different from the Greek east. Roman society in the last two centuries of the Republic accepted the ideas on which deification rested in Greece. The theory of the superman, whose soul's destiny is different from that of ordinary people, was attractive; but at the same time the practices of Hellenistic monarchy were distasteful to the nobles. The ruler cult in Hellenistic cities was wholly personal; in contrast, the imperial cult had an independent worth as an expression of belief in the unity of the

88. See P. M. Fraser, "The Foundation Date of the Alexandrian Ptolemaieo," *HTR* 54 (1961):141-45 for 280/279 as the date when Ptolemy Soter was honored as a god and Philadelphus still as a king.

89. In this section I follow Festugière, *Le monde gréco-romain au temps de notre-Seigneur* (Paris, 1935), 2:23-34.

90. Horace, *Carm.* 4.5. Cf. inscription quoted on p. 46.

empire, due to the fact that there was a Roman state as such and that the Greeks had worshiped the personified Roman state under the Republic before there was an emperor (p. 23). Thus Rome followed Greek precedents in this as in so much else, but with reservations and with distinctions of its own.

Julius Caesar provided the model for the official cult of Augustus.[91] The people in the east called Caesar "god" and honored him as such in his lifetime. A statue was dedicated to him in the temple of Quirinius in 45 B.C. with the words "To the invincible god." Before his death he had his own temple under the name "Jupiter Julius"; this was the first step in establishing the cult, by honoring a living hero according to the Greek idea as it had developed in the honors by Greek cities to Hellenistic rulers. The second step in the cult of Caesar was taken with his official apotheosis after his death. As a dead hero he was transferred to the number of the gods. The senate and people declared him a god and during the celebration in honor of the *divus Julius*[92] the appearance of a comet was taken as proof that his soul had been received into the number of the immortals.[93] Some Romans protested against the apotheosis of Caesar, and we should note that he was not officially recognized as a god in Rome until it was decreed by the senate: that was all according to proper Roman legal form.

These two stages are also found in the cult of Augustus. His own attitude and policy differed according to whether he was dealing with the provinces or with Rome itself. In his decrees to the provinces he called himself "son of god" (*divus filius*, i.e., the adopted son of Caesar who had been recognized as a god). Temples, altars, priests, and games in his honor were found in the provinces. He did insist that Rome be joined with him in the expressions of cult. Thus he allowed the Greeks in Asia to build temples to *dea Roma et Augustus*, but at Rome he refused a temple and allowed the Romans only to build a temple to *dea Roma et divus Julius*. Augustus did not want to antagonize further the conservative elements, and he made a show of restoring the old republican religion. There were three significant testimonies, nevertheless, to Rome's devotion: (1) The very name Augustus, conferred in 27 B.C., recognized a numinous quality in the young ruler. Without making specific claims it declared him to be something more than an ordinary man and as possessing a special sanctity. It represented the compromise between divine and human that *princeps* did between king and citizen. (2) Rome instituted a festival in honor of his fortune to which were added games (the *Augustalia*). (3) A month was dedicated to him in 8 B.C. as had earlier been done to Caesar when he reorganized the calendar; hence we have the months of July and August added to those which bear the names of Roman deities and numbers.

---

91. S. Weinstock, *Divus Iulius* (Oxford, 1971), goes too far in making Caesar the true founder of the imperial cult.

92. *Divus* in Latin meant *theios*, but was taken as *theos* in the east.

93. Pliny, *Natural History* 2.24.

From about 12 B.C. Augustus showed signs of less fear of the appearances of worship and took steps to initiate the cult of the ruler and Rome in the western provinces. The *genius* of the *princeps* was included with the gods in oaths. He instituted the offices of *Seviri* and *Augustales*. The former were quasi-magistrates and the latter were strictly religious, but both alike were associated with games in honor of the *princeps* and with municipal benefactions but not specially with temples. These offices were not primarily concerned initially with the worship of the *princeps* but were one of the ways Augustus's system sought to find a special function within the state for all classes. There were careers already for senators, knights, and wealthy provincials; these new offices were for freedmen. For provincials and freedmen the cult chosen as the focus of loyalty was that of the ruler. In the west the emotion was political — devotion to the Roman commonwealth and to the man who was the personal expression of its solidarity; it was not an outburst of gratitude for a heaven-sent savior as it was in the eastern cities.[94]

Augustus himself took steps even in Rome to include the element of religious devotion within loyalty to his rule. The populace had little active participation in the traditional Roman state cults. Hence, part of Augustus's program to revitalize religious life included the involvement of knights, freedmen, and slaves in religious exercises, and these new cultic expressions were connected with the emperor. For instance, when he reorganized the urban districts and the cult of the *lares compitales* (p. 180), he enjoined a sacrifice to the *genius* of the emperor as part of the ceremonies. This associated him with the domestic divinities and solidified his position with those classes not bound to the past, yet it was not deification, for the *genius* of a private person (as the life spirit of the family) commonly received sacrifice on his birthday.

What Augustus accepted in his lifetime in Rome involved a more than human status but not divinity. It was still necessary to grant to him divine honors. *Caelestes honores* was the official phrase, and from the constitutional point of view these could be given only by the vote of the senate. On Augustus's death in A.D. 14 this occurred. He was transferred among the celestial gods by apotheosis. Deification at Rome as in Greece was a conferring of status; cult was a supreme form of honor. By official act the senate included the new god in the list of Roman divinities and decreed that he receive in Rome (as he had elsewhere) a temple and priests.

All of the first-century emperors equally favored the cult of the dead emperor. Tiberius and Claudius did not encourage the marks of adoration; Vespasian, although skeptical about divine honors, introduced the imperial cult into the west; but Caligula, Nero, and Domitian permitted or even provoked them. The Antonines generally admitted the cult of the living divine em-

---

94. A. D. Nock, "Seviri and Augustales," in *L'Annuaire de l'Institut de Philologie et d'Histoire Orientales* (Brussels, 1934), 627-38 (*Essays*, 348-56).

CLAUDIUS AS ZEUS, from Lanuvium
One aspect of giving divine honors to emperors was portraying them as deities.
Here Claudius has the attributes of Zeus: a staff and an eagle.
(© Scala/Art Resource, NY)

peror but primarily as a manifestation of loyalty. The consecrations of their deceased wives Faustina the elder and Faustina the younger by Antoninus Pius and Marcus Aurelius respectively were prompted by genuine feeling and were efforts to breathe a more personal spirit of devotion into the cult but went no further.[95]

"Rome" was an abstraction, but the *divus Augustus* was visible, and he received the gratitude of the provinces, "free and peaceful." It is important to note that until the third century the imperial religion was not imposed by the Roman government. The provincial ruler cult showed some diversity from province to province, but was particularly promoted by Vespasian. The vitality of the imperial cult in the province of Asia during the reign of Domitian provides the setting for the Book of Revelation (pp. 602-3).

Forms of the Imperial Cult

The modes of the imperial cult varied according to the nature of the organizations that practiced it — provinces, a group of individual cities, professional corporations, military corps, colleges of freedmen. Although direct worship of the living emperor with temples, altars, priests, and sacrifices was contrary to official policy in Rome and the western provinces, the imperial cult was advanced in various ways: offering cult to the emperor's accompanying *genius* or the divine *numen* within him, elevating the imperial family to a divine status, making dedications to a deity and to the emperor, relating various divinities to the emperor as his protectors and helpers, and personifying the qualities and benefactions of the emperor.

At Rome both Caesar and Augustus had temples dedicated to them as gods of Rome. The temple to Caesar was dedicated under Augustus in 29 B.C., and the temple to Augustus was dedicated under Caligula. Under Hadrian a sanctuary to Rome and Venus (the mother of the race of Aeneas) was erected near the arch of Titus. It was only then that the civic cult, which previously in the capital was addressed to the Capitoline triad of Jupiter, Juno, and Minerva, was referred essentially to the Caesars as descendants of Venus.

Away from Rome honors advanced more rapidly. Even in the west altars at which a *sacerdos* officiated were erected to *Roma et Augustus* and from the time of Tiberius temples were dedicated to the divinized Augustus, presided over by a *flamen*.[96] A temple to Rome and the emperor was ordinarily situated at the center of the province — at the provincial capital where the assembly

95. Harold Mattingly, "The Consecration of Faustina the Elder and her Daughter," *HTR* 41 (1948):147-51.

96. Duncan Fishwick, "The Development of Provincial Ruler Worship in the Western Roman Empire," *ANRW* II, *Principat,* 16.2 (Berlin and New York, 1978), 1201-53.

(*koinon, concilium;* see p. 44) met and in the east often at other cities as well. The imperial cult was an important function of the *koinon.* Divine honors (continuing Hellenistic precedents) included identification with some god, re- naming old festivals, making sacrifices, erecting statues in temples and else- where, erecting temples, instituting games, naming months for the benefactor, etc.

In accordance with the practices of the civic religion, the high priest of the provincial imperial cult was an official who had ordinarily reached the top of the municipal *cursus honorum.* He was always a citizen of one of the cities of the province and usually of Rome. He was called *archiereus* in Asia and *flamen* or *sacerdos* in the west. The position required wealth. The high priest also func- tioned as president of the provincial assembly (p. 44), which had two objects — to discuss the affairs of the province and to manifest its devotion to the em- peror by public honors, embassies, religious ceremonies, feasts, and games. This fusion of material interests and religious sentiment was the strength of the empire. Rome protected the assemblies as the focus of loyalty.

The municipal devotion was manifested especially in wealthy cities that profited from Roman rule. The classes who benefited the most were the landed aristocracy, commercial interests, and military veterans.

The worship of personified powers, or virtues, a vital religious phenome- non under the Republic, became attached to the imperial cult.[97] Virtues such as Victoria, Concordia, Clementia, Pax, etc. were now represented as Victoria Augusti, Virtus Augusti, etc., and the surviving inscriptions attest to a popular devotion at all levels of society. The imperial virtues were viewed concurrently as supernatural beings capable of bestowing benefits on humankind or as pow- ers embodied in the emperor and expressed in his deeds. The first-century Romans worshiped these virtues of the emperor (as they did his *genius*) before they worshiped him personally.

The strength and popularity of the imperial cult is testified to by the large number of private associations that took as their patron the emperor instead of one of the traditional deities. The extent of religious devotion is indicated by the presence in some places of mysteries as part of the imperial cult.[98] The im- perial cult was so strongly bound to the monarchy that the Christian emperors could not abolish its trappings — bowing, extravagant language of compli- ment, homage to the imperial insignia and images.

What was suggested by art, sung by poets, and stated in private dedica- tions went beyond what was declared or done in the official cult.

97. Harold Mattingly, "The Roman 'Virtues,'" *HTR* 30 (1937):103-17.
98. H. W. Pleket, "An Aspect of the Emperor Cult: Imperial Mysteries," *HTR* 58 (1965):331- 47.

PERSONAL RELIGION

This section will bring together a variety of loosely related personal religious beliefs and practices. Many of the items included were features of officially established civic cults (e.g., oracles), but the basis for inclusion here is their place in the religious life of ordinary persons. Separate sections will look at the mystery religions and Gnosticism — those aspects of personal religion (again in the case of the mysteries frequently a part of civic religion) which have drawn most attention in relation to the setting of Christianity.

The increased concern with the individual and with chosen relationships (pp. 14-15, 325) in the period after Alexander may be observed in the greater prominence of personal involvement in religious activities and individual choice about participation.

Certain psychological-religious needs came to prominence in the early centuries of the Christian era: a feeling of helplessness before Fate, uncertainty of the hereafter, and inquisitiveness about the supernatural. These concerns found expression in the popularity of mystery initiations, magic, growth of private cult associations, and interest in revelation literature.

Bibliography

Festugière, A. J. *Personal Religion among the Greeks.* Berkeley, 1954.

Oracles

A popular religious activity was to make a pilgrimage to a famous sanctuary and consult its oracle. This was a common way of determining the will of the gods — by cities as well as individuals. The great oracular sites were part of the civic cult of the community where they were located. Requests from cities were made by official delegations and concerned political, economic, and official religious questions. In Hellenistic times, however, the oracles no longer determined political and religious development but were still consulted on local sacral business. Private individuals continued to seek advice from the oracles in matters of personal life. During the last stages of paganism (third–fourth centuries A.D.) the oracles were appealed to for answers to theological questions.

Delphi. There were many local oracle sites and procedural details would have varied from one to the other, but the oracle of Apollo at Delphi was representative. Its greatest influence was in classical times, but the most important oracle sites of Hellenistic and Roman times were in a sense its daughter sanctuaries. Also, the literary and archaeological evidence permits a fuller picture of Delphi than of any other oracle.

According to legend Zeus wanted to determine the center of the earth, so

TEMPLE OF APOLLO, Delphi
Delphi is a spectacular example of the dramatic setting of Greek sanctuaries.

he released two eagles from opposite ends of the world. They met over Delphi. The omphalos stone at Delphi marked it as the navel of the earth, and Delphi became the spiritual center of the Greek world.

The site of Delphi was a cult center of the earth goddess from very early times. Apollo (with the coming of the Greeks) killed the she-serpent (sacred to the earth goddess in earlier Minoan religion) known as the Python, from which the site got its name. The word continued to be associated with oracular utterances (cf. Acts 16:16 where the deranged girl who was used by her owners as a kind of fortune-teller is described as possessed by a "Pythian spirit"). Apollo became the god of prophecy and spokesman for Zeus. A priestess seems to have been a normal feature of the cult of Apollo, and she was the instrument of the god's revelations at Delphi.[99] Delphi was the center of Apollo's worship. The impressive ruins there include the stadium for the celebration of the Pythian games every four years (eight years at some periods of its history), a gymnasium, a theatre, and the dedications of many cities as an advertisement of their power and of their devotion to Apollo. The main attraction of Delphi was its oracle, located under the temple of Apollo.

99. K. Latte, "The Coming of the Pythia," *HTR* 33 (1940):9-18.

During classical times Delphi was the arbiter of religious matters in the Greek world and wielded a great influence in political affairs. Apollo made known the will of the gods on the whole field of ancient religion. Through the oracle at Delphi he prescribed particular features of cult for all the deities: what sacrifices and purifications were to be performed, under what titles a deity was to be approached, where a new temple was to be erected, whether a new festival was to be instituted or an older worship revived, what foreign deities were to be introduced (Delphi requested admission of Dionysus into Greek cities) and which new heroes honored (Delphi sponsored Asclepius).

The oracle also had a great influence on moral as well as ritual questions. It identified the evil intent with the evil deed, and the good intent with the good deed. The oracle was reported to have said that a tiny drop of water sufficed to purify a good man, but an ocean could not wash a bad man.[100] Responses to several inquiries show an opposition to ostentation: the gods preferred simple offerings, given regularly and piously, to costly gifts (Porphyry, *On Abstinence* 2.16, quoting Theopompus). Two inscriptions at Delphi became famous maxims: "Know Thyself" (as a human and not a god, but given a philosophical meaning by Socrates) and "Nothing Too Much" (a typically Delphic maxim counseling moderation).[101]

Delphi had an "international" information-gathering system through the coming of important persons from all over the Greek world to consult it. This knowledgeableness made it a potent political influence. Its sympathies were usually aristocratic and against the interests of Greek democracy, counseling submission to Persia (but also issuing the oracle that Themistocles turned to advantage in how to resist the invasion), favoring Sparta, and supporting Philip of Macedon. Such decisions did not help the oracle's standing in the Hellenistic age. Nevertheless, Delphi's decline was due not so much to its failures as to the changes in Greek society.

Ordinarily the decisions by the oracle were quite unambiguous, as in making decisions on ritual questions. But there were some famous instances reported in antiquity where ambiguity was of the essence of the response. The oracle told Croesus, king of Lydia, that if he made war on Persia he would "destroy a mighty empire." When he lost the war, it was explained that he did not inquire as to whose empire would be destroyed. In keeping with Delphi's interest in bloodguiltiness and retribution, it was said that Croesus paid for a sin of an ancestor of the fifth generation.[102] The oracle's function was rarely original; rather, it authorized what was already claiming recognition.

Political questions were out of place after Rome came to power, but the

---

100. *Greek Anthology* 14.71; cf. 14.74.

101. Plutarch, *Letter to Apollonius* 28 (*Moralia* 116C-D); cf. also *Moralia* 385D, 511B; Plato, *Protagoras* 343B and *Charmides* 164E-65A; Pausanias 10.24.1.

102. Herodotus 1.91; cf. 1.53.

questions of everyday life, which had been the stock-in-trade of other oracles, continued to be asked at Delphi. Frequent questions concerned whether to get married, to venture on a voyage, to risk a loan, or to buy a slave.[103] Women asked whether they would have a child and of what sex, and men asked whether the child a woman was bearing was his or another's.

The practice of freeing a slave at the temple of Apollo in Delphi existed after 200 B.C., when there begins a long series of inscriptions recording the manumission of slaves at the sanctuary. A typical expression was "The Pythian Apollo purchased so and so for freedom." The deity thus served as a third party, made necessary by the fact that in Greece a slave could not enter into a legal contract with his master. The purchase in the name of the god had the further advantage that the deed was properly registered for all time (see p. 60).

Oracle Procedures. For the procedures in consulting the god at Delphi we have only allusions, and it seems that these varied at different periods of the oracle's existence. The most common method of inquiry and the least expensive was the lot-oracle. There is inscriptional evidence for drawing beans as the normal system of obtaining an answer in the fourth century B.C. (cf. the drawing of lots as a way of obtaining an answer from the Lord in the Old Testament: Num. 33:54; 1 Sam. 28:6; 1 Chron. 24:7; etc.).

Direct prophecies of the prophetess (known as the Pythia) seem to have been uttered only once a month. On the seventh day of each month the Pythia had a ceremonial bath and a fumigation of laurel leaves. The priests presented a goat to Apollo; if it trembled when sprinkled with cold water the day was auspicious and the victim was offered. The prophetess entered the underground chamber of the temple and took her seat upon a tripod. Proper contact with Apollo's tripod was supposed in itself to inspire the Pythia. There is abundant evidence that she was in some kind of trance, but the explanations offered of what induced her ecstasy are unsatisfactory: breathing vapors (apparently not possible at Delphi but perhaps true at some places in Asia Minor), drinking from the sacred fountain (a central feature at Claros), chewing laurel leaves (laurel was sacred to Apollo, but the evidence for eating it is late), or taking some intoxicant (for which evidence is lacking). The inquirers and temple officials purified themselves in water from the springs nearby. The inquirers offered on the main altar before the temple a sacred cake whose cost was fixed at a high price and on the inner hearth sheep or goats. They were then admitted to the inner sanctuary (with the exception of women) with the warning to "think pure thoughts and speak well-omened words." There was some manner of separation between the Pythia and the inquirers, who sat on seats at one end of the room. A temple official asked the inquirer's question. The exact words of the Pythia are not recorded in our sources. At best they give the answer returned by the prophet who interpreted the Pythia's message. This was often in

103. Plutarch, *Moralia* 386C, 407D, 408C.

hexameters, although the composition of verse oracles died out from 100 B.C. to A.D. 100. The preliminary contacts and carefully staged procedure seem to have been designed to give the priests prior notice of the questions, and they controlled the situation. The Pythia was a woman of mature age who after her appointment renounced all sexual relations (the sole motive for which seems to have been ritual purity).

The questions were presented in one of two forms: Is it better that such and such a course be adopted? (and the oracle would approve or disapprove with clear or ambiguous indications of the probable consequences), or What is the best means to attain some end? (the oracle prescribed the appropriate sacrifice or ritual and the deities to be approached). The oracle thus did not properly foretell the future but indicated what was the will of the gods or gave advice as to the best course of action. Very often the question would be phrased in such a way as to indicate the desired answer. The oracle was sometimes in a position to know or to influence the outcome. On some questions there was no "wrong" answer. Probably in only a few cases was it necessary for the oracle to rely on ambiguity or to say that the inquirer had misinterpreted the answer. The Pythia herself need not have been either a charlatan or self-deceived; the "ecstasy" may have been real, whether induced by an outside influence or the product of a psychological state or mental condition. The priestly interpreters may be more culpable.

An inscription records the procedure for consulting the oracle of Apollo Koropaios at Demetrias in 100 B.C.[104] A sacrifice was offered, and if the omens were favorable, the consultation proceeded. The names of those making inquiry were written on a white tablet that was set up before the temple. The persons' names were called in order and they entered the sanctuary and took a seat. The inquirers had to be ceremonially clean and clad in festival garments and crowned with laurel crowns. Each submitted his question in writing on a sealed tablet. At dawn their names were called in order again, and their sealed tablets were returned with the reply of the oracle (cf. p. 219).

Other Oracles. The oracle at Delphi was in decline in late Hellenistic and early Roman times, but there are signs of a revival in the second century before the oracle fell silent in the third century. Plutarch discussed various explanations for the decline of the oracle.[105] Delphi's influence was picked up by other sanctuaries of Apollo: Didyma (favored by the Seleucid kings); Claros (interested in questions of theology and flourishing in the second century A.D.); Daphne near Antioch (which imitated Delphi).

Collections of oracles were made, the most important of which was the

---

104. Dittenberger, *Sylloge*³ 1157, trans. in Grant, *Hellenistic Religions* (New York, 1953), 34-37.

105. *On the Obsolescence of Oracles* (*Moralia* 409E-438E). S. Levin, "The Old Greek Oracles in Decline," *ANRW* II, *Principat*, 18.2 (Berlin, 1989), 1599-1649.

famous *Sibylline Books* in Rome; we will discuss them in Chapter 5 (pp. 461-62). The *Chaldean Oracles,* which have been called a pagan gnosis, are discussed under Gnosticism (pp. 315-16).

Many of the healing shrines (see further below) were properly oracles, because it was the response of the god that gave the prescription for healing: for example, the oracles of Amphiaraus at Oropus and of Trophonius at Lebadeia, and the sanctuary of Asclepius at Pergamum.

Oenomaus, a contemporary of Plutarch, was a Cynic who launched a vicious attack on the deception practiced by oracles.[106] For example, several sites give indications of architectural contrivances to permit a priest to give awesome responses from subterranean recesses — for example, at Didyma. Most of the oracles had honest origins, but the practice of consulting oracles provided opportunities for charlatans.

Alexander the False Prophet.[107] Lucian's treatise by this name shows the popular enthusiasm for oracles in the second century and his own rationalistic mood. It is notable for its account of the founding and functioning of an oracle and for an illustration of certain religious characteristics of the age, not to mention its testimony to how a clever charlatan could play on the hopes and fears of simple people.

Alexander and a colleague laid their plans well. They deposited in the temple of Apollo in Chalcedon bronze tablets foretelling that Apollo and his son, the healing god Asclepius, would take up residence in Abonuteichos (Alexander's hometown in Paphlagonia). After news of this reached the town, the citizens began to build a temple. Alexander appeared feigning fits of madness and uttering strange sounds. In a pool of water in the excavations for the temple he secretly hid a hollowed-out goose egg into which he had inserted a newborn snake. He then presented himself as the prophet of Asclepius and in a dramatic scene recovered the egg from the water and produced the small snake as the manifestation of the god Asclepius. He had earlier purchased a large, beautiful, harmless snake and had made a false head for it that looked like a man. He held an audience in a dimly lit room in which the god was shown as a full-grown snake with a man's head. The amazed populace was now ready for the purpose for which the whole scheme had been carried out: Alexander announced that the god would make prophecies and answer questions.

A flourishing oracle business ensued. At a charge of one drachma and two obols per question, Alexander reportedly brought in seventy or eighty thousand drachmae a year. Questions were submitted written on scrolls and sealed. Lucian tells of several ways by which the seals could be broken, the questions read, and the seals replaced so as not to appear broken. Sometimes the responses were written on the outside of the scrolls; sometimes Alexander

106. Eusebius, *Preparation for the Gospel* 5.19-36.
107. A. D. Nock, "Alexander of Abonuteichos," *Classical Quarterly* 22 (1928):160-62.

arranged for an assistant to speak the responses from another room through a tube connected with the false head of the snake so that it appeared that the serpent-god himself was speaking. Some responses were obscure and ambiguous, others unintelligible, most shrewd guesses. To some he gave favorable messages, to others unfavorable, and to still others he prescribed medical treatments; he "made predictions, discovered fugitive slaves, detected thieves and robbers, caused treasures to be dug up, healed the sick, and in some cases actually raised the dead" (chap. 24). The fame of the oracle spread so that business came from as far away as Rome. Alexander came to have a large staff and employed messengers in distant cities to bring him word of questions to be asked. No failures discouraged the believers. When asked by an inquirer who should be appointed tutor for his son, the oracle replied, Pythagoras and Homer. The boy died a few days later, but the father concluded that the oracle was right in naming those no longer alive as the lad's tutors.

Alexander not only combined healing instructions with the oracle, which was not uncommon, but also instituted mysteries. His chief opponents were Epicureans and Christians (chaps. 25 and 38).

BIBLIOGRAPHY

Homeric Hymn to Apollo (B).
Aeschylus. Prologue to *Eumenides.*
Euripides. *Iphigenia in Tauris.*
Lucan. *Civil War (Pharsalia)* 5.69-197.
Plutarch. *On the Obsolescence of Oracles* (*Moralia* 409E-438E). *The E at Delphi* (*Moralia* 384D-394C). *The Oracles at Delphi* (*Moralia* 394D-409D). *The Demon of Socrates* 21-22 (*Moralia* 589F-592E).
Pausanias. *Description of Greece* 1.34; 9.39.5-14; 10.39.4–40.2; 10.5.5–32.1.
Oxyrhynchus Papyri 1477.

Nock, A. D. "Religious Attitudes of the Ancient Greeks." *Proceedings of the American Philosophical Society* 85 (1942):472-82. Reprinted in *Essays*, pp. 534-50.
Parke, H. W., and D. E. W. Wormell. *The Delphic Oracle.* 2 vols. Oxford, 1956.
Fontenrose, Joseph. *Python: A Study of Delphic Myth and its Origins.* Berkeley, 1959.
Whittaker, C. R. "The Delphic Oracle: Belief and Behavior in Ancient Greece — and Africa." *HTR* 58 (1965):21-47.
Montegu, John C. "Oracles in Asia Minor under the Empire." Ph.D. diss., Harvard, 1966.
Parke, H. W. *The Oracles of Zeus: Dodona, Olympia, Ammon.* Oxford, 1967.
Parke, H. W. *Greek Oracles.* London, 1967.
Flacelière, R. *Greek Oracles.* Topsfield, Mass., 1977.
Fontenrose, Joseph. *The Delphic Oracle: Its Responses and Operations with a Catalogue of Responses.* Berkeley, 1978.
Parke, H. W. *The Oracles of Apollo in Asia Minor.* London, 1985.
Fontenrose, Joseph. *Didyma: Apollo's Oracle, Cult, and Companions.* Berkeley, 1988.

Robinson, Thomas L. "Oracles and their Society: Social Realities as Reflected in the
    Oracles of Claros and Didyma." *Semeia* 56 (1991):59-77.

Dreams and Divination

Dreams rivaled oracles as a source of divine commands. They figure promi-
nently in the healing cults (p. 225). Dreams were also a widely accepted means
of revealing the future. As Plutarch said, "In popular belief it is only in sleep
that men receive inspiration from on high" (*On the Sign of Socrates* 20
[*Moralia* 589D]). The ancients regarded dream experience as no less real than
other experience. Spontaneous dreams were especially significant and worthy
of interpretation, but persons also sought dreams that might give guidance and
instruction. Dreams were defended as divine communications or as the result
of the soul separating from the body during sleep and wandering about gaining information inaccessible while in the body. For the interpretation of a
dream one might consult "professional" interpreters, a mantis, or an oracle.
The lore of the professional dream interpreters was collected, systematized,
and rationalized (according to that day) by Artemidorus (late second century
A.D.). For comparison with dream revelations one may note the "visions" in
Acts 10:10-16; 16:9-10; 23:11; 27:23-24.

Divination was a broader category. Plutarch said that dreams are "our
most ancient and respected form of divination" (*Moralia* 159A). Divination
was defined as "the foreseeing and foretelling of events considered as happening by chance" (Cicero, *On Divination* 1.5.9; cf. 2.5.13ff.). Nearly everyone was
affected by the desire for signs about the future: "Heaven consorts directly with
but few [as in prophetic inspiration], and rarely, but to the great majority gives
signs, from which arises the art called divination" (Plutarch, *On the Sign of Socrates* 24 [*Moralia* 593D]).[108] The assumption was that information about what
to do and what would happen was available and humans only needed the
proper method of learning it. The ways of gaining the desired information
were numerous and varied: throwing dice in front of a temple, observing the
direction from which lightning came, examining the entrails of an animal,
watching the flight of birds, listening to a chance remark, etc. Contact with a
superhuman being might be sought for purposes of divination; the means employed in addition to dreams might be a direct vision, possession by using a
medium while in a trance, use of an object such as a container filled with water
in which a reflection would appear, or necromancy. Cicero divided divination
into two classes: (1) artificial, which depends on observation and deduction

---

108. Cf. Cicero, *On Divination* 1.1.2: "I am aware of no people . . . which does not think that
signs are given of future events, and that certain persons can recognize those signs and foretell
events before they occur." M. Schofield, "Cicero for and against Divination," *JRS* 76 (1986):47-65.

and includes oracles obtained by chance, astrology, augury, prophecies of soothsayers, and interpretation of portents, prodigies, and natural phenomena; (2) natural, which includes dreams and prophecies made by inspired persons, and so a direct communication without signs (*On Divination* 1.6.12; cf. 1.18.34; 33.72; 49.109-10; 2.11.26-27). He summarized the philosophical criticism of divination by saying it "is compounded of a little error, a little superstition, and a good deal of fraud" (*On Divination* 2.39.83). Omens (unlike astrology; see pp. 237ff.) were not so much indications of inevitable destiny nor causes of the outcome as tokens of luck or endorsements of a course of action. Mistakes in divination, like those in astrology, were explained the way mistakes in medicine were: the phenomena were there, but the practice was a human skill and one did not reject the reality because of mistakes. The desire to foretell the future is deep-rooted and not easily discouraged.

BIBLIOGRAPHY

Cicero. *On Divination*. Commentary in A. S. Pease, "M. Tulli Ciceronis De Divinatione libre duo," *University of Illinois Studies in Language and Literature* 6 (1920):161-500; 8 (1920):153-474; reprint Darmstadt, 1963.

Aelius Aristides. *Sacred Tales*. For his dream life see Behr, C. A. *Aelius Aristides and the Sacred Tales*. Amsterdam, 1968.

Artemidorus. *Interpretation of Dreams*. Translation and commentary by Robert J. White. *The Interpretation of Dreams: Oneirocritica by Artemidorus*. Park Ridge, N.J., 1975.

Lewis, Naphtali. *The Interpretation of Dreams and Portents*. Toronto, 1976.

Bouche-Leclercq, A. *Histoire de la divination dans l'antiquité*. 4 vols. Paris, 1879–1882.

Halliday, W. R. *Greek Divination: A Study of Its Methods and Principles*. London, 1913.

Hanson, John S. "Dreams and Visions in the Graeco-Roman World and Early Christianity." *ANRW* II, *Principat*, 23.2 (Berlin and New York, 1980), 1395-1427.

Healing Cults

Several healing gods were worshiped in the Hellenistic world. One of them was the hero Amphiaraus, who along with his chariot was swallowed up by the earth near Thebes. After becoming a god he reappeared on earth at Oropos where he was worshiped as a healing god. Most of the constructions at Amphiareion date from the fourth century B.C., but the sanctuary was still actively consulted for oracles and cures well into Roman times. The cult of Amphiaraus was local, but divine cures were attributed to universal gods as

ASCLEPIUS,
Unlike other Greek
gods, Asclepius
was sympathetic to
human suffering.
A serpent around
a walking stick
evolved into the
modern symbol of
the medical profes-
sion. *(© Vanni/Art
Resource, NY)*

well, such as Sarapis and Isis in Hellenistic times. However, the principal deity associated with healing was Asclepius, and we will discuss him as representative of the healing aspect of Greek and Roman religion.[109]

Asclepius. The divine cult of Asclepius spread from Epidaurus (despite rival claims to his birthplace), but it was his acceptance at Athens to counter a plague in 420 B.C. that turned the local healer of Epidaurus into a widely honored god of helpfulness. As A. D. Nock observed, "The rise of Asclepius reflects also a tendency for a religion of emergencies to become prominent, as contrasted with a religion of normality."[110] Asclepius's subsequent acceptance elsewhere was the most remarkable new development in Greek religion since the rise of Dionysus.

Scholars have held various theories of Asclepius's origin: that he was a faded god, that he was a historical personage who as a hero was divinized (before the time of Homer a legendary physician by the name of Asclepius was known), or that he was the archetypal doctor, that is, the personification of the ideal physician and incarnation of the divine power of healing (in his case, unlike that of other heroes, there was no mention of the locality of his death and no ascent to heaven). Asclepius was regarded as a god at Epidaurus from the end of the sixth century. Legends about Asclepius show many variations. According to the version at Epidaurus Asclepius was the son of Apollo and the mortal Coronis, who came to Epidaurus to give birth to her divine child. Healing had been one of Apollo's functions, but the influence of Delphi transferred this function to his son. The only details of Asclepius's life included in the divine legend are that "he healed the sick and revived the dead." His worshipers saw in him one of the many human beings of half-divine origin who had risen to the dignity of a god because of his accomplishments. He chose to live on earth and never became one of the Olympians. He died as a mortal and then came to life again. As a divinity, he was in charge of one specific function. His wife and children, with whom he acted as a unity in his cures, personified abstract concepts related to medicine. His wife's name, Epione, is from the Greek word for "mild." Of his children Hygeia was the most important and was often associated in art with her father; she symbolized the preservation of health.

Asclepius was the god of physicians, who were known as Asclepiads or "sons of Asclepius." His staff, with which he was normally portrayed, was perhaps originally the walking stick of the traveling doctors, but later received symbolic meanings of helpfulness or wisdom. The snake that twines around the staff in the ancient sculptures had been one of the attributes of Apollo but became associated with Asclepius. In the modern symbol of the medical profession the staff and snake have been adapted to the caduceus of Hermes. The

---

109. I follow largely the work of the Edelsteins listed in the bibliography.
110. Review of E. J. and L. Edelstein, *Asclepius,* in *Classical Philology* 45 (1950):48.

medicine practiced by Asclepius differed from human medicine only in that as a god he was better versed in his art. His treatment was distinguished from that of other healing deities in being more rational and empirical.

Asclepius was presented as the most human-loving of the gods. His only restriction was that he would not heal those who were not virtuous. The entrance inscription at Epidaurus read: "Pure must be he who enters the fragrant temple; purity means to be wise in holy things." Faith was not required. *Aretē* ("glorious deed") was the term used to describe his cures. His influence is seen in certain features of the Sarapis cult, and his portraiture influenced artists in depicting both Sarapis and Christ. His own statues imitated those of Zeus but with a milder countenance and eyes turned upward. His mildness and benevolence made him the most Christlike of the pagan deities. The Asclepius cult flourished in the early centuries of the Roman empire, and Asclepius held out against Christianity longer than did the Olympian gods. When the Parthenon in Athens was being used as a Christian church, the Asclepeion on the south slope of the Acropolis was still frequented. But Asclepius was a savior from sickness and danger, not from sin and damnation.

Sanctuaries. Asclepius had major sanctuaries at Epidaurus[111] and on the island of Cos from Hellenistic times and at Pergamum from Roman times, and smaller sanctuaries at Athens,[112] Corinth,[113] and other places. He was received in Rome under the name Aesculapius (one of the first foreign gods to be invited in) after a plague in 293 B.C., with a temple dedicated to him in 291 B.C. on an island in the Tiber where today are the Church of St. Bartholomew and a modern hospital.

The rhetor Aelius Aristides valued healing as a religious act. His comparison of healing with the mystery religions suggest that he viewed healing as an initiation that brought him into personal contact with the god.[114]

The three essentials of a healing sanctuary were a temple, a well or spring for purifications, and a place for sleeping (the *abaton*). Since Asclepius was concerned with intellectual as well as physical health, supplicants at his major sanctuaries could spend their days in rest or exercise in healthful and beautiful surroundings. The sacred precincts included trees, baths, a theatre, a gymnasium, and sometimes a library — similar to a modern health or resort spa. The remains at Epidaurus include a "hotel" of 160 chambers to accommodate visitors. However, since birth and death desecrated a place, a person about to give birth or to die was expelled from the sacred enclosure. Another feature of sanc-

111. R. A. Tomlinson, *Epidauros* (Austin, 1983); L. R. LiDonnici, *The Epidaurian Miracle Inscriptions: Text, Translation and Commentary* (Atlanta, 1995).

112. S. B. Aleshire, *Asklepios at Athens: Epigraphic and Prosopographic Essays on the Athenian Healing Cults* (Amsterdam, 1991).

113. M. Lang, *Cure and Cult in Ancient Corinth: A Guide to the Asklepieion* (Princeton, 1977).

114. Steven C. Muir, "Touched by a God: Aelius Aristides, Religious Healing, and Asclepius Cults," *Society of Biblical Literature 1995 Seminar Papers* (Atlanta, 1995), 362-393.

tuaries of Asclepius was the pit for keeping the sacred (nonpoisonous) snakes. Snakes were sacred to many deities, but their prominence in the cult of Asclepius added to the feeling shared by Jews and Christians that there was a demonic element in pagan religion.

The Healings. The procedure followed in visiting a healing sanctuary is indicated by both literary sources (e.g., Aelius Aristides, *Sacred Tales*) and inscriptions. The patient purified himself or herself at the sacred fountain and offered a sacrifice. Honey cakes, cheese cakes, and figs are frequently mentioned. At night that person took bedclothes and after leaving a small gift for the god reposed on a pallet in the *abaton* (halls built for incubation). The person would dream that the god appeared. We should not wonder at this, in view of the religious excitement of a pilgrimage to a famous shrine (cf. the atmosphere at such modern healing sites as Lourdes), the regimen of diet and exercise imposed, and sleeping in new surroundings. The god either healed directly or gave instructions to be followed in order to effect the cure. These instructions were told to the priests, who interpreted their meaning and gave the medical prescriptions — which often agree with what is known of medical practice of the day. The temple of Asclepius at Cos, home of the famous medical school of Hippocrates,[115] in particular seemed to combine religious healing with current medical practice. Custom called for a gift of thanksgiving to the god for the healing, although Asclepius required no more than what was in a person's power. A cock is the sacrifice most often mentioned.[116] The gift might be a work of art showing the god and his family or the scene of the cure, an inscription commemorating the cure and/or the offering that was brought, a literary piece (a hymn or prose encomium comparable to a sermon), or a reproduction of the part of the body that was healed (the collection from the Asclepeion at Corinth includes legs, arms, feet, hands, and sexual organs).

Some of the cures are reported as miracles of the most astounding kind.

> Cure effected by Apollo and Asclepius. Ambrosia of Athens, blind in one eye. She came with supplications to the god, and as she walked round the temple she smiled at the accounts of some of the cures which she found incredible and impossible, accounts which related how the lame and the blind had been cured by a vision which came to them in a dream. She fell asleep and had a vision. The god appeared before her, telling her that she would be cured and that she had to dedicate in the sanctuary a pig made of silver as a token of her ignorance. Having said this he cut out the bad eye and immersed it in a medicine. She awoke at dawn, cured.[117]

115. On his school of medicine, see Owsei Temkin, *Hippocrates in a World of Pagans and Christians* (Baltimore, 1991).

116. E.g., Herondas, *Mime* 4 (see p. 188 above) and Socrates at the close of Plato's *Phaedo*.

117. *Inscriptiones Graecae* (Berlin, 1902), vol. 4, no. 951, ll. 33-41. Translation from Grant, *Hellenistic Religions* (New York, 1953), 57.

A man with an ulcer in his stomach. While he slept he had a dream. The god appeared to him and ordered his assistants to hold him so that the god could cut out the affected part. The man tried to escape but he was seized and fastened to a door. Asclepius then opened up his stomach, cut out the ulcer, sewed him up again and finally released him. The man awoke cured, but the floor of the *abaton* was covered with blood.[118]

Several reports mention the licking of the diseased spot by a snake or a dog. Some cures can be accounted for on psychological grounds or from the medical practice of the time. In the early period the priests employed surgery, drugs, and hypnosis; later, they effected cures by courses of treatment, including beneficent prescriptions like diet, exercise, baths, and medicines. In some cases the treatment prescribed was contrary to all ancient medical theory.

The cures at the healing sanctuaries are in a totally different frame of reference from the healings by the spoken word or touch of Jesus recorded in the Gospels. For a somewhat closer parallel to Jesus' cures one must look to the wandering wonder-workers of the Hellenistic world. We will consider them through their best-known representative, Apollonius of Tyana, in the next chapter (pp. 384-86). Magic was also employed for healing purposes.

BIBLIOGRAPHY

Pindar. *Pythian Odes* 3.47-56.
Aristophanes. *Plutus* 653-748.
Herondas. *Mime* 4.
Aelius Aristides. *Orations* 38 and 47-52 (esp. 48), *Sacred Tales.* See Behr, C. A. *Aelius Aristides and the Sacred Tales.* Amsterdam, 1968.
Pausanias. *Description of Greece* 1.34.1-5; 2.26.1–29.1.
Edelstein, Emma J., and Ludwig Edelstein. *Asclepius: A Collection and Interpretation of the Testimonies.* 2 vols. Baltimore, 1945; reprint in 1 vol., 1998.
Cotter, Wendy. *Miracles in Greco-Roman Antiquity: A Sourcebook for the Study of New Testament Miracles.* London, 1999.

Kerényi, C. *Asklepios: Archetypal Image of the Physician's Existence.* New York, 1959.
Kee, H. C. *Miracle in the Early Christian World.* New Haven, 1983.
Kee, H. C. *Medicine, Miracle, and Magic in New Testament Times.* Cambridge, 1986.
Jackson, Ralph. *Doctors and Diseases in the Roman Empire.* Norman, Okla., 1988.
Coffman, Ralph J. "Historical Jesus the Healer: Cultural Interpretation of the Healing Cults of the Graeco-Roman World as the Basis for Jesus Movements." *Society of Biblical Literature 1993 Seminar Papers.* Pp. 412-443.
Wells, L. *The Greek Language of Healing from Homer to New Testament Times.* Berlin, 1998.

---

118. Ibid., no. 952, ll. 38-45. Translation from Giulio Giannelli, ed., *The World of Classical Athens* (New York, 1970), 156.

Magic and Maledictions

Magic refers to efforts to control supernatural forces for one's own ends by means that rest on some peculiar and secret wisdom. It differs from science in representing a different view of causality, supernatural versus natural; it differs from religion in involving an element of constraint in contrast to religion's attitude, "Thy will be done." One can argue that in origin magic is more nearly akin to science than to religion. Magic and science have in common the view that the same actions, the same "formulas," under the same circumstances will produce the same results.[119] These theoretical distinctions do not hold in practice. The boundaries between religion and magic are not sharply marked in the ancient world, and the distinction between manipulation and supplication was often blurred. Pliny the Elder said magic incorporated three arts: medicine, religion, and astrology (*Natural History* 30.1-2). Magic was a part of religion, and the two became one in later Neoplatonism.

There was no generally accepted definition of magic in Greco-Roman culture, and the meaning of "magic" changed in different contexts. Because of the ambiguity in ancient texts between what was religion and what was magic, the student must take account of the social setting. Accusations of magic were made against persons suspected of unacceptable or unexplained behavior. The factor of social deviance must be considered in descriptions of magic. Laws against magic assumed it to be efficacious and widely practiced; it was the doing of evil ("black magic") that was proscribed. What was regarded as religious by one person might be regarded as magic or superstition by another, and often there is little difference in procedures between the two.[120]

There was similar conflict in the ancient world over the interpretation of what was considered to be supernatural. Belief in miraculous deeds was common in antiquity: if done by one's own hero, they were attributed to divine power; if done by an opponent, they were attributed to magic (cf. the discussion concerning Apollonius of Tyana, pp. 384-86).[121] Jews and pagans said Jesus performed his deeds by magic.[122] Christians in turn attributed pagan marvels to the working of demons (pp. 236-37).[123] One person's miracle was another person's magic.

Magic, according to traditional analysis, comes in two major forms: sym-

119. B. Malinowski, *Magic, Science, and Religion* (New York, 1954), 85-90.

120. Alan F. Segal, "Hellenistic Magic: Some Questions of Definitions," in R. van den Broek and M. J. Vermaseren, eds., *Studies in Gnosticism and Hellenistic Religions Presented to Gilles Quispel on the Occasion of his 65th Birthday* (Leiden, 1981), 349-75.

121. Harold Remus, "'Magic or Miracle'? Some Second-Century Instances," *The Second Century* 2 (1982):127-56; idem, *Pagan-Christian Conflict over Miracle in the Second Century* (Cambridge, Mass., 1983).

122. Mark 3:22; Justin, *Apology* 1.30; Origen, *Against Celsus* 1.38; Ps.-Clement, *Recognitions* 1.42.4; 58.1; 70.2; b. Shabbath 104b.

123. 2 Thess. 2:9-10; Rev. 13:11ff.; 19:20.

HECATE,
2d/3d c. A.D.
The goddess of magic
was shown in triple
form. The restored
attributes of keys and
cords denote her
as a keeper of the
underworld.
(British Museum)

pathetic (imitative) and contagious. In the former, similarities or imitations are thought to have an identity with or influence on something else. An example of this would be the practice of throwing a lead curse tablet (see p. 233) into a well to disappear and become cold, imitating the fate desired for the person whose name was inscribed on the tablet.[124] In contagious magic the part stands for the whole; what is done to a part affects the whole from which it comes or what is like to it. For this reason parts of the human body were employed in magical rituals.[125]

The word *magic* (*mageia;* Acts 8:11; cf. 8:9) is derived from the name of a Persian priestly tribe and was borrowed as a loanword in Greek *(magos).*[126] It was given an extended, typical meaning, probably from the impression made on uncomprehending Greeks by the rites and formulas of Persian priests. Thus *magos* came to have a range of meanings from Persian priest, to a person representing the wisdom of the east (Matt. 2:1), to a charlatan, to a magician (Acts 13:6, 8). The professional magicians adopted the word because it had a dignified history for those with some control over the supernatural, in preference to *goēs* (2 Tim. 3:13), which commonly meant a quack.

The root idea in magic was that by employing the proper means the gods or demons could be forced to do something for you. Vital was the belief in the two different planes of visible and supernatural reality and in the possibility of transferring a thing from one to the other. Magic continued ideas from older, primitive strata of religion that were given up elsewhere. Hecate, the early goddess of ghosts and the uncanny, became the favorite of magicians.[127] She was depicted in triple form to express the three realms of her influence — earth, sea, and heavens.[128] Magic continued to flourish in Hellenistic and imperial times. Apuleius expected the readers of his *Metamorphoses* to take as much or more interest in his stories about magic as about amorous escapades. Magic came to rule supreme in late antiquity, receiving philosophical support from the Neoplatonist Iamblichus[129] on the basis of the philosophical doctrine of universal sympathies (see Chap. 4, esp. p. 362).

A number of "Magical Papyri" from the second to the sixth centuries A.D. (most are third–fourth century) have survived; "some are brief recipes for magical processes or exorcisms; others are collections of such recipes with

124. Cf. G. W. Elderkin, "An Athenian Maledictory Inscription on Lead," *Hesperia* 5 (1936):43-49.

125. Apuleius, *Metamorphoses* 3.

126. For this paragraph see A. D. Nock, "Paul and the Magus," in *The Beginnings of Christianity,* ed. F. J. Foakes-Jackson and K. Lake (London, 1933), 5:164-88 (*Essays,* 308-30).

127. A. D. Nock in "The Orphic *Argonautica,*" *Journal of Hellenic Studies* 46 (1926):50-52, elucidates a ceremony of sacrifice to Hecate.

128. Hesiod, *Theog.* 411ff.; Pausanias 2.30.2. Plutarch, *Moralia* 937F (cf. 944C), reflects the association of Hecate with the phases of the moon, but 416E refers to her dominion over the earth and the heavens.

129. *On the Mysteries* 4.2.

ABRAXAS, from Switzerland, 3d c. Since the letters of the name Abraxas had a numerical value of 365, it became an important magical symbol in late antiquity. *(Museum of Roman Germany, Mainz; original in Zurich)*

more ambitious invocations and methods of securing control over supernatural forces."[130] Those containing extensive collections of magical formulas may be the actual working copies of practicing magicians. For the users of this material magic was religion. All the religious views characteristic of late antiquity are found in the magical papyri: cosmic (astral) religion (cf. pp. 238-39), the highest god, belief in power and demons (cf. pp. 235ff.), search for wonders, occultism, designating magic as a "mystery," and acceptance of *heimarmenē* (fate; see pp. 241-43), whose power the magician as the "adept" can break. The texts contain invocations of the gods in which the divine epithets are multiplied. Included in the Paris Magical Papyrus, for instance, is the invocation of "the god of the Hebrews Jēsu, Jaba, Jaēa, Jaē, Abraōth, Aia, Thōth, Ele, Elō . . ."[131] No deity who might be effective in gaining the desired end was omitted. The motivation was the conviction, a commonplace in magic, that the knowledge of someone's true name gives one power over that person.[132] The syncretism of names

130. A. D. Nock, "Greek Magical Papyri," *Journal of Egyptian Archaeology* 15 (1929):219 (*Essays*, 176).

131. G. A. Deissmann, *Light from the Ancient East* (repr.; Grand Rapids, 1965), 260; cf. PGM 4.277.

132. Cf. Acts 19:11-20 for the assumption that the knowledge of the name is to control its power; cf. Origen, *Against Celsus* 1.25, for the claim that the power of an incantation is in the words themselves.

and formulas reflects the tendencies to a blending of deities and rites in the Hellenistic and Roman periods. A characteristic feature of the papyri is the use of threats against the deities and the compelling of a deity by a greater power. Precision of formula is another feature of magical texts: one binds the spirits by semijuristic phrases and repetitions that leave no loopholes or ambiguity. Other features are the use of incomprehensible formulas and the ascription of supernatural effects to the materials used.

The magical ceremony involved two activities: the invocation of the supernatural power (the "formula") and the ritual practice (the employment of material means, the "recipe"). The treatment in the magical texts is quite regular: invoke a higher power to compel it to assist the invoker in procuring what is wished — healing, fame, wealth, or power, or to obtain the affections of a loved object (which frequently included dissolution of an existing amatory bond). One magical text offers a progression to a climax: prayer to the materials employed in the magic treated as divine things, adjuration of the material by a great god, prayer to that great god, constraint of that god by the unnameable god, constraint by necessity.[133]

The collections of magical spells and charms represented in the magical papyri may be comparable to the books the practitioners of magical arts burned in Ephesus in Acts 19:19. Ephesus was in fact considered one of the centers for the practice of magic. Formulas used in magic were known as *Ephesia grammata* ("Ephesian Letters").[134]

The Jewish element is prominent in the magical papyri, and the Jews enjoyed considerable notoriety as magicians in the ancient world[135] — a fact reflected in several New Testament texts (Matt. 12:27; Acts 13:6; 19:13-14). Of interest in connection with Jewish magic is the fragmentarily preserved book of *Jannes and Jambres* (2 Tim. 3:8), written by a Jew in Greek probably in Egypt about the beginning of the first century. The work begins, "This is the book of the words of Jannes and Jambres the magicians," who are identified as withstanding Moses and Aaron, and it makes reference to Jambres' use of necromancy in bringing up the shade of his brother Jannes from Hades.[136] While some pagans regarded Moses as a magician,[137] the Jewish magician *par excellence* was Solomon, as seen in the *Testament of Solomon* (from the early centuries of the common era), in which Solomon uses his magical power over demons to construct the temple.[138] A document in Hebrew from the third or

133. H. I. Bell, A. D. Nock, and Herbert Thompson, "Magical Texts from a Bilingual Papyrus in the British Museum," *Proceedings of the British Academy* 17 (London, 1931):235-87.

134. C. C. McCown, "The Ephesia Grammata in Popular Belief," *Transactions and Proceedings of the American Philological Association* 54 (1923):128-31.

135. Pliny, *Natural History* 30.2.11.

136. Albert Pietersma, *The Apocryphon of Jannes and Jambres the Magicians* (Leiden, 1994).

137. John G. Gager, *Moses in Greco-Roman Paganism* (Nashville, 1972), 134-61.

138. Louis Ginzberg, *The Legends of the Jews* (Philadelphia, 1954), 4:149-54, 165-72, and ac-

fourth century A.D., *Sepher-ha-Razim* ("Book of Secrets"),[139] contains requests and recipes ("If you want this or that, do and recite the following") similar to those found in Greek magical papyri, only all is set in a very Jewish context — for example, the spirits invoked are angels subordinated as ministers and emissaries of the Supreme God.[140] The reserved notices of magic in rabbinic literature preserved monotheism and asserted power only over matter, human beings, and perhaps angels but not God.[141] Other representatives of Jewish magic are the Aramaic magic incantation bowls.[142]

Some of the magical papyri contain elements of an elevated mystical piety in their prayers. This aspect of personal religion is evident in the so-called Mithras Liturgy contained in the Paris Magical Papyrus codex.[143] Neither a liturgy nor specifically Mithraic, it is a magical text that borrowed some Mithraic features. It contains directions on how one's soul in ecstatic ascent may pass through the zones of heaven to the supreme God.[144] There was use of the language and practices of initiation into the mysteries to describe learning to be a magician.

Most of the magical texts are concerned with much more mundane things. In fact, most of the magical spells have nothing to do with religion at all. Four major concerns of magical texts are erotic spells, protection from evil, curses on others, and prognostications. Magic was also used in healing, in efforts to influence the weather, the outcome of judicial decisions, athletic contests, and economic competition, for protection against slanderers and thieves, and in connection with astrology. Among the many charms that have to do with affairs of love is the following incantation from the second century: "To Aphrodite to kindle love in a certain Ammonius, son of Helene, for Serapicus, son of a slave woman."[145]

---

companying notes. For the text of the *Testament of Solomon* see C. C. McCown, *The Testament of Solomon* (Leipzig, 1922) and for introduction and English translation D. C. Duling in James Charlesworth, ed., *The Old Testament Pseudepigrapha* (Garden City, 1983), Vol. 1, pp. 935-987.

139. Ed. M. Margalioth (Jerusalem, 1966). Trans. Michael A. Morgan, *Sefer Ha-Razim: The Book of Mysteries* (Chico, Calif., 1984).

140. On Jewish magic see Joshua Trachtenberg, *Jewish Magic and Superstition* (repr.; New York, 1979); Peter Schäfer, "Jewish Magic Literature in Late Antiquity and Early Middle Ages," *JJS* 41 (1990):75-91.

141. Brigitte Kern-Ulmer, "The Depiction of Magic in Rabbinic Texts: The Rabbinic and the Greek Concept of Magic," *JSJ* 27 (1996):289-303.

142. Charles D. Isbell, *Corpus of the Aramaic Incantation Bowls* (Missoula, Mont., 1975); idem, "The Story of the Aramaic Magic Incantation Bowls," *BA* 41 (1978):5-16.

143. Hans Dieter Betz, *The "Mithras Liturgy": Text, Translation, and Commentary* (Tübingen, 2003).

144. Cf. the section on Hermetic Literature and Gnosticism below, pp. 300ff.; for Mithraism, pp. 287ff.

145. In the Ashmolean Museum, Oxford, and published in the *Journal of Egyptian Archaeology* 15 (1929):155-57. On the subject in general, see Christopher A. Faraone, *Ancient Greek Love Magic* (Cambridge, Mass., 1999).

Some scholars have overlapped magic and popular Gnosticism. Although the two circles share some common elements (e.g., the *Pistis Sophia* contains magical prayers of constraint) and some Gnostics performed magic (as Marcus in Irenaeus, *Against Heresies* 1.13), the two phenomena are quite distinct. Yet many magical amulets are catalogued in museums as "Gnostic gems," although they have nothing to do with the religious movement now technically called Gnosticism. An amulet is an object that by its nearness to the person who possesses it keeps evil away or brings good luck.[146] Amulets of vegetable or animal matter obviously have not survived, but charms written on papyrus and carried on the person have survived. Most abundant are stone or metal amulets inscribed with deities or sacred symbols and magical words or letters that were worn as rings or pendants. A common formula is "Protect from every evil"; some are inscribed for a specific purpose, but many contain formulas or letters now unknown, or that even at their time of use were supposedly more potent because mysterious. The amulets show one aspect of the popular side of magic: they were important as protective devices because magic could be used to place a malediction upon someone.

A special kind of magical document that has survived is the curse tablet.[147] The binding spell written on the tablet was intended to subject another person to one's will. Most were written on lead and many were rolled up and pierced with a nail. The nail did not represent a weapon but symbolized the immobilizing or holding fast the object of the binding spell. The lead tablet was usually placed in a grave, and the fate of the victim of the spell was compared to the dead person in whose grave the spell was placed or to the lead tablet itself. Some were protected from prying eyes by the words being written retrograde. Such is the following curse, which is unusual in that the object (a thief) is presented to Jupiter, who when he forces the repayment will enjoy a tithe of the sum recovered:

> To the god Jupiter optimus maximus there is given that he may hound
> . . . through his mind, through his memory, his inner parts [?], his intes-
> tines, his heart, his marrow, his veins . . . whoever it was, whether man or
> woman, who stole away the denarii of Canius [?] Dignus that in his own
> person in a short time he may balance the account. There is given to the
> god above named a tenth part of the money when he has [repaid it?].[148]

146. C. Bonner, "Magical Amulets," *HTR* 39 (1946):25-54; idem, *Studies in Magical Amulets, Chiefly Graeco-Egyptian* (Ann Arbor, Mich., 1950); R. Kotanshy, *Greek Magical Amulets*, Part 1: *Published Texts of Known Provenance* (Opladen, 1994).

147. Collection by A. Audollent, *Defixionum Tabellae* (Paris, 1904); for others see the bibliography in the articles in the next note and David R. Jordan, "A Survey of Greek Defixiones not Included in the Special Corpora," *Greek, Roman, and Byzantine Studies* 26 (1985):151-97. A selection in Eng. trans. and notes in J. G. Gager, *Curse Tablets and Binding Spells from the Ancient World* (Oxford, 1992).

148. E. G. Turner, "A Curse Tablet from Nottinghamshire," *Journal of Roman Studies* 53 (1963):122-24. For texts, translations, and commentary on three curse inscriptions out of forty-

The Guildhall Museum in London holds a tablet with the following curse:

> I curse Tretia Maria and her life and mind and memory and liver and
> lungs mixed up together, and her words, thoughts, and memory; thus may
> she be unable to speak what things are concealed nor be able . . .

In order to counteract the effects of a spell one must find and destroy the magical object or employ a counter-spell against the magic.

Bibliography

Theocritus 2.
Virgil. *Aeneid* 4.
Horace. *Epodes* 5 and 17. *Satires* 1.8.23-45.
Ovid. *Metamorphoses* 7.
Lucan. *The Civil War (Pharsalia)* 6.413-830.
Pliny the Elder. *Natural History* 28.21; 30.1-20.
Apuleius. *Apology.*
Lucian. *Menippus; Lover of Lies.*
Preisendanz, Karl. *Papyri graecae magicae: Die griechischen Zauberpapyri.* Edited by
    A. Henrichs. Stuttgart, 1973–1974.
McCown, C. C. *The Testament of Solomon.* Untersuchungen zum Neuen Testa-
    ment, vol. 9. Leipzig, 1922. Translated by D. C. Duling in James H. Charles-
    worth, ed. *The Old Testament Pseudepigrapha.* Vol. 1. Garden City, 1983.
Luck, Georg. *Arcana Mundi.* Baltimore, 1985.
Daniel, R. W., and F. Maltomini, eds. and trans. *Supplementum Magicum,* vol. 1.
    Cologne, 1990.
Betz, H. D., ed. *The Greek Magical Papyri in Translation.* 2d ed. Chicago, 1992.
Gager, J. G. *Curse Tablets and Binding Spells from the Ancient World.* Oxford, 1992.
    (Translates more than 100.)
Meyer, Marvin and Richard Smith, eds. *Ancient Christian Magic: Coptic Texts and
    Ritual Power.* San Francisco, 1994.

Bonner, C. *Studies in Magical Amulets.* Ann Arbor, 1950.
Annequin, Jacques. *Recherches sur l'action magique et ses representations (Ier et
    IIème siècles après J. C.).* Paris, 1973.
Hull, John M. *Hellenistic Magic and the Synoptic Tradition.* Studies in Biblical The-
    ology, 2d ser. London, 1974.
Smith, Morton. *Jesus the Magician.* San Francisco, 1978.
Aune, D. "Magic in Early Christianity." *ANRW* II, *Principat,* 23.2. Berlin and New
    York, 1980. Pp. 1507-57.

---

five found in the Athenian Agora, see G. W. Elderkin, "An Athenian Maledictory Inscription on
Lead" (note 124 above) and "Two Curse Inscriptions," *Hesperia* 5 (1936):382-95. See also J. M. R.
Cormack, "A Tabella Defixionis," *HTR* 44 (1951):25-34.

Tupet, A. M. "Rites magiques dans l'Antiquité romaine." *ANRW* II, *Principat*, 16.3. Berlin and New York, 1986. Pp. 2591-2675.

Garrett, S. R. *The Demise of the Devil: Magic and the Demonic in Luke's Writings.* Minneapolis, 1989.

Faraone, C. A., and D. Obbink, eds. *"Magika Hiera": Ancient Greek Magic and Religion.* Oxford, 1991.

Meyer, M., and P. Mirecki. *Ancient Magic and Ritual Power.* Leiden, 1995.

Ritner, Robert K. "Egyptian Magical Practice under the Roman Empire: The Demotic Spells and their Religious Context." *ANRW* II, *Principat*, 18.5. Berlin and New York, 1995. Pp. 3333-3379.

Graf, Fritz. *Magic in the Ancient World.* Cambridge, Mass., 1997.

Luck, Georg. "Recent Work on Ancient Magic." *Ancient Pathways and Hidden Pursuits.* Ann Arbor, Mich., 2002. Pp. 203-222.

Janowitz, Naomi. *Magic in the Roman World: Pagans, Jews, and Christians.* London, 2001.

Klutz, Todd. *Magic in the Biblical World: From the Rod of Aaron to the Ring of Solomon.* Sheffield, 2003.

Brashear, Wm. M. "The Greek Magical Papyri: An Introduction and Survey. Annotated Bibliography (1928-1994)." *ANRW* II, *Principat*, 18.5. Berlin and New York, 1995. Pp. 3380-3684.

Imprecations and Oaths

Imprecations against grave robbers occur commonly on tombs, calling upon the gods to punish anyone who violates the tomb. For example, "Whoever does anything counter to the injunctions set forth above shall be held responsible to the authorities; and in addition may he have no profit from children or goods, may he neither walk on the land nor sail on the sea, but may he die childless, penniless, and ruined before death, and all his seed perish with him; and after death may he find the underground gods angry avengers."[149] Such imprecations are often confused with magical curses, but the only common element is the malediction against another. Although the grave inscriptions call upon the deity, there is no attempt to force an outcome by magical action.

A special kind of imprecation was the confession of sin hung up in a temple. The violator denounced himself for his faults, especially oversights of ritual precepts (the faults confessed are not moral and may have been involuntary). He called upon the god in the presence of all.

Imprecations against grave robbers and public confessions of transgression had in common with oaths a malediction upon the transgressor. They

---

149. CIG 3915. Trans. Richmond Lattimore, *Themes in Greek and Latin Epitaphs* (Urbana, Ill., 1962), 115-16; on the subject cf. André Parrot, *Malédictions et violations de tombes* (Paris, 1939); John S. Creaghan, "*Violatio Sepulchri*: An Epigraphical Study," Ph.D. diss., Princeton, 1951.

shared a belief that gods were the guarantors of justice and would punish those who violated sacred duties. The oath *(horkos)* held a preponderant place in the political, social, and religious life of the ancient world. Oaths were the very foundation of society; they were taken by magistrates, judges, and citizens and possessed a religious character (the gods gave the guarantee). The oaths contained a malediction pronounced against the self if the oath was not carried out. Faith in oaths was shown by both those wronged who made appeal to the gods for punishment and by perjurers in the confessions.

Demons and Superstition

The word *daimōn* ("demon") underwent important changes of meaning. In general it referred to a power that accompanies persons and dispenses destiny. In Homer it is used of impersonal power or of the gods collectively and indefinitely ("the divine") as the dispenser of individual events. Hesiod classified rational beings as gods, demons, heroes, and people; by demons he meant men of the golden age translated to blissful immortal life. His classification prepared the way for demons to be considered lesser divinities (cf. Acts 17:18) or heavenly intermediaries between the gods and human beings. Socrates referred to a demon that warned him against certain actions (Plato, *Apology* 31D, 40A), thus giving to the demon a function almost like the conscience. (Antiquity could not imagine an abstract force with no starting point.) Plato's varied use of the term influenced its future development. One work says that the demons are the sons of gods by nymphs or other mothers, serving as interpreters between gods and people ([?] *Epinomis* 984E); in this sense *demon* is a generic term for divine intermediaries. Plato's writings also regard the demon as a destiny spirit somewhat like a guardian angel as a companion of persons (*Phaedo* 107D; *Republic* 617D; *Statesman* 271D, 272E) or of cities as well as of individuals (*Laws* 713C, 738D). He also refers "demon" to the highest and divine element in a person.[150] From the idea of a demon accompanying each person came the use of the word as virtually equal to "fate" (but as referring to the personal destiny of an individual and without the capriciousness of Tychē).

Xenocrates, Plato's student, systematized demonology. He and later philosophers listed three classes of demons: permanently disincarnate beings, souls of the deceased, and the soul "in" or intelligence accompanying us. He ascribed human passions to them and made the distinction that some demons were good and some bad. From this came the idea that each person has two demons, one good and one bad. By the fourth century B.C. the word was deteriorating into use only for unlucky happenings. Since one avoided putting the blame for evil

---

150. Here Plato's true mind is brought out in *Timaeus* 90A: "God gave the sovereign part of the human soul to be the divinity of each one" (trans. B. Jowett).

happenings on the gods, they were attributed to the demons. Thus was the way prepared for regarding demons as evil beings. Xenocrates and Chrysippus allowed for evil as well as good demons, but Plutarch most developed the idea. He and Apuleius provide us with the developed demonology of early Christian times. Demonic forces were everywhere and were constantly affecting human life. Demons were important as intermediaries between human beings and the gods, who were increasingly made transcendent, and as a way of reconciling the philosophical movement toward monotheism with the polytheism of popular religion. The admission that the gods of polytheism were "demons" played into the hands of Christian apologists.[151] Also, to the demons could be transferred everything that philosophy regarded as unfitting in the gods. The apologists' claim that pagan religion was inspired by demons, who had a gross enjoyment of animal sacrifices, corresponded to the later Greek philosophical view that attributed the sacrifices of popular religion to the demons but reserved a rational worship for the immaterial gods (see Porphyry and Iamblichus, p. 393).

Pre-Christian Judaism had already begun to take over the word *demon* in that sense of intermediate evil beings which is so evident in the Christian Gospels. Belief in demon possession of individuals was widespread and led to the practice of exorcism to expel demons — by pagans,[152] Jews,[153] and Christians.[154]

Deisidaimonia, "fear of the demons" ("God-fearing" or "fearful" according to one's viewpoint), was the word that corresponded to "superstition." It is significant for the debasement of the idea of demon that this form and not *deisitheos* was coined for the excessive, irrational fear of the spiritual world. The word *Deisidaimonia*, unlike *superstitio*, did not, it seems, include magic. Theophrastus's caricature of "superstitiousness" (*Characters* 16) presents an almost pathological idea, a "religious hypochondriac," but by itself each instance in his description was not abnormal in Greek religion. Plutarch's *On Superstition* presents superstition as the excess on one side of the mean of proper reverence for the gods in contrast to atheism on the other extreme; it is worse than atheism in his view. The treatises by Theophrastus and Plutarch on superstition give many details of popular religious feeling and practice and testify to how widespread it was.

Exegetes and translators dispute how much of this negative philosophical connotation to *deisidaimonia* is intended by the use of the word in Acts 17:22. Could it have a neutral meaning of "very careful in the expression of religious feelings," or is the negative connotation intended in order to identify with the philosophical criticism of elements in the popular religion?

151. Plutarch, *Moralia* 361B-C, 415A-19A. Already in Paul, 1 Cor. 10:20 (following Ps. 96:5, LXX); cf. Justin, *Apology* 2.5; 1.5; Origen, *Against Celsus* 7.69; Tertullian, *Shows* 13.

152. Plutarch, *Table Talk* 5 (*Moralia* 706E); Philostratus, *Life of Apollonius* 4.20; Lucian, *Lover of Lies* 16.

153. Josephus, *Ant.* 8.2.5 [46-49]; b. Shabbath 67a.

154. Justin, *Apology* 2.5; *Acts of Peter* 11.

The Latin use of *superstitio* included Christians in the term (see pp. 593ff.).

BIBLIOGRAPHY

Theophrastus. *Characters* 16.
Plutarch. *On the Obsolescence of Oracles. On Superstition.*
Apuleius. *On the God of Socrates.*
Lucian. *Lover of Lies.*

Dibelius, M. *Die Geisterwelt im Glauben des Paulus.* Göttingen, 1909.
MacGregor, G. H. C. "Principalities and Powers: The Cosmic Background of Paul's Thought." *NTS* 1 (1954):17ff.
Caird, G. B. *Principalities and Powers.* Oxford, 1956.
Eitrem, S. *Some Notes on the Demonology of the New Testament.* 2d ed. Oslo, 1966.
Ferguson, E. *Demonology of the Early Christian World.* Lewiston, N.Y., 1984.
Wink, Walter. *Naming the Powers: The Language of Power in the New Testament.* Philadelphia, 1984.
Arnold, C. E. *Powers of Darkness: Principalities and Powers in Paul's Letters.* Downers Grove, Ill., 1992.

Astrology, Astral Religion, and Fate

Components of Astrology. The Greeks developed astrology in Egypt during the Hellenistic Age. Initially a learned product, welcomed by upper classes who had "lost piety without shedding superstition,"[155] it required an "intellectual" class to discover and record its findings. About the first century, however, astrological ideas began to be popularized. Three components went into its development: astronomical observations, especially by the ancient Babylonians but also by the Greeks; Greek science (especially the penchant for generalization) and philosophy (the Stoic view of the interrelationships of all parts of the universe); and religion, particularly the linking of the heavenly bodies with a special god and the transfer of the attributes of this god to the planets. The distinctive thought of astrology was that the movements of the heavenly bodies in absolute regularity control earthly events to the smallest detail.

Astrologers were called *mathematici* or *Chaldaei.* The former term testifies to the importance of mathematical calculations in the development of astrology; number relations were the basis for an extravagant symbolism. The term *Chaldaeans* had different meanings at different times: the inhabitants of Mesopotamia, members of the Babylonian priesthood, Greeks who had studied in Babylonia or proclaimed themselves disciples of the Babylonians, and fi-

155. A. D. Nock, review of W. Gundel, *Neue astrologische Texte des Hermes Trismegistos,* in *Gnomon* 15 (1939):365 (*Essays,* 499).

nally a professional term for those who claimed to foretell the future according to the stars.

Babylonian Astral Religion. The term *Chaldaean* would seem to point to Babylon for astrology's point of origin. The Babylonians had studied astronomy carefully and maintained careful records of their observations. Moreover, they had connected the stars with religion and developed a learned theology based on this connection. The Babylonian gods were given an abode in the stars and identified with them. Thus Babylonia was one source of the widespread star worship of the Hellenistic Age (the other was philosophy). The sun and moon did not receive cult among the early Greeks; only after Plato and Aristotle did the Greeks widely believe the heavenly bodies to be gods.[156]

The Babylonian astral religion infused many cults (e.g., see below, pp. 291ff., 316-18). It also contributed several influential ideas: notably that the spheres of the universe are each under the control of a deity, and that souls descend through these spheres, acquiring the characteristics of each, and must ascend through these realms. From the identification of the gods with the stars could be deduced the eternity of the world and of the sidereal gods. Moreover, the stars were not only eternal gods but were also universal. Their power was unlimited by time or space. The term *elements (stoicheia)* was applied to the heavenly bodies, a usage reflected in several New Testament passages (Gal. 4:3, 9; Col. 2:8, 20).[157] The astral religion placed the abode of the blessed in the heavenly realm rather than in the underworld.[158] The soul of the deceased had to pass through the spheres of the different planets and their ruling powers. Who these were, how this was done, and how the condition of the blessed was conceived were questions answered differently in the different cults (see esp. Gnosticism below, pp. 309-12).[159] Under the form of solar monotheism the astral religion received the patronage of the Roman emperors in the third century (see pp. 316-17).

Aspects of this astral theology have left a permanent cultural deposit: our names for the planets are the English form of the Latin equivalent of the Greek gods that were identified with the Babylonian deities. The seven-day week, with the days named for the seven planets supposed to preside over each, estab-

156. M. P. Nilsson, "The Origin of Belief among the Greeks in the Divinity of the Heavenly Bodies," *HTR* 33 (1940):1-8.

157. G. B. Caird, *Principalities and Powers* (Oxford, 1956), chap. 3; G. H. C. MacGregor, "Principalities and Powers: The Cosmic Background of Paul's Thought," *NTS* 1 (1954):17-28.

158. For this development and astral mysticism in general see Cicero's "Dream of Scipio," in *On the Republic* 6.13ff.

159. Alan F. Segal, "Heavenly Ascent in Hellenistic Judaism, Early Christianity and Their Environment," *ANRW* II, *Principat*, 23.2 (Berlin, 1980), 1333-94; James Tabor, *Things Unutterable: Paul's Ascent to Paradise in its Greco-Roman, Judaic, and Early Christian Contexts* (New York, 1986).

lished itself in the Roman world in the first century B.C. Christianity with its seven-day Jewish week confirmed this division of time.[160]

Greek Contributions to Astrology. Babylonia provided the starting point for astrology: the identification of the heavenly bodies with a special god and transfer of the attributes of this god to the heavenly body. This identification was the basis for astrological fortune-telling. On the other hand, astral religion was not astrology, and several features of Hellenistic-Roman astrology cannot be found in Babylonia: in particular that the movements of the heavenly bodies control earthly events up to the smallest detail. This is the defining characteristic of astrology, yet it has no early Babylonian evidence.[161] That omens could be obtained from heavenly signs is different, and the Greeks did this too. Whether the stars caused or signified events was crucial in the debate over astrology.

Furthermore, the Greek order of the planets and not the Babylonian (e.g., giving the sun and not the moon the first importance) is the presupposition of the astrological systems. The systematic development and mathematical exactitude given to the Babylonian basis, moreover, was the work of Greek science. Egyptian contributions to astrology seem to be minimal, but it was Greeks living in Egypt who seem to have had the major role in its development.

To what extent Stoic philosophy influenced the development is debated. The doctrine of universal sympathy, especially as developed by Posidonius (pp. 361-63), plus the determinism of Stoicism (pp. 359-60) would have been congenial to astrology and could have been used to defend it.

Characteristics of Astrology. Astrology remained doubleminded in antiquity: both scientific and religious. It appeared as scientific, and the ancients failed to make a distinction between astronomy and astrology. Astronomy was a popular science because of its importance in agriculture and sailing. This fact plus the belief that the stars influenced the weather prepared the ground for the rule of astrology. Giving the stars the names of gods introduced the mythological element into astrology. It was the character of the respective deities that determined the kind of influence the different planets exercised over human beings. The modern revival of astrology avoids this completely discredited connection with pagan religion that was the original basis for the system.

The worldview with which astrology worked was developed in the Hellenistic age (third–second century B.C.). The celestial world was divided into two regions. The highest was the sphere of the fixed stars, which did not move in relation to each other. The lower region was that of the seven planets. Their order varied in different lists, but from the second century B.C. it was established

---

160. F. H. Colson, *The Week* (Cambridge, 1926); W. Rordorf, *Sunday* (Philadelphia, 1968). See p. 318n.263.

161. M. P. Nilsson, "The Origin of Belief among the Greeks in the Divinity of the Heavenly Bodies," *HTR* 33 (1940):1-8, contra Cumont.

as Saturn (farthest from the earth), Jupiter, Mars, the Sun, Venus, Mercury, and the Moon (nearest the earth). Astrology divided the heavens into twelve compartments ruled over by twelve constellations; hence the twelve signs of the zodiac. It made the sublunary world subject to the influence of the heavenly bodies. The universe was thought of as something like a giant machine whose wheels are geared into each other; if one knew the movements of one wheel, the rest could be calculated.

Astrological ideas and symbolism were so pervasive that Judaism, although generally resistant to astrological beliefs, was yet influenced by imagery drawn from astrology.[162] The presence of the zodiac and the representation of the sun god in his chariot in synagogue floor mosaics from early Byzantine times (as at Hammath Tiberias [illustration, p. 507] and Beth Alpha) reflect an openness to astrological symbols in some circles, if only to the extent of affirming the subordination of the stars and the natural order to God and his law.[163] Such representations of the sun, stars, and seasons were part of the common iconography of the time, so the artists knew no other way of representing these heavenly bodies and cosmic forces. Since Jews regarded the temple as a symbol of the universe, the presence of cosmic symbols agrees with the many temple motifs in synagogues. (An alternative interpretation relates the twelve signs of the zodiac in Jewish art to the twelve tribes of Israel.) An earlier Jewish interest in astrology is attested by the *Treatise of Shem* (first century B.C.).[164]

Astrological Determinism. Astrology provided the ultimate justification for an absolute determinism. It applied the law of causality strictly and without exceptions. This fatalism affected many in the ancient world. That it should have been a source of religious feeling is surprising to the modern rationalistic mentality. Yet our picture of astrology as oppressive is overdrawn by the false psychological reasoning of "how I would feel." The ordinary Greek was always something of a fatalist, but his attitude was to accept this and go on anyway. To escape fate was not an overruling desire (but see above, p. 176 and below, pp. 241-43). Astrology, by strengthening a feeling of dependence, was a source of piety. The eagerness to surrender to fate inspired a devotion of submission to destiny. Some, as Tiberius, "fully convinced that everything is ruled by Fate, neglected the practice of religion" (Suetonius, *Life of Tiberius* 69). Probably most regarded the planetary powers as gods who could be appeased like the rest. A few, like Vettius Valens, deciding that the traditional religion was useless, found in fate a substitute religion. For him absolute determinism gave emotional sat-

162. James H. Charlesworth, "Jewish Astrology in the Talmud, Pseudepigrapha, the Dead Sea Scrolls, and Early Palestinian Synagogues," *HTR* 70 (1977):183-200.

163. Rachel Hachlili in "The Zodiac in Ancient Jewish Art," *Bulletin of American Schools of Oriental Research* 228 (1977):61-77, understands the mosaics as representing a liturgical calendar as a reminder of religious duties.

164. Translation by J. H. Charlesworth in *The Old Testament Pseudepigrapha* (Garden City, N.Y., 1983), 1:473-86.

isfaction and aroused an almost mystical feeling. Knowing that everything was already predetermined gave one a sense of freedom from anxiety and a sense of salvation (in this case, escape). Knowing that fate ruled all removed uncertainty:

> Whoever takes the trouble to learn about the future and to know the truth will possess his soul in freedom from this servitude, disregarding Chance *[Tychē]* and assigning no importance to Hope, not fearing death and living without distraction, having disciplined his soul to courage, and neither rejoicing over good fortune nor depressed by misfortune, but giving himself contentedly to the present. Since he does not long for things beyond his reach, he bears what is decreed for him with self-discipline and, renouncing both pleasures and penalties, becomes a good soldier of Fate. For it is impossible by means of prayer or sacrifice to overcome the destiny fixed from the beginning. . . . What has been assigned to us will happen without our praying for it, what is not fated will not happen for our prayers. So we too must don the masks and play as Fate requires of us, and accept the parts which time's conjunctions bring about, even when they do not suit us. (Vettius Valens 5.9.2)[165]

Words for Fate. Three words were used in Greek to express aspects of the English word *fate.* The Homeric word was *moira,* one's "appropriate share" (see p. 156); it was replaced in Hellenistic times by *tychē,* "chance" or "luck," a word referring to the change of destiny and not just the course of events.[166] The Hellenistic age was a time of rapid changes of fortune, and *tychē* described this capricious, erratic aspect of life. It could be neither controlled, predicted, nor understood. *Tychē* (like many other qualities and abstractions; see p. 176) was personified as a female goddess and worshiped. Cities especially were personified by their *Tychē* or *Fortuna. Tychē* was a popular deity, for her rule was universal. To worship unpredictable and capricious "luck" might seem inconsistent, yet it was an old Greek idea that one's skill counted for something and "luck" could be good or bad. Even more inconsistent might appear the practice of religion in the face of a belief in determinism, yet even this apparent contradiction was maintained. *Heimarmenē,* the word for fate in the astrological sense of determinism, referred to the chain of events linked as cause and effect so that they must happen. The Stoics used it for their view of determinism, and then it was used for the control exercised by the heavenly bodies. Pseudo-Apuleius defined it as necessity (*Asclepius* 39-40).

Several deities claimed power over or to be dispensers of fate. The mys-

---

165. Translation adapted from F. C. Grant, *Hellenistic Religions* (New York, 1953), 61-62.

166. Pliny, *Natural History* 2.22; Luther Martin, "The Rule of Tyche and Hellenistic Religion," *Society of Biblical Literature 1976 Seminar Papers,* ed. George MacRae (Missoula, Mont., 1976), 453-59.

tery religions offered their initiations as guaranteeing ultimate superiority over fate. Some Aristotelian philosophers found a solution to the problems posed by fate through saying that bodily existence is subject to destiny but the soul is free. Fate was one of the principal targets of Christian apologetics.[167] Here, as so often, the apologists followed philosophical arguments already used against the concept of fate.[168]

BIBLIOGRAPHY

Diodorus Siculus 2.2-31.

Cicero. *On Fate.*

Manilius. *Astronomica.*

Vettius Valens. *Anthologies.*

Seneca the Elder. *Suasoriae* 4.26.

Plutarch. *On Chance.*

Ps.-Plutarch. *On Fate.*

[Ps.?] Lucian, *On Astrology.*

Sextus Empiricus. *Against Mathematicians* 5 *(Against Astrologers)I.*

Alexander of Aphrodisias. *On Fate.* Text, translation, and commentary by R. W. Sharples. London, 1983.

Firmicus Maternus. *Mathesis.* Translated by Jean Rhys Bram. *Ancient Astrology: Theory and Practice.* Park Ridge, N.J., 1975.

Bouche-Leclercq, A. *L'Astrologie grecque.* Paris, 1889. Reprint. Brussels, 1963.

Cumont, F. *Astrology and Religion among the Greeks and Romans.* London, 1912.

Amand, D. *Fatalisme et liberté dans l'antiquité grecque.* Louvain, 1945.

Greene, W. C. *Moira, Fate, Good and Evil in Greek Thought.* Cambridge, Mass., 1948.

Cramer, F. H. *Astrology in Roman Law and Politics.* Philadelphia, 1954.

Neugebauer, O., and H. B. van Hoesen. *Greek Horoscopes.* Philadelphia, 1959.

Gundel, W., and H. G. Gundel. *Astrologumena: Die astrologische Literatur in der Antike.* Wiesbaden, 1966.

Lindsay, Jack. *Origins of Astrology.* New York, 1971.

Barton, Tamsyn. *Ancient Astrology.* London, 1994.

Death and the Afterlife

Funerary Rites. Two basic notions influenced ancient customs related to the deceased: (1) death brought pollution and demanded acts of purification; (2) to leave a corpse unburied had unpleasant repercussions on the departed soul.

---

167. Justin, *Apology* 1.43-44; Bardesanes, *The Book of the Laws of Countries* (or *Concerning Fate*).

168. Cicero, *On Fate;* Ps.-Plutarch, *On Fate.*

The funeral was on the day of death. The body was prepared for disposal by washing, anointing, clothing, and crowning with flowers. There followed lamentations, beating of breasts, pulling hair, and the wailing of the *aulos*. The essential rite involved throwing a little earth on the corpse (the minimum requirement when nothing more in the way of burial could be done). Even in cremations, a small part of the body was cut off for burial. The Greeks had sacrifices and meals for the dead on the third, seventh or ninth, and thirtieth day after the death; the Romans had a funeral meal on the day of burial (Lat. *silicernium*), on the ninth day, on the deceased's birthday, and annually on his birthday. There were also annual commemorations of all the dead at the festivals of *Parentalia* (Feb. 13-21) and *Lemuria* (May 9, 11, and 13). The graves, whether for inhumation or the remains of cremation, were equipped with holes or pipes through which food and drink could be poured down directly on the burial. Grave goods were deposited with the deceased to honor them and make them feel at home in the afterlife. The cult of the dead was not "worship" (p. 156) but had multiple purposes: it provided that the dead survived in memory (to be remembered was an important aspiration of the ancient world), and it appeased the spirits of the dead, and sought to ensure the comfort and refreshment of the deceased. Sacrifices on behalf of the dead, the funeral meal, and meals in commemoration of the dead were distinct but might blend these purposes. Wills of those who could afford it set up endowments to provide offerings of food, drink, and flowers. The poor banded together in burial clubs (see the "associations of the poor," p. 144) to provide for their burial and minimum remembrance.

The funerary meals were continued in Christianity, but with significant differences. The church provided for the family, especially for its martyrs; Christians met on the anniversary of the person's death, not of his birth (death was for the Christians the "birthday of immortality"); and the meal became a eucharist or love-feast.

Jewish funerary customs had many similar features.[169] The corpse was prepared for burial by anointing (Shabbath 23.5), washing (Acts 9:36-37), and wrapping in shrouds (John 19:39-40; Kilaim 9.4; b. Moed Katan 8b). Candles were lit at the head or feet of the corpse (Berakoth 8.6). Burial occurred before dark, on the day of death if possible. The bereaved employed professional pipers and wailers (Mark 5:38-39; Ketuboth 4.4). After the burial there was a ceremony of consolation. Mourning customs continued, with decreasing intensity, for seven days, thirty days, and a year.

Cremation or Inhumation.[170] Cremation was the normal practice in the

---

169. The extracanonical tractate Semahoth: see M. Higger, *Treatise Semahot* (New York, 1931), and D. Zlotnick, *The Tractate "Mourning"* (New Haven, 1966).

170. For this section I follow A. D. Nock, "Cremation and Burial in the Roman Empire," *HTR* 25 (1932):321-59 (*Essays*, 277-307).

JEWISH OSSUARIES
At the beginning of the Christian era secondary burial was common
among the Jews. After the body decayed, the bones were gathered
in stone containers for reburial. *(Dominus Flevit, Jerusalem)*

Roman world from 400 B.C. through the first century A.D. The Greek world
practiced cremation and inhumation side by side. Inhumation increased during the reign of Hadrian until by the mid–third century it had won its way
throughout the provinces. The change in the Roman world to inhumation
seems not to have been due to religion or to ideas of the afterlife, but may simply have been one of "fashion." Sarcophagi began to appear during the reign of
Trajan, and burial in these sculptured stone coffins (p. 248) offered the moderately rich a means of ostentation. Acceptance of inhumation among the poor
established it as the dominant custom. It could, moreover, have been felt to be a
more respectful way of laying to rest the habitation of the self and more appropriate to an individual's enjoyment of a blissful hereafter.

In the Semitic area burial was the usual practice. Often after the body decayed the bones were dug up for permanent preservation (secondary burial), a
very old practice in Palestine. Many small stone ossuaries for this purpose have
been uncovered from the late first century B.C. and the first century A.D.[171] In

---

171. Eric M. Meyers, "Secondary Burials in Palestine," *BA* 33 (1970):2-29; idem, *Jewish Ossuaries: Reburial and Rebirth* (Rome, 1971); P. Figueras, *Decorated Jewish Ossuaries* (Leiden, 1983);

Jewish thought the decay of the flesh had an atoning effect, and when it decomposed the soul of the deceased was finally at peace.[172] The secondary burial of the bones a year after death marked the end of the period of mourning by members of the family. To gather up the bones of the deceased could even be described as a day of joy,[173] presumably because of the end of the time of mourning. Niches hewn out of walls of caves were common burial sites in first-century Palestine. There are numerous examples of burial caves closed by a huge stone over the entrance, as in the tombs of Lazarus and Jesus (John 11:38; Mark 16:3-4). Graves in a field were marked to prevent a passer-by from becoming ritually defiled (Matt. 23:27).[174]

Among the Magi in Persia was the custom of exposing the body to be consumed by birds; considered strange to the Mediterranean world, this custom was due to a concern not to pollute either the earth or fire with a dead body.

Types of Tombs and Memorials. The last resting place of the dead took many forms. After cremation the ashes and burnt bones were placed in receptacles of various kinds and set up in tombs or buried in the earth. In inhumations the body might be placed directly in the earth or in coffins of marble, stone, terra-cotta, lead, or wood. These were then placed in chamber tombs, under tumuli, alongside the road, or in the earth. The dead were not buried within the city, so most cemeteries were found alongside roadways outside the city.

The simplest cremation or inhumation tombs were holes in the ground with a standing stone or large clay pot as a marker. Sometimes the body was enclosed in tiles or bricks set gable-wise in the ground. *Columbaria* is the name given to large tombs, wholly or partly underground, whose walls contain niches for the urns or chests in which the ashes of the dead were placed. Walled funerary enclosures open to the sky and housing several burials were a feature of the urban cemeteries in Italy. Some burial chambers, part subterranean and part above ground, were made to resemble the appearance of houses. The exteriors were austere, but the interiors were richly painted. The larger ones contained rooms for the funerary cult and family or club gatherings. The most wealthy

---

B. R. McCane, "Bones of Contention? Ossuaries and Reliquaries in Early Judaism and Christianity," *The Second Century* 8 (1991):235-46; L. Y. Rahmani, *A Catalogue of Jewish Ossuaries in the Collection of the State of Israel* (Jerusalem, 1994) (there are many in other collections).

172. Steven Fine, "A Note on Ossuary Burial and the Resurrection of the Dead in the First Century Jerusalem," *JJS* 51 (2000):67-76 connects the ossuaries with the economic impetus of Herod's rebuilding of the temple and the presence of well-trained artisans for its construction and not with a belief in resurrection or in atonement.

173. m. Mo'ed Qatan 1.5. See Byron R. McCane, "'Let the Dead Buy Their own Dead': Secondary Burial and Matt 8:21-22," *HTR* 83 (1990):31-43, who interprets the passage as reflecting the practice of secondary burial.

174. Samuel Tobias Lachs, "On Matthew 23:27-28," *HTR* 68 (1975):385-88.

GRAVE STELE, 4th c. B.C.
Such touching farewell scenes were common on early Hellenistic
funerary monuments. (© Vanni/Art Resource, NY)

built expensive mausolea above ground. These large circular or polygonal structures continued into Christian architecture, mainly in martyria. Large rooms
might be dug out underground *(hypogea)*. This practice provided a point of departure for the Jewish and Christian catacombs, which were burial sites and not
places of assembly or refuge. Burial holes *(loculi)* were cut into the walls of underground galleries and rooms. Some of the catacombs became quite large as
new passageways on different levels and in different directions were dug out.

A type of monument designed to win gratitude and remembrance for the
deceased was the exedra with a bench along the wall where passers-by could
rest. A common type of memorial was the grave altar *(cippus)*. Portrait reliefs
were often sculptured in shallow niches or placed on free-standing stelae.
Scenes of the deceased in everyday life were shown on some stelae. A particularly touching type of tombstone from Greece was the farewell scene, in which
one person clasps hands with the deceased, shown seated and often surrounded by his family. Also common is a portrayal of the funerary meal.

Scenes of everyday life frequently decorated the sarcophagi. Many funerary representations look backward to the dead person's life rather than forward
to his destiny.[175] Other common scenes shown on the sarcophagi were representations of qualities the deceased possessed or depictions of the joys of paradise (commonly in the form of Dionysiac revels). Many of the themes in funerary art were common in ordinary decorative art and may not carry symbolic
significance, although this is often claimed — such motifs as erotes, four seasons, battles with giants and centaurs, and hunting. Nevertheless, scenes from
mythology were most common, and of these three themes predominate —
death, love, and heroic achievements.[176] The "eastern" free-standing sarcophagi were carved on four sides and so may have stood in the open air along
roadsides or within the walls of a cemeterial precinct; the "western" type with
uncarved backs were placed in tombs against the wall or in niches.

Tomb markers often carried epitaphs and are a major source of surviving
inscriptions. The epitaphs reflect the desire to be remembered, and are often
worded in such a way as to seem to be an attempt to stay in conversation with
the living. Some, as noted, serve as warnings and pronounce curses on anyone
disturbing the grave. All possible moods in the face of death are reflected. The
epitaphs repeatedly emphasize the fact of death, although some feign indifference or trivialize it. The formula "I was not, I was, I am not, I care not" was
common enough that the Latin was simply abbreviated N F F N S N C *(non fui,
fui, non sum, non curo)*. Some faced death with resignation: the affirmation of
the democratic nature of death, "No one is deathless" (a sentiment as old as

---

175. A. D. Nock, "Sarcophagi and Symbolism," *AJA* 50 (1946):140-70 (*Essays*, 627) in review
of F. Cumont, *Recherches sur le symbolisme funéraire des romains*.

176. For religious themes from mythology see Michael Koortbojian, *Myth, Meaning, and
Memory on Roman Sarcophagi* (Berkeley, 1995).

Homer), was not necessarily a denial of immortality, but an acceptance that one does not live forever. Some epitaphs reflect a gloomy view, but the Hellenistic-Roman period was probably not any gloomier than other times. Menander's phrase that "those whom the gods love die young" reflects an early Greek idea that it is best not to be born and second best to die young.[177] A quiet confidence in the face of death and beliefs in various kinds of afterlife also find expression. To the latter we turn in the next section.

An extensive consolation literature was produced in Hellenistic and Roman times, much of it indebted to the now lost treatise of Crantor, *On Grief.* This literature is represented by Cicero, *Tusculan Disputations,* and Plutarch, *Letter to Apollonius.*

Afterlife. Death was defined as the separation of body and soul (however defined — see further below).[178] Two strands of thought were present in reference to the location of the dead. On one hand, the remains (whether buried, burned, or exposed) were localized in a particular place, important as the spot where the loved ones took their leave of the dead and where honor was appropriately shown to them. On the other hand, there was the possibility that the departed passed into a new plane of existence.

The belief that the departed lived on in the tomb is reflected in giving it the name "eternal house," in constructing tombs and the interior of sarcophagi to resemble a home, and in the offerings of food and drink placed in the tomb.

Quite widespread among Mediterranean peoples was the belief that the dead gather in a great cavity under the earth; the Hebrew *sheol,* Greek *hadēs,* and Latin *inferi* were basically the same conception. In earliest times no differentiation was made among the dead, who continued in a shadowy prolongation of human life in the same circumstances they had in human society. The "shades" *(repha'im)* of the Old Testament are similar to the "souls" in Homer. Orphic teaching modified the old Greek tradition and introduced distinct departments into the underworld. The resultant Greek view (cf. Ps.-Plato, *Axiochus* 371A-72) passed to the Romans and is seen in developed form in Virgil's *Aeneid,* Book 6. The souls or shades of the deceased are led by Hermes to the depths of the earth and in a provisional abode await a decision concerning their eternal lot. They cross the river Styx, conducted by the boatman Charon, and come to the court that judges them. The guilty are sent down the road to the left, which leads to dark Tartarus, the place of punishment (cf. 2 Pet. 2:4); the pious are led down the road on the right to the Elysian Fields, where all is bright and beautiful. The Orphics and Pythagoreans gave the specific content to these two places and assigned everyone to one place or the other.

177. Menander, *Sentences* 583; cf. Plutarch, *Letter to Apollonius* 27 (*Moralia* 115D-E); Theognis, *Elegies* 425; Sophocles, *Oedipus at Colonna* 1225; Cicero, *Tusculan Disputations* 1.48 (115). For death as the best gift of the gods see the stories collected in Plutarch, *Letter to Apollonius* 14 (*Moralia* 108F-109D).

178. Cicero, *Tusculan Disputations* 1 summarizes different interpretations of the soul.

Philosophical thought combined with the astral religion to transfer the abode of souls, clearly distinguished and now separated from bodies, to the celestial regions to enjoy immortality in the regions of either the moon, sun, or stars (pp. 238-39). The persistence of the idea of punishment and a separation of the virtuous from the wicked divided the atmosphere into upper and lower regions so that the whole of the former subterranean world was transported above the earth's surface. Cicero in the "Dream of Scipio" located the abode of blessed souls in the zone of the constellations.[179] That piece is a good description of the worldview of the time as well as of the afterlife (p. 381n.97).

A compromise was finally reached between these views. The celestial world became the home of the virtuous, whose spirits arose through the planetary spheres to the Supreme Being to dwell in luminous bliss, and the netherworld became the abode of the wicked, who were cast down to subterranean darkness in order to suffer eternal chastisement. An intermediate purgatory provided a posthumous purification for those stained with pardonable transgressions. The bliss of the righteous was commonly depicted under one of three images: repose or rest, a celestial banquet, or the vision of God. The threefold division of the universe and of souls was transmitted by antiquity to the Christian Middle Ages, providing the framework for Dante's *Divine Comedy*.

Outside of some Jews and the Christians, the only people of the ancient world to believe in a resurrection of the flesh were the Zoroastrians of Persia. Their typical teaching included the appearance of the good or evil conscience after death, the passing over a bridge, and the ultimate resurrection of the flesh and the kingdom of righteousness. (We will consider Jewish views of the afterlife in Chap. 5, pp. 554-55).

BIBLIOGRAPHY

Virgil. *Aeneid* 6.
Lucian. *On Funerals. Menippus or the Descent into Hades. The Ferry-Boat or the Tyrant. Charon or the Inspectors.*

Cumont, Franz. *After Life in Roman Paganism.* New Haven, 1922.
Richmond, I. A. *Archaeology and After-life in Pagan and Christian Imagery.* London, 1950.
Cullmann, O. *Immortality of the Soul or Resurrection of the Dead?* London, 1958.
Lattimore, Richmond. *Themes in Greek and Latin Epitaphs.* Urbana, Ill., 1962.
Dietrich, B. C. *Death, Fate, and the Gods.* London, 1965.
Stendahl, K., ed. *Immortality and Resurrection.* New York, 1965.
Hoffmann, Paul. *Die Toten in Christus: Eine religionsgeschichtliche und exegetische Untersuchung zur paulinischen Eschatologie.* Münster, 1966.
Toynbee, J. M. C. *Death and Burial in the Roman World.* Ithaca, N.Y., 1971.
Vermeule, Emily. *Greek Attitudes Toward Death.* Berkeley, 1979.

179. *On the Republic* 6.13ff.

Bremmer, Jan. *The Early Greek Concept of the Soul.* Princeton, 1983.

Garland, R. *The Greek Way of Death.* London, 1985.

Morris, I. *Death-Ritual and Social Structure in Classical Antiquity.* Cambridge, 1992.

Davies, Jon. *Death, Burial, and Rebirth in the Religions of Antiquity.* London, 1999.

Bremmer, Jan. *The Rise and Fall of the Afterlife.* New York, 2003.

Peres, Imre. *Griechische Grabinschriften und neutestamentliche Eschatologie.* Tübingen, 2003.

GREEK MYSTERIES AND EASTERN RELIGIONS

The mystery religions have occupied such an important place in the study of Christian origins that we will deal with them in a separate subdivision. They are placed here because they are being treated as part of "personal religion." Many of them, however, were bound to the traditional civic cult. Nothing was more official than the mysteries of Eleusis near Athens, Panamara in Caria, and Andania in the Peloponnesus (discussed below) and others such as of Apollo at Cyrene. Nonetheless, receiving initiation in a mystery was usually a matter of individual choice — although the initiation ceremony itself was collective, not individual — and so was a significant expression of personal religion. The great importance of the mysteries is seen in the words of a slave in a comedy by Theophilus (fourth century B.C.), who said his master conferred on him three benefits: knowledge of Greek customs, ability to read, and initiation in mysteries.

Mysteries were native to Greece, but many of the eastern cults adopted mystery initiations when they entered the Greek world, so this unit will provide the best place to introduce the cults from the east that attained international importance in Hellenistic-Roman times, becoming especially prominent from Flavian times onward. The eastern cults experienced progressive Hellenization in the Greek world and Romanization in the west. The Hellenization of a cult was a cultural matter; Romanization was largely a political matter.

The Greeks used the words *mystēria* and *teletē* without our present (valid) distinction between "mysteries" and other sacred ceremonies. In general Greek did not have technical terms that did not also continue their general meanings. *Mystērion* (sing.) meant "secret rite" but had the added sense of "something secret" without any ceremonial associations. It could be used of any secret — philosophy, magic, alchemy, even sexual intercourse ("the mysteries of Aphrodite") — and sometimes seems to be nothing more than a figure of speech. The verb *(myeō)* in the passive often means "to be initiated." The idea of secrecy is more prominent than in *teletē* ("performance" or "sacred rite"), but is not absolutely necessary. The Greeks had many annual or periodic ceremonies that were conducted in an atmosphere of secrecy and solemnity. "Mystery" is being used here in its technical sense of a secret cult in which the uninitiated could not participate. Initiation was an objective, not a subjective, experience; while other ceremonies could be repeated as needed when a person wished to be freed from defilement, initiation was received once for all. The important thing was, as Aristotle said, "not to learn, but to experience and be put into a state" *(diatethetai).*[180] We may define "mystery" as used here as a secret rite by which selected individuals were brought into a special relationship with a deity and assured of certain benefits. An initiate was given the special protection of the divinity by means of the ceremonies themselves, which worked automatically, and these ceremonies and their privileges were the exclusive property of a small group.

Authors ancient and modern classify three elements in the rites of initiation: (1) "things enacted" *(dromena),* (2) "things said" *(legomena),* and (3) "things shown" *(deiknymena)* — the most important part of the ceremony. These differed in each cult. Since they constituted the secret that gives the name "mysteries" to these cults, modern scholars are largely left to conjecture from tantalizing clues what may have been involved in each cult.

The mysteries may be classified into the local and the universal. At the beginning of the Christian era a number of local mysteries, some of great antiquity, flourished in Greece and Asia Minor. In the first century A.D. the only mysteries whose extension may be called universal were the mysteries of Dionysus and those of the eastern gods, especially Isis.

BIBLIOGRAPHY

Turchi, N. *Fontes mysteriorum aevi hellenistici.* Rome, 1930.

Meyer, M. W. *The Ancient Mysteries: A Sourcebook.* San Francisco, 1987. Reprinted 1999.

The series *Etudes préliminaires aux religions orientales dans l'Empire romain,* edited by M. J. Vermaseren, has many pertinent titles, some of which will be listed in the bibliographies to specific cults below.

Nock, A. D. "Mysteries." In *Encyclopedia of the Social Sciences,* edited by E. R. A. Seligman. New York, 1930. 11:172-75.

Nock, A. D. *Conversion.* Oxford, 1933. Reprinted Baltimore, 1998.

Cumont, Franz. *Oriental Religions in Roman Paganism.* Chicago, 1911. Reprint. New York, 1956. Translated from *Les religions orientales dans le paganisme romain.* 4th ed. Paris, 1929.

Bianchi, Ugo. *The Greek Mysteries.* Iconography of Religions, Section 17.3. Leiden, 1976.

Burkert, Walter. *Ancient Mystery Cults.* Cambridge, Mass., 1987.

Turcan, Robert. *The Cults of the Roman Empire.* Oxford, 1996. (Trans. of *Le Cultes Orientaux dans le monde Romain,* 1992.)

---

180. Aristotle, Frg. 15, from Synesius, *Dion* 10; for the thought cf. Dio Chrysostom, *Discourses* 12.33.

Metzger, Bruce. "A Classified Bibliography of the Graeco-Roman Mystery Religions 1924–1973 with a supplement 1978–1979." *ANRW* II, *Principat*, 17.3. Berlin, 1984. Pp. 1259-1423.

Local Mysteries

Mysteries in Greece were in earlier times dedicated to Demeter. The original Greek mysteries were rooted in the soil and related to the cycle of nature. Most of the local mysteries (a neglected aspect of the much studied mysteries) did not go beyond rites to assure fertility, safety, or the like.

An example of a local mystery was that of Panamara in southwest Asia Minor. This mystery was attached to the soil, dedicated to the deity of the city, of limited extension, and promised only terrestrial benefits. The Carians from early times worshiped a Zeus Warrior, and Zeus Panamaros appears in this form. As the native male god was Hellenized under the name Zeus, so his consort was Hellenized under the name of Hera. There were two sorts of festivals: the *komyria* reserved for men, and the *heraia* reserved for women. The essential element of the mystery was a sacred banquet (itself constituting the mystery) to which the divinity was invited to rejoice with his worshipers, who sacrificed oxen, chanted hymns, and together drank wine. The priest of Zeus officially invited the inhabitants of neighboring cities to come and pray to the god and receive initiation. The invitations do not exclude foreigners nor slaves and thus show the tendency to universalism in the religious sentiment of the first century, not characteristic of earlier times.

A long inscription dated 92/91 B.C. from Andania in the southwestern Peloponnesus gives the regulations for the external affairs of the Andanian mysteries. These regulations pertain to oaths, clothing, order of the procession, officials, management of funds, animals for sacrifice, musicians and dancers, use of the sacred area, and the sacred meal, but of course reveal nothing about the secret initiations themselves.[181]

A local mystery that acquired considerable fame and was even transplanted to other sites in Hellenistic and early Roman times was that of the "Mother of the gods" and the Cabiri at Samothrace.[182] Known as the "Great gods" by the Greeks, the Cabiri were non-Hellenic deities worshiped at several spots on the mainland and islands of the Aegean. Their numbers varied, but more frequently they were a pair and by Roman times they were often confused

---

181. English translation in Marvin Meyer, *The Ancient Mysteries: A Sourcebook* (San Francisco, 1987, 52-59.

182. K. Lehman, ed., *Samothrace: A Guide to the Excavations and Museum* (New York, 1960); Susan G. Cole, *Theoi Megaloi: The Cult of the Great Gods at Samothrace* (Leiden, 1983); idem, "The Mysteries of Samothrace during the Roman Period," *ANRW* II, *Principat*, 18.2 (Berlin, 1989), 1564-98.

with the Dioscuri. Like the latter they were general protective deities, particularly of seamen. It is possible, but unknown, that the Cabiri had a connection with the afterlife. Excavations have revealed their principal sanctuary at Samothrace where the mysteries were celebrated, but very little is known about the actual ceremonies. There is abundant evidence of sacrifices, and there was a meeting hall where initiates assembled for the rites. Ritual dances had some part in the ceremony.[183] There would have been the usual pattern of a purification *(myēsis)* followed by the initiation proper, evidently at night. A rigid inquiry was made into what sins the candidate had committed. Such a "confession of sins" was rare in pagan antiquity but became more common in Roman times.[184] Eleusis may have had an influence on the ancient rituals and their interpretation, but Samothrace offered the attraction over Eleusis that one could become both a *mystēs* (initiate) and *epoptēs* (higher grade of initiate) on the same day and at any time of year. Only a small percentage of the initiates, however, received the higher grade of initiation.

Eleusinian Mysteries

The Eleusinian mysteries provide a good transition from the local to the universal mysteries. They were local in the sense that one had to come to Eleusis in order to receive initiation.[185] They were universal in Roman times in being open to all who could come to Eleusis, afford the initiation, and meet the standards of purity. The Eleusinian mysteries are central to this unit because they were the most famous of the Greek mysteries and appear to have exercised a formative influence on the mysteries of the eastern cults.

The rites had originally been the property of one family at Eleusis and then became open to the town's citizens. When Eleusis was absorbed by Athens, the lesser mysteries were added to the greater, and initiation was opened to the people of Attica. With the increase in Athens' influence in the late sixth and fifth centuries the mysteries were opened to all who spoke Greek. They became truly universal after the conquests of Alexander, being expressly made available to citizens of the Roman Republic and then the empire. There was a great increase of interest in initiation at Eleusis from the first century B.C. to the second century A.D. An inscription at the sanctuary there, "All the Greeks to the Goddesses and the Emperor," shows the characteristic association of the imperial cult with the dominant local worship. Syncretism affected Eleusis at the end, for the last known hierophant (leader in the initiation) was also a priest of

---

183. A. D. Nock, "A Cabiric Rite," *AJA* 45 (1941):577-81.

184. Plutarch, *Moralia* 229D and 217C.

185. An Eleusinion built outside Alexandria for its Greek population was the location for erotic dramas. It was not protected by a rule of secrecy, and the church fathers handed down reports, incorrectly it seems, of these performances as elements of the Eleusinian Mysteries.

DEMETER AND PERSEPHONE, 5th c. B.C.
Demeter is seated; Persephone stands facing her.
(© Erich Lessing/Art Resource, NY)

Mithras. Mysteries were held on the site from the fifteenth or fourteenth century B.C. Christian burials of the fifth century A.D. show the site was then no longer in the hands of pagans.

Myth. Behind each of the important mysteries was a cult myth, which was not secret. The *Homeric Hymn to Demeter* has been taken as the official version from Eleusis,[186] but it may relate to the Thesmophoria and similar festivals of women.

Demeter was the Greek grain-goddess. She was a mother-goddess (note the last part of her name) associated with the fertility of the soil, particularly grain. Very early there was associated with her a daughter (Kore or Persephone), who is a younger double of Demeter and seems to have been the power in the grain itself, appearing or disappearing with it.

186. F. R. Walton, "Athens, Eleusis, and the Homeric Hymn to Demeter," *HTR* 45 (1952):105-14.

According to the myth, Hades, the god of the underworld, seized Kore and carried her off to the underworld. Demeter set out on a vain search for her daughter while the crops on earth dried up. Her wanderings brought her to Eleusis where, disguised as an old woman, she was received into the house of the king as a nurse for his son. Demeter put the child into the fire on the hearth each night in order to burn away his mortal nature. She was interrupted one night and so prevented from making him immortal. Demeter revealed herself, and the Eleusinians built her a temple. In return for their hospitality she taught the family of the king the mysteries that would assure a happy immortality and became the greatest boon of the Eleusinians. Meanwhile Zeus had persuaded Hades to allow Kore to return to her mother so that Demeter could return to Olympus and the earth could put forth grain once more. Kore had eaten a pomegranate seed in the other world and hence had to spend four months of each year underground with Hades. The agricultural basis of the myth seems to be the fact that in the Mediterranean world grain is planted in autumn (the time of the Great Mysteries), grows through the winter, and is harvested in the spring (the time of the Lesser Mysteries). During the hot, dry summer it does not grow but must be stored away underground in great grain-jars.

According to another myth Demeter and Persephone sent the Eleusinian hero Triptolemus, who was among the first initiates, to teach the arts of agriculture to the rest of humankind. The sending of Triptolemus on a winged chair is often depicted in art. This particular connection of Demeter and Eleusis with the production of grain, however, is not related to the Eleusinian mysteries proper.

Initiations. While the literary and artistic sources describe the public part of the cult, the initiation was a well-kept secret. There were three "degrees" of initiation: the Lesser Mysteries, the Greater Mysteries *(teletē),* and *epopteia* a year later.

MODEL OF SANCTUARY AT ELEUSIS
The sacred procession entered the sanctuary at the right and moved
to the *telestērion,* the large hall where the initiation into the
Eleusinian Mysteries occurred. *(Eleusis Museum)*

The Lesser Mysteries were carried out at Agrai, on the banks of the Illisos River outside the walls of Athens, in February/March. After 215 B.C. they were celebrated twice in years when a large number of foreigners came. We do not know exactly what took place, but the activities were designed to purify initiates in preparation for the Greater Mysteries. Fasting, sacrifices, sprinkling or bathing in the Illisos, singing of hymns, and bearing a sacred vessel (a firstfruit offering?) are referred to.

The Greater Mysteries in September attracted more attention, and more details of their public aspects are known. Thus, we may describe a day-by-day account from the standpoint of the Athenians.

14th of the month Boedromion: The *hiera* (sacred things) were taken from Eleusis to Athens in large round baskets *(kistai)* and deposited in the Eleusinion of Athens.

15th: The proclamation inviting initiation and stating the conditions marked this as the first day of the celebration proper.

16th: To the cry, "To the sea, O mystai [initiates]!" each candidate went to the ocean carrying a small pig to be washed along with himself. The pig was the principal sacrificial animal used for purification in the worship of Demeter. Its blood was considered capable of purifying whatever was impure in humans, so the pigs were probably sacrificed immediately after the bath in the sea. The application of water was a preliminary cleansing and not the initiation itself.

17th: A sow was officially sacrificed to Demeter and Persephone and prayer was made on behalf of the city.

18th: Those who arrived late made their preparations. Other initiates remained in their houses.

19th: This was the day of the great procession *(pompē)* to Eleusis and was the first day included in the term *mystēria*. Everyone saw this procession, and it is often alluded to in literature and art. The initiates were accompanied by friends and family. They wore festive clothes, were crowned with myrtle, and carried a thyrsus (see p. 261), a staff, and a sack for supplies. Priestesses led the procession carrying on their heads the baskets containing the sacred objects. It was night by the time the festive procession reached Eleusis, so they arrived by torchlight. Even after the fourteen-mile journey from Athens the people were excited enough to spend the rest of the night in singing and dancing.

20th–21st: The day of the twentieth was spent in resting and fasting, for the initiation proper began that night. The fast perhaps ended in drinking *kykeōn* ("mixture" — of barley, water, and mint), which marked the beginning of the initiation. Some of the sacred objects were revealed only to those initiated into the highest degree of *epopteia*. The initiates for the Greater Mysteries left before this ceremony, which may have occurred the following night.

22nd: There were libations and rites for the dead.

23rd: The initiates returned to Athens. With the end of the celebration one's obligations to the sanctuary and the goddesses were ended (except to preserve silence about what took place). There was no brotherhood of *mystai* to which one belonged after initiation. The initiation was individual, and so were its benefits.

Epopteia, the highest grade of initiation, could only be obtained one year after receiving the Greater Mysteries. A person went through the same preliminaries and ceremonies with the other initiates but remained to receive something more. As the name indicates, the chief feature would have been seeing something, and this appears to have been the most holy part of the Greater Mysteries also.

Initiation could be expensive, even for those who lived in Athens. An inscription sets the fee for a slave at fifteen drachmae; one also had to pay the price of the sacrificial animals. But initiation was considered worth the price. There are many ancient testimonies to the blessedness of the initiates at Eleusis. It was apparently the first of the mysteries to offer the promise of a happy afterlife in the underworld to those who received initiation.

The initiation took place in a large initiation hall, the *telestērion,* which differed in its ground plan from a regular Greek temple because it had to accommodate a large crowd of initiates at its services. At its largest the *telestērion* was fifty-four by fifty-two meters. Twenty-two interior columns supported the roof. Along the four walls were tiers of eight stone steps, probably designed for standing rather than sitting. Only initiates and those being initiated were permitted inside the hall. The most sacred part was the *anaktoron,* a small room covering an outcropping of rock. It remained unmoved throughout the seven successive enlargements and rearrangements of the initiation hall. The emperor Marcus Aurelius, who received initiation in 176, became the only layperson to be admitted to the *anaktoron.*

Interpretation. Many have suggested that the initiates participated in a sacred pageant of the story of Demeter and Persephone. Since the myth was presented to all in word and art, it is unlikely that a drama enacting the rape of Persephone or Demeter's search had anything to do with what was forbidden *(aporrhēton)* or the innermost secret *(arrhēton).* The Plutonion, a sanctuary in a cave near the initiation hall, has a hole giving access to an underground staircase, near a stepped platform that could have been used as stands. If this latter was not for the benefit of those watching the procession on the sacred way, then possibly some reenactment of the myth was done here, but not the initiation itself. The *Homeric Hymn* places the abduction of Persephone elsewhere, but the Eleusinians perhaps offered this hole as an alternative site where it occurred and could be restaged. The well beside which Demeter stopped to rest in her search for her daughter was also identified with a well in the sacred precincts. Even less likely as an interpretation of "the things enacted" is the mission of Triptolemus or a sacred marriage.

Due to a total lack of reliable evidence, we have no knowledge of what words might have been said. The suggestions are drawn from unreliable sources or from other cults.

The essential part of the ceremony was making something appear. *Hierophant*, the title given to the priest in charge of the initiation, means "he who makes things appear." He had a large chair that faced the small room (the *anaktoron*) where the *hiera* ("sacred things") were kept. What the hierophant made to appear came from the *anaktoron*. At the climax of the ceremony such a great fire was kindled that the light could be seen from some distance, and in the radiant light the hierophant exhibited the *hiera*. These may have been cult objects from Mycenaean times. A papyrus in Milan has Heracles say, in affirming that he was already initiated, "I have seen the Kore,"[187] implying that initiates saw some vision of the underworld goddess. Some have connected this with Hippolytus's report that cut wheat was shown (*Refutation of All Heresies* 5.8.38-41); however, Hippolytus has confused what was shown in the Phrygian mysteries, and cut wheat appears openly in Eleusinian art. The phallus is even less likely, for it was Dionysiac. Cut wheat, the sacred *kistai,* and poppy flowers (rosette shaped) are common cult emblems in surviving sculpture at Eleusis.

Bibliography

Foley, H. P., ed. *The Homeric* Hymn to Demeter: *Translation, Commentary and Interpretive Essays*. Princeton, 1994.
Cicero. *Laws* 2.36.
Ovid, *Metamophoses* 5.341-550.

Mylonas, George E. *Eleusis and the Eleusinian Mysteries*. Princeton, 1961.
Kerényi, C. *Eleusis: Archetypal Image of Mother and Daughter*. London, 1967.
Zuntz, G. *Persephone*. Oxford, 1971.
Clinton, Kevin. *The Sacred Officials of the Eleusinian Mysteries*. Philadelphia, 1974.
Alderink, L. J. "The Eleusinian Mysteries in Roman Imperial Times," and K. Clinton, "The Eleusinian Mysteries: Roman Initiates and Benefactors, Second Century B.C. to A.D. 267." *ANRW* II, *Principat*, 18.2. Berlin and New York, 1989. Pp. 1457-98, 1499-1539.
Clinton, Kevin. *Myth and Cult: The Iconography of the Eleusinian Mysteries*. Stockholm, 1992.

Dionysiac Mysteries

The Dionysiac mysteries were the only new mysteries of Greek origin that spread widely in Hellenistic-Roman times. They were practiced in general by private associations but under the control of the state. Their celebration was not confined to any one locality: they were very widespread in Asia Minor and the Greek islands but also are attested in Egypt and Italy.

Myth. Dionysus was the son of Zeus and Semele, a mortal. Hera, in her

187. C. Kerényi, *Eleusis: Archetypal Image of Mother and Daughter* (London, 1967), 83-84.

DIONYSUS,
Roman period
The drinking cup
(kantharos) turned
down was a sign
of drunkenness.
(© Alinari/Art
Resource, NY)

jealousy, craftily persuaded Semele to ask her lover to prove his deity by appearing in all his power and glory. Semele induced Zeus to give her whatever she asked for, and so he was tricked into granting a request that he knew would kill her. Zeus's lightning bolts destroyed Semele but made her unborn child immortal. Zeus placed the unborn child (Dionysus) in his thigh, from whence he was born at full term. Hermes then carried the child to a wise old silenus to rear him. After maturing, Dionysus descended to Hades and brought his mother up from the underworld. He gave people the gift of the vine and planted his worship everywhere (cf. this with the Orphic version of the myth recounted above, pp. 162-63). Although two aspects of the myth, the divinizing of Dionysus and his leading his mother from the underworld, could be connected with a belief in immortality, evidence is lacking that there was any enactment of the myth in the Dionysiac mysteries.

General Features. The orgiastic and ecstatic celebrations of Dionysus (Lat. Bacchus) in classical times are known from Euripides' play *The Bacchae*. A period of fasting preceded the winter festival. Weakened by the fasting, the devotees in wild ecstatic dance to the accompaniment of the *aulos* worked themselves into a delirium. In this frenzy, according to the prevalent interpretation, they ate the raw flesh with the blood in it of animals that were seized. Mainly women were affected. Known as maenads, they are depicted in art carrying a torch or a thyrsus (a staff with a pine cone on the end and entwined with vine or ivy leaves) and swirling in dance in the presence of sileni. Since Dionysus was believed to appear in animal form and to be present in the wine, eating the flesh from a living animal and drinking wine could be understood as incorporating the god and his power within.[188] The orgia in the milder form continued into later times and are distinct from the mysteries, which were added in Hellenistic times.

The ecstasy associated with Dionysiac worship evoked resistance from conservatives. The plot of *The Bacchae* revolves around the efforts of a Greek king to resist the introduction of the Dionysiac ecstasy into his realm and the impossibility of resisting the divine will.[189] Rome too at first opposed the spread of Dionysiac worship. An important landmark in the history of the cult and of our knowledge about it is Livy's report of the events surrounding the *senatus consultum* of 186 B.C. suppressing the Bacchanalia.[190] On the basis of charges of immorality and threat to the state the senate sought to confine the mysteries to a few persons acting under state supervision. An accommodation, however, was reached, and by the first century the new mysteries flourished among the wealthy in southern Italy, as inscriptions, wall paintings in villas, re-

188. Cf. Plato's phrase, "eternal drunkenness" (*Republic* 365D).

189. *Bacchae* 795; cf. Acts 26:14. E. R. Dodds, *Bacchae*, 2d ed. (Oxford, 1987).

190. Text and translation in Loeb Classical Library, Latin Series, *Remains of Old Latin*, 4:254-59.

HOUSE OF MYSTERIES, Pompeii
Flagellation followed by ecstatic dance depicted in the hall of paintings may be
related to a Dionysiac ceremony. (© Alinari/Art Resource, NY)

liefs, and decorations on sarcophagi show. The decree itself continued to exert
a negative influence on Roman attitudes toward foreign religions that did not
have official acceptance.

Despite opposition in some circles, Bacchus was very popular and held a
strong place in the imagination of the people. Thousands of images in all sizes
and every artistic medium have been found from all over the Roman influenced world. Dionysus/Bacchus is sometimes shown as an old, bearded man
(the archaic depiction but continued in later times), as youthful (the common
Hellenistic portrayal), and as a child (from the aspects of the myth of his
birth).[191]

An important inscription about the Dionysiac religion comes from Torre
Nova in Tuscany and is dated in the late second century A.D.[192] The inscription
is a record of the subscribers to the erection of a statue to "Agripinilla the

191. V. J. Hutchinson, "The Cult of Dionysus/Bacchus in the Graeco-Roman World: New
Light from Archaeological Studies," *Journal of Roman Archaeology* 4 (1991):222-230.

192. A. Vogliano and F. Cumont, "La grande inscription bachique du Metropolitan Museum," *AJA* 37 (1933):215-70.

SARCOPHAGUS WITH DIONYSIAC SCENES
On the left Dionysus and Ariadne recline in a cart pulled by two centaurs.
Other figures in the Dionysiac entourage include Pan, satyrs,
maenads, and Silenus. *(British Museum)*

priestess." Pompeia Agripinilla possibly learned the Dionysiac mysteries while her husband was proconsul of Asia in 165. The members of the society are probably listed according to their order in the sacred procession. The series of titles is extraordinarily long, but this fits the Greek practice of giving as many persons as possible a title. A family or individual could always found a religious association such as this one. While primarily women originally participated in Dionysiac rites, in time both sexes took part, as here.

Dionysiac worship had wider aspects than the mystery initiations, which is shown by another important inscription from the second century that lists the statutes of a Dionysiac association in Athens (quoted in part in the section on Greek associations, pp. 145-47). They indicate an association that did not differ in essentials from other private Greek clubs with a religious center. It appears primarily as a social and dinner club with burial responsibilities for its members, but presided over by a priest, performing cultic acts, and meeting on the days sacred to Dionysus. Its membership was drawn from the leading citizens of Athens.

Traveling guilds of actors that presented plays throughout the empire were organized as a religious association dedicated to Dionysus. They were considered "sacred" and granted immunity and special protection by the rulers.

Dionysiacs used the term *mysteries* loosely for their dances and for dramatic contests (both of which were public). The dances, masquerades, banquets and accompanying revelry, and singing were the main attraction for many. Nilsson suggests that the Dionysiac mysteries, as shown on the art monuments of well-to-do people in Italy, "appealed to those who loved a pleasant and luxurious life and from education and conservatism kept to the old culture and its religion and yielded less easily to the lure of foreign religions but wanted a little thrill of religion as a spice to the routine of life."[193]

Initiation. When mysteries were added to the Dionysiac cult in the Helle-

193. M. P. Nilsson, "The Bacchic Mysteries of the Roman Age," *HTR* 46 (1953):194-95.

nistic age, they were not hidden in the same secrecy as prevailed in regard to the old mysteries of Demeter. At least it seems that elements of the initiation were freely represented in art that survives from Italy in the early empire. Elements of the initiation may very well have differed from place to place, since the mysteries were added late and there was no central agency dictating uniformity.

The frescoes from the *Villa Item* ("House of the Mysteries") outside Pompeii are quite famous but their interpretation is much disputed, even as to their connection with a Dionysiac ceremony. One reads the pictures from left to right along the north, east, and south walls upon entering the room through the door in the west wall. The first scene shows a woman and a naked boy who is reading from a scroll. This perhaps represents certain instructions about the ritual or its meaning. The next group shows a seated woman, seen from the back, whose left hand uncovers a dish brought by a girl and whose right hand touches another dish in which a girl pours something from a small jug. This is usually interpreted as an offering: the first girl presenting a food offering and the second pouring a libation (or it may be a lustration). There follows a large silenus playing a lyre. A boy or young Pan plays a pipe while a girl (a Panisca) offers her breast to a kid. Next is a terrified woman running away. On the east wall a seated silenus (satyr) holds a bowl into which a boy is peering. Another boy holds a grotesque mask over the head of the silenus. Is the mask reflected from the bowl? Does it indicate that some participants in the initiation wore masks to impersonate sileni? The next group is the central scene, located opposite the entrance. Dionysus and Ariadne preside over the scene. Before them is a kneeling, veiled woman who is removing a covering from the sacred basket (a *liknon*, discussed below). Close to the basket stands a demonic female figure who wears a short cloth around her loins and high boots. She has powerful dark wings and holds in her right hand a staff with which she is ready to strike blows. Nilsson suggests that she represents *Dikē* (goddess of justice) or a personification of punishments in the underworld. The blows are aimed at a woman on the south wall whose back is bared and who kneels with her head in the lap of a seated woman who makes a protecting gesture toward the demon of punishment. After the terror of punishment comes the joyous abandon of celebration. Almost completely naked, the woman swirls in a dance and clashes cymbals above her head. She is the same woman who was whipped, for the scarf that waves around as she dances is the same scarf under her arms in the flagellation scene. She represents now the joyful aspect of the afterlife. In the background is another woman (priestess?) in a dark dress holding a thyrsus.

There are several recurrent features of Dionysiac art, many of which occur in the *Villa Item* frescoes. Most important is the *liknon* (Lat. *vannus*), the sacred wicker basket *(cista mystica)*. Originally an agricultural implement, it was adopted in the new Dionysiac mysteries. Looking into the sacred basket apparently was a central part of the initiation ceremony, but some of the representations show the basket placed on the head of the initiate. The *liknon,* covered with a cloth, was filled with fruit and a phallus. The latter was carried in Dionysiac processions and was a frequent Dionysiac symbol. In an agricultural setting it had been a symbol of fertility, but in the mysteries apparently was a symbol of life-giving power. Other frequently recurring symbols of the Dionysiac cult were dancing maenads, the thyrsus, masks, and satyrs — all from the old orgiastic background.

Infants or small children are sometimes pictured as initiated, unlike what is known from the other mysteries. The background for this practice was the sentimental view of children that began in the Hellenistic age, but the reason for its presence specifically in the Dionysiac mysteries perhaps was the prominence in his myths of Dionysus's childhood, interest in which is attested to by the art. The initiation of children shows that these were not mysteries in the strict sense of being hidden in secrecy. Some have connected the rise of infant baptism in Christianity with the practice of initiating small children as a safeguard against premature death. Probably the most that can be said in this regard is that similar feelings were at work.

The Dionysiac mysteries, it may be inferred, promised a happy afterlife. The ceremonies reminded one of the terror of punishment (Origen, *Against Celsus* 4.10) but presumably offered a life of bliss in the other world. Neither Dionysus nor the initiates were thought of as rising from the dead. Rather, the mysteries removed anxiety about death by depicting life in the other world as a Dionysiac revel. Such seems to be the significance of the many Dionysiac scenes on sarcophagi of the empire.

Bibliography

Homeric Hymn to Dionysus.
Euripides. *The Bacchae.* Translated with introduction and commentary by G. S. Kirk. Cambridge, Eng., 1979.
Livy 39.8-18.
Diodorus Siculus 4.3.3–4.6.5.

Festugière, A. J. "Les mystères de Dionysos." *Revue Biblique* 44 (1935):192ff., 366ff.
Nilsson, M. P. "The Bacchic Mysteries of the Roman Age." *HTR* 46 (1953):175-202. Expanded in *The Dionysiac Mysteries of the Hellenistic and Roman Age.* Lund, 1957.
Herbig, R. *Neue Beobachtungen am Fries der Mysterien-Villa in Pompeji.* Baden-Baden, 1958.
Zuntz, G. "On the Dionysiac Fresco in the Villa dei Misteri at Pompeii." *Proceedings of the British Academy* 49 (1963):177-201.
Matz, F. *Dionysike Telete: Archäologische Untersuchungen zum Dionysoskult in hellenistischer und römischer Zeit.* Wiesbaden, 1964.
Otto, Walter F. *Dionysus: Myth and Cult.* Bloomington, Ind., 1965.

Matz, F. *Die dionysischen Sarkophage*. Die antiken Sarkophag-reliefs, vol. 4, nos. 1-3. Berlin, 1968–1969.

Little, A. M. G. *A Roman Bridal Drama at the "Villa of the Mysteries."* Wheaton, Md., 1972.

Kerényi, C. *Dionysos: Archetypal Image of Indestructible Life*. Princeton, 1976.

Detienne, Marcel. *Dionysos at Large*. Cambridge, Mass., 1989.

Egyptian Deities: Isis, Osiris, and Sarapis

The Egyptian deities were the first of the eastern deities to become important in the Hellenistic world, and during the first two centuries of the common era they were the most popular and widespread of the non-Greek deities. Isis and Osiris were very old Egyptian gods: Osiris was important as the vegetation god and king of the underworld; Isis was his sister and wife and the mother of Horus. She took the leading role in the expansion of the Egyptian cult outside Egypt. The Greeks contributed two ideas of great importance to the success of Isis. They identified her with Demeter (and later with Aphrodite), so making her the most important of the mother goddesses of the Hellenistic world to whom culture and mysteries were attributed. Further, they elevated her to an all-encompassing cosmopolitan deity (although her cult preserved the appeal of the exotic from its Egyptian elements), and the propaganda for her claimed that other goddesses were but manifestations of her (see more below).

The distinguishing features of the artistic depictions of Isis include the Egyptian knot (or Isis knot) in her dress at the bosom, the Egyptian headdress (a disc for the sun, two feathers — symbols of royalty — and two ears of grain), and such cult instruments as the *sistrum* (a type of rattle) and *situla* (a small bucket for water or milk). A common portrayal of Isis shows her suckling sometimes an infant pharaoh or most often the infant Horus (Harpocrates, identified by a finger pointing to his mouth, symbolizing silence), which some have claimed to be the precedent for the Madonna and Child pictures in Christian art.[194]

Sarapis (Lat. Serapis) replaced Osiris in the Greek world. His name originated from Osorapis, a combination of Osiris with Apis, the bull god worshiped at Memphis. Ptolemy I established the cult at Alexandria and supplied Hellenistic features. Modern scholars see the cult, which spread from its famous temple (the Serapeum in Alexandria), as a focus to Ptolemy's Greco-Egyptian empire. Timotheus, an official of Eleusis, played a major role in the introduction of the Sarapis cult. Sarapis was portrayed with the features of Zeus, only with a milder and more kindly appearance (similar to Asclepius), and is often acclaimed on inscriptions as "one Zeus Sarapis." He is distin-

194. This has been disputed by V. Tran Tam Tinh, *Isis Lactans* (Leiden, 1973).

ISIS AND SARAPIS, from Gortys
The attributes of Isis included a rattle *(sistrum)* and Egyptian headdress. Sarapis
iconographically was a combination of Zeus (note the scepter), Asclepius
(a kindlier visage than Zeus), and Hades (the three-headed dog Cerberus,
who guarded the entrance to the underworld). *(Heraklion Museum)*

TEMPLE OF ISIS, Sarapeum C, Delos
The Hellenization of the Egyptian cult is seen in this Greek-style temple,
housing the cult image, with a horned altar in front.

guished from Zeus by his head-piece — identified as a *modius* (a container for measuring grain) or a *calathus* (a basket for carrying fruit), either of which served as a symbol of fertility. Sometimes he appears with Cerberus, the three-headed dog that was the attribute of Hades. Sarapis was a savior god, delivering from danger and healing the sick. In this he took over certain features of the cult of Asclepius.

Also sometimes associated with the Hellenized Egyptian cults were Harpocrates (Horus the child) and Anubis, the jackal or dog-headed god identified with Hermes.

The Sarapis inscriptions on the island of Delos provide a good illustration of how the eastern cults spread in the Greek world.[195] Apollonios, an Egyptian priest, arrived on Delos in the early third century B.C. and conducted worship to Sarapis in rented quarters. The cult grew and his grandson of the same name was commanded by the god in a dream to build an independent temple. The inscription he set up in the last quarter of the third century on a column in the temple (Sarapeum A) tells of the legal obstacles and the successful overcoming of all opposition to the building of the temple. Another private temple was also built (Sarapeum B) with various sodalities attached. The worship of Sarapis became an official civic cult about 180 B.C. and a public temple (Sarapeum C) was built, subscribed to by the private associations but now having priests elected annually in the Greek manner. Immigration and political considerations (in this case the influence of the Ptolemies in the eastern Mediterranean) were frequent factors in the spread of eastern cults. Dream instructions played a particularly prominent role in the cult of Sarapis (for which one may note the accounts in Acts 10:9-32; 16:9 for the importance of dream revelations in the spread of Christianity).

The Egyptian deities were thoroughly Hellenized, at least in externals — the statues, temples, and language — yet maintained the appeal of the foreign in their ceremonies. The Egyptian cults (notably Isis) never lost their Egyptian (foreign) atmosphere. That attracted some but repelled others (the situation of Judaism in this regard was somewhat analogous). The foreign aspects account for the occasional repressions. Authorities in Rome resisted the spread of the Egyptian gods, whose temples had a reputation for immorality.[196] More important was the political purpose: Isis and Sarapis represented the chief rival of Rome — Egypt. Even under the early empire there was fear of Egyptian influence. The Egyptian cult was suppressed repeatedly in the first century B.C. and A.D. A change in the official attitude came when Caligula erected a temple to Isis on the Campus Martius in A.D. 38, but it was only when Domitian made the temple one of Rome's most splendid monuments that Isis and Sarapis be-

---

195. A. D. Nock, *Conversion* (Oxford, 1933), 51ff.

196. Josephus, *Ant.* 18.3.4 (65-80); Ovid, *Art of Love* 1.77-78; Juvenal, *Satires* 6.486-89, 526-41; 9.22-26.

gan to enjoy uninterrupted imperial favor. Their cult had long since penetrated all the major cities.

Greek and Latin authors tended to see the Egyptian religion as either the highest or lowest of religions. On the one hand, they glorified the wisdom of ancient Egypt and said the Greeks had learned philosophy and the mysteries from them;[197] on the other hand, they considered the worship of animal forms the lowest form of religion.[198]

Myth. The myth of Osiris and Isis has been preserved in Hellenized form by Plutarch, *Isis and Osiris* 12-21 (*Moralia* 355D-59D). One must use Plutarch with caution, though; as was typical with philosophers, he gave a philosophical interpretation to the myth and found philosophical meaning in the ceremonies. Thus, we should not confuse Plutarch's use of philosophy with an "Egyptian" theology, despite his claim to derive some of his interpretations from Egyptian priests.

According to the myth, Osiris, after ruling over the Egyptians in a beneficent manner, was plotted against by his brother Set (Gk. Typhon). The latter made a chest and at a banquet promised to give it to anyone who exactly fit into it. As had been planned, when Osiris entered the chest, Set's men closed the chest and threw it into the Nile. Isis set out in search for the chest and her brother-husband. She found it at Byblos on the coast of Phoenicia and brought it back to Egypt. Typhon succeeded in getting possession of the body and cut it up into fourteen parts, which were scattered about Egypt. Isis then went through the country collecting the parts. She recovered all but the genitals, which she replaced by a gold image that was carried in procession. (This seems to combine two different traditions of the death of Osiris — that he was drowned and that he was murdered and dismembered.) Osiris became king of the underworld and helped his son Horus to gain a victory over Typhon. Osiris did not return to this world or experience a resurrection properly speaking; his continued existence was in the netherworld. The burial rites to make the deceased into an Osiris were a preparation for life in the underworld where Osiris ruled.

Ceremonies. There existed from of old in Egypt a sort of liturgical drama of Osiris and the search by Isis, but it does not seem that this was secret. The rites performed on the dead to make them a new Osiris were known only to the priests, and Greek writers used the terminology of mysteries to describe what was strange to them, but these rites applied only to the dead.

---

197. Diodorus Siculus 1.96 and 98. Plutarch, *Isis and Osiris* 9-10 (*Moralia* 354D-F).

198. Cicero, *On the Nature of the Gods* 1.16.43; Lucian, *Parliament of the Gods* 10; *Zeus Rants* 42. Cf. the Jewish and Christian appropriation of this — Josephus, *Against Apion* 1.225, 2.86 and passim; Philo, *Decalogue* 78; *The Contemplative Life* 8; Rom. 1:23; Aristides, *Apology* 12; Theophilus, *To Autolycus* 1.10; Athenagoras, *Plea* 1. See also K. A. D. Smelik, "'Who Knows Not What Monsters Demented Egypt Worships?' Opinions on Egyptian Animal Worship in Antiquity as Part of the Ancient Conception of Egypt," *ANRW* II, *Principat*, 17.4 (Berlin, 1984), 1852-2000.

The two great annual festivals in honor of the Egyptian gods and the daily rites at the temples were public. The great festival was a week-long commemoration at the end of October and beginning of November of the search for and finding of Osiris. It was connected with agriculture, fertility, and the cycle of the seasons. Set (Typhon) was the power of drought, Osiris the rising Nile, Isis the land awaiting the flooding of the waters. The other major annual festival came in early March to mark the opening of the sailing season. At seaports a ship consecrated to Isis was ceremonially launched.

One of the great attractions of the Egyptian cult was its eye appeal. There were daily ceremonies in the morning and evening at the Isis temples, a new feature in Greco-Roman paganism. Each morning the priests opened the temple, sprinkled with sacred Nile water the worshipers who gathered, lit lamps, awakened the goddess, dressed her statue, presented food to her, and chanted litanies. In the evening the temple was closed and the goddess undressed for the night. Processions were also an important part of the Egyptian cult, as may be seen from art monuments and from Apuleius's account of the spring festival (*Metamorphoses* 11). They had the air of a costume parade, but consisted of religious personnel, as follows: women crowned with flowers who scattered other flowers along the way; other women and a mixed company carrying lamps, torches, and candles; musicians playing pipes and a boys' chorus singing a hymn about the procession; the initiates wearing white linen and carrying sistra (the men's heads were clean shaven); priests

EGYPTIAN PROCESSION, relief, 2d c. A.D.
A priestess holding a *sistrum* and *simpulum,* a shaven-headed priest carrying a vessel of Nile water, a priest with falcon headdress, and a priestess with a lotus in her hair and carrying a snake and a *situla* are Egyptian characteristics.
(Gregorian Profane Museum, Vatican)

carrying various emblems of the goddess; and men dressed as various Egyptian deities.[199] Attention was also attracted by the devotees of Isis, on whom the goddess imposed acts of penitence and who bewailed their sins outside the temples.[200]

Some Egyptian temples in the Greek world exemplify a typical Greek temple, as Sarapeum C on Delos. Others show greater accommodation to the distinctive rites of the Egyptian cults. Native Egyptian temples were not just sanctuaries for an image, altar, and offerings, but each was a complex of buildings with facilities for lodging, meals, and other activities.[201] The well-preserved temple compound of Isis at Pompeii includes cells that may have been living quarters for the resident professional priesthood, a cistern for keeping Nile water, and a high platform (reached by a flight of steps) before the entrance to the cella.[202] A wall painting from Herculaneum illustrates either the daily ritual at such a temple or the preparation for a procession. At the top of the steps on the platform before the entrance stands the head priest holding a jar (probably containing Nile water). He is flanked by a priestess holding a sistrum and a situla, by a black priest holding a sistrum, and by two sphinxes. At the foot of the stairs a priest is fanning the flames on a horned and garlanded altar. Two choruses facing each other on the steps are being led in hymns by a priest and accompanied by a black musician playing on a pipe. In Egyptian temples hymns were sung daily by the general public gathered in outer halls. All the priests have shaven heads, and all except some in the choruses wear white linen (cf. Plutarch, *Isis and Osiris* 3-4 [*Moralia* 352C]).

Egyptian temples commonly had dining rooms that could be rented out. Cult meals were common in the religious associations (see pp. 145-47). Invitations to such religious meals have survived on papyri from Egypt. One such reads, "Chaeremon asks you to dine at the couch of the Lord Sarapis in the Sarapeum tomorrow, the 15th, beginning at the ninth hour."[203] Sarapis temples not uncommonly contained an underground chamber, which may have been used in the initiation (on the analogy of the Isis initiation described below).

Initiation. The Hellenization of the cult of Isis and Osiris included the addition of mysteries of the Greek type, patterned on Eleusis. These secret ceremonies of initiation belong only to the Hellenistic and later periods and to the cult outside Egypt.

Three classes of adherents comprised the Isiac religion: the ordinary

---

199. Clement of Alexandria, *Miscellanies* 6.4.35ff., describes another procession.

200. A. D. Nock, *Conversion* (Oxford, 1933), 80.

201. J. A. S. Evans, *Life in an Egyptian Temple in the Graeco-Roman Period* (New Haven, 1961).

202. V. Tran Tam Tinh, *Essai sur le culte d'Isis à Pompéi* (Paris, 1964).

203. *Oxyrhynchus Papyri*, ed. B. P. Grenfell and A. S. Hunt (London, 1898), 1.110. See Chan-hie Kim, "The Papyrus Invitation," *JBL* 94 (1975):391-402.

ISIS WORSHIP, wall painting from Herculaneum
In addition to the typically Egyptian elements, note the sacrifice on a horned
altar and the double choir singing hymns. The daily ceremony of opening an Isis
temple in the morning may be depicted. *(© Erich Lessing/Art Resource, NY)*

faithful who might attend the daily ceremonies and join a procession; the initiates who had the right to enter into the temple, were clothed in linen, and took an active part in the ceremonies; and the various levels of priests. The initiation was not for everyone but seems to have been required in order to enter the sacerdotal class, especially for one who was a foreigner. Initiation implied an intimate participation in the cult, qualifying one to perform certain functions and bringing him under the special protection of Isis. Most inscriptions were not set up by initiates, and they indicate that devotees were not primarily women.

The most substantial account that we possess of an initiation into a mystery cult comes from Apuleius in his *Metamorphoses,* Book 11. This is also a moving testimony to a deep, personal religious faith, almost unique in the surviving literature about Greco-Roman religion.[204]

The goddess appeared to Lucius in a dream:

> I am Nature, the Universal Mother, mistress of all the elements, . . . sovereign of all things spiritual, queen of the dead, queen of the immortals, the single manifestation of all gods and goddesses that are. [She recounts the names by which she is known among different peoples.] The Egyptians who excel in ancient learning and worship me with ceremonies proper to my godhead call me by my true name, namely, Queen Isis.

Lucius was assured by the high priest of Isis at Corinth that "her service is perfect freedom." He received three different initiations. The first was at Corinth into the cult of Isis. The priest explained to Lucius that one was not initiated without direct orders from Isis:

> The gates of the underworld and the guardianship of life are in her hands, and the rites of initiation approximate to a voluntary death from which there is only a precarious hope of resurrection. So she usually chooses old men who feel that their end is fast approaching yet are not too senile to be capable of keeping a secret; by her grace they are, in a sense, born again and restored to new and healthy life.

(Despite the interpretations put on these words they seem to be only metaphorical for the new kind of life to be taken up in the college of servants of Isis. The explanation that chastity was required perhaps explains the preference for older men.) Finally Isis in simultaneous dreams to Lucius and the high priest Mithras signified the day on which the initiation should take place. The priest took Lucius to the public baths for purificatory washing accompanied by prayers. (The close association with the priest ["father"] was typical of small religious associations and may be compared with the situation in 1 Cor. 1.) There followed a ten-day period of abstention from meat and wine. On the evening of the initiation the uninitiated withdrew. Lucius was clothed with a new linen robe, and led into the interior of the temple.

> It may be, my studious reader, that you would very much like to know what was said there and what was done. I would tell you if it were lawful for me to tell, and you would know all if it were lawful for you to hear. . . . Hear then and believe, for what I tell you is true. I drew near to the confines of death, treading the very threshold of Proserpine. I was borne through all the elements and returned to earth again. At the dead of night I saw the sun

204. Martin Dibelius, "The Isis Initiation in Apuleius and Related Initiatory Rites," in *Conflict at Colossae*, ed. Fred O. Francis and Wayne A. Meeks (Missoula, Mont., 1973), 61-121, attempts an understanding of certain passages in Colossians on the basis of Apuleius.

shining brightly. I approached the gods above and the gods below, and worshipped them face to face. See, I have told you things which, though you have heard them, you still must know nothing about.

The solemn rites ended at dawn, and Lucius emerged wearing twelve stoles, evidently representing his symbolic journey through the heavenly elements before his return to earth. A torch was in his right hand, and a crown of white palm leaves spread out like rays of light was on his head. So attired, he was led up on a wooden platform in the presence of an image of the goddess, curtains were pulled back, and he was presented to the gaze of the crowd. A banquet and three days of rejoicing celebrated his "birthday" as an initiate. The whole experience showed him that the underworld, the elements, and the heaven of the gods were under the protection of Isis; Lucius was no longer at the mercy of Fortune.

When Lucius went to Rome, though a foreigner, he was given the freedom of the Isis temple because of his initiation at Corinth. The goddess, however, instructed him in a dream that he must receive a second initiation, this time into the mysteries of Osiris. His expenses in Corinth and journey to Rome had used up all of Lucius's funds. At Osiris's instructions he sold the robe off his back in order to pay for the initiation. There was the same preliminary ten days of fasting plus a complete shaving of his head. No details of the initiation are given. It may have closely paralleled, although it was distinct from, that at Corinth to Isis, for it is described as a "nocturnal orgy" *(nocturnis orgius)*, after which he became the god's "illuminate."

After this, the goddess gave another vision requiring a third initiation. This time Lucius was inducted into the college of *pastophoroi*, the lower order of priests. He refers only to his fasting and keeping his head shaved, as was required for his priestly duties. It is not indicated that these inductions represent three different grades in which one penetrated deeper into the mysteries of the religion. The best explanation for the second initiation, which differed little from the first, was that evidently the priests at different temples found excuses to prescribe new initiations. The different initiations were not into different grades of membership.

The goddess prospered Lucius's legal practice, but the real theme of the *Metamorphoses* is that the initiation into Isis freed him from the control of fate and magic. It is only in Apuleius that Isis appears as ruler of the realm of the dead, but even here there is no explicit promise of immortality, only of bliss after death. Lucius now, unlike a Greek free before his god, was a slave, body and soul, to the goddess; this was an eastern conception.

Aretalogies.[205] The word *aretē* ("virtue") in Hellenistic Greek came to be

205. See the translations in F. C. Grant, *Hellenistic Religions* (New York, 1953), 128-36; V. F. Vanderlip, *The Four Greek Hymns of Isidorus and the Cult of Isis* (Toronto, 1972); H. Engelmann,

used of the manifestations and powers of the deity, his/her achievements and accomplishments (cf. 1 Pet. 2:9). Praises of the achievements of a deity were a propaganda device that began in the cult of Asclepius, but they seem particularly characteristic of the Egyptian gods. In all of the cults there was less concern with who a deity was or what his/her nature was than with what he/she did and what benefits he/she conferred.[206]

The aretalogies of Isis and Harpocrates follow a uniform style whether in prose or poetry. The pattern followed is that of the Hellenistic hymns (see pp. 194-95). The deity is identified by name, parentage, and places of worship. Many aretalogies, however, are in the first person, as the deity proceeds to relate his or her omnipotence and achievements. Isis in particular claims credit for all human civilization — temporal, political, social, moral, and religious. The social significance of her religion is strongly marked. Isis reigns supreme in the universe; the goddesses worshiped under other names are in reality Isis. The emphasis is on terrestrial benefits. Such praises served to promote the worship of the deity in the Greek world.

BIBLIOGRAPHY

Hopfner, T. *Fontes Historiae Religionis Aegyptiacae*. Bonn, 1922–1925.
Vanderlip, V. F. *The Four Greek Hymns of Isidorus and the Cult of Isis*. Toronto, 1972.
Zabkar, L. V. *Hymns to Isis in Her Temple at Philae*. Hanover, N.H., 1988.
Plutarch's De Iside et Osiride. Edited with an introduction, translation, and commentary by J. G. Griffiths. Swansea, 1970.
Apuleius of Maudauros. *The Isis Book* (*Metamorphoses*, Book 11). Edited and translated by J. G. Griffiths. Leiden, 1975.
Vidman, L. *Sylloge inscriptionum religionis Isiacae et Serapiacae*. Berlin, 1969.
Firmicus Maternus. *The Error of Pagan Religions* 2 and 22. Translated by C. A. Forbes in *Ancient Christian Writers*, vol. 37. New York, 1970.
Totti, M. *Ausgewählte Texte der Isis-und Sarapis-Religion*. Hildesheim, 1985.

Brady, T. A. *The Reception of the Egyptian Cults by the Greeks*. Columbia, Mo., 1935.
Youtie, H. C. "The Kline of Sarapis." *HTR* 41 (1948):9-30.
Festugière, A. J. "A propos des Arétalogies d'Isis." *HTR* 42 (1949):209-34.
Vidman, L. *Isis und Sarapis bei den Griechen und Römern*. Berlin, 1970.
Witt, R. E. *Isis in the Graeco-Roman World*. Ithaca, N.Y., 1971. Reprint Baltimore, 1997.
Roullet, A. N. *The Egyptian and Egyptianizing Monuments of Imperial Rome*. Leiden, 1972.

The Delian Aretalogy of Sarapis (Leiden, 1975). For studies of the possible relation of aretalogies to the Gospels see Morton Smith, "Prolegomena to a Discussion of Aretalogies, Divine Men, The Gospels, and Jesus," *JBL* 90 (1971):174-99 and H. C. Kee, "Aretalogy and Gospel," *JBL* 92 (1973):402-22.

206. Cf. Aristides, *Or.* 8.1.88 (Dindorf) = 2.356.15 (Keil). English trans. by C. A. Behr.

Stambaugh, John E. *Sarapis under the Early Ptolemies.* Leiden, 1972.

Dunand, Francois. *Le culte d'Isis dans le bassin oriental de la Meditérranée.* 3 vols. Leiden, 1973.

Kater-Sibbes, G. J. F., and W. Hornbostel. *The Monuments of Sarapis: A Preliminary Catalogue.* Leiden, 1973.

Heyob, Sharon Kelly. *The Cult of Isis among Women in the Graeco-Roman World.* Leiden, 1975.

Solmsen, Friedrich. *Isis among the Greeks and Romans.* Cambridge, Mass., 1979.

Griffiths, J. G. *The Origins of Osiris and his Cult.* Leiden, 1980.

Wild, R. A. *Water in Cultic Worship of Isis and Sarapis.* Leiden, 1981.

Wild, R. A. "The Known Isis-Sarapis Sanctuaries from the Roman Period." *ANRW* II, *Principat,* 17.4. Berlin and New York, 1984. Pp. 1739-1851.

Merkelbach, R. *Isis regina — Zeus Sarapis: Die griechisch-ägyptische Religion nach den Quellen dargestellt.* Stuttgart and Leipzig, 1995.

Takács, Sarolta A. *Isis and Serapis in the Roman World.* Leiden, 1995.

Phoenician Deities: Astarte and Adonis

The worship of a fertility goddess was widespread from very early times in the eastern Mediterranean. The Phoenician Astarte was essentially the same as the Syrian Atargatis and the Phrygian Cybele. The Greeks identified her with Aphrodite. Astarte was the consort of the supreme god of the Phoenician pantheon, *Baal Shamim* ("Lord of Heaven"). Many local pantheons included a youthful god, forming a family triad. One of these youthful gods, Adonis, became quite popular in the Greek world, but he was not nearly so important in Phoenicia as was Astarte.

There is not a great deal of information about the Phoenician cult for our time period and even less for the mysteries. The fertility cults of Phoenicia and Syria do not intersect Christian history very significantly despite the geographical proximity. The long-standing Old Testament polemic against the Canaanite fertility cult perhaps accounts for this.

Myth. Adonis was not a major deity in his own right and was always subordinated to a female divinity. The Adonis myth was told in several variations. A representative form is that Adonis was a beautiful youth loved by Aphrodite. While hunting he was killed by a wild boar. Aphrodite desired him back, but Persephone was also enchanted by his beauty and desired to keep him. They agreed to share him, a third of the year in the underworld, a third of the year with Aphrodite, and a third of the year as his own master, which he spent with Aphrodite. Adonis was originally a vegetation spirit who was mourned with the parching of vegetation in the hot, dry Mediterranean summer. In later forms of the myth his story was turned into a tragedy of hunting and love without reference to nature. There is no evidence of a "resurrection" of Adonis in sources before the second century A.D. and then probably under the influence of the Egyptian cult of Osiris.

Ceremony.[207] The center of the worship of Adonis was Byblos in Phoenicia, whence it spread to Greece and Italy. In the spring a boar was sacrificed as an act of personal atonement followed by a public procession to the temple by worshipers who lamented the death of Adonis. A summer festival (June–July),[208] observed only by women, was characterized by tending miniature gardens of Adonis and mourning for the god. Theocritus (*Idyll* 15) gives an account of the summer ceremony in Alexandria. There was a pageant of the wedding of Adonis and Aphrodite, and on the following day the wailing women carried an image of the dead Adonis to the sea and committed it to the waves.

Although mysteries of Adonis are claimed, the available evidence for them is insufficient.

Sacred Prostitution. A feature of the ancient Canaanite religion, sacred prostitution continued in the temples of Syria and Phoenicia. It was probably from this source (through the identification of the fertility goddess with Aphrodite) that the practice was adopted at the temple of Aphrodite at Corinth.[209] Young women gave themselves for a period of time to the service of the deity. Many explanations of the origin of the practice have been offered; it was perhaps connected with a fertility ritual.

BIBLIOGRAPHY

Theocritus, *Idylls* 3.46ff.; 15.86ff.
(Ps.)Apollodorus, *Bibliotheca* 3.14.4.
Ovid, *Metamorphoses* 10.298ff., 529ff.

Du Mesnil du Buisson, R. *Etudes sur les dieux phéniciens hérités par l'empire romain.* Leiden, 1970.
Teixidor, Javier. *The Pagan God: Popular Religion in the Greco-Roman Near East.* Princeton, 1977.
Soyez, Br. *Byblos et la fête des Adonies.* Leiden, 1977.

Syrian Deities: Atargatis and Others

Each city of Syria had its Baal ("Lord" or "Master") and his consort. The Baal was the master of the country and was responsible for its fertility, but he resided in the firmament. Because the female element was more closely associ-

---

207. Noel Robertson, "The Ritual of the Dying God in Cyprus and Syro-Palestine," *HTR* 75 (1982):313-59.

208. See F. R. Walton, "The Date of the Adonia at Athens," *HTR* 61 (1968):65ff. for the argument that at Athens it occurred in the spring.

209. Strabo, *Geography* 8.6.20; but see p. 70n.22.

JUPITER DOLICHENUS, 2d/3d c. A.D. The local Baal of Doliche in Commagene was a god of weather and fertility. Romanized, he was popular with soldiers, slaves, and merchants and had a temple in Rome, from which this image comes. The attributes combine features of Baal and Zeus. *(Capitoline Museum, Rome)*

ated with fecundity, the goddess often assumed a superior place, as is the case with Atargatis. Lucian identified Atargatis (the *Dea Syria*) with Hera and her consort Hadad with Zeus. Under the empire the Baal was associated with the sun and his consort with the moon. Syria was the source of the solar theology of the third-century Roman world (more on sun worship below, pp. 317-18). The most successful of the local Baals was the Jupiter of Doliche in Commagene, who from being god of lightning became a popular divinity of the Roman armies and was carried by them all over the empire.[210]

In the Roman world the best known of the Syrian goddesses (and better known than the Phoenician Astarte) was Atargatis of Hierapolis, identified simply as "the Syrian Goddess." Atargatis herself was a conflation of the three major goddesses of the older Canaanite Pantheon — Astarte, Anath, and Asherah — respectively goddesses of love, war, and fecundity, but often merging with each other. The great goddesses of the Near East — Astarte, Cybele, and Atargatis — were characterized as goddesses of nature, fertility, and motherhood and as rulers of animals.

The wandering Galli, mendicant priests whose name was perhaps given from the priests of Cybele (p. 284), themselves in turn deriving their name from the Gauls of central Asia Minor, provided the principal advertisement of the Syrian goddess in the Greco-Roman world. Syrian merchants and slaves introduced the cult into port cities. The Syrian goddess along with the god Hadad had a temple on the Janiculum hill in Rome under Nero, but in general the cult did not spread significantly in the western part of the empire.

Ceremonies. The principal seat of the worship of Atargatis was Hierapolis. At her temple there her statue was supported by lions, that of Hadad by bulls (long associated with the Baals of the region), as attested by coinage and other artistic representations. Atargatis may first have been portrayed as a fish; fish and doves remained sacred to her.

The worship at Hierapolis consisted of two daily sacrifices — one for Hadad in silence and the other for Atargatis to the accompaniment of singing, pipe playing, and shaking of rattles. The priests were clothed with white robes and tall caps. The high priest, an annual appointee, wore purple and a golden tiara. The statue of the goddess was taken to the lake on certain occasions, probably for bathing. If one is to judge from the tall phallic emblems outside the temple, the goddess had a marked naturalistic character.

A man who made a pilgrimage to the great festivals had first to shave his head and eyebrows. He then sacrificed a sheep, placed the fleece on the ground, and knelt on it and prayed. On the road to Hierapolis he used only cold water for bathing and drinking and always slept on the ground. Mysteries are attested at some places, but their nature is not known. In keeping with the

---

210. M. P. Speidel, *The Religion of Iuppiter Dolichenus in the Roman Army* (Leiden, 1978); M. Hörig and E. Schwertheim, *Corpus Cultus Iovis Dolicheni* (Leiden, 1987).

original elements of Syrian religion there might have been the exhibition of phallic symbols.

What attracted Greek and Latin authors of the early empire were the itinerant priests, the Galli. Apuleius (*Metamorphoses* 8, 27-28) tells how the image of the goddess was carried on an ass while the priests shouted and danced to the accompaniment of a pipe. One of their number, bewailing his sins, took a whip and beat himself until blood flowed freely. The priests took out their bags and began to collect contributions of money and produce. The itinerant feature of the Syrian cult is explained by the great number of Syrian slaves spread around the Mediterranean who were too poor to build a sanctuary and support priests and satisfied their devotion in the passing of the Galli.

Ritual Castration. Lucian's *On the Syrian Goddess* 51 tells how men became Galli. While the pipes were wailing and the men were dancing, frenzy seized many of them. The man who was seized stripped off his clothes, grabbed a sword, and castrated himself. He ran through the city and threw what was cut off into any house he chose and took from the house women's apparel. Thereafter he belonged to the goddess and wore woman's clothes. (See further on the Phrygian deities, below.)

Bibliography

Van Berg, Paul-Louis. *Corpus Cultus Deae Syriae*. Leiden, 1972.

Attridge, Harold W., and Robert A. Oden, trans. *The Syrian Goddess (De Dea Syria)*. Society of Biblical Literature Text and Translation, vol. 9. Missoula, Mont., 1976.

Lucian. *Lucius or the Ass* 35–41.

Firmicus Maternus. *The Error of the Pagan Religions* 4. Translated by C. A. Forbes in Ancient Christian Writers, vol. 37. New York, 1970.

Walton, F. R. "De Dis Syriis apud Graecos cultis." Ph.D. diss., Harvard, 1938.

Oden, Robert A. *Studies in Lucian's De Syria Dea*. Harvard Semitic Monographs. Missoula, Mont., 1977.

Phrygian Deities: Cybele and Attis

Pessinus near Mt. Ida in Phrygia was the most ancient site of the cult of Cybele and Attis. Cybele was the more important, and she was similar to the other mother goddesses of the Near East, who included Ma from Commagene (identified by the Romans with Bellona, goddess of war) and Bendis from Thrace (identified by the Greeks with Artemis). Hellenized, Cybele was assimilated to the "Mother of the Gods" of the Greeks, and in the Latin west she was known as the "Great Mother" *(Magna Mater)*. Cybele was occasionally called Agdistis, but the latter was sometimes worshiped separately. Attis was the youthful con-

CYBELE,
from Asia Minor, 2d/3d c. A.D.
Characteristics of the iconography
of Cybele included her crowned,
holding a dish *(patera)*, and seated
between two lions.

ATTIS
Attis, the consort of Cybele, was a
symbol of the renewal of life in nature.
(Chiaramonti Gallery, Vatican)

sort of Cybele, a mortal lover sometimes interpreted as a vegetation god. He
was at various times assimilated to Sabazius-Dionysus, the moon god Men,
and later Mithras. The high priest of Cybele at Pessinus and later the whole
priestly college wore the title Attis.

The cult of Cybele was the first of the eastern religions to be received officially into Rome,[211] at the time of the crisis posed to Italy by Hannibal. The
senate officially invited the Great Mother to Rome in response to a consultation of the *Sibylline Books*. Presumably the introduction of this foreign cult was
intended to gain added divine assistance to the Roman cause and to give the
people a new emotional outlet. An embassy was sent to Asia in 205 B.C. to bring
back the black meteorite that was identified as the image of the goddess. The

211. Livy 29.10-14.

cult statue arrived in Rome in 204 B.C., and a temple for it was erected on the Palatine in 191 B.C. Priests were brought in from Phrygia, because emasculation (shocking to Romans and Greeks) was prerequisite to the priesthood. The cult finally came out from under restriction under Claudius when Roman citizens (not eunuchs) could serve as priests and private associations worshiping the Phrygian deities were recognized. Claudius also publicly recognized Attis, but it was the second century before he became prominent in the cult.

Cybele in Hellenistic-Roman art is generally shown seated on a throne, wearing a mural crown (as city protectress) or the *calathus* (for fertility), carrying a patera and tympanum, and flanked by lions or holding one in her lap. Attis is frequently shown as a largely naked youth but wearing the Phrygian cap.

Myth. The myth of Attis and Cybele exists in several variant forms. According to one,[212] Zeus begat Agdistis, a wild creature half male and half female. Dionysus made it drunk and tied its male member to a tree so that on awakening suddenly from sleep it mutilated itself. From the severed male member an almond tree sprang up. Nana, the daughter of Sangarius, took fruit of the tree into her bosom and conceived Attis. The youth grew up and was about to be married to the daughter of the king of Pessinus, but Agdistis had fallen in love with him and to prevent the marriage caused Attis to castrate himself. According to another form,[213] Cybele was bound to Attis by chaste passion and made the youth take a vow of perpetual chastity. He became infatuated, however, with the nymph Sangaritis and broke his oath. Cybele killed the nymph, and Attis went mad and mutilated himself. In most versions Attis died (under a pine tree) as a result of the castration, but according to another tradition of the myth he was accidentally killed by a companion while hunting a wild boar[214] or by the boar itself (cf. the myth of Adonis above, p. 277). The majority versions, which make the castration central, are aetiological — to explain the rite of castration of the priests, a practice perhaps borrowed from the Syrian cult.

Apart from Firmicus Maternus (mid–fourth century A.D.), who interprets the myth according to the agricultural cycle, by which Attis is the grain cut down by the sickle and planted to grow again,[215] there is little in the ancient texts about a resurrection of the god. According to the first version cited above Agdistis repented of what she had done and asked Zeus to restore Attis to life. This was refused, but she was promised that his body would not decay and as token of this his hair continued to grow and his little finger would move itself.

Festivals. The *Megalensia* in Rome commemorated the introduction of

---

212. Pausanias 7.17, 10-12; Arnobius, *Against the Pagans* 5.5-7.
213. Ovid, *Fasti* 4.221-44.
214. Herodotus 1.34-45.
215. *The Error of the Pagan Religions* 3.2.

the Cybele cult there. Games, plays, sacrifices, banquets, and perhaps a ritual reenactment of the arrival of the goddess were held from April 4-10 annually. A graphic description of the excitement of a public procession in honor of Cybele is found in Lucretius 2.608ff.

We are better informed about the spring festival of Attis organized under Claudius. The program of events is recorded in the calendar of Philocalus for the year A.D. 354.[216] Since the festival had a long development, all of the fourth-century features may not go back to the first century.

March 15: *canna intrat.* The college of reedbearers *(cannophori)* brought bunches of reeds to the temple of Cybele. They and the *archigallus* (who supervised devotees) sacrificed a six-year-old bull. The initiates began a period of fasting and abstinence from sexual intercourse.

March 22: *arbor intrat.* The college of treebearers *(dendrophori)* cut down a pine tree, the symbol of Attis, brought it to the temple on the Palatine, and bedecked it with symbols of the Attis cult (including musical instruments and Attis figurines).

March 24: *sanguem.* The Galli scourged and wounded themselves to the point of shedding blood. The new candidates for the priesthood imitated Attis by castrating themselves and offering their genitals to the goddess.

March 25: *hilaria.* Often interpreted as a resurrection of Attis celebrated in a carnival spirit, this day in the cycle is only attested in later times and its significance is not revealed in the sources. The joy of the initiates may have reference not to Attis but to Cybele whose cult statue was about to be purified by the blood of the Galli.

March 26: *requetio.* This was a day of rest.

March 27: *lavatio.* The statue of the goddess and other cult objects were carried in procession to the river Almo to be purified. Some have seen this as a purification in connection with a holy marriage with the revivified Attis, but that seems fanciful.

The emasculation and shedding of blood in the Attis and Cybele cult may at one time have been associated with fertility magic. The emasculation, as an offering of blood, may also have been a means of purification or of expiation. Later the act may have been understood as identifying the priest with Attis and so with his destiny. There seem to be more grounds, however, for seeing the act as an assimilation to Cybele. The genitals were a gift to the goddess. The Galli assumed female dress and let their hair grow long. Whatever ideas were later incorporated, the most probable explanation of the castration is that the sacerdotal function implied continence during the charge (the idea was not moral but ritual purity).[217] The voluntary eunuch was always in the required state of

---

216. CIL I², no. 312; cf. H. Hepding, *Attis, seine Mythen und sein Kult* (Giessen, 1903), 51.
217. A. D. Nock, "Eunuchs in Ancient Religion," *Archiv für Religionswissenschaft* 23 (1925):25ff. (*Essays,* 1:7-15).

purity. However, this does not apply to the higher priesthood, who administered the temples, for they were not castrated.

Mysteries are attested, but how they relate to the other ceremonies of the cult is not known. The effort to parallel them with the spring festival when the Galli were consecrated is speculative. Two Christian authors have handed down a sacred formula or symbol by which a *mystē* was recognized as an initiate of the Attis cult. Clement of Alexandria[218] gives it, "I ate from the tympanum, I drank from the cymbal, I carried the *cernus* [a sacred basket, which in the taurobolium was used to carry the bull's testicles or blood], I entered the *pastos*." Since *pastos* can refer to a bridal chamber or bridal bed, some have understood this as a sacred marriage, but *pastos* could refer to the interior of the temple. That fits Firmicus Maternus's version,[219] "I ate from the tympanum, I drank from the cymbal, I was fully initiated into the secrets of religion."[220] The nature of the myth would seem to leave no place for a sacred marriage in the Phrygian cult.

Musical instruments were prominent in the cult and fit the frenzied nature of the rites. All the ceremonies refer to a naturalistic, very primitive religion, which could amuse the Roman people by its strange picturesqueness but in themselves carried no spiritual resource.

Taurobolium. In the study of New Testament backgrounds much attention has been drawn to the taurobolium in the cult of Attis, although nearly all of the evidence belongs to the second century and later. The word meant capturing a bull by throwing a rope around it, but the word came to mean a particular sacrifice of a bull. Most of the attestation for the taurobolium is inscriptional, but there is a description of it in Prudentius (*Crowns of Martyrdom* 10.1011-50), a Christian poet of the late fourth century, from which century comes most of the evidence. The person receiving the rite entered a deep underground pit that was covered with a wooden lattice work. A garlanded bull was brought to the planks covering the pit and killed with a spear. The blood ran through the openings and showered the initiate below, who held up his face so that the blood covered it and so that he could drink some. He was then exhibited to the worshipers, who praised him. The rite apparently meant the transfer of the energy of the bull to the person undergoing it or to the one for whom he performed it. The inscriptions fall into two large groups: most of the earlier ones pertain to a sacrifice, offered by individuals, associations, cities, or provinces for the welfare of the emperor, his household, his empire, or themselves; the later ones are predominantly acts of personal consecration, and Prudentius's account applies only to this situation. (When performed with a

---

218. *Exhortation* 2.15.3.

219. *The Error of the Pagan Religions* 18.1.

220. Firmicus quotes the Greek, in which the last phrase differs from his Latin, viz. Greek: "I became an initiate of Attis."

FOSSA SANGUINIS, 4th c. A.D., Neuss
This pit at a sanctuary of Cybele and Attis was apparently
for the performance of the taurobolium.

ram the rite was called criobolium.) The "initiatory" or "dedicatory" use of the
rite probably carried the idea of a purification, perhaps in preparation for the
afterlife. Hence, a few inscriptions speak of the person as "reborn," usually for a
period of about twenty years, although one (CIL 6.510 from A.D. 376) speaks of
the person as "reborn for eternity" *(in aeternum renatus).*

The addition of ideas of purification and rebirth to the bull slaying show
how even a naturalistic cult could receive more spiritual interpretations. The
code of moral purity for the household cult in Philadelphia (p. 187 above) illustrates the inclusion of moral elements within traditional Greek domestic religion allied with the naturalistic religion (Agdistis) of Asia Minor.

BIBLIOGRAPHY

Herodotus. *History* 1.34-35.
Dionysus of Halicarnassus. *Roman Antiquities* 2.19ff.
Diodore of Sicily. *Library of History* 3.58-59.

Catullus, *Carmen* 63.
Lucretius. *On the Nature of Things* 2.594ff.
Ovid. *Fasti.* 4.179-372.
Juvenal. *Satires* 6.511-21.
Pausanias. *Description of Greece* 7.17.9-12.
Arnobius. *Against the Pagans* 5.5-7.
Julian. *Oration* 5, "Hymn to the Mother of the Gods."
Firmicus Maternus. *The Error of the Pagan Religions* 3 and 18. Translated by C. A.
    Forbes in Ancient Christian Writers, vol. 37. New York, 1970.
Prudentius. *Crowns of Martyrdom [Peristephanon]* 10.1006-50.
Vermaseren, M. J. *Corpus Cultus Cybelae Attidisque.* 6 vols. Leiden, 1977-89.

Vermaseren, M. J. *The Legend of Attis in Greek and Roman Art.* Leiden, 1966.
Duthoy, R. *The Taurobolium, its Evolution and Terminology.* Leiden, 1969.
Vermaseren, M. J. *Cybele and Attis. The Myth and the Cult.* London, 1977.
Thomas, G. "Magna Mater and Attis." *ANRW* II, *Principat,* 17.3. Berlin and New
    York, 1984. Pp. 1500-1535.
Gasparro, G. S. *Soteriology and Mystic Aspects of the Cult of Cybele and Attis.* Leiden,
    1985.
Lane, Eugene N. *Cybele, Attis, and Related Cults: Essays in Memory of M. J.
    Vermaseren.* Leiden, 1996.
Roller, Lynn E. *In Search of God the Mother: The Cult of Anatolian Cybele.* Berkeley,
    1999.

A Persian Deity: Mithras

Students of Hellenistic and Jewish religion have often identified Persia as the source of important religious ideas, but only one god with a Persian name became important in the Roman empire — Mithra (in Latin and Greek, Mithras).

Among the few original Mithraic texts from antiquity are graffiti in the Mithraic sanctuaries at Dura Europus (Syria) and Santa Prisca (Rome). On the so-called "Mithras Liturgy" see p. 232. A fragmentary papyrus of the fourth century from Egypt may preserve instructions preparatory to initiation into Mithraism by giving answers to questions that will be asked, but the Mithraic connection is denied by some.[221] Literary references by others to Mithraism in the Roman period are meager, so the religion is known almost exclusively from the numerous Mithraic sanctuaries and their art that have been discovered.

Throughout most of the twentieth century the prevailing theory of the origins of Mithraism was that of Franz Cumont, who traced the religion to the ancient Persians. According to this theory, the Aryans, who worshiped Mithras,

---

221. The papyrus is now in Berlin — P. Berol. 21196. William M. Brashear, *A Mithraic Catechism from Egypt,* Tyche Supplementband 1 (Vienna, 1992).

carried him to India and Iran. He was a god of light, truth, and loyalty to covenants. In the Persian *Avesta* Mithras was an ally of the good god Ahura Mazda, in support of whom he fought against Ahriman, the evil power. He was thought of as mediating between Ahura Mazda and mortals. As the worship of Mithras spread into the Hellenized world, it borrowed from astrology and the mysteries. A weakness in this theory all along was that Roman Mithraism shows no evidence of including the cosmic dualism and eschatological conflagration and resurrection that were a part of the Persian religion. Moreover, the characteristics of the religion known from the monuments of the Roman pe-

MITHRAS, 3d c. A.D.
The bull slaying was the central cult image in each sanctuary of Mithras.
(© Erich Lessing/Art Resource, NY)

MITHRAEUM OF THE PAINTED WALLS, Ostia
Mithraic meeting places were narrow halls with couches on each side.

riod (cavelike sanctuaries, bull-slayings, and secret initiations) were unknown to the old Iranian god of light.

Recent studies of Mithraism have sought the explanation of Roman Mithraism not in old Iranian religion but in the astral religion of the Hellenistic and Roman periods. The central cult image of Mithraic sanctuaries was Mithras slaying a bull (tauroctony, not to be confused with the taurobolium — see below). The positioning of images in the scene has been shown to correspond to the location of constellations at a certain time (e.g., bull — Taurus, scorpion — Scorpio, snake — Hydra, raven — Corvus, dog — Canis minor, lion — Leo major). David Ulansey has brought the astronomical data and the scientific and philosophical thought together into an explanation of *The Origins of the Mithraic Mysteries*. On his theory Mithras was the Greek hero Perseus, who on a popular etymology of his name was known as "the Persian" and whose constellation was located above that of Taurus. Mithras's killing the bull had as one of its antecedents Perseus's killing of the Gorgon. In Mithraism, however, the scene had a cosmic significance, indicating the end of the Age of Taurus, when the spring equinox occurred in the constellation of the Bull, and the beginning of a new age when the spring equinox entered Aries. Mithras thus had the appeal of a deity powerful enough to move the cosmos and so a divinity superior to fate and able to offer immortality. Ulansey locates the origin of this new religion in Tarsus (Perseus was widely worshiped in Cilicia) near the beginning of the first century B.C. among intellectuals influenced by the astronomical discoveries of Hipparchus and the astral speculation of the Stoics. Mithraism, therefore, would have no more connection with Persia than the name given to its god and would be a product of the Hellenistic personification of the cosmos as conceived by a philosophical astrology. The identification of Perseus with Mithras was perhaps due to the influence of King Mithridates VI, who was named for Mithras and traced his ancestry to Perseus. The religion took the form of mystery initiations because only a few knew the secret of this newly discovered cosmic power.

Roger Beck has proposed a synthesis of the Iranian and astrological interpretations. He proposes that the founding group belonged to the military and civilian dependents of the ruling dynasty of Commagene about the time it came to an end in A.D. 72 and its members made the transition from client rulers to Roman aristocrats. This setting would account for the nearly simultaneous inscriptional and archaeological attestations of Mithraism in both the west and the east around the end of the first century A.D., the social and political acceptance of Mithraism (in contrast to the questionable status of other eastern cults), and the fusion of Persian religious tradition with a learned Greco-Roman tradition in which astrology was prominent.

Regardless of the origins of Mithraism and the question of continuity between the Persian deity and the Hellenistic-Roman mystery cult, the latter is our interest here. The first surviving notice of Mithraic mysteries concerns pirates on the Cilician coast whom Pompey suppressed in 67 B.C.[222] After the late first century A.D. archaeological evidence for Mithraism begins to increase; at the end of the second century the emperor Commodus was initiated; it was strongest during the third century; and it continued to be important in the fourth century, when it was a significant element in Julian's attempt to reestablish paganism (see p. 317). The main strength of Mithraism, according to the surviving monuments and sanctuaries, was among Roman soldiers and administrative officials along the frontier, from Hadrian's wall in Britain to Dura Europus on the Euphrates. Only men were admitted to the mysteries, and Mithras as a warrior and guardian of oaths appealed to manly pride. Mithraism also flourished at ports, as at Ostia where fifteen Mithraea have been found,[223] and it was well rep-

---

222. Plutarch, *Life of Pompey* 24.
223. Samuel Laeuchli, "Urban Mithraism," *BA* 31 (1968):73-99; Samuel Laeuchli, ed., *Mithraism in Ostia* (Evanston, Ill., 1967).

resented in and around Rome, thus indicating its appeal to merchants and city-dwellers. Mithraism largely skipped over Greece and is little attested in the Greek-speaking east. It seems never to have had much of a hold in Palestine, where to date only one Mithraeum has been discovered. At Caesarea one of the warehouses dated from the late first to the third century was used as a Mithraeum in the third century.[224] So chronologically and geographically any influence by Mithraism on the origins of Christianity seems excluded.

Sanctuaries and Art. The Mithraic sanctuaries were either caves or structures made to resemble caves, usually located near a source of water. Although there are individual differences, a general pattern prevails. They are oblong, with the long central "nave" flanked on each side by benches on which the members could recline at the sacred meals. Commonly the roof is vaulted, as a cave, but also to represent the sky. Sometimes the chamber terminated in an apse. All are small (fifty to sixty-five feet by twenty-five to thirty-five feet on the average), so each Mithraic society must have been restricted in size.

At the end of the nave, opposite the entrance, at the focal point of the meeting room was a representation of the cult symbol — Mithras slaying the bull. The scene might be in sculptured marble, molded in stucco, or painted. Mithras is in Persian dress with peaked cap. He is on the back of the bull with his left hand pulling the bull's head back by the nostrils while the right hand plunges a sword into its heart. The model for the scene appears to have come from classical art in which the goddess Nike is shown killing a bull in a similar manner.

The tauroctony is usually embellished by some or all of the following figures. The bull is flanked by two torchbearers, one holding his torch up (Cautes) and the other holding his torch down (Cautopates). On the astronomical interpretation these figures, appearing as smaller doubles of Mithras, represent respectively the passage of the sun from the southern to the northern hemisphere at the spring equinox and its passage from the northern to the southern hemisphere at the autumn equinox. Also witnessing the scene are personifications of the sun (Sol) and the moon (Luna) placed in the heaven above. The raven (messenger of the sun to Mithras?) is nearby. Underneath the bull, a dog and a snake are ready to lap up the blood from the wound. A scorpion attaches itself to the bull's genitals. The tail of the bull is sprouting grain. In some sanctuaries an image of the ocean god has been found accompanying the central group; this is perhaps a reference to the sun passing through the waters in its course around the world.

Although the bull-slaying was the central cult image, it was frequently accompanied by other pictures — a zodiac and other scenes involving Mithras. These include Mithras being born from a rock (sometimes witnessed by shep-

---

224. J. A. Blakely, *The Joint Expedition to Caesarea Maritima, Excavation Reports, The Pottery and Dating of Vault 1: Horreum, Mithraeum, and Later Uses* (Lewiston, N.Y., 1987).

herds), which may be interpreted as Mithras born in a cavern or as the sun rising from behind a mountain. Mithras was called *sol invictus* ("the unconquered sun"). Another incident involving a rock has Mithras shooting an arrow into a rock and thereby causing water to flow forth. Mithras brought not only light but also refreshing rain. The portrayal of water coming from a rock and men drinking it is strikingly similar to the portrayal of the water miracle in Christian art.

Next in importance to the bull-slaying for the Mithraists appears to have been the pact and sacred meal between Mithras and Sol (the sun). Sometimes Sol kneels before Mithras or in some way submits to him; sometimes Mithras and Sol are shown as equals, shaking hands or reclining at a meal. From one perspective Mithras was the superior deity; from another the two gods associated with the sun are united as world rulers. The meal shows them sharing bread,[225] drink (normally offered in a rhyton, a bull's horn cup), and other food. The meal could precede or follow an ascent of Mithras to heaven in a chariot (the journey of the sun was regularly shown in Hellenistic-Roman art as a rider in a chariot). The iconography of the ascent directly parallels the ascent of Elijah in Christian art.

The bull-slaying was not reenacted in the Mithraea, but initiations and cult meals were held there. The walls and benches of some Mithraea show scenes from an initiation.

Myth. No literary sources relate the cult myth of Roman Mithraism. The meaning of the art objects, therefore, must be reconstructed according to one's interpretation of the nature of Mithraism. This has been done by Cumont from Persian mythology and by Ulansey from astronomical data. The art objects likely contain several layers of meaning from different stages of interpretation and should not be pressed into an artificial consistency for every Mithraic community.

According to Cumont's reconstruction of the myth (unattested in this precise form in literature), Mithras was a hunter, horseman, and archer, as were his early worshipers in the Avesta, where one of his titles is "lord of the wide pastures." The tauroctony, his capturing of a bull and dragging it to a cave where he eventually killed it, was Mithras's greatest feat. Ahura Mazda had created a wild bull. The sun sent the raven to track it down, and Mithras and his hound found it. Mithras killed it in a cave, and from its blood sprang life and grain. The bull-slaying was a creative and beneficial act. Life and energy (symbolized by the bull) were captured and released for the benefit of nature and human beings by this act.

---

225. Cross marks on the bread are not significant. This was the normal incision made on the dough before baking Greek bread; it was given a Christian meaning in the Byzantine tradition. Justin Martyr, *1 Apology* 66, says that bread and a cup of water were given to initiates in the mysteries of Mithras.

MITHRAIC MOSAIC,
from Mithraeum of Felicissimus, Ostia. The pebble mosaic depicts symbols associated with the seven degrees of initiation into the cult of Mithras.

On the astronomical interpretation, instead of being mythological, the bull-slaying is a personification of cosmic forces and sidereal movements. Mithras is the world ruler *(cosmokrator)* who moves the universe and controls the stars, delivering souls from fate and protecting them in their journey after death through the planetary spheres. The initiations were the progressive revelation of this astral symbolism and its religious meaning.

According to both the Persian mythological and the Hellenistic astronomical interpretations the bull-slaying had cosmological significance. It represented a creative act, either as releasing life and energy or as demonstrating power over the stars and so over fate. Mithraism offered a form of salvation to its adherents. On the astronomical interpretation this may have meant protection for the soul during its journey after death through the planetary spheres (see above on astral religion and on the afterlife, pp. 238-50). An inscription in the Santa Prisca Mithraeum on the Aventine in Rome may be restored to read, "[And you saved us] by shedding [the eternal] blood."

Initiation. Roman Mithraism emphasized rank. We know the names of the seven grades of initiation into the Mithraic mysteries from Jerome *(Epistle* 107 *ad Laetam)* and from inscriptions on the walls of the Santa Prisca Mithraeum. The symbols of the different grades are found in a remarkable pebble mosaic on the floor of the mithraeum dedicated by Felicissimus in Ostia. The mosaic portrays three objects for each grade: one representing the grade itself, one an emblem for a function of the grade, and one for the planetary god associated with the grade.

(1) Raven. The first grade was under the protection of Mercury, whose role as messenger of the

gods was taken by the raven in the Mithraic myth. The symbols of this degree in the Ostia mosaic are the raven, a cup (perhaps because the ravens, wearing bird masks, served the sacred drink at the Mithraic meal, as appears in other art), and the caduceus of Mercury. The raven belonged to the element of air.

(2) Bride.[226] The second grade was under the protection of Venus. The mosaic at Ostia is damaged at this point, and the object standing for the degree itself is missing; but there are shown a lamp (to light the bridal chamber on the wedding night? Or did those who received this degree of initiation merely keep the lamps for the sanctuary?) and a crown (the symbol of Venus from the custom of crowning the wedding couple). Joining the right hands is known from the Roman wedding ceremony and the appearance of this gesture in Mithraic art suggests its presence in the initiation to this grade. Another possibility is the placing of a veil or a crown on the initiate. Furthermore, since there was a bridal bath, this grade may have been associated with the element of water and some purification by water may have occurred in the initiation.

(3) Soldier.[227] The third grade was under the patronage of Mars. The symbols from Ostia are the pouch that the soldier wore over his shoulder, a helmet, and a lance. There is evidence for a branding on the forehead. The soldier would have been associated with the element of earth.

(4) Lion. The fourth grade was connected with Jupiter. Its symbols as shown at Ostia were a fire shovel, sistrum (elsewhere associated with Isis but perhaps employed by the lions in some way), and thunderbolts (the attribute of Jupiter). This degree belonged to the element of fire. The inscriptions from the Santa Prisca Mithraeum describe incense burners, and in the paintings of an initiation at Santa Maria Capua Vetere torches are held close to the initiate, perhaps for some kind of purification by fire.[228]

(5) Persian. The fifth grade was under the protection of the moon. The symbols shown at Ostia are a hooked knife (with which Perseus cut off Medusa's head), a scythe or plow, and the moon and a star.

(6) Heliodromus. The sixth grade, the messenger of the sun, was under the protection of Sol, whose representative he was on earth. The symbols on the mosaic are a torch, the radiate crown, and a whip (with which Sol drives the horses of his chariot). The heliodromus and the father were the two most important members of a Mithraic society. At the Santa Prisca Mithraeum, next to a painting of the sacred meal shared by Sol and Mithras, is a raised podium on which the heliodromus and father of the society could recline at the cult meal in the role of their heavenly counterparts.

---

226. Jerome's text has sometimes but incorrectly been emended to read Cryphius ("hidden") — Bruce Metzger, "The Second Grade of Mithraic Initiation," *American Journal of Philology* 66 (1945):225-33 (repr. in *Historical and Literary Studies* [Grand Rapids, 1968], 25-33).

227. Tertullian, *On the Crown* 15.

228. M. J. Vermaseren, *Mithriaca* (Leiden, 1971) 1, plates XXII and XXVIII.

(7) Father *(Pater)*. The highest grade of Mithraic initiation was under the protection of Saturn, and the holder of this rank is portrayed at Santa Prisca dressed like Mithras himself. His symbols at Ostia are a ring (or is it a dish?) and staff, the Persian cap, and a sickle. For the ring and staff one may compare the symbols of the bishop's office in the Middle Ages, and for the title "father" the practice of calling the head of the Christian community this, attested as early as the third century.

The seven degrees of initiation thus corresponded to the order of the seven planets in astrology.[229] The initiate who had passed through all degrees could, on his death, pass through the planetary spheres to paradise. The Ostia mosaic shows before the seven grades a large vase, thought to refer to some preliminary purification by water, and the helmets of the Dioscuri (who were often understood as symbolizing the two celestial hemispheres). Following the seven grades is a final panel that contains cup and flowers, perhaps alluding to paradise.

According to the paintings at Santa Maria Capua Vetere and other pictures the initiate was led through the ceremonies naked (cf. the baptismal practice of the early church) and was at first blindfolded. The initiate took an oath of secrecy before admission to the society. The art further indicates such actions as a laying on of hands, pouring on of water, striking with the leg of a bull, placing a solar crown on the head, and fire held close to the body. Several sources indicate various ordeals through which the Mithraic initiate passed, but we do not know how much credence to put in some of these sources. Masks were worn for some ceremonies. A pretended slaying of the initiate has been thought probable. New discoveries and more study will perhaps give a clearer picture and permit a correlation with the different degrees.

Distinctive Features.[230] Mithraism, like other eastern cults, had no general organization, tolerated other gods, and allowed regional variations. Nevertheless, it differed in some significant ways: (1) it excluded women; (2) it made moral demands; (3) it did not spread on a national basis and never acquired civic status (although patronized later by emperors and government officials); (4) it had in the Roman world no priestly caste or professional clergy; (5) it had no public drama; (6) initiation was coextensive with its adherents; (7) its deity had a *vita,* a chain of events important for the world's drama, but also providing an example for his followers; (8) it had a consistent iconography.

On items (2) through (7) Mithraism was more like Christianity than were the other eastern cults. On the other hand, it had severe disadvantages in rela-

229. The order of the planets in Mithraism is given differently by Celsus in Origen, *Against Celsus* 6.21, 22, which follows the days of the week, beginning with Saturn, in reverse order. On the grades of initiation see R. L. Gordon, "Reality, Evocation, and Boundary in the Mysteries of Mithras," *Journal of Mithraic Studies* 3:19-99.

230. For this section see A. D. Nock, "The Genius of Mithraism," *Journal of Roman Studies* 27 (1937):109-13 (*Essays,* 452-58).

tion to Christianity: the exclusion of women, its limited appeal (it remained a religion of the few), its "manufactured" and mythical character, and its nonexclusiveness.

BIBLIOGRAPHY

Julian. *Oration 4, Hymn to King Helios*. (See p. 317n.261.)

Cumont, Franz. *Textes et monuments figurés relatifs aux mystères de Mithra*. 2 vols. Brussels, 1896, 1899.

Geden, A. S. *Select Passages Illustrating Mithraism*. London, 1925; repr. Hastings, 1990.

Vermaseren, M. J. *Corpus Inscriptionum et Monumentorum Religionis Mithriacae*. 2 vols. The Hague, 1956, 1960.

Cumont, Franz. *Les Mystères de Mithra*. 3d ed. Brussels, 1913. Eng. trans. *The Mysteries of Mithra*. From the 2d French edition. Reprint. New York, 1956.

Vermaseren, M. J. *Mithras: The Secret God*. New York, 1963.

Vermaseren, M. J., and C. C. van Essen. *The Excavations in the Mithraeum of the Church of Santa Prisca in Rome*. Leiden, 1965.

Betz, H. D. "The Mithras Inscriptions of Santa Prisca and the New Testament." *Novum Testamentum* 10 (1968):62-80.

Campbell, Leroy A. *Mithraic Iconography and Ideology*. Leiden, 1968.

Vermaseren, M. J. *Mithriaca*. Leiden, 1971–.

Gordon, R. L. "Mithraism and Roman Society: Social Factors in the Explanation of Religious Change in the Roman Empire." *Religion* 2 (1972):92-121.

Hinnells, J. R., ed. *Mithraic Studies*. 2 vols. Manchester, 1975.

Oikonomides, Al. *Mithraic Art*. Chicago, 1975.

Journal of Mithraic Studies. Edited by R. L. Gordon. 3 vols. London, 1976–1980.

Bianchi, V., ed. *Mysteria Mithrae*. Leiden, 1979.

Speidel, Michael P. *Mithras-Orion: Greek Hero and Roman Army God*. Leiden, 1980.

Lease, Gary. "Mithraism and Christianity: Borrowings and Transformations." *ANRW* II, *Principat*, 23.2. Berlin and New York, 1980. Pp. 1306-32.

Beck, R. "Mithraism since Franz Cumont." *ANRW* II, *Principat*, 17.4. Berlin and New York, 1984. Pp. 2002-2115.

Ulansey, D. "Mithras and Perseus," *Helios* 13 (1986):33-62.

Ulansey, D. "Mithraic Studies: A Paradigm Shift?" *Religious Studies Review* 13 (1987): 104-10.

Beck, R. *Planets and Planetary Orders in the Mysteries of Mithras*. Leiden, 1988.

Ulansey, David. *The Origins of the Mithraic Mysteries*. Oxford, 1989.

Hinnells, J. R., ed. *Studies in Mithraism*. Rome, 1990.

White, L. M. *The Social Origins of Christian Architecture*, Vol. II: *Texts and Monuments for the Christian Domus Ecclesiae in its Environment*. Valley Forge, Penn., 1997. Pp. 259-429. (Mithraic sanctuaries).

Beck, R. "The Mysteries of Mithras: A New Account of their Genesis." *JRS* 88 (1988):115-28.

Mystery Religions and Christianity

The study of Christian origins has been responsible for much of the study devoted to the mystery religions (see the bibliography at the beginning of this unit). Early researchers tended to make generalizations without regard to methodological problems. There was a tendency to interpret one cult by another and so construct a general "mystery theology" or common "mystery religion." Not uncommonly this was done by (unconsciously) starting with Christian ideas, using these to interpret data about the mysteries, and then finding the mysteries as the source of the Christian ideas. Early Christian authors, it seems, did this too, only their conclusion was that the similarities came from demonic imitation of Christian rites. The Christian writers of the early centuries may have exaggerated the similarities, either from defensiveness or from the same psychological process as modern researchers, or (as seems more likely) because they could make apologetical capital for the truth of Christianity by claiming demonic imitations in paganism.

Major methodological difficulties are the scarcity of our information (the initiates kept their secret) and the lateness of much that is preserved. Early Christian authors are, in fact, a major source. How well informed were they? Did they really know as much as they claimed, or did they pass on rumor and gossip? How reliable are they? Did they really understand even what they knew? Most important of all for the *origins* of Christianity, does the information (particularly interpretations of the meaning of the rites) hold for the pre-Christian period? The mysteries underwent changes in new environments. Where the Christian authors were not reading them through the eyes of the church, there is the possibility that the mysteries themselves adopted Christian ideas. Borrowing need not have been in only one direction. On the other hand, there definitely was, by the fourth century and in some cases earlier, Christian borrowing of outward gestures from the mysteries (e.g., the magical hands dedicated to Sabazius show the thumb and first two fingers raised and the other two fingers bent in the same position used by the Catholic clergy in blessing),[231] of terminology (for apologetic purposes by Clement of Alexandria and more extensively for interpretive purposes by the Cappadocian fathers in the fourth century), and of artistic motifs (e.g., meal scenes), even as there was borrowing from pagan religion in general of ceremonies (processions), of ideas (geography of Hades), of funerary practices (cult meals for the dead), and even of deities (now disguised as Christian saints).

Nevertheless, there is very little evidence for much Christian indebted-

---

231. Maarten J. Vermaseren, *Corpus Cultis Iovis Sabazii,* Vol. 1: *The Hands* (Leiden, 1983). The gesture was in wider use in the ancient world and may not have come into Christianity specifically from Sabazius. Other testimonies of the cult of Sabazius in E. N. Lane, *Corpus Cultus Iovis Sabazii,* Vol. 2: *The Other Monuments and Literary Evidence* (Leiden, 1985).

ness in the first century, and especially in Palestine. Hence, the search for pagan influences in early Christianity has focused on Hellenistic Christianity and especially on Paul as channels through which pagan ideas reached a religion that began on Jewish soil. This too has failed to be substantiated. Rather than deal only with Paul, we shall continue by discussing the larger question of primitive Christianity's relation to the mysteries on a conceptual basis, apart from the above-mentioned methodological considerations.

Parallels to the resurrection have been suggested in the "dying and rising savior-gods." But the "resurrection" of these gods is very different from what is meant by that word in Christian belief. There is nothing in the myth of Osiris that could be called a resurrection: the god became ruler over the dead, not the living. The myth of Attis contains no specific mention of a resurrection, though it has been thought that the gladness following mourning in his cult presupposed some such notion. The Adonis myth perhaps most clearly indicates the resuscitation of a god, but even here it is not strictly a resurrection. These beliefs are more closely allied to the cycle of nature, and the mysteries seem to have had their origin in the agricultural cycle. Even this element does not seem prominent in the mysteries of the Roman period where urban life had weakened the connection with the soil. But insofar as paganism offered "dying and rising gods," these gods are a world apart from Christ's resurrection, which was presented as a one-time historical event, neither a repeated feature of nature nor a myth of the past.

Initiation into the mysteries has been presented as a "pagan regeneration" in which there is a rebirth and a kind of mystical union with the deity. The terminology of regeneration is rare in connection with the mysteries and then as a metaphor for a new life. The idea of rebirth does not appear to be specifically connected with moral renewal. The salvation the mysteries brought was a deliverance from fate and the terrors of the afterlife, not a redemption from sins. The initiate was brought into the special favor of the deity and promised his or her protection in this life and often a blessed immortality in the afterlife. The union with the deity in the form of a sacred marriage, in spite of much that has been said, is not proved in the mysteries. There was no divinization, becoming children of the god, or receiving the divine nature.

There are no true parallels to baptism in the mysteries. Where water was applied it was done so for a preliminary purification, not as the initiation itself. The manner in which the initiation into the mysteries and baptism in the New Testament worked was entirely different: the benefit of the pagan ceremony was effective by the doing *(ex opere operato)*, whereas the benefit of baptism was a grace-gift of God given to faith in the recipient. (Ideas perhaps derived from the mysteries influenced the thinking and practice of some Christians, and that from a quite early period [e.g., the misunderstandings about baptism and the Lord's Supper reflected in the warnings of 1 Cor. 10:1ff.].) All converts to Christianity received baptism, whereas initiation in the mysteries was for an inner circle of adherents.

Sharing meals was a common religious activity in paganism, Judaism, and Christianity, and there are certain similarities in all these meals. The significance of the "communion," however, was different in each case. The weekly memorial of the death and resurrection of Jesus and the specific note of thanksgiving (eucharist) in the prayers of consecration provide no pagan counterparts.

Christian baptism was a "repentance" baptism and so connected with a moral transformation of the believer, who was promised the gift of the Holy Spirit as the power of a new life. Whereas Christianity welcomed the unworthy, the pagan mysteries were for those already pure individuals who met accepted social standards. Of the mystery religions only Mithraism seems to have offered a supernaturally sanctioned ethic and moral earnestness comparable in some way to Christianity. This is not to say that the mysteries were incapable of higher, spiritual aspirations, but that had nothing to do with their essence. There was, to be sure, a personal attachment to a god. The nearest thing to Christian conversion in the mysteries was that of Lucius to Isis (Apuleius, *Metamorphoses* 11); otherwise conversion was mainly to philosophy.[232] A Plutarch could find rich meaning in the myth and rites associated with Isis and Osiris, but any philosopher could find anything he wanted in the ceremonies, for no doctrine as such was involved. Thus, one could receive spiritual benefit and meaning from the rites, as well as emotional uplift, but that was largely a matter of what one brought with him or made of them, and not what inhered in the system.

The mysteries did not offer a god who came to earth to save humans. Their gods did not die voluntarily to save humankind. And there is no reason why they should, since the consciousness of sin was not so acute nor was there a strong desire for a new ethical life. The mysteries were not for everyone; for one thing they were expensive. Initiation was for the inner circle, not for the whole community of worshipers. The initiatory rites themselves were kept secret (one wants to keep a good thing at home), unlike the Christian "mystery" *(mystērion)*, which was an "open secret," something previously hidden but now revealed and proclaimed to all.

The New Testament did not use the technical vocabulary of the mysteries.[233] Although there are some superficial similarities of language, even these have different meanings (as the word *mystērion* itself). Christianity remained "intolerant": it was an exclusive faith, whereas one could accumulate all the initiations he could afford and adherence to one deity was not a denial of others. Christianity established a worldwide brotherhood to an extent that the myster-

---

232. See A. D. Nock, *Conversion* (Oxford, 1933), 138-55 for Lucius; 164-86 for conversion to philosophy.

233. A. D. Nock, "The Vocabulary of the New Testament," *JBL* 52 (1933):131-39 (*Essays*, 341-47).

ies did not. The initiations of Lucius at Corinth and then at Rome illustrate the limitations of the sense of brotherhood in the Isiac religion. Although initiates had formulas and signs by which they recognized one another, they did not form a community with a continuing life and organization such as was the church. Christianity imposed no racial or social bars. It became truly international. Although the mysteries moved in this direction, they never lost their identification with their national origin to the extent that Christianity was freed from Judaism: for example, Lucius shaved his head like an Egyptian priest upon his receiving initiation into the mysteries of Osiris; the initiate into Mithraism passed through the grade of "Persian."

BIBLIOGRAPHY

Nock, A. D. "Hellenistic Mysteries and Christian Sacraments." *Mnemosyne,* ser. 4, vol. 5 (1952):177-213. Reprinted in *Early Gentile Christianity.* New York, 1964. Pp. 109-45.

Rahner, Hugo. "The Christian Mystery and the Pagan Mysteries." *Papers from the Eranos Yearbooks.* Vol. 2, Bollingen Foundation 30. New York, 1955. Reprinted in *Pagan and Christian Mysteries,* edited by J. Campbell. New York, 1963. Pp. 146-210.

Metzger, Bruce. "Considerations of Methodology in the Study of the Mystery Religions and Early Christianity." *HTR* 48 (1955):1-20. Reprinted in *Historical and Literary Studies.* New Testament Tools and Studies. Grand Rapids, 1968. Pp. 1-24.

Wagner, Günther. *Pauline Baptism and the Pagan Mysteries.* Edinburgh, 1967.

Wiens, D. H. "Mystery Concepts in Primitive Christianity and Its Environment." *ARNW,* II, Principat, 23.2. Berlin, 1980. Pp. 1248-1284.

Wedderburn, A. J. M. "Paul and the Hellenistic Mystery-Cults: On Posing the Right Questions." In U. Bianchi and M. J. Vermaseren, eds. *La soteriologia dei culti orientali nell'imperio romano.* Leiden, 1982. Pp. 817-835.

Wedderburn, A. J. M. *Baptism and Resurrection: Studies in Pauline Theology against its Greco-Roman Background.* Tübingen, 1987.

Smith, J. Z. *Drudgery Divine: On the Comparison of Early Christianities and the Religions of Late Antiquity.* Chicago, 1990.

GNOSTICISM, HERMETIC LITERATURE, CHALDAEAN ORACLES

The Term Gnosticism

The Greek noun *gnōsis* means "knowledge," especially perception, insight, acquaintance. Plato coined the word *gnōstikos* for what gives intellectual knowledge in contrast to practical skill (*Statesman* 258E), and it remained for a long time a philosophical technical term.[234] The first attested use for persons as a distinct social entity occurs in the Christian anti-heretical writer Irenaeus in the late second century (*Against Heresies* 1.11.1). The word referred to a school of thought and then to its members. It was used in a complimentary sense as a self-designation by Sethians (see below) and others. Irenaeus extended the term to the Valentinians, whom he regarded as deriving from those who so described themselves, and this broader usage was continued by Christian opponents of those whose teaching they judged erroneous. The term Gnosticism is a modern designation for a group of systems of thought opposed by early Christian writers.

The use of Gnosticism as a general category is problematic, for not even Irenaeus and his successors constructed a single typology for the various groups now covered by this term. The teachings usually advanced as characterizing Gnosticism (see below) admit many exceptions. The most nearly common features of the sources treated under the heading of Gnosticism are a distinction between the creator(s) and controllers of the material world and the ultimate transcendent divine being, an interest in speculation about the nature of divinity and the heavenly realm, consideration of the cause of the human condition with a focus on the soul's eventual transcendence of the created order, patterns of spirituality consistent with this worldview, and the interpretation of Jewish or Christian Scripture traditions in advancing the viewpoint. The term Gnosticism seems so firmly established that whatever problems in generalization it provokes it is not likely to be replaced, and we continue to use it in this introduction with the understanding that readers must exercise caution.

Sources for Study

The study of Gnosticism was long hampered by the circumstance that it was known almost entirely from the writings of its orthodox Christian opponents. Fully developed Gnostic thought in the second century provided a major doctrinal challenge to the church and prompted the polemical writings of Irenaeus, Hippolytus, and later Epiphanius. The longest Gnostic work, which has been known for some years, is *Pistis Sophia*,[235] a work closely related in thought to some of the more recently discovered Gnostic documents.

The understanding of Gnosticism has been greatly advanced by the discovery of a "library of Gnostic writings" near Nag Hammadi (Chenoboskion)

234. This paragraph depends on Bentley Layton, "Prolegomena to the Study of Ancient Gnosticism," in L. M. White and O. L. Yarbrough, eds., *The Social World of the First Christians* (Minneapolis, 1995), 334-50; repr. E. Ferguson, ed., *Doctrinal Diversity, Recent Studies in Early Christianity*, Vol. 4 (New York, 1999), 106-122.

235. *Pistis Sophia*, ed. Carl Schmidt, trans. Violet Macdermot (Leiden, 1978).

NAG HAMMADI LIBRARY*

Number of Codex, Tractate, Page, and Lines	Name of Tractate	Literary Form	Affiliations
I,1 A,1-B,10	Prayer of Apostle Paul	Prayer	Valentinian
I,2 1,1-16,30	Apocryphon of James	Apocalypse set in an Epistle	
I,3 16,31-43,24	Gospel of Truth	Meditation or Homily	Valentinian
I,4 43,25-50,18	Epistle to Rheginus Treatise on the Resurrection	Epistolary Treatise	Valentinian
I,5 51,1-138,27	Tripartite Tractate	Theological Treatise	Valentinian
II,1 1,1-32,9	Apocryphon of John	Apocalypse–Revelation Discourse	Sethian
II,2 32,10-51,28	Gospel of Thomas**	Sayings Collection	
II,3 51,29-86,19	Gospel of Philip	Theological Statements	Valentinian
II,4 86,20-97,23	Hypostasis [Nature] of the Archons	Apocalypse (in part)	Sethian
II,5 97,24-127,17	On the Origin of the World	Theological Treatise	
II,6 127,18-137,27	Exegesis on the Soul	Exhortation	Valentinian?
II,7 138,1-145,19	Book of Thomas the Contender	Revelation Dialogue	
III,1 1,1-40,11	Apocryphon of John	(See II,1)	Sethian
III,2 40,12-69,20	Gospel of the Egyptians**	Theological Treatise-Liturgy	Sethian
III,3 70,1-90,13	Eugnostos the Blessed	Epistolary Treatise	Non-Christian
III,4 90,14-119,18	Sophia of Jesus Christ	Apocalypse – Dialogue	Christianized version of III,3
III,5 120,1-147,23	Dialogue of the Saviour	Revelation Dialogue	
IV,1 1,1-49,28	Apocryphon of John	(See II,1)	
IV,2 50,1-81,2	Gospel of the Egyptians	(See III,2)	
V,1 1,1-17,18	Eugnostos the Blessed	(See III,3)	
V,2 17,19-24,9	Apocalypse of Paul**	Apocalypse	Valentinian
V,3 24,10-44,10	First Apocalypse of James	Apocalypse – Dialogue	
V,4 44,11-63,32	Second Apocalypse of James	Apocalypse	
V,5 64,1-85,32	Apocalypse of Adam	Apocalypse	Sethian – Non-Christian
VI,1 1,1-12,22	Acts of Peter and the Twelve Apostles	Acts	
VI,2 13,1-21,32	Thunder, Perfect Mind	Revelation Discourse	Sethian
VI,3 22,1-35,24	Authoritative Teaching	Theological Treatise	Valentinian?
VI,4 36,1-48,15	Concept of our Great Power	Apocalypse	
VI,5 48,16-51,23	Plato, Republic 588B-589B		
VI,6 52,1-63,32	Discourse on the Eighth and Ninth	Revelation Dialogue	Hermetic
VI,7 63,33-65,7	Prayer of Thanksgiving	Prayer	Hermetic

VI,8 65,15-78,43	Asclepius 21-29	Apocalypse/Dialogue	Hermetic
VII,1 1,1-49,9	Paraphrase of Shem	Apocalypse	
VII,2 49,10-70,12	Second Treatise of the Great Seth	Apocalypse/Dialogue	
VII,3 70,13-84,14	Apocalypse of Peter**	Apocalypse	
VII,4 84,15-118,7	Teachings of Silvanus	Wisdom Sayings	Non-Gnostic
VII,5 118,10-127,27	Three Steles of Seth	Apocalypse – Hymnic Prayers	Sethian – Non-Christian
VIII,1 1,1-132,9	Zostrianos	Apocalypse	Sethian – Non-Christian
VIII,2 132,10-140,27	Letter of Peter to Philip	Apocalypse set in an Epistle	
IX,1 1,1-27,10	Melchizedek	Apocalypse	Sethian
IX,2 27,11-29,5	Thought of Norea	Hymn ?	Sethian
IX,3 29,6-74,30	Testimony of Truth	Homily	Valentinian sect
X,1 1,1-68,18	Marsanes	Apocalypse	Sethian – Non-Christian
XI,1 1,1-21,35	Interpretation of Knowledge	Homily	Valentinian
XI,2 22,1-44,37	Valentinian Exposition (including On Anointing, On Baptism, and On the Eucharist)	Catechism ?	Valentinian
XI,3 45,1-69,20	Allogenes	Apocalypse	Sethian – Non-Christian
XI,4 69,21-72,33	Hypsiphrone	Apocalypse ?	
XII,1 15,1-34,28	Sentences of Sextus	Wisdom Sayings	Non-Gnostic
XII,2 53,19-60,30	Gospel of Truth	(See I,3)	
XII,3	Fragments		
XIII,1 35,1-50,24	Trimorphic Protennoia	Revelation Discourse	Sethian
XIII,2 50,25-34	On the Origin of the World	(See II,5)	

The Berlin Gnostic Codex is closely related and contains the following:

BG 8502,1 7,1-19,5	Gospel of Mary	Resurrection Gospel/Dialogue and Revelation Discourse	
BG 8502,2 19,6-77,7	Apocryphon of John	(See II,1)	
BG 8502,3 77,8-127,12	Sophia of Jesus Christ	(See III,4)	
BG 8502,4 128,1-141,7	Acts of Peter	Acts	

*Adapted from George MacRae in *Interpreter's Dictionary of the Bible*, Supplementary volume, ed. Keith Crim (Nashville, 1976), 615f.
**Not to be confused with other works of the same name.

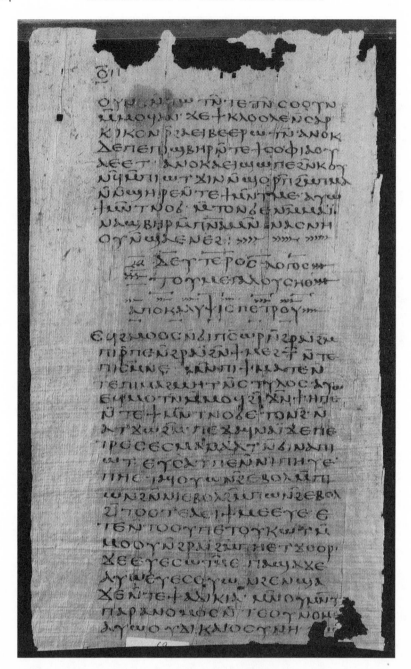

NAG HAMMADI MANUSCRIPT
This is the seventieth page of Codex VII, the end of the
Second Treatise of the Great Seth and the beginning of the *Apocalypse of Peter.*
(Courtesy of the Institute for Antiquity and Christianity, Claremont, California)

in upper Egypt.[236] The manuscripts are in Coptic and date from the mid–fourth century, but they contain writings that were originally in Greek and produced for the most part in the second and third centuries. The Nag Hammadi collection consists of twelve codices plus one loose tractate for a total of fifty-two tractates. Six are duplicates within the collection itself, and six were previously known works, leaving forty new documents, of which thirty are in relatively good condition.

The chart on pages 302-3 lists all of the tractates in the Nag Hammadi Library, with some indication of literary and doctrinal affinities. The Nag Hammadi documents are cited by codex number (in Roman numeral), tractate number in the codex (Arabic numeral), page, and line numbers of the manuscript.

The *Gospel of Thomas*[237] is a collection of 112 to 118 (according to different editions) sayings attributed to Jesus, some of which were already known in Greek from a collection in the Oxyrhynchus Papyri.[238] The *Gospel of Thomas* is perhaps the earliest of the new texts in the collection and demonstrates the existence of collections of sayings of Jesus (a sayings gospel) in the early church. It has a strong encratite or ascetic tone but otherwise is not so pronouncedly Gnostic, although clearly consistent with Gnostic understandings. Although scholarly opinion seems to incline toward emphasizing the extent of the independence of the *Gospel of Thomas* from the Synoptic Gospels, the age and originality of its individual sayings in relation to the canonical Gospels are much debated.[239]

The *Gospel of Truth*[240] may be identified with a work of that name that Irenaeus attributes to the followers of Valentinus (*Against Heresies* 3.11.9). It is not properly a "Gospel," but a meditation on the truth of redemption. Its theme is that the human state is ignorance, and salvation is by knowledge imparted by Jesus.

The *Gospel of Philip*[241] is another sayings or discourse gospel, also from Valentinian circles. It offers information on liturgical practices.

236. Michel Desjardins, "The Sources for Valentinian Gnosticism: A Question of Methodology," *Vigiliae Christianae* 40 (1986):342-347, offers cautions about the relative values of the patristic sources and Nag Hammadi texts.

237. F. F. Bruce, *Jesus and Christian Origins Outside the New Testament* (Grand Rapids, 1974), 110-56; Marvin Meyer, *The Gospel of Thomas,* trans. with int. and notes (San Francisco, 1992); Stephen J. Patterson and James M. Robinson with a new English translation by Hans-Gebhard Bethge et al., *The Fifth Gospel: The Gospel of Thomas Comes of Age* (Harrisburg, 1998); Bertil Gärtner, *The Theology of the Gospel According to Thomas* (New York, 1961).

238. B. P. Grenfell and A. S. Hunt, *Oxyrhynchus Papyri,* vols. 1 and 4 (London, 1898, 1904), nos. 1, 654, and 655.

239. K. V. Neller, K. R. Snodgrass, and C. W. Hedrick present three different views with extensive bibliographical notes in the special issue of *The Second Century* 7 (1989/90):1-56.

240. K. Grobel, *The Gospel of Truth* (New York, 1960).

241. R. McL. Wilson, *The Gospel of Philip* (New York, 1962).

The *Apocryphon of John*[242] appears to have been one of the most popular of the Gnostic works, for three copies of it were found at Nag Hammadi and one other was previously known. It provides a close parallel to the Gnostic system described in Irenaeus, *Against Heresies* 1.29.

The *Epistle to Rheginus, On the Resurrection*[243] sets forth a position close to that of the orthodox in terminology but emphasizes a resurrection of the soul.

The *Apocryphon of James*,[244] like many documents in the collection, is a postresurrection revelation of Jesus. He gives blessings and woes through Peter and James. It is argued that the work derives from a sayings collection independent of the New Testament.

The *Hypostasis of the Archons*[245] describes the efforts of the world rulers to deceive humankind in Genesis 1–6. The myth is close to that of the Ophites or Sethians in Irenaeus, *Against Heresies* 1.30.

The *Tripartite Tractate* is the most ambitious and comprehensive theological undertaking in the Nag Hammadi corpus. It has points of contact with the Valentinian teacher Heracleon and attempts to present Gnostic teaching, in response to orthodox criticism, in a way more acceptable to the great church.

Eugnostos the Blessed and *The Sophia of Jesus Christ* are two versions of the same document, the former a letter by a teacher to his disciples and the latter a revelation discourse of Jesus to his followers. The former is important as a non-Christian form of Gnosticism whereas the latter is a Christianized version of the same.

These writings give us more of the inner religious spirit of Gnosticism, whereas the heresiologists concentrated on the bizarre and on the outer structure of the Gnostic systems. Otherwise, the new finds correspond to the picture given by the Christian authors in its main outlines. The non-Christian nature of many tenets of Gnosticism is evident, although it attached itself to the Christian revelation. The concern with the Old Testament points to an area of proximity to Judaism if not to a specifically Jewish origin.

242. S. Giverson, *Apocryphon Johannis* (Leiden, 1963); M. W. Meyer, ed., *The Secret Teachings of Jesus: Four Gnostic Gospels* (New York, 1984).

243. Malcolm Lee Peel, *The Epistle to Rheginos* (Philadelphia, 1969); Bentley Layton, *The Gnostic Treatise on Resurrection from Nag Hammadi* (Missoula, Mont., 1979).

244. M. Melinine, H.-Ch. Peuch, G. Quispel, W. Till, and R. Kasser, *Epistula Iacobi Apocrypha* (Zurich, 1968); R. Cameron, ed., *The Other Gospels: Non-Canonical Gospel Texts* (Philadelphia, 1982); idem, *Sayings Traditions in the Apocryphon of James* (Philadelphia, 1984).

245. R. A. Bullard, *The Hypostasis of the Archons* (Berlin, 1967); Bentley Layton, "The Hypostasis of the Archons or *The Reality of the Rulers*," *HTR* 67 (1974):351-425 and 69 (1976):31-101.

Origins of Gnosticism

The questions of when and from what source Gnosticism arose have been hotly debated. Did Gnosticism originate as a Christian heresy, or did it originate as a non-Christian movement, whether pagan or Jewish? The Nag Hammadi documents give new evidence, but each position still has adherents. The new Gnostic texts do not solve the chronology of Gnosticism — none is demonstrably earlier than the New Testament. On the other hand, the collection witnesses to non-Christian expressions of Gnosticism and so reopens the question of the possibility that Christians in the formative period drew on external Gnostic concepts, imagery, and terminology to express their faith, even though at a later stage they found it necessary to combat extreme developments of Gnostic thinking.

Most forms of Gnosticism that we know seem to contain elements from pagan thought, Judaism, and Christianity. Elements of Gnosticism bear striking similarities to Neopythagoreanism (see pp. 382ff.) and Middle Platonism (pp. 387ff.), suggesting that some fusion of Greek speculative thought brought about Gnosticism. It has even been characterized as "Platonism run wild."[246] Here we may note the idea of a remote supreme being, the soul as immortal and in bondage to the body, and a disparagement of the material world: these were ideas for which Gnosticism found philosophical support although extending them to an extreme beyond what philosophers advocated. Plotinus (*Enneads* 2.9; cf. 3.2) debated with Gnostics over the interpretation of Plato, particularly with relation to the nature of the material world.[247] The *Hermetica* and *Chaldaean Oracles* (below, pp. 313-16) suggest Gnostic schemes in a non-Christian form. On the other hand, it is remarkable how many Gnostic speculations can be explained as arising from reflections on the early chapters of Genesis. The personification of Wisdom, the angelology, later speculations in Jewish mysticism[248] — these are some of the features that cause many to look to heterodox or esoteric expressions of Judaism or to Jews, who if not already in revolt against their religion and its God soon moved in that direction, for the origins of Gnosticism. Some of the possible combinations of elements drawn from Greek philosophy, Judaism, and Christianity are represented in the various groups rejected as heretical by the church. Since the groups called "Gnostic" do not represent one phenomenon, multiple origins are likely.

The church fathers traced Gnostic heresies back to Simon Magus in Sa-

246. A. D. Nock, "Gnosticism," *HTR* 57 (1964):267 (*Essays*, 949); A. H. Armstrong, "Gnosis and Greek Philosophy," in B. Aland, ed., *Gnosis: Festschrift für Hans Jonas* (Göttingen, 1978), pp. 87-124, argues that the influence of Greek philosophy on Gnosticism was superficial.

247. For the lines of connection, see R. T. Wallis and Jay Bregman, eds., *Neoplatonism and Gnosticism* (Albany, N.Y., 1992).

248. G. Scholem, *Jewish Gnosticism. Merkabah Mysticism and Talmudic Tradition* (New York, 1965).

maria (Acts 8); this artificial schematizing does fit the modern interest in circles in proximity to Judaism as the origin of Gnosticism. There seems to have been heavy contact of Gnostic thought with Judaism before its contact with Christianity. Any contribution from the rest of the Near East, at least to the Gnosticism combatted by the church fathers, was mediated through Greek or Jewish channels. Nevertheless, many of the new texts can be interpreted in a manner consistent with the church fathers' view of Gnosticism as a Christian heresy with roots in speculative thought, even if not a "Hellenization" of Christianity. Certainly, many things in the New Testament, especially in Paul, proved to be susceptible of a Gnostic interpretation.[249] There were non-Christian ideas in Gnosticism. The question is, did Christians take these ideas and put them together in order to interpret their faith, or did non-Christians put them together before Christians took them over? Even in the latter case, a non-Christian origin is not the same as pre-Christian.

In dealing with the question of Gnostic origins it is perhaps well to observe a distinction between Gnosis and Gnosticism. If we take *Gnosis* to refer to a wider atmosphere of ideas, we can then reserve *Gnosticism* for the developed systems known in the second century. Gnostic ideas were around and were gradually put together in various combinations around different organizing principles. Gnosticism seems to have grown up concurrently with Christianity in a similar environment (but from different roots), with the two having some interactions in the first century before Gnosticism developed into a separate religion in the second century. This could account for contacts and mutual influences and for Gnosticism's contributions, positive and negative, to the development of Christian theology. Modern scholars have delineated two principal expressions of Gnosticism — Valentinianism, which was more "Christian" and hence of special concern to the church fathers, and Sethianism, apparently an earlier form and possibly non-Christian in origin.

The principal pre-Christian feature that has been claimed as a decisive Gnostic contribution to the Christian framework of thinking has been the "redeemer myth." On this view a supernatural being, a cosmic Man, descended to earth to redeem the saved; this provided the category in which the meaning of Jesus' mission was explained in Christianity. But no pre-Christian document includes such a redeemer myth.[250] An alternative interpretation puts the influence the other way: "In general apart from the Christian movement there was a Gnostic way of thinking, but no Gnostic system of thought. . . . It was the emergence of Jesus and the belief that he was a supernatural being who had appeared on earth which precipitated elements previously suspended in solu-

---

249. Elaine Pagels, *The Gnostic Paul: Gnostic Exegesis of the Pauline Letters* (Philadelphia, 1975).

250. C. Colpe, *Die religionsgeschichtliche Schule: Darstellung und Kritik ihres Bildes vom Gnostischen Erlösermythus* (Göttingen, 1961).

tion."[251] (See the treatment of the Redeemer figure in the Introduction, pp. 2-3.) The essential character of Gnosticism has also been sought not in a redeemer but in a particular understanding of existence.

We know different expressions of Christian Gnosticism from the second century: one associated with Basilides, Christianized versions of Sethian Gnosticism, a Thomas tradition (not fully Gnosticized), and most important of all Valentinianism with its western branch represented by Ptolemy and Heracleon and its eastern branch represented by Theodotus. Elements of these various systems are known from the first century (or earlier), but so far as can be proved at present not as a developed Gnostic religion.

One Gnostic sect, the Mandaeans of southern Iraq, has survived to modern times.[252] It has been claimed that they are descendants of a pre-Christian baptizing sect in the Jordan valley associated with John the Baptist. Another interpretation sees the Zoroastrian element as the foundation and dates their origin much later, with Babylonian and Manichaean influences entering in.[253] An intermediate view allows an origin in the early centuries of the common era but suggests that the appropriation of an association with John the Baptist is a secondary development and allows for the influence of other ideas at a later date.

Characteristic Features

There were many teachers in the Hellenistic world, each in his own way combining religious, mythological, and philosophical ideas. Christianity added a new ingredient to a ferment already at work. Most of the earlier Hellenistic teachers are not known, but each gave his own twist to current ideas in the interest of originality — apart from continuing school traditions in philosophy. If Christianity had not been involved the names of the second-century Gnostic teachers and their ideas would have been left in a similar obscurity.

Each Gnostic teacher supplied his own constructions and variations, with the result that *Gnosticism* is now a general term that covers a variety of individual constructions. There is no single, uniform Gnostic system.

The most attractive system, and one of the better known, was that of Valentinus, who flourished in the mid–second century. His follower Ptolemy had an elaborate myth of origins. A perfect first principle generated by emission a spiritual universe made up of *aeons* (ages or realms). A "fall" in this di-

251. A. D. Nock, "Gnosticism," *HTR* 57 (1964):278.

252. E. S. Drower, *The Canonical Prayerbook of the Mandaeans* (Leiden, 1959); *The Mandaeans of Iraq and Iran* (Oxford, 1937; 2d ed. Leiden, 1962); K. Rudolf, *Die Mandäer*, 2 vols. (Göttingen, 1960, 1961); E. Yamauchi, *Gnostic Ethics and Mandaean Origins* (Cambridge, 1970); E. Lupieri, *The Mandaeans: The Last Gnostics* (Grand Rapids, 2001).

253. Edward T. Grabert, "The Vocabulary of Salvation in the Qolasta and the Fourth Gospel," Ph.D. diss., Drew University, 1963.

vine world *(plērōma)* resulted in matter coming into existence. A Demiurge (an inferior heavenly being) fashioned the world and humanity. However, some of the pure spiritual nature, a spark of the divine, was planted in some souls. A redeemer came from the divine world to reveal the way of escape for the divine spark out of the material world. The saved soul must pass through the realms of the world rulers (archons) in order to return to its proper spiritual home, but if it is among the elect it is easily able to do so.

Students of Gnosticism have been concerned with the following ideas:[254]

(1) The problem of evil. Several Gnostic systems "kicked the problem upstairs" by locating it ultimately in the divine rather than in human beings, and associated it somehow with the material world.

(2) Sense of alienation from the world. This was a part of the general despair over the world that characterized the early centuries of our era. A sense of alienation from the world is a better characterization than "anticosmic," which many scholars employ. Nevertheless, there was a tension in the attitudes toward society among the people involved in these groups. Many were moving more in the direction of social involvement with less estrangement toward their social environment than were more orthodox Christians, as may be seen in the avoidance of martyrdom, the efforts to reconcile the biblical tradition with Greco-Roman myths, practices, or philosophy, and the phenomenon characterized as syncretism.

(3) Desire for special and intimate knowledge of the secrets of the universe. The Gnostic salvation was from ignorance and not from sin. Knowledge was not just the means to salvation, it was the salvation. The knowledge was a knowledge of one's true self, one's home in the pleroma, and one's return there.

(4) Dualism. There are different kinds of dualism: for example, ethical dualism (good and evil — from Judaism, esp. Qumran, and with cosmic associations from Persian thought), eschatological or supernatural dualism (this age and the age to come — from Jewish apocalyptic and Qumran), and psychological dualism (body and soul — from Platonism). Gnosticism is an amalgam of psychological and ethical dualism with a cosmic dualism of this material world and the supercelestial spiritual world. Corresponding to this is the distinction between the Hidden God and the Creator God.

(5) Cosmology. The pleroma or divine world contains gradations of being that are emanations or devolutions from the first principle. These were arranged in masculine-feminine pairs in Valentinianism. The archons (intermediate beings) rule this world by fate.

---

254. Items (1) through (3) are taken from A. D. Nock, "Gnosticism," *HTR* 57 (1964):255-79 and items (4) through (8) from Hans Jonas, *Gnostic Religion* (2d ed.; Boston, 1963), 42-47, modified; see a related list in B. A. Pearson, *Gnosticism, Judaism, and Egyptian Christianity* (Minneapolis, 1990), 7-8. See also Kurt Rudolph, *Gnosis: The Nature and History of Gnosticism* (San Francisco, 1983), 53-272. The qualifications introduced in my summaries are based on Michael A. Williams, *Rethinking "Gnosticism": An Argument for Dismantling a Dubious Category* (Princeton, 1996).

(6) Anthropology. Valentinianism offered three classes of human beings according to their nature: the pneumatics or spirituals who had the divine spark in themselves and were destined for salvation, the psychics who could be saved by the ministrations of the church and good works, and the hylics who belonged to the material world and were hopelessly lost. On the other hand, extensive evidence speaks against a rigid determinism in Gnostic anthropology: extensive ethical paraenesis, an active interest in recruitment of new members, statements about the conditional nature of salvation and maturity, and language affirming liberation from determinism. These people appear to have been wrestling with the philosophical questions about providence and free will current in the second century.

(7) Radically realized eschatology. Gnosticism did not emphasize a futuristic eschatology of a cosmic or corporate nature; the kingdom of God was an interior kingdom. As a religion of personal salvation it taught that the pneumatic experienced his true condition now and at death went immediately to the pleroma.

(8) Ethical implications. As the pneumatic was free from fate, so he was free from the moral law. For some Gnostics this meant libertinism, though much of the evidence for this is suspect. One primary source, from Epiphanes (quoted by Clement of Alexandria, *Miscellanies* 3.4.6-9), advocates sexual promiscuity but does so on the basis of the goodness of creation. A more characteristic deduction from Gnostic premises, however, was asceticism. One sought to frustrate the flesh by denying it. The Nag Hammadi documents reflect the ascetic option. The main ascetic practices were abstinence from wine, from various foods, and from sex. Even so, the texts manifest a certain ambivalence toward the human body: The self is different from the physical body and must be rescued from it; yet the human body is the intersection of the divine image with defiled matter and represents a visible trace of the divine in the material world. Practices were not uniformly negative with regard to the body.

Some Christian Gnostics of the second century showed greater interest in leadership roles for women and less interest in a structured hierarchy than did their opponents. The prominence of feminine imagery for the divine in some of the documents has been thought to reflect a social context in which women were prominent, but proof of this is still lacking. In fact, there is a striking difference between the roles of females in Gnostic texts and the way Gnostics appear to have understood women. The prominence of feminine imagery in Gnostic literature, moreover, stands in contrast to the distrust of the feminine that is basic to Gnostic thought.[255]

---

255. Karen L. King, ed., *Images of the Feminine in Gnosticism* (Philadelphia, 1988; repr. Harrisburg, 2000), especially Frederik Wisse, "Flee Femininity: Antifemininity in Gnostic Texts and the Question of Social Milieu," 297-307.

Gnosticism in the New Testament

The false teachings opposed in some of the New Testament books bear similarities to the Gnosticism combatted in the second century and have been called "incipient Gnosticism" if not outright Gnosticism.[256] Simon Magus in Acts 8 was made by later church writers the arch-heretic from whom all later heresy derived. Acts presents nothing distinctively Gnostic about him but may not tell the whole story. If the church fathers' claim is not totally artificial, Simon's followers may have moved in a Gnostic direction, or later church writers may have confused him with a different Simon who was a Gnostic. Colossians and the Pastoral Epistles oppose errorists who served angelic mediators, practiced asceticism, had secret teachings, claimed a superior knowledge, and denied the Christian doctrines of creation and resurrection. First Timothy 6:20 even refers to the *gnōsis* "falsely so-called." The Johannine literature too opposes teachers who had left the Christian fold, denied the incarnation, held an individualistic and libertine view of salvation, and emphasized knowledge. The troubles at Corinth over the resurrection and enthusiastic spiritual gifts have also been traced to Gnostic thinking. There is enough to show that many of the materials with which the great Gnostic teachers of the second century worked were around in the first century. It is less clear that these ideas were present in the same combinations, in as developed a form, or within the same mythical framework. The New Testament errorists appear to combine Jewish, pagan, and Christian elements; but these ingredients provide an almost infinite variety of potential combinations.

BIBLIOGRAPHY

Haardt, R. *Gnosis: Character and Testimony.* Leiden, 1971.
Foerster, Werner, ed. *Gnosis: A Selection of Gnostic Texts.* 2 vols. Oxford, 1972, 1974.
The Department of Antiquities of the Arab Republic of Egypt in conjunction with UNESCO. *The Facsimile Editions of the Nag Hammadi Codices.* 12 vols. Leiden, 1972–1984.
Institute for Antiquity and Christianity. *The Coptic Gnostic Library.* Edited with an English translation, introduction, and notes. 15 vols. Nag Hammadi Studies. Leiden, 1975–.
Robinson, James, ed. *The Nag Hammadi Library in English.* 3d ed. San Francisco, 1988.
Layton, Bentley. *The Gnostic Scriptures.* Garden City, N.Y., 1987.
Robinson, James, ed. *The Coptic Gnostic Library.* 5 vols. Leiden, 2000. (Text, translation, and notes.)

Bianchi, Ugo, ed. *The Origins of Gnosticism.* Leiden, 1967.
Wilson, R. McL. *Gnosis and the New Testament.* Philadelphia, 1968.

256. C. A. Evans, et al., *Nag Hammadi Texts and the Bible: A Synopsis and Index* (Leiden, 1993) lists parallels between the Nag Hammadi documents and the Bible.

Yamauchi, Edwin. *Pre-Christian Gnosticism.* Grand Rapids, 1973.

Perkins, Pheme. *The Gnostic Dialogue: The Early Church and the Crisis of Gnosticism.* New York, 1980.

Layton, Bentley, ed. *The Rediscovery of Gnosticism.* 2 vols. Leiden, 1980–1981.

Rudolph, Kurt. *Gnosis: The Nature and History of Gnosticism.* San Francisco, 1983.

Logan, A. H. B., and A. J. M. Wedderburn. *The New Testament and Gnosis: Essays in Honour of Robert McL. Wilson.* Edinburgh, 1983.

Strousma, G. G. *Another Seed: Studies in Gnostic Mythology.* Leiden, 1984.

Hedrick, Charles W., Sr., and Robert Hodgson, Jr., eds. *Nag Hammadi, Gnosticism, and Early Christianity.* Peabody, Mass., 1986.

Tuckett, C. M. *Nag Hammadi and the Gospel Tradition.* Edinburgh, 1986.

Pearson, B. A. *Gnosticism, Judaism, and Egyptian Christianity.* Minneapolis, 1990.

Pétrement, Simone. *A Separate God: The Christian Origins of Gnosticism.* San Francisco, 1990.

Filoramo, Giovanni. *Gnosticism.* Oxford, 1990.

Goehring, J. E., et al., eds. *Gnosticism and the Early Christian World.* Sonoma, Calif., 1990.

Perkins, Pheme. *Gnosticism and the New Testament.* Minneapolis, 1993.

Scholer, David M., ed. *Gnosticism in the Early Church.* Studies in Early Christianity, ed. Everett Ferguson, Vol. 5. New York, 1993.

Williams, Michael A. *Rethinking "Gnosticism": An Argument for Dismantling a Dubious Category.* Princeton, 1996.

Turner, John D. and Anne McGuire. *The Nag Hammadi Library after Fifty Years: Proceedings of the 1995 Society of Biblical Literature Commemoration.* Leiden, 1997.

Roukema, Riemer. *Gnosis and Faith in Early Christianity: An Introduction to Gnosticism.* Harrisburg, 1999.

Turner, John D., and Ruth Majercik, eds. *Gnosticism and Later Platonism: Themes, Figures, and Texts.* Williston, Vt., 2000.

King, Karen L. *What Is Gnosticism?* Cambridge, Mass., 2003.

Markschies, Christoph. *Gnosis: An Introduction.* Edinburgh, 2003.

Scholer, David M. *Nag Hammadi Bibliography 1948–1969.* Leiden, 1971.

Scholer, David M. *Nag Hammadi Bibliography 1970–1994.* Leiden, 1997.

Scholer, David M. "Bibliographica Gnostica, Supplementum." *Novum Testamentum* 40 (1998):73-100, and continued annually in succeeding January issues.

The Hermetica

Hermes Trismegistus ("Thrice-Greatest Hermes") was the Greek translation of the Egyptian god "Thoth the very great," who was the reputed author of the religio-philosophical treatises known as the Hermetic Writings *(Hermetica* or *Corpus Hermeticum).* The works were produced in Egypt, but the authors were Greeks who sought to attribute their ideas to the reputed authority of Egyptian wisdom.

The *Corpus Hermeticum* consists of seventeen tractates in Greek, to which are to be added Apuleius's *Asclepius* (in Latin; an excerpt from it in Coptic is included in the Nag Hammadi collection) and the *Kore Kosmou* preserved in Stobaeus. Collections of Hermetic writings were made in antiquity; the one that survives was brought together in Byzantine times. Dating these writings is difficult, but the range is from the mid–first century to the end of the third century. Some of the tractates have a pantheistic and optimistic character (II, V, VIII, XIV, and *Asclepius*); some are dualistic and pessimistic in character (I, IV, VI, VII, XIII). Of most interest to New Testament scholars is Tractate I, the *Poimandres* (second century at the earliest), in which *Logos* and Creative Mind mediate between the transcendent God and the world and *Anthropos* descends through the seven planetary spheres to reveal God. The writer had a *mystērion* (an open secret) to reveal to the world.

The Hermetic writings have been described as the pagan branch of Gnosticism because of their scheme of individual redemption by knowledge without a cosmic conclusion to correct the original fault.[257] Their Redeemer is a Revealer. No consistent outlook is maintained, and it is the dualistic tractates that most nearly approximate Gnosticism. Yet the most distinguishing characteristic of the Hermeticist is that he was a mystic. True knowledge *(gnōsis)* is in inner enlightenment, the vision of God. Ecstasy produces the knowledge of God, and the result of *gnōsis* is the divinization of a person while alive, described as a rebirth *(palingenesia)*. Bodily things and things of the senses hinder ecstasy. A person, as a part of nature, is in a body and is by nature evil. God is the good. There are two kinds of human beings: those who participate in *gnōsis* and those confined by bodily lusts and concerns. The Hermeticist was full of a holy zeal to proclaim to all the way of salvation, yet not everyone can share in the *gnōsis*. Redemption is the recognition of the self, the knowledge that one came from "life and light" and will return. The way to salvation is putting to death the senses. Salvation is practically the contemplative ecstasy. The conception of the heavenly journey of the soul was patterned on astrological mysticism. Human beings in their descent through the planetary spheres were clothed with their properties and on return must remove them. Thus, the soul ascends through the seven planetary spheres, at each of which it sheds a vice, to the ogdoad (the eighth sphere, the realm of eternal perfection) where it passes into the heavenly powers and is at last absorbed into God. Hermeticism was not a theory or a philosophical system, but a way of spiritual progression. Some of the texts may refer to ceremonies of initiation to Hermetic brotherhoods.[258]

257. "For it is only knowledge of God that brings salvation to man." *Corpus Hermeticum* X,15. See G. Luck, "The Doctrine of Salvation in the Hermetic Writings," *The Second Century* 8 (1991):31-41.

258. J.-M. Mahé, "La voie d'immortalité à la lumière des *Hermetica* de Nag Hammadi et de découvertes plus récentes," *Vigiliae Christianae* 45 (1991):347-75 (with valuable European bibliography).

Even the pantheistic tractates, which employ Stoic terms, are much more mystical and personal than the writings of the Stoics. The mind of God governs *heimarmenē*, law, and all powers. The world is an image of God, and humans are an image of the world.

Jewish influence is certain in the *Hermetica*, where Genesis 1:28 is cited. Christian contacts are more indirect.[259] The Hermetic doctrine represented a small circle of students, and its redemption was individual. The new life in Hermeticism, as in some forms of Gnosticism, raised the person above the need for moral endeavor, whereas in Christianity it equipped the person for the moral struggle.[260]

BIBLIOGRAPHY

Nock, A. D., and A. J. Festugière, eds. *Corpus Hermeticum*. 2 vols. Paris, 1945. Reprint, 1960.

Copenhaver, B. P., ed. *Hermetica: The Greek "Corpus Hermeticum" and the Latin "Asclepius."* Cambridge, 1992. (Trans. with int. and notes.)

Festugière, A. J. *La Révelation d'Hermès Trismégiste*. 4 vols. 3d ed. Paris, 1950–1954.

Dodd, C. H. *The Bible and the Greeks*. London, 1954.

Van Moorsel, G. *The Mysteries of Hermes Trismegistus*. Utrecht, 1955.

Delatte, L., S. Govaerts, and J. Denooz. *Index du corpus hermeticum*. Rome, 1977.

Grese, W. C. *Corpus Hermeticum XIII and Early Christian Literature*. Leiden, 1979.

Iversen, E. *Egyptian and Hermetic Doctrine*. Copenhagen, 1984.

González Blanco, A. "Hermetism: A Bibliographical Approach." *ANRW* II, *Principat*, 17.4. Berlin and New York, 1984. Pp. 2240-81.

Fowden, G. *The Egyptian Hermes: A Historical Approach to the Late Pagan Mind*. Cambridge, 1986.

Segal, R. A. *The Poimandres as Myth: Scholarly Theory and Gnostic Meaning*. Hawthorne, N.Y., 1986.

Betz, H. D. "Hermetism and Gnosticism: The Question of the *Poimandres*." *Antike und Christentum: Gesammelte Aufsätze*, vol. 4. Tübingen, 1998. Pp. 206-21.

Chaldaean Oracles

The *Chaldaean* (or Chaldaic) *Oracles* was a collection made in the reign of Marcus Aurelius of verses in Greek allegedly based on divine revelations. It became the "Bible" of the later Neoplatonists and is known only from the some

---

259. C. H. Dodd, *The Interpretation of the Fourth Gospel* (Cambridge, 1953), 10-53, argues that the Fourth Gospel and the Hermetica represent kindred religious thought without substantial borrowing on either side.

260. A. D. Nock, "Early Gentile Christianity and its Hellenistic Background," in *Essays,* 127-29.

three hundred lines quoted by them. Its purpose was to justify theurgy. The old Greek belief in demons and magic was enriched by eastern beliefs and systematized by the demonology of philosophy.

The *Chaldaean Oracles* offer some elements of the Gnostic systems in a philosophical dress. They provide for the freeing of the imprisoned soul by purifications and ritual. However, they contain no fall nor prospect of an end of the present state. Although sharing with Gnosticism a similar stage in the development of Platonic thought, they are not "Gnostic" in the technical sense.

At the head of the system is Paternal Mind, which is fire (a Stoic feature in a system otherwise mainly indebted to Middle Platonism) and from which all proceeds. Through the Second Mind, who is the creator, he enters into contact with the world of sense. There is also a World Soul (identified with Hecate) that serves as Mediator. This much is similar to the philosopher Numenius (p. 386). A long series of powers, which is introduced between the highest god and the world, are vertically arranged in descending order and are paired as opposites. The soul is of a fiery nature and by fighting against the body strives to return to the father, the fire from which it came. Details of the rites are uncertain. The stars signify but do not cause events.

BIBLIOGRAPHY

Des Places, E. *Oracles Chaldaïques.* Paris, 1971.

Maajercik, Ruth, ed. *The Chaldean Oracles: Text, Translation, and Commentary.* Leiden, 1989.

Dodds, E. R. "Theurgy and Its Relationship to Neoplatonism." *Journal of Roman Studies* 37 (1947):55ff. Reprinted in *The Greeks and the Irrational.* Boston, 1951. Pp. 283-311.

Lewy, H. *Chaldaean Oracles and Theurgy.* Cairo, 1956. New edition by Michel Tardieu. Paris, 1978.

Dodds, E. R. "New Light on the 'Chaldaean Oracles.'" *HTR* 54 (1961):263-79.

LATER DEVELOPMENTS: MONOTHEISM AND SUN WORSHIP

The beginning of the tendency toward monotheism goes back to the philosophers Xenophanes and Antisthenes. Other philosophers reached the conclusion that there should be one supreme principle, albeit quite diversely understood in Platonism, Aristotelianism, and Stoicism. Many circumstances in addition to the influence of certain philosophies contributed to the full development of the tendency. The analogy with the monarchical government of the empire promoted the idea that there should be one Lord in heaven as on earth.

The new cosmology with its understanding of the orderly plan of the universe could only be explained by a supreme intelligence. The idea that all peoples worshiped the same gods under different names had long been held by the Greeks; syncretism in religion made it common in Roman times. Various deities were given the attributes of others, and this process was extended to merge the deities into one. The old polytheism was kept by regarding the deities as subordinate powers under the supreme god. Astral theology contributed a new concept of the universe, which identified this supreme god with the sun.

Monotheism in Greco-Roman paganism remained only a tendency. Its monotheistic gods were either an encompassing of all or many gods under one or else a philosophical principle. But a philosophical principle was no living god, and the philosophers' supreme god remained too abstract, too removed. The religious syncretism carried too much "excess baggage" from the old polytheism. The efforts to invest the supreme principle of philosophy with the personality of the god of religion was most nearly successful in the elevation of the sun god to the supreme position.

The rise of solar theology was perhaps the most significant development in paganism in late antiquity. Sun theology was the result of a fusion of Stoic philosophy (sun as reason = fire and divine power) and popular astrology in which the sun was the most important planet. When the Severan dynasty brought the Syrian sun god to Rome at the beginning of the third century, it gave a concrete expression of sun worship. The Syrian sun god was reinterpreted in accord with the new philosophical and popular ideas and was united with the imperial cult. This first official introduction was tentative and was placed alongside other cults, but in 274 the emperor Aurelian made *sol invictus* (the invincible sun) the imperial religion. The last pagan emperor, Julian (361–363), made the worship of Helios (the sun) the religious focus (as Neoplatonism provided the philosophical basis) of his efforts to revive paganism against Christianity.[261] All the other gods were powers or activities of the sun.[262]

Sun worship, however, remained largely a religion of the educated and ruling classes. The sun cult was the work of the emperor. "King Helios" did not win his way as a full god: he was too closely bound to the physical appearance of the sun, on one hand, and too dependent on a philosophical interpretation on the other. In mythology and art the sun was regularly presented as a charioteer who drove across the sky from east to west; by night he traversed the ocean that surrounds the earth in order to return to his starting place. Mithraism profited in the third and fourth centuries from the solar religion but supplied its deficiencies by giving a personal object of devotion in Mithras.

261. Julian's *Oration* 4 is the most comprehensive document of solar theology. For an interpretation in terms of Mithraism see Polymnia Athanassiadi, "A Contribution to Mithraic Theology: The Emperor Julian's *Hymn to King Helios,*" *JTS* 28 (1977):360-71.

262. Macrobius, *Saturnalia* 1.17.2ff.

Certain aspects of the solar religion had a popular impact, however. The planetary week gave the name Sunday to one of its days; the importance pagans attached to Sunday had implications for the significance the first day of the week held for Christians and encouraged the ascription of a cosmic significance to this day of redemption.[263] In addition, the solar calendar introduced by Caesar and Augustus encouraged sun festivals, especially the *dies natalis Solis invicti* (the birthday of the invincible sun) — December 25. The popularity of this festival, the Saturnalia, in late pagan times appears to have been the decisive factor in the church's choice of December 25 as the day to celebrate the birth of Jesus.[264]

BIBLIOGRAPHY

Halsberghe, G. H. *The Cult of Sol Invictus.* Leiden, 1972.
Smith, John Holland. *The Death of Classical Paganism.* New York, 1976.
Geffcken, J. *The Last Days of Greco-Roman Paganism.* Amsterdam, 1978.
Athanassiadi, Polymnia and Michael Frede, eds. *Pagan Monotheism in Late Antiquity.* Oxford, 1999.

263. The influence of paganism on the Christian Sunday is developed by Samuele Bacchiocchi, *From Sabbath to Sunday* (Rome, 1977), 236-68, but a better account of the origins of the selection of Sunday as the day of Christian assembly is provided in D. A. Carson, ed., *From Sabbath to Lord's Day* (Grand Rapids, 1982).

264. For some of the customs associated with the pagan festival, including gifts to the poor, see Lucian, *Saturnalia.* For the church's reaction see Oscar Cullmann, "The Origin of Christmas," in *The Early Church* (Philadelphia, 1956), 21-36.

4. HELLENISTIC-ROMAN PHILOSOPHIES

Bibliography

Collections of Sources

Lucian. *Philosophies for Sale.*

Diogenes Laertius. *Lives of Eminent Philosophers.*

Smith, T. V. *Philosophers Speak for Themselves.* Vol. 2, *Aristotle to Plotinus.* Chicago, 1956.

Oates, W. J. *The Stoic and Epicurean Philosophers.* New York, 1957.

De Vogel, C. J. *Greek Philosophy.* Vol. 3. Leiden, 1959.

Long, A. A., and D. N. Sedley. *The Hellenistic Philosophers,* 2 vols. Cambridge, 1987-1988.

Basic Secondary Works

Guthrie, W. K. C. *A History of Greek Philosophy.* 6 vols. Cambridge, 1962-1981.

Zeller, E. *Stoics, Epicureans, and Sceptics.* New York, 1962.

Brehier, E. *The History of Philosophy.* Vol. 2, *The Hellenistic and Roman Age.* Chicago, 1963.

Armstrong, A. H. *The Cambridge History of Later Greek and Early Medieval Philosophy.* London, 1967.

Goulet, Richard, ed. *Dictionnaire des Philosophes Antiques.* Paris, 1989–.

Erler, Michael. *Die Hellenistische Philosophie.* Vol. 4.1 of *Die Philosophie der Antike.* Munich, 1994.

Algra, K., J. Barnes, J. Mansfeld, and M. Schofield, eds. *The Cambridge History of Hellenistic Philosophy.* Cambridge, 1999.

Supplementary Works

Nock, A. D. *Conversion.* Oxford, 1933. Chap. XI.

Dill, S. *Roman Society from Nero to Marcus Aurelius.* Reprint. New York, 1956. Book III.

Long, A. A. *Hellenistic Philosophy: Stoics, Epicureans, Sceptics.* London, 1974; 2d ed., Berkeley, 1986.

Meyer, Ben F., and E. P. Sanders, eds. *Jewish and Christian Self-Definition.* Vol. 3, *Self-Definition in the Greco-Roman World.* Philadelphia, 1982.

Reale, G. A. *A History of Ancient Philosophy.* Vol. 3, *The Systems of the Hellenistic Age.* Albany, N.Y., 1985. Vol. 4, *The Schools of the Imperial Age.* Albany, N.Y., 1990.

Kristeller, P. O. *Greek Philosophers of the Hellenistic Age.* New York, 1993.

Sharples, R. W. *Stoics, Epicureans and Sceptics: An Introduction to Hellenistic Philosophy.* London, 1996.

Sterling, Gregory E. "Hellenistic Philosophy and the New Testament." In Stanley E. Porter, ed. *Handbook to Exegesis of the New Testament.* Leiden, 1997. Pp. 313-358.

INTRODUCTION

Philosophy in the Hellenistic and Roman periods was not the critical discipline it is in our day nor the theoretical and metaphysical study it has been through much of its history. It was a way of life.[1] Hellenistic-Roman philosophy exhibited certain characteristics that set it apart from earlier Greek philosophy as well as from later philosophical endeavors. Some of these characteristics of special interest for the student of early Christianity may be noted here before giving a historical survey of the major philosophers and philosophical schools of thought.

Philosophy as Religion

The religion of many in the Hellenistic and Roman periods, especially among the educated, was philosophy. Philosophy provided a criticism or reinterpretation of traditional religion and offered its own moral and spiritual direction. Each philosophical school had its own way of life *(agōgē)* with distinctive beliefs and practices.

The various schools of philosophy formed communities of "believers" around a revered master and his teachings. They had their "interdenominational" rivalries and conversion stories. Philosophy even had its holy men ("saints") and martyrs (notably Socrates). The various schools provided the

---

1. Lucian's treatise "Philosophies for Sale," according to the title in the Loeb translation, is literally "The Sale of Lives," that is, kinds of life represented by the different types of philosophies.

worldview and practical guidance for life that religion does for many today. A person did not normally go to the priest of the local cult for an interpretation of the nature of reality or for moral advice. One turned more often than not to a philosopher for an answer to these questions. Although the popular religion did not give much ethical guidance, poets and philosophers provided a conscience for the age. Some even saw philosophy as bringing a kind of conversion and cleansing of the soul,[2] although it was a redemption worked by one's own strength. Philosophy contributed to the impulse toward monotheism, but in general the god of Hellenistic-Roman philosophy was impersonal.

Philosophers developed significant criticisms of the popular religion.[3] Although there was no uniform approach, it was not uncommon to criticize the anthropomorphism and immorality of the traditional mythology, polytheism, superstitious religious practices, and the grosser features of sacrifice. In turn, an emphasis was placed on the proper attitudes in sacrifice, worthy conceptions of the gods, rational worship, and upright conduct. Such material could be, and was, appropriated by Jewish and Christian writers in the early centuries in their attack on the established pagan religion.[4]

Stoicism (see below) developed in a way that could give support to many traditional religious practices. In late Roman times, Neoplatonism became thoroughly religious in spirit, looking to religious literature as a source of inspiration for its speculations and incorporating religious ritual into its practices. This was the result of tendencies present in some of the philosophical thinkers earlier.

Philosophy as Ethics[5]

Ethics was the principal concern of the leading Hellenistic philosophies. Their aim was to teach people how to live. Moral instruction was quite specific about what is right and wrong and what one's duties in various social relationships were. Apuleius in the second century could describe the function of the philosopher as to rebuke the vices of mankind (*Apology* 15). The similarities of this popular philosophical moral instruction with that found in Judaism and early

---

2. The most famous example of conversion to philosophy was Polemon (p. 336) in Diogenes Laertius 4.3.16; also Lucian, *Double Endictment* 17. See also Lucian, *Nigrinus* 1 and *The Downward Journey, or the Tyrant* 24.

3. Harold W. Attridge, "The Philosophical Critique of Religion under the Early Empire," *ANRW* II, *Principat*, 16.1 (Berlin and New York, 1978), 45-78.

4. Josephus, *Against Apion* 2.33-35, 239-57; Justin, *Apology* 1.24-25; Athenagoras, *Plea* 8, 13-23.

5. Abraham J. Malherbe, *Moral Exhortation: A Greco-Roman Sourcebook* (Philadelphia, 1986); idem, "Hellenistic Moralists and the New Testament," *ANRW* II, *Principat*, 26.1 (Berlin, 1992), 267-333.

Christianity provide a closer affinity than any other aspect of the ancient world does to the New Testament. (See below on Popular Philosophy and on the individual philosophies for the content of philosophical ethics.)

Three modes of moral exhortation employed by the philosophers have been identified. Each resulted in corresponding literary expressions but could be found within other literary forms. *Protrepsis* was an exhortation to adopt a particular viewpoint. As used by philosophers it was an invitation to follow the philosophical life. This rhetorical category was put to use by philosophers and became a full treatise with Aristotle's *Protrepticus*; it had an influential Latin representative in Cicero's *Hortensius* (both works largely lost) and is represented in early Christian literature by apologetic works such as Clement of Alexandria's *Protrepticus*. In the New Testament, Romans has been described as a protreptic letter.[6] Protreptic works urged people to convert to the philosophical way of life, to join a particular school, or to adopt the moral conduct taught by philosophy. These goals often required turning the readers or hearers from an alternative course of action, refuting objections to what was being advocated, or censuring flaws in the person that hindered attainment of the new life.

Paraenesis is a broader term for moral exhortation to follow a given course of action or to abstain from a contrary behavior. It thus consisted of encouragement and dissuasion. Rules of conduct are prominent. Paraenesis presupposed some positive relationship between the parties or that the one giving instruction was a moral superior, and it involved habits of behavior already accepted within the society or community of which the parties were members. Common techniques of paraenesis were reminding of what was known, complimenting what was done that was good, censuring wrong conduct, offering examples for imitation, stringing together brief precepts and admonitions, and giving reasons for the recommended conduct. The concerns of early Christianity made paraenesis virtually ubiquitous in its literature. One of the best examples of a paraenetic letter is 1 Thessalonians.[7]

The *diatribe* was a popular treatment of ethical subjects aimed at moving people to action. The word is used for the moral discussions in philosophical schools, written records of that activity, and literary imitations of that kind of pedagogic activity. The earliest examples of the diatribe style are found in the fragments of Teles (p. 349). The diatribe set up a brief but lively dialogue. An imaginary interlocutor raised objections to a teaching or drew false conclusions that the speaker rejected with a strong negative ("By no means!") or corrected with censure or persuasion. Involved in the style were direct address,

6. Stanley K. Stowers, *Letter Writing in Greco-Roman Antiquity* (Philadelphia, 1986), 114.

7. Abraham J. Malherbe, "Exhortation in First Thessalonians," *Novum Testamentum* 25 (1983):238-56 = *Paul and the Popular Philosophers* (Minneapolis, 1989), 49-66; cf. 74; idem, *Paul and the Thessalonians* (Philadelphia, 1986), chap. 3; idem, "Hellenistic Moralists and the New Testament," *ANRW* II, *Principat*, 26.1 (Berlin, 1992), 287-93.

rhetorical questions and answers, short parallel or antithetical statements, interjections, appeal to examples, and quotations from poetry or other authorities.[8] The diatribe style finds examples in the New Testament (cf. Rom. 2–4; 1 Cor. 6:12-20; 15:29-35; Jas. 2:14ff.). The diatribe's home was in the discourses and discussions of the philosophical schools, where it was addressed to students with an imperfect understanding, but it was adapted for literary works. The term *diatribe* has often been used loosely for the characteristics of Cynic and Stoic popular preaching (or harangues) in the marketplace, but the latter was a separate phenomenon with a different setting and purpose, aimed at drawing hearers to a consideration of the serious questions of life.

Hellenistic moralists reinforced their teaching by use of the literary and rhetorical conventions of personal examples, lists of virtues and vices (exceptional is Philo's list of 147 characteristics of the lover of pleasure — *Sacrifices of Cain and Abel* 5.32), tables of duties (cf. p. 71 on the *haustafeln* or "household codes"), and lists of hardships.[9]

Popular Philosophy[10]

The activities of the philosophers in the various social settings noted below contributed to a popularization of philosophical ideas, particularly moral teachings, at various levels of society. Although the old school labels were maintained and despite the bitter polemic of the philosophical schools against one another, the Hellenistic-Roman age showed an increasing tendency toward a philosophical *koinē*, not just among educated laymen but even among more professional philosophers. Philosophy, at least from the first century, appeared to society as a unity (Juvenal, *Satires* 13.19-22) with the purpose of helping humanity. The different schools shared common elements and concerns (such as the individualism discussed below). Certain themes recur among the philosophical moralists with enough frequency to show what were matters of interest — marriage and sexual conduct, consolation, covetousness, and anger — and what the ideals were — virtue, friendship, civil concord and responsibility for the welfare of the state, and freedom.

Despite their sharp differences, to be delineated in the subsequent sections, the major Hellenistic philosophical schools had much in common. The purpose of philosophy was to teach people how to live. This entailed the as-

8. Stanley K. Stowers, *The Diatribe and Paul's Letter to the Romans* (Chico, Calif., 1981).

9. J. T. Fitzgerald, *Cracks in an Earthen Vessel: An Examination of the Catalogues of Hardships in the Corinthian Correspondence* (Atlanta, 1988).

10. Abraham J. Malherbe, *Paul and the Popular Philosophers* (Minneapolis, 1989); cf. David Balch, et al., eds., *Greeks, Romans, and Christians: Essays in Honor of Abraham J. Malherbe* (Minneapolis, 1990), for studies illustrating the use of the philosophical literature in interpreting the New Testament.

sumption that virtue is teachable. Virtue is related to knowledge, and reason is the means of attaining it. For all the schools, self-sufficiency *(autarkeia)*, freedom *(eleutheria)*, and happiness *(eudaimonia)* were goals, but they differed in the specific ways of attaining them. The virtuous life meant a detachment (in varying degrees) from the affairs and concerns of this life — a self-sufficiency with regard to all external circumstances. "If you become a philosopher, you will live not unpleasantly, but you will learn to subsist pleasantly anywhere and with any resources."[11] It was common to emphasize freedom from passion through renunciation. The virtuous life, furthermore, was a life lived according to nature, although the definition of nature varied considerably from one school to another. This kind of life brought an inner freedom and happiness.

Hellenistic philosophies sought spiritual freedom for people now living under kings, no longer in self-governing cities. Their paths were different, but all had the goal of spiritual autonomy — how one could be free within, regardless of external circumstance.

The message of the philosophers was for people to turn from luxury and self-indulgence and from superstition to a life of freedom, discipline, and sometimes contemplation. Cebes in the first century A.D. wrote a moral dialogue describing the good life and the bad life, depicted as the choice between two ways. One's goal should be deliverance from the bad life, achieved only by repentance.

> [The good man] will not be troubled in the least either by Pain or Grief, Incontinence, Avarice, Poverty or by any other vice. For he is master of all things and is superior to everything that formerly caused him distress. . . . No longer does anything cause distress to this man because he has an antidote. (26.3)[12]

An important contribution to moral thought — the concept of conscience — is often attributed to Stoicism but seems really to have belonged to popular thought.[13]

A fairly common stock of illustrations came to be employed in order to commend the proper approach to life. Especially frequent among all the schools was the comparison of persons to actors in a play. The part was prescribed by "fate"; the person's task was to play well the part assigned.[14] Other

---

11. Plutarch, *Virtue and Vice* 4 (*Moralia* 101D).

12. John Fitzgerald and L. Michael White, *The Tabula of Cebes* (Chico, Calif., 1983), 101, 103.

13. C. A. Pierce, *Conscience in the New Testament*, Studies in Biblical Theology, vol. 15 (London, 1955), 13-20; Hans-Joachim Eckstein, *Der Brgriff Syneidesis bei Paulus* (Tübingen, 1983); Ernesto Borghi, "La notion de conscience dans le Nouveau Testament: Une proposition de lecture," *Filologia Neotestamentaria* 10 (1997):85-98; Philip Bosman, *Conscience in Philo and Paul* (Tübingen, 2003).

14. Edwyn Bevan, "Hellenistic Popular Philosophy," in *The Hellenistic Age* (Cambridge, 1925), 86-89, 102.

common illustrations were drawn from athletics, warfare, and from medical practice.[15]

Popular philosophy was an expression of the eclecticism of the age (see pp. 379-82).

Philosophy and Individualism

The Hellenistic philosophical schools were an expression of the individualism of the period after Alexander the Great and in turn further encouraged it. In this regard they represented a break from the viewpoint of Plato and Aristotle who, from the perspective of the classical city-state, constructed universal systems of thought. The Sophists of the fifth century B.C. (pp. 326ff.) had already begun to weaken the foundations of traditional Greek life by distinguishing nature from custom and raising questions about the relativity of the latter. Then the conquests of Alexander effectively broadened the concept of the world and at the same time broke down the sense of security within the narrow confines of the old city-state. In the fourth century especially, the traditional religion, morality, and way of life no longer seemed to be assured by the customs of a close-knit community. Many persons were looking for new foundations of conduct and a new sense of community. Individuals were on their own. The Hellenistic philosophers spoke to individuals to fill their needs. They drew on Socrates' view that the soul is intellectual and moral personality and that the first duty of a person is to cultivate his own soul (pp. 327-30). This became the perspective from which different Hellenistic philosophical schools developed various responses to the new situation. The philosophies originating after Alexander's time, in a more universal setting, concentrated on the individual and his or her place in the cosmos.

Philosophy in Its Social Setting

Philosophers taught in many social settings.[16] Some were supported by wealthy patrons as almost house "chaplains." Others gave invited lectures at the public baths, gymnasia, or other public buildings. Some (especially Cynics) spoke on their own in the marketplaces and on street corners. Others (like Epictetus) taught in formal schools. The Epicureans formed their own communities,

---

15. Abraham J. Malherbe, *Paul and the Popular Philosophers* (Minneapolis, 1989), 78-89, 91-119, 121-36.

16. Samuel Dill, *Roman Society from Nero to Marcus Aurelius* (New York, 1905; repr. Meridian, 1956), identified three types of activity by philosophers: the philosophic "director of souls," e.g., Seneca; the philosophic "missionary," e.g., Dio Chrysostom; and the philosophic "theologian," e.g., Plutarch.

meeting in private homes. Under the empire some philosophers were supported out of state funds. Hellenistic philosophies were more "schools of thought" than institutions, although some did have a formal institutional embodiment.

In addition to public speeches, philosophers used other means of instruction: letters, epitomes (systematic summaries of larger works), and compilations of the teaching of a philosopher or of advice on a particular subject. Gnomes (pithy sayings), *chreiai* (especially apt and instructive anecdotes, differing from gnomes in giving a narrative setting to the saying),[17] and poetry were used to spread philosophical teachings.

SOPHISTS AND SOCRATES

The Sophists

Ancient writers traced all of the Hellenistic philosophical schools back to Socrates (p. 327). In order to place Socrates in his intellectual setting some notice must be taken of the Sophist movement.

The Sophists appeared in the fifth century B.C. during the golden age of Athens. Their name in origin was nothing derogatory and referred to "one who could make you wise." The Sophists came into being to satisfy the need for knowledge of the art of speech in Greek public life. In the assemblies of citizens, the army, and law courts persuasion was important. Failure to argue successfully on your feet could even end in taking a drink of hemlock (as Socrates learned).

The Sophists were essentially wanderers, cosmopolitan types. They gave public lectures to demonstrate their skill and so gain business. They earned their living as private tutors, teaching others the art of public speaking. The successful ones were known for their elegance in speaking and ability in reasoning. They taught their pupils how to argue on general grounds as opposed to specific evidence, to put new interpretations on the facts and turn them to their advantage.

The Sophists raised the antithesis of "custom" (*nomos,* "law") and "nature" *(physis).* As the Greeks became aware of other peoples, they realized that their traditional customs were not a matter of universal validity. Hence, the Sophists made a distinction between things that are so by convention and things that are so by nature. This cut at the root of tradition and led to the notion of moral relativity. The Sophists did not set out to subvert traditional morality, but their pupils began extending the range of conclusions that could be drawn from the approach.

17. Ronald F. Hock and Edward N. O'Neil, eds., *The Chreia in Ancient Rhetoric: The Progymnasmata* (Atlanta, 1986). Idem, *The Chreia and Ancient Rhetoric: Classroom Exercises* (Atlanta, 2002).

The Sophists began to raise general questions. The tendency to rationalism may be illustrated from thoughts about the existence of the gods. Protagoras said, "Concerning the gods I cannot know for certain whether they exist or not, nor what they are like in form. There are many things that hinder certainty — the obscurity of the matter and the shortness of human life" (Frg. 4).[18] Others advanced rationalistic theories of the origin of the gods. Prodicus said that the gods were the deification of things found useful.[19] Critias put in a play *(Sisyphus)* a speech in which it was suggested that the gods were invented as a check against human wrongdoing[20] (one might avoid human detection but the unseen gods see all). Euhemerus advanced the view that the gods were great persons who had been deified.[21] As a testimony to the influence of Euhemerus's view, his was the first Greek work translated into Latin by Ennius in the second century B.C. Christian apologists used the theory against paganism.[22]

The Sophistic movement was not the birth of thought, but it was the birth of conscious intellectualism. The Sophists raised questions that were central to the Hellenistic philosophical schools, and they provide the background to Socrates and Plato.

Socrates (469–399 B.C.)

The pre-Socratic philosophers were primarily natural philosophers.[23] Socrates decided the main problem was the human person and turned his attention to practical affairs of daily living. To paraphrase Cicero, Socrates brought philosophy down from heaven to earth.[24] Hence, it is no accident that we make a distinction between pre-Socratic and post-Socratic philosophy.[25] He was responsible for philosophy becoming concerned with the conscience and personal religion. The stress on individualism in Hellenistic philosophy found its basis

18. From Eusebius, *Preparation of the Gospel* 14.3.7; Diogenes Laertius, *Lives of Eminent Philosophers* 9.51.

19. Sextus Empiricus, *Against Mathematicians* 9.18; Cicero, *On the Nature of the Gods* 1.37.118.

20. Sextus Empiricus, *Against Mathematicians* 9.54.

21. Diodorus Siculus 6.

22. Athenagoras, *Plea* 28 (without reference to Euhemerus); Lactantius, *Divine Institutes* 1.15.

23. W. Jaeger, *The Theology of the Early Greek Philosophers* (Oxford, 1947); W. K. C. Guthrie, *History of Greek Philosophy*, vols. 1 and 2 (Cambridge, 1978); G. S. Kirk, et al., *The Pre-Socratic Philosophers: A Critical History with a Selection of Texts* (Cambridge, 1983); A. A. Long, ed., *The Cambridge Companion to Early Greek Philosophy* (Cambridge, 1997).

24. Cicero, *Academica* 1.4.15.

25. Pre-Socratic philosophy was not forgotten, however, and note will be made below of some of its elements in the Hellenistic schools. It also had an influence on early Christian thinkers; see R. M. Grant, "Early Christianity and Pre-Socratic Philosophy," *Harry Austin Wolfson Jubilee Volume* (Jerusalem, 1965), 376ff.

SOCRATES

Socrates was the hero of philosophers to whom the philosophical schools of
the Hellenistic age traced their origin. His popularity is shown by the large
number of representations that survive. (© Erich Lessing/Art Resource, NY)

and an exemplar in Socrates. And the various Hellenistic schools of philosophy traced their descent from him. Socrates made the human being — not some principle — central. The occasion for this interest was the questioning carried on by the Sophists.

Socrates was not himself a Sophist: he did not give public lectures nor take private pupils for pay. In fact he reacted against the "know-it-all" Sophists as well as against the old naiveté about willful, amoral deities. He realized that Athens could not turn the clock back and that the questions raised by the Sophists had to be dealt with and could not simply be avoided. On the other hand, he sought for something true and secure in place of the relativism to which the Sophists were tending. Yet the populace identified him with the Sophists because of his method of questioning and the circle of young men gathered around him.[26]

Socrates spent most of his time outside talking with people and seems to have known almost everyone in Athens. He had a sense of mission: to ask questions. His vocation was to serve people in this way. He tried to get people to give as much attention to their souls as they did to their bodies. (The *psyche* was now definitely the personality.) He challenged them to define justice and piety and other concepts about which they talked.

Socrates' basic idea was that if you know what is right, you will do it. Wrongdoing is the result of wrong thinking and wrong information. It has been said that "the trouble with Socrates was that he credited other people with his own strength of will." It would be a mistake, however, to regard Socrates as a pure rationalist. He claimed to have a *daimon* that guided him, always functioning negatively (somewhat like a conscience) in giving premonitions against doing certain things.

Socrates never gave his associates an answer. He steered the conversation in such a way that the person could give better answers to himself. His "philosophy" was an attitude, a discipline, not a system. He did not write anything; the important thing was not what he said, but how he said it. He proved to be very productive of thought in others. A major problem in the study of Socrates is that the two major sources about him — Plato's *Dialogues* and Xenophon's *Memorabilia* — give quite diverse pictures of the man. Likewise, quite varied philosophical schools claimed to derive from him. Not only did Plato, and through him Aristotle, claim succession from Socrates, but also linked to Socrates were Eucleides, founder of the Megarian school, whose sophistries promoted a skepticism about logic; Antisthenes, associated with the beginnings of the Cynics, who in turn influenced the Stoics; and Aristippus, leader of the Cyrenaic school, whose hedonism of bodily pleasure was modified by Epicurus into intellectual pleasures. This illustrates the point that the important thing

---

26. Aristophanes' *The Clouds* is a parody that illustrates the atmosphere in which Socrates moved (but not his teaching).

was the method and not the content. Most scholars have thought that Plato represents the direction in which Socrates' thought was heading but that his positive philosophical system certainly was not already formulated by his master. An inner circle of friends was devoted to Socrates. He had an uncanny power to attract disciples without seeking them, and his importance in the history of philosophy was his influence on them.

Socrates was not as popular as he might have been. People do not like mavericks, especially in bad times, and the war with Sparta was a bad time for Athens. Socrates seemed to be one of those ripping apart the fabric of public life, and among his pupils and friends were critics of the democracy. He was accused of not worshiping the gods but introducing a new *daimōn* and of corrupting the youth. The court was in effect a town meeting, and these meetings were temperamental in character. Plato's *Apology* probably represents Socrates' attitude and line of argument, though there would not have been such a lengthy speech in court and it would not have been written down. It was not the type of defense expected; hardly a defense, it was more a defiance: Socrates could not give up his mission. What the people really wanted was to get rid of him through exile, not death. Even in prison he was given an opportunity to escape, but his sense of duty led him to refuse. He accepted the sentence of drinking poison without fear of death. In dying as he did, Socrates was not really killed: he became a martyr.

BIBLIOGRAPHY

Ferguson, John. *Socrates: A Sourcebook*. London, 1970.

Taylor, A. E. *Socrates*. New York, 1933. Reprint. Garden City, N.Y., 1953.
Jaeger, W. *Paideia*. New York, 1939. Book 2, chap. 3; book 3, chap. 2.
Gulley, Norman. *The Philosophy of Socrates*. New York, 1968.
Beckman, James. *The Religious Dimension of Socrates' Thought*. Waterloo, Ont., 1979.
Navia, Luis E. *Socrates: The Man and His Philosophy*. Lanham, Md., 1985.
De Romilly, Jacqueline. *The Great Sophists of Periclean Athens*. Oxford, 1992.
Taylor, Christopher C. W. *Socrates*. Past Masters Series. Oxford, 1998.
Smith, Nicholas D. and Paul B. Woodruff, eds. *Reason and Religion in Socratic Philosophy*. Oxford, 2000.

PLATO AND THE ACADEMY TO THE FIRST CENTURY

Life of Plato (429–347 B.C.)

Plato came from an aristocratic family in Athens; if it were not for Socrates' death, he might have been a poet or a statesman. Plato's whole life had been

PLATO
Plato was the greatest of Socrates' pupils and has had
a major influence on Western intellectual history.
(© Erich Lessing/Art Resource, NY)

opened up by personal contact with Socrates, and the latter's death (399 B.C.) changed the course of his life. He could not serve Athens or advocate a democracy that would put such a man as Socrates to death. That death caused a kind of religious awakening in Plato, and he set himself to perpetuating his teacher's memory.

Plato left Athens and traveled for about twelve years; he returned to Athens and after 387 began teaching near the grove sacred to the deity *Akademos*. He organized a fellowship, a corporation like many of the associations of the time, dedicated to the muses. The building where he taught, and so his school, came to be called the Academy. Teaching was Plato's main occupation for the last forty years of his life. Some scholars have seen the *Seventh Letter* as perhaps the most illuminating source for what Plato was like.[27]

The Dialogues

Plato chose the dialogue form of writing as nearest to the teaching method of Socrates. He brought into literary expression what had been his own experience in listening to Socrates: arrive at truth through conversation, not lecture. He sought to reproduce in writing the question-and-answer method Socrates employed in talking with people so as to lead them to think and find answers for themselves.

The *Dialogues* fall roughly into three periods. The early dialogues (such as *Euthyphro, Crito,* and *Protagoras*) and the *Apology* most nearly approximate the Socratic method. There is a concern with the definitions of qualities: what is courage, self-control, holiness, justice? The typical approach is to ask: "What is such-and-such?" then break down foolish arguments and refute all suggested answers, ending on the note "I do not know."

This effort to arrive at concepts led to the rather complicated theory of "ideas" *(idea)* or "forms" *(eidos)*. Previously, if one wanted a definition of courage, a courageous person was pointed to. Plato came to think in terms of what is characteristic of all courageous persons. He then separated the ideas of courage, etc., more and more from the world. At the height of the middle period a new thought was being presented: the real world is "pure form." Plato wavered between the view that the world of the senses was an imitation of (and completely separated from) the real world of ideas and the view that the world participates in the ideas (see below, pp. 333-34). To this middle group of dialogues belong the *Republic, Phaedo,* and *Symposium*. With them the dialogue became an art form of the highest order.

The examination of the relationship of the just man to the idea of justice and of one idea to another (justice to courage, etc.) led to a criticism of the the-

---

27. But L. Edelstein, *Plato's Seventh Letter* (Leiden, 1966), argues that it cannot be genuine.

ory of ideas. During this time Plato's interest in mathematics (the relations of numbers and the relation of mathematics to the sensible world as illustrations of the relation of forms to this world) grew. In this later period Plato had returned to what is for us the real world, but for a reason — to learn the relations between things. His interest now was in logic, mathematics, and the relations of the forms. By this time Plato had become so scientific and so far-removed from the usual ethical interests of people that few outside his school could understand him. To the late period belong the *Sophist, Statesman, Philebus, Timaeus,* and *Laws.* Dialogues were now used for exposition.

Although the *Republic* has been Plato's acknowledged masterpiece and the most important of his works for the study of his philosophy, two works of the later period are actually more important for the student of the backgrounds of early Christianity — the *Laws* and *Timaeus.* Whereas the *Republic* offers a theory of the ideal state, the *Laws* presents the actual detailed prescriptions for public and private life — including a great concern with religion. Consequently, the *Laws* is a more valuable historical source about how things were done or might be done. The *Timaeus* provided the starting point for the Hellenistic and later Platonic worldview. The Middle Platonists (pp. 387-88) found in it three ultimate principles: the Demiurge or Maker of all things; preexistent matter out of which the world is made; and the ideas as the patterns by which things are made. The World Soul is intermediate between the intelligible and sensible worlds.

Plato's Thought

Theory of Ideas. This is the real crux of Plato's philosophy, but difficult because it goes so much against "common sense." "Ideas" for us are something in the mind. For Plato in his most distinctive period (e.g., *Parmenides*) ideas are neither physical nor mental; they are outside space and time. *Ideas* are real; the physical world is but a poor imitation. The idea is independent of its exemplification in the copies or images observed in space and time. To actualize something is to degrade it. The things in the physical world are imperfect imitations of the form or idea. For example, the idea of the circle is of something perfectly round, but no actual circle is truly perfect.

All forms or ideas are summed up in the one ultimate ideal, which he calls the idea of the Good (principle of perfection). The idea of the Good has been thought to be the nearest approximation in Plato to the biblical idea of God, but the Good for Plato was a "form," not a "god," and for the biblical "living God," one must turn to the Platonic "World Soul," which was not the supreme being. Plato does not have a personal God. His thought is deeply religious, but it is the impersonal principle of perfection that he worships. Nevertheless, in pointing to a First Principle — absolute, unchanging, and true

Being — and to the divine principle of order in the cosmos he prepared for the religious thought of the empire.

The "Myth of the Cave" in the *Republic* 7 (514A-19A) is one of the great myths of literature. We may see this allegory of life as a summary of Plato's philosophy of ideas and his mission as a philosopher. Human beings, according to the myth, live in a cave, where from birth they are chained facing the inside wall. Outside the mouth of the cave a fire is burning. Between the fire and the entrance to the cave other beings pass by and cast their shadows on the inside wall. We never see anything but the shadows, hence we mistake that for reality. We know only shadows of reality and shadows of ourselves. We cannot turn around to look at each other. To "know thyself" is to get out of the cave. Some break their chain and turn around. The light from outside after the darkness of the cave is dazzling. Those who cannot stand the light prefer to remain in the cave. A few overcome the initial dazzlement and march out past the fire. These climb a steep hill and finally reach the top where they can see the sun. After an experience of ecstasy they return to the cave, because they have a duty to their fellow prisoners. As they return, they experience a second bewilderment. Accustomed to the light, they stumble in the darkness of the cave. Those who remained in the cave laugh at them and are so impatient with their stumbling that they may put them to death.

The meaning of the allegory is that the philosopher who has seen the world of ideas can explain the realities better than those who know only this shadowy world of sense. Some who have seen the light, however, cannot stand the truth. But those who know only darkness treat harshly those who have come from the world of light. The chains that blind people are their prejudices and appetites. The real truth is represented by the sun, not by man-made fire. The highest life is a combination of contemplation (the mountaintop) and action (returning to instruct others), of theory and practice. Unfortunately, this beautiful and powerful myth leaves one important question inadequately answered. What breaks the chain? What makes conversion possible? Here the Christian religion offered a significant point of contact and correction to Platonic philosophy.

The Soul. Plato's thought about the soul was perhaps the most influential part of his philosophy in the period of concern in this book. His emphasis on a spiritual reality distinct from the body, his doctrine of immortality, and his analysis of the soul with the related ethical theory had an acceptance his theory of ideas did not receive.

Plato drew on earlier Orphic and Pythagorean thought to establish a nonmaterial reality in humanity. The human has two distinct realities: the body is the vehicle of the invisible soul. Only the soul can comprehend ideas, so it belongs to the realm of ideas. The soul's relation to bodies is analogous to the relation of ideas to material manifestations. The familiar dichotomy in Western thought between body and soul is a product of the Platonic tradition. Thus in the modern world the clumsy word *psychosomatic* (from *psychē*, "soul," and *sōma*, "body") has had to be coined in order to put back together two things that from the biblical perspective never should have been separated.

For Plato the soul is immortal, possessing both preexistence and continued postexistence. The *Phaedo,* set as a conversation between Socrates and his friends in his last hours, is an argument for the immortality of the soul. By definition the soul is life *(psychē),* and life is antithetical to death. The soul, therefore, does not die but survives the body. Plato draws on the older ideas of transmigration, rewards, and punishment. The real self possesses something divine. The home of the soul is not earth but the sphere of the planets. Plato's immortality of the soul is a natural immortality, something that is true of the soul by reason of its very nature. This philosophical doctrine of the immortality of the soul is to be distinguished from the Jewish and Christian doctrine of a resurrection of the body and from the patristic doctrine of a created or a conditional immortality of the soul dependent on the grace and power of God.

Plato's theory of knowledge (epistemology) is related to his view of the soul. Knowledge is recollection. Persons can have concepts only because they had them previously. Ideas are a priori, known independently of experience. The soul saw and learned the ideas before it came to dwell in a body. Experience reminds, but it does not prove and validate. Knowledge is innate and must be evoked by the teacher as a midwife drawing it out of a person.

Plato divided the soul into three parts: the intellectual or rational, the vibrant or spirited, and the desirous or appetitive. His ethics is related to this threefold analysis, as he saw a virtue for each part: wisdom for the intellectual part, courage for the spirited part, and self-control for the desirous part. When there is harmony and balance between the three parts of the soul, with the rational in firm control, then the person reflects the virtue of justice. These four virtues — justice, self-control, courage, and wisdom — were given prominence in the Hellenistic age and became the four natural virtues to which were added the three supernatural virtues (faith, hope, and love) to form the seven cardinal virtues of the Middle Ages.

Plato's Influence

Although Plato did not hold a dominant place in the philosophy of the Hellenistic age, he came to that position in the early centuries of the Christian era. Patristic theology took shape largely in the framework of Platonic philosophy. Not only Christian thought but also some Jewish (notably Philo) and later Islamic philosophy owed much to him. Plato's emphasis on nonmaterial reality, a deathless soul distinct from the body, the idea of a cosmic religion (beauty of the celestial order above), and a just society has been enormously influential.

The Old Academy[28]

Plato designated his nephew *Speusippus* (c. 407–339 B.C.) to succeed him as head of the Academy on his death in 347 B.C. Speusippus was a capable thinker who continued Plato's work on definitions and mathematics.

Xenocrates (head from 339 to 314 B.C.) continued an interest in numbers and in formalizing Plato's thought. He was more significant, however, for systematizing the nature of the gods and demons (p. 236) and turning attention to practical morality.

Polemon (head 314–270) was converted from a dissolute life to philosophy by Xenocrates. The story was told that while drunk and garlanded from a party he stumbled into Xenocrates' lecture room. He was moved to change his ways and took up the study of philosophy so eagerly that he became the next head of the school.[29] He was mainly interested in ethics, and under his headship Crantor wrote *On Grief*, a work always considered in the later consolation literature of antiquity.

Crates (head 270–268) was the last head of the "Old" Academy; his successor gave up the defense of Plato's system and changed the Academy.

The Skeptical Academy

Arcesilas or Arcesilaus (316–241 B.C.) became head of the Academy in 268, beginning the period variously called the Middle, New, or Second Academy. In order to meet the challenge presented by the new popular teaching of Stoicism, Arcesilas adopted a questioning attitude. He went back to what he said was the real Socrates. True Socratism is "suspension of judgment." Socrates apparently did not dogmatize; he questioned.

According to Arcesilas we cannot tell what actual experience is, we cannot say one perception is clearer and more certain than another (against the Stoic theory of knowledge; see p. 358). Hence, the proper philosophical position is the withholding of judgment. There is, however, what is probable and reasonable (e.g., the sun will rise tomorrow) and other things are persuasive (e.g., a bull coming at you). Therefore, there is enough basis on which to develop a system for daily life. Although he said that we cannot know absolute truth, on this point of probability he differed from the true Skeptics (pp. 346-48).

Carneades (214–129, head of the Academy c. 180–136) carried the Academy further into skepticism, introducing what was called the New or Third Academy. Like Arcesilas, he wrote nothing, but his views were collected by his pupil Clitomachus and are known through Cicero and others. The arguments

28. I am indebted in the following section, as in the whole chapter, to Zeph Stewart's lectures at Harvard University on Hellenistic philosophy.

29. A. D. Nock, *Conversion* (Oxford, 1933), 173.

of Arcesilas against the Stoa were answered by Chrysippus (p. 355), so that it was said, "If there were no Chrysippus, there would be no Stoa." Carneades responded to the challenge and added, "If there were no Chrysippus, there would be no Carneades." He was a great intellect — "widely quoted, often opposed, never refuted." He resembled Socrates in skill and method of arguing and in being an intellectual gadfly, asking awkward questions that continued to bother people.

Carneades could affirm that we do not even know that Socrates did not know. The "presentations" to the mind may give true or false information, and since we can never be certain about any presentation, we must never give our assent. Yet he too granted a realm of the probable and analyzed three degrees of probability: (1) the merely probable, (2) the probable and not contradicted, and (3) the probable, not contradicted, and examined. He waged war on all absolutes, but he did not attack convention as such.

The most famous event in Carneades' life was a political embassy to Rome on behalf of Athens along with the Peripatetic Critolaus and the Stoic Diogenes of Babylon. Carneades demonstrated his skill as a public speaker and dialectician when he gave speeches on successive days for and against justice. This had an electrifying effect on the Romans. His suggestion that Rome give back what she had conquered in order to be just set back the cause of philosophy in Rome for a century.

The Eclectic Academy[30]

Philo of Larissa (160–80 B.C.) became head of the Academy about 110 B.C., succeeding Clitomachus. With him begins what is sometimes termed the Fourth Academy. Others dispute the fact that Philo departed from the skepticism of Arcesilas, but there does seem to be a change in emphasis. Since we cannot know that we do not know, Philo said we should assume that the probable is true. The concern of all the schools by this time was ethics, and life was considered unlivable if nothing could be determined. This attitude could lead to a break with skepticism, which certainly occurred with Antiochus of Ascalon. The Academy as an institution appears to have ceased after 88 B.C.

Antiochus of Ascalon (c. 130–c. 68 B.C.) brought about a full shift from skepticism, sometimes called the Fifth Academy. He claimed that Plato, Aristotle, and the Stoics said about the same things, so one should select their common points. The true successors of Plato, he said, were the Stoics and not the skeptical Academy. Zeno changed a few names (he spoke of preferred things for Plato's good things; see pp. 359-60) and although he rejected an incorporeal soul, the essential thing was the duality of an active and passive part in human

---

30. Charles Brittain, *Philo of Larissa: The Last of the Academic Sceptics* (Oxford, 2001); J. Glucker, *Antiochus and the Late Academy* (Göttingen, 1978).

beings. Moreover, the Stoics accepted certainty, although basing it on the senses. Aristotle, too, was essentially a Platonist, although he modified the ethics.

Thus the Academy was moving toward the Stoa at a time when (as will be seen below) the Stoa was becoming Platonic. This development contributed to the rise of Middle Platonism and Neoplatonism, the histories of which will be taken up in the last sections of this chapter.

BIBLIOGRAPHY

Plato. *Letter 7.*
Diogenes Laertius. *Lives of Eminent Philosophers 3.*
Fox, Adam. *Plato and the Christians.* London, 1957.

More, P. E. *The Religion of Plato.* Princeton, 1921.
Shorey, P. *What Plato Said.* Chicago, 1933.
Demos, Raphael. *The Philosophy of Plato.* New York, 1939.
Cherniss, Harold. *The Riddle of the Early Academy.* New York, 1945.
Taylor, A. E. *Plato: The Man and His Work.* 6th ed. London, 1949.
Ross, David. *Plato's Theory of Ideas.* Oxford, 1951.
Crombie, I. M. *An Examination of Plato's Doctrines.* 2 vols. New York, 1962, 1963.
Werkmeister, W. H., ed. *Facets of Plato's Philosophy.* Atlantic Highlands, N.J., 1976.
North, Helen F., ed. *Interpretations of Plato: A Swarthmore Symposium.*
    Mnemosyne Supplements, vol. 50. Leiden, 1977.
Melling, D. J. *Understanding Plato.* Oxford, 1987.

ARISTOTLE AND THE PERIPATETICS

Life of Aristotle (384–322 B.C.)

Aristotle was born at Stagirus in Chalcidice (hence his epithet "the Stagirite"). His father was a doctor, which may explain why Aristotle had an interest in biology. When Aristotle came to the Academy at age seventeen, Plato was in his last stage of development, interested in logic and the criticism of the theory of ideas. At Plato's death Aristotle (and Xenocrates) withdrew from Athens. He spent time at Assos and Mytilene before Philip of Macedon invited him to come to his court in Pella to tutor the young Alexander. In 334 B.C. Aristotle returned to Athens and taught in the rented buildings of a gymnasium (the Lyceum). His successor, Theophrastus, formally founded a school at a complex of buildings that included a *peripatos,* a colonnaded walkway, that gave the name Peripatetic to the school.[31] An outbreak of anti-Macedonian feeling in Athens

---

31. This is contrary to the story in Diogenes Laertius 5.2 that the name came from Aristotle's walking while he lectured; everyone walked while lecturing.

and a charge of impiety against Aristotle caused him to leave Athens ("lest the Athenians sin twice against philosophy") for Chalcis, where he died.

Aristotle's Thought

Aristotle saw himself, at least initially, as a true successor of Plato. Picking up the last phase of Plato's thought, he criticized the ideas as not separate but within things themselves. Individual objects develop toward their own perfection. Thus Aristotle had an interest in this world and in individual things. Whereas Plato started with the forms and moved to specifics, Aristotle started with specifics and tried to group them into ever higher genera. He set his students to the task of collecting all of the objects they could. Since each object is striving for the fulfillment of its own nature, that is, perfection for itself, it is possible to learn the ideal from studying individuals and what they have in common. Thus, by studying the parts one may understand the whole. For example, in preparation for his *Politics* Aristotle had his students collect the constitutions of the different Greek cities. Of the 158 they collected, only that of Athens survives.

Aristotle divided things two ways: as substance, when we see nature in a moment; and as motion, when we see it as a world of change. Moreover, we may analyze nature into potentiality and actuality.

World as Substance. When one looks at things in a moment, as they are in themselves, he sees that everything in nature is a particular substance. Substance is what something is in itself; its "accidents" are its attributes, how it is perceived. The distinction between substance and accidents became important to the clarification of certain theological thoughts in the Middle Ages.

Substance is divisible into form and matter (or pattern and possibility). In the world of nature everything is composed of "stuff" and its arrangement or ordering. For example, a statue is marble to which the sculptor has given a shape. It is matter that has been given a form. Matter does not exist without form, nor form without matter.

For Aristotle it is impossible that all the individuals in a category be destroyed while the forms (ideals) still exist. This is because the forms exist only in matter, in the concrete individuals. This is not so for Plato in his characteristic thought, for in his theory the ideas (forms) exist outside and apart from the individuals. Aristotle's criticism of Plato was that he confused the process of knowing with the nature of reality. To be able to think we must make abstractions. Plato confused the necessary abstractions of thought with the way things really are.

World as Motion. Change is a fact that all observe. While Plato wanted to go beyond the world of change to the unchangeable ideas, Aristotle studied change itself. Change has a pattern that we can understand. There are four causes of motion or change. These are not causes in the modern sense of causality, but Aristotle, using the language of common sense, states the necessary elements in order to explain a change. First is the *material cause* — the matter out of which something is produced. Today we would not call this a cause, for it is only necessary that it be there. It does not do anything, but it is the *sine qua non* of change. Second is the *efficient cause* — the active, producing cause. This is "cause" in the modern sense. Aristotle used the illustration of parents who produce children (the seed is the material cause). Third is the *formal cause* — the technique or way of doing something, the pattern followed. In nature this is the law of development — for example, an acorn grows into an oak according to the laws of nature. The fourth is the *final* (or telic) *cause* — the goal or purpose intended. For Aristotle, everything in nature has an end or purpose. Here Aristotelian science conflicts with modern science, which has given up the question of "Why?" and asks "How?" There is a goal toward which everything is moving — for example, a kitten to become a cat, an acorn to become an oak. The final cause is the cause of causality in the other causes. As with human beings, nothing in nature is done without a purpose (although for most things this may be unconscious). For Aristotle purpose is immanent, not transcendent. An illustration of the four causes may be seen in the work of a sculptor: the marble on which he works is the material cause; the sculptor himself is the efficient cause; the pattern for the statue is the formal cause; and the purpose for which the work is undertaken is the final cause.

World as Potentiality. We may consider change as the development or transition from potentiality to actuality. There are active and passive potentialities. Not all possibilities are realized. A potency becoming actual can mean that something new comes about or that something which is a part of an object is activated.

Aristotle comes close to Plato when he considers the underlying factor responsible for the movement of all things. This factor is their form *(eidos)*, which is the mover. Everything has in itself a power, a potency (e.g., the pupa of a butterfly has the potency to fly). Only in the act itself *(en energeia)* is the thing perfect. The goal toward which the activity moves is the entelechy (*entelecheia*, complete reality) of that thing. The perfection of things is immanent in them, and they move toward actuality. (This explains Aristotle's close investigation into everything.) The most perfect entelechy is thought, hence the prime mover is thought *(nous)*. This supreme mind is transcendent; it has to think about itself, or it would not be perfect. The prime mover is not a causal agent in an active sense — it moves other things by being an object of their desire: they desire its supreme perfection and thus are moved.

God.[32] Late in his life Aristotle allowed for a multiplicity of unmoved movers, but his surviving work does not explain how they would have been related to the prime mover. Even without this complication, Aristotle's view of "God" was quite unlike the biblical conception. The eternal mind, always con-

---

32. A. H. Armstrong, *Ancient Philosophy* (Boston, 1963), 90.

templating its own thinking, was the logical culmination of the hierarchy of substances and the ultimate explanation of motion and change — but it was not a person exercising providence or revealing his will. It affected the universe only through the desire for its unattainable perfection that it inspired, but was not in any sense the creator of the universe. Aristotle's thought was centered in the universe; and his "God" was a part of the structure of reality, at its pinnacle to be sure, but not outside it or its cause.

Souls. Aristotle preferred to speak of powers of the soul rather than parts. He found three kinds of souls: (1) Nutritive or vegetative souls. These lowest souls simply possess the principle of life: nutrition, repair, and reproduction. This is sheer biological life shared by all living things. (2) Sensitive or animal souls. In addition to possessing the principle of life, the middle level possesses sensations: senses, impulses, instincts. The sensitive faculty is the source of desire and motion, which separates animal life from plant life. (3) Thinking or rational souls. The highest level of life possesses reason or intellect, in addition to all the faculties of the lower souls. This level is found in human beings alone.

Aristotle's view of form and matter was ready-made to fit his view of humanity. Soul and body are related as form and matter, with the soul as the organizing principle of the body. Soul and body can be distinguished only in thought, not in fact. For Plato, following Pythagorean thought (p. 382), the body is the instrument or vehicle of the soul: "I am a soul; I have a body." This is not so for Aristotle: there cannot be body without soul, or soul without body. His view had the advantage of preserving the human being intact, but it created problems for Christian thought in the later Middle Ages. Aristotle allowed that a part of the intellect might survive death, but his followers developed this in reference to the universal soul shared by individuals, and not as allowing an individual immortality.

Theory of Knowledge. Aristotle reversed Plato's epistemology, as he did most other things. Knowledge depends on sense experience. By sensation a person grasps the particular; by the intellect that person learns the universal. Knowledge is abstraction. Sensations provide the beginning or basis of knowledge, but not its end. Since the universal is in the particular, the intellect can go beyond sense experience and abstract the form from matter, the universal from the particular. The mind has no form or structure of its own to impose on the things perceived. It finds the universal by taking the common elements from all the individuals.

Ethics.[33] Since human beings are distinguished from other life by rational faculties, the supreme good for them is a rational life. Persons have both theoretical reason and practical reason. Theoretical reason is the capacity to think, understand, and contemplate, while practical reason is reason applied to conduct. For a human being, therefore, happiness will include both intellectual and moral

---

33. *Eudemian Ethics* and *Nicomachean Ethics.*

virtues. The fulfillment of theoretical reason is knowledge, learning the truth; the fulfillment of practical reason is moral virtue. This analysis influenced Hellenistic philosophical thought and through it Christian categories for many centuries. Aristotle's successors classified philosophers as theoretical or practical. Christian thinkers spoke of theoretical (contemplative) and practical (active) lives.

Moral virtue requires that actions possess three qualities: that they be voluntary, chosen, and in conformity to the mean. A voluntary action is a willing action. An unwilling action involves external compulsion or ignorance of the circumstances (here Aristotle distinguishes culpable from inculpable ignorance). A chosen act is a product of reflection, of deliberation. The doctrine of the mean identifies virtue as the middle term between the extremes of excess and deficiency. For example, courage is the mean between foolhardiness (excess) and cowardice (deficiency).

Aristotle did not define happiness in terms of externals, but unlike succeeding Hellenistic moralists he allowed that some goods were instrumentally necessary to the good life. Of great importance for the future was his association of happiness with the highest part of human nature. If the intellect is divine in comparison with the rest of human nature, the life of contemplation will be divine in comparison with human life in general and will possess in the highest degree the quality of self-sufficiency.[34]

Aristotle's Influence

Aristotle has influenced thought to such an extent that it has been said that even if one disagrees with him, his language must be used in the attack. That was not so in antiquity. His pupil Alexander the Great ushered in such changes in the world that succeeding philosophies turned their attention to practical morality, and the ordered metaphysical worlds of Plato and Aristotle receded into the background. Plato's thought had a revival about the beginning of the Christian era, but Aristotle's great influence on Christian thought was only to come centuries later. In the meantime, Aristotle's school made its contribution as a research institution, as his students continued the task to which he had set them in collecting materials on a wide range of subjects.

Theophrastus (370–285 B.C.)[35]

Theophrastus remained the truest of Aristotle's students to their master. He continued the study of plants that Aristotle had assigned him, and two books

---

34. *Nicomachean Ethics* 10.7-8.

35. W. W. Fortenbaugh, et al., trans. and ed., *Theophrastus of Eresos: Sources for His Life, Writings, Thought, and Influence* (Leiden, 1992–).

on this subject survive. Three other works by Theophrastus, however, are of more importance for our purposes.

On Piety (now known from quotation in Porphyry, *De abstinentia* 2.32) opposed animal sacrifice and argued that the gods were more pleased with right thinking. This idea of spiritual sacrifice appealed to some Neoplatonists and was welcomed by Christian apologists as a weapon against idolatry.

The *Characters* attempts to give its readers a real slice of life. It contains thirty descriptive sketches of funny or evil characteristics (cf. "Superstitiousness," referred to on p. 237). Theophrastus divides human nature into types or categories, as plants are divided in the natural world, thus placing the characters in the context of Aristotelian philosophy. *Charactēr* in Greek meant the stamp used in minting coins, so the characters of Theophrastus are those with a distinctive stamp. The value of this work for learning about customs and attitudes is supplemented by its usefulness for language studies. Inasmuch as Theophrastus gives conversations as well as descriptions of the persons, he makes an effort to reproduce colloquial speech. Furthermore, he describes the characters by their traits rather than by adjectives. Menander, the founder of New Comedy in the Hellenistic age, shows much the same interest in character traits, and there was a report that he studied under Theophrastus.

Characters was one of the most influential books from the Hellenistic age on modern European literature. Another work by Theophrastus, now lost except for fragments, was more influential in ancient times. *Opinions of the Philosophers* shaped the way later generations viewed the preceding philosophers. It is now almost impossible to break away from the forms in which Theophrastus put the history of thought (and that was in Aristotelian categories). The work itself, however, was too long and complicated, so it was very soon excerpted. The practice grew up of compiling handbooks on different subjects, and a favorite type summarized the views of different philosophers on different subjects. Eventually there were handbooks of the handbooks so that on a given topic or situation there was given a man's name and a one-word statement of his opinion (e.g., Origin of Matter: Thales — water; Anaximenes — air; etc.). The condensations of Theophrastus made it easy to continue his work, which was brought up-to-date by various writers (see p. 344).

Strato

Strato succeeded Theophrastus as head of the Peripatetic school from 287 to his death in 269. Strato gave up completely the idea of metaphysics, working mainly on mechanics. Nature became a blind force, no longer controlled by a divine *nous* outside itself. Nature develops, but it is not going anywhere in particular. The school of Aristotle became purely scientific, marking a major break, comparable to the turn from dogmatism to skepticism near the same time in the Academy. Neither the Academics nor the Peripatetics maintained their founders' emphases in the Hellenistic period, and both gave way in importance to new schools.

Later History and General Character

Strabo (13.54) relates the story that Aristotle's library was willed by his successor Theophrastus to Neleus, who, not having the headship of the school, returned to his home in Asia Minor. When the Attalids were collecting books for their library at Pergamum, Neleus's family hid the manuscripts of Aristotle in order to keep the Attalids from confiscating them. Then in the first century B.C. the manuscripts were sold and taken to Rome. Here they were edited by Andronicus of Rhodes, who laid the basis for future study of Aristotle and the tradition of scholarly commentaries on Aristotle that has continued to the present. Modern scholars question this story, however, for there is evidence that Aristotle's thought was known in the third and second centuries B.C. (although this may have come from works now lost) and there was likely more than one copy. The story may have been invented in order to explain the fact that Aristotle's school was not "Aristotelian" for those two hundred years.

After Strato the Peripatetics in Athens by the mid–third century became concerned with ethics and rhetoric. The scientists went to Alexandria, the greatest center of scientific knowledge in the Hellenistic world. The school of Aristotle became known as a research institution. As soon as his followers lost sight of Aristotle's conviction of a goal *(telos)* toward which each of the sciences moved, their efforts became knowledge for its own sake — encyclopedianism. Anyone interested in the natural world for its own sake tended to be called a Peripatetic. The Peripatetics were the source of facts for nearly everyone.

Aspects of the Peripatetic Legacy

Soul. The understanding of the soul was important to philosophers and religious teachers. Aristotle's *De Anima* (p. 341) received a number of commentaries in the period from approximately 200-600.[36] His followers maintained an alternative to Plato's view of the soul that was continued in Neoplatonism.

Worldview. The Peripatetic interest in the natural world, but with religious overtones, may be seen in the Pseudo-Aristotelian treatise *On the Cosmos,* variously dated to the first century B.C. or A.D. The cosmology is a devel-

---

36. H. J. Blumenthal, *Aristotle and Neoplatonism in Late Antiquity: Interpretations of the* De Anima (Ithaca, N.Y., 1996.)

opment within the Peripatetic school, although borrowing from others. The world is seen as the expression of the cosmic deity. God is not the immanent deity of the Stoics nor simply the unmoved mover of Aristotle; "it is more noble, more becoming, for him to reside in the highest place, while his power, penetrating the whole of the cosmos," maintains its order. This is done immediately: "The divine nature with a single movement of the nearest element distributes its power to the next part and then to the more remote parts until it permeates the whole." "God is mightiest in power, outstanding in beauty, immortal in life, and supreme in excellence, because though he is invisible to every mortal thing he is seen through his deeds."[37]

History of Philosophy. The Peripatetic interest in the lives of philosophers, the history of philosophical schools, and the classification of thought on particular problems flowed into the work of Diogenes Laertius, a major source for the history of Greek philosophy. (In his *Lives of Eminent Philosophers* [third century A.D.], Diogenes Laertius drew on so many predecessors [whose works are now largely lost] that he is not a consistent representative of any one type of biography. However, we may cite him here as a beneficiary of the Peripatetic contributions to biography — see p. 121.)[38] He covers philosophers from the pre-Socratics to the Stoics and Epicureans, grouping them by schools, but he combines the various kinds of handbook information into a biographical treatment. His *Lives* follows this pattern: a summary of the life, anecdotes about the person, his philosophy in general, some particular points from the philosophy, a list of works, an account of his death, and a poem that Diogenes himself wrote about the philosopher. Diogenes Laertius preserved the gossip on everyone and so must be used with caution, but he is still the first place to begin for information about the various Greek philosophers. In his approach he drew on the literary tradition fashioned by Theophrastus and the Peripatetics.

BIBLIOGRAPHY

Ackrill, J. L., ed. *New Aristotle Reader.* Oxford, 1987.

Cherniss, H. *Aristotle's Criticism of Plato and the Academy.* Baltimore, 1944.
Jaeger, W. *Aristotle.* 2d ed. Oxford, 1948.
Ross, W. D. *Aristotle.* New York, 1964.
Grayeff, F. *Aristotle and his School.* London, 1974.
Gottschalk, H. B. "Aristotelian Philosophy in the Roman World from the Time of Cicero to the End of the Second Century A.D." *ANRW,* II, *Principat,* 36.2. Berlin, 1987. Pp. 1079-1174.

37. *On the Cosmos* 6 (398b, 399b). Cf. Rom. 1:20.
38. J. Mejer, *Diogenes Laertius and his Hellenistic Background,* Hermes-Einzelschr. Heft 40 (1978).

SKEPTICISM

The Greek word *dogma* meant opinion or view, and was the position to which one came after examining something. To examine without necessarily coming to a decision was *skeptesthai*. Plato and Aristotle, after examining, dogmatized. But if one cannot come to a conclusion, then that person suspends judgment. The word for this was *epochē*, reservation of opinion or suspension of judgment.

We have seen how the Academy passed through an extended period of skepticism (pp. 336-37). There was an earlier expression of skepticism that had periodic revivals in antiquity. The Skeptics proper had more practical than theoretical aims and adopted a more thoroughgoing skepticism than did the Academy. To the Skeptics all the other schools were dogmatic, and this was the chief philosophical illness needing a cure.

Pyrrho (c. 360–c. 270 B.C.)

All the philosophers were looking for the purpose of life. Pyrrho too searched and searched but could not find it. So he gave up the search and "suspended judgment." When he did, he discovered that he had reached the goal he sought. His experience was like that of the painter who could not make the picture come out right, gave up, and threw the paint at the canvas — and then it was just right.[39] Everyone was looking for peace of mind *(ataraxia)*, and Pyrrho found it in a skeptical suspension of judgment. Skeptics were consistent in entertaining doubts about everything including their own denials. Pyrrho was characterized by gentleness (*praotēs;* cf. *praeis* in the New Testament) and by a remarkable indifference (or apathy) because there was nothing to get excited about in life. He arrived at this kind of life because he did not have strong opinions about anything.

Pyrrho wrote nothing, but something of his approach is known from the surviving fragments of Timon of Phlius, one of his principal pupils. Pyrrho did not develop a systematic philosophy but represented a view of life, and his followers imitated his life rather than his teachings. Since he did not form a school in the organizational sense, this early phase of Skepticism died out after the second generation. The next phase was associated with the Academy from Arcesilas up to Antiochus and has been treated above (pp. 336-37).

39. This illustration is an old one; see Pliny, *Natural History* 35.36.103; Dio Chrysostom, *Orations* 63.4; Plutarch, *On Chance* 4 (Moralia 99B); Valerius Maximus 8.11.7.

Aenesidemus

About 50 B.C. Aenesidemus revived Pyrrhonism apart from the Academy. He reduced the arguments against knowledge to ten tropes, all very much alike. For a positive approach, he says to follow as a criterion what appears to be real.

The two principal arguments used by the Skeptics were (1) "nothing is more this than the other"; that is, nothing is more probable than anything else, and (2) "all is equal"; that is, to any argument there is a counterargument. The result of such reasoning was to make no judgment. We may illustrate this approach from the question of the existence of God. Instead of attacking God's existence, the Skeptics attacked the possibility of knowing God's existence. They were very Socratic in this and concluded that there were insuperable obstacles to any conception of God advanced up to that time.

Sextus Empiricus (c. A.D. 200)[40]

A late flowering of true Skepticism occurred with Sextus Empiricus, a Greek with a Latin name. "Empiricus" identifies him as a physician of the Empiric school of medicine. Modern knowledge of Skepticism is due to his interest in it, for he compiled what was known about the Skeptics and their arguments. Unlike the situation in regard to earlier Skeptics his writings survive: *Outlines of Pyrrhonism*,[41] *Against Dogmatists (Logicians, Physicists, Ethicists)*, and *Against the Professors* or *Adversus Mathematicos*, a composite title for six books covering separate works against various professions (Grammarians, Rhetoricians, Geometricians, Arithmeticians, Astrologers, and Musicians).[42]

Influence of Skepticism

Skepticism never became an effective school, for it was always negative. It was not influential on a continuing basis, and the last flowering came at a time when the world was turning to religion.

The Skeptical approach may have been all right as far as the external world and theoretical questions were concerned, but how does one live? The

40. Ph. P. Hallie and S. G. Etheridge, *Skepticism, Man, and God: Selections from the Major Writings of Sextus Empiricus* (Middletown, Conn., 1964).

41. Julia Annas and Jonathan Barnes, *Outlines of Scepticism: Sextus Empiricus* (Cambridge, 1994) (trans. with int. and notes); Benson Mates, *The Skeptic Way: Sextus Empiricus' Outlines of Pyrrhonism* (Oxford, 1996) (trans. with int. and commentary).

42. Richard Bett, *Sextus Empiricus: Against the Ethicists (Adversus Mathematicos XI)* (Oxford, 1997) (translation with introduction and commentary); David L. Blank, *Sextus Empiricus: Against the Grammarians (Adversus Mathematicos I)* (Oxford, 1998) (translation with introduction and commentary).

Skeptics answered by saying, To live according to the society in which one finds oneself. Why not steal? It is easier to live by the norms and stay out of trouble. The Skeptics turned out to be the most conservative people in the ancient world. This conservatism in practical life left Skepticism with no message and thus led to its downfall.

The reason that Sextus Empiricus and through him so much of the Skeptical material has survived, surprisingly, is that Christians preserved it. Christians used it against all the ancient dogmas: here was a fully developed arsenal of arguments against all the other ancient philosophical schools.

BIBLIOGRAPHY

Diogenes Laertius. *Lives of Eminent Philosophers* 9.11-12.
Annas, Julius, and Jonathan Barnes. *The Modes of Scepticism: Ancient Texts and Modern Interpretations.* Cambridge, 1985.
Hankinson, R. J. *The Sceptics.* London, 1998.

CYNICISM

Beginnings of Cynicism

Diogenes of Sinope (c. 400–c. 325 B.C.)[43] is usually credited with founding the Cynic way of life. He was influenced in his outlook by Antisthenes, a devoted follower of Socrates, who taught in a gymnasium in Athens known as Cynosarges ("Park of the Agile Dog") and himself apparently known as the "dog" (Greek *kyōn,* "dog," which gave the name Cynic to the movement), but Diogenes became the one primarily known by that epithet. The name "Diogenes the Dog" was given him because of his shamelessness *(anaideia)* in public (cf. the behavior of dogs). Whatever is natural, he felt, is not indecent even in public. Diogenes advocated a life of self-sufficiency in which needs were kept to a minimum. He gave away everything in order to attain independence. To live according to nature meant to live simply. Like Pyrrho, he did not found a school, but others imitated his life-style. The Cynics represented a way of life more than a doctrine or a school of thought.

The caustic wit and drastic actions of Diogenes gave rise to many famous anecdotes in the ancient world.

> One day, observing a child drinking out of his hands, he cast away the cup from his wallet with the words, "A child has beaten me in plainness of living." (Diogenes Laertius, *Lives of the Philosophers* 6.37)

43. Luis E. Navia, *Diogenes of Sinope: The Man in the Tub* (Westport, Conn., 1998).

When he was sunning himself in the Craneum, Alexander came and stood over him and said, "Ask of me any boon you like." To which he replied, "Stand out of my light." (Ibid., 6.38)

He claimed that to fortune he could oppose courage, to convention nature, to passion reason. (Ibid., 6.38)

These anecdotes convey a type and were more influential than was the real man. Such pointed stories with a moral *(chreiai)* became a characteristic of Cynic preaching.

Crates (c. 365–285 B.C.) was the most faithful disciple of Diogenes. He led a wandering life preaching voluntary poverty and an independent life-style. He was highly regarded for his peace-making efforts and for consoling those in distress.

Bion (c. 325–c. 255 B.C.) and *Menippus* (first half of third century B.C.) are credited with developing the diatribe style, but the evidence is lacking and the earliest extensive material that permits study is found in the fragments of *Teles,* a mid–third-century-B.C. follower of Bion.[44] Teles commended the life that exists with a minimum of needs, making use of whatever is available. Such a person plays his role with happiness, because his heart is not set on luxury. Teles represented a milder form of Cynicism, better known from Dio (p. 352).

Zeno, the founder of Stoicism (p. 354), was a disciple of Crates. Whereas Stoicism developed in the direction of upholding the norms of society, the Cynics shocked the Greeks by abandoning manners and saying and doing whatever they wanted when they wanted. Not being a formal school, Cynicism itself was open to whoever chose to appropriate the name and so became more moderate in some of the popular preachers of Roman times.

Cynic Characteristics

The Cynics carried to an extreme the Sophists' contrast between custom and nature (p. 326). They tried to dispel the illusions they saw in human attitudes and conduct and to attain "clarity of mind." They sought to free themselves from luxuries and so inure themselves to hardship by ascetic practices. In order to excite censure they exposed themselves to scorn by deliberately acting against the conventions of society: using violent and abusive language, wearing filthy garments, performing acts of nature (defecation, sex) in public, and feigning madness. The Cynics alone among the Greeks did not view life as lived

---

44. J. F. Kindstrand, *Bion of Borysthenes: A Collection of the Fragments with Introduction and Commentary,* Acta Universitatis Upsaliensis, Studia Graeca Upsaliensia 2 (Uppsala, 1976). Edward O'Neil, *Teles (The Cynic Teacher)* (Missoula, Mont., 1977); R. Nickel, *Epiktet. Teles. Musonius. Ausgewählte Schriften* (Darmstadt and Zurich, 1994).

in society as a life of ruling and being ruled. By rejecting pleasure and seeking dishonor the Cynics sought to attain hardness, apathy, and freedom. They claimed that this action benefited the public; it shamed the people more than it shamed the Cynic. The Cynic's behavior showed the truth and so effected an ethical cure on the populace.

The basic instruction of the Cynics was as follows:

> Take care of your soul, but take care of the body only to the degree that necessity requires, and of externals not even that much. For happiness is not pleasure, on account of which we need externals, while virtue is complete without any externals. (Pseudo-Crates, *Epistle* 3)[45]

It was summed up in this way: "But I deem it enough to live according to virtue and nature, and that this is in our power" (Pseudo-Diogenes, *Epistle* 25).[46] The reasoning in support of begging may be cited as an example:

> Socrates used to say that sages do not beg but demand back, for everything belongs to them, just as it does to the gods. And this he tried to infer from the premises that the gods are masters of all, that the property of friends is held in common, and that the sage is a friend of god. Therefore, you will be begging for what is your own. (Pseudo-Diogenes, *Epistle* 10)[47]

The Cynics believed that the life of virtue could be attained by one's moral effort, and thus they rejected the claims of fate over an individual's life. At the same time they were impatient of Stoic dogma and were sharply and consistently critical of the traditional religion. Yet they believed in the divine and some were monotheists. Indeed, the Cynic sage could be thought of as attaining the divine life. Cynics differed from Stoics in their rejection of dogma and of popular religion and in their insistence that the ideal of the wise man was attainable.[48]

A particular feature of the Cynics was their boldness or frankness of speech (*parrhēsia;* cf. 1 Thess. 2:2), which they took to mean the freedom to speak the truth. This word had been used of the privilege of citizens in Greek cities to speak freely in the assemblies; the Cynics appropriated it to express their independence in reviling others with insolent invective; Christians used it to describe the relationship that they now had with God and one another by reason of the revelation in Christ.[49]

45. Abraham J. Malherbe, *The Cynic Epistles* (Missoula, Mont., 1977), 55; cf. *Epistle* 18 (p. 69).

46. Ibid., 117.

47. Ibid., 105; cf. Ps.-Crates, *Ep.* 26.

48. A. J. Malherbe, "Pseudo Heraclitus, Epistle 4: The Divinization of the Wise Man," *Jahrbuch für Antike und Christentum* 21 (1978):42-64.

49. W. C. Van Unnik, "The Christian's Freedom of Speech in the New Testament," *BJRL* 44

The picture sketched above represents mainly the harsh, austere Cynics, who attracted the most attention. They stressed their radical individualism and their moral superiority over the mass of evil humanity, characteristics expressed by deliberately choosing a hard life, by begging, by harsh speech, and by offensive public acts. There were, however, milder Cynics, represented by the pseudo-Socratic *Epistles* from the beginning of the Christian era. These Cynics were less prideful and less pessimistic about the human condition and about reforming society. They were willing to accept social roles, associating with political leaders, living as residents in cities rather than wandering about, and developing circles of friends. They were still conscious of their mission as social critics and emphatic in their sense of self-sufficiency.[50]

The wandering Cynic philosophers became a common feature of the early empire. Their distinctive appearance — woolen cloak, walking stick, beggar's bag, and long beard — identified them throughout the Mediterranean world (Apuleius, *Apology* 22). The ancients differed as to who originated the attire (Antisthenes, Diogenes, or others). Many without education adopted the Cynic dress and way of life and passed for philosophers, going from city to city living off alms from those attracted to but not adopting their "freedom" or only amused by them. The Cynics exercised much influence, not in getting people to adopt their way of life but in practical guidance in the affairs of life.

The Cynics contributed much to popular philosophy (pp. 323-24) and popularized certain key themes of the moralists (pp. 321-23). They provided the background to the development of Stoicism and influenced the discourses of Dio of Prusa and the satires of Lucian of Samosata, two authors who reflect Cynic concerns and tell us much about Cynics. Not much is heard about Cynics in the second and first century B.C., but from the first century A.D. to the end of antiquity the Cynic beggar philosophers were a common feature in the cities of the Roman world. Popular philosophers could be found haranguing the people in marketplaces and wherever people gathered. By renouncing possessions, wearing a philosopher's cloak, and practicing self-affliction, the Cynics were one of the important strands leading to the Christian monk.

The interpretation of Jesus as a Cynic teacher rests primarily on superficial parallels undocumented in a Palestinian setting.[51]

(1962):466-88; John T. Fitzgerald, ed., *Friendship, Flattery, and Frankness of Speech: Studies on Friendship in the New Testament World* (Leiden, 1996); see now the Epicurean treatise by *Philodemus: On Frank Criticism*, introduction, translation, and notes by David Konstan et al. (Atlanta, 1998).

50. A. J. Malherbe, "Self-Definition among the Cynics," in *Paul and the Popular Philosophers* (Minneapolis, 1989), 11-24.

51. Paul Rhodes Eddy, "Jesus as Diogenes? Reflections on the Cynic Jesus Thesis," *JBL* 115 (1996):449-469; David Seeley, "Jesus and the Cynics Revisited," *JBL* 116 (1997):704-712.

Dio of Prusa (A.D. 40 to after 112)[52]

The orations of Dio, later called Chrysostom ("Golden-mouth"), have been preserved and give us the fullest collection of speeches by a Greek popular philosopher, albeit a much better educated and more moderate one than the typical Cynic. The Cynic way of life attracted deadbeats and imposters who loved the notoriety and alms. Dio and later Lucian had much to say distinguishing the "true" Cynic from other types (Dio, *Discourse* 32.9; cf. 1 Thess. 2 for Paul distinguishing himself from other street preachers and the use of *spermologos* in Acts 17:18 to describe him).[53]

Dio was a native of Prusa in Bithynia and practiced rhetoric in Rome until he fell under Domitian's wrath and was banished. Thereafter he traveled around the eastern Mediterranean, preaching the moral philosophy that was the common property of all the schools. His conversational style was aimed to reach the people, but he reflected the classical tradition and the culture of the upper classes of the eastern half of the empire. His theology was Stoic (perhaps especially dependent on Posidonius). Thus he did not represent the anti-traditional attitude of most Cynics and did not identify himself with any school, but he adopted many of the Cynic themes and insisted on the philosopher's right of free speech and his role as critic.

Dio addressed a wide range of topics reflecting the life of his times. For example, *Discourse* 12 ("The Olympic Oration") discusses the philosophical justification of images in paganism as part of a treatment of ideas of deity and the place of art in religion.[54] *Discourse* 1 sketches the ideal ruler, with an implied contrast of Trajan with Domitian. The main thrust of Dio's messages was to raise the moral level and increase the civic virtues among his hearers. He sought to improve people through his speeches and heal their sickness of soul. He imparted a warmth of religious feeling to his teaching.

Lucian of Samosata (c. A.D. 120 to after 180)[55]

Lucian was not himself a philosopher or an adherent of a particular philosophical school (see p. 118), but his satires on religious and philosophical topics re-

52. G. Mussies, *Dio Chrysostom and the New Testament*, Studia ad Corpus Hellenisticum Novi Testamenti, vol. 2 (Leiden, 1972); S. Dill, *Roman Society from Nero to Marcus Aurelius* (repr., New York, 1956), 334-83; C. P. Jones, *The Roman World of Dio Chrysostom* (Cambridge, Mass., 1978); R. Koolmeister and T. Tallmeister, *An Index to Dio Chrysostomus* (Uppsala, 1981).

53. Abraham J. Malherbe, "'Gentle as a Nurse': The Cynic Background to I Thess ii," *Novum Testamentum* 12 (1970): 205-17.

54. F. F. Harris, "The Olympian Oration of Dio Chrysostom," *Journal of Religious History* 2 (1962).

55. H. D. Betz, *Lukian von Samosata und das Neue Testament* (Berlin, 1961); D. Clay,

peat certain common themes. His dialogues were indebted in form and occasionally in content to Menippus's satires. The *Dialogues of the Gods* hold up to ridicule the popular mythology in regard to the gods; other works such as *Zeus Catechized, Zeus Rants* (Tragedian) — both indebted to Menippus — and *The Parliament of the Gods* show the destructive effect of philosophical criticism on popular beliefs.

Philosophers were a major target of Lucian's satire, and he spares none of the schools. One may note his *Hermotimus* for his attack on philosophers, in this case through the Skeptic criticism of Stoicism. Representatives of all the schools get rough treatment for their unphilosophical behavior at the *Banquet* (Carousal) *or the Lapiths. Philosophies for Sale* (or better "Kinds of Lives") reflects the popular understanding of the different schools and the life-style advocated by each. He defended the work later in *The Dead Come to Life or the Fisherman,* which contrasts the ancient philosophers and their unworthy successors. Lucian could be devastating in his mockery of pseudo-philosophers, especially Cynics *(On the Death of Peregrinus* and *Runaways),* but occasionally he drew the picture of a true one — as in *Nigrinus* and *Demonax. Nigrinus* illustrates the conversion to philosophy, which was the nearest parallel to Christian conversion. The work also illustrates themes of popular philosophy — the imagery of the theatre and other descriptions of life — and the contrast between the true philosopher and the one looking for a living. *Demonax* was an eclectic, but was nearest to the Cynics, without renouncing ordinary life. He illustrates the Cynic boldness of speech (or insolence) and the way in which Socrates was the hero of philosophy.

Lucian preserves some of the Cynic themes — as in *The Dream or the Cock* (against wealth; cf. *Timon or the Misanthrope*), *Charon or the Inspectors,* and *The Downward Journey or the Tyrant* (follies of human life since all are equal in death). He also preserves themes from popular philosophy — as *Toxaris or Friendship.*

BIBLIOGRAPHY

Attridge, Harold W. *First Century Cynicism in the Epistles of Heraclitus.* Introduction, Greek text, and translation. Harvard Theological Studies, vol. 29. Missoula, Mont., 1976.

Malherbe, A. J. *The Cynic Epistles: A Study Edition.* Missoula, Mont., 1977.

Dio Chrysostom. *Discourse* 13 (which may be based on Antisthenes) and 33 (First Tarsic, as typical of moral rebuke in public lecture).

Diogenes Laertius. *Lives of Eminent Philosophers* 6.

Perry, B. E. *Secundus the Silent Philosopher.* Ithaca, N.Y., 1964.

"Lucian of Samosata: Four Philosophical Lives (Nigrinus, Demonax, Peregrinus, Alexander Pseudomantis)," *ANRW* II, *Principat,* 36.5 (Berlin, 1992), 3406-50. For further bibliography on Lucian, see p. 118n.87.

Epictetus. *Discourses* 3.22.

Dudley, D. R. *A History of Cynicism from Diogenes to the Sixth Century* A.D. London, 1937.

Sayre, F. *The Greek Cynics.* Baltimore, 1948.

Höistad, R. *Cynic Hero and Cynic King.* Uppsala, 1948.

Downing, F. G. *Christ and the Cynics: Jesus and Other Radical Preachers in First-Century Tradition.* Sheffield, 1988. (See the criticism by C. M. Tuckett, "A Cynic Q?" *Biblica* 70 (1989):349-76.)

Downing, F. G. *Cynics and Christian Origins.* Edinburgh, 1992.

Branham, R. Bracht, and Marie-Odile Goulet-Cazé, eds. *The Cynics: The Cynic Movement in Antiquity and Its Legacy.* Berkeley, 1996.

Navia, Luis E. *Classical Cynicism: A Critical Study.* Westport, Conn., 1996.

Downing, F. G. *Cynics, Paul, and the Pauline Churches.* London, 1998.

Navia, Luis E. *The Philosophy of Cynicism: An Annotated Bibliography.* Westport, Conn., 1995.

STOICISM

The two principal philosophical schools of the Hellenistic Age were the Stoics and Epicureans (cf. Acts 17:18). Both were primarily interested in ethics but developed comprehensive explanations of reality that were influential beyond their own circles of adherents. (For comparison of the two, see pp. 377-78.)

Early Stoa

Zeno (335–263 B.C.). Stoicism was founded by Zeno of Citium (Cyprus), perhaps a Phoenician by race, who came to Athens about 313 B.C. The story was told that he read Xenophon's *Memorabilia* of Socrates and asked where he could find a man like him. He was directed to the Cynic Crates, and followed him.[56] Whatever the truth of the anecdote, Zeno's early outlook was very much influenced by Cynicism. Stoicism was ambiguous about its Cynic origins. Panaetius (pp. 360-61) was embarrassed by them and denied that Zeno studied under the Cynics. But other Stoics did not forget their Cynic origin, and Epictetus spoke of himself as a Cynic (pp. 366-67).

Zeno began teaching in the *Stoa Poikilē* (the Painted Porch, which served as a public hall) in Athens; hence the name of the school (as with some other philosophical schools) was derived from the place of teaching. Zeno started the scientific study of Greek grammar and vocabulary. He developed a complete

---

56. Diogenes Laertius, *Lives of Eminent Philosophers* 7.1.2-3.

philosophical system of three branches — logic and theory of knowledge, physics and theology, and ethics (see pp. 356ff.). His main concern was securing humanity from fear and disturbance. According to Zeno, the goal of life is virtue; everything else is indifferent. Since no one can deprive the wise person of virtue, that person is always in possession of the only true good and is therefore happy.

Cleanthes (331–232 B.C.). Zeno was succeeded as head of the Stoic school by Cleanthes of Assos from 263 to 232. He was the only true Greek among the early leaders of the school. Cleanthes looked at Zeno's description of the world as altogether material in a much more religious way. He developed the comparison of the universe to a human being. As the human body has a leading part, a greater concentration of soul, in the chest (where the voice comes from), so there is a leading part of the universe in the realm of the fixed stars. This greater concentration of spirit could be worshiped, as Cleanthes did in his "Hymn to Zeus," which had enough influence on antiquity that it has been preserved.[57] The hymn emphasized "God's universal law," providence, and the individual's need to praise the universal law. The Stoa at this time came under heavy attack from the Academy. Cleanthes was a good man, but he could not handle the logical problems. Zeno had said of him that he was a slow learner but when he got something it stuck.

Chrysippus (c. 280–207 B.C.).[58] Chrysippus of Soli (Cilicia) succeeded to the headship of the Stoa in 232, and saw a rebirth of Stoicism. He was interested in psychology and logic. His efforts to show that Homer and Hesiod were really Stoics gave an impetus to allegorizing. Chrysippus became the Stoic par excellence to the ancient world. Zeno and Cleanthes were absorbed into him and their ideas given a new foundation. Through him Stoicism assumed a more academic and technical character. It was largely in the form given by Chrysippus that Stoicism was transmitted in the ancient world. Hence, we must take the first three leaders of the Stoic school together in examining the system. None of their writings has survived intact, so we are dependent on quotations and fragments. Chrysippus had the reputation in antiquity of being the best logician and having the worst style among the philosophers. If the latter is true, there may be some consolation for the loss of source material in the seven hundred works attributed to him but not preserved.

Aratus of Soli (c. 315–240 B.C.). Although not the head of the Stoic school, Aratus deserves special mention because he was quoted in the New Testament. After coming to Athens, Aratus was a pupil of Zeno in the latter's old age. When Antigonus Gonatas invited Zeno to come to the Macedonian court, the old man instead sent two of his pupils, Persaeus, a regular philosopher, and his

57. Stobaeus, *Eclogae* 1.1.12. Trans. in F. C. Grant, *Hellenistic Religions* (New York, 1953), 152-54. See E. H. Blakeney, *The Hymn of Cleanthes* (London, 1921).

58. J. B. Gould, *The Philosophy of Chrysippus*, Philosophia Antiqua, vol. 17 (Leiden, 1970).

friend Aratus, a poet. While at Pella, Aratus put into verse a textbook of astronomy, *Phaenomena*.[59] Simple astronomy took the place of our calendars for everyone in that time outside of urban and court life. (The preoccupation with astronomy in ancient authors was a simple matter of knowing the days and seasons, which was essential for agriculture and sailing.) Aratus's poem became a textbook in the schools; it was easier to remember the astronomical information in verse form. Everyone read Homer and Aratus. When the Romans translated something from Greek into Latin, Aratus was one of the first (Varro, Cicero, and Germanicus translated his work). Aratus gave a Stoic coloring to his poem, and so he was important in the spread of Stoic ideas. When Paul (Acts 17:28) wanted to quote something religious from the Greek poets, the opening lines of Aratus' *Phaenomena* came to mind. The statement "We are also his offspring" is similar to a statement in Cleanthes' "Hymn to Zeus," but Cleanthes uses the second person in direct address to Zeus whereas Aratus's statement is third person, as is Paul's quotation. Everyone would know Aratus's poem, and this particular idea was a Stoic commonplace, so this quotation does not of itself necessarily indicate any extensive knowledge of Greek literature. Aratus more than the founders of Stoicism made its ideas a part of the common Greek tradition.

The Stoics borrowed from Xenocrates a threefold division of philosophy into physics, logic, and ethics.

Stoic Physics

Since, as we noted, it is difficult to distinguish the views of the first Stoics, we will look at a composite picture, recognizing that Zeno was the originator and making some distinctions where it seems significant to do so.

Materialism. According to the Stoic view, nothing is immaterial. God, the world, and even words are material. For each thing that one describes three things really exist: the word, the idea, and the physical object (e.g., the word *horse*, the idea of a horse, and the animal called "horse"). Even emotions are material things because they have a physical manifestation (e.g., shame causes a person to blush).

Pantheism. There are two basic kinds of matter: the grosser matter and the finer matter called breath or spirit *(pneuma)* that is diffused throughout reality. This special form of matter holds everything together and is given various names: *logos* (reason), breath *(pneuma)*, providence *(pronoia)*, Zeus, or fire (the element considered most akin to reason). Stoicism was pantheistic in that

59. Text and translation in Loeb Classical Library volume with Callimachus and Lycophron and by Douglas Kidd, *Aratus: Phaenomena*, Cambridge Classical Texts and Commentaries 34 (Cambridge, 1997).

it found the divine reality in everything. Thus Zeus is everywhere, as the Greeks had said. The Stoic god has been described as a "perfectly good and wise gas" or more exactly as "intelligent, fiery breath."

Soul and Providence. The human being consists of these two kinds of matter: the heavier matter of the physical body and the lighter matter of the soul. The soul stretched through the body has eight parts: the five senses, voice, generative power, and the "leading part" *(hēgemonikon),* the mind, which is concentrated in the heart. Later Stoics, because of advances in medicine, placed it in the head.

The universe is like a giant living body with its own leading part. (Posidonius [pp. 361-63] later placed it in the sun.) All parts of the universe are connected; thus, what happens in one place is affected by what happens elsewhere. On this basis divination and oracles were defended. Another basis for their defense was the principle of providence. Since the universe is rational, it does take thought for humanity. Chrysippus wrote voluminously to show that this is the best of all possible worlds. Everything is directed toward a good goal, and even evil exists for a good purpose.

Allegory. The Stoics sought to find their physical theories in the ancient mythology and in so doing promoted the allegorical method of interpretation. Even as Zeus was said to pervade all, so other features of the popular religion were justified. Mythology was seen as a crude expression of truth, presented on the level of the people of the time. The gods did not actually do the things attributed to them, which were descriptions of natural events. In particular this approach served to account for immoral actions by the gods in the myths. The common people might continue to believe these things, but the philosopher knew their true meaning. They were accounts of Stoic philosophy in story form. As an example of the way the allegorizing was done at an early stage, note the following: rearranging the letters in the name of the goddess Hera *(ERA)* gives the word for air *(AER);* or an easy semantic change in *DEMETER* gives *GE METER* (Earth Mother).

The allegorical method of interpreting sacred literature was adopted by the Jewish philosopher Philo of Alexandria (pp. 478ff.), who harmonized the Mosaic religion with philosophy. From Philo the method passed to such Alexandrian Christian scholars as Clement of Alexandria and Origen.

Conflagration and Regeneration.[60] Stoicism went back to Heraclitus (c. 500 B.C.) for its view of the world. Heraclitus thought that the world was essentially fire in various forms. Fire turned into air, air into water, water to earth, and back again. This constant change is balanced by an interchange. He called this principle of balance, stability, or order *logos.* The *logos* became an-

---

60. A. A. Long, "The Stoics on World Conflagration and Everlasting Recurrence," in R. H. Epp, ed., *Spindel Conference 1984: Recovering the Stoics, The Southern Journal of Philosophy* 23 (1985), 13-37.

other word in the Stoic system for god, since it maintains order. This impersonal reason that gives order to the world is thus unlike the Christian conception found in John 1.

From Heraclitus Zeno got the principle of "creative fire" — once all was
fire and all will become fire again. The world goes through a period of stability, followed by the conflagration (*ekpyrōsis;* cf. the language of 2 Pet. 3:10-12).
The cycle will then be repeated (the regeneration — *palingenesia;* cf. Matt.
19:28; Titus 3:5). Since the world is perfect, if it is done over again it must be
done the same way. There was no idea in Stoicism that the soul survives the
conflagration. Cleanthes said the soul lives until the next conflagration, but
Chrysippus said only the souls of the wise do so. Later Stoics allowed a kind of
limited immortality in that the soul is part of the World Soul and will reap-
pear in the new world, but a personal immortality does not seem to have been
a real possibility.

Stoic Logic and Epistemology

If reality is rational, it must be possible to represent it rationally. A fundamental principle of Greek thought was that the universe is orderly. Problems in understanding it are logical problems and can be solved if one works on them.
Hence, the Stoics gave a lot of attention to logic.

The Stoic epistemology took as its criterion of truth a "perception that
lays hold" *(kataleptic phantasia)* — something that must be believed because it
is so compelling. It is not clear whether the mind lays hold of something or the
object lays hold of the mind. If it is the latter, the view is very near to that of
Epicurus (pp. 374-75), but the Stoics would never have admitted this.

Zeno said an emotion was an unnatural movement of the mind. The human soul is basically a thinking apparatus. There was no place in the Stoic system for the desirous part of the soul or spirit, as in Plato. An emotion therefore
was either a superabundant wish (a reaching out of the mind) or an exaggerated impulse (something coming in from the outside and moving the mind
more than it should). If the mind is an undifferentiated unity, how can impulses override the rational? Chrysippus answered by saying that emotions are
false judgments. He made all things intellectual. When the soul thinks, that is
one aspect; when it makes a judgment, it turns to another aspect, but it is the
same entity functioning in different ways. An illustration used was this: to feel
fear if you see a lion is a false judgment, since the only thing to fear is an evil
life. It is all right to save your life, but do not feel terror. Or, to experience grief
when one's parent dies is a false judgment. Everyone loses parents. If one
adopts this explanation of emotions, however, there must be an explanation of
how the emotions stopped. Chrysippus had a complicated answer involving a
seeping back in of a true judgment.

Stoic Ethics[61]

Virtue. For the Stoics the goal or end of life is being happy, but this consists in living in accord with virtue, which is living in accord with nature (Stobaeus 6e = 2.77). Since human beings are rational, and the rational principle pervades the universe, the virtuous person lives in accord with reason *(logos).* The common formulation of this conception was "to live according to nature." This is the best of all possible worlds, and nature is the perfect environmment into which all are born. All people should live in accord with the *logos* that runs throughout the world. Thus to live in accord with nature means to live reasonably. Zeno apparently often stated the principle as simply "to live in accord"; that is, "to live harmoniously." Sometimes he added a word to clarify the concept, and it seems that later Stoics fastened on the phrase "to live in accord with nature" (nature understood according to the Stoic perception of reality). Virtue or perfection, then, is to live in accord with rational nature.

Since virtue is a matter of making the right judgments, it comes down to practical judgment *(phronēsis).* One either has or does not have this capacity to make right judgments. A person is either wise or foolish, completely virtuous or nonvirtuous. This proved to be the hardest part of the ethical theory to defend, but the Stoics stuck to it because they did not want to divide the virtues into little boxes. If a person makes a wrong choice, it is evident that he does not have proper training. One wrong judgment is as bad as any other. The perfect or wholly right act arising from a perfect judgment was called *katorthōma.* A person who does this is the really wise person. Once one has the power to make right decisions, the power is never lost. Thus the Stoic ethics were in theory quite intellectual.

Was there ever any such a man as the Stoic wise person? By the second generation it was decided that such was only in the past. Not even Socrates survived this attack. Thus, being the wise person, a reality to the first Stoics and a goal they strived to attain, became ideal. But admitting that no one truly wise ever actually existed proved to be very damaging. The Stoics initially made a division between the wise and the foolish, then presented the wise person as an ideal, and finally admitted that everyone was quite bad. The other schools made fun of the Stoic wise man.

Indifferent Things. At this stage another category in early Stoic thought became important. Zeno had spoken of what is indifferent *(adiaphoron),* which for him was a very large category that included everything except virtue or vice. He further divided the indifferent things *(adiaphora)* into two groups: things preferred (e.g., family, house, health) and things not preferred. In between are the truly indifferent things that make no difference at all in life (e.g.,

61. Damianos Tsekourakis, *Studies in the Terminology of Early Stoic Ethics* (Wiesbaden, 1974); B. Inwood, *Ethics and Human Action in Early Stoicism* (Oxford, 1987).

whether the number of one's hairs is even or odd). When asked on what basis some things are preferred, the reply was that they must have something to do with life. With that the Stoics had a basis for bringing the whole social structure back in and so departed from their Cynic origins. The Stoics thus became concerned with preserving society, because it was to be preferred to uncivilized conditions, although it was not part of virtue. Later Stoics figured out a whole series of actions that were fitting or suitable in relation to the "preferred" conditions. A fitting or suitable action was termed *kathēkon*. As perfect actions became impossible, interest shifted to what was practicable. Stoicism increasingly showed an interest in what it considered secondary. It did allow for a class of persons on the way to becoming wise (those who live according to the fitting), and in those terms did not lose sight of its ideal altogether.

Determinism.[62] If everything is leading toward the best, as the Stoic theory of providence affirmed, then everything is determined in advance. The Stoic cyclical theory also pointed to the same conclusion. After the next conflagration, Socrates will gather the youth about him and teach as in the preceding cycle. (And students will be taking the same courses and reading this same textbook — a thought that should deter any potential converts to Stoicism!) Nevertheless, Stoicism believed in "free will." How is that possible within a deterministic system? Freedom has to do with the internal disposition. The Stoics used the illustration of a river with eddies in its current. A person is being carried along the river to perfection. The eddy is the free will when it resists, but like the stream one eventually will be carried along anyway. The wise will submit to the providence of the *logos*. Since one is going to be swept along regardless, it is better to do so voluntarily. The fundamental problem is how persons can resist at all if everything is determined. This is especially acute for Stoics, since for them the divinity is within. How can one resist what one is a part of?

Middle Stoa

Panaetius (c. 185–109 B.C.).[63] Chrysippus was succeeded in the headship of the Stoa by Zeno of Tarsus, Diogenes of Seleucia, and Antipater of Tarsus. Panaetius studied under the latter two before himself succeeding to the headship in 129 B.C. He was from a noble family in Rhodes, but by the time he was grown Rhodes had fallen to a second-rate power and was a protectorate of Rome. Panaetius turned to philosophy instead of a political career. After studying in Athens he went to Rome about 144 B.C., where he became a part of the circle that gathered around Scipio and included the Greek historian of Rome, Polybius. Panaetius was one of the first Greeks to appreciate the new role and

---

62. Susanne Bobzien, *Determinism and Freedom in Stoic Philosophy* (Oxford, 1998).
63. M. van Straaten, *Panaetii Rhodii Fragmenta*, Philosophia Antiqua, vol. 5 (Leiden, 1962).

power of Rome, and was fortunate to be in the circle of Romans who for the first time were interested in Greek culture. Since he came from a leading family of what had been a great power and was an ally of Rome, it was easy for Panaetius to have access to leading Romans. He returned to Athens to head and rejuvenate the Stoic school for the last twenty years of his life.

Panaetius adapted Stoicism to the Romans, making it suitable for a people ruling the world. He gave up the idea of a world conflagration and accepted the eternity of the world. (Since providence makes for the good, there is no destruction.) Panaetius returned to a more Platonic understanding of the body and soul which make up a human being. The mind is not a single part, as Chrysippus had said, but two parts — the drives and the *logos*. The emotional life is separate from the intellectual life; thus, the virtuous person is the one whose drives are controlled by the *logos*. Panaetius turned attention in ethics to the practical things of life. The correct act (*to kathēkon*, the fitting) is any act that reflects the control of the *logos*.[64]

With Panaetius the natural law became the standard of reference. He said that there are four great natural drives: toward community (political), toward knowledge (intellectual), toward ambition (perfection for oneself), and toward beauty (aesthetic). All four drives are to be directed by the *logos*. This was a return to a more Greek concept than had characterized the Stoa and brought back into its philosophy some sense of the beauty of the world.

It is possible that Panaetius developed the idea that the best constitution is a mixed kind, combining elements of oligarchy, democracy, and monarchy. Polybius set forth this view in his history of Rome as an explanation of its greatness.

Panaetius suggested that there were three kinds of gods: those of the philosophers (the natural gods), which are true; those of the poets (the mythical gods), which are false; and those of the state (the political gods), which are somewhat in the middle for they tie the others together and are to be worshiped for their value to society. Varro developed this idea in the first century B.C. in a work Augustine selected as the best philosophical defense of paganism for refutation in his *City of God*.

Posidonius (c. 135–c. 50 B.C.).[65] Decorum is the word for Panaetius; enthusiasm is the word for Posidonius. For achievements in both science and philosophy Posidonius may be compared with Aristotle. Since unfortunately

---

64. Panaetius wrote a treatise "Concerning the One Who Acts Correctly." Cicero used it in his ethical treatise *De officiis* (Eng. trans. *On Duties*, but *officium* was the Latin for *kathēkon*). That work in turn was Christianized by Ambrose, fourth-century bishop of Milan, in his work *On the Duties of the Clergy*.

65. W. Theiler, *Poseidonios: Die Fragmente*, 2 vols. (Berlin, 1982); J. G. Kidd and L. Edelstein, eds., *Posidonius*, vol. 1: *The Fragments*, 2d ed. (Cambridge, 1989); Vol. 2: *The Commentary* (Cambridge, 1988); Vol. 3: *The Translations of the Fragments*, by J. G. Kidd (Cambridge, 1999); A. D. Nock, "Posidonius," *Journal of Roman Studies* 49 (1959):1-15 (*Essays*, 853-76).

nothing of his writings survives, it is difficult to judge the extent of his influence, which some modern scholars have seen as considerable. Posidonius was
born in Apamea in Syria and studied under Panaetius at Athens. After travels
in the western Mediterranean he went to Rhodes and started a school there. He
was never head of the Stoic school in Athens and indeed was regarded as somewhat of a renegade by them. Strabo said he was always Aristotelianizing, which
meant that he had an interest in scientific observation of the natural world and
in causation. Some aspects of Posidonius's worldview may be reconstructed
from ideas attributed to him and related passages that seem to be dependent on
him. Three of these will be noted for discussion.

(1) The source of life, growth, and differences in the world is the sun.
Whereas the earlier Stoics had spoken of a "fashioning [or creative] fire,"
Posidonius spoke of a "life-giving force." The greatest concentration of heat
and fire in the universe is the sun. The heat of the sun is responsible for different animals and precious stones. Life comes from the force of the sun. The sun
is also responsible for the differences in human races. Different peoples live in
different zones, and their characteristics are derived from the sun. The
Scythians live to the north and are blonde. The Ethiopians live to the south and
are black. The Mediterranean peoples live in the intermediate zone and are intermediate in color. People who stay in their own zone develop; when they
move away from their natural zone they degenerate. The starting point of the
thought is good Stoic doctrine, but Posidonius developed it in an original way
and combined it with ethnographic theory.

(2) There is a sympathetic relationship between all parts of the world.
Posidonius discovered the effect of the moon on the tides in one of the great
methodical studies of antiquity. He went to Cadiz on the Atlantic coast of
Spain, marked the heights of the tide, and correlated these with the phases of
the moon. Seeing the effect of the sun and moon on the world, Posidonius developed the theory of sympathy, a mutual affecting of the parts of the world.
This was quite consistent with the Stoic worldview.

From this theory of sympathy Posidonius elaborated a theory of unity.
There are three kinds of unity: the kind an army has — separate individuals
functioning in harmony; the kind a building has — each part connected
(joined) to the other; and the kind a living being has — what affects one part
affects all.[66] What type of unity is the cosmos? The third kind, because of the
effect of sun and moon on the earth. This view has been brought into discussions of Paul's views of the unity of the church as a body, but recent studies
point to an Old Testament and Jewish background as more probable.[67]

---

66. Cf. the summary without reference to Posidonius in Plutarch, *Advice to Bride and
Groom* 34 (*Moralia* 142F).

67. See J. A. T. Robinson, *The Body: A Study in Pauline Theology* (London, 1952), 55, for a
listing of interpretations and bibliography; R. H. Gundry, *Sōma in Biblical Theology* (Cambridge,
1976); cf. Eduard Schweizer, *The Church as the Body of Christ* (Richmond, Va., 1964).

(3) The cosmos is an ordered world with graduated levels of being. Each level or grade of being has its own "power." As in Aristotle, the first level has the power of growth and nourishment, the next level adds the power of motion, and humans add the power of reason and speech. So, Posidonius spoke of powers of the soul (as Aristotle), not parts of the soul. Each part of the universe is interconnected with the rest through gradations. A characteristic concept of Posidonius is that the whole universe is a being and is "nourished." A human being is a microcosm of the macrocosm. It has been conjectured that the "chain of being" in Neopythagoreanism (e.g., Numenius; p. 386) is derived from Posidonius. Posidonius wrote a work on beings intermediate between human and divine — demons and heroes. Not a mystic himself, his worldview inspired mysticism in others.

What is original in Posidonius and how much is old Stoicism simply reworked by him is a difficult problem in the history of philosophy in this period. Posidonius shared with Panaetius the Platonic thought that there is a separate emotional life rooted in the soul. He carried further a "Platonizing Stoicism." This return to Plato and Aristotle was typical of the century beginning around 50 B.C. Posidonius wrote on so much that he gave his age almost an encyclopedia of knowledge. Many characteristics of the ensuing worldview seem to be derived from him.

Later Stoa: Roman Stoicism[68]

The Roman representatives of Stoicism in the first and second centuries A.D. show an exclusively ethical and practical concern. They illustrate many of the themes that are part of the common philosophical outlook of the time (see above, pp. 323-25). They also represent the broad range of Stoicism's appeal — from the slave Epictetus to the emperor Marcus Aurelius.

Arius Didymus was a philosopher in Alexandria who accompanied Augustus into the city in 30 B.C. Although the identification with the companion of Augustus is questioned, Arius Didymus compiled epitomes of Stoic and Peripatetic ethics that are extensively preserved in Stobaeus.[69] He says that the Stoics define virtue as "a disposition of the soul in harmony with itself concerning one's whole life" (Stobaeus 5b1 = 2.60). The person who is ready for philosophy is not the one who listens to philosophers but the one who lives by the prescriptions of philosophy (Stobaeus 11k = 2.104).

Seneca (c. A.D. 1-65).[70] Lucius Annaeus Seneca was born near the begin-

---

68. E. V. Arnold, *Roman Stoicism* (Cambridge, 1911).

69. Arthur J. Pomeroy, ed., *Arius Didymus Epitome of Stoic Ethics* (Atlanta, 1999). From Stobaeus, *Eclogues* 2.7.5-12.

70. H. B. Timothy, *The Tenets of Stoicism Assembled and Systematized from the Works of L. Annaeus Seneca* (Amsterdam, 1973); J. N. Sevenster, *Paul and Seneca* (Leiden, 1962); C. D. N.

ning of the Christian era at Cordoba, Spain. He was from an equestrian family and his brother Gallio was the proconsul of Achaea mentioned in Acts 18:12. His future in Rome was made when he became the tutor of the young Nero. When Nero became emperor in 54, Seneca joined with the praetorian prefect Burrus to give good guidance to the government for eight years. On Burrus's death in 62 Nero came completely under the influence of evil counselors and Seneca retired from public life. An offer to relinquish his great wealth to Nero failed to save his life, and he was forced to commit suicide in 65 for alleged participation in a conspiracy against the emperor.[71]

Seneca's principal philosophical writings are the ten ethical treatises preserved under the name "Dialogues." Similar in content, and most popular through the ages, is the collection of 124 *Moral Epistles*, which are not real letters. Even the *Natural Questions* evidence a moralizing interest. Also of interest is the *Apocolocyntosis*, a satire on the deification of Claudius. The nine tragedies are of less significance for our purpose.

In Seneca's psychology and metaphysics the Stoic monism is modified in the direction of Platonic dualism, and in his ethics Stoicism is tempered by eclecticism, human experience, and common sense. He does not hesitate to quote from Epicurus. Although he sometimes speaks in the tones of traditional Stoicism, in many passages he speaks of God in warm, personal ways. The organizing principle of his thought continued to be Stoicism. His writings, however, subordinate philosophy to moral exhortation and show a philosopher who was a director of souls.[72] His ascetic advice and realistic assessment of human nature appear irreconcilable. He exposes the deepest and darkest secrets of human souls. By showing the folly of indulgence he sought to set people free from the bondage of desire. As admirable as are the sentiments in his works, Seneca does not rise above the limitations of Stoicism (see pp. 368-69). Added to this is the evidence[73] that Seneca's life fell far short of his exhortations to others: after heaping slavish flattery on the living Claudius, he poisoned his memory with malicious satire; if he did not connive at the crimes of Nero, he did not restrain them; while preaching an indifference to material wealth he allowed himself to be enriched while in office; his writings describe in detail moral impurities and violence, so that whatever their author's practice the influence of some of his writings would have stimulated baser instincts.

On the positive side, Seneca's sentiments have more nearly approximated Christian teaching than those of any other classical philosopher. Tertullian de-

---

Costa, *Seneca* (London, 1974); Léon Herrmann, *Sénèque et les premiers chrétiens* (Brussels, 1979); Villy Sørensen, *Seneca: The Humanist at the Court of Nero* (Chicago, 1984); J. M. Rist, "Seneca and Stoic Orthodoxy," *ANRW* II, *Principat*, 36.3 (Berlin, 1989), 1193-2012; A. L. Motto and J. R. Clark, *Essays on Seneca* (Frankfurt, 1993).

71. Tacitus, *Annals* 14.64.

72. S. Dill, *Roman Society from Nero to Marcus Aurelius* (repr. New York, 1956), 289-333.

73. Dio Cassius 61.10 and Tacitus, *Annals* 13.4 and 14.52.

scribed him as "always our Seneca" (*On the Soul* 20),[74] and the similarities in thought at places prompted the Christian invention of an apocryphal correspondence between Paul and Seneca.[75] J. B. Lightfoot has compiled an impressive list of parallels in thought and language between Seneca and the New Testament (Paul in particular) with a judicious assessment of their fundamental differences.[76]

Cornutus (b. c. A.D. 20).[77] Cornutus was a freedman of Seneca or of one of his relatives. He began teaching philosophy in Rome about A.D. 50 but was exiled in the mid-60s. His literary work included critical studies of logic, rhetoric, and poetry. His principal philosophical work was "Summary of the Traditions concerning Greek Theology," in which he gives an allegorical explanation of the myths along the lines of Chrysippus's natural theology. Cornutus found a truth behind the myths (but not a hidden wisdom in them). His etymological interpretation of the deities was based on the premise that the knowledge of the meaning of a name revealed the real nature of the person or object. He explained that he was writing in order to teach the young to worship in piety and not in superstition. He believed that the soul was annihilated at death.

Musonius Rufus (A.D. 30–101).[78] Because of his association with philosophical criticism of the emperors, Musonius Rufus was twice banished from Rome. We do not know of his having written books, but many of his apothegms and discourses have been preserved by others.

Musonius considered the most important part of philosophical education to be the practical exercise of virtue. Several features of his moral teaching are of interest to students of early Christianity: he is the clearest of any ancient writer on the equality of man and woman (Frgs. 3 and 4); he believed marriage to be a complete partnership, with sexual intercourse to be confined to the marriage relationship and then only for the purpose of procreation (Frgs. 12-14); furthermore, parents should bring up all their children (Frg. 15); in addition, he advocated vegetarianism and opposed luxury so as to harden the body (Frgs. 18-20).

74. Less favorable comments are in *On the Soul* 42; *Apology* 12, 50; *On Resurrection* 1.

75. Cornelia Römer, "The Correspondence between Seneca and Paul," in *New Testament Apocrypha*, rev. ed., ed. E. Hennecke and W. Schneemelcher (Louisville, 1992), 2:46-53; A. J. Malherbe, "Seneca on Paul as Letter Writer," in *The Future of Early Christianity*, ed. B. A. Pearson, et al. (Minneapolis, 1991), 414-21.

76. J. B. Lightfoot, "St. Paul and Seneca," in *Saint Paul's Epistle to the Philippians* (London, 1913; repr. Grand Rapids, 1953), 270-333.

77. P. W. van der Horst, "Cornutus and the New Testament," *Novum Testamentum* 23 (1981):165-72; G. W. Most, "Cornutus and Stoic Allegoresis: A Preliminary Report," *ANRW* II, *Principat*, 36.3 (Berlin, 1989), 2014-65.

78. C. E. Lutz, *Musonius Rufus, "The Roman Socrates"* (New Haven, 1947); A. C. van Geytenbeek, *Musonius Rufus and the Greek Diatribe* (Assen, 1963); P. W. van der Horst, "Musonius Rufus and the New Testament," *Novum Testamentum* 16 (1974):306-15; R. Nickel, *Epiktet, Teles, Musonius: Ausgewählte Schriften* (Darmstadt and Zurich, 1994), 399-537.

Musonius was directly appropriated by the Christian moralist, Clement of Alexandria.

Epictetus (c. A.D. 55–c. 135).[79] The son of a slave woman, Epictetus was born at Hierapolis in Phrygia. Perhaps through sale he came to Rome where he grew up in the household of Epaphroditus, one of Nero's powerful freedmen who was secretary to the emperor. Epictetus was crippled and showed an interest in philosophy, so his master allowed him to attend the lectures of Musonius Rufus and then granted him his freedom. Epictetus began teaching philosophy on the street corners and in the marketplace. Banished from Rome with other philosophers in 89, Epictetus went to Nicopolis, Greece, and conducted his own school. Students came from Rome and Athens to attend his lectures.

Among Epictetus's students in his later years was Flavius Arrian from Rome. Arrian published his notes on Epictetus's teachings under the title *Discourses,* of which four books survive complete. He also arranged a brief summary of the basic ideas of Epictetus in the *Enchiridion* (Manual).[80] The *Discourses* present a vivid picture of the living philosopher; the *Enchiridion* the finished product of the Stoic spirit.

Epictetus tried to reach the masses with his message. He taught that the universe is the product of Divine Providence, which continues to be manifest in the world's order and unity. He saw the philosopher as an ambassador of the Divine with a mission to teach people how to live, as a physician of souls (*Discourses* 3.23.30), a witness for God (3.22.23; 1.29.46), a scout (3.22.24-25; 1.24.3-10). He emphasized indifference to all things that are not within one's own self and will as the way to inner freedom.

A few quotations from the *Enchiridion* illustrate the Stoic emphasis in Epictetus.

> There are things which are within our power, and there are things which are beyond our power. Within our power are opinion, aim, desire, aversion, and in one word, whatever affairs are our own. Beyond our power are body, property, reputation, office, and in one word, whatever are not properly our own affairs. . . . If [something] concerns anything beyond our power, be prepared to say that it is nothing to you. (No. 1, pp. 17-18 of the Higginson and Salomon trans.)

79. Douglas Sharp, *Epictetus and the New Testament* (London, 1914); A. Bonhöffer, *Epiktet und das Neuen Testament* (Giessen, 1911; repr. Berlin, 1964); J. N. Sevenster, "Education or Conversion: Epictetus and the Gospels," in *Placita Pleiadia* (Leiden, 1966); J. P. Hershbell, "The Stoicism of Epictetus: Twentieth Century Perspectives," *ANRW*, II, *Principat,* 36.3 (Berlin, 1989), 2148-63; A. Bonhöffer, *The Ethics of the Stoic Epictetus: An English Translation* (New York, 1996; German original, 1894); Robert F. Dobbin, *Epictetus: Discourse, Book 1* (Tr. and comm.) (Oxford, 1998).

80. Gerard Boter, *The* Encheiridion *of Epictetus and its Three Christian Adaptations: Transmission and Critical Editions* (with English translation) (Leiden, 1999); translation by T. W. Higginson and Albert Salomon (New York, 1948).

Men are disturbed not by things, but by the views which they take of things. (No. 5, p. 19)

Wish things to be only just as they are. (No. 33, p. 32; cf. no. 8, p. 20)

Remember that you are an actor in a drama of such sort as the author chooses — if short, then in a short one; if long, then in a long one. If it be his pleasure that you should enact a poor man, see that you act it well; or a cripple, or a ruler, or a private citizen. For this is your business — to act well the given part; but to choose it belongs to another. (No. 17, p. 23)

The will of nature may be learned from things upon which we are all agreed. As, when our neighbor's boy has broken a cup, or the like, we are ready at once to say, "These are casualties that will happen"; be assured, then, that when your own cup is likewise broken, you ought to be affected just as when another's cup was broken. Now apply this to greater things. Is the child or wife of another dead? There is no one who would not say, "This is an accident of mortality." But if anyone's own child happens to die, it is immediately, "Alas! how wretched am I!" It should always be remembered how we are affected on hearing the same thing concerning others. (No. 26, p. 26)

The last quotation presents in close focus the difference between Christianity and Stoicism. Stoicism said, "Feel toward yourself as you feel toward others"; Christianity said, "Feel toward others as you would feel toward yourself."[81]

Marcus Aurelius (A.D. 121–180).[82] Stoicism ascended the throne in the person of the emperor Marcus Aurelius (see p. 39). He deserves added mention here because of his *Meditations* (lit. "To Himself"), the last great written expression of the Stoic view of life. These meditations are in no particular order and seem to have been transcribed from the emperor's personal notebooks as he put down thoughts for his private guidance. They represent the Stoicism that had been recast by Posidonius according to Plato's psychological dualism and transmitted to Marcus Aurelius in the writings of Epictetus. These aphorisms and reflections are often obscure, but they reflect the sober conservatism of a great-souled and somewhat ascetic man who was wrestling with great responsibilities. There is a mood of melancholy about the work, but the intensity of religious and moral feeling has made the *Meditations* a book much read through the ages.

---

81. Origen gives a positive Christian evaluation of Epictetus: "Epictetus is admired by persons of ordinary capacity, who have a desire to be benefitted; and who perceive the improvement which may be derived from his writings" (*Against Celsus* 6.2).

82. F. W. Bussell, *Marcus Aurelius and the Later Stoics* (Edinburgh, 1910); R. B. Rutherford, *The Meditations of Marcus Aurelius: A Study* (Oxford, 1989); *The Meditations of Marcus Aurelius,* tr. A. S. L. Farquharson and int. by R. Rutherford (Oxford, 1990); Pierre Hadot, *The Inner Citadel: The* Meditations *of Marcus Aurelius* (Cambridge, Mass., 1998).

The reign of Marcus Aurelius was a difficult time for Christians, and the emperor could not understand their readiness for martyrdom (see p. 600), although his own Stoic belief allowed for suicide. But the Stoic took his life as a rational decision, not (as the emperor saw it) in rash abandonment of life.

The End of Stoicism. Marcus Aurelius was the last of the great Stoics. Stoicism came to an end, as it has been expressed, "because everyone became a Stoic": not that everyone gave adherence to the Stoic creed, but in the sense that everything Stoicism had to say became common property. What was of value in Stoicism was absorbed into the Neoplatonic synthesis.

Stoicism and Christianity

Christianity used some of the same terminology that was at home in Stoicism: Spirit, conscience, *Logos,* virtue, self-sufficiency, freedom of speech, reasonable service, etc. The biblical injunctions concerning the units of society (Eph. 5:21–6:9; Col. 3:18–4:1; 1 Pet. 2:13–3:7; etc.) in both form (the reference to stations in society) and content (e.g., "it is fitting") show Stoic influence. The similarities go deeper than individual items to a general atmosphere: humankind's persistent evil, the need for self-examination, humanity's kinship with the divine, denial of the world's values, and emphasis on inner freedom from external circumstances. The Stoic natural theology, transmitted via Hellenistic Judaism (cf. Wisdom of Solomon 13–14), influenced Romans 1–2 and Acts 17. Paul was familiar with philosophical, especially Stoic, idioms and assumptions and used these to express his own arguments.[83]

Whatever the similarities in Christian and Stoic ethical thought and household maxims, these instructions are placed in such a fundamentally different worldview as to give them a different significance. Despite some of the language (as in Epictetus), Stoicism did not have a fully personal God; it knew only an immanent god. The God of the Bible is the Creator of the world, never equated with it as in Stoic pantheism. In Christianity the universe has a beginning, purpose, and end; in Stoicism none of these. The only incarnation in Stoicism is that each one of us has part of the *logos* within.

Stoicism's consciousness of sin did not reach the depths of Jewish and Christian thought. Conscience has little significance unless there is a Person to whom it must answer. Stoicism shared the limitations of all philosophies in comparison to religion: A knowledge of universal ethical precepts, as such, is seldom sufficient to call out and organize a corresponding conduct. This only follows when a special religious motive or ground of obligation is united with

83. Abraham J. Malherbe, "Determinism and Free Will in Paul: The Argument of 1 Corinthians 8 and 9," in Troels Engberg-Pedersen, ed., *Paul in His Hellenistic Context* (Minneapolis, 1994), 231-255.

the knowledge of the universal principle. Thus Stoicism, although denying the reality of the world's distinctions, remained a philosophy for the few, because the basis of its ethics was intellectual. Not all persons can live on a high plane because the divine spark flickers but feebly in most. Christianity, on the other hand, appealed to the masses. It did so by relating all classes of people to a personal Savior with moral power.

Stoicism had no personal immortality. When one died, his divine part went back into the Whole. Stoicism was a creed of despair and acquiescence; it looked down on the Christian virtues that depend upon the affirmation "God is love." Stoicism's apathy basically denied the emotional side of human experience. Christianity by contrast brought joy and hope into the world.

Again, even where the teaching on social ethics was similar, the motivation was fundamentally different. Christians, ideally, act benevolently not merely in fulfillment of the obligation of a common kinship in the universe or even in God, but because they have learned self-sacrifice and active love from God in Christ. Self-respect, not love, was Stoicism's driving force. For Stoicism, as for all Greek philosophy before Neoplatonism, the goal of humanity is self-liberation, and this goal is attainable. It did not know the redemptive love of a merciful God.[84]

BIBLIOGRAPHY

Diogenes Laertius. *Lives of Eminent Philosophers* 7.
Arnim, H. F. A. von. *Stoicorum veterum fragmenta*. 4 vols. Leipzig, 1903–1924. Reprint. Stuttgart, 1968.

Pohlenz, M. *Die Stoa*. 2 vols. Göttingen, 1948–1949.
MacMullen, Ramsey. *Enemies of the Roman Order*. Cambridge, Mass., 1966.
Rist, J. M. *Stoic Philosophy*. London, 1969.
Sandbach, F. H. *The Stoics*. London, 1975.
Engberg-Pederson, Troels. *The Stoic Theory of Oikeiosis: Moral Development and Social Interaction in Early Stoic Philosophy*. Aarhus, 1990.
Colish, Marcia L. *The Stoic Tradition: From Antiquity to the Early Middle Ages*. 2 vols. Leiden, 1985-1990.
ANRW II, *Principat*, 36.3. Berlin, 1989. Whole volume on Stoicism.
Colish, Marcia L. "Stoicism and the New Testament: An Essay in Historiography." *ANRW* II, *Principat*, 26.1. Berlin, 1992. Pp. 334-79.
Ierodiakonou, Katerina, ed. *Topics in Stoic Philosophy*. Oxford, 1999.
Engberg-Pedersen, Troels. *Paul and the Stoics*. Louisville, 2000.

---

84. W. R. Halliday, *The Pagan Background of Early Christianity* (Liverpool, 1925; repr. New York, 1970), 132-38.

EPICUREANISM

Epicurus and His School

Epicurus was born in 341 B.C. at the Athenian colony of Samos. In 307/306 he settled in Athens, where he bought a house with a garden that gave to his school its name, "the philosophy of the Garden." Epicurus died in 270 B.C.

Epicurus gathered disciples of more intense loyalty than any other philosopher in antiquity. He was also the most controversial figure in ancient philosophy, with bitter enemies as well as devoted followers. His disciples formed a close-knit group, living on Epicurus's property a life of austere contentment withdrawn from the world. This seclusion and avoidance of public activities contributed to their unpopularity. Epicurus admitted women (including courtesans) and slaves to his community, and this along with his professed hedonism probably was the source of some of the stories that circulated about his school.

Actually, as we will see more fully below (pp. 375-77), Epicurus did not teach an "eat, drink, and be merry" philosophy. (The Cyrenaic school founded by Aristippus advocated this sensual view of pleasure.) Epicurus's philosophy promoted the placid pleasures of the mind, friendship, and contentment. For him there was no reason to eat, drink, and be merry today if you are going to have a headache from it tomorrow. Poor health imposed on Epicurus himself a frugal life.

Epicurus was a father figure to his followers. He formed communities of his followers and wrote letters of instruction to them. They celebrated his birthday and gave him honors as to a god. No later figure of importance and influence arose in his school. Thus the Epicurean school did not have the changes noted in the others; rather, there was a conservative tendency in preserving Epicurus's teachings.

According to Diogenes Laertius, Epicurus wrote about three hundred rolls, but little of this survives. However, he has preserved three of Epicurus's letters (to Herodotus, to Pythocles, and to Menoeceus — the latter most important as a clear, elementary summary of his ethics) and the collection of forty maxims known as "Principal Doctrines" (*Kyriae doxai*). Similar to the latter is the "Vatican Sayings," a collection of eighty-one short sayings discovered in a Vatican manuscript.

A remarkable find at Herculaneum in the mid–eighteenth century — a library of papyrus scrolls covered by lava and charred on the outside — added to the understanding of Epicureanism. About one-half had been burned by explorers as fuel before it was discovered that books were inside the lava. Others were destroyed in learning how to unroll the scrolls. The papyri come from a villa, probably that of Lucius Calpurnius Piso Caesoninus, but now popularly called the Villa of the Papyri. The contents of the scrolls turned out to be the li-

EPICURUS
Epicurus had more loyal followers than any other Hellenistic philosopher and created close-knit communities with similarities to Christian communities.
(© Erich Lessing/Art Resource, NY)

brary of Philodemus, a first-century-B.C. Epicurean.[85] His works, still being edited and translated, include "On Piety,"[86] "On Signs," "On Household Economy," "On Vices," "On Music,"[87] "On Poems," and "On Rhetoric." These works and other papyri from the site add to our knowledge of Epicureanism just prior to the life of Jesus.

In approximately the 120s a follower of Epicurus, Diogenes of Oenoanda in Lycia, set up a huge inscription setting forth the basic ideas of Epicurus. Much of the inscription remains buried, but the recovered parts give extensive material from Epicurus himself and from Diogenes' own writings.[88]

Hence, we have a clearer picture of Epicurus than of any of his contemporaries. And that is fitting, as he was more of a personality in the ancient world than any other philosopher with the exception of Socrates.

Lucretius (94–55 B.C.)[89]

For modern times the most important and influential exposition of the Epicurean system has come from the Latin poet Lucretius. He demonstrates the continuity of Epicurean teaching to the first century B.C. and its appeal even in Rome. Lucretius's only work is the philosophical poem "On the Nature of Things" *(De rerum natura).* The poem consists of six books expounding the physical theory of Epicurus with a view to abolishing superstitious fears of interference by the gods in the world and of punishment in an afterlife. Lucretius was the ideal convert — having found "the truth," he wanted others to find it. The poem provides a good outline of Epicurean philosophy.

Epicurean Physics

Epicurus depended on the pre-Socratic philosopher Democritus for his physical theory. The whole of nature consists of matter and space ("the void"). Mat-

85. Marcello Gigante, *Philodemus in Italy: The Books from Herculaneum* (Ann Arbor, Mich., 1995); Clarence E. Glad, *Paul and Philodemus: Adaptability in Epicurean and Early Christian Psychagogy* (Leiden, 1995); J. T. Fitzgerald et al., eds., *Philodemus and the New Testament World* (Leiden, 2003).

86. Dirk Obbink, *Philodemus on Piety: Critical Text with Commentary* (Oxford, 1997) (includes translation).

87. Everett Ferguson, "The Art of Praise: Philo and Philodemus on Music," in J. T. Fitzgerald et al., eds., *Early Christianity and Classical Culture: Comparative Studies* (Harrisburg, 2003).

88. M. F. Smith, *Diogenes of Oinoanda: The Epicurean Inscription: Edited with Introduction, Translation, and Notes* (Naples, 1993); Pamela Gordon, *Epicurus in Lycia: The Second-Century World of Diogenes of Oenoanda* (Ann Arbor, 1997).

89. Diskin Clay, *Lucretius and Epicurus* (Ithaca, N.Y., 1984); K. Summers, "Lucretius and the Epicurean Tradition of Piety," *Classical Philology* 90 (1995):32-57; David Sedley, *Lucretius and the Transformation of Greek Wisdom* (Cambridge, 1998).

ter is divisible, but not infinitely, for then we would have nothing. We finally reach the atom (which in Greek means the "indivisible"). Atoms are the invisible "building blocks" out of which the world is made. They are neither created nor destroyed. They are solid with no void within (unlike modern atomic theory). Atoms do not have color, sound, taste, or smell, but they do have shape (and come in a variety of shapes), size (for they are not mathematical points), weight, and motion.

Atoms together with space constitute the whole of the universe, which is unbounded and infinite. The atoms are in motion in the void. Space is infinite and the number of atoms is infinite: both must go together. The atoms move downward, always at an incredible speed since they meet no resistance. Here is a difficulty, however: if the universe is infinite, what is down? Epicurus recognized there could be no "down," but he had to say "fall" to express motion. There is another difficulty: if movement is all downward and at the same speed, how can the atoms meet to form objects? But they do meet, since there is matter. Here Epicurus introduces the spontaneous swerve. This is contrary to his law of motion, but he brings in an inexplicable factor to explain why things are the way they are. The swerve made room for free will in his morals also.[90]

Epicurus was a materialist. The physical world comes from atoms that operate according to law (with the one exception mentioned above). Therefore, nature has no purpose. Moreover, there is no creation — the world is eternal, for atoms are indestructible though they may be changed. For Epicurus this physical theory was the fall of religion.

Epicurus, however, did believe in the gods, who are made of refined material atoms. But the gods never interfere in nature or the affairs of humans. Their existence is something of a paradox, for they have no pragmatic function and do not explain anything in Epicurus's system. A most important consequence of his views on which he insists is that there is no providence. But the visions of gods in dreams and the universal opinion of humankind prove their existence. The gods have bodies, but they never dissolve and so are immortal. They live in the interstellar spaces completely outside the world and have no contact with it. The gods are supremely happy and serene, for they are not bothered by humans. There is no place for prayer or answer to prayer in his system: since each person prays against the interests of another, it would disturb the gods to settle these petitions. The picture given of the gods is that of an Epicurean society, conversing in Greek, enjoying celestial pleasures. We might say that Epicurus had a theology without a religion. Nevertheless, Epicurus counseled his followers to participate in sacrifices and other acts of homage. There is more than conformity here. The gods as supremely perfect beings deserve worship and honor. People receive the benefit of aesthetic pleasure from contemplating their perfect existence. However, since they have nothing to do with

---

90. W. G. Englert, *Epicurus on the Swerve and Voluntary Action* (Atlanta, 1987).

us, we have no responsibilities to them and should not expect anything from them. The Epicureans were called "atheists" by the ancients. The word was not theoretical; it was used because the Epicureans did not believe in providence and because many did not follow through with participation in the public cults.

Epicurus's goal was to achieve peace of mind and tranquility *(ataraxia)* for all. He reacted against those who, like Theophrastus's superstitious person (*Characters* 16), lived in constant fear of the divine powers (p. 237). He wanted to get across the idea that the world is a garden, not a jungle. His interest was practical; while the Greeks believed in gods that interfered capriciously in human affairs, Epicurus believed that there are no gods who scare you.

Another consequence of his physical theory was the belief that there was no future life to worry about. The soul is a type of body, a physical object, since the soul too is composed of atoms. The physical body is a house for the subtler atoms of the soul, which is a kind of body within the body. There is also a kind of "soul of the soul" inasmuch as the organ of thinking and willing is the most refined part of the soul. Body and soul must be joined to give life. When the physical body dies, the soul also disintegrates. When a person is dead, he or she is dead all over. Therefore, there is nothing to fear in death. There is no future punishment.

Epicurus wanted to save humanity from the darkness of religion. Oracles, divination, magic, etc., are humbug. He saw religion as a source of fear; therefore the banishing of the gods brought peace and the possibility of a good life. Epicurus was something of a strange materialist from the modern standpoint in that he believed in the swerve (and so free will) and in the gods. His views did secure the independence of nature, the happiness of gods, and (as he thought) the happiness of humanity.

Epicurean Epistemology

Epicurus divided philosophy into physics and ethics. Although he wrote a work entitled "Canonic" on how to tell whether things were true or false, he said that this did not have independent importance and made it a part of his physics. His theory of knowledge is very closely related to his physical theory.

For Epicurus sense perception is the basis of all reason. Sensation is immediate confrontation, hence it is infallible. Sense experiences cannot be refuted by reason, for reason is built on them. For Aristotle the reason uses the senses, but for Epicurus reason is something constructed out of the senses. If one perceives something often enough, he has a concept (*prolēpsis;* lit. "anticipation") of it. In other words, a series of perceptions build up an anticipation or idea of something so that it is possible to think and reason about it. The soul forms general concepts from the particular objects seen. For example, the concept "horse" is a composite picture of the horses one has seen. When one thinks of "horse," the thought is of what one expects to see *(prolēpsis)*. All mental operations, therefore, are accumulated experiences.

The other schools criticized this theory by pointing to examples where things are not as they appear to be to the senses. But the Epicureans had a ready reply to this criticism. An oar in the water should look bent; the mistake comes in supposing that it really is bent. A tower at a distance should look smaller than it really is; the mistake is to think that that is its real size. Thus the Epicureans turned the objections on their critics: the mistakes were not in the senses but in the reason, which made a mistaken inference from the sense data. The only way to know things is through perception *(aisthēsis)*.

Hearing, vision, and smell do not immediately touch their objects. At this point Epicurus had a doctrine of effluences or emanations. From every object there emanate *eidōla* ("idols"; i.e., images or films) of itself. These come to the eyes (or other sense organs), which reproduce the pictures. As fire gives off smoke, so objects are perpetually giving off *eidōla*. (This may sound crude but is comparable to the modern theory that objects send out waves.) If there is trouble in the atmosphere or if the person receiving the image is troubled, the image is distorted. Errors do not arise in seeing, but in applying the wrong concept *(prolēpsis)* to the image, such as mistaking a donkey for a horse. The idea of mythical monsters arose from the images given off by creatures bumping into each other and getting mixed up so that someone perceived the combination. The belief in composite creatures such as centaurs arose in this way. The gods too give off images, so they have appeared to people in visions and dreams and do really exist. If someone has perceived something, there is something there, for nothing comes from what does not exist.

Epicurean Ethics[91]

Epicurus's physics and canonics existed for the sake of his ethics. The goal *(telos)* of life was formulated in various ways: Tranquility *(ataraxia)*, happiness *eudaimonia)*, or especially as pleasure *(hēdonē)*. But pleasure as Epicurus defined it was not self-indulgence. We must discount the modern content of "Epicurean" if we would understand him.

In addition to the senses is feeling. This too is part of experience and therefore infallible. Epicurus's hedonism was an extension of his empiricism. There are immediate feelings of pain and pleasure. It is human nature to seek pleasure and avoid pain, since all pleasure is good and all pain is bad. One seeks the maximum of pleasure and the minimum of pain. What is the criterion for this? He had to have, as any hedonist must, a standard for measuring pleasure.

---

91. Philip Mitsis, *Epicurus' Ethical Theory: The Pleasures of Invulnerability* (Ithaca, 1988).

Plato and Aristotle had external criteria, but Epicurus could judge pleasure and pain only by each person's experience. Hence, he measured pleasure and pain by intensity (strength of the feeling), duration (length of the feeling), and purity (i.e., pleasure unaccompanied by pain). We do not choose every pleasure, because it may be accompanied by pain; nor do we avoid every pain, because it may be necessary to a greater pleasure.

Epicurus divided pleasures into the kinetic (active) and the static (pertaining to a state or condition, passive). Pleasures of the body and pleasures of the soul are of both kinds. In each case the static pleasures are superior to the kinetic.

The lowest pleasures are those of the body. He begins with the pleasures of the stomach. Their source is in desire; we get pleasure in satisfying the desire. They start from a privation, as in the pains of hunger and thirst. Pleasure that has its source in desire is attended by pain, which precedes the pleasure. Satisfaction involves activity, hence the designation kinetic. When the desire is satisfied, the person reaches equilibrium.

Pleasures of equilibrium are static, in contrast to kinetic pleasures. Bodily pleasures of this kind would include rest, good health, and the like. These pleasures are "pure" because they are unattended by pain. Hence, they are preferable to the pleasures of desire. For Epicurus, the absence of pain is an ideal to strive for; for example, getting drunk would not be worth the hangover the next day. Thus, his ideas are not identical to modern ideas of hedonism.

Epicurus classified pains into three types: the natural and necessary, as hunger; the natural but unnecessary, such as sex, which involves turmoil and so would not be one of the highest pleasures and can be abstained from; and the unnatural and unnecessary, as sadism.

There are pleasures of the soul and mind, since the soul has some feelings independent of the body. The kinetic pleasures here include such things as wealth and power. One starts with the pain of poverty and seeks to satisfy the need through activity. The pain of ambition is satisfied by power. Economic, political, and social action involve an attendant pain. Therefore, Epicurus recommended avoiding the kinetic pleasures of the mind, such as ambition and public life. This would enable one to avoid fear caused by others. He counseled his followers to "live secretly," "live keeping hidden." He advised against taking on any responsibilities in public life (holding office) or social life (getting married). This was one of the first philosophical responses to the new situation created by Alexander's conquests. Plato and still Aristotle could not conceive of life apart from the context of the Greek city. Epicurus created a substitute community among the circle of "friends" who made up his school.

The pleasures one should seek pertain to the equilibrium of the soul. Tranquility, the absence of agitation (*ataraxia* — the same word used by Pyrrho, p. 346), was the highest good. The absence of pain and fear was achieved, in large part, as seen above through the absence of the gods (banished from the world by his physics). Peace of mind was achieved by removal of divine intervention and realizing that there is no pain in death because the soul does not survive to feel anything.

The positive aspect of the pleasures of the soul is the enjoyment that comes from a society of good friends. For Epicurus friendship is the basic pleasure, replacing ambition and other desires. One is a stranger in the world and needs friends, who shelter the fearful and give pleasure. Epicurus apparently made up for the loss of the gods and of civic life by introducing the bond that exists among friends. The friendship of Epicurean groups was the chief attraction of the school. The "Garden of Epicurus" became a symbol of aloofness. Here the pleasures of the body were simple. Hedonism had undergone a transformation. Epicurus was not (in its modern connotation) an Epicurean.

Estimate and Comparisons

The main points, and the practical appeal, of Epicureanism may be seen in the following summary of the philosophy:

> Nothing to fear in God;
> Nothing to feel in Death;
> Good [pleasure] can be attained;
> Evil [pain] can be endured.[92]

The establishment of a community of men and women where all were equal, had a common way of life, were isolated from the world, and were held together by reverence for a master was an ideal that had a great influence. Christians and Epicureans were sometimes lumped together by pagan observers because of their common rejection of traditional religion ("atheists"; see pp. 219, 594ff.) and the separation of their communities from ordinary life (1 Thess. 4:9-12 employs words used by Epicureans to describe a life of quietness withdrawn from public affairs). It has been suggested that the Epicurean communities served as a pattern for the Christian communities (cf. the title "friends" in John 15:15; 3 John 15),[93] but this would not extend beyond externals and there would seem to be more immediate analogues in the Judaism of Jesus' day.

92. Quoted by Gilbert Murray, *Five Stages of Greek Religion* (Garden City, N.Y., 1955), 205. The summary must have been something of an Epicurean commonplace; cf. Philodemus, "The fourfold remedy: 'God presents no fears, death no worries; and while good is readily attainable, evil is readily endurable'" (*Against the Sophists* 4.9-14). These formulations go back to Epicurus — Diogenes Laertius 10.139-140.

93. N. W. De Witt, *St. Paul and Epicurus* (Toronto, 1954), 9, 44, suggests that Paul avoided the words "friend" and "friendship" because of Epicurean associations, but his interpretations are often one-sided.

The Epicureans and Stoics were the chief rivals for the allegiance of educated people in the Hellenistic age (cf. Acts 17:18). Both had a primary emphasis on ethics and made philosophy a way of life that could be its own religion with converting power. As Epicureanism had an extreme antecedent for its hedonism in the Cyrenaic philosophy, so Stoicism had an extreme antecedent for its denial of the world in Cynicism. As Epicureanism drew its physical theory from the pre-Socratic philosopher Democritus, so Stoicism was indebted for part of its physical theory to the pre-Socratic philosopher Heraclitus. Both Epicureans and Stoics sought to liberate humans from fate, to make them self-sufficient and indifferent to externals. Their major concerns — undisturbedness *(ataraxia)* in Epicureanism and passionlessness *(apatheia)* in Stoicism — were similar, but Stoicism was more stolid. Stoicism said in effect, "Let us neither eat nor drink, for tomorrow we die." Both had a continuing influence, but Epicureanism changed little (though its polemic against other schools did) whereas Stoicism absorbed elements from others and underwent significant changes. Epicureanism advocated a quiet and peaceful life, the life of "the Garden"; it took no interest in public affairs. Stoicism, as indicated by its name, "the Porch," was set in the middle of public life and affairs. Stoicism developed in the direction of upholding the structures of society and the traditional religion. Its more active creed appealed to more persons, especially among the Romans, and exerted more influence. Nevertheless, one anecdote is revealing. A Stoic was asked once why Stoics sometimes became Epicureans, but Epicureans never became Stoics. He replied, "Men may become eunuchs, but eunuchs cannot become men."[94] The question is more significant than the reply and indicates that there was a strong cohesion and religious power about the Epicurean way of life.

BIBLIOGRAPHY

Plutarch. *That Epicurus Actually Makes a Pleasant Life Impossible. Reply to Colotes. Is "Live Unknown" a Wise Precept? (Moralia,* 1086C-1107C; 1107D-1127E; 1128B-1130E)

Diogenes Laertius. *Lives of Eminent Philosophers* 10.

Bailey, Cyril. *Epicurus: The Extant Remains.* Oxford, 1926. Reprint. Hildesheim, 1970.

Strodach, G. K. *The Philosophy of Epicurus.* Evanston, Ill., 1962.

Geer, Russel M. *Letters, Principal Doctrines, and Vatican Sayings.* Indianapolis, 1964.

Inwood, Brad, and L. P. Gerson, eds. *The Epicurus Reader: Selected Writings and Testimonia.* Indianapolis, 1994.

De Witt, N. W. *Epicurus and his Philosophy.* Minneapolis, 1954.

---

94. Diogenes Laertius, *Lives of Eminent Philosophers* 4.43.

Festugière, A. J. *Epicurus and his Gods.* Oxford, 1955.

Farrington, Benjamin. *The Faith of Epicurus.* New York, 1967.

Rist, J. M. *Epicurus: An Introduction.* Cambridge, 1972.

Frischer, Bernard. *The Sculpted Word: Epicureanism and Philosophical Recruitment in Ancient Greece.* Berkeley, 1982.

ECLECTICISM

Characteristics

Eclecticism means to pick and choose. It refers to the tendency to select elements from different philosophical schools and integrate them into one's own system of thought or to put them together in new combinations. Eclecticism is the opposite of Skepticism; instead of an irreducible antagonism, it posits that at bottom all philosophy is in agreement. The term "eclecticism" has been used by historians of philosophy in a pejorative sense for what is judged to be a lack of originality in philosophy during the period from about 50 B.C. to A.D. 200. That is not the intention of the label here. There was in antiquity "an eclectic school,"[95] but it was a minor school, and "eclecticism" is used by modern historians of philosophy, and so here, more broadly of a tendency or attitude characteristic of Hellenistic-Roman times.

School affiliations and loyalties continued, but representatives of different philosophical schools learned from one another. This is evident in the admiration and quotation of Epicurus by the Stoic Seneca, admittedly unique in this regard. Notice has been taken of Panaetius and Posidonius, who incorporated elements of Platonism and Aristotelianism into their Stoicism, and of Philo of Larissa and Antiochus of Ascalon, who as members of the Academy moved toward Stoicism. The difficulty of identifying Dio Chrysostom (Stoic or Cynic?) and Numenius (Platonist or Neopythagorean?), not to mention lesser known figures, is symptomatic of the situation.

The popular philosophy of Hellenistic-Roman times owed much to the common elements (especially in ethical thought) of the various schools. When carried through in a systematic way, this process of amalgamation produced Middle Platonism and Neoplatonism. No single combination is representative of the eclectic tendency. For example, Philo of Alexandria (pp. 478-83) belongs in the broad spectrum of Middle Platonism, but may justly be termed an eclectic for the way in which he drew especially on Platonism and Stoicism (while knowledgeable of the other schools) to construct an apologetic for Judaism. He is unique among philosophers in the way he used Scripture to interpret philos-

---

95. Diogenes Laertius, *Lives of Eminent Philosophers* 1.21.

ophy and philosophy to interpret Scripture. The eclectic tendency of later Hellenistic philosophy will be illustrated in more detail here from the work of Cicero. Although his philosophical affiliation was with the Academy, he drew much from other schools, especially the Stoics. Cicero deserves special attention for the further reason that he provides an excellent summary of the status of philosophical thought, both theoretical and practical, at the threshold of the New Testament era.

BIBLIOGRAPHY

Zeller, E. *A History of Eclecticism in Greek Philosophy.* London, 1883.

Dillon, J. M., and A. A. Long, eds. *The Question of "Eclecticism": Studies in Later Greek Philosophy.* Berkeley, 1988.

Cicero (106–43 B.C.)

Cicero had the asset and liability of not being born in Rome. The small town of Arpinum spared him the corroding influences of Rome, but he had to struggle hard to gain acceptance by the Roman nobility. Cicero learned the Greek technique of speech. His education included instruction in Rome from Phaedrus (an Epicurean), Diodotus (a Stoic), and Philo of Larissa (under whose tutelage he became an Academic). In Athens on a foreign tour he attended the lectures of Antiochus of Ascalon (an Academic) and Zeno of Sidon (an Epicurean), and in Rhodes he became intimate with Posidonius (a Stoic). At this time Cicero's interest in philosophy was limited to what could contribute to his career as an orator. He could advise that one should learn the precepts of philosophy but live as a citizen. Cicero passed through three stages in his philosophical development: (1) an initial adherence to Philo of Larissa's moderate skepticism, (2) affiliation during his public career with the doctrinaire Platonism of Antiochus of Ascalon from 79-46 B.C., during which time were written the works indebted to Plato — De republica (On the Republic) and De legibus (On Laws), and (3) a return in his final years of philosophical composition to the Fourth Academy of Philo of Larissa. He took refuge in "suspension of judgment" in questions of knowledge, but on moral questions he was willing to "dogmatize." The general conscience of humankind provided him with an arbiter of right and wrong. The Roman respect for good order is prominent in his strictures against the Epicureans, but he could never go all the way with the harsh features of Stoicism. In summary of his eclectic approach it has been said that his intellect was with the Academy, his conscience with the Stoa, and his information with the Peripatetics. He brought together oratory and philosophy, and he disseminated a theory of natural law.

Caesar's rise to power forced Cicero into retirement, and in his free time he gathered philosophical material. The death of his daughter Tulia in 45 B.C. made philosophy an existential concern. He sought a home or refuge in philosophy, which at that time provided the consolation supplied by religion in our times. Moreover, he formed the idea of an encyclopedic collection of philosophical writings as a patriotic service to his countrymen. He was concerned to take what of Greece could be used for the benefit of Rome, and thus intended to introduce the study of the major points of philosophy to readers who knew no Greek. During 45 and 44 B.C. he wrote on epistemology — *Academica;* ethics — *De finibus (On the Ends of Goods and Evils), Tusculum Disputations,*[96] and *De officiis (On Moral Duties);* and theology — *De natura deorum (On the Nature of the Gods), De divinatione (On Divination),* and *De fato (On Fate),* as well as the lost *Consolatio* and *Hortensius.* The earlier philosophical treatment of politics in *On the Republic* is largely lost, but one part of it has been preserved separately — the "Dream of Scipio" *(Somnium Scipionis),* which expresses the Platonic idea of philosophy guiding the state. It is important for the development of later ideas concerning the soul and the hereafter.[97]

On the Nature of the Gods[98] introduces the positions and arguments of the Stoics, the Epicureans, and the skeptical Academy. Dedicated to Brutus, the work is in dialogue form. The Platonic dialogue involved real participation in the discussion by several of those present, with comparatively short speeches and frequent expressions of assent or dissent, and made the emerging opinion so far as possible the result of their common thought. This form of dialogue was adapted to a polemical work but not to one of a descriptive character. Aristotle had invented another kind of literary dialogue, no longer involving questions and answers but pitting monologue against monologue and introducing himself as a character. Using this style the author states "fully from the standpoint of those who hold them views which are finally rejected."[99] This is the device that Cicero adopted. The assumed date of the dialogue is between 77 and 75 B.C. The participants are Cicero himself, whose part is minimal, Cotta (another Academic) the host, Velleius (an Epicurean), and Balbus (a Stoic).

After a prooemium defending philosophical studies and setting the stage, Book I gives Velleius's case for Epicureanism and Cotta's refutation. Book II is Balbus's exposition of Stoicism, and Book III is Cotta's refutation. At the end Cotta votes for Velleius's argument and Cicero for Balbus's as more probable. Various explanations of this have been advanced but most probable is the view that underlines the descriptive rather than polemical aim of the work. Cicero

---

96. *Tusc. Disp.* 5.5 shows some of the deepest piety of ancient times.

97. Cf. Georg Luck, "Studia Divina in Vita Humana: On Cicero's 'Dream of Scipio' and its Place in Greco-Roman Philosophy," *HTR* 29 (1956):207-18.

98. A. S. Pease, ed., *M. Tulli Ciceronis De Natura Deorum* (Cambridge, 1955); P. G. Walsh, tr., *Cicero: The Nature of the Gods* (Oxford, 1997); Philip Levine, "The Original Design and the Publication of the *De Natura Deorum,*" *Harvard Studies in Classical Philology* 62 (1956):7-36.

99. Pease, Introduction; I follow him throughout this section.

wanted to show that the classic arguments against various theological views were as proper for study as the views themselves. He was concerned to show the Academic method and freedom to accept material from any school. An Academic dogma might be implied if both Academics in the dialogue had voted together.

Up to Cicero's time philosophy at Rome had been a hobby. He made it popular and so had a great influence on intellectual life. Cicero's philosophical works adapted the Latin language for abstract thought. This made possible a theology in Latin, and without this preliminary phase it is difficult to imagine development of a Latin Christian theology. In that regard his writings are comparable in importance to the Septuagint (which translated Hebrew ideas into Greek). He is a prime source for Greek thought and the status of philosophy at the close of the Republic.

BIBLIOGRAPHY

Reiley, Katharine. *Studies in the Philosophical Terminology of Lucretius and Cicero.* New York, 1909.
Rolfe, John C. *Cicero and his Influence.* New York, 1963.
Bailey, D. R. Schackleton. *Cicero.* London, 1971.
Goar, R. *Cicero and the State Religion.* Amsterdam, 1972.
Rawson, Elizabeth. *Cicero: A Portrait.* London, 1975.
Glucker, John. "Cicero's Philosophical Affiliations." In *The Question of "Eclecticism": Studies in Later Greek Philosophy.* Berkeley, 1988. Pp. 34-69.
Powell, J. G. F., ed. *Cicero the Philosopher.* Oxford, 1995.

NEOPYTHAGOREANISM

Pythagoras

The historical Pythagoras of the sixth century B.C. remains a shadowy figure,[100] but he is associated with four ideas of importance for the history of philosophy and religion. (1) Pythagoras had the brilliant idea that *number* is related to the structure of the universe. This idea came from his discovery of the numerical ratios of the principal intervals in the musical scale. The idea that the universe obeys mathematical laws has been of profound importance, apart from the more dubious speculation about number symbolism encouraged by this idea. (2) Pythagoras taught the theory of *metempsychosis,* or transmigration (the passing of a soul at a body's death into another body). He shared with the

---

100. Walter Burkert, *Lore and Science in Ancient Pythagoreanism* (Cambridge, Mass., 1972), and Peter Gorman, *Pythagoras, a Life* (London, 1979), represent two different approaches.

Orphics the idea of a cycle of existence. Pythagoras apparently was an important source for Plato's distinction between soul and body. (3) Pythagoras formed a close group of *disciples* with the cohesion of a religious group, whose patron deity was Apollo. This religious enthusiasm was something new among pre-Socratic philosophers. Other philosophers were lone thinkers, but Pythagoras created a brotherhood (the first thing approaching a "church") and gave his followers a distinctive way of life. (4) He established an ascetic *discipline*. A member of his group had to live by rules. Purifications were to improve the soul. The Pythagoreans became complete vegetarians.

Pythagoreans remained a group apart and their ideas were somewhat exotic in classical Greece. Heraclitus, who abhorred rituals and purifications, said of Pythagoras, "Much learning does not teach wisdom, or it would have taught Pythagoras." The early Pythagoreans are thought to have almost completely disappeared in the fifth century B.C., but a date of 350-300 B.C. is argued for the *Golden Verses,* a gnomic poem of basic moral, religious, and philosophical doctrines that appears to have been an introduction to the teachings of a Pythagorean group (see Bibliography below). Such Pythagorean literature produced a revival of Pythagorean ideas and sodalities in the first century B.C., which in turn contributed to Neoplatonism.

The Pythagorean Revival

Nigidius Figulus (d. 45 B.C.), friend of Cicero and supporter of Pompey, was led by his scholarly and mystical interests to a revival of Pythagorean ideas.

An underground basilica near the Porta Maggiore in Rome, built in the first century A.D., has been identified by some as a Neopythagorean cult hall.[101] The basilica is adorned with stuccos of mythical, religious, and secular themes, the overall interpretation of which is debatable.

The Neopythagoreans continued Pythagoras's interest in numbers and asceticism and his understanding of philosophy as religious. They were also interested in the stars and intermediary demons between the transcendent God and humankind, contributing to the concept of a "chain of beings." In addition, they seem to be the principal philosophical source for the view that the material world is bad, an idea that colored Gnostic thinking and was influential in the general pessimism about the world that began to spread in the second century A.D.

The Neopythagoreans speculated on the occult meaning of numbers, were vegetarians, had their own passwords and signs of recognition, and were often linked with occult and magical practices. The rule of life — not philosophical

---

101. J. Carcopino, *La Basilique pytagoricienne de la Porte Majeure* (Paris, 1927); Salvatore Aurigemma, *La basilica sotterranea neopitagorica di Porta Maggiore in Roma* (Rome, 1974).

speculation — was its chief attraction. The Pythagorean life-style became the ideal representation of the holy, wise man — Christian lives of saints who were not martyrs (e.g., Athanasius, *Life of Antony*) follow the pattern of Pythagoras. We know the ideal best from Philostratus's portrayal of Apollonius of Tyana.

Apollonius of Tyana[102] and Philostratus[103]

The most significant Neopythagorean for New Testament studies has been Apollonius of Tyana (in Cappadocia), whose life spanned the first century A.D., and who died in the principate of Nerva. As presented by his biographer Philostratus, he was an ascetic wandering teacher and reformer who visited many of the prominent cities of the Roman world and traveled as far as India. He was known as a wise man and wonder-worker. As with other philosophers, he was persecuted under Nero, but charges of magical practices were also involved. His reported miraculous powers and his life-style have made him the principal first-century representative of the "divine man" *(theios anēr)*[104] concept — both of the sage and wonder-worker types — which has come to prominence in Gospel studies as the background for the portrayal of Jesus.[105]

Rival traditions about Apollonius were circulated in the ancient world, but the only full account to be preserved is the *Life of Apollonius* by Flavius Philostratus (c. A.D. 170–249).[106] Behind Philostratus are two older views of Apollonius — as a magician and charlatan or a wonder-worker and theosoph.

102. Translation of Philostratus, *Life of Apollonius* by C. P. Jones (Baltimore, 1970; now in LCL); see F. W. G. Campbell, *Apollonius of Tyana: A Study of his Life and Times* (Chicago, 1968); G. Petzke, *Die Traditionen über Apollonius von Tyana und das Neue Testament,* Studia ad Corpus Hellenisticum Novi Testamenti, vol. 1 (Leiden, 1970). Ewen Lyall Bowie, "Apollonius of Tyana: Tradition and Reality," *ANRW* II, *Principat,* 16.2 (Berlin and New York, 1978), 1652-99 (with comprehensive bibliography) is skeptical of Philostratus's portrait; Maria Dzielska, *Apollonius of Tyana in Legend and History* (Rome, 1986); Erkki Koskenniemi, *Apollonios von Tyana in der neutestamentlichen Exegese* (Tübingen, 1994).

103. G. Anderson, *Philostratus: Biography and Belles Lettres in the Third Century A.D.* (London, 1986).

104. See Apollonius's *Epistle* 48; Philostratus, *Life of Apollonius* 2.17; 8.15 for the phrase. It refers to a man with divine power or wisdom (or both — as Apollonius), but especially the latter.

105. D. L. Tiede, *The Charismatic Figure as Miracle Worker* (Missoula, Mont., 1972); Morton Smith, "Prolegomenon to a Discussion of Aretalogies, Divine Men, the Gospels, and Jesus," *JBL* 90 (1971):174-99; Gail P. Corrington, *The "Divine Man": His Origin and Function in Hellenistic Popular Religion* (New York, 1986). Carl Holladay's dissertation *Theios Aner in Hellenistic Judaism* (Missoula, Mont., 1977) makes it very doubtful that Hellenistic Judaism mediated the divine man concept from Hellenism to Christianity. See also Barry Blackburn, *Theios Anēr and the Markan Miracle Traditions* (Tübingen, 1991); G. Anderson, *Sage, Saint and Sophist: Holy Men and their Associates in the Early Roman Empire* (London, 1994).

106. See also *The Letters of Apollonius of Tyana,* ed. with prolegomena, translation, and commentary by Robert J. Penella (Leiden, 1979).

A principal thrust of Philostratus's work is to defend Apollonius from charges of magic[107] and to attribute his miracles to supernatural power (cf. the charge that Jesus was a magician; p. 227). He wrote the *Life* at the instigation of Julia Domna, wife of the emperor Septimius Severus, whose family was interested in religious teachers and philosophers. Alexander Severus kept statues (in place of Roman gods) of Alexander, Orpheus, Apollonius, Abraham, and Christ.[108] Later Hierocles, a provincial governor, used the *Life* to parallel Apollonius with Christ as a polemic against Christianity in a work that called forth a reply by Eusebius, bishop of Caesarea in the early fourth century.[109] Some of the apparent parallels between Philostratus's picture of Apollonius and Christ may be due to syncretistic tendencies already present in Severan circles. Indeed, Apollonius may be the spokesman of Philostratus's own religious views and so represent third-century thought rather than the first century.[110] Philostratus's Apollonius describes his practices as follows:

> My own system of wisdom is that of Pythagoras who taught me to worship the gods in the way you see . . . and to dress myself . . . in linen. And the very fashion of letting my hair grow long, I have learned from Pythagoras as part of his discipline, and also it is a result of his wisdom that I keep myself pure from animal food. I cannot therefore become either for you or for anybody else a companion in drinking [wine] or an associate in idleness and luxury. (*Vita* 1.32)

Apollonius also rejected marriage for himself. He condemned animal sacrifice, substituting prayer and meditation.[111] His closeness to the gods supposedly gave him a knowledge of the past and the future. He renounced monetary advantage and recommended to others a kind of communism. Despite his professed adherence to Pythagoras, there are Stoic, Cynic, and Platonic elements in Apollonius.

Among the features of Apollonius's life that may be paralleled with Jesus

---

107. Cf. Origen, *Against Celsus* 6.41.

108. According to the unreliable *Historia Augusta, Alexander* 29.2. Cf. the earlier practice of certain Gnostics mentioned by Irenaeus, *Against Heresies* 1.25.

109. *The Treatise of Eusebius . . . Against the Life of Apollonius of Tyana Written by Philostratus*, trans. F. C. Conybeare in Loeb Classical Library, vol. 2, *Philostratus. The Life of Apollonius of Tyana* (London, 1912).

110. Erkki Koskenniemi, "Apollonius of Tyana: A Typical ΘΕΙΟΣ ΑΝΗΡ?" *JBL* 117 (1998):455-467, who notes that with Apollonius removed from consideration, there is no "pattern" for the concept of *theios anēr*. Another work by Philostratus expresses his religious thought: *Flavius Philostratus: Heroikos, Translated with an Introduction and Notes* by J. K. Berenson Maclean and E. B. Aitken (Atlanta, 2001).

111. Cf. the quotation from his "On Sacrifices" in Eusebius, *Preparation of the Gospel* 4.13: "We should make use in relation to him [God] solely of the higher speech, I mean of that which issues not by the lips; and from the noblest of beings we must ask for blessings by the noblest faculty we possess, and that faculty is mind, which needs no organ."

are: his miraculous birth (1.4, 5); the gathering of a circle of disciples, of whom one (Damis) was in a position to transmit authentic information; itinerant teaching; collection of miracle stories (demoniacal boy, lame man, blind man, paralytic; 3.38ff.); and disappearance at his trial (8.5).

As a travel romance of a saint and a wonder-worker and as a collection of lore from many places the *Life of Apollonius* is of a piece with the Christian apocryphal Acts.

Numenius[112]

The last and best philosopher of the Pythagorean revival was Numenius of Apamea (late second century A.D.), whose classification is disputed and who has been termed a "Pythagorizing Platonist." He exerted influence on Plotinus (pp. 391-93) and had contacts with Jews and Christians. He anticipated Plotinus's absolutely transcendent One as the first principle of reality, with Mind and World Soul providing potential contact with the human soul.

The difficulty of classifying Numenius (as a Neopythagorean or Middle Platonist) testifies to the flowing together of different philosophical currents in the second century A.D., which prepared for the new synthesis known as Neoplatonism. This confluence was anticipated by the eclectic spirit of later Hellenistic and popular philosophy.

BIBLIOGRAPHY

Diogenes Laertius. *Lives of Eminent Philosophers* 8.
Thesleff, H. *An Introduction to the Pythagorean Writings of the Hellenistic Period.* Acta Academiae Aboensis, Humaniora, vol. 24, no. 3. Abo, 1961.
Thesleff, H. *The Pythagorean Texts of the Hellenistic Period.* Acta Academiae Aboensis, Humaniora, vol. 30, no. 1. Abo, 1965.
Städele, Alfons. *Die Briefe des Pythagoras und der Pythagoreer.* Meisenheim, 1980.
Navon, R., ed. *The Pythagorean Writings: Hellenistic Texts from the 1st c. B.C.–3rd c. A.D. on Life, Morality, Knowledge, and the World.* New Gardens, N.Y., 1986.
Guthrie, K. S. et al. *The Pythagorean Sourcebook and Library: An Anthology of Ancient Writings Which Relate to Pythagoras and Pythagorean Philosophy.* Grand Rapids, 1987.
Thom, Johan C. *The Pythagorean* Golden Verses: *With Introduction and Commentary.* Leiden, 1995. (Text and trans.)
Iamblichus: On the Pythagorean Life. Trans., with notes and int., by G. Clark. Liverpool, 1989.
Iamblichus: On the Pythagorean Way of Life. Ed. and trans. John Dillon and Jackson Hershbell. Atlanta, 1992.

112. K. S. Guthrie, *Numenius of Apamea: The Father of Neoplatonism* (London, 1917).

Festugière, A. J. *L'ideal Religieux des Grecs et l'Evangile*. Paris, 1932.

Carcopino, J. *De Pythagore aux apôtres*. Paris, 1956.

Vogel, C. J. de. *Pythagoras and Early Pythagoreanism*. Philosophical Texts and Studies, vol. 12. Assen, 1966.

Philip, J. A. *Pythagoras and Early Pythagoreanism*. Toronto, 1966.

Thesleff, H. "The Pythagoreans in the Light and Shadow of Recent Research." *Mysticism*. Scripta Instituti Donneriani Aboensis, vol. 5. Stockholm, 1970.

Balch, David L. "Neopythagorean Moralists and the New Testament Household Codes." *ANRW* II, *Principat*, 26.1. Berlin, 1992. Pp. 380-411.

MIDDLE PLATONISM

Characteristics

The Platonism from the first century B.C. to the second century A.D. is called Middle Platonism. It seems to have begun in Alexandria about 50 B.C. The development had been prepared for in the move from skepticism to eclecticism by Antiochus of Ascalon. At this time, when the Academy was moving toward Stoicism, the Stoa was becoming more Platonic (Posidonius). The first century B.C. saw a revival in the study of Plato and Aristotle, who returned to a position of predominance they have not lost since. The idea of the soul as distinguished from the body reappeared and became the basis of patristic and medieval philosophy. The thinkers included among the Middle Platonists — Plutarch, Apuleius, Albinus, Alcinous, Maximus of Tyre — provide the bridge to Neoplatonism, the dominant philosophy at the end of paganism. Middle Platonism provided the intellectual background for the work of the Christian apologists of the second century — Justin Martyr,[113] Tatian,[114] Athenagoras,[115] and Clement of Alexandria.[116] Even in the New Testament Platonism has been seen reflected in the Epistle to the Hebrews.[117]

Middle Platonism was Platonism influenced by Stoic ethics, Aristotelian

---

113. L. W. Barnard, *Justin Martyr: His Life and Thought* (London, 1967); J. C. M. van Winden, *An Early Christian Philosopher* (Leiden, 1971); E. F. Osborn, *Justin Martyr* (Tübingen, 1975).

114. Gerald F. Hawthorne, "Tatian and his Discourse to the Greeks," *HTR* 57 (1964):161-81.

115. L. W. Barnard, *Athenagoras: A Study in Second Century Christian Apologetic* (Paris, 1972); A. J. Malherbe, "The Structure of Athenagoras, 'Supplicatio pro Christianis,'" *Vigiliae Christianae* 23 (1969):1-20.

116. E. F. Osborn, *The Philosophy of Clement of Alexandria* (Cambridge, 1957); S. R. Lilla, *Clement of Alexandria, A Study in Christian Platonism and Gnosticism* (London, 1971).

117. L. K. K. Dey, *The Intermediary World and Patterns of Perfection in Philo and Hebrews* (Missoula, Mont., 1975); James W. Thompson, *The Beginnings of Christian Philosophy: The Epistle to the Hebrews* (Washington, 1982).

logic, and Neopythagorean metaphysics, religion, and number symbolism. Roots of its metaphysics may be found in Xenocrates (head of the Academy 339–314 B.C.). Given the different elements from which the Middle Platonists drew, it is understandable that there are many issues on which different positions were taken by philosophers bracketed under this name. Some common elements, however, may be discerned. The Middle Platonists started with the idea that it might be possible to reconcile Plato's and Aristotle's views about the universe and divine things. Alcinous, for instance, identified Aristotle's Supreme Mind (the Unmoved Mover) with Plato's Good (which became the first principle of the world of forms). The Platonic ideas or forms became the thoughts within the divine mind. Philo of Alexandria is the first extant author explicitly to give this formulation: the ideas are the thoughts in the reason of the Supreme God of Judaism (*On the Creation of the World* 15-20). In view of Philo's general lack of philosophical originality and incorporation of existing philosophical commonplaces it is conjectured that this reconciliation of Plato and Aristotle may go back to Antiochus.

The Middle Platonists exalted the absolute transcendence of the Supreme Mind (God). This is the head of a hierarchy of being, reached only through intermediary powers. The universe is animated by a World Soul. Direct knowledge of the transcendent Mind is impossible, but a "negative theology" gives an indirect knowledge of God. Direct contemplation may bring a few brief flashes of intuition even in this life. Some, influenced by Neopythagoreans, gave a negative judgment on matter as evil. Others, closer to Plato, saw evil as the result of the embodiment of ideas. Another emphasis of the Middle Platonists was the immortality of the soul.

Middle Platonists derived from Plato (*Theaet.* 176B) their doctrine that the goal of life as happiness consists in "likeness to God, so far as is possible."

Whereas philosophers from the fifth century B.C. onward had kept a certain distance between themselves and religious tradition, even when friendly toward it, from the end of the first century A.D. they increasingly looked to religion as a source of enlightenment.

Three figures affiliated in varying degrees with various forms of the Platonic tradition — Cicero (pp. 380-82), Philo of Alexandria (pp. 478-83), and Plutarch (pp. 389-90) — reflect the eclectic tendencies of the time and the capacity of Platonism to absorb many other elements and be the integrating framework for new syntheses, a capacity that enabled it to be the leading force in the last stages of paganism and the major philosophical influence in the formulation of patristic theology. These three figures, who bracket the first century (Cicero at the end of the first century B.C. and Philo at the beginning of the first century A.D., and Plutarch at the end of the first century A.D.), by the broad nature of their writings give a fairly complete picture of the state of philosophy (the major schools and issues) at the time of the beginning of Christianity.

Bibliography

Trapp, M. B., ed. *Maximus Tyrius: Dissertationes.* Stuttgart and Leipzig, 1994.

Koniaris, G. L., ed. *Maximus Tyrius, Philosophumena — ΔΙΑΛΕΞΕΙΣ.* Berlin: DeGruyter, 1995.

Trapp, M. B. *The Philosophical Orations by Maximus of Tyre.* Oxford, 1997. (Translation with introduction and notes)

Tobin, Thomas H. *Timaios of Locri, On the Nature of the World and the Soul: Text, Translation, and Notes* (Chico, Calif., 1985). (Also identified as a Pythagorean)

Dillon, John. *Alcinous: The Handbook of Platonism.* Oxford, 1993. (The *Didaskalikos* — Translation with introduction and commentary)

Witt, R. E. *Albinus and the History of Middle Platonism.* Cambridge, 1937. Reprint. Amsterdam, 1971. (The attribution of the *Didaskalikos* to Albinus rather than to Alcinous, to whom the manuscripts assign the work, is now rejected.)

Dillon, John M. *The Middle Platonists: A Study of Platonism 80 b.c. to a.d. 220.* London, 1977.

Wittaker, J. "Platonic Philosophy in the Early Centuries of the Empire." *ANRW,* II, *Principat,* 36.1. Berlin, 1987. Pp. 81-123.

Dillon, John M. *The Golden Chain.* Aldershot, 1999. (Reprints three studies on the history of the Academy and one on Plutarch as a Platonist.)

Plutarch (c. a.d. 50–after 120)

The most extensive corpus of writings by an author included among the Middle Platonists comes from Plutarch. This quantity plus his proximity in time to the New Testament writings make him an extremely important person for the study of Christian backgrounds. Most literary and historical studies of Plutarch have been concerned with his *Parallel Lives;* for philosophical, cultural, social, and religious matters much greater importance attaches to his *Moralia.* These seventy-eight miscellaneous essays and letters include short treatises on themes of popular philosophy (e.g., *On Tranquility, On Brotherly Love, On Envy and Hate*), major dialogues on the Delphic Oracle *(On the E at Delphi, On the Pythian Oracle, On the Decline of Oracles),* a major treatise on religious speculation *(On Isis and Osiris),* treatises on technical philosophy *(The Platonic Questions, On the Procreation of the Soul in the Timaeus),* antiquarian works *(Roman Questions, Greek Questions),* and the nine books of *Table Talk.*

Plutarch was a citizen of Chaeronea in central Greece. He came from a prominent family and had contacts with some of the leading men of his time. He was privileged to spend time in Athens, Egypt, and Italy. For the last thirty years of his life he was a priest at Delphi; he combined piety and respect for the old ways with a moderate rationalism.[118] Devoted to public duties, he advo-

118. Cf. A. D. Nock, "Religious Attitudes of the Ancient Greeks," *Proceedings of the Ameri-*

cated a partnership of Greek culture and Roman statesmanship. A genial and perceptive man with tendencies to monotheism and with practical moral interests, Plutarch has maintained popularity with Christian readers.

For Plutarch, the crown of philosophy is to form true and worthy conceptions of God and to give him pious worship. His description of God sounds like that of the Christian apologists, but he supported the traditional religion and sought to resolve its contradictions. With "reverent rationalism" he plotted a middle way between atheism and superstition (see *On Superstition*).[119] The latter he uses for a faith derived from a pious but obsessive neurotic fear. He reconciled the spiritualized view of the unity of God with the popular polytheism by seeing the traditional gods as subordinates and by interpreting mythology as a poetic expression of truth for a more primitive age. His works *On the Decline of Oracles, The Oracles at Delphi,* and *On the Demon of Socrates* are major sources for the doctrine of demons. Philanthropy is Plutarch's favorite virtue. He maintained a quiet optimism that good is stronger than evil.

We have already mentioned Plutarch several times in this book either as a source or an illustration of the political, social, cultural, religious, and philosophical thought of the early Roman empire. He has many points of contact with the New Testament.

BIBLIOGRAPHY

Almquist, H. *Plutarch und das Neuen Testament, ein Beitrag zum Corpus Hellenisticum Novi Testamenti.* Uppsala, 1946.

Dill, S. *Roman Society from Nero to Marcus Aurelius.* Reprint. New York, 1956. Pp. 401-40.

Barrow, R. H. *Plutarch and his Times.* London and Bloomington, Ind., 1967.

Jones, C. P. *Plutarch and Rome.* Oxford, 1971.

Russell, D. A. *Plutarch.* London, 1972.

Betz, H. D. *Plutarch's Theological Writings and Early Christian Literature.* Corpus Hellenisticum Novi Testamenti. Leiden, 1974.

Betz, H. D. *Plutarch's Ethical Writings and Early Christian Literature.* Corpus Hellenisticum Novi Testamenti. Leiden, 1977.

Brenk, Frederick E. *In Mist Apparalled: Religious Themes in Plutarch's Moralia and Lives.* Mnemosyne Supplement, vol. 48. Leiden, 1977.

Lamberton, Robert. *Plutarch.* New Haven, 2001.

can *Philosophical Society* 85 (1942):472 (*Essays,* 534); Frekerick E. Brenk, "An Imperial Heritage: The Religious Spirit of Plutarch of Chaironeia," *ANRW,* II, *Principat,* 36.1 (Berlin, 1987), 248-349.

119. H. Moellering, *Plutarch on Superstition: Plutarch's De Superstitione, its Place in the Changing Meaning of Deisidaimonia and in the Context of His Theological Writings,* 2d ed. (Boston, 1963); H.-J. Klauck, "Religion without Fear: Plutarch on Superstition and Early Christian Literature," *Skrif en Kerk* 18 (1997):11-26.

PLOTINUS AND NEOPLATONISM

The Hellenistic philosophical developments we have surveyed found their climax in Neoplatonism. The eclecticism of philosophy in the early empire was brought into an ordered system by Plotinus, the creator of Neoplatonism. Neoplatonism was the last form of spiritual Greek religion, although some of its representatives (Iamblichus) combined it with magic and theurgy. Neoplatonism provided the focus for the last intellectual challenge to Christianity in the paganism of the fourth century. On the other hand, as a metaphysical system it had enormous influence on Christian thought. Origen was educated in the same thought-world from which Neoplatonism came. This philosophy was the background of the work of the Cappadocians in the fourth century and through them influenced Greek Orthodox theology, and it was decisive in the intellectual development of Augustine and so through him had a great impact on the medieval Latin development. Some later thinkers such as Pseudo-Dionysius the Areopagite and John Scotus Erigena appropriated its views directly.

Life of Plotinus (A.D. 205–270)

Plotinus was born in Egypt and studied in Alexandria under Ammonius Saccas. Plotinus traveled to the east, and at age forty settled in Rome. A number of pupils gathered around him, for whom he began to write essays based on their philosophical discussions. These were collected by his pupil Porphyry, who arranged them in six groups of nine treatises, the *Enneads,* the major source of his philosophy. Porphyry prefaced the *Enneads,* published c. A.D. 300, with a *Life of Plotinus.* Plotinus has been a major source of western mysticism, and Porphyry says that he experienced union with the divine on four occasions.

Plotinus's System

Plotinus has been called the greatest thinker between Aristotle and Spinoza. His system consisted of Platonism with Aristotelian, Stoic, and Neopythagorean elements. The dualistic outlook of the period is expressed within a framework of ultimate unity.

The highest principle is wholly transcendent. It is the One, an immaterial and impersonal force that is the ground of all existence and source of all values. The One is neither subject nor object, neither self nor the world. The One is what is left by transcending all duality. As the number one is different from all other numbers and yet is their source, so is this first principle. A description is possible only by negation: whatever one thinks of, the One is not that, but yet the One is all. Plotinus goes beyond Plato in positing a transcendence that encompasses not only all being but also nonbeing.

Creation is impossible in Plotinus's thinking, for it implies that God is involved in this universe. There is an essential difference between the One and matter, which is at the bottom of reality. Instead of creation, Neoplatonism speaks of emanations that provide the connection between the One and matter. The doctrine of emanations made Neoplatonism something of a dynamic pantheism, although not a pantheism in the ordinary sense.

Out of the One came Mind *(Nous)*, which resembles Aristotle's Unmoved Mover. This supreme intellectual principle, however, is not for Plotinus the highest reality. The World Mind was not created but emanated from the One. *Nous* is the ideal Mind, the principle of divine intelligence. The Mind was emanated so that the Eternal could consider itself. The One is not changed by the radiating of intelligence from itself. The Mind is the highest really knowable entity. This element in the system is already marked by duality, for consciousness already contains the knower and the known.

The next emanation is the World Soul, the principle at work in the moving stars, animals, plants, and humanity. It is the moving power behind the whole universe. The World Soul is between Mind and bodily reality. It exercises itself in individual souls. There are three phases of the World Soul in human souls: the intellectual, intuitive soul; the reasoning soul; and the unreasoning animal life. The human soul is an element of the divine, but it can turn itself to the Good or to evil. Existence by the very fact that it exists lacks something. The soul descends from the World Soul and desires ascent to the One; manifoldness longs to be reunited. But the soul as a dynamic force can turn toward nonbeing as well as toward Being.

The increasing manifoldness of the emanations is expressed in Nature, the immanent laws of the working of the world. At the lowest level is bare matter. A person is a microcosm, containing all these principles: there is a link between individual minds and *Nous*, individual souls and the World Soul, between the body and the laws of nature.

Evil is not an ontological reality. Nothing is evil in its nature. Evil is nonbeing, the term or limit of being.

The longing of the soul to return to the source of all being is a desire for union. For Plotinus, this unity is salvation. The return to the One is not achieved easily. It requires asceticism — restraining from actions and desires and purifying the self from the influences of the finite world. A person must concentrate on contemplation of the One. The final step, the realization of Ultimate Reality, is an experience of ecstasy, of rapture, which is the goal of contemplation. It occurs very rarely. Unlike Christian mysticism, this experience of union with the divine is not a matter of grace but is the result of prolonged effort by the will and understanding. Nevertheless, one cannot determine when it will occur. Plotinus thus thinks in a circular way. As the One through emanations has produced manifoldness, the manifold returns to the One. Nothing gets lost in this circular movement of devolution and return. There is no personal survival in the Christian sense.

Later Neoplatonists

Neoplatonism was so successful because it brought to fruition and systematized the conceptions of the time and united theology and philosophy. The later Neoplatonists made it a scholasticism and took superstition and theurgy into its doctrine.

Porphyry (A.D. 232–c. 305)[120] was born in Tyre, studied under Longinus in Athens, and became a devoted disciple of Plotinus in Rome. He is important not only for preserving Plotinus's work but for a wide range of other writings, unfortunately much of which is lost. His *Introduction to the Categories of Aristotle* (in a Latin translation by Boethius) became the textbook of logic in the schools of the Middle Ages. He wrote fifteen books entitled *Against the Christians,* which were burned in 448.[121]

Iamblichus (c. A.D. 250–c. 325)[122] studied under Porphyry and wrote a *Life of Porphyry.* His *On the Mysteries* is a fundamental work for late antique religion.[123] In his own school in Syria he introduced theosophical tendencies into Plotinus's system. He was attracted by theurgy, the practice of inducing the presence of divine powers by magic.[124] Theurgy makes it possible for humans to enter into relations with the gods. The soul, according to Iamblichus, has a double life — part united with the body and part separated from it.

Sallustius was a friend of the emperor Julian, and during the latter's reign (A.D. 361–363) wrote *Concerning the Gods and the World* to support his effort to

120. Alice Zimmern, trans., and int. by D. Fideler, *Porphyry's Letter to His Wife Marcella* (Grand Rapids, 1986); K. S. Guthrie, trans., and int. by M. Hornum, *Porphyry's Launching-Points to the Realm of the Mind* (Grand Rapids, 1988).

121. Amos Barry Hulen, "Porphyry's Work against the Christians: An Interpretation," *Yale Studies in Religion* 1 (Scottsdale, 1933); Robert Grant, "Porphyry among the Early Christians," *Romanitas et Christianitas,* ed. W. den Boer, et al. (Amsterdam, 1973); Robert L. Wilken, "Pagan Criticism of Christianity; Greek Religion and Christian Faith," in *Early Christian Literature and the Classical Intellectual Tradition,* ed. W. R. Schoedel and R. L. Wilken (Paris, 1979), 117-34; Anthony Meredith, "Porphyry and Julian against the Christians," *ANRW* II, *Principat,* 23.2 (Berlin and New York, 1980), 1119-49.

122. T. M. Johnson, trans., *Iamblichus: Exhortation to Philosophy* (Grand Rapids, 1988); D. J. O'Meara, *Pythagoras Revived: Mathematics and Philosophy in Late Antiquity* (Oxford, 1989); Gregory Shaw, *Theurgy and the Soul: The Neoplatonism of Iamblichus* (University Park, Penn., 1995).

123. Emma Clarke et al., trans. and eds., *Iamblichus on the Mysteries* (Atlanta, 2003).

124. E. R. Dodds, "Theurgy and its Relationship to Neo-Platonism," *JRS* 37 (1947):55ff.

reestablish paganism.[125] The book is a brief manual of Neoplatonic piety and gives an excellent summary of pagan thought at the time of the last major conflict between Christianity and paganism.

Julian (332–363),[126] emperor 360–363, attempted to reestablish paganism and so earned from Christians the designation "Julian the Apostate." Despite his claim to revive the old Greek religion, he was the champion of a late form of paganism interpreted in Neoplatonic terms, especially in the form given by Iamblichus. Although he was conservative about religious ceremonies and myths, his view blended the gods in syncretism. He worshiped the sun as the supreme deity. A warmly spiritual man, he was aristocratic in outlook and superstitious as well as philosophical.

Macrobius was an important transmitter of Neoplatonism to the Middle Ages. He wrote before 410 a *Commentary on the Dream of Scipio* (see pp. 250, 381n.97) that covered topics appealing to later periods: classification of dreams, number symbolism and musical concords, classification of virtues, description of the afterlife, immortality and nature of the soul, how humans differ from animals and plants, celestial bodies, the harmony of the spheres, and the zodiac.[127]

Proclus (A.D. 410–485)[128] was head of the Academy in Athens. He was the last great systematizer of the Greek philosophical inheritance, but his system is in reality mystic. Of his vast literary output special mention may be made of the *Elements of Theology,*[129] a concise summary of Neoplatonic metaphysics.

The Academy had not had a continuous institutional existence through antiquity, and the school was closed by the emperor Justinian in A.D. 529. By that time this was not so much an act of religious persecution as a decent burial.

Bibliography

MacKenna, S. J., trans. *Plotinus: The Enneads.* 4th ed. with notes. Burdette, N.Y., 1992. Reprint.

Dodds, E. R. *Select Passages Illustrating Neoplatonism.* New York, 1923.

Sleeman, J. H., and G. Pollet, eds. *Lexicon Plotinianum.* Leiden, 1980.

Armstrong, A. H. *The Architecture of the Intelligible Universe in the Philosophy of Plotinus.* Cambridge, 1940. Reprint. Amsterdam, 1967.

125. A. D. Nock, ed., *Sallustius Concerning the Gods and the Universe* (Cambridge, 1926; repr. Hildesheim, 1966).

126. G. W. Bowersock, *Julian the Apostate* (Cambridge, Mass., 1978).

127. William Harris Stahl, trans., *Macrobius: Commentary on the Dream of Scipio* (New York, 1952).

128. L. J. Rosan, *The Philosophy of Proclus: The Final Phase of Ancient Thought* (New York, 1949); Lucas Siovanes, *Proclus: Neo-Platonic Philosophy and Science* (New Haven, 1997).

129. E. R. Dodds, *Proclus: Elements of Theology* (2d ed.; Oxford, 1963).

Pistorius, P. V. *Plotinus and Neoplatonism: An Introductory Study.* Cambridge, 1952.

Rist, J. M. *Plotinus: The Road to Reality.* Cambridge, 1967.

Wallis, R. T. *Neo-Platonism.* London, 1972.

Geffcken, J. *The Last Days of Greco-Roman Paganism.* New York, 1978.

O'Meara, D. J., ed. *Neoplatonism and Christian Thought.* Norfolk, Va., 1982.

Gersh, Stephen. *Middle Platonism and Neoplatonism: The Latin Tradition.* Vols. 1 and 2. Notre Dame, 1986.

Finan, Thomas, and V. Twomey, eds. *The Relationship between Neoplatonism and Christianity.* Dublin, 1992.

Gerson, Lloyd P. *Plotinus.* London, 1994.

Gerson, Lloyd P., ed. *The Cambridge Companion to Plotinus.* Cambridge, 1996.

5. JUDAISM

BIBLIOGRAPHY

Collections of Sources

Alexander, P., ed. *Judaism*. Textual Sources for the Study of Religion Series. Manchester, 1984.

Nickelsburg, George W. E., and Michael E. Stone. *Faith and Piety in Early Judaism: Texts and Documents*. Philadelphia, 1991.

Feldman, L., and M. Reinhold. *Jewish Life and Thought among Greeks and Romans: Primary Readings*. Minneapolis, 1996. (With rich bibliographies.)

Schiffman, Lawrence H. *Texts and Traditions: A Source Reader for the Study of Second Temple and Rabbinic Judaism*. Hoboken, 1998.

(See further the section on Jewish Literature.)

Reference Works

The Jewish Encyclopedia. 12 vols. New York, 1901–1910.

Encyclopedia Judaica. 16 vols. Jerusalem, 1971–1972.

Cambridge History of Judaism. Vol. 1: *Introduction: The Persian Period*, W. D. Davies and L. Finkelstein. Vol. 2: *The Hellenistic Age*, ed. W. D. Davies and L. Finkelstein. Vol. 3: *The Early Roman Period*, ed. William Horbury, W. D. Davies, and John Sturdy. Cambridge, 1984, 1989, 1999.

Dictionary of Judaism in the Biblical Period, 450 B.C.E. to 600 C.E. Ed. Jacob Neusner and William Scott Green. 2 vols. New York, 1996. 1 vol. Peabody, 2000.

Basic Secondary Works

Schalit, A., ed. *World History of the Jewish People*. Vols. 6-8. New Brunswick, N.J., 1972–.

Schürer, Emil. *The History of the Jewish People in the Age of Jesus Christ (175 B.C.–*

A.D. *135*). Revised and edited by Geza Vermes and Fergus Millar. 3 vols. Edinburgh, 1973–1987.

De Jonge, M., and S. Safrai, eds. *Compendia Rerum Iudaicarum ad Novum Testamentum.* Section One, *The Jewish People in the First Century.* 2 vols. Edited by S. Safrai and M. Stern. Assen, 1974, 1976.

Hengel, Martin. *Judaism and Hellenism.* 2 vols. Philadelphia, 1974. See review by L. Feldman in *JBL* 96 (1977):371-82.

Kraft, Robert, and George Nickelsburg. *Early Judaism and Its Modern Interpreters.* Philadelphia, 1986.

Sanders, E. P. *Judaism: Practice and Belief, 63 B.C.E.–66 C.E.* Philadelphia, 1992.

Neusner, Jacob, ed. *Judaism in Late Antiquity.* Leiden, 1995–.

Supplementary Works

Davies, W. D. *Paul and Rabbinic Judaism.* London, 1955.

Schoeps, H. J. *Paul, the Theology of the Apostle in the Light of Jewish Religious History.* Philadelphia, 1961.

Neusner, J. *A History of the Jews in Babylonia.* 5 vols. Leiden, 1965–1970.

Alon, G. *Jews, Judaism, and the Classical World.* Jerusalem, 1977.

Sanders, E. P. *Paul and Palestinian Judaism: A Comparison of Patterns of Religion.* Philadelphia, 1977.

Oppenheimer, A. *The 'Am Ha-aretz, A Study in the Social History of the Jewish People in the Hellenistic-Roman Period.* Leiden, 1977.

Green, Wm. S., ed. *Approaches to Ancient Judaism: Theory and Practice.* Missoula, Mont., 1978.

Sandmel, S. *Judaism and Christian Beginnings.* New York, 1978.

Stone, M. *Scriptures, Sects, and Visions: A Profile of Judaism from Ezra to the Jewish Revolts.* Philadelphia, 1980.

Sanders, E. P., ed. *Jewish and Christian Self-Definition.* Vol. 2, *Aspects of Judaism in the Greco-Roman Period.* Philadelphia, 1981.

Cohen, Shaye J. D. *From the Maccabees to the Mishnah.* Philadelphia, 1987.

Neusner, Jacob and William Scott Green, eds. *The Origins of Judaism: Religion, History and Literature in Late Antiquity: A 20-Volume Collection of Essays and Articles.* Hamden, Conn., 1990.

Otzen, Benedikt. *Judaism in Antiquity: Political Development and Religious Currents from Alexander to Hadrian.* Sheffield, 1990.

Riches, John. *The World of Jesus: First-Century Judaism in Crisis.* Cambridge, 1990.

Talmon, S., ed. *Jewish Civilization in the Hellenistic-Roman Period.* Philadelphia, 1991.

Grabbe, L. L. *Judaism from Cyrus to Hadrian.* Vol. 1: *The Persian and Greek Periods.* Vol. 2: *The Roman Period.* Minneapolis, 1991.

Schiffman, Lawrence H. *From Text to Tradition: A History of Second Temple and Rabbinic Judaism.* Hoboken, 1991.

Schwartz, D. R. *Studies in the Jewish Background of Christianity.* Tübingen, 1992.

Stern, Sacha. *Jewish Identity in Early Rabbinic Writings.* Leiden, 1994.

Chilton, Bruce, and Jacob Neusner. *Judaism in the New Testament: Practices and Beliefs.* London, 1995.

Rousseau, J. J., Ravi Arav, and C. Meyers. *Jesus and His World: An Archaeological and Cultural Dictionary.* Minneapolis, 1995.

Scott, J. Julius, Jr. *Jewish Backgrounds of the New Testament.* Grand Rapids, 1995.

Winter, Bruce W., ed. *The Book of Acts in Its First Century Setting.* Vol. 4. *The Book of Acts in Its Palestinian Setting,* ed. Richard Bauckham. Grand Rapids, 1995.

Grabbe, L. L. *An Introduction to First Century Judaism: Jewish Religion and History in the Second Temple Period.* Edinburgh, 1996.

Trebolle Barrera, Julio. *The Jewish Bible and the Christian Bible: An Introduction to the History of the Bible.* Grand Rapids, 1998.

Levine, Lee I. *Judaism and Hellenism: Conflict or Confluence?* Peabody, Mass., 1999.

VanderKam, James C. *An Introduction to Early Judaism.* Grand Rapids, 2000.

Murphy, Frederick J. *Early Judaism: The Exile to the Time of Jesus.* Peabody, Mass., 2002.

Nickelsburg, George W. E. *Ancient Judaism and Christian Origins.* Minneapolis, 2003.

Tomasino, Anthony J. *Judaism Before Jesus: The Events and Ideas That Shaped the New Testament World.* Downers Grove, 2003.

Marcus, R. "A Selected Bibliography of the Jews in the Hellenistic-Roman Period." *Proceedings of the American Academy for Jewish Research* 16 (1946–47):97-181.

Neusner, J., ed. *The Study of Judaism: Bibliographical Essays.* New York, 1972.

Bokser, Baruch M. "Recent Developments in the Study of Judaism, 70–200 C.E." *The Second Century* 3 (1983):1-68.

Bourquin, D. R. *First Century Palestinian Judaism: A Bibliography of Works in English.* San Bernardino, Calif., 1990.

Boccaccini, G. *Portraits of Middle Judaism in Scholarship and Arts: A Multimedia Catalog from Flavius Josephus to 1991.* Turin, Italy, 1993.

Jewish Quarterly Review
Journal of Jewish Studies
Journal for the Study of Judaism

JUDAISM was hardly a single entity in the first century, any more than was Greek philosophy. The variety of expression goes beyond the traditional distinction between Palestinian Judaism and Diaspora Judaism. In fact, this distinction is often only a geographical one, not a language or religious description, for there were Diaspora Jews who maintained the Hebrew language and, like Paul, received a strict Pharisaic upbringing, and there were strong Hellenistic influences in Palestine, even in conservative rabbinic circles. The Jewish matrix of early Christianity was itself already Hellenized. In giving special, and more extensive, treatment to Judaism, we are moving to the study of one particular people that was a part of the larger Greco-Roman world. The varied nature of Hellenistic influence on the Jews, and the variety of their reactions to Hellenism (pp. 428-29), provided only part of the variety in first-century Judaism. There were, moreover, many strands of thought in Judaism — the Wisdom tradition, apocalypticism, messianism, legalism, Hellenism — that frequently overlapped and intermingled. We will make an effort to present this variety by introducing the available sources. We will also make an effort to identify the entity of Judaism by noting its common (if not universal) characteristics. As a very broad generalization, subject to many qualifications, one can say that Palestinian Judaism is the most important background for the ministry of Jesus and the Gospels,[1] and the Judaism of the Greek Diaspora is the most important background for the ministry of Paul and his Epistles and the Book of Acts.

The concern of this chapter is Judaism in the Hellenistic and Roman periods. Various other designations have been given to Judaism in this time span. Christians have often used the designation "intertestamental," terminology obviously unacceptable to Jews. The description "post-Biblical" fails to give a *terminus ad quem*. Jewish scholars prefer "Second Temple Judaism," and the period after 70 does begin a new era of Jewish history, but for our purposes the rabbinic literature (all post-70) needs to be included, so a strict definition of this title is inadequate.

We begin by sketching the history of the Jews, especially in Palestine, within the framework of the general history outlined in Chapter 1.

JEWISH HISTORY, 538 B.C. TO A.D. 200

The Persian Period (538–332 B.C.)[2]

Cyrus and the Dispersion. The Persian period is one of the more obscure periods of Palestinian Jewish history because of the paucity of extrabiblical source material. Nevertheless, the importance of this period is undoubted, for the foundations of postbiblical Judaism were laid during this time. This was the achievement of those Jews who returned to Palestine from their exile in

---

1. David Flusser, *Jewish Sources in Early Christianity* (New York, 1987), is a popular treatment putting the life of Jesus in its Jewish context as well as illustrating the value of the New Testament as a source for Judaism in the first century. More extensive is his collection of articles, *Judaism and the Origins of Christianity* (Jerusalem, 1988); a synthesis of his work in *Jesus* (Winona Lake, Ind., 1997). See also Martin McNamara, *Palestinian Judaism and the New Testament* (Collegeville, Minn., 1983), and F. J. Murphy, *The Religious World of Jesus: An Introduction to Second Temple Palestinian Judaism* (Nashville, 1991); Geza Vermes, *Jesus in His Jewish Context* (Minneapolis, 2003).

2. Ephraim Stern, *The Material Culture of the Land of the Bible in the Persian Period — 538– 332 B.C.* (Warminster, England, 1979); K. G. Hoglund, *Achaemenid Imperial Administration in Syria Palestine and the Missions of Ezra and Nehemiah* (Atlanta, 1992).

Babylonia under the auspices of their new Persian rulers. The very name "Jews" (derived from Judah) attests the importance of the survivors of the southern kingdom for the continued existence of the chosen people. Cyrus reversed the policies of the Assyrians (cf. 2 Kings 17) and Babylonians (cf. 2 Kings 24–25) by encouraging peoples to return to their homelands and by supporting local institutions under the oversight of the royal administration. Since the Hebrew order of the Old Testament books places Chronicles last, the Jewish Bible closes with Cyrus's proclamation of 538/537 allowing the Jews to go up to Jerusalem to rebuild the temple (2 Chron. 36:22-23; cf. Ezra 1:1-4). Although the decree has no extrabiblical attestation, it accords with Cyrus's general claim to be the servant of the gods of his conquered peoples.[3]

Many Jews, however, chose to remain in Babylonia. They had followed the advice of Jeremiah (chap. 29, which became something of a charter to dispersion Judaism) and settled down and sought "the welfare of the city" to such an extent that they prospered, some even becoming high goverment officials (as were Daniel, Mordecai, and Nehemiah). The Babylonian Jewish community grew in influence over the centuries. The Babylonian Talmud (c. A.D. 500) shows the great prestige later attained by the rabbinic scholars there.

Some Jews at the time of the Babylonian conquest had fled to Egypt, where there continued to be sizable Jewish settlements. Aramaic papyri from 495 to 399 contain the correspondence of a Jewish military colony at Elephantine (which dates back to 594–589) with Persian and Jewish officials in Palestine.[4] There was a Jewish temple at Elephantine, which the Jerusalem priesthood could not have looked on with much favor. An anti-Jewish riot in 410 B.C. destroyed the Elephantine temple; after considerable correspondence the Persian authorities granted permission for its rebuilding. When Egypt secured its independence from Persia for a time in 400, this shrine to the Lord disappeared from history, perhaps suppressed by the new native rulers.

Temple and Torah. The two great accomplishments of the returned exiles were the rebuilding of the Lord's house in Jerusalem and the collecting and studying of the law *(Torah)* with a view to regulating the life of the people by it.

Those who returned from the Babylonian captivity under the leadership of Zerubbabel the governor and Joshua the priest were not themselves wealthy, but they had the support of their countrymen and of the royal treasury. They were zealous for the worship of God but were soon discouraged in their efforts

3. The Cyrus Cylinder attests the general policy of Cyrus; see translation in James B. Pritchard, *Ancient Near Eastern Texts Relating to the Old Testament* (Princeton, 1955), 315-16.

4. A. E. Cowley, *Aramaic Papyri of the Fifth Century B.C.* (Oxford, 1923); E. G. Kraeling, *The Brooklyn Museum Aramaic Papyri* (New Haven, 1953); G. R. Driver, ed., *Aramaic Documents of the Fifth Century B.C.* (Oxford, 1954); Bezalel Porten, *Archives from Elephantine: The Life of an Ancient Jewish Military Colony* (Berkeley, 1968); Bezalel Porten and A. Yardeni, *Textbook of Aramaic Documents from Ancient Egypt Newly Copied, Edited, and Translated into Hebrew and English* (Jerusalem, 1986, 1989, 1993).

to rebuild the temple. With the encouragement of the prophets Haggai and Zechariah the Second Temple was completed and dedicated in 515 B.C. (Ezra 1–6).[5] Thus began what is called the period of the "Second Temple" or the "Second Jewish Commonwealth."

A second group of exiles returned under the leadership of Ezra (Ezra 1–7), whose dates are much disputed. Ezra is termed "a scribe skilled in the law of Moses" (7:6), and with him we are introduced to a new class of religious leaders who were to assume great importance in the subsequent period. Previously the religious leaders were the priests, prophets, and wise men; but prophecy was soon to cease, and while there were still priests, they were concerned with the temple ritual and its affairs. A different kind of "wise men" arose — scholars in the sacred writings. Scribes replaced priests as the interpreters of the law, and in the absence of prophetic revelation, scribal interpretation became the authority.[6]

The great work of Ezra was the restoration of the law (cf. Neh. 8–10). The postexilic community was dedicated to the study of the law, and its piety revolved around the law so that the Jews were a unique people in the ancient world in their effort to educate a whole nation in a book religion.

The restoration of the temple and the law needed a physical security. This was attained with the restoration of the walls of Jerusalem by Nehemiah, who came to Jerusalem in 445/444 B.C. as governor under Artaxerxes I.

The religious problems of the restoration community, as the books of Ezra, Nehemiah, Haggai, Zechariah, and Malachi indicate, were usury, profaning the Sabbath, nonpayment of tithes, and intermarriage with foreigners. Not to minimize the significant developments in the Second Temple period, the reader who goes from Malachi to Matthew recognizes some of the same elements in the spiritual atmosphere: the concern to "remember the law" (Mal. 4:4), waiting for Elijah (4:5), pride that would "tread down the wicked" (4:3), an externalism in religion that would "rob God" (3:8). One problem the postexilic community did not have, which had plagued its ancestors, was idolatry. The avoidance of idolatry did not characterize Jews everywhere, however, as Jewish papyri from Elephantine show.

The Persian period after the time of Nehemiah is almost a silent century as far as Judea is concerned. The province of Judah formed a very small area extending no more than twenty miles in any direction from Jerusalem. It would have appeared to the outsider as simply another one of the temple-states so nu-

---

5. b. Yoma 21b lists five things in the first temple lacking in the second: the sacred fire, the ark, the Urim and Thummim, the oil for anointing, and the holy spirit. Despite such questions about the second temple's legitimacy, most Jews remained loyal to it.

6. *Seder Olam Rabba* 30: "Until [Alexander of Macedon] the prophets prophesied in the holy spirit, from now on turn your ear and hear the words of the sages." Cf. D. E. Orton, *The Understanding Scribe: Matthew and the Apocalyptic Ideal* (Sheffield, 1989); Christine Schams, *Jewish Scribes in the Second-Temple Period* (Sheffield, 1998).

merous in the Near East. The local government was, as Josephus says, "aristo-cratic and oligarchic"; for "the high priests were at the head of affairs" (*Ant.* 11.4.8 [111]), subject to but not appointed by the local governor, who in turn was satrap of the region "beyond the river," that is, west of the Euphrates. "Satrap" was the title given the governors of the large administrative areas (20 to 29 in number) and of the smaller subdivisions (of which there were about 120). The high priest remained the leader of the Jewish community in Judea through Ptolemaic times.

Samaritan Schism. We will discuss the Samaritans in more detail in the section "Parties and Sects" (pp. 534ff.), but the background to the separation of Jews and Samaritans (if not the actual break itself) falls in the Persian period. The exiles who returned from Babylonia felt a social superiority to the "people of the land" who remained around Jerusalem (Jer. 24; 2 Kings 24:14; 25:12) and a religious and racial superiority to their neighbors to the north around the old capital of the northern kingdom, Samaria (2 Kings 17:24ff.; Ezra 4:1ff.). Author-ities in Samaria opposed the rebuilding of the temple and city walls (Ezra 4:1ff.; Neh. 6:1ff.). Nehemiah relates that the grandson of the high priest at the time he came to Jerusalem married the daughter of Sanballat, the governor of Sa-maria, and that he drove out this Samaritan sympathizer (Neh. 13:28). Josephus tells a similar story, adding that Sanballat promised the grandson (Manasses) a priesthood and temple on Mt. Gerizim; only Josephus puts the incident a cen-tury later in connection with Alexander the Great (*Ant.* 11.8.1-2 [304-312]). It may be that Josephus has confused two similar sets of circumstances and that there was a history of intermarriage between the noble families of Samaria and the high-priestly family of Jerusalem.

A reform movement purified the Samaritan religion, perhaps at the same time as Ezra and Nehemiah, for later the Jewish-Samaritan religious rivalry had to do with the place of worship, not its ritual, and the Samaritans have continued to recognize the same law book as the Jews (the Pentateuch). It is hard to date the building of the Samaritan temple on Mt. Gerizim, but Josephus may be right in putting it in the period of Alexander the Great. That event would have put a strain on relations, if it was not the cause or confirma-tion of the break (see pp. 534-35). The dating of the Samaritan schism is con-troversial, because there is no agreement on what constituted the definitive break during a long history of strained relations.[7]

---

7. A. D. Crown, "Redating the Schism Between the Judaeans and the Samaritans," *Jewish Quarterly Review* 82 (1991):17-50, argues that the process of separation began after Bar Kokhba and was completed in the third century A.D. as exclusive claims broke the limits of tolerance.

The Greek Period (332–167 B.C.)[8]

The Coming of Alexander. The conquests of Alexander the Great of Macedon brought him into possession of Palestine in 332 B.C. Josephus (*Ant.* 11.8.4-5 [326-39]) records a story of Alexander meeting with the high priest Jaddua, prostrating himself before him, and then offering a sacrifice at the temple under his directions — a story legendary in details if not in entirety. The Jews, as other peoples, would have appeared before Alexander and made submission to him, at which time Alexander would have confirmed their permission "to live according to their ancestral law"; but this would not have occurred at Jerusalem, which was off Alexander's line of march.

The coming of the Macedonians accelerated a process of Hellenization already under way in the eastern Mediterranean. Colonies of Greek soldier-settlers were established and cities were founded on Greek patterns. The gymnasium, stadium, hippodrome, theatre, and celebration of Greek festivals spread the Greek way of life. Coinage followed the Attic standard. Greek language spread, and with it Greek literature and education. Although Aramaic continued to be spoken in the old Persian domains and Hebrew continued in limited use (just how much is disputed) among the Jews, Greek became the language for commerce, government, and literature. Greek culture came to hold sway throughout the eastern Mediterranean, at least in the cities and upper levels of society, among the Jewish aristocracy as well as among other peoples.

Not only did the Greeks penetrate Palestine, but during the Hellenistic period the Jewish dispersion expanded. Egyptian Jewry received a new center with large numbers settling in the new city of Alexandria. Syria became another significant numerical center, especially at the trading metropolis of Antioch. Fairly large numbers of Jews were moved by Hellenistic monarchs to Asia Minor. The Jews in a Greek world, both in and out of Palestine, reacted to the new situation in the variety of ways possible to foreigners in an alien environment, either resisting or accommodating to Greek culture (see pp. 428-29).

The Rule of the Ptolemies (301–198 B.C.).[9] On Alexander's death in 323 B.C. his empire began to break up. For a time his generals maintained the fiction of a regency while maneuvering for strategic advantages. The Diadochi (Alexander's successors) struggled for control of Palestine, which changed hands between Antigonus (who controlled Asia Minor) and Ptolemy (who ruled Egypt) before the latter held it.[10] Ptolemy occupied the country in 320, 312, and 302. Although Antigonus seemed to have the best opportunity of securing Alexander's realm, the other generals combined against him and before the battle of Ipsus (301 B.C.) agreed that Ptolemy would receive Palestine. Ptolemy's troops

8. E. J. Bickerman, *The Jews in the Greek Age* (Cambridge, Mass., 1988).
9. Martin Hengel, *Jews, Greeks, and Barbarians* (Philadelphia, 1980).
10. Diodorus Siculus 18.43.1-2; 19.80.3; 19.93; 20.73.2; 20.113.1; 21.1.4.

were late; so Seleucus, who held Syria then, claimed the agreement was void. However, Ptolemy had already occupied Palestine, and Seleucus was indebted to him for sheltering him on another occasion, so Seleucus did not press his claim and after 301 the Ptolemies were in effective control in Palestine for a century. Palestine (sometimes included in Coele-Syria) nevertheless remained a point of contention between the Egyptian and Syrian rulers, and four wars were fought over it. Daniel 11 traces the external history of the Ptolemaic-Seleucid rivalry for Palestine.

The century of Ptolemaic rule in Palestine appears not to have been unpleasant for the Jews. Politically it was a time of peace, for the Egyptian-Syrian rivalry did not greatly affect the interior. The economic and administrative circumstances are illuminated by the Zenon papyri for the period after 259 B.C.[11] Hellenization in the economic and social spheres may be seen in Josephus's story of Joseph, son of Tobiah, who secured (in place of the high priest) the right of collecting taxes for the Ptolemies and of being the representative of the Jewish people (*Ant.* 12.4.1-5 [154-85]). The continuation of traditional Jewish ideals in Palestine is seen in the Wisdom of Jesus the Son of Sirach, or Ecclesiasticus (discussed below under Apocrypha, pp. 444-45). The author, a sage and teacher, wrote in Hebrew about the time of the change to Seleucid rule in Palestine. The Hellenistic influences may perhaps be seen in the fact that the author's grandson translated the work into Greek in Egypt about 118 B.C. Sirach (chap. 50) celebrates the virtues of the high priest Simon II (c. 220–198 B.C.), whose piety was to shine even more illustriously in contrast with the high priests of succeeding centuries.

Ptolemy I transported many Jews to Egypt, and Alexandria became a major center of the Jewish dispersion. The Jews in Egypt flourished during most of the Ptolemaic period, playing a not inconsiderable role in the political and economic life of the country and supplying a significant part of its military force. During the Ptolemaic period one of the most significant events in religious history was undertaken: the translation of the Old Testament into Greek (pp. 432ff.).

The Rule of the Seleucids (198–167 B.C.). Antiochus III the Great (223–187 B.C.) brought the period of peace to an end in 219. After several attempts he finally wrested Palestine from Egypt about the turn of the century. The Jews readily changed allegiance and welcomed Antiochus. It proved to be a tragic mistake to expect better conditions. Antiochus's expansion of his realm was checked when the Romans defeated him at Magnesia in 190 B.C. and imposed such a heavy tribute that the Seleucids thereafter were in financial difficulties.

---

11. C. C. Edgar, *Zenon Papyri,* 4 vols. (Cairo, 1925–1931); idem, *Zenon Papyri in the University of Michigan Collection* (Ann Arbor, 1931); W. L. Westermann and E. S. Hasenoehrl, *Zenon Papyri: Business Letters of the Third Century B.C.,* 2 vols. (New York, 1934–1940); V. Tcherikover and A. Fuks, *Corpus Papyrorum Judaicarum* (Cambridge, 1957), 1:115-46.

During this time there was a rivalry between the Oniads and Tobiads, two leading Jewish families that were related by marriage. The house of Onias held the high priesthood in succession from Zadok, and the house of Tobias held the right of collecting taxes for the Ptolemies and presumably for the Seleucids. Against this background the Jewish Hellenizers attempted to promote more openly their cultural and political objectives.

The high priest Onias III was in Antioch to answer calumnies by the Tobiads against him, when in 174 B.C. his brother Jason appeared and with the payment of a large bribe secured appointment as high priest from Antiochus IV (175–163 B.C.). It seems Onias III was murdered in Antioch (2 Macc. 4:33ff.) and that his son, Onias IV, who would have been the legitimate high priest, fled to Egypt and continued a pro-Egyptian policy by founding a temple for the military colony of Jewish settlers at Leontopolis/Heliopolis (contrast Josephus, *Ant.* 12.3.1 [62ff.] and *War* 7.10.2 [423ff.]).[12] This event was not important to Egyptian Jewry as a whole, and the temple was closed by the Romans in A.D. 73.

The process of Hellenization in Jerusalem accelerated under Jason. He changed the constitution of Jerusalem from that of a temple-state to a Greek city-state with council, citizen list, gymnasium, and *ephebeia*. To dramatize these changes the city was renamed Antioch. The high priest was now a Seleucid official. The old orthodox Jews were scandalized to see the young aristocrats in Jerusalem wearing the broad-brimmed Greek hat ("by their hats you shall know them"), to hear of the young priests hastening to finish their duties at the temple so that they could go exercise naked in the Greek manner at the gymnasium, and worst of all to learn that some youths underwent an operation to hide their circumcision so as not to be ridiculed by Greeks (1 Macc. 1:13-15; 2 Macc. 4:10-17).

The Seleucids needed money, and rich Jews wanted power in Jerusalem. Menelaus (Menahem) represented the extreme Hellenizers who could not be content with the Oniad Jason. Menelaus, presumably on no ancestral grounds but with Tobiad support, offered a higher sum of money for the high priesthood. Such "piety" could not go unrewarded and he was appointed. The law-loving Jews were exasperated. A clear division appeared between the Hellenizers, who supported Greek culture, and the Ḥasidim (the "pious"), leaders among the people who were loyal to the law and the covenant. The course of events soon eroded any middle ground.

Antiochus IV, escorted by Menelaus, plundered the temple at Jerusalem in 169 B.C. to help finance his plans against Egypt.[13] Plundering temples was

12. A different reconstruction on Onias III is given by Joan E. Taylor, "A Second Temple in Egypt: The Evidence for the Zadokite Temple of Onias," *JSJ* 29 (1998):297-321.

13. For the order of events I follow Victor Tcherikover, *Hellenistic Civilization and the Jews* (Philadelphia, 1961), 152-234; but see Martin Hengel, *Judaism and Hellenism* (Phildelphia, 1974), 1:267-309 for supplement and revision.

TETRADRACHM OF ANTIOCHUS IV, 167 B.C.
The obverse portrays the king, and the reverse (not pictured) Zeus.
The inscription reads "Of King Antiochus, god made manifest and victorious."
(© Erich Lessing/Art Resource, NY)

standard policy, but in this act the Jews saw an early stage of Antiochus's proceedings against their religion. In 168 B.C. Antiochus was on the verge of securing his designs on Egypt and restoring Seleucid power when Rome intervened and forced his withdrawal. Rumor in Jerusalem had it that Antiochus had died in Egypt, so Jason attempted to drive out Menelaus, who fled to the king for support. Faced with an attack from the Syrian army, Jason abandoned the city; after his rebuff in Egypt Antiochus was in no mood to be conciliatory and took a harsh vengeance for the revolt. The walls of Jerusalem were broken down, a new citadel (the Acra) was erected to dominate the temple area, and a garrison was stationed there converting the city into a military settlement. Menelaus and the Jewish Hellenizers collaborated with the military settlers in modifying the temple service into the worship of the Semitic "Lord of Heaven" *(Baal Shamayim),* who was identified with Zeus.

According to Jewish sources Antiochus IV in 168 or 167 B.C.[14] issued decrees prohibiting the practice of the Jewish religion: the Scriptures were to be destroyed, the Sabbath and festivals were no longer to be observed, the food laws were to be abolished, and circumcision was no longer to be practiced (1 Macc. 1:41-64). Moreover, at the end of 168/167 a smaller altar was erected on the top of the great altar of burnt offering, and as the supreme insult to Judaism swine were sacrificed on it. (Feasts of Dionysus included the sacrifice of pigs, and there

---

14. For the change from the traditional 167 and 164 (next page) to 168 and 165, see L. L. Grabbe, "Maccabean Chronology: 167-164 or 168-165 BCE," *JBL* 111 (1991):59-74.

was an identification of the Jewish God with Dionysus.)[15] Although the Jews saw these attempts to promote one cultural policy throughout his realm as a religious persecution, Antiochus's aims may have been strictly political. Actually, it is likely that the initiative for these decrees came not from Antiochus, but from Jews with extreme pro-Hellenistic sympathies, who saw that the only way to maintain their position was to eliminate the traditional religion and win the cooperation of the king or his ministers. Nevertheless, there was justification for Antiochus's contemporaries making a pun on his title *Epiphanes* ("God Manifest") by referring to him as *Epimanes* ("the mad man").[16]

The Maccabean or Hasmonean Period (167–63 B.C.)[17]

Although many Jews followed the decrees against the law, there was also violent resistance to them. The influences of Hellenism had been slower reaching rural districts. The resistance movement came from the people there, augmented by the pious who fled Jerusalem. The books of 1 and 2 Maccabees give an extensive account of the Jewish revolt against the Seleucids and the early years of independence.

When representatives of the government came to the Judean village of Modin and sought to persuade the priest Mattathias as the leading citizen to set an example by sacrificing to the pagan gods, Mattathias not only refused but also killed a Jew who stepped forward to comply with the royal request; in addition he killed the king's officer. Mattathias and his sons then fled to the hills of Judea and called upon all those zealous for the law of their fathers to rally to them. This family soon gained leadership of an organized resistance movement.

Judas (d. 160 B.C.).[18] Before his death Mattathias in 166 or 165 B.C. gave the leadership to Judas, one of his five sons. Judas bore the nickname "Maccabee" (the "hammerer"?), a name that was popularly given to his brothers and their descendants and the resistance movement as a whole. The family, however, is more accurately named Hasmonean from an ancestor Hashmon, and their period may be better termed the Hasmonean period.

From their strongholds in the wilderness Judas and his followers carried on a guerrilla campaign, raiding villages, overthrowing pagan altars, killing Jews who were Hellenist sympathizers, and circumcising children by force. Af-

---

15. Cf. Plutarch, *Moralia* 671C-72C.

16. Polybius 26.1a (10); Athenaeus 10.439a.

17. D. J. Harrington, *The Maccabaean Revolt: Anatomy of a Biblical Revolution* (Wilmington, Del., 1988); Joseph Sievers, *The Hasmoneans and Their Supporters: From Mattathias to the Death of John Hyrcanus I* (Atlanta, 1990).

18. B. Bar-Kochva, *Judas Maccabaeus, The Jewish Struggle against the Seleucids* (Cambridge, 1989).

ter a group of faithful Jews were killed on the Sabbath because they judged it a violation of the commandments to fight on that day, even the Ḥasidim decided to dispense with Sabbath observance when it was necessary for self-defense. For better or worse the *pious* cast their lot with Judas, and the resistance movement assumed the character of a holy war.

Judas proved himself a master of guerrilla tactics. With a knowledge of the countryside and fresh support with each new success, he defeated every Syrian detachment sent after him. The need for troops in the east against the Parthians and internal conflicts kept the Syrians from throwing their full force against the Jewish insurgents.

Finally, in 165 or 164 B.C. Antiochus IV withdrew the ban on the Jewish religion but left Menelaus in the high priesthood and the garrison on the Acra. Nevertheless, Judas's troops moved into Jerusalem and kept the Syrians occupied while the temple area was rededicated. The idol altar was dumped in an "unclean place" (valley of Hinnom?), and the sacred furniture was restored. According to the sad note of 1 Maccabees 4:40 the altar of burnt offering that had been defiled was dismantled and the stones deposited "in a convenient place on the temple hill until there should come a prophet to tell what to do with them." This was one indication of the realization during this period that prophecy had ceased. A new altar built according to the directions in the law was set up. On the twenty-fifth of Kislev (Dec. 14), 165/164 B.C., the third anniversary of the profanation of the altar, the daily burnt offering was resumed. In commemoration of the event a new festival was added to the Jewish religious calendar, *Ḥanukkah* (or "Dedication"; John 10:22), commonly called the Feast of Lights.

When Antiochus IV died the following year, Judas laid siege to the Syrian garrison in Jerusalem. The Syrian regent, Lysias, led an army southward. As he was on the point of crushing Judas's forces, news of trouble for him in Antioch caused him to stop the attack. He confirmed the restoration of the temple service according to ancient practice but ordered the destruction of the fortifications the Maccabees had erected in the temple area. He further deposed Menelaus and nominated Alcimus for the high priesthood.

The Hasmoneans were not content with their achievements and rejected the Syrian-appointed Hellenizer, Alcimus. The Ḥasidim, however, at first accepted Alcimus in return for his recognition that they represented the correct interpretation of the ancestral laws. They withdrew from the revolt once the narrow religious aims had been accomplished, but Judas continued the struggle, undertaking campaigns for religio-political purposes. Judas also began a policy of concentration of the Jewish population, bringing groups of Jews from out-lying regions into Judea for their protection and for the strengthening of his position.

Fresh disturbances by Judas led Alcimus and the Hellenizers to appeal for Syrian help. Judas was killed in an engagement against an overwhelming Syrian army in 160 B.C.

Jonathan (160–143 B.C.). For a time Syrian military power kept Judea quiet, but Judas's brother Jonathan did not give up. Finally, dissension over the Seleucid throne played into his hands.

The pretender Alexander Balas claimed to be the son of Antiochus IV. He won the support of Jonathan's partisans in 152 B.C. by allowing him to maintain a military force and appointing him to the high priesthood, vacant since the death of Alcimus. The Hasmonean period offers many ironies, but one of the strangest was that a Hasmonean, whose family rose in revolt against Antiochus IV for his intervention in Jewish religious affairs that began with deposing and appointing high priests, would accept the high priesthood from one who based his right to bestow it on a claim to be the son of that same Antiochus.

Jonathan had neither the military genius of Judas nor the statesmanship of his successor Simon, but he succeeded in playing off the rival claimants to the Syrian throne until the Syrian general Trypho, acting as regent for the infant son of Alexander Balas, used treachery to imprison and finally kill him.

Simon (143–134 B.C.). The last survivor of the five brothers was Simon. With strong Jewish backing he supported the cause of the Seleucid king Demetrius II against Trypho. In return, Demetrius in 142 B.C. lifted tribute from the Jews, a decision that implied complete independence. The following year the garrison on the Acra was starved out, and the last vestige of Seleucid control was removed from Judea.

An assembly of the Jewish people in 140 B.C. formally proclaimed Simon commander of the army, ethnarch of the nation, and high priest. The last office was confirmed to his family "forever until a trustworthy prophet should arise" (1 Macc. 14:41) to declare the will of God. Up to this time Jonathan and Simon had technically been Seleucid officials; now was laid the legal foundation for the rule of a new dynasty.

Efforts to reassert Syrian authority were repulsed, but Simon (perhaps the worthiest of the sons of Mattathias) was not immune to internal troubles. In 134 B.C. he was assassinated and two of his sons were imprisoned by his son-in-law Ptolemy. The Maccabees had captured the imagination of many people, but later religious leaders were more inclined to examine their conduct in the priesthood. The books about them were not included in the Jewish canon of Scripture.

John Hyrcanus (134–104 B.C.). From the securing of religious freedom under Judas (162 B.C.) to the supplanting of the priestly aristocracy under Jonathan (152 B.C.) to the gaining of political independence under Simon (142 B.C.), the house of Hashmon was to go on to military conquest under John Hyrcanus and to kingship under his sons.

John acted swiftly on the death of his father Simon. He routed Ptolemy, who killed John's two brothers and mother (whom he held before fleeing the country), and was acclaimed by the people as his father's successor.

Beginning in 133 B.C. Antiochus VII succeeded in imposing Seleucid overlordship once more on Judea for five years. With his death no other strong ruler came to the Syrian throne, and the internal weakness of Syria was such that no further threat to Jewish independence came from there. John Hyrcanus was free to embark on a policy of expansion, and he began to use hired mercenaries. He subjugated the Idumeans to the south (Idumea is Latin for Edom) and by compelling them to be circumcised formally incorporated them into the Jewish nation. To the north he destroyed the Samaritan temple on Mount Gerizim (c. 128 B.C.) and captured Samaria (109 B.C.).

Josephus mentions the Pharisees as an opposition group to the Hasmonean high priesthood in connection with the reign of John Hyrcanus (*Ant.* 13.10.5-6 [288-98]). John, however, received the support of another group, the Sadducees, the dominant party in the Sanhedrin (cf. pp. 519-20).

The rule of John Hyrcanus brought stability and security to Judean affairs so that he was remembered as the outstanding Hasmonean leader. Josephus says, "He was accounted by God worthy of three of the greatest privileges — the rule of the nation, the office of high priest, and the gift of prophecy" (*Ant.* 13.10.7 [299]). The last was ascribed to him because of some instances of his allegedly knowing at a distance the outcome of events in which he was vitally interested. Coins attributed to him emphasized the priesthood and associated the people with him: "John the high priest and the congregation of the Jews" (but see p. 92).

Aristobulus I (104–103 B.C.). John's son Aristobulus I was the first of his family to take the title "king" after the fashion of the Hellenistic monarchies (Josephus, *Ant.* 13.11.1 [301] is to be preferred over Strabo 16.2.40, who says Alexander Jannaeus). This is but a further indication of the increasing acceptance of Hellenization by the dynasty that had come to power in reaction against Hellenism. He made conquests in "Galilee of the Gentiles" (the "region" of the Gentiles) and began the settlement of new Jewish colonists in that region. That Joseph of Bethlehem dwelt in Nazareth may be the result of the expansionist policy of the later Hasmoneans, who in order to secure their new conquest settled Jewish colonists in the conquered regions.

Alexander Janneus (103–76 B.C.). Aristobulus's widow, Salome Alexandra, designated his oldest brother, Alexander Janneus, as high priest and king and then married him. Of all the Hasmoneans he acquired the worst reputation.

Alexander extended his conquests to the greatest extent of any Jewish ruler since Solomon. To do this he had to make extensive use of foreign mercenaries. He issued bilingual coins: in Hebrew, "Yehonathan the king," and in Greek, "King Alexander." Alexander was frankly a Hellenistic monarch without scruples who had little regard for the spiritual dignities of his priestly office.

Strained relations soon developed between king and people. We are told how at one Feast of Tabernacles as Alexander was about to offer sacrifice the people began to throw at him the citrons they carried with the palm branches at the festival (Josephus, *Ant.* 13.13.5 [372]). The people finally raised a rebellion against him, which he was compelled to put down with mercenaries. The rebels called in the Seleucid king Demetrius III to aid them. This was the irony of ironies: the Jews who had supported the Hasmoneans in order to throw off the Seleucid yoke now invited a Seleucid king to help rid them of the oppressions of a Hasmonean! Alexander was defeated in the battle, but at the moment of victory the Jews deserted Demetrius and went over to Alexander. Josephus says the strange conduct was due to pity at the sight of their own king helpless (*Ant.* 13.14.2 [379]). There is evidence, however, that the Syrian king attempted to enter the temple, and, more likely, the Jews were roused to resist this sacrilege.

This was the turning point in Alexander's fortunes, and he took gruesome revenge on his most die-hard opponents. While he caroused with his concubines, eight hundred men hung on crosses as their wives and children were butchered at their feet. This introduction of mass crucifixion among the Jews had the desired terrifying effect on dissidents.

The Pharisees were the major antagonists of Alexander Janneus, but according to Josephus (*Ant.* 13.15.5–16.1 [398-406]), the king on his deathbed advised his wife to make peace with them.

Salome Alexandra (76–67 B.C.). Alexander bequeathed his kingdom to his wife, to whom he owed it in the first place. Israel's only queen in second-temple times, she had a better record than did the Old Testament queens. She appointed her elder son, Hyrcanus II, high priest. He was retiring and pliable enough to permit her to run mundane affairs. Under her reign the Pharisees came to dominance in the Sanhedrin.

Hyrcanus II and Aristobulus II (67–63 B.C.). Aristobulus II, the younger son of Alexandra, was ambitious and had allied himself with the Sadducees. On his mother's death, he defeated Hyrcanus II and assumed the kingship and high priesthood. Hyrcanus may have been willing to retire, but Antipater, governor of Idumea, saw an opportunity to use Hyrcanus to advance his own interests and kept strife and suspicion stirred up between the brothers. Civil war broke out between Aristobulus and Hyrcanus, the latter supported by Aretas III, king of the Nabatean Arabs.

The armies of the Roman general Pompey appeared in Syria after having overcome Asia Minor, Armenia, and the last vestiges of Seleucid power. Both Jewish claimants presented their cases to the Romans.

The Roman Period (from 63 B.C.)

The Roman Conquest. The year 63 B.C. was eventful: Cicero was consul; Augustus was born; and Pompey took Jerusalem. When Pompey approached Jerusalem, he sided in favor of Hyrcanus. Aristobulus's followers barricaded themselves in the temple but could not withstand the siege. Josephus records that the priests in the temple court went on with their duties as if nothing were happening (*Ant.* 14.4.3 [65-68]). Pompey entered the Holy of Holies and was amazed to find only emptiness. The shock of his action is reflected in the nearly contemporary *Psalms of Solomon,* the first Jewish writing to express complete hostility toward Rome. The author expresses the ardent expectation of a righteous Davidic king-messiah who would deliver the holy land from unholy enemies. Pompey confirmed Hyrcanus in the high priesthood, but his rule (without the title of king) was confined to Judea and Idumea, a region made tributary to Rome and subject to the oversight of the governor of Syria. The above-mentioned Antipater, who resolved on a course of friendship to whoever represented Roman authority, held the substance of power. During Pompey's time the Greek cities in the region of the Decapolis ("ten cities") were given independence; afterward more cities than ten were included in the designation. Pompey carried many slaves to Rome; later emancipated, they added significantly to the Jewish community in Rome.

Aristobulus II and his two sons revolted unsuccessfully three times against Roman rule between 57 and 55 B.C. Hyrcanus was deprived of civil rule so that the land could be brought under the closer jurisdiction of the governor of Syria.

The last century of the Roman Republic was beset by civil wars, and after Pompey's time Jewish affairs were complicated by these troubles. Antipater and his sons, Phasael and Herod, successfully changed allegiance with each change in Rome — to Julius Caesar, to Mark Antony, and to Octavian. One notable bit of assistance to Caesar brought the Jews to Roman favor. After Pompey's assassination in 48 B.C. Caesar landed in Egypt; but the supporters of Ptolemy XII blockaded him in Alexandria. Timely aid from Antipater enabled Caesar to defeat his enemies, and he responded with favors to the Jews.

According to 1 Maccabees 8, Judas had made an alliance with Rome; and in view of the Roman policy to weaken the Seleucids this is plausible. The Hasmoneans had continued this alliance. Now Caesar granted new privileges, including a reduction in tribute and an exemption from military service. He made Antipater a Roman citizen with the title of procurator of Judea, and he named Hyrcanus ethnarch ("ruler of a people").

Antipater was poisoned in 43 B.C., but Mark Antony made Herod and Phasael joint tetrarchs, once more terminating Hyrcanus's political authority. The title "tetrarch" was used in Roman times to denote the ruler of any part of a province and was inferior in dignity to ethnarch.

Antigonus, son of Aristobulus II, gained power in Judea in 40 B.C. on the strength of a Parthian invasion in which Phasael was killed. For three years he held the titles of king and high priest, the last Hasmonean to do so. He imprisoned his uncle, Hyrcanus II, and bit off his ears (Josephus, *War* 1.13.9 [270]) so as to disqualify him from the high priesthood, since according to the Old Testament the high priest must be without physical defect.

BRONZE COIN OF HEROD THE GREAT

Bronze coins were minted in Judea, but silver and gold coins only at imperial mints. The coin of "Herod the king" shows an incense altar on the reverse *(left)* and a helmet and star between palm branches on the obverse *(right)*.

(Courtesy British Museum)

Herod the Great (37–4 B.C.).[19] Fleeing to Rome, Herod was declared king of the Jews by the senate in 40 B.C. The not-so-easy task of actually winning his kingdom was accomplished in 37 B.C. Herod persuaded Antony to put Antigonus out of the way. He was bound to a cross and flogged — "a punishment no other king had suffered at the hands of the Romans" (Dio Cassius 49.22) — and then killed.[20] Although Herod was officially "friend and ally of the Roman people," as a client king he was bound to carry out the will of Rome.

Herod proved to be an able king. His firm rule brought peace and order to his realm and successfully put down brigandage. He brought great wealth to his kingdom through agricultural and commercial enterprises. He spent these funds in a lavish building program — not only in his own realm but in other cities as well. Most notable for Jewish history was his massive rebuilding of the temple, planned so that the building of the sanctuary was done by trained priests without the interruption of the worship. The rabbis paid tribute to Herod's work by saying, "He who has not seen Herod's temple has not seen beauty" (b. Baba Bathra 4a). Herod had many Gentile subjects as well, and he built temples and other structures for them too. He also built a theatre and am-

---

19. A. H. M. Jones, *The Herods of Judaea* (Oxford, 1938); M. Avi-Yonah and Z. Baras, *The Herodian Period* (New Brunswick, 1977); Peter Richardson, *Herod: King of the Jews and Friend of the Romans* (Columbia, S.C., 1996); Nikos Kokkinos, *The Herodian Dynasty: Origins, Role in Society and Eclipse* (Sheffield, 1998).

20. Josephus, *War* 1.18.3 [357], says he "fell beneath the axe."

phitheatre in Jerusalem; and on the site of Strato's Tower he built the city of Caesarea as the port of entry to his realm.

Although Herod was a Jew by religion, his racial descent was Edomite; and in spite of his efforts to appease the Jews he was never popular. Jewish hostility is expressed in the almost contemporary *Assumption of Moses* 6:2-7. Among his wives was the Hasmonean princess Mariamne, granddaughter of both Hyrcanus II and Aristobulus II. Not only was this marriage politically advantageous for legitimating Herod's position in the eyes of the Jews, he also seems to have had a strong affection for Mariamne. There was constant friction, however, between the Idumean and Hasmonean branches of his family.

Though it may be true that Herod was an extremely able ruler, it is also true that he was intensely jealous of his position. The story of his family and dynastic troubles would make a tragic opera. He killed the two sons of Mariamne when his suspicions were aroused that they might become the rallying point for Jewish patriotism. Mariamne herself was killed when his mind was poisoned against her by his sister. The slaughter of the infants of Bethlehem (Matt. 2) finds no independent confirmation in sources outside the New Testament, but the incident fits well the reign of terror of Herod's last years. A man who killed a large part of his own family and arrested large numbers of the most prominent citizens with orders for their execution when he died so there would be mourning at his death (Josephus, *Ant.* 17.6.5 [173-75], but not carried out — 8.2 [193]) would not have caused much of a stir by liquidating a score of children in an obscure village. Knowing of Herod's conduct and the Jewish scruples about pork, the emperor Augustus was reported to have said that he would rather be Herod's pig than Herod's son.[21]

Herod's Sons.[22] On Herod's death in 4 B.C., in spite of Jewish pleas that the former temple-constitution be restored with internal autonomy under a governor appointed by the emperor, his kingdom was divided by Rome basically according to his will (cf. Matt. 2:22; Luke 3:1).

Archelaus received Judea, Samaria, and Idumea as ethnarch. He possessed his father's bad qualities without his abilities. Protests from the Jews and Samaritans finally secured his dismissal in A.D. 6 (Luke 19:11-15 seems to draw details from what happened to him).

Philip was made tetrarch of Iturea and Trachonitis, northeast of the Sea of Galilee. Until his death in A.D. 34 he governed justly and conscientiously. He rebuilt his capital of Panion (modern Banias) and named it Caesarea (Caesarea Philippi). Philip married Salome, daughter of his half-brother Herod Philip by Herodias. Josephus's judgment was that "in his conduct of the government he showed a moderate and easy-going disposition" (*Ant.* 18.4.6 [106]).

---

21. Macrobius, *Saturnalia* 2.f.11. Although reported in Latin, the saying depends on a pun in Greek — *hyn* (pig) and *huion* (son).

22. S. Perowne, *The Later Herods* (London, 1958).

Herod Antipas[23] was made tetrarch over Galilee and Perea. The most capable and astute of the brothers, he ruled for some forty years. He divorced the
daughter of the Nabatean king Aretas IV (9 B.C.–A.D. 40; cf. 2 Cor. 11:32) in order to marry his niece Herodias, the wife of his half-brother Herod Philip (not
to be confused with Philip the tetrarch). John the Baptist's condemnation of
this union led to his execution (Mark 6:17-28). Josephus, who also relates the
story (*Ant.* 18.5.2 [116-19]; see p. 487), says that a heavy defeat inflicted on
Antipas by Aretas was interpreted as divine retribution for his treatment of
John.[24]

The Early Governors (A.D. 6-41).[25] In A.D. 6 the territory of Archelaus was
made a Roman province and placed under imperial governors known as prefects and after 44 as procurators (see pp. 43-44). The governors established
their residence at Caesarea on the coast and went up to Jerusalem only on the
feast days and other special occasions, but a strong Roman military presence
was maintained in Jerusalem at all times. Whereas Herod had made frequent
changes in the high priesthood to keep the office under his control, the governors did so to enrich themselves. The man who held the office the longest in
the first century was Joseph Caiaphas,[26] son-in-law of Annas, who officiated
from A.D. 18 to 36. The Sanhedrin, the council of seventy presided over by the
high priest, had considerable, if limited, authority over internal affairs. The
Romans in general showed great respect for Jewish religious scruples: for example, Jews were exempted from appearing before a magistrate on a Sabbath
or holy day; a sacrifice offered at the temple "for Caesar and the Roman nation"
was taken as a sufficient expression of loyalty; and copper coins minted in the

---

23. H. W. Hoehner, *Herod Antipas* (Cambridge, 1972).

24. Douglas A. Campbell, "An Anchor for Pauline Chronology: Paul's Flight from 'the
Ethnarch of King Aretas' (2 Corinthians 11:32-33)," *JBL* 121 (2002):279-302 argues the case that this
was the occasion when Aretas IV gained control of Damascus and appointed an ethnarch as governor of the city with the result that the date for Paul's flight from Damascus is late A.D. 36 or early
37.

25. The early governors were as follows:
      Coponius, A.D. 6–9 (*War* 2.8.1 [117])
      Marcus Ambibulus, A.D. 9–12 (*Ant.* 18.2.2 [31])
      Annius Rufus, A.D. 12–15 (*Ant.* 18.2.2 [32-33])
      Valerius Gratus, A.D. 15–26 (*Ant.* 18.2.2 [33])
      Pontius Pilate, A.D. 26–36 (see below)
      Marcellus, A.D. 36–37 (*Ant.* 18.4.2 [89])
      Marullus, A.D. 37–41 (*Ant.* 18.6.10 [237])

26. An ossuary apparently bearing his name has been found in Jerusalem. Final report on
the excavations by Zvi Greenhut, "The Caiaphas Tomb in North Talpiot, Jerusalem," *Antiqot* 21
(1992); popular report by idem, "Burial Cave of the Caiaphas Family," and Ronny Reich,
"Caiaphas Name Inscribed on Bone Boxes," *Biblical Archaeology Review* 18 (1992):28-36, 76 and 38-
44, 76. William Horbury, "The 'Caiphas' Ossuaries and Joseph Caiaphas," *Palestine Exploration
Quarterly* 126 (1994):32-48 points out that the ossuary inscription does not correspond exactly to
the name attested in Josephus and the New Testament.

country carried no human portrait but only the emperor's name and inoffensive emblems, as did the Roman standards.

The best known of the early governors (p. 43) is the one of most interest to readers of the Gospels, Pontius Pilate[27] (A.D. 26–36). Some scholars see a contrast between the portrayal of Pilate's attitude toward the Jews in Philo and Josephus (harsh) and in the Gospels (weak and accommodating). One explanation for the apparent difference is that Pilate changed from arrogance in his early years as governor to deference at the trial of Jesus because of the fall from power of his powerful patron in Rome, Sejanus, prefect of the praetorian guard. Another view denies a fundamental discrepancy between the Jewish and Christian sources: Pilate, ignorant and insensitive to Jewish concerns, was provocative toward them, but he was ultimately indecisive and had a knack for getting into trouble and having to back down.[28] The general picture that emerges is of a governor loyal to Rome, intent on preserving order, trying to avoid excessive bloodshed, and flexible in the face of demonstrations. He was the first of the governors seriously to antagonize the Jewish populace.

Four episodes from Pilate's governorship are reported outside the Gospels. Shortly after assuming office, under cover of night he introduced into Jerusalem Roman standards to which were attached images of the emperor (Josephus, *Ant.* 18.3.1 [55-59]; *War* 2.9.2-3 [169-74]). Large numbers of Jews appeared before Pilate in Caesarea imploring him to remove the standards from Jerusalem. When he refused, they fell prostrate around his house and remained in that position for five days and nights. On the next day Pilate took his seat on the tribunal in the stadium and summoned the Jews. He then had soldiers surround them and threatened to cut them down unless they admitted the images of Caesar. The Jews, however, fell to the ground and as one man bared their necks to the sword. The astonished Pilate relented and ordered the standards removed from Jerusalem.

In a later incident Pilate did not yield to the Jews. He had taken funds from the sacred treasury known as Korban (cf. Matt. 27:6) to pay for the construction of an aqueduct into Jerusalem (*Ant.* 18.3.2 [60-62]; *War* 2.9.4 [175-77]), from his standpoint a normal thing to do. When he visited Jerusalem, a crowd of Jews protested this use of money devoted to the purchase of sacrificial animals. Pilate had interspersed among the crowd soldiers in civilian dress armed with cudgels. On an agreed signal they began to beat the rioters. A large number perished, and the protest was silenced.

In an incident that probably occurred toward the end of his governorship,

---

27. Paul L. Maier, *Pontius Pilate* (Garden City, N.Y., 1968); Jean-Pierre Lémonon, *Pilate et le gouvernement de la Judée: Textes et monuments* (Paris, 1981); Helen Bond, *Pontius Pilate in History and Interpretation* (Cambridge, 1998); Anne Wroe, *Pontius Pilate* (New York, 2001).

28. The former view is stated by Paul L. Maier, "Sejanus, Pilate, and the Date of the Crucifixion," *Church History* 37 (1968):3-13; the latter is argued by Brian C. McGing, "Pontius Pilate and the Sources," *CBQ* 53 (1991):416-438.

COPY OF PILATE INSCRIPTION
The only inscription found containing the name of Pontius Pilate is important for establishing that his correct Latin title was "Prefect." The original, now in the Israel Museum, Jerusalem, was found at the theatre in Caesarea. Transcribed on p. 44n.35.
(Milan Archaeological Museum)

Pilate dedicated in Herod's palace in Jerusalem some shields coated with gold, inscribed with his name and Tiberius's (which presumably included his title as "son of the deified Augustus"), "not so much to honor Tiberius as to annoy the multitude" (Philo, *Embassy to Gaius* 38.299-305).[29] The Jews asked for them to be removed as an infringement of their traditions. Pilate, "naturally inflexible, a blend of self-will and relentlessness," refused. The Jews then threatened to send a petition to Tiberius. Pilate feared that an embassy to the emperor would "expose the rest of his conduct as governor by stating in full the briberies, the insults, the executions without trial constantly repeated, the ceaseless and supremely grievous cruelty." Letters finally were sent, and Tiberius ordered the shields removed from Jerusalem and set up in the temple of Augustus at Caesarea.

Pilate's wrath was not limited to the Jews. A Samaritan convinced a number of his countrymen that if they accompanied him to Mount Gerizim he would show them the sacred vessels Moses had buried there (Josephus, *Ant.* 18.4.1-2 [88-89]). The people showed up armed, but Pilate blocked their ascent with a detachment of soldiers, who killed many of the assembled Samaritans. A council of the Samaritans went to Vitellius, governor of Syria, to protest that their purposes were religious, not rebellious. Vitellius removed Pilate from office and dispatched him to Rome to give an account to the emperor Tiberius, who died before Pilate arrived.

Herod Agrippa I.[30] One of Mariamne and Herod's sons left a child who became known to history as Herod Agrippa. He was sent to Rome by Herod for an education. There he lived a dissolute life but made an important friend, the future emperor Gaius Caligula (see p. 32).

When Caligula came to the throne in A.D. 37, he gave Agrippa the former tetrarchies of Philip and Lysanias (Luke 3:1) with the title of king. Herodias, Agrippa's sister and now wife of Herod Antipas, urged her husband to secure the title of king for himself. When Antipas went to Rome for this purpose, intimations of disloyalty from Agrippa led to his banishment in A.D. 39. To Herodias's credit she chose to accompany her husband into exile. Antipas's tetrarchy was now given to Agrippa.

Caligula, indignant at the Jewish attitudes, conceived the mad idea in A.D. 40 of ordering his statue to be erected at the temple in Jerusalem (Josephus, *Ant.* 18.8.2-9 [261-309]; *War* 2.10.1-5 [184-203]; Philo, *Embassy to Gaius* 29.184-42.348; Tacitus, *History* 5.9). He sent Petronius, governor of Syria, with two legions to enforce the order. Generally, as noted above, the Romans had respected Jewish feelings, but Caligula was not an ordinary Roman ruler. Agrippa's intercession convinced Caligula to send further word that if the stat-

---

29. Some consider this incident a variant account of the first, but see Paul L. Maier, "The Episode of the Golden Roman Shields at Jerusalem," *HTR* 62 (1969):109-21, and Gideon Fuks, "Again on the Episode of the Gilded Roman Shields at Jerusalem," *HTR* 75 (1982):503-7.

30. D. R. Schwartz, *Agrippa I: The Last King of Judaea* (Tübingen, 1990).

ues had not yet been erected to take no further action. Petronius, however, had already written to the emperor that it was impossible to carry out the order without exterminating the Jewish people. For this insubordination Caligula commanded Petronius to commit suicide. Due to wind currents, however, the ship bearing the news of Caligula's assassination at Rome reached Syria twenty-seven days before the suicide order did.

When Claudius became emperor in A.D. 41, he continued to favor Agrippa, this time by adding the province of Judea to his territory. Outwardly Agrippa took every care to court the favor of the Jews, not only observing the customs of the people but also beheading James the son of Zebedee and imprisoning Peter (Acts 12). According to the Mishnah, when at the Feast of Tabernacles in A.D. 41 he read from Deuteronomy according to custom and came to the passage, "You may not put a foreigner over you" (Deut. 17:15), he wept; but the people cried out, "Grieve not, Agrippa; you are our brother! You are our brother!" (Sotah 7.8). On the other hand, he struck coins bearing the image of the Caesars and pagan scenes and participated in pagan ceremonies.

Agrippa's gruesome death in A.D. 44 is recounted by Josephus (*Ant.* XIX.viii.2 [343-52]) as well as in Acts 12:20-23.

Herod Agrippa II. At seventeen, Agrippa's son was not judged ready to rule in his father's place. About A.D. 50, however, he succeeded his uncle, Herod king of Chalcis, on the latter's death. This kingdom was exchanged in A.D. 53 for his father's former holdings north and east of the Sea of Galilee. Although he never ruled over Jewish territory, he was given supervision of the temple services and the right of appointing the high priest, and the Romans looked to him as an expert in Jewish affairs. In the latter capacity he heard Paul's defense (Acts 26). He was accompanied on the occasion by Bernice, his sister and widow of his uncle Herod; his relations with her were the subject of widespread scandal (Josephus, *Ant.* 20.7.3 [145]; Juvenal 6.156-60). Bernice later lived for a time with Titus (Tacitus, *History* 2.2; Suetonius, *Titus* 7). Agrippa strongly supported the Romans and sought to dissuade the Jews from continuing the revolt that broke out in 66. With his death about 92/93 the last Herodian territory was incorporated into the province of Syria, and the Herodian family passed from history.

The Later Governors (A.D. 44–66).[31] With the death of Agrippa I the gov-

---

31. The later governors were as follows:

    Cuspius Fadus, A.D. 44-46 (*Ant.* 19.9.2 [363]; *War* 2.11.6 [220])

    Tiberius Julius Alexander, A.D. 46-48 (*Ant.* 20.5.2 [100])

    Ventidus Cumanus, A.D. 48-52 (*Ant.* 20.5.2 [103]; *War* 2.12.1-7 [223-46])

    Antonius Felix, A.D. 52-59 or 60? (*Ant.* 20.7.1 [137]; *War* 2.12.8 [247]; Suetonius, *Claudius* 28)

    Porcius Festus, A.D. 59 or 60-61 or 62? (*Ant.* 20.8.9 [182]; *War* 2.14.1 [271])

    Albinus, A.D. 61 or 62-64 (*Ant.* 20.9.1 [197]; *War* 2.14.1-2 [272-77])

    Gessius Florus, A.D. 64-66 (*Ant.* 20.11.1 [252-53]; *War* 2.14.2 [277])

ernment of Judea reverted to governors (procurators). The later governors were a bad lot; and if Josephus is to be believed, they became steadily worse. Mention may be made of Tiberius Alexander,[32] the nephew of Philo but an apostate from Judaism who later as prefect of Egypt took the lead in declaring Vespasian emperor, and Felix and Festus, before whom Paul made appearances (Acts 24, 25). Felix, although only a freedman, had three wives of royal birth, the last of which, Drusilla, was a sister of Agrippa II and Bernice. According to Tacitus's oft-cited characterization of him, "practicing every kind of cruelty and lust, he exercised royal power with the instincts of a slave" (*Histories* 5.9). About the year 62 when Festus died and Albinus had not arrived, the high priest Ananus (or Annas) II, son of the Annas of the Gospels, took advantage of the opportunity to kill James the brother of Jesus and the leading Christian in Jerusalem.[33]

The First Jewish Revolt (A.D. 66–70).[34] The request by the Jews at the trial of Jesus for the release of Barabbas, a revolutionary (Mark 15:6-15), and not Jesus, the prince of peace, was symbolic of the next century of Jewish history; they got what they asked for — many false messiahs and revolutionaries. The word for the "robbers" *(lēstai)* crucified with Jesus is often used by Josephus in reference to "revolutionaries." The instances of insurrection mentioned in Acts 5:36-37 and 21:38 also are recounted by Josephus: Theudas, although placed at a different date (*Ant.* 20.5.1 [97-99]), Judas the Galilean (*Ant.* 18.1.1 [4-10]; *War* 2.8.1 [118]), and the Egyptian (*Ant.* 20.8.6 [169-72]; *War* 2.13.5 [261-63]). And these insurrections represent only a small part of the disturbances in first-century Palestine. Even good governors had to contend with Jewish resentment against foreign rule and memories of independence. Revolutionary ideology (see below on Zealots, pp. 532-53) had a considerable following, and even moderates in the populace could be provoked by incidents.

The seizure of seventeen talents from the temple treasury by the governor Florus, coming after a string of incidents in an atmosphere of seething unrest, precipitated the revolt of A.D. 66. The legate of Syria advanced on Jerusalem to put down the disturbance, but he was put to flight, and Zealot leaders were convinced the hour of deliverance had come. Moderates tried to stave off the revolt, but to no avail.

Nero appointed Vespasian to put down the revolt. By the end of 67 Gali-

32. E. G. Turner, "Tiberius Iulius Alexander," *JRS* 44 (1954):54-64.

33. Josephus, *Ant.* 20.9.1 [200]; see pp. 458-59; Eusebius, *Church History* 2.23.1-18; *Second Apocalypse of James* (Nag Hammadi Library V, 4) 61-62.

34. David M. Rhoads, *Israel in Revolution 6–74 C.E.* (Philadelphia, 1976). R. A. Horsley and J. S. Hanson, *Bandits, Prophets, and Messiahs: Popular Movements at the Time of Jesus* (Minneapolis, 1985); M. Goodman, *The Ruling Class of Judaea: The Origins of the Jewish Revolt Against Rome, A.D. 66-70* (Cambridge, 1987); Edwin Yamauchi, "Christians and the Jewish Revolts Against Rome," *Fides et Historia* 23 (1991):11-30; J. J. Price, *Jerusalem under Siege: The Collapse of the Jewish State, 66-70 C.E.* (Leiden, 1992); Neil Faulkner, *Apocalypse: The Great Jewish Revolt Against Rome* (Stroud, 2002).

SHEKEL OF FIRST JEWISH REVOLT
Coins of the Jewish revolt use Jewish symbols and Hebrew inscriptions.
This "shekel of Israel" shows a chalice and is dated year one of the
revolt, A.D. 66. *(Courtesy British Museum)*

lee was subdued. Its command had been held by Josephus, who has left a very
detailed account of the progress of the war *(The Jewish War)*. He went over to
the Romans and won the patronage of Vespasian by predicting he would become emperor. By 68 Judea was subjugated, but Nero's death brought a suspension of operations. According to a report in Eusebius (*Church History*
3.5.3), Christians abandoned Jerusalem and took refuge in the Transjordan,
principally at Pella in the Decapolis.[35] The year A.D. 69 was the year of the
"four emperors" in Roman history. Out of the civil war Vespasian emerged
victorious.

In the meantime Vespasian had left his son Titus to lay siege to Jerusalem.
The siege was pressed in earnest in A.D. 70. Three rival factions among the rebels contested for leadership, and the internecine strife of the Jews hastened the
fall of the city. In July Herod's fortress of Antonia was captured. On the ninth
day of the fifth month (August 5), the anniversary of the destruction of the first
temple by the Babylonians, the sanctuary was set on fire by the invaders. A
month later the whole city was in Titus's hands. The arch of Titus on the east
end of the Forum in Rome depicts the table of showbread and seven-branched
lampstand from the temple being carried in the triumphal procession. Some
strongholds held out longer. The last to fall was Masada (possibly as late as 74),
where the defenders chose suicide to surrender (Josephus, *War* 7.8.1-7 [252-
388]). Judea was made a full province governed by a legate of praetorian rank.

35. Reservations on the historicity of this tradition are set forth by Gerd Lüdemann, "The
Successors of pre-70 Jerusalem Christianity," in *Jewish and Christian Self-Definition*, Vol. 1, ed.
E. P. Sanders (Philadelphia, 1980), 161-73.

ARCH OF TITUS, Rome
Inside the Arch of Titus on the Forum in Rome the suppression of the Jewish revolt was celebrated in the representation of the triumphal procession carrying the seven-branched lampstand from the temple to Rome. *(Courtesy B. K. Condit)*

The organization and worship of Jewry were profoundly affected. The Sanhedrin was dissolved, and the temple could no longer serve as a center of unity.

Jewish Reorganization. During the height of the siege of Jerusalem, according to one story (*Aboth R. Nathan* 4.11b-12a), Rabbi Johanan ben Zakkai was smuggled out of the city in a coffin and secured permission from Roman authorities to reestablish his academy at Jamnia (Yavneh). Johanan was a leader of the school of Hillel, lenient in the interpretation of the law, and in favor of submission to Rome. He was a colorful figure, had been a priest but not a Sadducee, was reputed to be the only survivor from the pre-70 Sanhedrin, and was learned in the oral tradition (see further p. 491). Although other rabbinic academies grew up after the destruction, that of Johanan became the dominant one and later received official authorization from Rome as representing the Jewish people.

The academy at Jamnia became the administrative seat of Jewish life. Its council, *bet-din* (lit. "house of judgment"), became a successor to the Sanhedrin at Jerusalem. Under Johanan and Gamaliel II, grandson of Paul's teacher, postdestruction Judaism took shape. The Jamnia period marks the beginning of the change from a temple-oriented Judaism comprising a variety of sects to a more united Judaism centered around the local synagogues.[36] The rabbis at Jamnia discussed the canonicity of certain Old Testament books (Ecclesiastes, Song of Songs), but these discussions had more of the nature of settling doubts as to why these books were recognized than they were a determination of the canon. They were debating a canon they received, not creating one (p. 540). Acceptance by the community was determinative in making books authoritative. At least, there was nothing like a "Council of Jamnia" comparable to the later Christian councils that listed the New Testament books.[37]

Later Revolts and Results. Vespasian ordered the closing of the temple at Leontopolis lest it become a rallying point. Nevertheless, there was an uprising of Jewish communities in Cyrene, Egypt, and Cyprus in A.D. 115 during the reign of Trajan.[38] The fighting was savage, and the revolt was not put down until 117. This was the only known Jewish rebellion in the Diaspora, and it seems

36. S. J. D. Cohen, "The Significance of Yavneh: Pharisees, Rabbis, and the End of Jewish Sectarianism," *Hebrew Union College Annual* 55 (1984):27-53.

37. Jack Lewis, "What Do We Mean by Jabneh?" *Journal of Bible and Religion* 32 (1964):125-32; idem, "Jamnia After Forty Years," *Hebrew Union College Annual* 70-71 (1999-2000):233-59. See p. 540n.274 for bibliography on the Hebrew canon.

38. S. Applebaum, "Notes on the Jewish Revolt under Trajan," *JJS* 2 (1950):26-30; idem, "The Jewish Revolt in Cyrene in 115–117 and the Subsequent Recolonisation," *JJS* 2 (1951):177-86; idem, "Cyrenensia Iudaica: Some Notes on Recent Research Relating to the Jews of Cyrenaica in the Hellenistic and Roman Periods," *JJS* 13 (1962):31-43; A. Fuks, "The Jewish Revolt in Egypt (A.D. 115–117) in the Light of the Papyri," *Aegyptus* 33 (1953):131-58; idem, "The Jewish Revolt of 115–117," *Journal of Roman Studies* 51 (1961):98-104; V. Tcherikover, "The Decline of the Jewish Diaspora in Egypt in the Roman Period," *JJS* 14 (1963):1-32; S. Applebaum, *Jews and Greeks in Ancient Cyrene* (Leiden, 1979).

AERIAL VIEW OF MASADA
Herod built a palace and fortress at this easily defensible site near the Dead Sea.
Sicarii occupied the site in the first revolt against Rome and held out at least
three years after the temple in Jerusalem fell. *(Courtesy Werner Braun)*

to have been prompted more by the Jewish quest for greater rights and civil status than by messianic aspirations.

The Jews still had not fully learned their lesson.[39] Two edicts of the emperor Hadrian, not aimed at the Jews, caused them to revolt in Palestine in 132: imposing the death penalty for castration, which was worded to include circumcision (*Historia Augusta, Life of Hadrian* 14.2), and planning to rebuild Je-

39. S. Applebaum, *Prolegomena to the Study of the Second Jewish Revolt (A.D. 132–135)* (Oxford, 1976); Joseph A. Fitzmyer, "The Bar Cochba Period," in *Essays on the Semitic Background of the New Testament* (Missoula, Mont., 1974), 305-54; Peter Schäfer, ed., *The Bar-Kokhba War Reconsidered* (Tübingen, 2003).

COIN OF BAR KOKHBA

The religious ideology of the second Jewish revolt is shown by the representation
of the temple and the ark of the covenant on this silver shekel.
(Courtesy British Museum)

rusalem as Aelia Capitolina with a temple to Zeus on the site of the old temple
(Dio Cassius 69.12).[40] A leader arose by the name of Simon, who was recognized by Rabbi Akiba, a student of Johanan's at Jamnia, as the Messiah.[41] He
was designated Bar Kokhba, "son of a star," from Numbers 24:17. Later, when
his revolt failed, he was called Bar (or Ben) Koziba, "son of a lie." Since some of
his correspondence during the revolt has been discovered in connection with
the neighboring Dead Sea Scrolls, we know that both were puns on his proper
name, Simon (Shimeon) ben Koseba. The villages that were destroyed and the
numbers of Jews killed or sold into slavery left Judea no longer Jewish, ended
Jewish nationalism, and marked the end of accommodations to Hellenism. After the suppression of the Bar Kokhba revolt in 135 Judea was devastated and
the center of Jewish life became Galilee. The principal rabbinic academy was
now located at Usha, but eventually the center of learning became Tiberias.[42]

40. Some have argued that these actions by Hadrian were the result rather than the cause
of the rebellion; see H. Mantel, "The Causes of the Bar Kokba Revolt," *JQR* 58 (1968):224-42. Recently discovered coins seem to confirm Dio Cassius on the founding of Aelia Capitolina before
the revolt — Hanan Eshel, "Aelia Capitolina: Jerusalem No More," *Biblical Archaeology Review*
23.6 (1997):46-48, 73.

41. Y. Yadin, *Bar-Kokhba: The Rediscovery of the Legendary Hero of the Last Jewish Revolt
against Imperial Rome* (London, 1971).

42. For the later history, see M. Avi-Yonah, *The Jews of Palestine: A Political History from the
Bar Kokhba War to the Arab Conquest* (Oxford, 1976); G. Alon, *The Jews in Their Land in the Talmudic Age*, 2 vols. (Jerusalem, 1980, 1984); Lee Levine, ed., *The Galilee in Late Antiquity* (Cambridge, Mass., 1992).

The execution of the two Jameses, the Christians' flight from Jerusalem, the excommunication of Christians from the synagogue under Gamaliel II (but see pp. 491-92), and the Bar Kokhba revolt — these events marked a century of increasing alienation between Jews and Christians. The separation of Christianity and Judaism was a process over a period of time.

By now the Romans had learned their lesson. With the suppression of the revolt in 135 Hadrian proceeded with his plans for Jerusalem: the official name of the city became Colonia Aelia Capitolina, and a temple to Jupiter Capitolinus was erected on the site of the former temple and a statue of Hadrian set up. Hadrian forbade Jews to set foot there, and so Jerusalem became the pagan city (but not of the same kind) envisioned in the days of Antiochus IV.

Rome dealt with the Jews through a patriarch.[43] The patriarchate was hereditary in the family of Hillel until it was abolished in the fifth century. The patriarchs claimed descent from David and so were termed *Nasi* by the Jews, a title with royal connotations. Otherwise, Judaism was detached from nationalism until the founding of the modern Israeli state. Judaism had already been set on its course as a religion of the synagogue and law, divorced from temple and land. The Judaism that emerged in the period between A.D. 70 and the compiling of the Talmuds became normative for Judaism until modern times.

BIBLIOGRAPHY

1 and 2 Maccabees.
Josephus. *The Jewish War. Jewish Antiquities.*
Smallwood, Mary. *The Jews under Roman Rule from Pompey to Diocletian.* Leiden, 1976. Rev. ed. 1981.

Ben-Sasson, H. H., ed. *A History of the Jewish People.* Cambridge, Mass., 1976.
Hayes, J. H., and J. M. Miller. *Israelite and Judean History.* Philadelphia, 1977.
Freyne, Sean. *Galilee from Alexander the Great to Hadrian: 323 B.C.E. to 135 C.E.* Notre Dame, 1980.
Schalit, A. *The Hellenistic Age: Political History of Jewish Palestine from 332 B.C.E. to 67 B.C.E.* New Brunswick, 1972.
Jagersma, H. *A History of Israel from Alexander the Great to Bar Kochba.* Philadelphia, 1986.
Bickerman, E. *The Jews in the Greek Age.* 4th ed. Cambridge, Mass., 1988.
Millar, F. G. B. *The Roman Near East 31 B.C.–A.D 337.* Cambridge, Mass., 1993.
Schäfer, Peter. *The History of the Jews in Antiquity: The Jews of Palestine from Alexander the Great to the Arab Conquest.* Luxembourg, 1995. (German original, 1983.)

43. Lee Levine, "The Jewish Patriarch (Nasi) in Third Century Palestine," *ANRW* II, *Principat*, 19.2 (Berlin and New York, 1979), 649-88; M. Goodman, *State and Society in Roman Galilee, A.D. 132-212* (Totowa, N.J., 1983); Ephrat Habas, *The Patriarchs — a Jewish Dynasty in Roman Palestine* (Leiden, 1995).

Tcherikover, V. *Hellenistic Civilization and the Jews*. Reprint ed. with preface by J. J. Collins. Peabody, 1999.

Sacchi, Paolo. *The History of the Second Temple Period*. Sheffield, 2001.

Satre, Maurice. *D'Alexandre à Zenobie: Histoire du levant antique IVe siècle avant J. C.–IIIe siècle après J. C.* Paris, 2001.

JEWS IN THE EARLY ROMAN EMPIRE

The Jewish dispersion, which had its origin in the Assyrian and Babylonian captivities of Old Testament times and had been furthered by the Hellenistic and Roman rulers (pp. 399-400, 404-5) and the normal movement of families in the mobile conditions of Hellenistic and Roman times, had by the beginning of the Christian era covered the Roman empire and the Parthian empire to the east. Strabo could say that "it is not easy to find a place in the inhabited world which this tribe has not penetrated and which has not been occupied by it."[44] As many as two-thirds of the Jews in the first century were living outside Palestine. Besides the large and important communities in ancient Babylonia (pp. 399-400, 496-97) now under Parthian rule, the largest concentrations of Jews outside Palestine were in Syria and Egypt, but sizeable groups were found throughout Asia Minor and not insignificant numbers in Phoenicia, Cyrene, Greece, and Rome, with probably lesser numbers farther west. By the first century the Jewish population had grown enormously.[45] Estimates of the total numbers of Jews are little more than guesses and range from three to eight million, but even minimum estimates put the number of Jews at about 7 percent of the population of the Roman empire.[46] The large numbers of Jews would have been due not only to reproduction but also to conversions, whether by force, as during the Maccabean wars (pp. 409-11), or by attraction (pp. 549-50). A notable development in the first century was the conversion of the king of Adiabene, Izates, and his mother, Helena (p. 546).[47]

The problem of numbers is complicated (apart from the lack of statistical information) by the difficulty of defining a Jew. We have a general idea of what is meant today, but when racial, religious, or even political aspects are considered, a precise definition is hard to give. We have even less confidence about the viewpoints from which Jews were being perceived in the Roman world. See

44. Quoted by Josephus, *Ant.* 14.7.2 [115]; other statements in *Sibylline Oracles* 3.271-72; Philo, *Embassy to Gaius* 36.281-83 (cf. 214, 245); *Against Flaccus* 7.45-46; Josephus, *War* 2.16.4 [398]; 7.3.3 [43].

45. Diodorus Siculus 40.3.8 (citing Hecataeus of Abdera); Strabo, *Geography* 16.2.28; Philo, *Life of Moses* 2.42.232.

46. V. Tcherikover, *Hellenistic Civilization and the Jews* (Philadelphia, 1961), 292-93.

47. Josephus, *Ant.* 20.2.1-5 [17ff.].

p. 537 for a certain minimum definition in terms of common practices and beliefs. Even allowing for exceptions to the few common features noted there, they are a reminder that Judaism was a single if by no means uniform phenomenon. Nevertheless, Josephus himself wavers on the status of Herod (*Ant.* 14.1.3 [8-9]; 11.4 [283]; 15.2 [403]; 20.8.7 [173]) and is not fully consistent on the Samaritans (*Ant.* 9.14.3 [288-91]; 11.8.6-7 [340-46]). Compromises were made on such minimum matters as circumcision (see on Izates, p. 546). When the varieties within first-century Judaism in Palestine alone are considered (pp. 513ff.), we are warned against simplistic definitions.

Most cultivated Greeks and Romans expressed a negative attitude toward Jews (pp. 512-13). Various reasons lay behind this judgment: Jews shared the opprobrium in which easterners in the Greco-Roman cities were held; the Jewish religion and customs were strange according to Greek standards; the Jews were resented for their privileges and their efforts to secure further political advancement. The other side of the picture was the attraction to Judaism (pp. 546, 550).

The Jews themselves in the early empire, whether in Palestine or abroad, experienced the impact of Greek culture.[48] This was felt more strongly in their western dispersion, but even in Greek cities it was more a matter of degree than something providing a difference in substance between "Hellenistic" and "Palestinian" Judaism. The use of Hellenistic literary forms in the New Testament (pp. 120-27) was already present in Judaism. As the Greek language, literature, education, and customs became known and to a degree accepted, Judaism felt the influence of universalism and individualism (pp. 9, 14-15). The Jews responded in a variety of ways to Hellenistic and Roman cultural influences. In this they were no different from other peoples transplanted from one culture to another or brought into contact with another culture: some "go native" and reject their traditions for the customs of the new culture; some withdraw into a mental, if not neighborhood, "ghetto"; and others make various intermediate compromises with the new situation. Jews may be found representing the whole range of reactions. Some turned to their own traditions and customs with a fiercer and more uncompromising loyalty than before. Many who joined the Maccabean revolt (pp. 407-8) opposed any compromise with Hellenism. An unusual but probably not unique example of the opposite reaction of assimilation to Hellenism was the Jew reported by Clearchus of Soli to have been "Greek not only in his language, but also in his soul."[49] And there were prominent Jews who apostatized from the law, such as Tiberius Alexander (p. 420). Others simply did not stress their Jewishness. More often the as-

48. S. Lieberman, *Greek in Jewish Palestine* (New York, 1942); idem, *Hellenism in Jewish Palestine* (New York, 1950); Martin Hengel, *The "Hellenization" of Judaea in the First Century after Christ* (Philadelphia, 1990); John J. Collins and Gregory E. Sterling, eds., *Hellenism in the Land of Israel* (Notre Dame, 2000).

49. Quoted by Josephus, *Against Apion* 1.180.

similation, it seems, was of the forms of Hellenism and not of its spirit and content. Rabbi Meir could say, "When in Rome do as the Romans do" (*Gen. Rab.* 48). Although there were varying degrees of accommodation to the new environment, the Jews maintained their distinctiveness more successfully than did any other people of the Mediterranean world. Jewish writers in Greek stressed certain characteristics of Judaism: monotheism and an aniconic cult, compliance with the law of Moses and ancestral customs, moral ideals, Sabbath observance, circumcision, and abstinence from pork. Indeed, an emphasis on certain distinctives may have been more characteristic of the dispersion than of Palestinian Jewry, perhaps because this was necessary. Even where much else might be given up, the Sabbath, circumcision, and the law were emphasized.

Judaism enjoyed a privileged position in the Roman empire. The Jews were an ancient people with a traditional religion, had been allied with Rome during the Maccabean age, and had rendered important assistance to Roman leaders such as Julius Caesar. Consequently the Jews had free exercise of their religion and were exempted from worshiping the deities of the Roman state. They could regulate life within their own communities by their law. (No central authority in Jerusalem possessed legal authority outside Palestine.) Many concessions were granted locally from time to time in deference to Jewish scruples: exemption from military service,[50] protection in observing the Sabbath[51] (including nonappearance in court on Sabbath days), and protection for messengers who carried the annual temple tax to Jerusalem.[52] A daily sacrifice on behalf of the emperor was accepted as proof of loyalty (see p. 567). Josephus may sometimes have stretched the meaning of documents he quotes in order to make it appear that Jews had citizen status when they did not (cf. p. 41), but it seems clear that the Jews were recognized and accorded a distinctive place in many cities of the Mediterranean world.[53] The political condition of the Jews in the empire appears to have remained unaffected by the revolts of their countrymen in Judea, although the diversion of the temple tax to the royal coffers after 70 did cause unrest.

Some Jews became prominent in the Roman administration and in international politics — the Herods (pp. 412-14, 418-19), Philo (pp. 478-79), Tiberius Alexander (p. 420). Jewesses, of race or of religion, reached even higher circles: Drusilla, wife of the governor Felix (p. 420); Bernice, consort of Titus (p. 419), and Poppaea, wife of Otho and then of Nero (p. 34; Josephus, *Ant.* 10.8.11 [195]).

Most Jews found themselves in less prominent, and less exposed posi-

---

50. Josephus, *Ant.* 14.10.6 [204], 12 [227], 13 [230].
51. Ibid., 14.10.20 [242], 21 [245], 23 [258], 25 [264].
52. Ibid., 16.6.2 [163], 3-7 [166-72]. See p. 564.
53. V. Tcherikover, *Hellenistic Civilization and the Jews* (Philadelphia, 1961), 296-332.

tions. In fact, they are found in nearly every occupation and circumstance of life known from the ancient world, and cannot be stereotyped as to wealth or employment. On one end of the economic scale was Alexander, the brother of Philo, who was able to lend large sums of money.[54] On the other end were the poor and beggars.[55] The percentage of Jewish slaves (before the enslavement of the rebels by Titus in 70) appears to have been less than among other peoples. In between the extremes, many occupations are explicitly attested, with farming the most widely represented — not only in Palestine and Syria, but also in Egypt and Asia Minor.

BIBLIOGRAPHY

Williams, Margaret. *The Jews among the Greeks and Romans: A Diasporan Sourcebook.* Baltimore, 1998.

Juster, J. *Les Juifs dans l'Empire romain.* Paris, 1914.

Rabello, A. M. "The Legal Condition of the Jews in the Roman Empire." *ANRW* II, *Principat,* 13. Berlin and New York, 1980. Pp. 662-762.

Reinhold, Meyer. *Diaspora: The Jews among the Greeks and Romans.* Sarasota, Fl., 1983.

Kasher, Aryeh. *The Jews in Hellenistic and Roman Egypt: The Struggle for Equal Rights.* Tübingen, 1985.

Linder, A. *The Jews in Roman Imperial Legislation.* Detroit, 1987.

Kasher, Aryeh. *Jews and Hellenistic Cities in Eretz-Israel: Relations of the Jews in Eretz-Israel with the Hellenistic Cities during the Second Temple Period (332 BCE–70 CE).* Tübingen, 1990.

Trebilco, Paul. *Jewish Communities in Asia Minor.* Cambridge, 1991.

Lieu, Judith, John North, and Tessa Rajak, eds. *The Jews Among Pagans and Christians in the Roman Empire.* London, 1992.

Feldman, Louis H. *Jew and Gentile in the Ancient World: Attitudes and Interactions from Alexander to Justinian.* Princeton, 1993.

Barclay, John M. G. *Jews in the Mediterranean Diaspora from Alexander to Trajan (323 BCE–117 CE).* Edinburgh, 1996.

Winter, Bruce W., ed. *The Book of Acts in Its First Century Setting.* Vol. 5. Irina Levinskaya. *The Book of Acts in Its Diaspora Setting.* Grand Rapids, 1996.

Goodman, Martin, ed. *Jews in the Graeco-Roman World.* Oxford, 1998.

Rutgers, Leonard V. *The Hidden Heritage of Diaspora Judaism.* Leuven, 1998.

Gruen, Erich S. *Heritage and Hellenism: The Reinvention of Jewish Tradition.* Berkeley, 1998.

Collins, John J. *Between Athens and Jerusalem.* 2d ed. Grand Rapids, 1999.

Gruen, Erich S. *Diaspora: Jews amidst Greeks and Romans.* Cambridge, Mass., 2002.

54. Josephus, *Ant.* 18.6.3 [159-60].
55. Juvenal, *Satires* 3.14-16, with an anti-Jewish motivation.

JEWISH LITERATURE AND OTHER SOURCES IN THE HELLENISTIC AND ROMAN PERIODS

The literature produced by Jews testifies to the geographical extent, social differences, and religious variety among Jews of the Greco-Roman period. Some of the great variety of kinds of literature and some examples of each are as follows:

Rewritings of the Bible

Jubilees, *Genesis Apocryphon,* Pseudo-Philo's *Biblical Antiquities,* Josephus's *Jewish Antiquities;*

Interpretations of the Bible

Qumran pesharim, Philo's commentaries, rabbinic midrashim;

Legal texts

Qumran Temple Scroll, rabbinic Mishnah and Talmuds;

Testaments

Testaments of the Twelve Patriarchs, Assumption of Moses, Testament of Job;

Narratives

Tobit, Judith, Additions to Daniel, Joseph and Aseneth;

Histories

1 and 2 Maccabees, Josephus's *The Jewish War;*

Apocalypses

(pp. 475-78);

Wisdom writings

Sirach, Wisdom of Solomon, Epistle of Aristeas, Pseudo-Phocylides;

Apologies

Philo's *Against Flaccus* and *Embassy to Gaius,* Josephus's *Against Apion;*

Philosophical treatises

Philo;

Hymns

Song of the Three Young Men in Greek Daniel, Qumran *Thanksgiving Hymns,* Psalms of Solomon;

Prayers

Prayer of Azariah in Greek Daniel, Prayer of Manasseh, Additions to Esther.

These literary categories cut across the different groups among the Jews. Rather than following a classification according to these literary forms, we will introduce the sources according to their traditional groupings. The literature surfaces from nearly every part of the empire, documents the varieties within early Judaism, and witnesses to the concerns that provided the context in which Christianity was born and grew up. When the archaeological sources and pagan literary references are added, yet more details can be included in the picture.

BIBLIOGRAPHY

Delling, G. *Bibliographie zur judisch-hellenistischen und intertestamentarischen Literatur, 1900–1970.* Berlin, 1975.

Rost, Leonhard. *Judaism Outside the Hebrew Canon: An Introduction to the Documents.* Nashville, 1976.

Nickelsburg, G. W. E. *Jewish Literature Between the Bible and the Mishnah.* Philadelphia, 1981.

Musaph-Andriesse, R. C. *From Torah to Kabbalah: A Basic Introduction to the Writings of Judaism.* Oxford, 1982.

Collins, John J. *Between Athens and Jerusalem: Jewish Identity in the Hellenistic Diaspora.* New York, 1983.

McNamara, Martin. *Intertestamental Literature.* Wilmington, Del., 1983.

DeJonge, M., and S. Safrai, eds. *Compendia Rerum Iudaicarum ad Novum Testament.* Section Two, *The Literature of the Jewish People in the Period of the Second Temple and the Talmud.* 3 vols., edited by M. J. Mulder, M. E. Stone, and S. Safrai, respectively. Philadelphia, 1984-88.

Evans, Craig A. *Noncanonical Writings and New Testament Interpretation.* Peabody, Mass., 1992. (About two-thirds is Jewish literature.)

Denis, Albert-Marie. *Introduction à la littérature religieuse judéo-hellénistique.* Turnhout, 2000.

Carson, D. A., Peter T. O'Brien, and Mark A. Seifrid, eds. *Justification and Variegated Nomism.* Vol. 1: *The Complexities of Second Temple Judaism.* Grand Rapids, 2001.

The Old Testament in Greek

Septuagint

The name *Septuagint* (from the Latin for seventy, thus often abbreviated LXX) derives from the legend that the translation of the books of Moses was the product of seventy (-two) Jewish scholars sent by the high priest from Palestine to Alexandria to provide a Greek translation of the law for the library in Alexandria at the request of Ptolemy II Philadelphus. This traditional theory is recounted in the *Epistle of Aristeas* (p. 450) and was often repeated.[56] Eventually Greek translations were provided for the remainder of the Hebrew Bible and other books; these are popularly included also under the name Septuagint, but since the legend of seventy translators does not apply to these later works, the whole of the Greek Old Testament is more accurately described as the Old Greek.

Modern scholars have suggested other theories of origin. Twentieth-century controversy centered around Paul Kahle's theory that the Septuagint originated as a "targum," not as a translation proper.[57] According to this theory, in various Greek-speaking synagogues oral paraphrases of the Hebrew Scriptures were in use before being written down, in the same way that there were extempore, oral translations into Aramaic before the official Targums (see pp. 498-500) were reduced to writing. Thus the history of the text of the Greek Bible is not that of one "official" or standard text undergoing change in the process of copying and revision, but of a variety of texts to which Christians later brought a measure of standardization.

Kahle's theory seems reasonable, and the initiative for a Greek translation of the Hebrew Scriptures probably did come from the needs of Greek-speaking Jews to have the Scriptures in their language, particularly in synagogue worship. Scholars, however, have found the textual evidence decisive against this theory. While rejecting the claims for supernatural inspiration of the Septuagint, most students of it accept with the *Epistle of Aristeas* the view that the Pentateuch was translated at Alexandria in the third century B.C. as at least a semiofficial undertaking. They consider it the work, however, of Alexandrian Jews, initiated within the Jewish community, whatever encouragement may have come from Ptolemaic officials and whatever approbation may have been given the project by temple authorities in Jerusalem. Translation of the prophets and writings (see p. 540 on the three parts of the Hebrew canon) would have followed in time, and various parts of the Old Greek Bible had different textual histories. The prologue to the Greek translation of Sirach, by the author's grandson, indicates that all three parts of the Hebrew canon were available in Greek by the end of the second century B.C. (although not necessarily all of the books in the second and third part):[58]

> You are urged therefore to read with good will and attention, and to be indulgent in cases where, despite our diligent labor in translating, we may seem to have rendered some phrases imperfectly. For what was originally

---

56. Philo, *Vita Mosis* 2.5–7.25-44; Josephus, *Ant.* 12.2.1-15 [11-118]; Justin, *Apology* 1.31; Irenaeus, *Against Heresies* 3.21.2.

57. *The Cairo Geniza* (Oxford, 1959).

58. For the qualification see G. B. Caird, "Ben Sira and the Dating of the Septuagint," *Bulletin of IOSCS* 7 (1974):21-22. Contrast Roger Beckwith, *The Old Testament Canon of the New Testament Church* (Grand Rapids, 1986), 110-11.

expressed in Hebrew does not have exactly the same sense when translated into another language. Not only this work, but even the law itself, the prophecies, and the rest of the books differ not a little as originally expressed.

The process of transmission produced different local texts with variant readings. Scholarly activity at Christian centers tried to establish the text. At the end of the fourth century A.D. Jerome knew three different recensions (*trifaria varietas*) of the Septuagint: those attributed to Hesychius (Egypt), Lucian (Antioch), and Origen (Caesarea).[59] Only the latter two have been identified in the surviving manuscripts. Origen (early third century) produced the greatest piece of textual criticism in the ancient church in compiling his Hexapla, parallel columns containing the Hebrew text, a Greek transliteration, and the translations of Aquila, Symmachus, the Septuagint, and Theodotion (see pp. 437-38). The fifth column was the important one, where Origen supplied critical notations marking which passages were not represented by the Hebrew and where there were omissions from the Hebrew. The Hexapla was too bulky to be copied in its entirety, so it is known now only from fragmentary copies and quotations.[60] (To add to the confusion in the transmission of the Septuagint the fifth column was copied without its critical markings.) The number of manuscripts of the Septuagint, complete and fragmentary, reaches nearly 2,000, a total greater than for any other Greek work except the New Testament.

The work of Paul Anton de Lagarde lies behind the modern critical study of the Septuagint. Lagarde sought to reconstruct the threefold form of the Septuagint text known to Jerome as the best method of getting back to the text of the proto-(original) Septuagint. Lagarde attempted to classify manuscripts according to these three families and to establish the form of the text associated with each recension, and then by comparing these readings work back to the original. But mounting evidence of major revisions of the Septuagint that antedate these later Christian recensions have caused scholars to question this enterprise. Most important of these revisions are the so-called proto-Lucian and Kaige (a kind of proto- or Ur-Theodotion), although there are serious doubts that the latter is a discrete recension at all. Manuscripts associated with these revisions reflect pre-Masoretic readings of the Hebrew text and indicate that the later translators and revisers used readings already in circulation. Some of the variations in Old Testament citations by the New Testament, church fathers, and Jewish Hellenistic literature may be explained by these early recensions. A more serious problem for reconstructing the original Greek ac-

---

59. Jerome, *Preface to Books of Chronicles*. Cf. his different statement in *Epistle* 106, "To Sunnias and Fretela," 2.2. See *Bulletin of IOSCS* 11, p. 44 and Bruce Metzger, "Lucian and the Lucianic Recension of the Greek Bible," *NTS* 8 (1962):191-92.

60. F. Field, *Origenis Hexaplorum quae supersunt*, 2 vols. (Oxford, 1875; repr. Hildesheim, 1964).

cording to Lagarde's method is that comprehensive textual criticism of the extant manuscripts of certain Old Testament books shows no trace of the supposed recension of Hesychius or even of Lucian (the supposed Antiochian text being nothing other than the Byzantine text). Nevertheless, although a process of revision of the Old Greek began quite early, Lagarde was probably right to assume one original translation, except that for some books there were two distinct translations (Esther, Daniel, Judges).

The two major critical editions of the Septuagint in the twentieth century were influenced by Lagarde and presupposed an original, uniform Septuagint. The two projects were associated with Cambridge, England, and Göttingen, Germany. Both are represented by student "handbook" editions and major critical editions. The Cambridge scholars printed the text of the Septuagint as it is known to have existed in one time and place, with variant readings given in the critical apparatus. This has meant printing the text of Codex Vaticanus (B) or where it is missing that of one of the other great uncial manuscripts (Alexandrinus, Sinaiticus). H. B. Swete, *Introduction to the Old Testament in Greek,* and A. E. Brooke, N. McLean, and H. St.-J. Thackeray, *The Old Testament in Greek,* used this method. The Göttingen scholars, continuing directly the work of Lagarde but profiting from his mistakes, have printed an eclectic text with variants in the apparatus. A. Rahlfs, Lagarde's successor, brought out a manual edition based on Vaticanus, Sinaiticus, and Alexandrinus, entitled *Septuaginta,* the most widely used student edition. The major Göttingen edition constitutes a more extensive examination of manuscripts. The Cambridge project has unfortunately been suspended, so the Göttingen project is now the standard work.[61]

Differences between the Septuagint and the Hebrew result from various causes: employing a different Hebrew text from the one that became the Masoretic text, theological and apologetical interpretations of the Hebrew, exegetical interpretations, socio-political concerns of the translators, failure sometimes to understand the Hebrew. Semitic influence, nonetheless, is felt at places in the vocabulary and syntax. Different translators who worked on the Greek version had different techniques: Some are quite literal (as in Samuel-Kings, Song of Solomon, Lamentations), some are moderately literal (Pentateuch, Joshua, Isaiah), and some use freer renderings (Esther, Job, and Proverbs). Greek Jeremiah has considerable difference from the Masoretic text in total length (shorter) and arrangement of contents.

The New Testament professor who advised those of his students who did not own a Septuagint to sell their commentaries and buy one had a good point. Much of the grammar, vocabulary, and thought-world of the New Testament finds its best parallel and illustration in the Septuagint. The distinctive reli-

---

61. The International Organization for Septuagint and Cognate Studies is sponsoring a New English Translation of the Septuagint.

gious meaning of many New Testament words (e.g., *ekklēsia*, *baptisma*, *presbyteros*, *psallō*, *cheirotonia*) is to be found not from etymology or classical usage but from the adaptations already made by Greek-speaking Jews, as known from the Septuagint, Philo, Josephus, the Apocrypha, and the Pseudepigrapha. On such theological and religious terms and on ways of thinking, the influence of the Septuagint on New Testament vocabulary and theology is extensive; on other matters, such as structure of the language, the influence is not so much.

As the first translation of a sacred book into another language, the Septuagint is one of the most significant events in all religious history. The putting of Hebrew religious ideas into the Greek language was an important transitional step that prepared the way for Christian preaching. Moreover, most of the New Testament citations of the Old Testament follow the Septuagint.[62] The Bible of the early church, except for some Jewish believers and a few scholars, was the Greek Old Testament. The Septuagint was the most important literary event, perhaps the most important single development of any kind in the Hellenistic period, for the background of early Christianity.

BIBLIOGRAPHY

Brooke, A. E., N. McLean, and H. St.-J. Thackeray, *The Old Testament in Greek*. Cambridge, 1906–.
Swete, H. B. *Introduction to the Old Testament in Greek*. Cambridge, 1914. Reprint. New York, 1968. Reprint. Peabody, Mass., 1989.
Septuaginta: Vetus Testamentum Graecum. Göttingen, 1931–.
Rahlfs, A. *Septuaginta*. Stuttgart, n.d.

Hatch, Edwin, and Henry A. Redpath. *Concordance to the Septuagint*. 2 vols. Oxford, 1897. Reprint. Graz, 1954.
Lust, Johan, E. Eynikel, and K. Hauspie. *A Greek-English Lexicon of the Septuagint*. 2 vols. Stuttgart, 1992, 1996.
Muraoka, T. *A Greek-English Lexicon of the Septuagint: Twelve Prophets*. Louvain, 1993.

Dodd, C. H. *The Bible and the Greeks*. London, 1935. Reprint, 1954.
Hill, D. *Greek Words and Hebrew Meanings*. Cambridge, 1967.
Jacques, Xavier. *List of LXX Words Sharing Common Elements*. Rome, 1972.
Walters, P. *The Text of the Septuagint: Its Corruptions and their Emendation*. Cambridge, 1973.
Klein, R. W. *Textual Criticism of the Old Testament*. Philadelphia, 1974.
Jellicoe, S., ed. *Studies in the Septuagint: Origins, Recensions, and Texts*. New York, 1974.

62. Henry Shires, *Finding the Old Testament in the New* (Philadelphia, 1974); E. Earle Ellis, *Paul's Use of the Old Testament* (Edinburgh, 1957); Krister Stendahl, *The School of St. Matthew* (Uppsala, 1954).

O'Callaghan, J. "Lista de los papiros de los LXX." *Biblica* 56 (1975):74-93.

Pietersma, Albert, and Claude Cox, eds. *De Septuaginta: Studies in Honor of John William Wevers on his Sixty-fifth Birthday*. Mississauga, Ont., 1984.

Wevers, J. W. "An Apologia for Septuagint Studies." *Bulletin of IOSCS* 18 (1985):16-30.

Harl, M., G. Dorival, and O. Munnich. *La Bible Grecque des Septante: Du Judaïsme hellénistique au christianisme ancien*. 2d ed. Paris, 1994.

Hengel, M., and A.-M. Schwemer, eds. *Die Septuaginta zwischen Judentum und Christentum*. Tübingen, 1994.

Tov, Emanuel. *The Greek and Hebrew Bible: Collected Essays on the Septuagint*. Leiden, 1999.

Wevers, J. W. "Apologia pro Vita Mea: Reflections on a Career in Septuagint Studies." *Bulletin of IOSCS* 32 (1999):65-96.

Fernández Marcos, Natalio. *The Septuagint in Context: An Introduction to the Greek Version of the Bible*. Leiden, 2000.

Jobes, Karen H., and Moisés Silva. *Invitation to the Septuagint*. Grand Rapids, Mich., and Carlisle, England, 2000.

Hengel, Martin. *The Septuagint and Christian Scripture: Its Prehistory and the Problem of Its Canon*. Edinburgh, 2002.

McLay, R. Timothy. *The Use of the Septuagint in New Testament Research*. Grand Rapids, 2003.

Brock, S. P., C. T. Fritsch, and S. Jellicoe, eds. *A Classified Bibliography of the Septuagint*. Leiden, 1973.

Dogniez, C. *Bibliography of the Septuagint/Bibliographie de la Septante (1970-1993)*. Leiden, 1995.

Bulletin of the International Organization for Septuagint and Cognate Studies. 1968–.

Other Greek Translations

Aquila made his translation during the Jamnia period and completed it in the early second century.[63] It was an official translation supervised by the rabbis Joshua ben Hananiah, Eliezer ben Hyrcanus, and Akiba[64] for the use of Jews in the Greek Diaspora. Aquila was a proselyte to Judaism and came from Pontus; some identify him with the Onqelos of the Aramaic Targums. The translation may have been designed in part to replace the Septuagint, which had been appropriated by Christians. The Jewish-Christian debate over Aquila and the Septuagint is already reflected in Justin, *Dialogue with Trypho,* in the mid–second century. Aquila's work was extremely literal, even word-for-word. It was also designed to enable Greek-speaking Jews to follow the rabbinic exegetical methods that interpreted every word, even particles. It followed the text of the

---

63. A. E. Silverstone, *Aquila and Onqelos* (Manchester, 1931); D. Barthélemy, *Les Devanciers d'Aquila* (Leiden, 1963); J. Reider and N. Turner, *Prolegomena to a Greek-Hebrew and Hebrew-Greek Index to Aquila* (Leiden, 1966).

64. j. Megillah 1.71c; j. Kiddushin 1.59a.

Hebrew Bible, which was being standardized in this period (corresponding to what is now called the Masoretic text).

Symmachus was an excellent Greek stylist. Christian sources state that he belonged to the Jewish Christian sect of Ebionites.[65] The date of his translation is usually put in Caesarea in the early third century, but his position in the Hexapla and one statement from Epiphanius[66] would put him earlier than Theodotion.

Theodotion was a Jewish proselyte from Ephesus.[67] His version is midway between the literalness of Aquila and the stylistic excellence of Symmachus. It was produced in the second half of the second century. The version of Daniel associated with the name of Theodotion supplanted the Old Greek version in nearly all Christian manuscripts. Origen preferred Theodotion's Daniel, and it was shortly after his time that the transition occurred. Many readings identified with Theodotion are known from the New Testament and other sources earlier than Theodotion. The traditional Theodotion, therefore, may have been simply a reviser of an earlier version from the late pre-Christian age produced in western Asia Minor.[68]

Alexandrian Canon

Since the Septuagint manuscripts contain books outside the Hebrew canon of the Old Testament (see p. 440 on the Apocrypha), it has been commonly supposed that the Jews in Alexandria accepted a wider canon than that of the Jews in Palestine. Actually, there is no evidence for an "Alexandrian canon," or for any other Jewish canon larger than the traditional one. Philo, the most extensive literary representative of Alexandrian Jewry, gives no indication of accepting as authoritative any of the books included in the Apocrypha. Moreover, the Septuagint manuscripts and the early Christian lists do not agree on which if any books beyond the Hebrew canon are to be accepted. This lack of agreement suggests that in Christian circles varying books out of the Jewish heritage were found valuable and included in biblical manuscripts and employed in study and teaching. They thus passed into the tradition of the church, but it was very much later before any authoritative decision was reached in the Christian church about these books which lay outside the Hebrew canon. The debates between Origen and Julius Africanus over the Additions to Daniel[69] (p. 446) and between Augustine and Jerome over the extent of the canon are indicative

---

65. Eusebius, *Church History* 6.17. Alison Salvesen, *Symmachus in the Pentateuch* (Manchester, 1991) concludes that Symmachus's translation does not reflect Samaritan or Ebionite elements but does show awareness of rabbinic exegesis.

66. *De Mens. et Pond.* 16-18, but there is an internal contradiction in the passage.

67. Irenaeus, *Against Heresies* 3.21.1, and Eusebius, *Church History* 5.20.6.

68. Barthélemy (n.63 above) argues for Palestine.

69. Julius Africanus, *Epistle to Origen*, and Origen, *Epistle to Africanus* in *Ante-Nicene Fathers* 4.385-92.

of the situation. But there was no Jewish canon other than the one in Hebrew that has come down to us.[70]

Jewish Literature in Greek: Fragments

The first literary productions of Greek-speaking Jews after the Septuagint survive only in fragmentary form through quotations made by later writers. Most of these were compiled by Alexander Polyhistor (c. 80–35 B.C.), whose book *On the Jews* strung together extracts from various authors concerning the Jews. Alexander's work is lost, but many of his quotations are preserved in Eusebius of Caesarea's *Preparation for the Gospel.* A few passages are found in other writers, especially Josephus and Clement of Alexandria. These fragments show that quite early in their contact with Hellenism the Jews were attempting, not very successfully at first, to communicate their religion and culture through Greek literary conventions. The first Jewish authors in Greek were forerunners of the historical work of Josephus and the philosophical work of Philo in the first century. They were important for the creation of apologetic material that held a central place in Jewish propaganda and then in Christian preaching and apologetics.

The fragmentary Hellenistic Jewish authors were especially active in producing historical writings.[71] These works developed the argument for the superiority of the Jewish people on the basis of their great antiquity. The Jews had introduced alphabetical writing (Eupolemus), and even all important aspects of civilization (Artapanus). Some Jewish authors attempted to appropriate Greek poetry in order to tell the Jewish story in epic and drama: for example, Theodotus (c. 100 B.C.) — a poem *On Shechem;* Philo (the Elder) the Epic Poet (c. 100 B.C.) — *On Jerusalem;* Ezekiel the Tragic Poet (181-145 B.C.) — *The*

---

70. Albert C. Sundberg, *The Old Testament of the Early Church* (Cambridge, Mass., 1964); B. F. Westcott, *The Bible in the Church* (London, 1891; repr. Grand Rapids, 1979); Roger Beckwith, *The Old Testament Canon of the New Testament* (Grand Rapids, 1986); E. E. Ellis, *The Old Testament in Early Christianity: Canon and Interpretation in the Light of Modern Research* (Grand Rapids, 1991). See pp. 423, 539-41.

71. Note the following:
  Demetrius the Chronographer (c. 215 B.C.) — *On the Kings in Judea*
  Eupolemus (c. 150 B.C.) — *On the Kings in Judea;* and Pseudo-Eupolemus, a Samaritan of about the same date
  Artapanus (c. 100 B.C.) — *On the Jews*
  Cleodemus Malchus (c. 100 B.C.) — a history of the Jews (untitled)
  Aristeas (c. 100 B.C.) — *On the Jews*
  Pseudo-Hecataeus (c. 100 B.C.) — *On the Jews* and *On Abraham*
  Thallus (under Tiberius, A.D. 14–37) — a universal history
  Justus of Tiberias (first century A.D.) — *Chronicle of the Jewish Kings* and *History of the Jewish War*
Texts, translations, and notes in Carl R. Holladay, *Fragments from Hellenistic Jewish Authors,* vol. 1, *Historians* (Chico, Calif., 1984).

Exodus and other dramas.[72] They were not too proficient in breathing life into Greek hexameters (epic) and iambic trimeters (drama). A few Jewish authors went beyond the use of Greek literary forms to a blending of Jewish and Greek thought in philosophical writings that employed an allegorical interpretation of the Scriptures. The argument for Jewish priority and superiority in history and culture was extended to include the claim that Greeks had learned philosophy from Moses.[73] Jews also promoted their ideas under the names of legendary pagan figures, as in the *Sibylline Oracles* (see under Pseudepigrapha below) and Pseudo-Orpheus.[74]

Apocrypha

The books Protestants call the "Apocrypha" are called by Roman Catholics "Deuterocanonical." Those so designated in modern translations are an arbitrary selection out of the considerable Jewish literature produced in pre-Christian and early Christian times. They include the seven books (eight if Baruch and the Letter of Jeremiah are separated) and the Additions to Esther and three additions to Daniel (Greek versions) accepted as canonical by the Council of Trent (1546), plus 1 Esdras, 2 Esdras (4 Ezra), and the Prayer of Manasseh that Catholics treat as an appendix to the Bible.[75] The collection thus does not correspond even with the Catholic canon, much less with the contents of any ancient list or manuscript. The need for "handles" on convenient groupings within Jewish literature in Hellenistic and Roman times is so great that the arbitrary distinction between Apocrypha and Pseudepigrapha (terms that could apply to books in both classifications with equal appropriateness) will no doubt continue (pp. 448-49).

Although the historical accuracy and moral tone of some of these books is doubtful (the value of 1 Maccabees for history and Sirach for moral teaching is quite high), their neglect in most Protestant circles is regrettable for the loss in perspective this entails for understanding the background of New Testament times. Only a few words of introduction to each may be offered here with the encouragement that they be read.

72. Texts, translations, and notes in Carl R. Holladay, *Fragments from Hellenistic Jewish Authors*, vol. 2, *Poets* (Atlanta, 1989).

73. Aristobulus (181–145 B.C.) — *An Explanation of the Mosaic Law*. Texts, translations and notes in Carl R. Holladay, *Fragments from Hellenistic Jewish Authors*, Vol. 3: *Aristobulus* (Atlanta, 1995).

74. Texts, translations, and notes in Carl R. Holladay, *Fragments from Hellenistic Jewish Authors*, Vol. 4: *Orphica* (Atlanta: 1996). Holladay summarizes the recensional history in "Pseudo-Orpheus: Tracking a Tradition," in A. J. Malherbe, et al., *The Early Church in Its Context: Essays in Honor of Everett Ferguson* (Leiden, 1998), 192-220.

75. The Prayer of Manasseh and 4 Ezra are included in the Pseudepigrapha in James H. Charlesworth, ed., *The Old Testament Pseudepigrapha* (Garden City, N.Y., 1983, 1985).

1 Esdras [76]

Greek Ezra is based on material in Chronicles, Ezra, and Nehemiah. It is written in much better Greek than the Septuagint translation of those books, which is later and is translated from a different recension of the Hebrew text. It relates the history from 621 B.C. to Ezra's reading of the law after the return from captivity. The only major addition to the Hebrew books is the court tale of three youths in the bodyguard of King Darius (3:1–5:6).[77] Each young man argued on behalf of what he considered the strongest thing in the world: the first said wine, the second (a good politician) said the king, and the third (Zerubbabel) said women. Then Zerubbabel added that "truth prevails over all" and gave a further discourse on behalf of truth. The addition by the same speaker is a giveaway that the story originally circulated without the "moral" and was included for its own sake but was given a "religious" conclusion by the addition of the words about truth. The outcome was that Zerubbabel was honored by the king and given royal assistance to carry out the rebuilding of Jerusalem.

2 Esdras [78]

Second Esdras is also known as 4 Ezra, because the Latin Vulgate (the Latin version alone preserves the entire book) counted Ezra, Nehemiah, 1 Esdras, and 2 Esdras 3–14 as 1, 2, 3, and 4 Ezra, respectively. Some modern scholars designate chapters 1–2 as 5 Ezra[79] and 15–16 as 6 Ezra.[80] Fourth Ezra, therefore, properly applies only to chapters 3–14 of the present work; 2 Esdras is in more common use for the whole work. The Syriac and other eastern versions contain only chapters 3–14. The original work (probably in Hebrew or Aramaic), consisting of seven visions (chaps. 3–14), was an apocalypse written about A.D. 100. Because of its date, it is treated in Catholic Bibles as an appendix to the New Testament and thus might more appropriately be placed in the Pseudepigrapha. As the same genre of literature (apocalypse) and coming from about the same date, it is instructive for comparison with the Christian book of Revelation. Written in terms of Judah's exile to Babylon, the book struggles with theodicy in the face of the destruction of Jerusalem thirty years before and the

76. Jacob M. Myers, *I and II Esdras: Introduction, Translation, and Commentary,* Anchor Bible (Garden City, N.Y., 1974); R. J. Coggins and M. A. Knibb, *The First and Second Books of Esdras,* Cambridge Bible Commentary (Cambridge, 1979); Zipora Talshir, *1 Esdras: From Origin to Translation* (Williston, VT, 1999); idem, *1 Esdras: A Text-Critical Commentary* (Williston, Vt., 2001).

77. F. Zimmermann, "The Story of the Three Guardsmen," *JQR* 54 (1963/64):179-200 argues for an Aramaic, non-Jewish original of the story, worked over by the Jewish editor.

78. M. E. Stone, *Fourth Ezra: A Commentary on the Book of Fourth Ezra* (Minneapolis, 1990); idem, *Features of the Eschatology of IV Ezra* (Atlanta, 1990); Bruce Longenecker, *2 Esdras* (Sheffield, 1996).

79. T. A. Bergren, *Fifth Ezra: The Text, Origin, and Early History* (Atlanta, 1990).

80. T. A. Bergren, *Sixth Ezra: The Text and Origin* (Oxford, 1998).

apparent collapse of Jewish hopes.[81] Its response to those circumstances was quite different from the response by the rabbis at Jamnia. Christians added to the Greek version chapters 1–2 in the late second century and 15–16 in the third century. The Greek (except for fragments) is now lost, but the Latin is a faithful rendering of the Greek. The book is notable for its tendency to blame Adam for human sinfulness (3:20-26; 4:30; 7:118), its scheme of eschatology (a special curiosity is its messianic kingdom of four hundred years preceding the resurrection and judgment — 7:28-29), its vision of the man rising from the sea (called God's son) who delivers the world (chap. 13), and the tradition it preserves about the place of Ezra in transmitting the Old Testament Scriptures and seventy secret writings reserved for the wise (14:22, 42-48).

Tobit [82]

This edifying short story has been transmitted in three quite different Greek recensions, which poses a considerable problem in textual criticism.[83] Aramaic and Hebrew fragments discovered at Qumran[84] confirm a Semitic original for the work and support the long recension. It seems to date from the early second century B.C., before the Maccabean revolt.

Tobit is one representative of the piety of Judaism in the dispersion, the story being set in the exile of the northern tribes among the Assyrians, but maintains a strong national identity (separation from Gentiles) and reverence for the temple in Jerusalem. It is particularly notable for its prayers[85] and its emphasis on burying the dead as the foremost charitable work. Against the background of Tobit, the sharp challenge of Jesus, "Let the dead bury their dead" (Matt. 8:22; Luke 9:60), takes on added significance: the duty to follow him and respond to the message of the kingdom took precedence over the highest obligation of contemporary religion. Angels play a prominent role, reflecting the more developed angelology of the post-Persian period. One may wonder about the morality of the angel who presents himself under false pretenses (5:4-12); otherwise there is much sound moral advice.

The story employs the motifs of "the grateful dead" and "the dangerous bride" from folk literature. The pious Tobit sent his son Tobias to collect a de-

---

81. A. L. Thompson, *Responsibility for Evil in the Theodicy of IV Ezra* (Missoula, Mont., 1977).

82. F. Zimmermann, *The Book of Tobit*, Jewish Apocryphal Literature (New York, 1958); C. A. Moore, "Scholarly Issues in the Book of Tobit before Qumran and After: An Assessment," *Journal for the Study of the Pseudepigrapha* 5 (1989):65-81; Benedikt Otzen, *Tobit and Judith* (Sheffield, 2001).

83. J. D. Thomas, "The Greek Text of Tobit," *JBL* 91 (1972):463-71.

84. J. T. Milik, "La patrie de Tobie," *Revue Biblique* 73 (1966):522-30.

85. N. B. Johnson, *Prayer in the Apocrypha and Pseudepigrapha*, JBL Monograph Series 2 (Philadelphia, 1948).

posit. On his journey he stayed with a kinsman whose daughter had lost seven husbands in the bridal chamber.[86] Tobias's traveling companion, the angel Raphael disguised as a relative, instructed him to burn with incense the liver, heart, and gall of a fish that had been caught earlier on the journey, promising that the smoke would drive away the demon who had caused the death of the previous bridegrooms. (A fish kept without "refrigeration" for a long period of time should drive away even demons!) The presence of magic alongside a strict observance of the law is notable. Tobias married the girl and accomplished his mission. The historical background given the story is quite confused and obviously fictitious, used as a vehicle to express moral and religious ideas of great interest and importance.

Judith [87]

Judith exists in a Greek translation from Hebrew. There is little firm indication of date, but it would fit the period around the middle of the second century B.C. It emphasizes patriotic loyalty to the law, which will effect deliverance from foreign invaders. The work is historical fiction: Holofernes, the general of the Assyrian [sic] king Nebuchadnezzar, was besieging a Jewish town where a beautiful and wealthy widow named Judith resided. When the siege became severe, Judith undertook a plan to save her people. She was very scrupulous about the ritual law, but one may wonder about her regard for the moral law. Judith presented herself to Holofernes and by her intelligence and beauty won his favor. She was provided with quarters and given permission each night to go outside the armies' lines to a stream to perform her ritual ablutions and to pray, so her going and coming evoked no notice from the troops. One night after Holofernes was overcome with wine, she cut off his head, hid it in a bag, and returned to the city. The head of Holofernes was hung on the city wall, and at the sight of it the next morning the besieging army fled.

Additions to Esther [88]

The colophon to the Greek text of Esther gives a date of 114 B.C. for the Greek translation, but this does not necessarily guarantee that all the additions were made at this time. The Septuagint Esther contains six pieces not found in the Hebrew, mainly official decrees and prayers. The latter give expression to Jewish religion, and in general the additions amply supply the name of God, which

86. Is this the background for the Sadducees' question in Matt. 22:23ff.?

87. Morton S. Enslin and Solomon Zeitlin, *The Book of Judith* (Leiden, 1972); Toni Craven, *Artistry and Faith in the Book of Judith* (Chico, Calif., 1983); J. C. VanderKam, ed., *"No One Spoke Ill of Her": Essays on Judith* (Atlanta, 1992).

88. Carey A. Moore, *Daniel, Esther, and Jeremiah: The Additions*, Anchor Bible (Garden City, N.Y., 1977).

was so conspicuously absent from the Hebrew book. Some of the additions may have originated in a Semitic language.

Wisdom of Solomon [89]

The Wisdom of Solomon was written in Greek, probably by an Alexandrian Jew about 50 B.C. or thereafter. It is one of the most important works in the Apocrypha, both as representing an early effort to reconcile Hellenistic philosophy to the Hebrew Wisdom tradition and as incorporating ideas important for the background of the New Testament (ideas with which [and likely the book itself] Paul was familiar).

Addressed to the "rulers of the earth" and "kings," the book calls for justice and praises wisdom. Wisdom is seen as the guiding force in Israel's history. It was present (9:9) when God created the universe by his spoken word out of formless matter (11:17). As his imperishable breath continues in all that lives (12:1), so Wisdom is preexistent (7:26) and permeates the universe (7:24; cf. the divine reason or breath in Stoicism). Wisdom, however, is not hypostatized, although Christians reading the book with their understanding of Christ as preexistent Wisdom found much to support their Christology in the book, which became very popular among Christians especially in Alexandria. Wisdom brings immortality of the soul (8:17); not Plato's doctrine of a natural immortality but an immortality based on the eternal nature and moral character of God (2:23; 3:1ff.; 15:3). The penetrating analysis of pagan religion includes a denunciation of the folly of idolatry and its moral consequences (13–14) that has similarities with Romans 1. Philosophical views are reflected in the explanation that idolatry originated either in regarding the elements and stars as gods or in affection for the deceased and devotion to a distant king. The author considers the Egyptian worship of animals as the lowest form of religion. Typically Jewish is the claim that idolatry is the root of immorality (14:12, 27). The four cardinal virtues of Hellenistic philosophy are said to be Wisdom's teaching and of greatest value in life (8:7).

Sirach (Ecclesiasticus)[90]

"The Wisdom of Jesus the Son of Sirach" (Greek title) or "Ecclesiasticus" (Latin title) is cited simply as Sirach, Ben Sira, or the Wisdom of Sirach. Joshua (Jesus) ben Sira (his Hebrew name) wrote the work in Hebrew between 190 and 175 B.C. According to the Prologue (pp. 433-34), his grandson went to Egypt

---

89. J. M. Reese, *Hellenistic Influence on the Book of Wisdom and its Consequences* (Rome, 1970); David Winston, *The Wisdom of Solomon*, Anchor Bible (Garden City, N.Y., 1979).

90. J. G. Snaith, *Ecclesiasticus*, Cambridge Bible Commentary (Cambridge, 1974); Jack T. Sanders, *Ben Sira and Demotic Wisdom* (Chico, Calif., 1983); P. W. Skehan and A. A. DiLella, *The Wisdom of Ben Sira*, Anchor Bible (New York, 1987).

in 132 B.C. and there translated the work into Greek. Ben Sira was a teacher and scholar in Jerusalem, and his work invited students to study under him. His book is a worthy continuation of the Wisdom literature of the Old Testament. About two-thirds of the work is represented in medieval Hebrew manuscripts and most of chapters 39–43 is contained in a scroll discovered at Masada.[91] The Hebrew manuscripts represent two different recensions; the main Greek manuscripts follow the shorter.

Sirach continued the conservative religious views of the Old Testament but was aware of and tried to meet the challenges of Hellenism. His book employs Hellenistic motifs to promote the traditional piety and wisdom of Judaism. He uses Torah (law) ordinarily with reference to the Pentateuch. The law is identified with Wisdom and is eternal. "If you desire wisdom, keep the commandments, and the Lord will supply it for you" (1:26; cf. 1:9-10; 19:20). Wisdom has three aspects: secular, moral, and religious. The author includes such traditional Wisdom themes as relations to various classes of people (parents, children, women, wives, slaves, friends, the poor), use of the tongue, money, food and wine, and the dignity of work. Motives for obedience range from self-interest to obedience for its own sake. Reward and retribution are in this life; there is no developed concept of the afterlife. Sirach strongly emphasizes freedom of the will. He recognized in human beings an evil impulse, a *yezer*, to sin. God created it, since God is Creator of everything, but human beings are free and are not enslaved to the impulse. Moral conduct and prayer are the essence of religion; nevertheless, Sirach was interested in the priesthood, sacrifice, and the temple service. His special section in "Praise of the Fathers" in chapters 43–50 concludes with a eulogy on the high priest Simon II, who is perhaps the same as Simon the Just of rabbinic tradition.

Baruch [92]

Baruch purports to have been written during the Babylonian captivity by Baruch, the secretary of Jeremiah, and sent to Jerusalem to be read on feast days as a confession of sins. The book is a composite work: 1:1–3:8 is in prose and constitutes an elaborate introduction confused in its history and little related to the author's message (1:1-14), and a confession of sin (1:15–3:8); 3:9–4:4 is a poetic piece in praise of Wisdom (similar to Job 28); and 4:5–5:9 is a poetic piece of comfort. The parts may come from different periods but the general opinion is that they date between 150 and 60 B.C.

---

91. Y. Yadin, *The Ben Sira Scroll from Masada* (Jerusalem, 1965).

92. Carey A. Moore, "Toward the Dating of the Book of Baruch," *CBQ* 36 (1974):312-20; Emanuel Tov, ed. and trans., *The Book of Baruch also called I Baruch (Greek and Hebrew)* (Missoula, Mont., 1975); J. Edward Wright, *Baruch ben Neriah: From Biblical Scribe to Apocalyptic Seer* (Columbia, S.C., 2003).

Letter of Jeremiah

The Letter of Jeremiah in some Greek and Syriac manuscripts and in the Latin version is attached to Baruch and so is sometimes treated as chapter 6 of that book. It was, however, a separate work in the oldest Greek manuscripts. The original language was Hebrew (or Aramaic). The letter purports to have been sent by Jeremiah in 597 B.C. to those Jews going into Babylonian captivity; it actually seems to date from the Hellenistic period, before 100 B.C. It is a denunciation of Babylonian idolatry, identifying the image with the god. The author shows little real knowledge of Babylonian religion, and follows the stock Jewish apologetic against paganism as this was applied to Greek idolatry. Jeremiah 10:11 provided the text. The theme, "From this you know that they are not gods," is repeated nine times.

Additions to Daniel

Prayer of Azariah and Song of the Three Young Men. Both the Septuagint and Theodotion insert this material between 3:23 and 24 of the Hebrew text of Daniel. The prayer (vv. 3-22) and the song (vv. 29-68) are poetry, preceded by brief prose introductions. The Prayer of Azariah suggests that prayer replaces sacrifice for those deprived of a place for sacrifice. The song calls upon all creation to praise God. The author was influenced by Psalms 136 and 148 and may have written first for a liturgical context. This and the other Greek additions to Daniel have been dated about 100 B.C., as a round figure, but there is actually very little to go on in determining their date.

Susanna. The story of Susanna is one of the most familiar from the Apocrypha and was popular among early Christians. The Septuagint and the Vulgate placed it after chapter 12 of the Hebrew Daniel as a thirteenth chapter, but Theodotion placed it at the beginning of Daniel as an introduction to the book.

Susanna is a marvelously told short story about the beautiful and pious wife of the wealthy Joakim. Two elders who frequently came to the house developed a passion for her. She refused their advances, however, and in reprisal they claimed to have caught her in adultery with a young man. She was condemned to death, but Daniel came forward and cross-examined the two elders separately. He was able to convict them of perjury, and they were killed instead of the virtuous Susanna.

Bel and the Dragon. These two tales were designed to ridicule idolatry in contrast to the worship of the living God. In the first, the king claimed that the image of the Babylonian god Bel ate the huge amounts of food and drink set out as offerings to the god each day. Daniel placed ashes in the temple in order to reveal the footprints of the priests who came during the night to take the food. In the other story, Daniel destroyed a great serpent that was an object of worship by putting lumps of pitch, fat, and hair in its mouth. For punishment, he was placed in the lions' den. An angel of the Lord took the prophet Habakkuk by the hair and carried him to Babylon so he could take food to Daniel, who remained unharmed by the lions.

Prayer of Manasseh

The Prayer of Manasseh is justly famous as one of the finest pieces in this literature. It is a penitential prayer supplying what 2 Chronicles 33:11-13 (cf. 18-19) refers to but does not include. The earliest use is the Christian *Didascalia* 7 [2.22] (Syriac, mid–third century A.D.), which incorporates it. Septuagint manuscripts beginning with Codex Alexandrinus included it in the collection of biblical odes appended to the Book of Psalms. It has been dated as early as 250 B.C., but again there is little indication of date in the contents. Since it is not included in the Catholic canon, it can be included in the Pseudepigrapha.

1 Maccabees [93]

First Maccabees was originally composed in Hebrew around 100 B.C.,[94] and the Greek translation in which the work survives probably followed shortly thereafter. The author was a Jew living in Jerusalem who supported the Hasmoneans. He tells the history from the accession of Antiochus IV Epiphanes, 175 B.C., to the death of Simon, 134 B.C. The author gives a straightforward, if patriotic, account of the careers of the three Hasmonean brothers — Judas, Jonathan, and Simon. His chief bias is national achievement. There is good reason why all of the secondary accounts of the Maccabean period sound very similar: ever since Josephus they have relied on 1 Maccabees as their principal source. There is nothing of the miraculous in the narrative, but the author clearly sees the providence of God in the victories of his people. The author recognized the cessation of prophecy in his time.

2 Maccabees [95]

Jason of Cyrene wrote a five-volume history of the Maccabean revolt in Greek about 100 B.C. A Jewish historian well schooled in Hellenistic rhetoric, Jason nonetheless adhered to the law and held to the viewpoint of his countrymen in Palestine. His history survives only through the epitome known as 2 Maccabees. The epitomist, besides abbreviating Jason's work, added chapters 1–2,

93. J. A. Goldstein, *I Maccabees: A New Translation with Introduction and Commentary,* Anchor Bible (Garden City, N.Y., 1974); John R. Bartlett, *1 Maccabees* (Sheffield, 1998).

94. S. Schwarz, "Israel and the Nations Roundabout: 1 Maccabees and the Hasmonean Expansion," *JJS* 42 (1991):16-38, says it should be dated 130 B.C.

95. Robert Doran, *Temple Propaganda: The Purpose and Character of 2 Maccabees* (Washington, 1981); J. A. Goldstein, *II Maccabees: A New Translation with Introduction and Commentary,* Anchor Bible (Garden City, N.Y., 1983).

15:37-39, and a few comments throughout the work. This popular summary of Jason's work covers the history from about 176 B.C. to 161 B.C.

The work is independent of 1 Maccabees and varies in content, sequence, and details from the latter. On most matters historians have preferred 1 Maccabees, but allowing for some misunderstandings and displacement of material, 2 Maccabees is a useful source. The differing outlooks of the two books may be compared on several points. First Maccabees extols patriotism and the national power; 2 Maccabees expects a celestial reward for pious martyrs. In 1 Maccabees the Jews suffered persecution because of the wickedness of the heathen; in 2 Maccabees it is because of their own sins. First Maccabees talks about the achievements of the Hasmoneans; 2 Maccabees makes much of God's care for the temple and his people. First Maccabees has nothing of God's direct intervention; in 2 Maccabees there are supernatural manifestations.

As can be expected from the foregoing, 2 Maccabees is more interested in theology than 1 Maccabees, and it makes some significant statements for the history of theology. The book contains the first explicit statement of creation *ex nihilo* (7:28). It is the only book in the Apocrypha to teach the resurrection of the flesh (12:43-45). It recounts intercession made for the dead (ibid.), but it should be noted that nothing is said about purgatory and the context is that of the Old Testament doctrine of atonement and has only a remote connection with the Reformation controversies that made the Apocrypha a battleground because of this passage.

BIBLIOGRAPHY

Zeitlin, et al., eds. *Jewish Apocryphal Literature*. Published for Dropsie College by Harper, New York, 1950–.

Metzger, Bruce, ed. *The Oxford Annotated Apocrypha*. New York, 1977.

The Holy Bible Containing the Old and New Testaments with the Apocryphal/ Deuterocanonical Books: New Revised Standard Version. New York, 1989.

The Revised English Bible with the Apocrypha. Oxford Study Bible. New York, 1992.

Pfeiffer, R. H. *History of New Testament Times with an Introduction to the Apocrypha*. New York, 1949.

Metzger, Bruce. *An Introduction to the Apocrypha*. New York, 1957.

Brockington, L. H. *A Critical Introduction to the Apocrypha*. London, 1961.

Harrington, Daniel J. *Invitation to the Apocrypha*. Grand Rapids, 1999.

Pseudepigrapha

Since Roman Catholics use "Deuterocanonical" for the books Protestants call the Apocrypha, they call "Apocrypha" what Protestants have called Pseudepigrapha. Actually both terms are arbitrary: there is much "hidden" about the

Pseudepigrapha, and some writings in the Apocrypha are pseudepigraphical. Although Jude quotes from 1 Enoch and apparently the Assumption of Moses and some of the Pseudepigrapha enjoyed a certain measure of authority in limited circles, none of these books seems ever to have been a serious contender for canonical status. That is the main reason for leaving them in a separate category.

The Pseudepigrapha has been a catchall for the Jewish literature that did not fall in some other category. Many types of literature are represented: Wisdom (4 Maccabees), edifying expansion of Hebrew Scriptures (Jubilees, Martyrdom of Isaiah), apocalypses proper (1 and 2 Enoch, 2 Baruch), testaments (Testaments of the Twelve Patriarchs, Testament of Job; the Testament of Abraham is a narrative and not a testament), prayers and psalms (Psalms of Solomon, Prayer of Joseph), and others.

A comprehensive listing of the "Extrabiblical Books" is found in Charlesworth (see bibliography, p. 462). A few introductory words will be said here about some of the better-known books in this classification and those with the greatest relevance for the backgrounds of early Christianity.

3 Maccabees [96]

There is general agreement that 3 Maccabees was written in Greek in Egypt, probably in the first century B.C. Third Maccabees is pseudo-history. Its alternate title, *Ptolemaica,* would be more appropriate, for it is set in the reign of Ptolemy Philopator after he defeated Antiochus III at Raphia in 217 B.C. Ptolemy desired to enter the holy place of the temple at Jerusalem, but God prevented him by striking him down with convulsions and paralysis. When the king returned to Egypt, he instigated a persecution of the Jews. They were assembled in the hippodrome, where a herd of elephants who had been maddened with drugs was to be turned loose. But God frustrated the king's plans several times, and then in response to the prayer of the righteous Eleazar two angels appeared and turned the elephants back upon the Egyptian troops. The king's mind was changed, and he gave the Jews a banquet and other honors and allowed them to kill apostates from the law.

4 Maccabees [97]

Fourth Maccabees is usually dated in the first century A.D. and placed in Alexandria, but good arguments can be made for Syrian Antioch. Fourth Macca-

---

96. M. Hadas, *The Third and Fourth Books of Maccabees,* Jewish Apocryphal Literature (New York, 1953).

97. R. Renehan, "The Greek Philosophical Background of Fourth Maccabees," *Rheinisches Museum für Philologie* 115 (1972):223-38; M. Schatkin, "The Maccabean Martyrs," *Vigiliae Christianae* 28 (1974):97-113; S. K. Williams, *Jesus' Death as Saving Event: The Background and Origin of a Concept* (Missoula, Mont., 1975); David A. deSilva, *4 Maccabees* (Sheffield, 1998).

bees is a discourse in Greek on the theme "Whether the Inspired Reason Is Supreme Ruler over the Passions." Although the author introduces his work as a philosophical diatribe, from 3:19 on the closest rhetorical parallels are to the encomium on those who died in the service of the state.

The Jewish author has drawn heavily on Greek philosophy, especially Stoicism, for his theme and many of his ideas. He employs the four cardinal virtues the Stoics took from Plato: prudence, justice, courage, and temperance (1:18). Preeminence is given to temperance (moderation) or self-control as the means through which the reason masters (but does not extirpate) the passions (3:5). The author speaks of the immortality of the soul instead of a resurrection (18:23; cf. 17:12; 14:5f.). The standpoint, however, remains that of a Jew loyal to the law of Moses (there is none of Philo's allegorizing). God gave the law to guide the reason (2:23). The Greek ideal of virtue is attainable only by Judaism.

The author refers to Old Testament heroes Joseph, Moses, and David as examples of the reason ruling the passions. But his principal examples (5:1–17:6) are Eleazar and the seven young men and their mother whose steadfastness to death was told in 2 Maccabees 6:18–7:42. The death of the martyrs is seen as a ransom for the nation's sins (17:22). Fourth Maccabees had its principal circulation in Christianity and influenced Christian ideas of martyrdom.

Epistle of Aristeas [98]

The Epistle of Aristeas purports to be an account by an official in the court of Ptolemy II Philadelphus to Philocrates. The actual date is disputed, but most scholars put it at least a century later, sometime in the second century B.C. Aristeas gives an account of his embassy to Eleazar, high priest of the Jews, to secure the service of elders and scholars to make a translation of the Hebrew law into Greek and of the things he learned about the Jews. The framework of the account is the request from the chief librarian to have a translation of the Hebrew Scriptures in the library at Alexandria, the king's provisions for this enterprise, the work of the seventy-two translators (six from each tribe) who completed the task in seventy-two days, and the acceptance of the translation by the Jewish people and Ptolemy. The association of the letter with the Septuagint has meant that about two dozen manuscripts survive in Greek.

The story of the translation, however, actually occupies only a small part of

98. Moses Hadas, *Aristeas to Philocrates* (New York, 1951); André Pelletier, *Lettre d'Aristée à Philocrate*, Sources Chrétiennes, vol. 89 (Paris, 1962); V. Tcherikover, "The Ideology of the Letter of Aristeas," *HTR* 51 (1958):59-85; O. Murray, "Aristeas and his Sources," *Studia Patristica* 12 (Berlin, 1975):123-28; D. W. Gooding, "Aristeas and Septuagint Origins," *Vetus Testamentum* 13 (1963):357-79; A. F. J. Klijn, "The Letter of Aristeas and the Greek Translation of the Pentateuch in Egypt," *NTS* 11 (1964/65):154-58; S. Jellicoe, "The Occasion and Purpose of the Letter of Aristeas: A Re-Examination," *NTS* 12 (1965/66):144-50; George Howard, "The Letter of Aristeas and Diaspora Judaism," *JTS* B.C. 22 (1971):337-48.

the whole. Also included are an account of the release of the Jewish prisoners who had been deported to Egypt by Ptolemy I, a description of Judea and Jerusalem, an explanation of some features of the law (i.e., a moral interpretation of the food laws) by the high priest Eleazar, and (the longest section) the table conversations of Ptolemy II with the Jewish translators in which the king asked each man a question about kingship, philosophy, or the good life. The letter thus is an important source for Jewish propaganda in the Diaspora from circles open to accommodation to Hellenistic ideas. The whole work serves not only to commend the Septuagint as an official translation but also to commend more liberal Hellenistic Judaism: either to inquiring pagans or to more conservative countrymen.

Jubilees [99]

The Book of Jubilees was apparently written around the mid–second century B.C. The text survives in entirety only in Ethiopic translation, but the discovery at Qumran of fragments from nine or ten manuscripts of the work confirms that the original language was Hebrew. Although R. H. Charles with the limited information available in his time postulated that the author was a Pharisee, a priest, and an upholder of the Maccabean priesthood (a strange combination), the popularity of the work at Qumran shows that it was at least acceptable to the Essenes, and the large number of parallels to other documents from Qumran suggest that the author was an Essene or a representative of the type of piety out of which that movement developed. Prominent among these similarities is the polemic on behalf of a solar calendar of 364 days a year in which the feasts would fall on the same day of the week each year.

Jubilees is a rewriting of history from creation to the giving of the law on Sinai. The book is presented as a revelation from an "angel of the presence" to Moses while he was on the mount, and the mediation of angels is prominent throughout. The history is dated by Jubilee periods (forty-nine years) and weeks of years (or Sabbath years, i.e., seven years). The book emphasizes the absolute supremacy of the law. It traces the origin of various ordinances to incidents in the lives of the patriarchs. Even the angels observe the Sabbath, but it is said to have been given to Israel alone among the nations. The sins most frequently and strongly opposed are fornication, idolatry, and eating blood (cf. Acts 15:20, 29). Angels who sinned are led down to a place of punishment and imprisonment (as in Jude 6; cf. 1 Pet. 3:19).

---

99. The standard critical text and translation is J. C. VanderKam, *The Book of Jubilees*, 2 vols., *CSCO* 510-11 (Louvain, 1989). For studies see L. Finkelstein, "The Book of Jubilees and the Rabbinic Halaka," *HTR* 16 (1923):39-61; E. Wiesenberg, "The Jubilee of Jubilees," *RQ* 3:1 (1961):3-40; G. L. Davenport, *The Eschatology of the Book of Jubilees* (Leiden, 1971); J. C. VanderKam, *Textual and Historical Studies in the Book of Jubilees* (Missoula, Mont., 1977); John C. Endres, *Biblical Interpretation in the Book of Jubilees* (Washington, 1987); J. C. VanderKam, *The Book of Jubilees* (Sheffield, 2001).

1 Enoch [100]

First Enoch is a composite work with a most complicated history. The present work, extant in its entirety only in Ethiopic, is composed of five parts: (1) The Book of Watchers (1–36) — introductory visions and parables of Enoch, including his journeys through the heavens, underworld, and earth, perhaps third century B.C.; (2) Book of the Similitudes (37–71) — of uncertain date, perhaps first century B.C. or A.D.;[101] (3) Book of Heavenly Luminaries or Astronomical Book (72–82) — an astronomical treatise in support of the solar year of 364 days, third century B.C. at the latest; (4) Dream Visions (83–90, including the Animal Apocalypse, 85–90) — in which Enoch relates to his son Methuselah in symbolic form the history from antediluvian times to the founding of the messianic kingdom in Maccabean times, c. 166–161 B.C.; (5) The Two Ways of the Righteous and the Sinner (91–107) — Enoch's admonitions to his children, beginning of the first century B.C., if not earlier, followed by a Conclusion (108).

The contents are actually much more complex than this outline; the final editor apparently rearranged and combined material from several sources in all of the sections except possibly the fourth. R. H. Charles identified in the first section before the journeys of Enoch (17–36) a parable on the future condition of the wicked and the righteous (1–5), a fragment from a Noah book (6–11), and an announcement of doom to the fallen angels (12–16). And he found in the fifth section in addition to the admonitions giving blessings upon the righteous and pronouncing woes upon sinners an Apocalypse of Weeks (93; 91:11-

---

100. M. Black, ed., *Apocalypsis Henochi Graece* (Leiden, 1970); J. T. Milik, *The Books of Enoch: Aramaic Fragments of Qumran Cave 4* (Oxford, 1976); review by E. Ullendorff and M. Knibb in *Bulletin of the School of Oriental and African Studies* 40 (1977):601-2; also reviewed in *JTS* 29 (1978):517-30; M. A. Knibb and E. Ullendorff, *The Ethiopic Book of Enoch: A New Edition in the Light of the Aramaic Dead Sea Fragments,* 2 vols. (Oxford, 1978); M. Black, "The Eschatology of the Similitudes of Enoch," *JTS* B.C. 3 (1952):1-10; J. P. Thorndike, "The Apocalypse of Weeks and the Qumran Sect," *RQ* 3:1 (1961):163-84; S. Aalen, "St. Luke's Gospel and the Last Chapters of I Enoch," *NTS* 13 (1967):1-13; J. T. Milik, "Problèmes de la Littérature Hénochique à la Lumière des Fragments Araméens de Qumrân," *HTR* 64 (1971):333-78; Jonas C. Greenfield and Michael E. Stone, "The Enochic Pentateuch and the Date of the Similitudes," *HTR* 70 (1977):51-65; M. A. Knibb, "The Date of the Parables of Enoch: A Critical Review" and C. L. Mearns, "Dating the Similitudes of Enoch," *NTS* 25 (1979):345-69; D. W. Suter, *Tradition and Composition in the Parables of Enoch* (Missoula, Mont., 1979); G. W. E. Nickelsburg, "The Book of Enoch in Recent Research," *Religious Studies Review* 7 (1981):210-17; J. C. VanderKam, *Enoch and the Growth of an Apocalyptic Tradition* (Washington, 1984); M. Black, *The Book of Enoch or I Enoch: A New English Edition with Commentary and Textual Notes* (Leiden, 1985); Margaret Barker, *The Lost Prophet: The Book of Enoch and Its Influence on Christianity* (Nashville, 1989); George W. E. Nickelsburg, *1 Enoch 1: A Commentary on the Book of 1 Enoch, Chap. 1-36, 81-108,* Hermeneia (Minneapolis, 2001).

101. The absence of the "Similitudes" from the Dead Sea Scrolls and the similarities of this section to the New Testament (e.g., the "Son of Man" passages) have led some scholars to argue that it is Christian in origin (Milik dates it as late as the third century); but most scholars are convinced that the "Similitudes" are Jewish and pre-70 in date.

19) from pre-Maccabaean times, and another fragment of the book of Noah (106–7). Recent study has also identified an "Animal Apocalypse."[102] J. T. Milik has argued that the original five parts were as follows: (1) Book of Watchers (1–36); (2) Book of Giants (37–71); (3) Astronomical Book of Luminaries (72–82, but the Ethiopic has lost a long part of the original Aramaic work); (4) Book of Dreams (83–90); and (5) Epistle of Enoch (91–107). There were later incorporated in part one the Visions of Enoch (6–19) and part of the Book of Giants, when the position of the latter was replaced in the Christian era by the Book of Similitudes.

Fragments of eleven Aramaic manuscripts containing parts of four of the sections of the Ethiopic book (missing is the Similitudes) have been found at Qumran; one of these (from the Book of Heavenly Luminaries) was copied about 200 B.C. The original language may have been Hebrew or Aramaic, or (as Daniel) a combination of the two. Also existing are fragments of the Greek. The work was not only popular at Qumran, exhibiting definite similarities with the Essene calendar and angelology, but was used in early Christianity (Jude 14-15 quotes 1 Enoch 1:9, and Tertullian considered the work inspired Scripture — see *On the Apparel of Women* 1.3; cf. *On Idolatry* 4 — although he recognized that others did not accept it).

The Similitudes offer some of the most interesting material in 1 Enoch for the study of the New Testament, especially the Gospels. The titles "Son of man," "Elect One," and "the Anointed" appear to be used almost interchangeably. Associated with this figure are his people, spoken of as elect ones, holy ones, and righteous ones. The usual name for God is Lord of Spirits. The four angels of the presence are Michael, Gabriel, Raphael, and Phanuel. The resurrection is taught in chapter 51.

The different sources in 1 Enoch have not been harmonized into a consistent eschatology. Noteworthy is the description in chapter 22 of Sheol with its four divisions — one for the righteous and three for different classes of sinners. The demonology of 1 Enoch is similar to that of Jubilees and provides part of the background for the New Testament view of angels and demons. The angels who kept not their first estate (cf. Jude 6; 2 Pet. 2:4 for the phrase, if not the incident) are watchers who fell from lusting after the daughters of men and have been imprisoned in darkness (1 Enoch 6–16). Demons are disembodied spirits of the giants; they work moral ruin until the final judgment (1 Enoch 16). Satan is the ruler of the kingdom of evil, but he is subject to the "Lord of Spirits." The functions of the Satans are tempting to evil (69:4-6), accusing the fallen (40:7), and punishing the condemned (53:3; 56:1). In the first part of the work the origin of evil is traced to the fallen angels, but in the last part man is himself the source of moral evil (98:4-5).

---

102. Patrick Tiller, *A Commentary on the Animal Apocalypse of* 1 Enoch (Atlanta, 1993).

2 Enoch [103]

Second Enoch is also called the Book of the Secrets of Enoch or Slavonic Enoch, because the book survives only in longer and shorter Slavonic recensions, translated from Greek. The place and date of composition cannot be determined, but modern study favors the first century, suggests a possible Hebrew original and points to antecedents or connections to Merkabah mysticism.[104]

According to the work, an elaboration on Genesis 5:21-32, Enoch was led through the ten heavens — the tenth being the throne of God. God gave Enoch an account of creation. The fall of Eve is given a sexual interpretation, for it is said that the Devil seduced her. History corresponds to creation: the world will last for seven thousand years and there will follow an eighth eternal period in which there will be no counting of time. Enoch returned to earth to give his children final instructions. These include certain close parallels to the teachings of Jesus: judgment on those who revile, are angry with, or spit on a person (44:1-3; cf. Matt. 5:22); God's demand of pure hearts, with outward sacrifice only to test the heart (45:3; cf. Matt. 12:7; 23:23); swearing with "yes, yes" and "no, no" (49:1; cf. Matt. 5:34-35); feeding the hungry, clothing the naked, etc. (51:1; 63:1; 9:1; cf. Matt. 25:34).

Testaments of the Twelve Patriarchs [105]

The Testaments of the Twelve Patriarchs is the principal representative of the literary genre of testament, the formal setting in which an ancient worthy on his deathbed bequeathed a spiritual message to his descendants. Two major

---

103. K. Lake, "The Date of the Slavonic Enoch," *HTR* 16 (1923):397-98; A. Rubenstein, "Observations on the Slavonic Book of Henoch," *JJS* 13 (1962):1-21; S. Pines, "Eschatology and the Concept of Time in the Slavonic Book of Enoch," *Types of Redemption*, Supplement to *Numen* 18 (Leiden, 1970).

104. Andrei Orlov, "Titles of Enoch-Metatron in *2 Enoch*," *Journal for the Study of the Pseudepigrapha* 18 (1998):71-86; idem, "The Origin of the Name 'Metatron' and the Text of 2 (Slavonic Apocalypse of) Enoch," *Journal for the Study of the Pseudepigrapha* 21 (2000):19-26; idem, "Secrets of Creation in 2 (Slavonic) Enoch," *Henoch* 22 (2000):45-62.

105. M. de Jonge, *Testamentum XII Patriarchum* (2d ed.; Leiden, 1970); M. de Jonge, et al., *The Testaments of the Twelve Patriarchs: A Critical Edition of the Greek Text* (Leiden, 1978); G. R. Beasley-Murray, "The Two Messiahs in the Testaments of the 12 Patriarchs," *JTS* 48 (1947):1-12; Jürgen Becker, *Untersuchungen zur Entstehungsgeschichte der Testamente der Zwölf Patriarchen* (Leiden, 1970); M. de Jonge, *Studies on the Testaments of the Twelve Patriarchs: Text and Interpretation* (Leiden, 1975); G. W. E. Nickelsburg, Jr., ed., *Studies in the Testament of Joseph* (Missoula, Mont., 1975); H. Dixon Slingerland, *The Testaments of the Twelve Patriarchs: A Critical History of Research* (Missoula, Mont., 1977); M. de Jonge, "The Main Issues in the Study of the Testaments of the Twelve Patriarchs," *NTS* 26 (1980):508-24; H. W. Hollander and M. de Jonge, *The Testaments of the Twelve Patriarchs: A Commentary* (Leiden, 1985); M. de Jonge, "The Testaments of the Twelve Patriarchs: Central Problems and Essential Viewpoints," *ANRW* II, *Principat*, 20.1 (Berlin and New York, 1986), 359-420; Robert A. Kugler, *The Testaments of the Twelve Patriarchs* (Sheffield, 2001) (studies the Christian form of the text).

concerns of testamentary literature are ethical paraenesis and apocalyptic fore-
casts of the future. (New Testament examples of testaments are John 13–17, Acts
20, 2 Timothy, and 2 Peter.) This work purports to be the last words of each of
the twelve sons of Jacob as they gathered their own families about them, each
in turn, before their death. It survives in several Greek manuscripts containing
Christian passages; therefore it has been claimed as a Christian work incorporating Jewish traditions (and so is translated in the *Ante-Nicene Fathers*, Vol.
VIII, pp. 9-38). The case for the alternative hypothesis that this was a basically
Jewish work to which Christian scribes made interpolations has been strength-
ened by the discovery of Aramaic fragments of a Testament of Levi in Caves 1
and 4 at Qumran and a Hebrew fragment of a Testament of Naphtali in Cave 4.
These fragments do not prove the case for a Jewish original, since they are not
identical with the Greek testaments; but their discovery opens up a new perspective on the study of the transmission and compilation of this literature.
There evidently were several stages of rewriting and borrowing, and the process requires much more study. It is safe to say that there was a Jewish original
and that the present form is Christian, but what lies in between is not clear.
There is a consensus that the clearly Christian elements belong to the second
century, but there is no general agreement on the Jewish stages of the work.

The testaments of Levi and Naphtali, the ones for which fragments have
been found at Qumran, do not follow the same pattern as the rest. Most of the
testaments follow the form of a narrative section about an event in the patriarch's life (especially as related to Joseph), an ethical admonition based on a
key word from the narrative, and an account of eschatological blessings and
curses. The Testament of Reuben warns against fornication, a sin with which
the testaments show considerable preoccupation. The Testament of Simeon
warns against envy. The Testament of Judah has a longer historical narrative,
stressing the prowess of Judah (perhaps to justify his military leadership as the
royal tribe), but the ethical section warns against the dangers of wine, fornication, and the love of money. The Testament of Issachar commends the virtue of
singleness of heart (integrity), the Testament of Zebulun the quality of mercy.
The Testament of Dan warns against lying and anger, that of Gad against hatred. Asher presents his ethical teaching in terms of "two ways [of good and
evil] and two inclinations" (1:3; cf. *Didache* and Barnabas). The testaments of
Joseph and Benjamin are less focused on one key idea but continue the exaltation of Joseph as the pious Jew who keeps the law and obeys God at all times.[106]
The Testament of Joseph is compiled from two sources: 3:1–9:5 recounts Joseph's avoidance of the temptations of Potiphar's wife, commending his chastity and piety; 11:2–16:6 is a narrative about Joseph's early life with a commen-
dation of the patient love that does good to those who wish you evil and hides

---

106. Harm W. Hollander, *Joseph as an Ethical Model in the Testaments of the Twelve Patriarchs* (Leiden, 1981).

the faults of others.[107] In its present form it teaches that God exalts those with endurance, humility, and fear of God. The Testament of Benjamin says to "fear the Lord and love your neighbor" (3:3). The teachings of the testaments about love for God and neighbor, forgiveness, and universalism provide close parallels to the New Testament.

Several testaments in the pseudepigraphal literature commonly emphasize a foretelling of future history,[108] an element in the Testament of Levi (third in the group) and the Testament of Naphtali (eighth), which include dreams that prefigured the future. The Testament of Joseph is one of the longest, and the way the other testaments take the relationship to Joseph as the point of departure would argue that it was the nucleus, or part of the nucleus, around which the collection grew. On the other hand, there is a unifying thread of exhortations to the families to follow Levi and Judah. Normally, it is stressed that the priesthood was given to Levi and the kingship to Judah (Simeon 7:1-2; Issachar 5:7; Naphtali 5:3; 8:1; Joseph 19:11; Benjamin 11:2). Since the former was valued more highly (Judah 21:2), Levi is given preeminence, which in some places extends to giving him the kingship as well (Reuben 6:7, 11-12; cf. Levi 8:4-5).

The ideological associations of the testaments show further the complexity of this work and add to the difficulty of tracing its history. Some passages seem to support the Maccabean ideology, as in the promise of sovereignty as well as priesthood to Levi. On the other hand, there are even more points of contact with the thought-world at Qumran. The assigning of the kingship to Judah and the priesthood to Levi corresponds to the two messiahs at Qumran. The doctrine of the "two spirits in man" (Judah 20; cf. Asher 1) and the role of Beliar (cf. 2 Cor. 6:15, Belial) are particularly close contacts. There are also frequent references in the testaments to the Enoch literature. Although some of the ethical teaching may have received Christian glosses, the principal signal of a Christian hand is doctrinal assertions relative to Christ. The messianic-apocalyptic sections present us with the Christ of the Gospels.

Testament of Job [109]

The Testament of Job is of uncertain date and provenance, perhaps about the beginning of the Christian era in Egypt. It praises the virtue of patience as superior to everything (27:7). The prominence of women, mystical tendencies,

107. H. Dixon Slingerland, "The Testament of Joseph: A Redaction-Critical Study," *JBL* 96 (1977):507-16. Others begin and end the two sections at different places. If the second story was the original form of the Testament of Joseph, it would be brought into close conformity with the other testaments.

108. A. B. Kolenkow, "The Genre Testament and Its Use for Forecast of the Future in Hellenistic Judaism," *JSJ* 6 (1975):57-71.

109. S. P. Brock, *Testamentum Iobi* (Leiden, 1967); R. A. Kraft, *The Testament of Job* (Missoula, Mont., 1974); M. A. Knibb and P. W. van der Horst, eds., *Studies on the Testament of Job* (Cambridge, 1990).

references to the language of angels, and information on burial practices have drawn the attention of modern scholars.

Assumption of Moses [110]

The work which goes under the name Assumption of Moses is primarily the Testament of Moses; most of the Assumption proper is missing at the end. The work survives only in a sixth-century Latin palimpsest manuscript. References by Greek authors to the Assumption (Clement of Alexandria, *Frg. in Ep. Jude* 9, and Origen, *On First Principles* 3.2.1) make almost certain that Jude 9 cited the now lost section of the Assumption. Jude 16 also seems influenced by the Assumption of Moses 5:5; 7:7, 9.[111] The original language apparently was Hebrew or Aramaic. Majority opinion is that the document was written during the lifetime of Jesus; at the least the present form of the work belongs to his time because it refers to the sons of Herod ruling. It has been argued that the Testament of Moses in its present form is a redaction of a work from the time of the Maccabean revolt. The Testament and Assumption originally may have been separate works that were united under the latter title.

The Assumption of Moses is a rewriting of Deuteronomy 31–34. Moses commissioned Joshua as his successor and foretold the history of the Jewish people to the first century of our era. The author has harsh things to say about the Hellenizers, the Maccabees, the priesthood, and Herod. He commends the example of Taxo, who led his seven sons into a cave to die rather than transgress the commands of God. He expects God shortly to usher in his kingdom to avenge the blood of such faithful men. The author thus represents a pacifist stance opposed to militant nationalism. He rejects the validity of present cultic acts but not of sacrificial cultus as such. There is a great exaltation of Israel, for whom the world was created, and of Moses, who is so great that all the world is his sepulchre. Moses is not, however, supernatural, and is presented primarily as a prophet.

Ascension of Isaiah [112]

The present form of the Ascension of Isaiah, which survives entire only in an Ethiopic version, contains three separate works: (1) Martyrdom of Isaiah (1:1–3:12; 5:1-14); (2) Testament of Hezekiah (3:13–4:18); and (3) Vision of Isaiah (6–

110. J. Licht, "Taxo, or the Apocalyptic Doctrine of Vengeance," *JJS* 12 (1961):95-103; G. W. E. Nickelsburg, ed., *Studies on the Testament of Moses: Seminar Papers* (Cambridge, Mass., 1973); A. Schalit, *Assumptio Mosis* (Leiden, 1985); J. Tromp, *The Assumption of Moses: A Critical Edition with Commentary* (Leiden, 1993).

111. Josephus, *Ant.* 4.8.48 [326], from near the same date as Jude, is also aware of the work.

112. Robert G. Hall, "The *Ascension of Isaiah:* Community, Situation Date and Place in Early Christianity," *JBL* 109 (1990):289-306; C. Detlef and G. Müller, "The Ascension of Isaiah," in *New Testament Apocrypha*, rev. ed., ed. E. Hennecke and W. Schneemelcher (Louisville, 1992), 2:603-620; J. Knight, *The Ascension of Isaiah* (Sheffield, 1995).

11). The first part is Jewish in origin, probably written in Hebrew, and perhaps from the second century B.C. It tells of the accession of Manasseh to the throne of Judah, his wickedness, Isaiah's withdrawal to the wilderness, and finally of Isaiah being sawed in two. Isaiah's death in this manner apparently is referred to in Hebrews 11:37 and is also included in the pseudepigraphal *Lives of the Prophets*, the Talmud (b. Yebamoth 49b; j. Sanhedrin 10), and *Testimony of Truth* from the Nag Hammadi library (IX.3,40, 21).

The other two parts of the book are Christian in origin, written in Greek perhaps as early as the end of the first century. The Testament of Hezekiah relates Isaiah's vision of the descent of the Beloved, his crucifixion and resurrection, the establishment of the church, and subsequent departures from the teaching of the Twelve. The Vision of Isaiah relates Isaiah's journey through the seven heavens; from the seventh heaven he watches the descent of Christ, his life, and his reascent to the right hand of Glory.

2 Baruch [113]

Second Baruch, or the Syriac Apocalypse of Baruch, survives in entirety in a single Syriac manuscript and in Arabic. Chapters 78–86, Baruch's epistle to the nine and one-half tribes in the dispersion, circulated separately and were included in the Syriac Bible. The Syriac is a translation from the Greek, of which a fragment of chapters 12–14 was found in the Oxyrhynchus Papyri. A Hebrew original is likely. Second Baruch was written (or compiled) about A.D. 100 or shortly thereafter. It has close contacts with the concerns of 2 Esdras.

The book recounts the destruction of Jerusalem by the Babylonians and more successfully maintains the standpoint of the assumed date of writing than most of the pseudepigrapha do, but it would seem that the destruction of A.D. 70 is what the author really had in mind. When Jerusalem was about to fall, angels caused the earth to swallow up the sacred vessels to hide them until the messianic age and broke down the walls of the city so that the heathen could not boast of doing so. As in other apocalypses, a survey of history in symbolic form is included; an interpretation is also provided. God explained to Baruch the justice of his judgments. The advice to the people is "not to withdraw from the way of the law" (44:3). Second Baruch is particularly noteworthy for its descriptions of the messianic age (the marvelous productivity of the earth in 29:5 was picked up by the Christian writer Papias) and of the resurrec-

---

113. S. Dedering, *Apocalypse of Baruch* (Leiden, 1973); A. F. J. Klijn, "The Sources and the Redaction of the Syriac Apocalypse of Baruch," *JSJ* 1 (1970):65-76; Gwendolyn Saylor, *Have the Promises Failed: A Literary Analysis of 2 Baruch* (Chico, Calif., 1984); F. J. Murphy, *The Structures and Meaning of Second Baruch* (Atlanta, 1985); F. Leemhuis, A. F. J. Klijn, and G. J. H. van Gelder, *The Arabic Text of the Apocalypse of Baruch* (Leiden, 1986); Rivka Nir, *The Destruction of Jerusalem and the Idea of Redemption in the* Syriac Apocalypse of Baruch (Atlanta, 2002) (Gives the book a Christian context).

tion body (the earth gives up the dead as it received them and they have the same shape but then they are transformed; 50:2; 51:1-6; cf. 1 Cor. 15).

Between the opening announcement of the destruction of Jerusalem (1–5) and the concluding Epistle of Baruch (78–86), the contents are structured by seven revelations to Baruch (6–7; 10:1-3; 13–20; 22–30; 36–43; 48–51; 53–76), five of which are prepared for by fasts (5:7; 9:2; 12:5; 21:1; 47:2) and three of which are followed by addresses to the people (31–34; 44–46; 77).

The Psalms of Solomon [114]

We can date the Psalms of Solomon from the allusions in chapter 2 to Pompey's appearance in Jerusalem (63 B.C.) and death in Egypt (48 B.C.). The collection of eighteen psalms exists in Greek and Syriac, but the original language was Hebrew. They are the product of a single author, or at least reflect similar thought from the same period of time. The occasion for the association with Solomon is unknown, since the contents make no connection or allusion to him. The Psalms of Solomon have commonly been identified with the Pharisees, but the discovery of the *Thanksgiving Hymns* at Qumran has opened up the possibility of comparison with the Essenes; thus, we cannot at this time confidently assign them to any group. The Psalms of Solomon testify to a common Jewish piety and are a reminder that individuals do not stay in a box for the convenience of later historians.

The headings use the terms *psalm, hymn,* and *ode* interchangeably (cf. Col. 3:16; Eph. 5:19). The author makes a sharp distinction within the nation between the righteous, who are frequently called the "poor" (cf. the Gospels and Qumran), and the unrighteous sinners who are charged with oppressing the righteous, pleasing men, profaning the sanctuary, and setting up a worldly monarchy. The author rejects the Hasmonean monarchy and advocates a Davidic king (chaps. 17–18). This Son of David will be a righteous king, the anointed of the Lord:

> Gird him with strength that he may shatter unrighteous rulers, and that he may purge Jerusalem from nations that trample her down to destruction. . . . He shall destroy the godless nations with the word of his mouth. (17:24-25)

He will gather together a holy people who are like a firstborn, only-begotten son (18:4; 13:8). The righteous will be raised to eternal life (3:16). The apparent

114. J. O'Dell, "The Religious Background of the Psalms of Solomon," *RQ* 3:2 (1961):241-58; R. B. Wright, "The Psalms of Solomon, the Pharisees, and the Essenes," *1972 Proceedings: International Organization for Septuagint and Cognate Studies and the Society of Biblical Literature Pseudepigrapha Seminar,* ed. R. A. Kraft (Missoula, Mont., 1972), 136-47; Joachim Schüpphaus, *Die Psalmen Salomos* (Leiden, 1977); Robert Hann, *The Manuscript History of the Psalms of Solomon* (Atlanta, 1982); Joseph L. Trafton, *The Syriac Version of the Psalms of Solomon* (Atlanta, 1985).

"mission" language in chapter 11 pertains to the gathering in of the saints from all over the world.

Joseph and Aseneth [115]

Joseph and Aseneth is the story of the conversion of the daughter of a priest of Heliopolis to Judaism and her marriage to Joseph. It is a Jewish work written in Greek, probably in Egypt, perhaps near the beginning of the common era. The work shows a certain accommodation to a Gentile setting and an acceptance of proselytes but at the same time a strong emphasis on a distinctive Jewish identity as demonstrated by the polemic against idolatrous practices. The language of "bread of life," "cup of blessing," and "ointment of incorruption" have provoked discussion whether a possible ritual meal is intended or if these are formulas describing a Jewish way of life. Practices mentioned that are relevant for the study of early Christianity include the emphasis on virginity and avoidance of pre-marital sex, the removing of the veil to indicate availability for marriage, Aseneth's washing of Joseph's feet, Pharaoh placing his hands on the heads of the couple, the black dress and ashes to show mourning, and the beautiful prayers. Joseph is called a "son of God."

Pseudo-Phocylides [116]

A gnomic poem with contacts with Jewish Wisdom literature and Hellenistic gnomic literature, Pseudo-Phocylides may be included among the Jewish

---

115. E. W. Brooks, *Joseph and Asenath* (Translations of Early Documents, Series 2, London 1918); Edgar W. Smith, Jr., "Joseph and Aseneth and Early Christian Literature: A Contribution to the Corpus Hellenisticum Novi Testamenti," Ph.D. diss., Claremont, 1975; R. I. Pervo, "Joseph and Asenath and the Greek Novel," and H. C. Kee, "The Socio-Religious Setting and Aims of Joseph and Asenath," in *Society of Biblical Literature 1976 Seminar Papers* (Missoula, 1976), 171-181, 183-192; C. Buchard, "The Importance of Joseph and Aseneth for the Study of the New Testament," *NTS* 33 (1987):102-34; R. Chesnutt, "The Social Setting and Purpose of Joseph and Aseneth," *Journal for the Study of the Pseudepigrapha* 2 (1988):21-48; A. Standhartiner, *Das Frauenbild im Judentum der hellenistischen Zeit: Ein Beitrag anhand von Joseph und Aseneth* (Leiden, 1995); R. Chesnutt, *From Death to Life: Conversion in Joseph and Aseneth* (Sheffield, 1995); Gideon Bahak, *Joseph and Aseneth and the Jewish Temple in Heliopolis* (Atlanta, 1996); Ross S. Kraemer, *When Aseneth Met Joseph: A Late Antique Tale of the Biblical Patriarch and His Egyptian Wife* (Oxford, 1998) (argues the work is late antique, not early Roman Egypt); Edith M. Humphrey, *Joseph and Aseneth* (Sheffield, 2001).

116. P. W. van der Horst, *The Sentences of Pseudo-Phocylides* (Leiden, 1978); idem, "Pseudo-Phocylides and the New Testament," *Zeitschrift für die neutestamentliche Wissenschaft* 69 (1978):187-202; idem, "Pseudo-Phocylides Revisited," *Journal for the Study of the Pseudepigrapha* 3 (1988):3-30; the latter two reprinted in idem, *Essays on the Jewish World of Early Christianity* (Freiburg, 1990), 19-34, 35-62; Walter T. Wilson, *The Mysteries of Righteousness: The Literary Composition and Genre of the Sentences of Pseudo-Phoclides* (Tübingen, 1994) (includes text and new translation).

pseudepigrapha. It was written, it seems, by a Jew, probably early in the first century, possibly in Alexandria under the name of Phocylides of Miletus, a gnomic poet of the sixth century B.C. It is a summary of Jewish ethical teaching for Greek-speaking Jews living in a Hellenistic environment. This didactic poem supplements the Decalogue with the four cardinal virtues of Hellenistic philosophy and other non-biblical materials consistent with the Jewish Law. These teachings have affinities with early Christianity.

Sibylline Oracles [117]

The Greeks and Romans applied the term *Sibyls* to aged, inspired women not attached to a particular oracular shrine who, in a state of ecstasy, prophesied coming events. The ancient testimony regarded Sibyl as a proper name, and the earliest writers mention only one Sibyl. Soon as many as ten are mentioned, but the most famous was at Erythrae in Ionia. She was rivaled by the Sibyl at Cumae near Naples, who sold three Sibylline books to King Tarquin of Rome.[118] A special commission in Rome had charge of these Greek oracles and consulted them on request of the magistrates at times of crisis for the state. This official collection burned with the Capitoline Temple in 83 B.C. A commission was then dispatched to collect oracles wherever they might be found. This apparently became the occasion for a great increase in the production of spurious oracles. There were already in existence certain private collections. So many "Sibylline oracles" were found, often of a politically subversive nature, that Augustus had two thousand volumes destroyed; and it was still necessary to carry out a weeding process. The Jews found the circulation of oracles attributed to the Sibyl an effective propaganda device, and the Christians imitated them in this. The surviving collection was edited about the fifth or sixth century A.D. in fifteen books, of which books 9, 10, and 15 are missing, and there are gaps in the others. Books 3–5 are Jewish, and there is a Jewish base for the Christian redaction in most of the rest (although some pagan elements have been kept).[119]

Book 3, despite being quite heterogeneous, is the oldest, probably coming

---

117. Texts by J. Geffcken, *Die Oracula Sibyllina* (Leipzig, 1901), and A. M. Kurfess, *Sibyllinische Weissagungen* (Munich, 1951); and J.-D. Gauge, *Sibyllinische Weissagungen* (Düsseldorf/Zurich, 1998); translations by M. S. Terry, *The Sibylline Oracles* (New York, 1899), and J. J. Collins in *The Old Testament Pseudepigrapha*, ed. James H. Charlesworth (Garden City, N.Y., 1983), 1:317-472; studies by J. J. Collins, *The Sibylline Oracles of Egyptian Judaism* (Missoula, Mont., 1974); idem, "The Development of the Sibylline Tradition," *ANRW* II, *Principat*, 20.1 (Berlin, 1987), 421-59; H. W. Parke, *Sibyls and Sibylline Prophecy in Classical Antiquity* (London, 1988).

118. Dionysius of Halicarnassus, *Roman Antiquities* 6.42.

119. Some of the main Christian passages are translated in Ursula Treu, "Christian Sibyllines," in *New Testament Apocrypha*, rev. ed., ed. E. Hennecke and W. Schneemelcher (Louisville, 1992), 2:656-84.

from the second century B.C. Book 4 comes shortly after the destruction of Jerusalem and the eruption of Vesuvius, to which it refers. Book 5 was written under Hadrian before the Bar Kokhba revolt, but there are later insertions. The Jewish Sibyllines emphasize the unity and sovereignty of God over against the various practices of idolatry and the moral corruptions of paganism. Much attention is given to the history of the world and God's judgments on the different peoples. The hatred for Rome is intensified in the Christian books. Some scholars have seen Essene influence, especially in book 4 where there is a repudiation of animal sacrifice and temples and reference to grace before meals and purification by washing in water,[120] but this connection is rather tenuous.[121] The eschatological portions are quite similar to what one reads in apocalyptic writings.

BIBLIOGRAPHY

Denis, A.-M., ed. *Fragmenta pseudepigraphorum quae supersunt graeca.* Leiden, 1970.

Charlesworth, James H., ed. *The Old Testament Pseudepigrapha.* 2 vols. Garden City, N.Y., 1983, 1985.

Sparks, H. F. D., ed. *The Apocryphal Old Testament.* Oxford, 1984.

De Jonge, M., ed. *Outside the Old Testament.* Cambridge, 1985.

Denis, A.-M., and Y. Janssens. *Concordance Grecque des Pseudépigraphes d'Ancien Testament.* Louvain-la Neuve, 1987.

Denis, A.-M. *Introduction aux pseudépigraphes grecs d'Ancien Testament.* Leiden, 1970.

Reeves, John C., ed. *Tracing the Threads: Studies in the Vitality of Jewish Pseudepigrapha.* Atlanta, 1994.

Charlesworth, James H. *The Old Testament Pseudepigrapha and the New Testament: Prolegomena for the Study of Christian Origins.* Harrisburg, Pa., 1998.

Stone, Michael E., and Theodore A. Bergen, eds. *Biblical Figures Outside the Bible.* Harrisburg, Pa., 1998.

Di Tommasio, Lorenzo. *A Bibliography of Pseudepigrapha Research 1850-1999.* Shefield, 2002. (This comprehensive bibliographical guide replaces an extensive list in this book.)

Journal for the Study of the Pseudepigrapha.

120. B. Noack, "Are the Essenes Referred to in the Sibylline Oracles?" *Studia Theologica* 17 (1963):90-102.

121. V. Nikiprowetzky, "Réflexions sur quelques problèmes de quatrième et du cinquième livre des Oracles Sibyllins," *Hebrew Union College Annual* 43 (1972):29-76, esp. 55-58.

Dead Sea Scrolls

The Dead Sea Scrolls have had a major impact on recent interpretations of Judaism and Christian origins. They have enlarged the understanding of Judaism in Palestine, especially in regard to messianism, eschatology, and religious observances. In making accessible new evidence for variety in first-century Judaism, they have required a modification of descriptions projecting "normative" Judaism on this period. This in turn has supplied new configurations in the background of Christianity (see pp. 526-30).

Following the discovery in 1947 of manuscripts hidden in caves in the vicinity of Khirbet ("ruin") Qumran on the northwest shore of the Dead Sea, explorations in the general area produced other manuscript discoveries. The finds range from excellent, well-preserved manuscripts to masses of fragments. The documents include biblical manuscripts, previously known apocryphal and pseudepigraphal works, and previously unknown documents, both sectarian and non-sectarian (especially para-biblical texts). More than 850 manuscripts have been identified (mostly fragmentary), over 200 of which come from books in the Hebrew Bible. Our interest will be in the nonbiblical texts, but it should be noted that the biblical manuscripts among the Dead Sea Scrolls demonstrate that various text types circulated among Jews prior to the second revolt. Three known text types are represented in Qumran's biblical manuscripts: the text standardized later as the Masoretic text, the Hebrew text behind the Septuagint where it differs from the Masoretic text, and readings agreeing with the Samaritan version. Before we concentrate our attention on the finds at Qumran, however, we will briefly note discoveries made at other sites.

Two caves in the *Wadi* (a seasonal stream) *Murabba'at*, some eleven miles south of Qumran, have yielded documents related to the rebellion of Bar Kokhba in 132–135, including letters from the leader of the revolt himself. Most of the fragmentary biblical works, legal documents, and letters belong to the period from 70 to 135, but an eighth- or seventh-century-B.C. papyrus in Hebrew is the earliest papyrus in that language ever found. The major find is a well-preserved scroll of the Twelve Minor Prophets. Since the text agrees with the traditional Hebrew text and the earlier manuscripts of the Twelve from Qumran do not, there is firm evidence that the so-called Masoretic text was standardized in the period between 70 and 135.

South of En Gedi at *Naḥal Hever* and *Naḥal Se'elim* a more extensive collection of letters from Bar Kokhba has been found along with other documents from his era.[122] Receiving greatest interest among the biblical materials is a fragmentary copy of the Twelve Minor Prophets in Greek from the first century A.D.

---

122. N. Lewis, ed., *The Documents from the Bar Kokhba Period in the Cave of Letters: Greek Papyri* (Jerusalem, 1989).

A DEAD SEA SCROLL
The process of unrolling one of the fragile Dead Sea Scrolls was a delicate
operation. *(Courtesy Israel Department of Antiquities and Museums)*

The ruins of the Byzantine monastery at *Khirbet Mird,* east of Bethlehem,
have yielded late Byzantine and early Arabic documents.

The *Wadi Daliyeh,* north of Jericho, has been the source of important legal papyri from 375 to 335 B.C.[123] The documents are in Aramaic and apparently were brought to the cave by persons from Samaria fleeing before soldiers
of Alexander the Great in 331 B.C.

Masada, the fortress built by Herod and occupied by the Sicarii during
the first revolt, has yielded some important manuscripts: a text of Sirach in Hebrew, fragments of biblical books, and some works previously known only
from Qumran (e.g., the "Angelic Liturgy").

For most people, however, reference to the Dead Sea Scrolls means the
remains of the library of the community that lived at Qumran from the second century B.C. until its destruction in A.D. 68. Eleven caves in the vicinity of
Qumran have produced manuscripts or fragments. The official method of
designation and citation for one of these documents is to give the Arabic nu-

---

123. Frank M. Cross, "The Discovery of the Samaria Papyri," *BA* 26 (1963):110-21.

meral for the cave in which it was found, Q for Qumran, the abbreviation for the (Hebrew) title of the document (unidentified fragments are given a number), and, if more than one copy is represented, a lower case letter as a superscript, followed by the Roman numeral and Arabic numerals to designate the column and lines of the manuscript. Thus 4QpIsa^c 4-7 ii 2-4 refers to Cave 4, Qumran, a pesher (commentary) on Isaiah, the third copy, fragments 4-7, column 2, lines 2-4. The major documents are also known popularly by their modern titles.[124]

Cave 1 produced the initial excitement and was the source of the principal complete (or nearly so) documents on which much of our knowledge of the Qumran community rests: two scrolls of Isaiah and five sectarian documents (1QS, 1QM, 1QH, 1QpHab, and 1QapGen; see below) — all now housed in the Shrine of the Book in Jerusalem. There are in addition seventy-two numbered fragments from this cave.

Caves 2, 3, and 5-10 have been designated *Minor Caves* because of the paucity of finds, both in extent and quantity, totaling 130 pieces. Most notable is the *Copper Scroll* (3Q15), a list of temple treasures with their hiding places (apocryphal?), from Cave 3. The claim that some of the Greek fragments from Cave 7 represent part of the Gospel of Mark has been sensational because the paleography would date about A.D. 50.[125] Christian works would not be out of the question, because these fragments may have been deposited on another occasion. Dating on paleographical grounds has to allow for at least some decades of variance. Critical response has not been favorable to the claim, however, and it seems likely that the fragments are in fact from the Greek Old Testament.[126]

Cave 4, near the ruins of the ancient settlement, has proved to be the main depository of the Qumran library. Fragments numbered to 579 have been recorded; unhappily most are in a poor state of preservation. Of the over 120 biblical manuscripts identified in this number, all of the books of the Hebrew canon except Esther are represented. 4QEx-Lev^f dates from the mid–third century B.C., making it at present the oldest biblical manuscript in existence. A considerable number of previously known apocryphal and pseudepigraphal works are included (e.g., 1 Enoch, Jubilees, Tobit), plus a large number of previously unknown sectarian works.

Cave 11 has furnished from its over thirty works a large Psalms scroll,

124. Patrick H. Alexander, David L. Petersen, et al., *The SBL Handbook of Style* (Peabody, 1999), 176-233 (Appendix F: Texts from the Judean Desert) lists the abbreviations, documents, and publication for the texts from Qumran and twelve other sites; cf. the earlier listing with bibliography by J. A. Fitzmyer, *The Dead Sea Scrolls: Major Publications and Tools for Study* (Atlanta, 1990).

125. Jose O'Callaghan, "New Testament Papyri in Qumran Cave 7?" Supplement to *JBL* 91/2 (1972):1-14.

126. Jerry Vardaman, "The Earliest Fragments of the New Testament?" *Expository Times* 83 (1971–72):374-76; Gordon Fee, "Some Dissenting Notes on 7Q5 = Mark 6:52-53," *JBL* 92 (1973):109-12.

which contains some Psalms not in the Hebrew canon,[127] a Targum on Job, and a copy of Leviticus in paleo-Hebrew script.

We will discuss the beliefs and practices of the community that produced the Dead Sea Scrolls in the section on Jewish parties and sects (pp. 521-30). In the present section our discussion is limited to brief introductions to some of the principal writings that originated with the Qumran community. All mentioned here are in Hebrew, except the *Genesis Apocryphon*. The texts in general include community rules, scriptural commentaries,[128] liturgical works,[129] and wisdom texts.[130]

Rule of the Community (or Manual of Discipline — 1QS)[131]

The abbreviation S is from the Hebrew *Serek* ("Rule"). This document is of fundamental importance for understanding the structure and ideology of the Qumran community and will be drawn on for the description of the sect later. In addition to 1QS and its supplements (see below) cave 4 yielded at least ten copies dated between 125 B.C. and A.D. 50 in four different recensions of the *Rule of the Community.*

The *Rule of the Community* comes from the early years of the sect in the second century B.C. Some have thought that the sect's founder, "The Teacher of

---

127. Patrick Skehan, "The Biblical Scrolls from Qumran and the Text of the Old Testament," *BA* 28 (1965):87-100; J. A. Sanders, *The Psalms Scroll of Qumran Cave 11* (Oxford, 1965); idem, *The Dead Sea Psalms Scroll* (Ithaca, N.Y., 1967); idem, "The Variorum in the Psalms Scroll (11QPsª)," *HTR* 59 (1966):83-94; Robert Polzin, "Notes on the Dating of the Non-Massoretic Psalms of 11QPsª," *HTR* 60 (1967):468-76; Patrick Skehan, "Qumran and Old Testament Criticism," *Qumran: sa piété, so théologie et son milieu*, ed. M. Delcor (Gembloux, 1978), 163-82; R. T. Beckwith, "The Courses of the Levites and the Eccentric Psalms Scrolls from Qumran," *RQ* 11 (1984):499-524 (offering an intriguing explanation for the extra Psalms); G. H. Wilson, "The Qumran Psalms Scroll Reconsidered: Analysis of the Debate," *CBQ* 47 (1985):624-42; E. M. Schuller, *Non-Canonical Psalms: A Pseudepigraphic Collection* (Decatur, Ga., 1986); Peter W. Flint, *The Dead Sea Psalms Scrolls and the Book of Psalms* (Leiden, 1997). Was the Qumran Psalter different from that of the rest of Judaism, were the contents of the Psalter not fixed in Judaism as a whole at this time, or was the scroll a hymnbook containing a selection of canonical psalms plus others?

128. James H. Charlesworth, *The Dead Sea Scrolls*, Vol. 6b: *Pesharim, Other Commentaries, and Related Documents* (Louisville, 1994); James H. Charlesworth, ed., *The Pesharim and Qumran History* (Grand Rapids, 2002); Timothy H. Lim, *Pesharim*, Companion to the Dead Sea Scrolls (Sheffield, 2002).

129. James H. Charlesworth, ed., *The Dead Sea Scrolls*, Vol. 4A: *Pseudepigraphic and Non-Masoretic Psalms and Prayers* (Louisville, 1997); James R. Davila, *Liturgical Works*, Eerdmans Commentaries on the Dead Sea Scrolls 6 (Grand Rapids, 2001).

130. D. J. Harrington, *Wisdom Texts from Qumran* (Sheffield, 1996).

131. J. Murphy-O'Connor, "La genèse littéraire de la Règle de la Communauté," *Revue Biblique* 78 (1969):528-49; James H. Charlesworth, ed., *The Dead Sea Scrolls: The Rule of the Community* (New York, 1996) (color plates of text and transcription and translation into six languages); Philip S. Alexander and Geza Vermes, eds., *Discoveries in the Judean Desert, Vol. XXVI, Qumran Cave 4 — XIX: Serekh Ha-Yahad and Two Related Texts* (Oxford, 1998).

Righteousness," is its author, but more likely he only inspired it, or perhaps wrote just part of it. As a working manual for the organization and discipline of the group, it was modified during the sect's history.

We may outline the contents as follows: i.1-15 — Introduction; i.16–iii.12 — Admission of new members and annual renewal of vows with a strong denunciation of those who refuse to enter the covenant; iii.13–iv.26 — Doctrine of the two spirits, light (truth) and darkness (perversity) with their respective works,[132] appointed by God to preside over humankind; v.1–vi.23 — Purpose of the community and regulations for its communal life; vi.24–vii.25 — Penal code for various transgressions; viii.1–ix.26 — Ideal community; x.1–xi.22 — Praise of God and concluding hymns.

Rule of the Congregation (or Messianic Rule — 1QSᵃ)[133]

One leaf with two columns of text originally belonging to the same scroll as 1QS was broken off through use and is designated 1QSᵃ. It is closely related to 1QS but is an independent work, now badly preserved. As the opening words say, it is "a rule for all the congregation of Israel at the end of days." Column i sets forth ages at which certain duties are to be assumed. Principal interest attaches to column ii with its description of a meal at which the priest and the Messiah of Israel are present. At the blessing of the bread and wine precedence belongs to the priest who first extends his hand over the bread; then the Messiah of Israel extends his hand over the bread, and then all the congregation utter a blessing.

Book of Blessings (1QSᵇ)[134]

The scroll containing 1QS originally contained a collection of benedictions, of which five columns survive, designated 1QSᵇ. The benedictions carried introductory statements. The blessings that survive are for the Faithful, the High Priest, the Sons of Zadok the Priest, and the Prince of the Congregation. Since the last sentence is incomplete, there was at least one more column.

Damascus Document (CD)[135]

The *Damascus Document* has been known since 1910 when Solomon Schechter published two manuscripts he had found in 1896 in the storeroom *(geniza)* of a

---

132. P. Wernberg-Møller, "A Reconsideration of the Two Spirits in the Rule of the Community (1QSerek III,13–IV,26)," *RQ* 3 (1961):413-41.

133. L. H. Schiffman, *The Eschatological Community of the Dead Sea Scrolls: A Study of the Rule of the Congregation* (Atlanta, 1990).

134. S. Talmon, "The 'Manual of Benedictions' of the Sect of the Judaean Desert," *RQ* 2 (1960):475-500.

135. Chaim Rabin, *The Zadokite Documents* (Oxford, 1958); S. Schechter, *Documents of Jew-*

Cairo synagogue. He called the manuscripts "Fragments of a Zadokite Work" from the prominence given to the priests as descendants of Zadok. Manuscript A contains eight leaves of parchment written on both sides (sixteen columns) and was written about the tenth century B.C.; manuscript B is a single leaf written on both sides from about two centuries later, overlapping columns 7 and 8 of A but containing at the end material not found in A. The abbreviation CD stands for Cairo (place of discovery) and Damascus (name of the document, because of prominence given in the contents to a migration to Damascus — whether literal or metaphorical). The discovery of extensive fragments at Qumran and similarities to 1QS show that the document belongs to the same circles, although perhaps from a different settlement or reflecting a later development in the sect. The Qumran fragments supply the introduction and conclusion to the work and some additional matter as well as paralleling the Cairo fragments.

The Damascus Document has two principal parts: Exhortation and Prescriptions. The former includes a brief history of the sect. Three hundred ninety years after the destruction of the temple by Nebuchadnezzar, God "caused a root of planting to spring from Israel and Aaron to possess his land." They were "like blind men and like men groping to find their way for twenty years." Then God "raised up for them a Teacher of Righteousness to lead them in the way of his heart." The group entered into a new covenant (actually a renewal of the old covenant) and went out from the land of Judah to the land of Damascus. They pledged to keep the commandments of the Teacher until "the coming of the Anointed out of Aaron and Israel" (Ms. B ii.1) or "until the arising of him who will teach righteousness at the end of the days" (Ms. A vi.10-11), which some have interpreted (but without good reason) as referring to an expected resurrection and return of the Teacher of Righteousness. The Prescriptions offer information about the community, which we will look at later. As examples of the interest of the document for New Testament studies we may note that the sect was more strict in their Sabbath interpretation than were the Pharisees. Their consistency in not lifting a beast out of a pit on the Sabbath (xi.13-14; but a man could be helped out, 16-17) would have avoided the force of Jesus' argument directed to the Pharisees in Matthew 12:11. An argument against polygamy in the exhortations prohibits "marrying two women during their lifetime" (iv. 21); it is based on Genesis 1:27, the text (combined with 2:24) on which Jesus based his argument for monogamy (Matt. 19:4).

ish Sectaries (repr.; New York, 1970); Louis Ginzberg, An Unknown Jewish Sect (New York, 1976); P. R. Davies, The Damascus Covenant, in Journal for the Study of the Old Testament, Supplement 25, and Winona Lake, Ind., 1983; M. Broshi, ed., The Damascus Document Reconsidered (Jerusalem, 1992); James H. Charlesworth, ed., The Dead Sea Scrolls, vol. 2: Damascus Document, War Scroll, and Related Documents, ed. J. Baumgarten and D. R. Schwartz (Louisville, 1995); Charlotte Hempel, The Damascus Texts (Sheffield, 2000).

War Scroll (1QM)[136]

The *War Scroll*, which gives the "Rule for the War of the Sons of Light against the Sons of Darkness," is one of the best preserved of the Dead Sea Scrolls. The scroll contains five sheets joined together and has nineteen columns of writing. It is nine and one-half feet long with the end missing. The *War Scroll* or "War Rule" (*milchamah*, "war") is a unique document from the ancient world. The author was well informed on Roman military science (which he integrated with the biblical instructions for holy war), as well as on Jewish liturgical practices (he was evidently a priest). There is little indication of date, but late first century B.C. or early first century A.D. seems likely.

We may outline the contents as follows: i — Identification of the sons of light and of darkness and announcement of the eschatological war that shall destroy the latter; ii.1-14 — Duties of the priests, mobilization of fighting men, and list of enemies in each year of the war (a forty-year period is envisioned but no service during the Sabbath years [5] and six years of preparation, so only twenty-nine years of fighting); ii.15–iii.11 — Instructions concerning the priests' trumpets; iii.12–v.2 — Instructions concerning the standards of the different units; v.3–ix.18 — Array, weapons, and maneuvers of the infantry and cavalry and the role of the priests and Levites; x.1–xiv.16 — Exhortation by the high priest and prayers, blessings, and curses; xv.1–xix.13 — Exhortation by the high priest and description of the last battle against the Kittim.

The "sons of light" are the "exiles of the wilderness." The "sons of darkness" are the traditional enemies of Israel in the Old Testament, plus their Jewish allies ("the wicked of the covenant") and the Kittim. Scholars have debated whether those identified in the scrolls as the Kittim are the Greeks or the Romans. The Nahum Commentary (4QpNah) refers to "kings of Greece from Antiochus to the appearance of the rulers of the Kittim" and seems conclusive for the Romans, unless the term was used with a different reference in different works. The reference to three kinds of holy days as "feasts, new moons, and Sabbaths" (ii.4) provides a parallel to Colossians 2:16 (but cf. also 1 Chron. 23:31). The four chief angels are Michael, Gabriel, Sariel, and Raphael (ix.15-16). Some of the passages are quite moving; others display a blatant militancy.

Thanksgiving Hymns (1QH)[137]

The Thanksgiving Scroll contains eighteen columns of text, with some thirty-two separate hymns (many quite defective). The hymns date from the middle

---

136. Y. Yadin, *The Scroll of the War of the Sons of Light against the Sons of Darkness* (Oxford, 1962); Philip R. Davies, *1QM, The War Scroll from Qumran, Its Structure and History* (Rome, 1977); James H. Charlesworth, ed., *The Dead Sea Scrolls*, vol. 2: *Damascus Document, War Scrolls, and Related Documents*, ed. J. Duhaime (Louisville, 1995).

137. J. Baumgarten and M. Mansoor, "Studies in the Thanksgiving Hymns," *JBL* 74

of the second century B.C. to the early first century A.D. There are additional fragments of the same scroll, and fragments from Cave 4 reflect other collections of hymns. Since nearly all of the hymns begin, "I give thee thanks, O Lord," the collection has been entitled *Hodayot* (Thanksgivings).

The hymns are written in the first person singular and contain many autobiographical reflections on the author's sufferings and experiences of the grace of God. (A liturgical setting and use are nonetheless possible.) There is a note of predestination and of the author's duty, in spite of his human frailty, as one to whom God has revealed his mysteries to be the bearer and interpreter of God's truth. It seems likely that at least some, if not all, of the hymns were written by the Teacher of Righteousness himself. The author was surely an early leader of the sect. The depth of piety reflected in the *Hymns* would explain how the Teacher of Righteousness, if he is the author, had such spiritual power. It was out of such spiritual experience and personal conviction that the Qumran sect was created.

Habakkuk Commentary (1QpHab)[138]

This is the major surviving representative of a genre of writing much employed at Qumran — interpretations of segments of Scripture. Other important commentaries from Qumran represented by substantial fragments are on Psalms 37, 57, 68, Isaiah, and Nahum.[139] The particular kind of commentary produced at Qumran has been called *pesher* (hence the abbreviation pHab), because after giving the biblical text the writer used the word *pesher* ("the interpretation or meaning [lit., presaging] is"). This word was used in Daniel, an influential book at Qumran, for the interpretation of dreams (e.g., Dan. 4:9). The *pesher* may be defined as a revealed interpretation of inspired mysteries with reference to history. Characteristic of the *pesher* commentary at Qumran is the interpre-

---

(1955):115-24, 188-95; *JBL* 75 (1975):107-13; *JBL* 76 (1957):139-48; S. Holm-Nielsen, *Hodayot: Psalms from Qumran*, Acta theologica danica 2 (1960); M. Mansoor, *The Thanksgiving Hymns: Translated and Annotated with an Introduction* (Grand Rapids, 1961); B. Thiering, "The Poetic Forms of the Hodayoth," *JSS* 8 (1963):189-209; Paul Rotenberry, "A Translation and Study of the Qumran Hodayot," Ph.D. diss., Vanderbilt Univ., 1968; E. H. Merrill, *Qumran and Predestination: A Theological Study of the Thanksgiving Hymns* (Leiden, 1975); B. P. Kittel, *The Hymns of Qumran: Translation and Commentary* (Chico, Calif., 1981); D. Dombkowski Hopkins, "The Qumran Community and 1QHodayot: A Reassessment," *RQ* 10 (1981):323-64.

138. K. M. T. Atkinson, "The Historical Setting of the Habakkuk Commentary," *JSS* 4 (1959):238-63; F. F. Bruce, "The Dead Sea Habakkuk Scroll," *Annual of Leeds University Oriental Studies* 1 (1959):5-24; L. H. Silberman, "Unriddling the Riddle: A Study in the Structure and Language of the Habakkuk Pesher (1QpHab)," *RQ* 3 (1961):323-64; J. G. Harris, *The Qumran Commentary on Habakkuk*, Contemporary Studies in Theology, vol. 9 (London, 1966); William H. Brownlee, *The Midrash Pesher of Habakkuk: Text, Translation, Exposition with an Introduction* (Missoula, 1979).

139. Gregory L. Doudna, *4QPesher Nahum: A Critical Edition* (Sheffield, 2001); J. H. Charlesworth, *The Pesharim and Qumran History: Chaos or Consensus?* (Grand Rapids, 2002).

tation of the biblical text as foretelling contemporary events of importance to the community, thus giving the text a present application as if it had been written literally with reference to their own time. Techniques employed include giving a different grammatical form to the word in the text, using synonyms, making a pun by rearranging the letters or words, using a different textual tradition, or connecting the statement with earlier or following passages. The methods of dealing with the biblical text are an important background to early Christian interpretation of the Old Testament, about which more will be said under the Qumran community.

The *Habakkuk Commentary* comments on chapters 1 and 2. We cannot determine whether the author's text lacked the prayer of chapter 3 or whether as a liturgical piece chapter 3 did not suit the author's purpose of interpreting prophecy in terms of contemporary events.

The various interpretations of the text were quite explicit to the sect but are not to the modern reader. Thus, while the author identifies the Chaldaeans of Habakkuk as the Kittim, we are uncertain who they are — an important part of efforts to date the scrolls (see above on *War Scroll*). The Kittim will destroy the Wicked Priest, who "betrayed the statutes for the sake of wealth," "defiled the temple of God," and "persecuted the Teacher of Righteousness." He was assisted by other priests "who gathered wealth from the spoil of the peoples," the Man of Falsehood who "rejected the Law," and the House of Absalom "who kept silent when the Teacher of Righteousness was reproached." The Teacher was the one to whom "God revealed all the mysteries of the words of his servants the prophets." His followers were "men of truth, the doers of the Law." Since no names are given, the *pesher* itself is in need of a modern scholar with the Teacher of Righteousness's gift of insight into divine mysteries in order to understand. With a proper interpretation, a fairly detailed account of the origins of the sect would emerge.

Precise dating depends on exact interpretation, but the late second century B.C. is the most likely range.

Genesis Apocryphon (1QapGen)[140]

Rewriting and supplementing Genesis seems to have been a popular thing to do in late Judaism.[141] The scroll containing the *Genesis Apocryphon* is badly damaged. The early columns concern the story of Noah, with parallels to the Noah book in 1 Enoch. The best-preserved part, columns 19-22, concerns Abraham in Genesis 12–15. The story is told by Abraham, who speaks in the first per-

---

140. N. Avigad and Y. Yadin, *A Genesis Apocryphon: A Scroll from the Wilderness of Judaea* (Jerusalem, 1956); J. A. Fitzmyer, S.J., *The Genesis Apocryphon of Qumran Cave I: A Commentary* (Rome, 1971).

141. *Jubilees*, Pseudo-Philo, *Joseph and Asenath*, *Testaments of the Twelve Patriarchs*, rabbinic midrashim.

son throughout, as does Lamech in the early part. The author was not a particularly effective storyteller, but the work is valuable for providing a sample of Aramaic at the beginning of the Christian era.

Copper Scroll (3Q15 or 3QTreasure)[142]

Perhaps better named the *Copper Plaque,* this work consists of two parts rolled up to resemble scrolls inscribed in Hebrew similar to that of the Mishnah. Containing a list of treasures with topographical descriptions of their hiding places, it was enough to turn scholars into treasure hunters. The work may have had nothing to do with the Qumran community. Some have thought it a list of the temple treasures hidden at the time of the Roman siege; others consider the contents imaginary.

Temple Scroll (11Q19-21 or 11QTemple)[143]

Three copies of the Temple Scroll have been identified, one of which at twenty-eight feet is the longest of the scrolls and is the basis of our brief remarks. There are points of contact with the Qumran community in regard to calendar and strictness in interpreting the law. Yadin dates the scroll to the last third of the second century B.C., but this is disputed. The handwriting of the scroll is that of the early first century. God is presented as speaking in the first person, giving Torah (a new Deuteronomy) to the people. Although some claim the *Temple Scroll* was intended as a replacement or completion of the Pentateuch, it seems rather to present itself as the revealed and therefore only valid interpretation of the law. There are four major sections: festivals, with their respective offerings; regulations pertaining particularly to ritual uncleanness and purification; a description of the temple (almost one-half of the scroll), corresponding to neither Solomon's nor Herod's temple, so the temple as the author thinks it should be until it is replaced by one created directly by God; and instructions for the king's bodyguard and for mobilization in war.

---

142. J. T. Milik, "The Copper Document from Cave III of Qumran: Translation and Commentary," *Annual of the Department of Antiquities of Jordan* 4-5 (1960):137-55; Al Wolters, *The Copper Scroll* (Sheffield, 1996).

143. Y. Yadin, *The Temple Scroll,* 3 vols. (Jerusalem, 1983); idem, *The Temple Scroll: The Hidden Law of the Dead Sea Sect* (London, 1985); Johann Maier, *The Temple Scroll: An Introduction, Translation, and Commentary,* Journal for the Study of the Old Testament Supplements 34 (Sheffield, 1985); G. J. Brooke, ed., *Temple Scroll Studies* (Sheffield, 1989); D. D. Swanson, *The Temple Scroll and the Bible: The Methodology of MQT* (Leiden, 1994); Sidnie White Crawford, *The Temple Scroll and Related Texts* (Sheffield, 2000).

Halakhic Letter (4QMMT)[144]

A letter in Hebrew from the members of what became the Qumran sect to the leader (high priest?) of the people in Jerusalem is preserved in six manuscripts (4Q 394-399), all incomplete, totalling 130 lines and dating from 75-50 B.C. The work itself is probably from 159-152 and, if so, is addressed to the Hasmonean political leader Jonathan before he assumed the high priesthood. It is given the title *Misqat Ma'ase Ha-Torah* ("Some Precepts of the Torah") from a phrase in its concluding section that describes its contents. After the now lost opening there are three sections: exposition of the calendar of 364 days, legal rulings, and an explanation of the sect's separation with an appeal to the addressee to adopt the sect's legal views. The document sets forth some twenty points on which the sect differs from the Jerusalem establishment over the interpretation of the laws governing sacrifices and rituals of purification. The conclusion, "And it will be reckoned for you as righteousness when you perform what is right and good before Him," may be contrasted with Paul (Rom. 4:1-12). There are significant parallels to the Temple Scroll. More important, some of the interpretations agree with positions that rabbinic literature ascribes to the Sadducees, reinforcing the Zadokite, priestly origins of the Qumran sect.

BIBLIOGRAPHY

Discoveries in the Judaean Desert. Oxford, 1955–.

Biblical Archaeology Society. *A Facsimile Edition of the Dead Sea Scrolls.* Washington, 1991.

Israel Antiquities Authority, E. Tov, ed. *The Dead Sea Scrolls on Microfiche.* Leiden, 1993. E. Tov, ed., with S. J. Pfann. *Companion Volume to the Dead Sea Scrolls Microfiche Edition.* Leiden, 1995.

Charlesworth, J. H., ed. *The Dead Sea Scrolls: Hebrew, Aramaic, and Greek Texts with English Translations.* 10 vols. planned. Louisville, 1994–.

García Martínez, Florentino, and E. J. C. Tigchelaar, *The Dead Sea Scrolls Study Edition.* 2 vols. 2d ed. Leiden, 1997, 1998. Paperback, Grand Rapids, 2000.

Dupont-Sommer, A. *The Essene Writings from Qumran.* Oxford, 1961.

Knibb, M. A. *The Qumran Community.* Cambridge, 1987.

García Martínez, Florentino. *The Dead Sea Scrolls Translated: The Qumran Texts in English.* 2nd ed. Grand Rapids, 1996.

Wise, M., M. Abegg, and E. Cook. *The Dead Sea Scrolls: A New Translation.* San Francisco, 1996.

Vermes, G. *The Complete Dead Sea Scrolls in English.* New York, 1998.

Parry, D. W., and E. Tov. *Dead Sea Scrolls Reader.* (Trans. of all nonbiblical texts.) 6 parts. Leiden, 2003–.

144. E. Qimron and J. Strugnell, *Qumran Cave 4, V. Miqsat Ma'ase Ha-Torah,* Discoveries in the Judaean Desert X (Oxford, 1994); John Kampen and Moshe J. Bernstein, *Reading 4QMMT: New Perspectives on Qumran Law and History* (Atlanta, 1996).

Charlesworth, J. H., ed. *The Graphic Concordance to the Dead Sea Scrolls.* Louisville, 1991.

Schiffman, Lawrence H., and James VanderKam, eds. *Encyclopedia of the Dead Sea Scrolls.* 2 vols. Oxford, 2000.

JQR 85 (1994):1-273, special issue on "Qumran Studies."

Schiffman, Lawrence H. *Reclaiming the Dead Sea Scrolls: The History of Judaism, the Background of Christianity, the Lost Library of Qumran.* Philadelphia, 1994.

Stegmann, Hartmut. *The Library of Qumran: On the Essenes, Qumran, John the Baptist, and Jesus.* Grand Rapids, 1998.

VanderKam, James C. *The Dead Sea Scrolls Today.* Grand Rapids, 1994.

Charlesworth, J. H., and W. P. Weaver, eds. *The Dead Sea Scrolls and Christian Faith.* Harrisburg, 1998.

Flint, Peter W., and James C. VanderKam. *The Dead Sea Scrolls after Fifty Years: A Comprehensive Assessment.* 2 vols. Leiden, 1998.

Kugler, Robert A., and Eileen M. Schuller. *The Dead Sea Scrolls at Fifty.* Atlanta, 1999.

Ulrich, Eugene. *The Dead Sea Scrolls and the Origins of the Bible.* Grand Rapids, 1999.

Near Eastern Archaeology 63 (2000):120-176, special issue on "Qumran and the Dead Sea Scrolls."

Vermes, Geza. *An Introduction to the Complete Dead Sea Scrolls.* Minneapolis, 2000.

Flint, Peter E., ed. *The Bible at Qumran: Text, Shape, and Interpretation.* Grand Rapids, 2001.

Magness, Jodi. *The Archaeology of Qumran and the Dead Sea Scrolls.* Grand Rapids, 2002.

Lim, T. H., et al., *The Dead Sea Scrolls in their Historical Context.* Edinburgh, 2000.

Washburn, David L. *A Catalogue of Biblical Passages in the Dead Sea Scrolls.* Atlanta, 2002.

Burchard, C. *Bibliographie zu den Handschriften vom Toten Meer.* 2 vols. Berlin, 1957, 1965.

Jongeling, B. *Bibliography of the Finds in the Desert of Judah, 1958–1969.* Leiden, 1971.

Fitzmyer, J. A., S.J. *The Dead Sea Scrolls: Major Publications and Tools for Study.* Rev. ed. Atlanta, 1990.

Dimant, Devorah, and Uriel Rappaport, eds., *The Dead Sea Scrolls: Forty Years of Research.* Leiden, 1992.

García-Martínez, Florentino, and Eibert J. C. Tigchelaar. "Bibliography of the Dead Sea Scrolls." *RQ* 18 (1988):459-490, 605-619.

Reed, S. A., M. J. Lundberg, and M. B. Phelps. *The Dead Sea Scrolls Catalogue: Documents, Photographs, and Museum Inventory Numbers.* Atlanta, 1994.

Lim, T. H., P. S. Alexander, et al. *The Dead Sea Scrolls Electronic Reference Library, 2* vols. Oxford and Leiden, 1997, 1999.

Revue de Qumran.

Dead Sea Discoveries: A Journal of Current Research on the Scrolls and Related Literature. Ed. G. J. Brooke, L. H. Schiffman, and J. C. VanderKam. 1995–

(See further the bibliography on the Qumran Community; p. 531.)

Apocalyptic Writings

Apocalyptic writings are found in four of the artificial (from a literary standpoint) categories of literature falling in our period: the Jewish and Christian canons of Scripture (Daniel, Revelation), the Apocrypha (2 Esdras), the Pseudepigrapha (Ethiopic Enoch, Syriac Apocalypse of Baruch, to name only the purest representatives), and the Dead Sea Scrolls *(War Scroll)*. They were not the particular expression of any one religious group. Although apocalyptic literature has a prehistory in Isaiah 24–27, Ezekiel, and Zechariah, the earliest canonical apocalypse was Daniel.

We should keep in mind several distinctions, as failure to do so has further complicated the study of this subject, so strange to many readers of the Bible. First of all, the term *apocalyptic* is to be distinguished from the term *eschatological.* Eschatology, which means "the last things," is a broad term and refers to whatever is influenced by a doctrine of the end of the ages. *Apocalypse* means revelation or unveiling and normally refers to the kind of writing that gives a revelation of hidden knowledge, particularly of God's control over when and how history ends. The literary form of an apocalypse, however, could be employed for subjects having little or nothing to do with eschatology proper (as the Gnostic apocalypses that reveal the Gnostic understanding of existence, the *Shepherd of Hermas* that deals with Christian living and repentance, or even the *Apocalypse of Peter* with its revelations of the condition of the damned, although it deals with "eschatology" but does not contain the characteristic apocalyptic concern with the imminent end of history). Further, the symbolism of apocalypses could be employed in messages of another type (some would argue that this applies to the Book of Revelation).

These comments already suggest another important distinction. One should distinguish between the literary character of an apocalypse and the world of ideas in apocalyptic literature. Confusion would be reduced if we use "apocalyptic" as an adjective for a "mode of revelation" or the content of the revelation, and instead of "apocalyptic" as a noun we use "apocalypse" for the literary genre, "apocalyptic eschatology" for a set of ideas, and "apocalypticism" for a social ideology. Here we must describe these phenomena in generalizations to which there are frequent exceptions and varying degrees of purity in type (there was no "manual of style" of what must go in an apocalypse).

As to literary form, an apocalyptic writing was normally pseudonymous.

(Revelation is an obvious exception, written by a prophet in his own name to communities to whom he was well known and with no effort to present his message as a revelation from the ancient past; Rev. 1:1-2.) An apocalypse usually is presented as a vision, dream, or supernatural journey received by one of the great men of Israel's past (Enoch, Ezra, etc.), written down, then sealed and hidden according to God's decree, and now made known to the generation that must experience the things foreseen. Apocalypses are commonly classified as either "cosmic" or "historical." Often there is an angelic interpreter. Apocalypses based on an otherworldly journey include 1 Enoch 1–36; 37–71; 72–82; 2 Enoch; Testament of Abraham; Testament of Levi 2–5; Apocalypse of Zephaniah. Part of what is presented as prediction is often a symbolic survey of history up to the real author's own time. This plus the "scientific" material about the structure of the cosmos apparently functioned to give credence to the message concerning the end. The survey of history in future form is a common feature of apocalyptic but is not present in all, just as an otherworldly journey is often but not always present.[145] "Historical" apocalypses include Daniel; 1 Enoch 85–90; 93; 91:11-19; 4 Ezra; and 2 Baruch. The account of the revelation is set in different literary forms in different books: some present the material within the framework of a farewell discourse (testament), others as a predictive discourse, and still others as an account of a vision. Other literary forms employed are the oracular utterance, interpretive rewriting of the Bible (midrash), prayer, and paraenesis. Often more than one of these literary forms is employed in the same work. There is frequent use of repetition and recurring patterns. All is told with a supernatural coloring. The highly figurative language is most striking. The imagery is drawn from Near Eastern mythology, the Old Testament, and Hellenistic syncretism. Foreign nations are depicted as wild and ravenous beasts, Israel as domesticated animals, rulers as horns, angels and supernatural beings as stars. Numbers also have symbolic meaning.

Modern writers often mean the thought-world rather than the literary genre when they refer to apocalyptic. Apocalyptic eschatology may be said to present a philosophy of history. It is concerned with universal history, but especially as it affects God's people. Although much study of apocalyptic literature has centered on its eschatology, its authors' main concern was with revelation (as the word apocalypse indicates) rather than eschatology. Events are marching toward a predetermined goal; but while history is under divine control, individual decisions are not. There is both a universalism and an individualism in apocalypticism. God's plans are universal, but the individual (not the nation as a whole) decides whose side he is on and so where he will stand in the final

145. John J. Collins, "Apocalypse: Towards the Morphology of a Genre," *Society of Biblical Literature 1977 Seminar Papers* (Missoula, Mont., 1977):359-70 (*Semeia* 14 [1979]:1-20), suggests a typology of apocalyptic writings according to whether or not they contain an otherworldly journey with three subdivisions of each according to content: a "historical" review, a cosmic and/or political eschatology, or only a personal eschatology.

cataclysm. An apocalyptic view of history is very pessimistic. Only an act of God working from the outside and bringing history to a close will deliver his people and defeat evil. The end is expected imminently. Human hopes are focused on the beyond. There is thus a dualism of the two ages,[146] the present evil age (Gal. 1:4) and the age to come (Heb. 6:5). In addition to this doctrine of two ages, apocalyptic literature developed two other contrasts from its Jewish heritage — the ethical dualism between good and evil and the "spatial" dualism between heaven and earth, God and the world. The divine transcendence stands out. This is perhaps related to the well-developed angelology and demonology of apocalyptic thought: the distance between God and humanity was filled up with intermediate beings, good and bad.

Apocalypticism had roots in Israelite priestly and Wisdom sources, and especially in prophecy. Pseudonymity in apocalyptic literature points to the absence of prophecy at this time in Israel: only by appeal to a holy name in the past could the claim to revelation be maintained. There are apocalypticlike passages in various prophetic books; nevertheless there are some definite differences between classical Hebrew prophecy and apocalypticism. These can be overdrawn, for there are gradations and exceptions, but in general we may note these differences: (1) In prophecy the future grows out of the present and salvation and fulfillment are looked for in history, but in apocalypticism the future represents a radical break for there is a pessimism about history and God must intervene from without and bring history to an end. (2) Prophecy is conditional and contingent: Jonah said, "Forty days and Nineveh will be overthrown," but it was not; yet he was not a false prophet nor was his message untrue. Something else — the repentance of Nineveh — intervened. By contrast, apocalypticism presents history as predetermined from the beginning. (3) The prophetic messages were largely preached messages, but apocalypses were a literary product, so far as we can determine, though their actual sociological setting is yet to be fully established. (4) Prophetic oracles were often poetic in form, whereas apocalypses were in prose (although it is difficult to determine this because the apocalypses are mainly preserved in translations).

Were the apocalypses accounts of real visionary experiences, or were they learned literary productions based on earlier motifs? It is difficult to know now, but likely there survive apocalypses in both categories.

More study is needed on the social setting of apocalypticism. It originated and recurred in times of oppression and among groups experiencing alienation, but its eschatological perspective was widely influential, affecting many Pharisees and rabbis as well as sectarian groups like the Qumran community. Apocalypticism flourished especially in the times of trial imposed by

---

146. *Dualism* is a much abused word, and students need to watch in what sense it is being used. See John G. Gammie, "Spatial and Ethical Dualism in Jewish Wisdom and Apocalyptic Literature," *JBL* 93 (1974):356-85.

foreign occupation of Palestine. It was written to meet the issue of how continued persecution could be squared with Israel as the chosen people and God as just and merciful. The writers sought to strengthen faith and instill hope. They did so through a symbolic universe that emphasized what God is doing on the cosmic level in contrast to mundane existence. It seems to be a feature of apocalyptic writings that the eschatological message was followed by exhortation to a kind of life appropriate to the situation; the same is found in the New Testament (Mark 13; 1 Thess. 4–5; 1 Pet. 4:7ff.).

BIBLIOGRAPHY

Reddish, M. G., ed. *Apocalyptic Literature: A Reader.* Nashville, 1990.

Collins, J. J. ed., *The Origins of Apocalypticism in Judaism and Christianity,* Vol. 1 of *The Encyclopedia of Apocalypticism.* New York, 2000.

Rowley, H. H. *The Relevance of Apocalyptic.* New York, 1963.

Schmithals, Walter. *The Apocalyptic Movement: Introduction and Interpretation.* Nashville, 1975.

Barr, James. "Jewish Apocalyptic in Recent Scholarly Study." *BJRL* 58 (1975):9-35.

Hanson, P. D. *The Dawn of Apocalyptic.* Philadelphia, 1975.

Collins, J. J., ed. *Apocalypse: The Morphology of a Genre. Semeia* 14 (Missoula, Mont., 1979).

Greunwald, Ithamor. "Jewish Apocalyptic Literature." *ANRW* II, *Principat,* 19.1. Berlin and New York, 1979. Pp. 89-118.

Rowland, Christopher. *The Open Heaven: A Study of Apocalyptic in Judaism and Early Christianity.* New York, 1982.

Hellholm, D., ed. *Apocalypticism in the Mediterranean World and the Near East.* 2d ed. Tübingen, 1988.

Collins, J. J. *The Apocalyptic Imagination: An Introduction to the Jewish Matrix of Christianity.* New York, 1984.

Russell, D. S. *Divine Disclosure: An Introduction to Jewish Apocalyptic.* Minneapolis, 1992.

García Martínez, F. *Qumran and Apocalyptic.* Leiden, 1992.

VanderKam, James C., and William Adler, eds. *The Jewish Apocalyptic Heritage in Early Christianity.* Compendia Rerum Iudaicarum ad Novum Testamentum, Section 3, Volume 4. Minneapolis, 1996.

Philo

In every way the opposite of apocalyptic thinking is Philo, who lived between approximately 30 B.C. and A.D. 50. The one incident from his life that is known involved a crisis for the Alexandrian Jewish community that occurred when he was an old man. Flaccus, the prefect of Egypt, instigated a series of anti-Jewish measures in A.D. 38 that resulted in a pogrom against the Jews (see p. 32). The events of this year are the subject of Philo's *In Flaccum* ("Against Flaccus"). After Flaccus was sent to Rome for trial and peace was restored in Alexandria, two rival delegations from Alexandria went to Rome to plead their case before the emperor Gaius Caligula. They were concerned about the responsibility for the recent riots and the civic status of Jews in Alexandria. Apion (p. 486) led the delegation from the Greek citizens, and Philo led the Jewish delegation. His *Legatio ad Gaium* ("Embassy to Gaius") relates the frustrations of the Jewish embassy in the years 39–41 while praising Augustus and Tiberius in contrast to the policies of Caligula.[147] The troubles in Alexandria had to be settled by the new emperor Claudius.[148] Philo, therefore, was a leader and respected member of the Alexandrian Jewish community.

Philo had received a thorough Greek education (see pp. 109-12). He advocated for his fellow Jews a system of education similar to that of the Hellenistic schools of Alexandria and was able to integrate his appropriation of such an education into his Jewish religion and life *(On the Preliminary Studies)*. Since his brother was wealthy (p. 430), we may assume that Philo was financially independent, allowing him the leisure for acquiring a thorough familiarity with pagan culture. It may be that a private school he conducted provides the context from which Philo's treatises were written.[149]

Philo's educational background and social position as a member of the Jewish aristocracy, with time and money to indulge in intellectual pursuits, led him to respond to the atmosphere of Alexandria with a large literary output (see below, pp. 480-81). The extent of his writings plus the lack of biographical detail has resulted in a variety of characterizations. From his works he emerges first of all as a biblical commentator, next as an apologist for Judaism, and only third as a philosopher. He presents the modern reader with the concrete phenomenon of a person who apparently fully assimilated Hellenistic culture while remaining immovably loyal to his Jewish heritage.

In his literary work Philo sought to promote a middle way between the rejection of the law by Jewish Hellenizers (cf. his own nephew; p. 420) and the naive, literal interpretation of the law he found among most of its adherents. He insisted that the outward forms of the law were to be observed, but he sought a philosophical interpretation of the meaning of its ceremonies and provisions.[150] Philo was widely read in the Hellenistic philosophers and drew eclectically what suited his purposes in commending Judaism as a rational reli-

---

147. Philo Alexandrinus, *Legatio ad Gaium*, ed. with intro., trans., and comm. by E. M. Smallwood (Leiden, 1970).

148. H. I. Bell, *Jews and Christians in Egypt* (London, 1924), 10-21, 27-29. See pp. 487-88 below.

149. Gregory E. Sterling, "'The School of Sacred Laws': The Social Setting of Philo's Treatises," *Vigiliae Christianae* 53 (1999):148-164.

150. *Migration of Abraham* 89-90.

The Loeb Classical Library arranges Philo's works according to the Pentateuchal order, except for the miscellaneous works and fragments. The following classification of
Philo's writings is based on E. R. Goodenough, *Introduction to Philo Judaeus* (New York,
1963), 30-51, where he gives a suggested order for reading Philo's works. Abraham
Terian, "Had the Works of Philo Been Newly Discovered," *BA* 57 (1994):86-97 gives a
classification of Philo's works in chronological order (p. 41).

Apologetic Writings

1. Against Flaccus
2. Embassy to Gaius
3. On the Contemplative Life
4. Apology for the Jews (or *Hypothetica* — fragments in Eusebius)
5. Life of Moses

Exposition of the Law

1. On the Creation of the World
2. On Abraham
3. On Isaac (now lost)
4. On Jacob (now lost)
5. On Joseph
6. On the Decalogue
7. On the Special Laws (4 books)
8. On Virtues
9. On Rewards and Punishments

The Allegorical Interpretation

1. Allegorical Interpretation (3 books)
   a. Book I (Gen. 2:1-17)
   b. Book II (Gen 2:18–3:1)
   c. Book III (Gen. 3:8b-19)
2. On the Cherubim (Gen. 3:24 and 4:1)
3. On the Sacrifices of Abel and Cain (Gen. 4:2-4)
4. The Worse Attacks the Better (Gen. 4:8-15)
5. On the Posterity and Exile of Cain (Gen. 4:16-25)
6. On the Giants (Gen. 6:1-4)
7. On the Unchangeableness of God (Gen. 6:4-12)
8. On Husbandry (Gen. 9:20)
9. On Noah's Work as a Planter (Gen. 9:20b)
10. On Drunkenness (Gen. 9:21)
11. On Sobriety (Gen. 9:24)
12. On the Confusion of Tongues (Gen. 11:1-9)
13. On the Migration of Abraham (Gen. 12:1-6)
14. Who is the Heir of Divine Things? (Gen. 15:1-18)
15. On the Preliminary Studies (Gen. 16:6-14)
16. On Flight and Finding (Gen. 16:6-14)
17. On the Change of Names (Gen. 17:1-22)
18. On Dreams (2 books) (Gen. 28:12ff. and 31:11ff.)

Commentary
  1. Questions and Answers on Genesis
  2. Questions and Answers on Exodus

Miscellaneous Treatises
  1. On the Indestructibility of the World
  2. That Every Good Man Is Free
  3. On Providence
  4. Alexander (Whether Dumb Animals Have the Power of Reason)*

  * Not in the Loeb edition but now available in Supplements to *Studia Philonica*, Abraham
  Terian, *Philonia Alexandrini de Animalibus: The Armenian Text with an Introduction, Translation,
  and Commentary* (Chico, Calif., 1981).

gion and the source of the wisdom of the Greeks. Most of his works follow the order of the contents of the Pentateuch and show the philosophical wisdom found therein by means of allegorical exegesis. Philo used Hellenistic allegory to find cosmological information and ethical teaching in the law. He is useful to the modern student, therefore, for his method of exegesis and the philosophical materials he incorporated. There are often, moreover, important clues in his writings to features of the Hellenistic synagogue, and in this he is especially valuable.

Harry Wolfson has emphasized Philo's philosophical importance and yet his essential Jewishness, showing his contacts with the main streams of Judaism.[151] For instance, much of Philo's biblical interpretation has many points of contact with rabbinic exegesis. On the other hand, E. R. Goodenough has emphasized Philo's Hellenistic background, even finding in him a Jewish version of a Hellenistic mystery religion.[152] It is true that Philo uses mystery terminology, but he was doing no more than the philosophers did in comparing their teaching to the mysteries, so Goodenough has had few followers on this point. On the other hand, the clarity and organization of Wolfson's work is due to his abilities; these are not Philo's qualities. In his defense, part of the impression of muddleheadedness that Philo leaves is due to his method: instead of offering a systematic presentation (assuming he was capable of such), the presentation of his ideas is governed by the order of material in the Pentateuch.

Philo has an elaborate *Logos* speculation, and this has attracted students of the New Testament and Christology to his writings. According to Philo the Logos was the mind or reason of God, the locus of the ideas of Platonic philosophy (p. 333). The Logos was God in his rational aspect, but the Logos also

151. Harry Wolfson, *Philo*, 2 vols. (Cambridge, Mass., 1947).
152. E. R. Goodenough, *By Light Light: The Mystic Gospel of Hellenistic Judaism* (New Haven, 1935).

functioned as the head of the hierarchy of intermediaries between the world and God. An aspect of God himself, the Logos was not hypostatized as a person as in Christianity and certainly never became incarnate. What Philo said only hypothetically, "God would sooner change into a man than man into a god" (*Embassy to Gaius* 16.118), the Fourth Gospel affirmed as reality (John 1:14).

Three blocks of writings in the New Testament have been studied particularly for possible indebtedness to Philo. As indicated by his Logos speculation, the Gospel of John is one of these.[153] The prologue, however, goes so far beyond anything in Philo that there seems no reason to postulate any more dependence on him than on any other philosophical background that made use of the Logos idea for what gave rational structure to the world. That Philo was a Jew of the Diaspora and his use of the Logos is prominent and extensive are the main reasons for thinking that the author of John knew Philo or speculations like his. In fact, other parts of John may offer better parallels between Philo and the Gospel. Regarding Christology, Philo's picture of Moses corresponds to functions of Jesus in the Fourth Gospel.[154] The interpretation of the manna in the wilderness in John 6 has points of contact with interpretations found in Philo.[155]

Another place where some have advocated the dependence of a New Testament author on Philo is the Epistle to the Hebrews, which has some striking parallels in terminology, thought patterns, and interpretations of the Old Testament. But again, although there is no reason why there may not be a direct indebtedness, the situation seems to be that Philo illuminates Hellenistic Jewish thought that provides the common background for both Philo and the New Testament writer.[156]

We can also see a relationship based on a background with much in common in regard to Paul, whose place in time and space makes it a bold assumption that he gave much attention to reading Philo. Nonetheless, as Henry Chadwick expresses it, "Both men fished in the same pool."[157] As a Greek-speaking Jew living in the Diaspora, whose outlook and mode of life were de-

---

153. W. L. Knox, *Some Hellenistic Elements in Primitive Christianity* (London, 1944), 55-90; C. H. Dodd, *The Interpretation of the Fourth Gospel* (Cambridge, 1953), 54-73.

154. W. A. Meeks, *The Prophet-King: Moses Traditions and the Johannine Christology* (Leiden, 1967).

155. P. Borgen, *Bread from Heaven: An exegetical study of the concept of Manna in the Gospel of John and the writings of Philo* (Leiden, 1965). This has good Palestinian origins: Bruce J. Malina, *The Palestinian Manna Tradition* (Leiden, 1968).

156. S. G. Sowers, *The Hermeneutics of Philo and Hebrews* (Zurich, 1965); Ronald Williamson, *Philo and the Epistle to the Hebrews* (Leiden, 1970); L. K. K. Dey, *The Intermediary World and Patterns of Perfection in Philo and Hebrews* (Missoula, Mont., 1975); R. Nash, "The Notion of Mediator in Alexandrian Judaism and the Epistle to the Hebrews," *Westminster Theological Journal* 40 (1977):89-115; J. W. Thompson, *The Beginnings of Christian Philosophy* (Washington, 1982).

157. "St. Paul and Philo," *BJRL* 48 (1966):286-307; cf. W. L. Knox, *St. Paul and the Church of the Gentiles* (Cambridge, 1939).

termined by Jewish tradition and the Greek Old Testament, Philo provides an excellent counterpart to his younger contemporary Paul. The two men represent radically different responses to their urban cultures. Philo's lack of concern for messianism, eschatology, and missionizing throws the figure of Paul in bolder relief. On the positive side, some of the parallels between Paul and Philo have to do with the contrast of the Creator with idolatry, similar lists of virtues and vices, the notion of the conscience as a judge of past action, circumcision of the heart, and the similarities between Philo's Logos and Paul's idea of divine Wisdom.

Such similarities may have contributed to the Christian "tradition" that Philo met Peter in Rome and was converted to Christianity (known already to Eusebius, *Church History* 2.17.1).[158] As impossible as that may be, the Christian appropriation of the Jewish heritage included a virtual monopoly on Philo, whose works were preserved by Christians. Philo's synthesis of Hellenism and Judaism prepared for like efforts in Christian philosophy and theology, and his influence is even more direct and far more pervasive in early Christian thinkers after the New Testament. Alexandrian Christian authors such as Clement and Origen show a heavy dependence on Philo (the allegorical method of interpretation of the Old Testament, specific points of interpretation of the Old Testament, and general doctrinal viewpoint), and through them the whole stream of Christian theology, especially in its Greek branch, shows his influence and the questions he confronted.[159]

Philo's writings also are of interest for the study of Gnosticism. Although "Gnostic" would be an inappropriate category for describing Philo, his thought-world is similar to that out of which Gnosticism came and so invites comparison.

The *Biblical Antiquities*[160] attributed to Philo was actually written sometime after A.D. 70 and is related to 2 Esdras and the Apocalypse of Baruch. It survives in a Latin translation of a Greek version made from the Hebrew original. The contents are a history from creation to the time of Saul, supplementing the existing biblical narratives. Unfortunately, only a part of the whole is preserved.

158. J. Edgar Bruns, "Philo Christianus: The Debris of a Legend," *HTR* 66 (1973):141-45.

159. Henry Chadwick, "Philo and the Beginnings of Christian Thought," *Cambridge History of Later Greek and Early Medieval Philosophy*, ed. A. H. Armstrong (Cambridge, 1967), 137-92; Harry Wolfson, *Philosophy of the Church Fathers* (3d ed.; Cambridge, Mass., 1970).

160. Frederick J. Murphy, *Pseudo-Philo: Rewriting the Bible* (Oxford, 1993) (includes commentary); Howard Jacobson, *A Commentary on Pseudo-Philo's Liber Antiquitatum Biblicarum with Latin Text and English Translation*, 2 vols. (Leiden, 1996).

Bibliography

Cohn, L., P. Wendland, S. Reiter, and H. Leisegang. *Philonis Alexandrini Opera quae supersunt.* 7 vols. Berlin, 1896–1930.

Colson, F. H., G. H. Whittaker, J. W. Earp, and Ralph Marcus. *Philo.* 12 vols. Loeb Classical Library. Cambridge, Mass., 1929–1962.

Philon d'Alexandrie. Sources Chrétiennes. Paris, 1957–.

Winston, David, trans. *Philo of Alexandria; The Contemplative Life, the Giants and Selections.* Ramsey, N.J., 1981.

Williamson, R. *Jews in the Hellenistic World: Philo.* Cambridge, 1989.

Yonge, C. D., trans., with notes by David Scholer. *The Works of Philo: New Updated Edition.* Peabody, Mass., 1992.

Brill is planning a 20-volume series of translations and commentaries on the works of Philo under the general editorship of Gregory Seerling.

Mayer, G. *Index Philoneus.* Berlin, 1974.

Borgen, Peder, *et al.,* eds. *A Complete Concordance of Philo of Alexandria on CD-ROM.* Leiden, 1996.

Borgen, Peder, Kåre Fuglseth, and Roald Skarsten *The Philo Index.* Grand Rapids, 2000.

Cohn, L. *Einteilung und Chronologie der Schriften Philos.* Leipzig, 1899.

Goodenough, E. R. *The Politics of Philo Judaeus.* New Haven, 1938. Reprint, 1967. (The appendix contains an important bibliography.)

Wolfson, H. A. *Philo.* 2 vols. Cambridge, Mass., 1947.

Katz, Peter. *Philo's Bible.* Cambridge, 1950.

Bréhier, E. *Les idées philosophiques et religieuses de Philon.* 3d ed. Paris, 1950.

Goodenough, E. R. *Introduction to Philo Judaeus.* 2d ed. New York, 1963.

Philon d'Alexandrie. Colloques nationaux du Centre national de la recherche scientifique, Lyon, 11-15 Sept., 1966. Paris, 1967.

Nikiprowetzky, V. *Le Commentaire de l'Ecriture chez Philon d'Alexandrie.* Leiden, 1977.

Sandmel, S. *Philo of Alexandria: An Introduction.* Oxford, 1979.

Tobin, Tom. *The Creation of Man: Philo and the History of Interpretation.* Washington, 1983.

ANRW II, *Principat,* 21.1. *Hellenistisches Judentum in römischer Zeit: Philon.* Berlin and New York, 1984. Entire volume devoted to Philo, mostly in English, including a systematic bibliography.

Runia, David T. *Philo of Alexandria and the Timaeus of Plato.* Leiden, 1986.

Borgen, P. *Philo, John, and Paul: New Perspectives on Judaism and Early Christianity.* Atlanta, 1987.

Mendelson, Alan. *Philo's Jewish Identity.* Atlanta, 1989.

Runia, David T. *Philo in Early Christian Literature.* Assen, 1993.

Borgen, P. *Philo of Alexandria: An Exegete for His Time.* Leiden, 1997.

Sterling, Gregory, ed. *Philo of Alexandria Commentary Series.* Announced for 20 vols. by E. J. Brill, Leiden.

Feldman, Louis. *Scholarship on Philo and Josephus (1937–1962)*. New York, 1963.

Radice, R., and D. T. Runia. *Philo of Alexandria: An Annotated Bibliography 1937-1986*. Leiden, 1992.

Studia Philonica, 1972–1980; continued as *Studia Philonica Annual: Studies in Hellenistic Judaism*, ed. D. T. Runia. Vol. 1 (1989)–.

Josephus

Josephus was born 37/38 and died between 110 and 120. He was of royal blood (since his mother was a Hasmonean) and a priest who later gave his adherence to the Pharisees.[161] As an educated and energetic member of the aristocracy he was placed in charge of the defense of Galilee at the outbreak of the Jewish revolt in 66. During the siege of Jotapata he and forty followers made a pact not to fall into the hands of the Romans. They drew lots to establish the order in which they were to die, each at the hands of his comrade. Josephus drew the last lot. After the others had been killed, he persuaded the next to last to surrender with him (*War* 3.8 [340-98]). Josephus prophesied to Vespasian that he would become emperor; when that became true, his future was made. Josephus pled unsuccessfully with his compatriots to give up the revolt. He went with Titus to Rome, where he received citizenship and a pension, taking the name Flavius from his patrons, the Flavian dynasty. He gave himself to a literary defense of the Jewish people, extolling its antiquity and religious beliefs and blaming the revolt on a few extremists. Josephus is the principal source for Jewish history in the first century and hence exceedingly important for New Testament backgrounds.

Four works by Josephus survive, preserved and much read by Christians. He originally wrote *The Jewish War (Bellum Judaicum)* in Aramaic and then rewrote it in Greek with the assistance of collaborators; it was published between 75 and 82. (Unlike Philo, Josephus was not in his early work fluent in Greek; that he was writing for non-Jewish readers limits his usefulness for determining word usage by Jews.) The seven books begin with a survey in a book-and-a-half of Jewish history from the Maccabean revolt to A.D. 66. For the reign of Herod the Great Josephus employed the works of Nicholas of Damascus, court historian of Herod. For the war of 66–70 itself Josephus had his own notes and recollections plus official documents furnished by Vespasian and Titus. *The Jewish War* follows the tradition of military and political history represented by Polybius.

The twenty-volume *Jewish Antiquities (Antiquitates Judaicae)* was pub-

---

161. For the argument that Josephus never claimed to be a Pharisee (*Life* 2.12 is carefully worded) and was critical of them, see Steve Mason, *Flavius Josephus on the Pharisees* (Leiden, 1991).

lished in 93 or 94. It covers the history of the Jews from creation to A.D. 66, following the Old Testament, and preserving some current interpretations and some that are Josephus's own, for the early history. The account is fuller than the *War* for the period from the Maccabean revolt to the revolt against Rome, and the material on Herod the Great is supplemented by sources hostile to Herod in addition to Nicholas of Damascus. The *Jewish Antiquities* represents the rhetorical historiography exemplified in Dionysius of Halicarnassus's *Roman Antiquities,* on which the book is modeled. Whereas in the *War* Josephus spoke for the Roman empire and the Flavian dynasty, in the *Antiquities* he spoke as the apologist for Judaism.

The *Life (Vita)*[162] is not an account of his whole career, but defends his activities as commanding officer in Galilee in 66–67 against criticisms by Justus of Tiberias about his conduct of the war. It was written as an appendix to the *Antiquities* and published shortly after 100.

Against Apion (Contra Apionem), the latest of Josephus's works, is a two-book apology for Judaism.[163] The title refers to an Alexandrian grammarian contemporary with Philo who had spoken derogatorily of the Jews. Josephus's work goes further than a response to Apion and corrects the prejudices, ignorance, and malignant statements about Judaism made by other writers. After answering accusations concerning Jewish history, conduct in Alexandria, and temple rites and laws generally, Josephus gives a positive account of Jewish precepts: one God, one temple, sanctity of marriage and family, education of children, hospitality, afterlife as a reward for living in accord with the law. *Against Apion* is a valuable source for quotations from writers whose works are now lost and for Jewish apologetics and propaganda in the Hellenistic-Roman world.

Josephus' biases have often been noted by later historians: he was pro-Roman and sought to whitewash Titus; he defended the Jews by blaming the rebellion on a succession of incompetent governors and a few extremists among his own people; he praised himself and slandered his opponents; he was pro-priestly and pro-Hasmonean (he was identified with both groups), so his writings reflect an aristocratic outlook; he favored a strong government that would promote order and peace; and he incorrectly interpreted the legal position of the Jews throughout the empire in order to claim special privileges for them. As an apologist he interpreted Judaism in terms familiar to his Gentile readers — for example, presenting the parties in Judaism as philosophical schools. These biases are to be expected and generally it is easy to discern Josephus's special pleading in contrast to the facts. With proper allowance made for his special in-

---

162. Steve Mason, *Flavius Josephus: Life of Josephus: Translation and Commentary* (Leiden, 2001).

163. Louis H. Feldman and John R. Levison, *Josephus's* Contra Apionem: *Studies in its Character and Context, with a Latin Concordance to the Portion Missing in Greek* (Leiden, 1996).

terests and recognition that he was sometimes misinformed, the reader will find Josephus an invaluable resource not to be neglected.

Three passages in Josephus bear directly on Christian origins. They pertain to John the Baptist, James the Just, and Jesus. Concerning John, Josephus says:

> He was a good man and exhorted the Jews to lead righteous lives, practice justice towards one another and piety towards God, and so to join in baptism. In his view this was a necessary preliminary if baptism was to be acceptable to God. They must not use it to gain pardon for whatever sins they committed, but as a consecration of the body, implying that the soul was thoroughly purified beforehand by right behavior. When many others joined the crowds about him, for they were greatly moved on hearing his words, Herod feared that John's great influence over the people would lead to a rebellion (for they seemed ready to do anything he might advise). Herod decided therefore that it would be much better to strike first and be rid of him before his work led to an uprising, than to wait for an upheaval, become involved in a difficult situation and see his mistake. Accordingly John was sent as a prisoner to Machaerus, the fortress mentioned before, because of Herod's suspicious temper, and was there put to death. (*Ant.* 18.5.2 [117-19])

In most respects this account complements and supplements the New Testament reports.[164] Two differences call for comment. The New Testament, although also emphasizing the call to an inner change of heart and reformation of life (Luke 3:1-20; Matt. 3:1-12), gives the forgiveness of sins as the purpose of John's baptism (Mark 1:4; Luke 3:3; and note the problem this caused in regard to the baptism of Jesus as reflected in Matt. 3:13-15) and connected it with eschatology (Matt. 3:7, 11-12). Josephus's words about the baptism administered by John actually describe quite well the significance of the washings administered by the Qumran community (1QS v.13-14). A plausible hypothesis would be that Josephus (who was acquainted with Essene teaching; *Vita* 10) has elaborated the meaning of John's baptism in terms familiar to himself and has omitted its eschatological orientation (as part of his general toning down of eschatological expectations among the people at large) in favor of its moral significance.

A similar discrepancy but one of wider significance concerns the background and occasion of John's imprisonment. The New Testament says the motive was John's denunciation of Herod Antipas for marrying Herodias, his brother's wife (Mark 6:17-20; Matt. 14:3-5; Luke 3:19-20). Josephus says nothing of this personal matter but speaks only of Herod's fear of political unrest.

164. J. P. Meier, "John the Baptist in Josephus: Philology and Exegesis," *JBL* 111 (1992):225-37.

However, the two may be closely related. The denunciation of Herod's marriage could have aroused the discontent of the people, and Josephus relates that Herod's divorce of his wife, the daughter of King Aratas of Nabatea, in order to marry Herodias eventually brought on war with the Nabateans in A.D. 36 (*Ant.* 18.5.1 [109-15]).

Josephus provides valuable supplementary information concerning James, the brother of Jesus, and his death at the hands of the Jews in A.D. 62:

> Possessed of such a character, Ananus thought that he had a favorable opportunity because Festus was dead and Albinus was still on the way. And so he convened the judges of the Sanhedrin and brought before them a man named James, the brother of Jesus who was called the Christ, and certain others. He accused them of having transgressed the law and delivered them up to be stoned. Those of the inhabitants of the city who were considered the most fair-minded and who were strict in observance of the law were offended at this. (*Ant.* 20.9.1 [200])

A fuller account of the death of James was given in the later second century by Hegesippus, quoted by Eusebius, *Church History* 2.23.1-18. Josephus confirms the esteem in which James was held and that his condemnation was an assertion of Jewish presumption. There has been little question of the authenticity of this passage. Even the reference to Jesus as "called Christ" is too noncommital to be a Christian interpolation; but if Josephus identified James by reference to Jesus here, then presumably he had already identified Jesus. That would argue that the next passage to be considered is derived from some reference to Jesus in Josephus's original work.

Both of the above statements appear to be genuine, but the situation is quite different in regard to the third, the *testimonium Flavianum*:

> At about this time lived Jesus, a wise man, if indeed one might call him a man. For he was one who accomplished surprising feats and was a teacher of such people as accept the truth with pleasure. He won over many Jews and many of the Greeks. He was the Messiah. When Pilate, upon an indictment brought by the principal men among us, condemned him to the cross, those who had loved him from the very first did not cease to be attached to him. On the third day he appeared to them restored to life, for the holy prophets had foretold this and myriads of other marvels concerning him. And the tribe of the Christians so called after him has to this day still not disappeared. (*Ant.* 18.3.3 [63-64])

Some of these statements could not have been written by a Jew who did not believe in Jesus ("if one might call him a man," "He was the Messiah," "He appeared to them on the third day," "holy prophets had foretold this"). Indeed, there was a later legend to the effect that Josephus became a Christian and a bishop. There is no truth in this, and it is probably an outgrowth of reading texts of Josephus containing this passage. The passage is in all three existing Greek manuscripts of *Antiquities* 18, but these are later than the eleventh century and were preserved by Christians. Origen provides decisive external evidence that the passage was not in his copy of Josephus, for he says that Josephus did not believe in Jesus (*Commentary in Matthew* 10.17; *Against Celsus* 1.47). On the other hand, it seems that at this point Josephus did make some reference to Jesus, which was then corrected and supplemented by Christian scribes. It is easier to believe that this happened than that the passage was invented in its entirety and interpolated here. Moreover, several of the statements are quite in accord with what Josephus could have said ("a wise man," "Pilate upon an indictment by the principal men among us condemned him to the cross," "the tribe of the Christians"). It seems likely, then, that Josephus made some reference to Jesus that was revised by Christian scribes. That statement could have included reference to the crucifixion under Pilate as a consequence of charges by Jewish leaders, to his reputation as a miracle worker, to his claim to be the Messiah, and to his being the founder of Christians.[165] The Slavonic version of Josephus carried the Christianizing tendency further.[166]

BIBLIOGRAPHY

Thackeray, H. St.-J., R. Marcus, A. Wikgren, and L. H. Feldman. *Josephus.* 9 vols. Loeb Classical Library. Cambridge, Mass., 1926–1965.

Mason, Steve, ed. *Flavius Josephus: Translation and Commentary.* 10 vols. planned. Leiden, 2000–

Thackeray, H. St.-J., and R. Marcus. *A Lexicon to Josephus.* Vols. 1-4. Incomplete. New York, 1930–1955.

Rengstorf, K. H. *A Complete Concordance to Flavius Josephus.* 4 vols. Leiden, 1973-1983.

Thackeray, H. St.-J. *Josephus, the Man and the Historian.* New York, 1929. Reprint with introduction by S. Sandmel. New York, 1968.

---

165. For this view see E. Schürer, *The History of the Jewish People in the Age of Jesus Christ,* ed. G. Vermes and F. Millar (Edinburgh, 1973), 428-41; F. F. Bruce, *Jesus and Christian Origins Outside the New Testament* (Grand Rapids, 1974), 36-41. S. Pines, *An Arabic Version of the Testimonium Flavianum and its Implications* (Jerusalem, 1971), publishes an Arabic text of the passage in Josephus that lacks some of the suspicious phrases and therefore may be a witness to an original reference to Jesus by Josephus. G. Vermes, "The Jesus Notice of Josephus Re-Examined," *JJS* 38 (1987):1-10. J. P. Meier, "Jesus in Josephus: A Modest Proposal," *CBQ* 52 (1990):76-103, argues that if one brackets out the three clearly Christian affirmations, there remains a genuine reference to Jesus by Josephus; Alice Whealy, *Josephus on Jesus: The Testimonium Flavianum Controversy from Late Antiquity to Modern Times* (New York, 2003).

166. Bruce, *Jesus and Christian Origins,* 42-53.

Shutt, R. J. H. *Studies in Josephus.* London, 1961.

Montefiore, H. W. *Josephus and the New Testament.* London, 1962.

Attridge, H. W. *The Interpretation of Biblical History in the* Antiquitates Judaicae *of Flavius Josephus.* Missoula, Mont., 1976.

Cohen, S. J. D. *Josephus in Galilee and Rome: His* Vita *and Development as a Historian.* Leiden, 1979.

Yamauchi, Edwin M. "Josephus and the Scriptures." *Fides et Historia* 13 (1980):42-63.

Rajak, T. *Josephus: The Historian and his Society.* Philadelphia, 1984.

Feldman, Louis H. "Flavius Josephus Revisited: The Man, His Writings and His Significance." *ANRW* II, *Principat,* 21.2. Berlin and New York, 1984. Pp. 763-862.

Moehring, H. R. "Josephus ben Matthia and Flavius Josephus: The Jewish Prophet and the Roman Historian." *ANRW* II, *Principat,* 21.2. Berlin and New York, 1984. Pp. 864-944.

Villalba i Varneda, P. *The Historical Method of Flavius Josephus.* Leiden, 1985.

Feldman, Louis H., and Gohei Hata, eds. *Josephus, Judaism, and Christianity.* Detroit, 1987.

Bilde, Per. *Flavius Josephus: Between Jerusalem and Rome: His Life, His Works, and Their Importance.* Journal for the Study of the Pseudepigrapha, Supplement Series 2. Sheffield, 1988.

Feldman, Louis H., and Gohei Hata, eds. *Josephus, the Bible, and History.* Detroit, 1989.

Mason, Steven N. *Josephus and the New Testament.* Peabody, Mass., 1992.

Feldman, Louis H. *Josephus's Interpretation of the Bible.* Berkeley, 1998.

Mason, Steve, ed. *Understanding Josephus: Seven Perspectives.* Sheffield, 1999.

Von Schreckenberg, Heinz. *Bibliographie zu Flavius Josephus.* Leiden, 1968. Supplementband. Leiden, 1979.

Feldman, Louis H. *Josephus and Modern Scholarship (1937–1980).* Berlin and New York, 1984.

Feldman, Louis H. *Josephus: A Supplementary Bibliography.* New York, 1986.

Rabbinic Literature

Rabbinic literature developed in two major periods: after the collapse of the Bar Kokhba revolt in the 130s, and after the establishment of a Christian empire under Constantine and his successors in the fourth century. To the former period belong the formation of the Mishnah and the earliest Midrashim (second-third centuries), to the latter the compilation of the Talmuds (fifth-sixth centuries). Our treatment of this literature will not follow a strictly chronological order but will group the writings by their compilations and literary types.

At the beginning of the first century the two leading rabbis were Hillel

(c. 50 B.C.–A.D. 10)[167] and Shammai, and their schools dominated Pharisaic interpretation of the law until A.D. 70. The school of Shammai prevailed in the predestruction era, but after 70 the school of Hillel took the lead in the reorganization of Judaism and so assumed the ascendancy in Jewish life. In general, the school of Shammai adhered to a stricter interpretation of the law, so that the Mishnah takes special note of those instances where they were more lenient than the school of Hillel. When similarities to the attitude of Jesus are found in rabbinic literature, one should remember that this literature reflects the later development when the more lenient views of Hillel prevailed and that the stricter views of Shammai prevailed during Jesus' ministry.

The corpus of rabbinic literature was shaped by Hillelites. The leader of the school of Hillel during the mid–first century was his grandson Rabban Gamaliel the Elder, Paul's teacher (Acts 22:3; cf. 5:34ff.). The mishnaic tractate Sotah 9.15, which preserves tributes to outstanding rabbis, says that "when Rabban Gamaliel the Elder died, the glory of the law ceased and purity and abstinence died." His younger contemporary Johanan ben Zakkai[168] (pp. 423-25) took the lead in the reorganization of Jewish life after the destruction of the temple through the rabbinical academy at Jamnia.[169] "When the Rabban Johanan ben Zakkai died, the splendor of wisdom ceased." Also active at this time was Rabbi Eliezer.[170] Gamaliel's grandson, Rabban Gamaliel II (active c. 80–120)[171] did not take so open a view toward Christianity. He introduced into the Eighteen Benedictions the curse, "Let the Nazarenes and the heretics perish as in a moment, let them be blotted out of the book of the living and let them not be written with the righteous," which effectively excommunicated Christians from the synagogues and formalized the break between the two faiths.[172]

Rabbi Akiba[173] was a leading figure in the period from A.D. 120 to 140. We have already noted his alleged recognition of Simon bar Kosibah as the Mes-

---

167. Nahum N. Glatzer, *Hillel the Elder* (New York, 1970).

168. J. Neusner, *A Life of Rabban Yohanan Ben Zakkai* (Leiden, 1962); idem, *Development of a Legend: Studies on the Tradition Concerning Yohanan ben Zakkai* (Leiden, 1970); idem, *First Century Judaism in Crisis* (Nashville, 1975).

169. Jacob Neusner, "The Formation of Rabbinic Literature: Yavneh (Jamnia) from A.D. 70 to 100," *ANRW* II, *Principat*, 19.2 (Berlin and New York, 1979), 3-42.

170. Ben Zion Bosker, *Pharisaic Judaism in Transition: R. Eliezer the Great and Jewish Reconstruction after the War with Rome* (New York, 1935); J. Neusner, *Eliezer ben Hyrcanus: The Tradition and the Man* (Leiden, 1973).

171. Shammai Kanter, *Rabban Gamaliel II: The Legal Traditions* (Chico, Calif., 1980).

172. Such is the usual interpretation of the twelfth benediction in the Jewish daily prayer (see pp. 578-79), but the heretics there cursed may not have been Christians — see Reuven Kimelman, "*Birkat Ha-Minim* and the Lack of Evidence for an Anti-Christian Jewish Prayer in Late Antiquity," *Jewish and Christian Self-Definition*, vol. 2, *Aspects of Judaism in the Greco-Roman Period*, ed. E. P. Sanders (Philadelphia, 1981), 226-44; D. Instone-Brewer, "The Eighteen Benedictions and the *Minim* Before 70 CE," *JTS* n.s. 54 (2003):25-44, argues the curse was originally directed against Sadducees.

173. L. Finkelstein, *Akiba: Scholar, Saint, and Martyr* (New York, 1936).

siah in the abortive rising under Hadrian (p. 425). Of him too it was said, "When Rabbi Akiba died, the glory of the law ceased." Akiba and his disciple Rabbi Meir made important contributions toward codifying the oral law. "When Rabbi Meir died, there were no more makers of parables." The authoritative compilation of the oral law in the Mishnah was the achievement of Rabbi Judah the Patriarch (or Prince) at the end of the second century. He was the great-great-grandson of Gamaliel the Elder and is often cited simply as "Rabbi." Thus, "When Rabbi died, humility and the shunning of sin ceased."

Rabbi Judah's compilation of the oral law in written form and with a few minor additions is the Mishnah, a topical collection of legal rulings. The word comes from a verb meaning "to repeat," and so means "study." The *Tannaim* (lit. "repeaters") were the rabbinic scholars of the first and second centuries whose interpretations are collected in the Mishnah. More specifically, the Mishnah is a codification of the *Halakah* (pl. *Halakoth*). The verb *halak* means "to walk," and *halakah* referred to an authoritative legal decision on how one was to conduct himself according to the law. (Note the frequency of "to walk" in the practical, ethical sections of the New Testament Epistles — e.g., Gal. 5:16; Eph. 4:1, 17; 5:2, 8, 15; Col. 4:5; 1 Thess. 4:1.)

The process of interpreting the Scriptures, the written law, was called *midrash* (exposition). Whereas Mishnah was the law codified in topical form, midrash was commentary that stated rabbinic interpretation of the laws arranged according to the order of the biblical text. Not all midrash was *halakic,* or legal; it also includes *haggadah,* which refers to all biblical interpretation that is nonhalakic, that is, all edifying and informative commentary.

When the Mishnah itself was commented upon, the result was *Talmud,* derived from a word for "study," or "instruction." The commentary on the Mishnah was called *Gemara,* from the verb *gemar* ("to complete"). The *Amoraim* ("speakers") were commentators on the Mishnah of Rabbi Judah.

Since the rabbinic materials were not reduced to writing until later than the New Testament, the earliest apparently not until the second century, the use of this literature for the backgrounds of early Christianity is problematic. Much material from the first century and earlier is certainly preserved in rabbinic literature, but determining precisely the extent of such traditions is not easy. The presence among the Dead Sea Scrolls of interpretations of law debated in the rabbinic literature strengthens the case for continuity between the rabbinic tradition and Judaism in the pre-70 period. Many decisions and sayings are attributed to rabbis whose dates are known, but even here one is not always on firm ground. When the same statement is attributed to more than one person, it is clear that even these attributions do not give a secure basis for the date and origin of a tradition. Some traditions, moreover, will be older still than their first attribution to a given teacher. Sometimes early traditions have been modified in transmission so that they contain details of later date. Form-critical analysis and the inherent logic of the development of the teachings help in arranging the traditions in chronological order.[174] The quantity of *reliable* historical information for the pre-70 period in rabbinic literature is not great: even what is attributed to that period actually depends for its formulation on the second- and third-century situation. This question of dating has often left even specialists in dispute, but the difficulties do not mean that one should ignore the rabbinic literature. When used carefully in comparison with other sources the rabbinic writings often help to fill out the picture.

The relation of some of these writings was expressed in this way: "The reading of the *Miqrā'* [vocalized text of Scripture] leads to the Targum, the Targum to the Mishnah the Mishnah to the Talmud and the Talmud to action" (*Sifre, Deuteronomy* 17:19).

Mishnah [175]

The Mishnah originated about 200 or shortly thereafter. It comprises sixty-three tractates *(massekoth)* arranged in six divisions or orders *(sedarim)* dealing respectively with laws pertaining to agricultural produce (*Zeraim*, "seeds"), the holy days and festivals (*Moed*, "set feasts"), women *(Nashim)*, property rights and legal proceedings (*Nezikin*, "damages"), the holy things related to the temple (*Kodashim*, "hallowed things"), and uncleanness and purification (*Tohoroth*, "cleannesses"). They are thus concerned, in order, with the holiness of the land of Israel, the holiness of time (proper conduct on holy days), the holiness of family life (with special reference to the transfer of women from the father's house to the husband's), the sanctification of property (the stable conduct of civil life), the holy place (stable conduct of the cult), and the bounds of holiness (purity in an unholy world). The Mishnah thus focuses on the sanctification of Israel, distinguishing her from the world and establishing order and stability.

The Mishnah is concerned only with life lived in the Holy Land; it leaves out of account life in the Diaspora. That in large measure accounts for older

---

174. See the pioneering work of Jacob Neusner, e.g., *Judaism: The Evidence of the Mishnah* (Chicago, 1981), 14-22, which summarizes what is worked out in detail in his histories of mishnaic law. Note the discusson of dating of rabbinic materials by D. Instone-Brewer, "Review Article: The Use of Rabbinic Sources in Gospel Studies," *Tyndale Bulletin* 50 (1999):281-298 (esp. 281-284, 292).

175. H. Danby, trans., *The Mishnah* (London, 1933); J. Neusner, *The Mishnah: A New Translation* (New Haven, 1991); text by J. Hutner, director, and N. Sacks, ed., *The Mishnah with Variant Readings* (Jerusalem, 1972–); H. Albeck and H. Yalon, *Shisha Sidre ha-Mishnah* (an edition with commentaries in Hebrew), 6 vols. (Jerusalem, 1952–1958); text and literal translation by P. Blackman, *Mishnayoth*, 7 vols. (New York, 1965); J. Neusner, *The Modern Study of the Mishnah* (Leiden, 1973); E. J. Lipman, *The Mishnah: Oral Traditions of Judaism* (New York, 1974); J. Neusner, *Judaism: The Evidence of the Mishnah* (Chicago, 1981); Charles R. Gianotti, *The New Testament and the Mishnah: A Cross-Reference Index* (Grand Rapids, 1983); A. J. Avery-Peck, "Judaism without the Temple: The Mishnah," in H. W. Attridge and G. Hata, eds., *Eusebius, Christianity, and Judaism* (Detroit, 1992), 409-431; J. Neusner, *The Mishnah: Introduction and Reader* (Philadelphia, 1992); J. Neusner, *Making God's Word Work: A Guide to the Mishnah* (New York, 2003).

The Orders and Tractates of the Mishnah[176]

Zeraim ("Seeds")

Berakoth ("Benedictions")
Peah ("Gleanings")
Demai ("Produce not certainly tithed")
Kilaim ("Diverse Kinds")
Shebiith ("Seventh Year")
Terumoth ("Heave Offerings")
Maaseroth ("Tithes")
Maaser Sheni ("Second Tithe")
Hallah ("Dough-offering")
Orlah ("Fruit of Young Trees")
Bikkurim ("First-fruits")

Moed ("Set Feasts")

Shabbath ("Sabbath")
Erubin ("Sabbath Limits")
Pesahim ("Passover")
Shekalim ("Shekel Dues")
Yoma ("Day of Atonement")
Sukkah ("Tabernacles")
Yom Tob or Betzah ("Festivals")
Rosh ha-Shanah ("New Year")
Taanith ("Days of Fasting")
Megillah ("Scroll of Esther")
Moed Katan ("Mid-Festival Days")
Hagigah ("Festival Offering")

Nashim ("Women")

Yebamoth ("Sisters-in-Law")
Ketuboth ("Marriage Deeds")
Nedarim ("Vows")
Nazir ("Nazirite Vow")
Sotah ("Suspected Adulteress")
Gittin ("Bills of Divorce")
Kiddushin ("Betrothals")

Nezikin ("Damages")

Baba Kamma ("The First Gate")
Baba Metzia ("The Middle Gate")
Baba Bathra ("The Last Gate")
Sanhedrin ("Sanhedrin")
Makkoth ("Stripes")
Shebuoth ("Oaths")
Eduyoth ("Testimonies")
Abodah Zarah ("Idolatry")
Aboth ("Fathers")
Horayoth ("Instructions")

Kodashim ("Hallowed Things")

Zebahim ("Animal Offerings")
Menahoth ("Meal-offerings")
Hullin ("Animals killed for food")
Bekhoroth ("Firstlings")
Arakhin ("Vows of Valuation")
Temurah ("Substituted Offering")
Kerithoth ("Extirpation")
Meilah ("Sacrilege")
Tamid ("Daily Whole-offering")
Middoth ("Measurements")
Kinnim ("Bird-offerings")

Tohoroth ("Cleannesses")

Kelim ("Vessels")
Oholoth ("Tents")
Negaim ("Leprosy-signs")
Parah ("Red Heifer")
Tohoroth ("Cleannesses")
Mikwaoth ("Immersion-pools")
Niddah ("The Menstruant")
Makshirin ("The Predisposers")
Zabim ("They That Suffer a Flux")
Tebul Yom ("He That Immersed Himself That Day")
Yadaim ("Hands")
Uktzin ("Stalks")

176. For standard abbreviations, see *The SBL Handbook of Style*, ed. Patrick H. Alexander, David L.Petersen, et al. (Peabody, Mass., 1999), 79-80. See J. Neusner's *A History of the Mishnaic Law of . . .* on the different orders in five parts and forty-three volumes for the series "Studies in Judaism in Late Antiquity" (Leiden, 1974-1985).

scholars making a sharp distinction between Palestinian and Diaspora Judaism and for those who have studied Judaism primarily through the Mishnah and related materials taking it as "normative" for all Judaism. The tractates within each division are in general arranged according to length, the longest first. Passages from the Mishnah are not cited by the orders but by the name of the individual tractate followed by the chapter and section (paragraph) numbers. The language of the Mishnah is Hebrew.

The Mishnah prescribes a form of Judaism that will continue in the aftermath of the destruction of the temple. What the temple stood for — holiness and the presence of God — would now be actualized in a code of everyday conduct for family and town. The cult and sanctification were removed from the sole control of priests and given to the rabbis, who would regulate a life of holiness lived by the ordinary Israelite.

Since the Mishnah is primarily interpretations of the legal and cultic laws of the Pentateuch, much of it is of marginal interest to the student of early Christianity. Some, however, is of great importance for understanding the Judaism out of which Christianity arose and against which it reacted. The gem of the Mishnah is the tractate Aboth (Sayings of "the Fathers"), a collection of moral and practical wisdom that has maintained perennial interest.[177] The entire second division with its instructions about the observance of the Sabbath and the annual feasts is important for understanding the public expression of Judaism in the early Christian period. Berakoth gives the Jewish practice in regard to prayer. Tamid ("Daily Whole-offering") and Middoth ("Measurements") in the fifth division give information about the temple and its daily routine. Sanhedrin (fourth division)[178] describes the various law courts and some of the rules for their functioning. Nedarim ("Vows") in the third order and Shebuoth ("Oaths") in the fourth provide the background for Jesus' teaching on oaths, and Ketuboth ("Marriage Deeds"), Gittin ("Bills of Divorce"), and Kiddushin ("Betrothals") the background on marriage and divorce customs.

Tosefta [179]

Tosefta ("Supplement") is a collection of interpretations contemporary with those included in Rabbi Judah's Mishnah but excluded from it (called *baraita,*

---

177. R. T. Herford, *The Ethics of the Talmud: Sayings of The Fathers* (repr.; New York, 1962); B. T. Viviano, *Study as Worship: Aboth and the New Testament* (Leiden, 1978).

178. S. Krauss, *The Mishnah Treatise Sanhedrin,* ed. with intro., notes, and glossary in English and German (Leiden, 1909).

179. Text by M. S. Zukermandel, *Tosefta* (Jerusalem, 1937; repr. 1970), and S. Lieberman, *The Tosefta According to Codex Vienna,* 4 vols. (New York, 1955–1989); idem, *Tosefta Ki-fshutah: A Comprehensive Commentary on the Tosefta,* 9 vols. (New York, 1955–1989); Jacob Neusner, *The Tosefta* (Peabody, 2002); J. Neusner, *The Tosefta: An Introduction* (Atlanta, 1992).

"external"). Arranged after the Mishnah and based on it, but adding other material and other rules, the Tosefta may be considered the first commentary on the Mishnah. It may be dated after the Mishnah but before about 300. Since it did not have the authoritative status of the Mishnah, it has been less studied, but for historical purposes it is of equal (or greater) value with the Mishnah. The Tosefta is arranged in orders and tractates parallel to those of the Mishnah; only four tractates of the latter are not represented. It is cited T. or Tos. (for Tosefta), then the name of the tractate, as with the Mishnah.

Talmud [180]

The Mishnah plus Gemara ("completion") equals *Talmud*. Thus the Talmud includes the text of the Mishnah by sections and commentary on it. Two different Talmuds were produced, the Palestinian or Jerusalem (Yerushalmi) and the Babylonian (Babli). The Jerusalem Talmud comments thirty-nine of the Mishnah's tractates, from divisions one through four, and the Babylonian comments on thirty-six and one-half of the tractates, from divisions two through five; but the Babylonian Talmud is three to four times as long as its Palestinian counterpart. The Yerushalmi contains textual criticism, exegesis, and harmonization of the Mishnah as well as interpretations of Scripture and stories of rabbis. The Babli too is concerned with harmonization of the Mishnah and com-

---

180. Text of the Babylonian Talmud by I. Epstein, ed., *Hebrew-English Edition of the Babylonian Talmud* (London, 1960–); J. Hutner, dir., and M. Hirschler, ed., *The Babylonian Talmud with Variant Readings* (Jerusalem, 1972–). Text of the Jerusalem Talmud in *Talmud Yerushalmi* [Hebrew] (New York, 1948); an edition including the traditional commentaries in Hebrew was published in 7 vols. (Vilna, 1922; repr. New York, 1959). H. W. Guggenheimer, *The Jerusalem Talmud: Edition, Translation, and Commentary* (Berlin, 2000–). The old standard English translation of the Babylonian Talmud is I. Epstein, *The Babylonian Talmud*, 18 vols. (London, 1935–1948), with good indices; two other translations are in progress: J. Neusner, *The Babylonian Talmud: An American Translation* (Atlanta, 1984–); A. Steinsaltz, *The Talmud: The Steinsaltz Edition* with extensive commentary (New York, 1989–). Neusner has also translated the Jerusalem Talmud, *The Talmud of the Land of Israel*, 35 vols. (Chicago, 1982–1989). For introductions and study aids: H. J. Kasouwski, *Thesaurus Talmudis* (Jerusalem, 1954–); L. Goldschmidt, *Subject Concordance to the "Babylonian Talmud"* (Copenhagen, 1959); M. Mielziner, *Introduction to the Talmud* (4th ed.; New York, 1968); M. Zevin and J. Hutner, eds., *Encyclopedia Talmudica* (Jerusalem, 1969–); J. Neusner, *The Formation of the Babylonian Talmud* (Leiden, 1970); idem, *Invitation to the Talmud: A Teaching Book* (San Francisco, 1984); A. Carnell, *Aids to Talmud Study* (Jerusalem, 1975); A. Corré, *Understanding the Talmud* (New York, 1975); Baruch M. Bosker, "An Annotated Bibliographical Guide to the Study of the Palestinian Talmud," *ANRW* II, *Principat*, 19.2 (Berlin and New York, 1979), 139-256; David Goodblatt, "The Babylonian Talmud," *ANRW* II.19.2, 257-336; J. Neusner, *Judaism in Society: The Evidence of the Yerushalmi* (Chicago, 1983); L. Jacobs, *The Talmudic Argument: A Study in Talmudic Reasoning and Methodology* (Cambridge, 1984); J. Neusner, *Judaism — The Classical Statement: The Evidence of the Bavli* (Chicago, 1986); D. Kraemer, *The Mind of the Talmud: An Intellectual History of the Bavli* (Oxford, 1990); J. Neusner, *The Talmud: A Close Encounter* (Minneapolis, 1991).

mentary on Scripture but is especially characterized by essays on theoretical questions and giving scriptural basis for laws.

The Jerusalem Talmud was actually the product of rabbinic schools in Palestine, particularly Tiberias, and was compiled around 400 or shortly thereafter. According to traditional theory, the Babylonian Talmud was basically complete around the year 500, but recent study puts some of its material as much as a century or so later. The Gemara of both are in Aramaic, but there were dialectical differences between Babylonia and Galilee. The Babylonian Talmud has enjoyed the greater authority of the two in Jewry as a whole.

Although the Talmuds are the work of later generations of Jewish scholars, they nonetheless often contain traditions of greater antiquity (i.e., a *baraita*, "outside," referring to material of equal date not included in the Mishnah), and even where not of such age are still of importance in preserving the Jewish interpretation from an age close to the beginnings of Christianity. Passages are cited by j (Jerusalem) or (more frequently) y (Yerushalmi) for the Palestinian Talmud and b (Babli or Babylonian) for the Babylonian Talmud, followed by the title of the tractate and the folio number and column of the first complete printed edition.

Extracanonical Tractates [181]

At the end of the fourth *seder* of the Talmud are seven tractates compiled in the post-Talmudic period and of lesser authority. The first of these, *Aboth de Rabbi Nathan,* gives additional biographical information and sayings of the rabbis of the Tannaitic period.[182] *Derek Eres* ("Moral Conduct") may also date from Mishnaic times; it and *Derek Eres Zuta* ("small," containing instructions for scholars) have been used to elaborate on Paul's moral teaching.[183]

There are seven other "small tractates"[184] that did not attain "canonical" authority among the Jews. One of these, *Gerim* ("Proselytes"), is of special interest to students of early Christianity due to its subject.

Midrashim[185]

The term "midrash" can refer to the exegetical process of interpreting a text, the actual interpretation given to a passage, or the collected works of interpre-

---

181. A. Cohen, ed., *The Minor Tractates of the Talmud,* 2 vols. (London, 1965; repr. 1971).

182. J. Goldin, *The Fathers according to Rabbi Nathan* (Leiden, 1955), translates Version A; A. J. Saldarini, *The Fathers according to Rabbi Nathan* (Leiden, 1975), translates Version B.

183. E.g., W. D. Davies, *Paul and Rabbinic Judaism* (3d ed.; London, 1970); for more detail, Daniel Sperber, *A Commentary on "Derech Eres Zuta" Chapters Five to Eight* (Ramat Gani, 1990).

184. M. Higger, *Seven Minor Treatises* (New York, 1930).

185. See pp. 544-45 below on Jewish scriptural interpretation for bibliography pertinent to this literature in general. Gary Porton, *Understanding Rabbinic Midrash: Texts and Commentary*

tation (which is the meaning used here for a genre of literature). The midrashim are commentaries but not in the modern sense of historical explanation of the meaning of texts; rather they are explanations within the practice, liturgy, and teaching of the rabbis. We can note here only a sampling of the rabbis' extensive commentary literature, primarily from the early period, in order to indicate the richness available. The midrashim are sometimes classified as *halakic* or *haggadic*, with *halakah* predominating in the Tannaitic midrashim and *haggadah* in the later, but most of the midrashim contain both types of interpretation. A given midrash may be composed of close exegesis of each word or phrase, expansion of the meaning of a passage, illustration of a theme by various passages, or a collection of statements around a general topic.

Three works of Tannaitic midrashim form a group, offering mainly verse by verse comments: *Mekilta (of Rabbi Ishmael)* on Exodus 12–23,[186] *Sifra* on Leviticus,[187] and *Sifre* on Numbers 5–35 and on Deuteronomy.[188] They have been dated to the second century, but now are assigned to the second half of the third century. A second group of midrashim use the verses of the biblical text in the interest of significant propositions. These include *Genesis Rabbah (Bereshith Rabbah)*[189] and *Leviticus Rabbah*, which belong to the fifth century. A third group of midrashim from around 600 continue the trend of generalization by reading individual verses in order to make comprehensive, coherent statements (these deal with Lamentations, Esther, Song of Songs, and Ruth). The midrashim on the Pentateuch and the Five Scrolls (*Megilloth:* Song of Solomon, Ruth, Lamentations, Ecclesiastes, Esther), although they range in date from the fourth/fifth century to the twelfth, are sometimes treated together

---

(New York, 1985), translates and explains selected passages from the major rabbinic midrashim. He introduces Midrash, but from a limited standpoint, in "Midrash: Palestinian Jews and the Hebrew Bible in the Greco-Roman Period," *ANRW* II, *Principat*, 19.2 (Berlin and New York, 1979), 103-38; cf. A. Wright, *The Literary Genre Midrash* (New York, 1967); J. Neusner, *Midrash in Context: Exegesis in Formative Judaism* (Philadelphia, 1983); idem, *Invitation to Midrash: The Workings of Rabbinic Bible Interpretation: A Teaching Book* (San Francisco, 1989).

186. Text and translation by J. Z. Lauterbach, *Mekilta de Rabbi Ishmael*, 3 vols. (Philadelphia, 1949); W. S. Towner, *The Rabbinic "Enumeration of Scriptural Examples," A Study of a Rabbinic Pattern of Discourse with Special Reference to Mekhilta d'Rabbi Ishmael* (Leiden, 1973).

187. J. Neusner and R. Brooks, *Sifra: The Rabbinic Commentary on Leviticus — An American Translation* (Atlanta, 1985); Morris Ginsburg, *Sifra: With Translation and Commentary* (Atlanta, 1999).

188. W. S. Green and J. Neusner, *Sifre to Numbers* (Atlanta, 1986); L. Finkelstein, *Sifre on Deuteronomy* (New York, 1969 repr.); R. Hammer, *Sifre: A Tannaitic Commentary on the Book of Deuteronomy* (New Haven, 1986); J. Neusner, *Sifre to Deuteronomy: An Analytical Translation* (Atlanta, 1987); S. D. Fraade, *From Tradition to Commentary: Torah and Its Interpretation in the Midrash Sifre to Deuteronomy* (Albany, N.Y., 1991).

189. J. Neusner, *Genesis Rabbah: The Judaic Commentary to the Book of Genesis — A New American Translation*, 3 vols. (Atlanta, 1985); idem, *Genesis and Judaism: The Perspective of Genesis Rabbah — An Analytical Anthology* (Atlanta, 1985); idem, *Comparative Midrash: The Plan and Program of Genesis Rabbah and Leviticus Rabbah* (Atlanta, 1986).

under the name *Midrash Rabbah.*[190] Of the later midrashim mention may be made of the *Midrash on the Psalms (Midrash Tehillim)* — from the ninth century or later although the nucleus may be second to fourth century.[191]

Homiletic midrashim are collections of synagogue sermons (see p. 580). The three earliest are *Pesikta* (*de Rab Kahana*, fifth century) — homilies on the festivals and special sabbaths; *Pesikta Rabbati*[192] — also covering certain feasts and sabbaths; *Tanhuma* (or *Yelammedenu*) — a homiletic midrash on the whole Pentateuch.[193] The homilies are mainly of two types: (1) proem — from an introductory text chosen outside the Scripture readings of the day but linking them, with a key word tying the beginning to the end of the sermon;[194] (2) yelammedenu — based on a request for instruction. In both types texts of Scripture were strung together with interpretive material.

Targumim[195]

An important source for the way in which the Hebrew Bible was understood is found in the *Targumim* (plural of Targum). As knowledge of biblical Hebrew declined, the custom arose of following the Scripture reading in Hebrew in the synagogue with an Aramaic paraphrase (p. 580), the Targumim or Targums. They preserve the way passages were commonly interpreted, and stand midway between a literal translation and the longer midrashic commentaries. Since the people often remembered passages best according to the way they were paraphrased, it is not surprising that sometimes the text was quoted according to the meaning given in the Targum rather than according to its actual wording.

190. English translation by H. Freedman and M. Simon, *Midrash Rabbah,* 10 vols. (London, 1939–1951).

191. English translation by W. G. Braude, *The Midrash on Psalms* (New Haven, 1959).

192. English translation by W. G. Braude, *Pesikta Rabbati: Discourses for Feasts, Fasts, and Special Sabbaths* (New Haven, 1969).

193. John Townsend, trans., *Midrash Tanhuma* (New York, 1989).

194. J. Heinemann, "The Proem in the Aggadic Midrashim: A Form-Critical Study," *Studies in Aggadah and Folk-Literature: Scripta Hierosolymitana* 22 (Jerusalem, 1971), 100-200.

195. R. Le Déaut, *Introduction à la littérature targumique* (Rome, 1966); P. Nickels, *Targum and New Testament: A Bibliography together with a New Testament Index* (Rome, 1967); John Bowker, *The Targums and Rabbinic Literature: An Introduction to Jewish Interpretation of Scripture* (Cambridge, 1969); M. P. Miller, "Targum, Midrash and the Use of the Old Testament in the New Testament," *JSJ* 2 (1971):29-82; Martin McNamara, *Targum and Testament* (Grand Rapids, 1972); Bernard Grossfeld, *Bibliography of Targum Literature*, 2 vols., Biliographica Judaica 3 and 8 (Cincinnati, 1972, 1977); Martin McNamara, *The New Testament and the Palestinian Targum to the Pentateuch* (2d ed.; Rome, 1978); J. T. Forestell, *Targumic Traditions and the New Testament: An Annotated Bibliography with a New Testament Index* (Chico, Calif., 1979); R. Le Déaut, *The Message of the New Testament and the Aramaic Bible* (Chicago, 1982); Bruce D. Chilton, *A Galilean Rabbi and his Bible; Jesus' Use of the Interpreted Scripture of his Time* (Wilmington, Del., 1984). An English translation in 19 vols. of *The Aramaic Bible (the Targums),* ed. Martin McNamara, is in progress (Collegeville, Minn.). Pierre Grelot, *What Are the Targums?* (Collegeville, Minn., 1992).

Thus Ephesians 4:8 cites Psalm 68:18 according to a form known to us only from the Aramaic Targum (and the apparently related Syriac translation of the Psalms). For a long time the Targums were not written down, but eventually, as with the oral law, they were. The dates below pertain to the written texts; much earlier traditions of interpretation may be included.

Targums survive on all the books of the Hebrew Bible except Ezra-Nehemiah and Daniel. The two principal Targumim are *Targum Onqelos* to the Pentateuch, which perhaps originated in Palestine before being used at the end of the third century in Babylonia where it soon won high esteem;[196] and *Targum Jonathan* to the Former and Latter Prophets, in use in Babylonia in the early fourth century.[197] The names Onqelos and Jonathan are the equivalent of Aquila and Theodotion, and may have been transferred from their Greek versions to the Aramaic Targums. These were the Targums in use in Babylonia.

Most of the Palestinian Targums are later. That to the Torah came to be called also by the name of Jonathan (as in the Etheridge translation), but it is now commonly called *Targum Yerushalmi* or *Targum pseudo-Jonathan* to distinguish it from the Targum on the Prophets. The Targums to the Writings came later,[198] although that to the Psalms is fourth or fifth century. Fragments of earlier Palestinian Targums to the Pentateuch exist. One manuscript (Codex Neofiti I in the Vatican Library) contains a complete Palestinian Targum to the whole Pentateuch. Considerable attention has been given to the claim that it contains an early form of the Palestinian Targum, perhaps going back as early as the first century,[199] although the general view is that the linguistic usage of the Targums is not earlier than the second century.

Bibliography

Ginzberg, Louis. *The Legends of the Jews.* 7 vols. Philadelphia, 1909–1938. Reprint, Baltimore, 1998.

---

196. Text ed. A. Sperber, *The Bible in Aramaic,* vol. 1, *The Pentateuch according to Targum Onkelos* (Leiden, 1959); J. W. Etheridge, trans., *The Targums of Onkelos and Jonathan ben Uzziel on the Pentateuch with Fragments of the Jerusalem Targum* (repr.; New York, 1968); KTAV is publishing an English translation and commentary of *Targum Onqelos,* of which Genesis, Exodus, and Deuteronomy have appeared.

197. Text ed. A. Sperber, *The Bible in Aramaic,* vol. 2, *The Former Prophets according to Targum Jonathan* (Leiden, 1959), and vol. 3, *The Latter Prophets according to Targum Jonathan* (Leiden, 1962); text and trans. of Isaiah by J. F. Stenning, *The Targum of Isaiah* (Oxford, 1949); Bruce Chilton, *The Glory of Israel: The Theology and Provenance of the Isaiah Targum* (Sheffield, 1983); L. Smolar, M. Aberbach, and P. Churgin, *Studies in Targum Jonathan to the Prophets* (New York, 1983).

198. English translation by E. Levine, *The Targum to the Five Megillot* (Leiden, 1977).

199. See A. Díez Macho, *Neophyti I. Targum Palestinense de la Bibliotheca Vaticana* (Madrid, 1968), for text and translations into Spanish, French, and English.

Bonsirven, J. *Textes rabbiniques des deux premiers siècles chrétiens pour servir l'intelligence du Nouveau Testament*. Rome, 1955.

Montefiore, C. J. G., and H. Loewe. *A Rabbinic Anthology*. New York, 1960. Reprint, 1977.

Maccoby, H. Z. *Early Rabbinic Writings*. Cambridge, 1988.

Montefiore, C. J. G. *Rabbinic Literature and Gospel Teachings*. London, 1930. Reprint. New York, 1970.

Smith, Morton. *Tannaitic Parallels to the Gospels*. JBL Monograph Series, vol. 6. Philadelphia, 1951.

Strack, H. L., and P. Billerbeck. *Kommentar zum Neuen Testament aus Talmud und Midrasch*. 6 vols. Munich, 1961.

Neusner, J. *Early Rabbinic Judaism: Studies in Religion, Literature, and Art*. Leiden, 1975.

Green, W. S. *Persons and Institutions in Early Rabbinic Judaism*. Brown Judaic Studies, vol. 3. Missoula, Mont., 1977.

S. Safrai, ed. *The Literature of the Sages. First Part: Oral Torah, Halakha, Mishna, Tosefta, Talmud, External Tractates*. Compendia Rerum Iudaicarum ad Novum Testamentum. Philadelphia, 1987.

Lachs, S. T. *A Rabbinic Commentary on the New Testament: The Gospels of Matthew, Mark, and Luke*. New York, 1987.

Hilton, Michael, and Gordian Marshall. *The Gospels and Rabbinic Judaism: A Study Guide*. Hoboken, N.J., 1988.

Neusner, Jacob. *Are There Really Tannaitic Parallels to the Gospels? A Refutation of Morton Smith*. Atlanta, 1993.

Neusner, Jacob. *Introduction to Rabbinic Literature*. New York, 1994.

Strack, H. L., and G. Stemberger, *Introduction to the Talmud and Midrash*. 2d ed. Minneapolis, 1996.

Neusner, Jacob. *Four Stages of Rabbinic Literature*. London, 1999.

Jewish Mysticism

Although most of the literature for Jewish mysticism is late, its presence is a reminder of the variety in Judaism, even in the time of rabbinic literature and in some cases in rabbinic circles. The earliest surviving mystical Jewish literature (postmishnaic) are the *Hekhaloth* ("palaces") and *Merkabah* ("chariot") texts,[200] describing heavenly palaces to which one ascends in a heavenly journey comparable to that described in apocalyptic literature. The ascent was an ecstatic vision in an altered state of consciousness but without the mystic's loss of individuality. In rabbinic mysticism the Torah was contemplated with a view

---

200. Included in these is 3 Enoch: H. Odeberg, *3 Enoch* (New York, 1973 repr.); intro. and trans. by P. Alexander in James H. Charlesworth, ed., *The Old Testament Pseudepigrapha* (Garden City, N.Y., 1983), 1:223-315.

to achieving a visionary experience of God. Ezekiel and the Song of Solomon were the basis of esoteric speculations.

The person of God was protected by speaking of his Glory *(kabod)*, to which anthropomorphic features were assigned, or his Angel, who manifested his presence. One of the major themes of Jewish mysticism, which issued in the Kabbalah of the Middle Ages, was the mystery of the aspects or manifestations *(sefiroth)* of the infinite God *(Ein Sof)*. The ten *sefiroth* were described as "emanations," "garments," "lights," or "limbs" of the one God. The Infinite God clothed himself in the form of primordial man in order to create the material world.

The *Sefer ha' Zohar* ("Book of Splendor") is the crowning achievement of the Kabbalah. It is a running commentary on the Pentateuch composed 1280–1286. The *Sefer Yezirah* ("Book of Creation") from the third to the sixth century in Palestine is the oldest surviving text of systematic Jewish mystical speculation. According to it the twenty-two letters of the Hebrew alphabet were the instruments of creation. Although this work is late, it is contemporary with the Mishnah and Talmud and (as they do) could contain earlier speculations and so not be completely unrelated to New Testament backgrounds.

BIBLIOGRAPHY

Blumenthal, David R. *Understanding Jewish Mysticism: A Source Reader on the Merkabah Tradition and the Zoharic Tradition*. New York, n.d.

Schaefer, Peter, with M. Schlueter and H. G. Von Mutius. *Synopse zur Hekhalot-Literatur*. Tübingen, 1981.

Elior, R., trans. *Hekhaloth Zutartey*. Jerusalem, 1982.

Cohen, M., trans. *Shiur Komah*. Lanham, Md., 1983.

Gruenwald, Ithamar, and Morton Smith. *The Heikhalot Literature in English*. Chico, Calif., 1983.

Janowitz, N. *The Poetics of Ascent: Theories of Language in a Rabbinic Ascent Text*. Albany, N.Y., 1989. (Contains trans. of *Maaseh Merkabah*.)

Matt, Daniel C. *The Zohar* (trans. and comm.). Stanford, 2003.

Scholem, G. *Major Trends in Jewish Mysticism*. New York, 1946.

Scholem, Gershom G. *Jewish Gnosticism: Merkabah Mysticism and Talmudic Tradition*. New York, 1965.

Halperin, David J. *The Merkabah in Rabbinic Literature*. New Haven, 1980.

Gruenwald, Ithamar. *Apocalyptic and Merkabah Mysticism*. Leiden, 1980.

Chernus, I. *Mysticism in Rabbinic Judaism: Studies in the History of Midrash*. Berlin, 1982.

Tabor, James D. *Things Unutterable: Paul's Ascent to Paradise in Its Greco-Roman, Judaic, and Early Christian Contexts*. Lanham, Md., 1986.

Halperin, David. *The Faces of the Chariot: Early Jewish Responses to Ezekiel's Vision*. Tübingen, 1988.

Schäfer, Peter. *Hekhalot Studien*. Tübingen, 1988.

Morray-Jones, C. R. A. "Paradise Revisited (2 Cor. 12:1-12): The Jewish Mystical Background of Paul's Apostolate. Part 1. The Jewish Sources." *HTR* 86 (1993):177-217.

Schäfer, Peter, and Joseph Dan. *Gershom Scholem's 'Major Trends in Jewish Mysticism': 50 Years After.* Tübingen, 1993.

Laenen, J. H. *Jewish Mysticism: An Introduction.* Louisville, 2001.

Green, Arthur. *A Guide to the Zohar.* Stanford, 2003.

Archaeological Sources[201]

The literary sources for Judaism in the period surrounding the origins of Christianity are supplemented by archaeological sources. These are not extensive but are more numerous than is generally recognized and add a significant dimension to the understanding of Jewish history and religion. For instance, there were Jewish sarcophagi.[202]

Numismatics [203]

The study of coinage is adding significantly to the understanding of Jewish history from the first century before Jesus to the second century. The coins reflect titles and claims of rulers, ideas being promoted (pp. 91-92), and religious and political symbolism. They also often help determine chronology.

Inscriptions [204]

The basic collection of Jewish inscriptions from the Greco-Roman world was made by J.-B. Frey (Rome, 1936–1952) and has been reprinted with a supplement by Baruch Lifshitz to bring the collection up-to-date.[205] New collections of Jewish inscriptions are being prepared at Tübingen and Cambridge.[206] The

---

201. James F. Strange, "Archaeology and the Religion of Judaism in Palestine," *ANRW* II, *Principat*, 19.2 (Berlin and New York, 1979), 646-85; E. M. Myers and J. F. Strange, *Archaeology, the Rabbis, and Early Christianity* (Nashville, 1981); R. Hachlili, *Ancient Jewish Art and Archaeology in the Land of Israel* (Leiden, 1988).

202. A. Konikoff, *Sarcophagi from the Jewish Catacombs of Ancient Rome: A Catalogue Raisonné*, rev. ed. (Stuttgart, 1990).

203. See bibliography on coinage, p. 87, for Jewish coins.

204. L. H. Kant, "Jewish Inscriptions in Greek and Latin," *ANRW* II, *Principat*, 20.2 (Berlin and New York, 1987), 671-713; R. S. Kraemer, "Jewish Tuna and Christian Fish: Identifying Religious Affiliation in Epigraphic Sources," *HTR* 84 (1991):141-62; P. W. van der Horst, *Ancient Jewish Epitaphs* (Kampen, 1991).

205. J.-B. Frey, *Corpus of Jewish Inscriptions* (New York, 1975), reprint of *Corpus Inscriptionum Iudaicarum* with Prolegomenon by Baruch Lifshitz.

206. For the latter, W. A. Horbury and David Noy, eds., *Jewish Inscriptions of Graeco-Roman Egypt* (Cambridge, 1992); David Noy, *Jewish Inscriptions of Western Europe*, Vol. 1: *Italy, Spain, Gaul* (Cambridge, 1993); Vol. 2: *The City of Rome* (1995).

inscriptions from Palestine were collected by S. Klein, but many have been found since his time, and new collections are being published in Hebrew.[207] Most surviving Jewish inscriptions are either epitaphs or donations. The majority are in Greek, but some are in Latin, Hebrew, or Aramaic.

Necropolises

A principal source of archaeological information relative to Jews comes from excavations of Jewish burial sites. Palestine and Italy have provided the most abundant evidence. The necropolis of Hellenistic-Roman Jericho provides many tombs from the period before A.D. 70.[208] Significant finds include wooden coffins and evidence of primary and secondary burials (on ossuaries see pp. 245-46, 415n.26, 591-92) in the same context. Beth Shearim, between Haifa and Nazareth, was a principal burial place in the Holy Land in the third and fourth centuries, and many persons came from abroad to die there.[209] Thirty-one catacombs have been identified, including the family tomb of Rabbi Judah the Patriarch. The finds include many inscriptions and some ornate sarcophagi. Jewish catacombs have also been found at Venosa in Italy, including many inscriptions and a tomb with frescoed decoration. Of the seven Jewish catacombs discovered in Rome, only three are accessible — two under the Villa Torlonia on the Via Nomentana and the Vigna Randanini. They have produced many frescoes, inscriptions, sarcophagi, and artifacts that have been used to provide major studies of the Jewish community in Rome.[210]

207. S. Klein, *Jüdisch-pälastinisches Corpus Inscriptionum* (Vienna and Berlin, 1920); J. Naveh, *On Stone and Mosaic: The Aramaic and Hebrew Inscriptions from Ancient Synagogues* [Hebrew] (Jerusalem, 1978); J. A. Fitzmyer and D. J. Harrington, *A Manual of Palestinian Aramaic Texts* (Rome, 1978); J. Naveh, *On Sherd and Papyrus: Aramaic and Hebrew Inscriptions from the Second Temple, Mishnaic and Talmudic Periods* [Hebrew] (Jerusalem, 1992); R. C. Gregg and D. Urman, *Jews, Pagans, and Christians in the Golan Heights: Greek and Other Inscriptions of the Roman and Byzantine Eras* (Atlanta, 1997).

208. R. Hachli, "A Jerusalem Family in Jericho," *Bulletin of the American Schools of Oriental Research* 230 (1978):45-56; idem, "The Goliath Family in Jericho: Funerary Inscriptions from a First Century A.D. Jewish Monumental Tomb," ibid. 235 (1979):31-66; idem, "Jewish Funerary Customs During the Second Temple Period in the Light of Excavations at the Jericho Necropolis," *Palestine Exploration Quarterly* 115 (1983):109-32.

209. B. Mazar, M. Schwabe, B. Lifshitz, and N. Avigad, *Beth She'arim*, 3 vols. (Jerusalem, 1973–1976).

210. Harry J. Leon, *The Jews of Ancient Rome*, updated edition, with new introduction by Carolyn A. Osiek (Peabody, 1995); Leonard Victor Rutgers, *The Jews in Late Ancient Rome: Evidence of Cultural Interaction in the Roman Diaspora* (Leiden, 1995). See also George LaPiana, "Foreign Groups in Rome During the First Centuries of the Empire," *HTR* 20 (1927):183-403, but LaPiana is incorrect in assuming a central organization for the Jews in Rome. Note also E. S. Brettman's catalogue for the exhibition by the International Catacomb Society, *Vaults of Memory: Jewish and Christian Imagery in the Catacombs of Rome* (Boston, 1985).

Herodian Palestine

The intense archaeological excavations in modern Israel have revealed much from the period of Herod the Great and early Roman times.[211] In addition to the Herodian fortresses of Herodion near Bethlehem and Masada near the Dead Sea, the building activities of Herod the Great are manifest in many urban structures at Caesarea, Samaria, Jericho, and Jerusalem. In addition to Herod's work on the temple mount in Jerusalem, private homes and other evidence of everyday life in the first century have been found. Excavations are in progress at the capitals of two of his sons — Sepphoris (Antipas)[212] and Caesarea Philippi (modern Banias — Philip).

Papyri

Egypt is the major source of papyri, and with papyri pertaining to the Jews scholars have gained new insights about Jews in Alexandria and other parts of Egypt. The principal collection, with English translation and an important historical prolegomenon, is edited by V. A. Tcherikover, A. Fuks, and M. Stern.[213] The papyri have clarified in particular the legal status of Jews in the Hellenistic cities (pp. 42-43, 429-30). They have furthermore provided valuable data on the occupations and economic activities of Jews. The adoption by Jews of non-Hebrew names is sometimes a clue to the degree of cultural accommodation.

Synagogues [214]

The synagogue buildings that have been excavated provide a specific, physical setting for information supplied by literary sources about the synagogue service and related aspects of Jewish life (see pp. 573-82). Most of them date from the post–New Testament era. Synagogues of possibly pre-70 date have been found at Masada, Herodion, Magdala, and Gamala. Among the more impressive syna-

---

211. M. Avi-Yonah, ed., *Encyclopedia of Archaeological Excavations in the Holy Land,* 4 vols. (Jerusalem, 1975–1978).

212. Eric M. Meyers, Ehud Netzer, and Carol L. Meyers, *Sepphoris* (Winona Lake, Ind., 1992).

213. *Corpus Papyrorum Judaicarum,* vols. 1-3 (Cambridge, 1957–1964).

214. S. J. Saller, *Second Revised Catalogue of the Ancient Synagogues of the Holy Land,* Publications of the Studium Biblicum Franciscanum, Collectio Minor, vol. 6 (Jerusalem, 1972); A. T. Kraabel, "The Diaspora Synagogue: Archaeological and Epigraphic Evidence since Sukenik," *ANRW* II, *Principat,* 19.2 (Berlin and New York, 1979), 646-85; Hershel Shanks, *Judaism in Stone: The Archaeology of Ancient Synagogues* (Washington, 1979); L. I. Levine, ed., *Ancient Synagogues Revealed* (Jerusalem and Detroit, 1981); M. J. S. Chiat, *Handbook of Synagogue Architecture* (Chico, Calif., 1982); Dan Urman and Paul V. M. Flesher, eds., *Ancient Synagogues: Historical Analysis and Archaeological Discovery* (Leiden, 1995); Steven Fine, ed., *Sacred Realm: The Emergence of the Synagogue in the Ancient World* (Oxford, 1996); L. I. Levine, "The Nature and Origin of the Palestinian Synagogue Reconsidered," *JBL* 115 (1996):425-48. See further bibliography on p. 582.

SYNAGOGUE, Sardis, 4th c.

The most impressive Diaspora synagogue is at Sardis. The reading desk at the
front is at the opposite end from the double Torah shrine, where the scrolls of
the law were kept, between the three entrances on the east end.

gogues excavated in Palestine are those at Capernaum, Chorazin, Hammath
Tiberias, Bar'am, Beth Alpha, and Maaon; of those outside Palestine especially
notable are Ostia, Stobi, Delos, Sardis, and Dura Europus. There is no uniform
architectural plan, but they do share some common features. Synagogues were
commonly oriented toward Jerusalem (to the east; Josephus, *Against Apion*
2.10); but not with absolute consistency or accuracy. The Diaspora synagogues
were frequently built near a source of water (sea or river)[215] or had cisterns near
the entrance. The essential part of the furniture was an ark (chest) for keeping
the biblical scrolls. This ark or Torah shrine was originally a portable chest
(Taanith 2.1) brought in for the service; but later permanent structures appear,
usually on the wall facing Jerusalem, attached to a niche, aedicula, or apse. The
sanctity that came to be ascribed to synagogue buildings came from the Torah
scrolls placed in an ark that was framed in terms of temple architecture. Most
synagogues had a platform where there would have been a reading stand; other

215. Cf. Josephus, *Ant.* 14.10.23 (258).

MOSAIC FLOOR, synagogue at Hammath Tiberias, 3d/4th c. A.D.
Along with characteristically Jewish emblems — lions, ark of the covenant (or
Torah shrine), and menorahs — the signs of the zodiac and a personification of
the sun in his chariot occur on synagogue floor mosaics. These seemingly pagan
symbols apparently represented the universe as subject to God's law (p. 241).

features were benches lining the walls and a chief seat ("Moses' seat"; Matt. 23:2)
for the person presiding.[216] Many had guest rooms adjoining the assembly
room. Pictorial evidence indicates the use of a menorah (lampstand).

Jewish Symbols and Art [217]

Something of a surprise has been the presence of art in many of the synagogues. Apparently not all Jews applied the prohibitions in the Decalogue
(Exod. 20:4; Deut. 5:8) as strictly or extensively as rabbinic interpretation attempted.[218] In addition to sculptured architectural elements (column capitals,

216. Bernd-Jörg Dielner, "Zur literarischen und monumentalen Ueberlieferung der sog.
'Moseskathedra'," *Studien zur spätantiken und byzantinischen Kunst*, vol. 2 (Bonn, 1986), 147-55.

217. E. R. Goodenough, *Jewish Symbols in the Greco-Roman Period*, 13 vols. (New York,
1953–1968); J. Gutmann, "Early Synagogue and Jewish Catacomb Art and its Relation to Christian
Art," *ANRW* II, *Principat*, 21.2 (Berlin and New York, 1984).

218. C. Konikoff, *The Second Commandment and its Interpretation in the Art of Ancient Israel* (Geneva, 1973).

SYNAGOGUE WALL PAINTINGS, early 3d c., Dura Europus
The most nearly complete cycle of paintings from an ancient Jewish synagogue
was found at Dura Europus on the Euphrates. Biblical scenes and characters
are the theme, especially events associated with the ark of the covenant.
(Courtesy Yale University Art Gallery)

COLUMN CAPITAL
The *menorah* was the almost ubiquitous Jewish symbol, but it was
often accompanied by other symbols such as the *lulab* (palm branch) and *ethrog*
(citron). This capital came from the synagogue at Corinth. *(Corinth Museum)*

etc.) were mosaic floors with scenes from the Bible and nature (from the fifth
and sixth centuries; p. 241),[219] and wall paintings. (For Jewish funerary art, see
pp. 245, 504).

The most important of the early synagogues to be excavated from the
standpoint of pictorial art is at Dura Europus on the Euphrates.[220] The walls of
this third-century synagogue were lined with spectacular frescoes, including
scenes from the life of Moses, the career of Elijah, the anointing of David, the
vision of Ezekiel, the Book of Esther, a sequence dealing with the history of the
ark, and portraits (biblical characters?). Copies of the paintings are housed at
Yale; the originals are in Damascus.

Jewish religious emblems occur not only in synagogue architecture and

219. R. and A. Ovadiah, *Hellenistic, Roman, and Early Byzantine Mosaic Pavements in Israel*
(Rome, 1987). The Targum of Ps.-Jonathan to Leviticus 26:1 allows pictures and figures on the
floors of synagogues if they are not worshipped.

220. C. Kraeling, ed., *The Excavations at Dura Europos,* 8:1, *The Synagogue* (New Haven,
1956; New York, 1979); Jonathan Goldstein, "The Central Composition of the West Wall of the
Synagogue at Dura Europos," *Journal of the Ancient Near Eastern Society* 16/17 (1984/85):99-142;
Joseph Gutmann, *The Dura Europos Synagogue: A Reevaluation (1939-1992),* 2d ed. (Atlanta, 1992).

JEWISH GOLD GLASS
Symbols of religious festivals — water jars, palm branches, citron,
and ram's horns — as well as furnishings from the temple continued
to be important to the Jews. *(Courtesy Vatican Museum)*

decoration but also on objects of everyday use, such as lamps.[221] Objects associated with the festivals (palm branch, citron, menorah) are especially prominent.

The major collection of Jewish art and symbols by E. R. Goodenough should be used for its collection of evidence but not for Goodenough's interpretation, which involves a particular theory of the transfer of symbolic meanings and a speculative interpretation of Hellenistic Judaism.[222] The nearly

221. Varda Sussman, *Ornamented Jewish Oil-Lamps from the Destruction of the Second Temple Through the Bar-Kokhba Revolt* (Warminster, England, 1982); Rachel Hachlili, *The Menorah, the Ancient Seven-armed Candelabrum: Origin, Form and Significance* (Leiden, 2001).

222. Note 217. See reviews by A. D. Nock in *Gnomon* 27 (1955):558-72; 29 (1957):524-33; 32 (1960):728-36 (*Essays,* 877-918); and Morton Smith in *JBL* 86 (1967):53-68.

SCRIPTORIUM, Qumran
The Dead Sea Scrolls were written or copied in the Scriptorium. The buildings
at Qumran provided for the full needs of the community.

ubiquitous Jewish symbol was the menorah (the lampstand, usually but not always seven-branched).[223] It is found sculptured on the column capitals in synagogues and on sarcophagi, on mosaic pavements of synagogues, painted on
walls of catacombs, on gold glasses, on lamps, and on bone and ivory carvings.
The menorah held the place in Jewish symbolism occupied by the Chi-Rho
and later the cross in Christian symbolism. Other emblems occurring with
great frequency in various media in Jewish art include the Torah shrine containing scrolls of the Scriptures, the lion (of Judah), lulab (palm branch) and
ethrog (a citron) representing the Feast of Tabernacles, incense shovel for the
Day of Atonement, and the shofar for New Year's Day. The association of these
with the temple and its ritual and festivals is noteworthy for the self-
understanding of the synagogue and the transformation of older symbols into
a new setting.

Among biblical stories the sacrifice of Isaac occupied a special place in
Jewish art. Its frequency in synagogue art suggests that the *Aqedath Isaac*
("binding of Isaac") was emphasized. Did this come to prominence as a coun-

---

223. D. Sperber, "The History of the Menorah," *JJS* 16 (1965):135-59; Carol Meyers, *The Tabernacle Menorah* (Missoula, Mont., and Chico, Calif., 1976).

terpart to the Christian doctrine of redemption, or was this the background of Paul's formulation of the significance of Jesus' death?[224]

Pagan References to Jews

Pagan references to Jews in the Greco-Roman period do not add a great deal to what can be learned from Jewish literature about Judaism itself, but they are very important for how Jews and Judaism were perceived and thus are significant for various purposes. It is impossible here to provide a listing of the pagan sources for the study of Judaism, but fortunately there are extensive collections of these readily available. Varied motives lay behind comments on Jews, and various attitudes toward them were expressed. Some Gentile writers were favorable to Judaism and found it attractive, looking on the Jews as philosophers and as an ancient source of wisdom with pure concepts of the divine and how it is to be worshiped. Other men of affairs had very negative impressions of the Jews because of the struggles over citizen rights and the special privileges of the Jews in the empire.[225] The pagan sources do permit some conclusions about the impact of Jews in the Greco-Roman world and what features of the Jewish religion and way of life were prominent to outsiders: Sabbath, circumcision, abstention from pork, and the worship of the one God. Even the hostile statements indicate that the pagan sense of what constituted Jewish identity conformed closely to Jewish self-understanding (pp. 537ff.).

One of the more scurrilous accounts of Jewish history and religion is found in Tacitus, *Histories* 5.2-13, whose charges conform closely to those to which Josephus responded in *Against Apion* (p. 486). Tacitus's report correctly notes that Moses was the founder of the Jewish religion and mentions many of the details of Jewish practice: abstention from pork, use of unleavened bread, paying tribute to Jerusalem, loyalty to other Jews, general avoidance of intermarriage with non-Jews, circumcision, making proselytes, not exposing children, burial and not cremation of the dead, worship of one God, and absence of an image in the temple. His interpretations show the hostile attitude: the Jews were driven out of Egypt; they worship an ass (alluded to); the Sabbath rest is kept from indolence; the Jews hate other peoples; and they are lustful.

Apart from those with political reasons to oppose Jews, such negative opin-

224. The latter is the position of H.-J. Schoeps, *Paul: the Theology of the Apostle in the Light of Jewish Religious History* (Philadelphia, 1961), 141-49; cf. G. Vermes, *Scripture and Tradition in Judaism* (Leiden, 1983), 193-227, and R. Wilken, "Melito, The Jewish Community at Sardis, and the Sacrifice of Isaac," *Theological Studies* 37 (1976):53-69; but see P. R. Davies and Bruce Chilton, "The Aqedath: A Revised Tradition History," *CBQ* 40 (1978):514-46. The Jewish sources are compiled in S. Spiegel, *The Last Trial: On the Legends and Lore of the Command to Abraham to Sacrifice Isaac* (New York, 1967).

225. V. Tcherikover, *Hellenistic Civilization and the Jews* (Philadelphia, 1961), 357-77.

ions come primarily from a conservative circle of Roman literary figures. Anti-Semitism surfaced mainly where Jews appeared most alien — in race and particularly in customs — and would not conform to pagan society. Where Jews were most at home in society, attitudes were favorable. Jewish exclusivism appears repeatedly in the texts. Hostility from pagan traditionalists increased in proportion to the numbers of Gentiles attracted to Judaism. The pagan perception of Christianity, initially, was colored by the stereotypes of Jews (pp. 592-601).

BIBLIOGRAPHY

Stern, M. *Greek and Latin Authors on Jews and Judaism.* 2 vols. Jerusalem, 1974, 1980.
Whittaker, M. *Jews and Christians: Graeco-Roman Views.* Cambridge, 1984.

Gager, John. *Moses in Greco-Roman Paganism.* Nashville, 1972.
Sevenster, J. N. *The Roots of Pagan Anti-Semitism in the Ancient World.* Leiden, 1975.
Daniel, Jerry L. "Anti-Semitism in the Hellenistic-Roman Period." *JBL* 98 (1979):45-65.
Gager, John. *The Origins of Anti-Semitism.* Oxford, 1983.
Feldman, L. H. *Jew and Gentile in the Ancient World: Attitudes and Interactions from Alexander to Justinian.* Princeton, 1993.
Schäfer, Peter. *Judeophobia: Attitudes Toward the Jews in the Ancient World.* Cambridge, Mass., 1997.

PARTIES AND SECTS

That Judaism in the first century was far from a monolithic entity is evident from the divisions in Palestinian Judaism. The well-known groupings discussed in this section do not exhaust the varieties. Even within these groups were subdivisions, as is known from the controversies among the Pharisees. Modern scholars make a distinction between "parties" (groups that recognize the existence of others from whom they are separated as having a place in the total people; cf. modern Christian denominations or political parties in a country) and "sects" (groups claiming an exclusive right to represent the total people and having exclusive possession of the truth). According to this distinction the Pharisees and Sadducees were parties but the Essenes were a sect.

BIBLIOGRAPHY

Simon, Marcel. *Jewish Sects at the Time of Jesus.* Philadelphia, 1967.
Saldarini, A. J. *Pharisees, Scribes, and Sadducees in Palestinian Society: A Sociological Approach.* Wilmington, Del., 1989. Reprint with intro. by James VanderKam, Grand Rapids, 2001.

Stemberger, Günter. *Jewish Contemporaries of Jesus: Pharisees, Sadducees, Essenes.*
    Minneapolis, 1995 (German original, 1991).
Baumgarten, Albert I. *The Flourishing of Jewish Sects in the Maccabean Era: An Interpretation.* Leiden, 1997.

Pharisees

History

The name *Pharisee* is usually derived from the Hebrew *parush*, meaning "separate" but also "interpret." Those who agree on the former etymology do not agree concerning from whom or of what was the separation: of Israel from the nations? Of a select group, the Associates *(Haberim),* from the "people of the land" *('am ha-aretz* of the Mishnah)? Of themselves from ritual impurity? Of the tithes according to the Torah? The name Pharisee was used primarily by outsiders; the authors of Rabbinic literature referred to their predecessors as "sages."

Although Josephus's first reference to the Pharisees occurs in his discussion of Jonathan (*Ant.* 13.5.9 [171]), his first reference to their activities that connects with historical events falls in the reign of John Hyrcanus (13.10.5-6 [288-98]). It may be that they emerged out of the Hasidim at the time of the Maccabean revolt.[226] After the success of that revolt, if one did not choose to drop out of political life and withdraw to the wilderness as did the Qumranians, one of two courses could be followed with regard to the law. The traditional code might be expanded to meet new circumstances and be reinterpreted in accord with new beliefs; or these experiences could be left outside the scope of its authority and new ideas be left unrecognized. Those who accepted the first policy became the Pharisees, and those who adopted the second became the Sadducees.

According to Josephus the Pharisees rejected Hyrcanus's right to be both king and priest, so he gave his allegiance to the Sadducees. The Pharisees appear in Josephus as a political party who sought to impose their interpretation of the law upon the nation. Their conflict with the Hasmoneans became intense under Alexander Jannaeus, who severely persecuted them; however, they came to power under his widow Alexandra. They successfully wrested control of the governing council and, although lay scholars, supplanted the priests as interpreters of the law. Rabbinic literature credits Simeon ben Shetah with restoring the Torah at this time.

When Aristobulus turned once again to the priestly hierarchy, the Phari-

---

226. John Kampen, *The Hasideans and the Origin of Pharisaism: A Study of 1 and 2 Maccabees* (Atlanta, 1988).

sees began to lose some of their authority. With the coming of Roman rule and the establishment of the Herodian dynasty, the Pharisees' political power was limited and they concentrated on their own fellowships and on influencing the life of the nation on the local level. It may be that Hillel the Elder is significant in this change of approach. At any rate, in the New Testament and rabbinic literature the Pharisees appear principally as a table-fellowship who kept the same laws of ritual purity and so might eat together. Rabbinic literature's concern for agricultural law, Sabbath and festival regulations, and rules of cleanness agrees with the Gospels' picture of Pharisaic concerns. The Pharisees were likely both a table fellowship interested in purity and a political group at all periods, with one characteristic more prominent than the other depending of the circumstances. The New Testament, Josephus, and rabbinic literature agree in characterizing the Pharisees as those most concerned with accurate interpretation of the law and with promoting their own tradition.[227] Josephus gives their number in the first century as six thousand and attributes to them the greatest influence of any party on the common people. However, this claim, it has been argued, may reflect the situation only in the late first century (or be part of Josephus's campaign to commend the Pharisees to the Romans at the expense of other groups).[228] After 70 the Pharisees did take the lead in giving the Jewish people a new center of religious life apart from the temple.[229] The Pharisaic scholars at Jamnia and at Usha after the Bar Kokhba revolt were recognized by Rome as the governing body for the internal life of the Jewish people, so the Pharisees again became a party with political power as well as religious influence. The Judaism that survived was primarily Pharisaic Judaism.

The Pharisaic Program

The twin pillars of the Pharisaic system were "Torah and Tradition." Torah (teaching, or law) was primarily the five books of Moses. A written law must be interpreted and applied. The process of applying the teaching contained in the Torah involved new precepts. The Pharisees differed from the Sadducees in giving divine authority to the interpretation and application of the law. "It is more culpable to teach against the ordinances of the scribes than against the Torah itself" (Sanhedrin 11.3). The Sadducees answered the question "By what authority?" in terms of Deuteronomy 17:8-13, that the priests were to give the au-

---

227. A. I. Baumgarten, "The Name of the Pharisees," *JBL* 102 (1983):411-28; idem, "The Pharisaic *Paradosis*," *HTR* 80 (1987):63-77.

228. Steve Mason, "Pharisaic Dominance Before 70 CE and the Gospels' Hypocrisy Charge (Matt 23:2-3)," *HTR* 83 (1990):363-81, argues that Josephus shows antipathy to the Pharisees and their dominance in Jewish life even pre-70 and so is to be believed on their influence.

229. Jacob Neusner insists that post-70 rabbinism is not simply to be equated with pre-70 Pharisaism; see "The Formation of Rabbinic Judaism: Yavneh (Jamnia) from A.D. 70 to 100," *ANRW* II, *Principat*, 19.2 (Berlin and New York, 1979), 3-42.

thoritative applications of the Torah, but their instructions were not Torah. The Pharisees, on the other hand, felt that the Torah had been given to all Israel, not just to the priests, and therefore was open to all who were competent to interpret it. Here the scribes came in. They were not identical with the Pharisees, but there is good reason why scribes and Pharisees appear together so frequently in the Gospels. The scribes were the official scholars of the Torah. Most of the scribes accepted the principles of the Pharisees, and the Pharisees followed the teachings derived from scribal interpretations. Moreover, the Pharisees felt that if the applications of the law were to be binding, they had to have the force of Torah itself. The means to achieve this was the idea of oral law ("tradition of the elders"; Mark 7:3, 5), equally authoritative with the written law (for more about the oral law see pp. 542-43).

The Pharisees appear to have been for the most part non-priests. The concerns of the rabbis who succeeded them, as indicated by rabbinic literature, would indicate that their adherents included small landowners and the shopkeepers and artisans of the towns. The Pharisees' reputation for exactitude in the study and interpretation of the biblical law and their applications of it to areas of life where other Jews did not apply it distinguished them from other Jews. Their interpretations and applications were attributed to the "traditions of the elders."[230] It is estimated that two-thirds of the rabbinic traditions concern ritual purity, and this concern led to a great interest in the proper preparation of foods, careful observance of the agricultural laws, and meticulous tithing.

Because the Pharisees saw Torah as a developing, dynamic social force, they sought to keep the law of Moses from becoming a dead ritual and to give it new meaning and life. Thus they were also open to further doctrinal developments — resurrection of the body, last judgment, and rewards and punishment in the afterlife.

The flexibility of the Pharisees may also be seen in their approach to the problem of fate and free will. As characterized by Josephus, the three principal "philosophical schools" among the Jews were distinguished on this issue in this way: the Essenes assigned everything to fate *(heimarmenē)*; the Sadducees assigned everything to human freedom; and the Pharisees believed in both fate and free will *(Ant.* 13.5.9 [171-72]).[231] Josephus was borrowing the Greek philosophical terminology; for fate one should understand God's governance, or providence (cf. Gamaliel's advice in Acts 5:38-39). As Rabbi Akiba expressed it, "All is foreseen but freedom is granted" (Aboth 3.16).

---

230. E. P. Sanders, *Judaism: Practice and Belief 63 BCE–66 CE* (Philadelphia, 1992), 444.
231. George F. Moore, "Fate and Free Will in the Jewish Philosophies According to Josephus," *HTR* 22 (1929):371-89.

Jesus and the Pharisees

The sharp rebukes Jesus administered to the Pharisees and their frequent appearance as his antagonists have obscured the considerable area of agreement between them. Jesus lived as a loyal Jew and accepted the authority of the Torah (cf. such details as Mark 6:56; 1:40-45; 14:12; 12:36). He had many friendly contacts with certain Pharisees (Luke 7:36ff.; 11:37; 13:31-33; 14:1; Mark 12:28-34; Matt. 23:1-2). These verses, if nothing else, should have made unnecessary the lesson many Christians have had to learn from Jewish scholars that "Pharisee" was not synonymous with "hypocrite." Any way of life based on authoritative teaching or law has a tendency to hypocrisy, and no doubt there were hypocrites among the Pharisees. Yet just as Epicurus was not an "Epicurean," so the Pharisees were not "Pharisaical." The relationship between inner motive and outward conduct is often differently perceived by those who adhere to a given practice and those who disagree with it. Much of Jesus' ethical teaching finds parallels in rabbinic literature. Most often cited is the negative form of the "Golden Rule" attributed to Hillel. The effort to reduce the law to as few principles as possible (Matt. 22:36) was a rabbinic concern.[232] According to one story a Gentile volunteered to become a proselyte on the condition that he be taught the whole Torah while he stood on one foot. Hillel converted him with the teaching: "What is hateful to you, do not to your neighbor. That is the whole Torah, while the rest is commentary; go and learn" (b. Shabbath 30b).

Precisely because there was so much in common, the points on which Jesus took issue stand out boldly.[233] Four stories illustrate the underlying differences. (1) Jesus' association with "sinners" illustrates a different conception of separation from the world (Mark 2:15-17; Matt. 9:9-13; Luke 5:27-32). The Pharisees' attitude was well defined: the pious must keep apart from those neglectful of the law, ceremonial cleanness, and payment of tithes, especially in their meals. The Essenes took this a step further and practiced a spatial as well as moral separation from the world; the Pharisees did not attempt spatial withdrawal but tried to achieve the same kind of physical separation while living in the world. In contrast, Jesus was often in the homes of and ate with "publicans and sinners." He thus rejected the effort to extend the priestly regulations to the people as a whole. He defended his own conduct in terms of his sense of personal mission (Mark 2:17 and par.; cf. Luke 19:10). Jesus took a different model for the religious life — involvement with sinners while not partaking of their sins. Saving the world required contact with it.

(2) Ritual purity illustrates differences on the authority of tradition (Mark 7:1-23; Matt. 15:1-20). Behind the Pharisaic separation from sinners lay

---

232. b. Makkoth 23b-24a says Moses gave 613 laws; David reduced them to 11 (Ps. 15); Isaiah to 6 (Isa. 33:15-16); Micah to 3 (Mic. 6:8); Isaiah to 2 (Isa. 56:1); Amos to 1 (Amos 5:4) and Habakkuk to 1 (Hab. 2:4).

233. For this section see B. H. Branscomb, *Jesus and the Law of Moses* (New York, 1930).

their concern for ritual purity. The basis for their interpretation was the oral law ("the tradition of the elders"). Jesus not only rejected the emphasis on ritual purity (that which defiles is internal, not external), he also rejected the Pharisaic basis of authority. The oral law had actually contravened the written law in many instances.

(3) Sabbath-keeping illustrates a different set of priorities (Mark 2:23–3:6; Matt. 12:1-13; Luke 6:1-11). The scribal interpretations entered into the question of what constituted work on the Sabbath. The conduct of Jesus' disciples in picking and rubbing grain and Jesus' healings on the Sabbath did not contravene any specific text in the Old Testament but did run counter to the current Pharisaic interpretation. Mark's account defends the disciples on three bases: the Old Testament allowed exceptions in case of need; human values take precedence over ritual requirements;[234] and finally messianic authority determines the law. The priority of human needs also figures in Jesus' defense of his healings on the Sabbath.

(4) Divorce illustrates a difference in interpretation, whether by principle or by precept (Matt. 19:3-12; Mark 10:2-9). The practice involved here was the method of interpreting the law. Jesus was questioned in regard to a difference among the Pharisees themselves concerning the meaning of Deuteronomy 24:1 ("unseemly thing," "indecency," or "uncleanness"). Hillel allowed divorce for any cause, whereas Shammai limited it to sexual immorality and immodest behavior (Gittin 9.10). Jesus was closer to Shammai, but his answer went on to state the divine intention in regard to marriage. In so doing he repudiated the ultimate authority of the Mosaic legislation, appealing in its place to the divine purpose expressed in the order of creation. This interpretation of the law in terms of fundamental principles distinguishes Jesus from the rival groups in the Judaism of his day. According to him the Sadducees were right in exegesis — the Scriptures did not mean what the Pharisees made them mean — but they were wrong in relegating Scripture to the place of an archaic relic with less and less relevance to the present. The Pharisees were right in trying to keep Scripture applicable, but were wrong in their method by making tradition superior or equal to the written word. Jesus offered a corrective to both viewpoints. The written word is authoritative, but the great fundamental principles therein take precedence and provide the standard by which it is to be interpreted and applied.

BIBLIOGRAPHY

Josephus. *War* 1.5.1-3 [107-14]; 2.8.14 [162-66]. *Ant.* 13.5.9 [171-73]; 18.1.2-3 [11-15]; 13.10.5-6 [288-98] (the same story is told about Alexander Jannaeus in b. Qid. 66a); 13.15.5–16.3 [399-418].
Neusner, J. *The Rabbinic Traditions about the Pharisees before 70.* 3 vols. Leiden, 1971.
Bowker, J. *Jesus and the Pharisees.* Cambridge, 1973.

234. Cf. b. Yoma 85b.

(See the bibliographies on rabbinic literature, the product of later Pharisaism.)

Abrahams, I. *Studies in Pharisaism and the Gospels.* Cambridge, 1924. Reprint. New York, 1967.

Herford, R. T. *The Pharisees.* New York, 1924. Reprint. Boston, 1962.

Marcus, R. "The Pharisees in the Light of Modern Scholarship." *Journal of Religion* 32 (1952):153-64.

Davies, W. D. *Introduction to Pharisaism.* Philadelphia, 1967.

Rivkin, E., ed. *Judaism and Christianity.* 3 vols. New York, 1969.

Neusner, J. *From Politics to Piety: The Emergence of Pharisaic Judaism.* Englewood Cliffs, N.J., 1973.

Finkel, A. *The Pharisees and the Teacher of Nazareth.* Leiden, 1974.

Rivkin, E. *A Hidden Revolution.* Nashville, 1978.

Mason, Steve. *Flavius Josephus on the Pharisees: A Composition-Critical Study.* Leiden, 1991.

Deines, Roland. *Die Pharisäer: Ihr Verständnis im Spiegel der christlichen und jüdischen Forschung seit Wellhausen und Graetz.* Tübingen, 1997.

Sadducees

The derivation of the name *Sadducee* is not certain, but it is usually connected with Zadok, either the high priest under David or some later Zadok, or with "just ones" (either positively or ironically).

The Sadducees were the party of the wealthy priests (some priests were Sadducees but not all) and their friends in the aristocracy (Acts 5:17). They combined conservative religious attitudes with power politics. They rejected the Pharisees' innovations, and their interpretations were stricter than those of the Pharisees. Although Josephus claims the Sadducees had to follow the legal rulings of the Pharisees, this seems unlikely, for the Sadducees controlled the temple ritual. Their political position and practical sense of survival perhaps led them to an openness toward certain Hellenistic cultural influences, but we lack the sources to conclude that they were heavily Hellenized. They may be characterized as both conservative and compliant. After the coming of Rome, they encouraged collaboration with the ruling power and were interested in maintaining the status quo, which preserved the peace and their power and influence. Their center of strength was the temple. With its destruction and the collapse of their program and way of life after 70, they ceased to influence Jewish religious life. One of the high-priestly families was that of Boethus, which was so prominent that in Talmudic literature Boethusians is at times almost equivalent to Sadducees. The Boethusians, however, appear to have been originally distinct from the Sadducees, perhaps as one branch of them.

The Sadducees are known now only through the eyes of their opponents: Pharisees — Josephus and the traditions in rabbinic literature — and Christians

— the New Testament. Hence, they are known primarily for those points on which they differed from the Pharisees; that is, they are known negatively and not for positive things for which they stood. The Sadducees accepted only the written law of Moses as authoritative and rejected the oral law of the Pharisees. Of course, they had their own traditions of interpretation relative to the temple ritual and legal matters, but these were not Torah and were not binding. Even the prophets and writings, although not rejected, were not treated as a source of doctrine. Jesus, therefore, in responding to their question about the resurrection (Matt. 22:23-33 and par.) cited a passage from the Pentateuch (Exod. 3:6) in support of the idea of a resurrection and not one of the more obvious texts from Isaiah or Daniel. These would have carried no conviction for the Sadducees, given their understanding of authority, so Jesus met them on their own ground.

The question about the resurrection introduces another negative identifying belief of the Sadducees: their denial of the resurrection. Their question to Jesus presupposed the common Pharisaic understanding of a literal resurrection involving the same physical activities in the world to come as characterize human life now. Luke's account is more explicit in rejecting this understanding of the resurrection (20:34-36), but the main thrust of Jesus' answer was to put the emphasis on the nature of God, his power, and his relationship to humanity. He did so because the Sadducees apparently went beyond a rejection of a fleshly resurrection. According to Acts 23:8, "The Sadducees say there is no resurrection, neither angel nor spirit." The verse has created problems not only because there is no external confirmation of a Sadducee denial of angels and spirits but because there would seem to be enough about angels in the Pentateuch to satisfy even a skeptical literalist. Therefore, it has been suggested that the Sadducees did not deny all angels but the elaborate angelology and demonology developed in the postbiblical period and accepted by the Pharisees. Another possibility is that the latter two negatives in Acts 23:8 are distributive: they denied a resurrection (not only physical) whether in the form of an angel or a spirit. In this case Jesus' affirmation is even more to the point ("like angels") in affirming what the Sadducees rejected. Another possibility is that two questions are being dealt with and the phrase "nor angel nor spirit" refers to an intermediate state before the resurrection.[235] At any rate, Jesus' answer went to the heart of the Sadducees' problem: a temporal concern that gave inadequate (if any) attention to the spiritual side of human existence.

BIBLIOGRAPHY

Josephus. *War* 2.8.14 [164-65]. *Ant.* 18.1.4 [16-17]; 13.5.10 [173].

LeMoyne, J. *Les Sadducéens*. Paris, 1972.

---

235. David Daube, "On Acts 23: Sadducees and Angels," *JBL* 109 (1990):493-97.

Qumran Community, Essenes, and Therapeutae

History of the Qumran Community [236]

The principal Dead Sea Scrolls have been introduced in the "Jewish Literature" section of this chapter. The use of the scrolls for historical study depends upon their date. Although there has been debate over the exact age of the scrolls, several converging lines of evidence have convinced the great majority of scholars that they belong to the last two centuries of the Second Temple (second century B.C. to first century A.D.). (1) Paleography, the study of ancient handwriting, places the writing of the scrolls in this time period. (2) The carbon 14 test on the linen cloths in which some of the scrolls were wrapped gave a date of A.D. 33 and then of 20 B.C., both with a range of plus or minus two hundred years. (3) Linguistic studies place the kind of language employed in this time period. (4) The historical allusions fit the events of this period, although names are seldom given and the internal evidence is not so explicit as would be hoped. (5) Archaeology has provided the conclusive evidence. It has connected the manuscripts found in the caves near the Wadi Qumran with the ruins (Khirbet) of the settlement at Qumran. Jars of the same type in which the scrolls were stored when placed in the caves have been found in the ruins, one jar beside a coin dated A.D. 10. Dried ink in the scriptorium at Qumran matched exactly in chemical content the ink with which the scrolls were written. The evidence of the jars and coins unmistakably places the period of occupation at Qumran in the late Second Temple period.

Excavations at Qumran have revealed provisions for a complete community. The members of the sect apparently slept in tents, or perhaps in caves. They carried on farming activities at Ain (spring) Feshka to the south. But the center of all communal activities was at Qumran. There was an elaborate water system with canals and cisterns to provide water for the community and pools for its ritual washings. There were workshops and facilities for pottery making, a kitchen, and storerooms. There was an assembly hall and a library or scriptorium with writing tables where presumably the manuscripts were written.

By correlating the archaeological evidence with the internal evidence of the scrolls, it is possible to reconstruct a general outline of the history of the Qumran community.[237]

---

236. H. H. Rowley, "The History of the Qumran Sect," *BJRL* 49 (1966):203-32; Jerome Murphy-O'Connor, "The Essenes and their History," *Revue Biblique* 81 (1974):215-44; idem, "The Essenes in Palestine," *BA* 40 (1977):100-124; J. H. Charlesworth, "The Origin and Subsequent History of the Authors of the Dead Sea Scrolls: Four Transitional Phases among the Qumran Essenes," *RQ* 10.38 (1980):213-33; P. R. Callaway, *The History of the Qumran Community*, Journal for the Study of the Pseudepigrapha Supplement Series 3 (Sheffield, 1988).

237. This outline follows J. T. Milik, *Ten Years of Discovery in the Wilderness of Judaea* (London, 1959), 49-98.

Prehistory. The *Ḥasidim* initially supported the Hasmonean revolt, but after Judas restored the worship in Jerusalem, they withdrew from further involvement in political affairs. For about twenty years the group was leaderless.

Phase One — from the founding to the rule of John Hyrcanus. The date of the founding of the sect depends on the identification of the Wicked Priest, who persecuted the Teacher of Righteousness (better, "Righteous Teacher") and his followers. Proposed candidates have included Jonathan, Simon, and Alexander Jannaeus, with Jonathan appearing as the most likely candidate.[238] That there are several candidates for the title "Wicked Priest" is commentary on the religious situation in Jerusalem, but one must recognize the narrow definitions of the Qumran literature. When Jonathan assumed the high priesthood and pursued a secular policy in his civil rule, around the mid–second century B.C., one branch of the pious under the leadership of the Teacher of Righteousness withdrew into the wilderness of Judea. They advocated the rights of the Zadokite priesthood against the Hasmoneans. This was the period of the initial settlement at Qumran and of zealous Essenism.

Phase Two — from John Hyrcanus to Herod. John Hyrcanus's break with the Pharisees brought an influx of new recruits to Qumran. The archaeological evidence shows that during Hyrcanus's reign (134–104) the settlement entered its most flourishing stage. Other groups were formed, and Pharisaic influence may perhaps be seen in the interpretation of the law.

Phase Three — the reign of Herod. An earthquake in 31 B.C. has left clear signs of its destruction at Qumran, which the Essenes abandoned. During this period Essenes were prominent in support of Herod, the antagonist of the Essenes' old enemies, particularly the Hasmoneans.

Phase Four — from Archelaus to the Jewish revolt. About the beginning of the Christian era rebuilding and reoccupation began at Qumran. The unsettled conditions in first-century Palestine made the monastic-type life at Qumran once more attractive. As tensions with Rome increased, Zealot influences may have been felt at Qumran. The settlement was destroyed by Roman troops in A.D. 68, but not before the library had been hidden in nearby caves. Some of the Essenes apparently found refuge with the defenders of Masada and brought some of their literary works with them.

Identity: The Essenes

The debate over the proper identification of the Qumran community has centered on the Essenes. Of the previously known sects in Judaism the Qumran community has the closest affinities with the Essenes. The Qumran cove-

---

238. This assumes that the Wicked Priest was a reigning high priest; the case for his being the leader of a rival faction in the community is argued by B. E. Thiering, "Once More the Wicked Priest," *JBL* 97 (1978):191-205.

nanters were either Essenes, a branch of the Essenes, or a previously unknown sect similar to the Essenes. The derivation of the name *Essene* is unclear, but a likely suggestion is that this is a Grecizing of Aramaic *hasayya*, the "pious ones," and possibly equivalent to *Ḥasidim* in Hebrew.[239] The Essenes were known previously from Latin and Greek sources (listed below in bibliography).[240]

There are striking similarities between the accounts of the Essenes in these previously known sources and the information in the Dead Sea Scrolls about the community at Qumran: there was a one-year waiting period and two years of probation before full membership in the sect (*War* 2.8.7 [137-38]; 1QS vi.14-22 requires two stages of probation, of one year each, before full membership); oaths were sworn at initiation; there was a strict discipline (both *War* 2.8.9 [147] and 1QS vii.13 mention that spitting into the assembly was forbidden); purification baths were practiced regularly; a common meal was eaten together by the community; there was a community of goods; and the study of the Scriptures was a prominent activity.

Some of the very similarities, however, show discrepancies in details among the sources; yet those between the scrolls and the Greek sources are no greater than those between Josephus and Philo. The nature and extent of the community of possessions may not be the same in the Greek and the new Hebrew sources.[241] Philo states that the Essenes banned marriage altogether (*Hypothetica* 11.14), whereas Josephus knew both marrying and nonmarrying Essenes (*War* 2.8.13 [160]). The scrolls do not indicate a condemnation of marriage, and the Qumran cemetery contains bones of women and children as well as men (but recent anthropological examination indicates that these are recent, non-Israeli remains). It may very well be that celibacy was practiced by some (or most) but was not a general rule among the Essenes. Another area that is not clear is the attitude toward animal sacrifice. Philo implies a rejection of it (*Every Just Man Is Free* 75), and the manuscripts of Josephus have the Essenes sending votive offerings to the temple but performing their own sacrifices (*Ant.* 18.1.5 [19]). The situation seems to be that they objected to the Jerusalem cultus but not to sacrifice per se. What if any sacrifice they offered at Qumran remains unclear.

Some interpretations of the law by the Qumran community agree with interpretations given by the Sadducees. Connections with the Sadducees

---

239. Philo connects the name with *hosiotēs*, "holiness" (*Every Good Man Is Free* 75 and *Hypothetica* 11.1).

240. T. S. Beall, *Josephus' Description of the Essenes Illustrated from the Dead Sea Scrolls* (Cambridge, 1988); G. Vermes and M. G. Goodman, eds., *The Essenes According to the Classical Sources* (Sheffield, 1989); Roland Bergmeier, *Die Essener — Berichte des Flavius Josephus: Quellenstudien zu den Essenertexten in Werk des Jüdischen Historiographen* (Kempen, 1993).

241. M. Black, *The Essene Problem* (London, 1961), 19-26.

should not be surprising nor do they argue that the Qumran community was Sadducee, since both groups had a priestly connection.

It may be that *Essene* was a broad term including several similar sects, one segment of which was the Qumran community. Or, perhaps some modifications in practice were made over the years (the different forms of the *Rule of the Community* and its relations with the *Damascus Document* would confirm that this did happen, as is always to be assumed in regard to a living community). The discrepancies are not enough to overthrow the Essene hypothesis or weaken the broad areas of agreement and even detailed similarities. If the Qumran community was not an Essene group, it was a similar sect, active in the same time period and in the same location.

Organization, Beliefs, and Practices at Qumran

We have already alluded to some beliefs and practices, and some will be treated best in relation to Christianity. The Qumran sect was a closely structured community in which priests predominated. They called themselves the "sons of Zadok," but they provided for priests, Levites, Israelites, and proselytes in their membership. An annual examination assigned a rank to each member according to his knowledge and spiritual progress, and he sat and spoke in the assembly according to this rank. The organization included oligarchic, monarchic, and democratic elements. The supreme council of the community was a group of three priests and twelve laymen (elders?).[242] The administration of affairs was handled by an overseer *(mebaqqer* or *paqid)* who examined candidates for membership, had charge of finances, and directed the labor of the community.[243] A number of decisions were made by the sessions of the "Many," as the assemblies of the whole were called, although again the hierarchical structure dictated who could speak when. There was a tight system of discipline, and even minor infractions could result in exclusion from communal life for varying periods of time.[244]

One became a member, after a time of probation, by taking an oath to live by the law of Moses as interpreted by the "men of the covenant" and by being admitted to the water of purification. He turned his "knowledge, powers, and possessions" over to the sect.

The Qumran community lived under a strong eschatological expectation. They believed that they were living in the last days, and they interpreted the prophets as referring to their times. They looked forward to the coming of a

---

242. The *Damascus Document* provides for ten judges.

243. According to the *Damascus Document* the overseer, however, did not have the prestige of the presiding priest, who directed the study of the Bible.

244. M. Weinfeld, *The Organizational Pattern and the Penal Code of the Qumran Sect: A Comparison with the Guilds and Religious Associations of the Hellenistic-Roman Period* (Göttingen, 1986).

Prophet and the Messiahs (Anointed) of Aaron (the eschatological Priest) and of Israel (the messianic King), according to 1QS ix.9-11 and 4QTest.[245] The claim to find a "slain Messiah" in one of the Qumran scrolls appears to be a misreading: the Messiah will kill his enemy rather than the reverse.[246] They made a sharp distinction between the "sons of light" and the "sons of darkness."

As the community awaited God's action they spent their time in intense study of the Scriptures. Wherever ten members were together, someone was to be studying the law at all times, and the members took turns reading and praying together night and day (1QS vi.6-8). The interpretation followed the lines laid down by the Teacher of Righteousness, who was believed to have revealed the true knowledge of God and the correct understanding of the Bible. Various types of interpretation of Scripture are reflected in the manuscripts from Qumran: midrashic or halakhic rewriting of texts, *pesher* interpretation (p. 544), collection of texts *(testimonia)* on a topic, allegorical, and typological interpretations.

It is problematic, however, to think of a closed canon of Scripture at Qumran. The Law, Prophets, and some other writings presumably had a special status, as shown by numbers of copies, formula citations, commentaries, and summary statements about authoritative writings; yet inspiration and revelation were not necessarily thought of as ended. The *Temple Scroll* was a reworked Pentateuch, at the least an authoritative interpretation of it, and other works were on the border between Scripture text and commentary. Moreover, there was no single fixed text even of the Pentateuch at Qumran, and some works show considerable fluidity in their contents (Exodus and especially Psalms). The Qumran community took the written word seriously, but caution must be exercised lest anachronistic conclusions be drawn about its recognition of the limits of Scripture.

The meals of the community had a sacred character, and the proceedings were carefully regulated.

The community lived by a solar calendar, identical with that of Jubilees and 1 Enoch, rather than by the luni-solar calendar observed by the Jerusalem priesthood.[247] This calendar contained 364 days, divided into 52 weeks, with 12 months of 30 days and one extra day every three months. New Year's and the first day of each three-month period began on a Wednesday; festivals and Sabbaths always fell on the same day of the year. This meant that the festivals fell

245. J. J. Collins, *The Scepter and the Star: The Messiahs of the Dead Sea Scrolls and other Ancient Literature* (Garden City, 1995), who finds four paradigms of the Messiah: King, Priest, Prophet, and Heavenly Man; J. H. Charlesworth, H. Lichtenberger and G. S. Oegema, eds., *Studies in the Messianic Expectations in the Dead Sea Scrolls* (Tübingen, 1998); Israel Knohl, *The Messiah Before Jesus: The Suffering Servant of the Dead Sea Scrolls* (Berkeley, 2000).

246. Markus Bockmuehl, "A 'Slain Messiah' in 4QSerekh Milhamah (4Q285)?" *Tyndale Bulletin* 43 (1992):155-169.

247. S. Talmon, "The Calendar Reckoning of the Sect from the Judaean Desert," *Scripta Hierosolymitana* 4 (1958):162-99; E. Wiesenberg, "The Jubilee of Jubilees," *RQ* 3 (1961):3ff.

on different days at Qumran from those at Jerusalem. The difference over the religious calendar appears to have been a principal point of contention with the Jerusalem priesthood.

Qumran and the New Testament [248]

Of individuals known from the New Testament the strongest circumstantial case for a connection with Qumran can be made for John the Baptist.[249] As noted above, Josephus described John's baptism in terms of the Qumran washings (p. 487). Several facts support the theory that John lived at Qumran: he was of a priestly family, his parents were old at the time of his birth (Luke 1:7), the Essenes reared orphan children (Josephus, *War* 2.8.2 [120]), and the scene of his activity was the wilderness of Judea (Luke 3:2).

It might further be suggested that John learned the practice of baptism there, but his baptism was different from the Qumran ceremonial lustrations in important respects. John's was a "baptism of repentance for the forgiveness of sins" (Luke 3:3). It was a once-for-all act. The washings at Qumran — apparently by immersion (CD x.11 and the pools at Qumran) — were daily purifications; we may assume that the first ablution had a special meaning but we are not told this in the texts. The Qumran bath was noninitiatory, for one was admitted to the water only after taking the oath of membership. The roots of the Qumran practice were in the Old Testament washings for purification. It was presumably self-administered, as were Jewish washings, although we have nothing explicit on this. However, what made John's baptism unique was that he administered it himself, hence his name "the baptizer." Furthermore, John's baptism was related to the coming of the Messiah and saved one from the wrath to come (Matt. 3:6-7; Acts 19:4).

Another point of contact was the use of Isaiah 40:3. Once more there is a difference: Qumran, following the Hebrew text, emphasized the going into the wilderness to prepare the way for the Lord (1QS viii.13-14), whereas Christians interpreted John as the "voice crying in the wilderness" (Matt. 3:3, following

---

248. F. F. Bruce, "Qumrân and Early Christianity," *NTS* 2 (1956):176-90; K. Stendahl, ed., *The Scrolls and the New Testament* (New York, 1957); David Flusser, "The Dead Sea Sect and Pre-Pauline Christianity," *Scripta Hierosolymitana* 4 (1958):215-66; M. Black, *The Dead Sea Scrolls and Christian Doctrine* (London, 1966); F. F. Bruce, "The Dead Sea Scrolls and Early Christianity," *BJRL* 49 (1966):69-90; Jerome Murphy-O'Connor, ed., *Paul and Qumran* (Chicago, 1968); M. Black, ed., *The Scrolls and Christianity* (London, 1969); W. S. LaSor, *The Dead Sea Scrolls and the New Testament* (Grand Rapids, 1972).

249. J. A. T. Robinson, "The Baptism of John and the Qumran Community," *HTR* 50 (1957):175-92; John Pryke, "John the Baptist and the Qumran Community," *RQ* 4 (1964):483-96; B. G. Wood, "To Dip or Sprinkle? The Qumran Cisterns in Perspective," *Bulletin of the American Schools of Oriental Research* 256 (1984):45-60; Joan E. Taylor, *The Immerser: John the Baptist within Second Temple Judaism* (Grand Rapids, 1998), who debunks a facile association of John with Qumran.

the LXX text). Moreover, his asceticism if anything was stricter than Qumran's. These and other differences indicate that if John grew up at Qumran (and he may have), he made a break with it. Most significant is his prophetic role. A new impulse sent him forth "to make ready" the way of the Lord. The Qumran covenanters did not offer a public call to repentance in view of the imminent judgment, as did John. They were content to set an example and await the Lord's action. John actively undertook a call to repentance.

Even less may be made of possible associations of Jesus with Qumran.[250] Some of his teachings may parallel those of the Essenes, while even more have parallels in the Talmud. More will be said of such similarities later, but since Jesus, the Essenes, and the rabbis all accepted the same biblical revelation and addressed themselves to similar problems in the same period of time, it would be more surprising if no affinities were found. However, the structure of thought within which the teachings were placed is significantly different, as are some particulars. For example, Jesus refers to the teaching "Love your neighbor and hate your enemy" (Matt. 5:43), a teaching for which we have no previous record, and such may only have been Jesus' way of formulating the effects of some interpretations of the Old Testament command. However, now a similar statement is known from Qumran (1QS i.9-11; ix.21-22).[251] Furthermore, Jesus did not forsake the temple and religious life of the people, nor did he practice the asceticism of Qumran. He also had a different understanding of the Sabbath.

Various books of the New Testament have been closely studied for contacts with Qumran. Curiously, the Gospel exhibiting the closest similarities is the one considered the most Hellenistic of the New Testament, the Fourth Gospel.[252] Many of the ideas thought to be Greek (e.g., the dualism of light and darkness) can be seen as quite Jewish. This has led even to the suggestion that John is the earliest of the Gospels. As unlikely as this is, that the suggestion could be made shows how thoroughly at home the Fourth Gospel is in first-century Palestine.

Others have sought the background for the ideas in the Epistle to the Hebrews in Qumran, but this endeavor has not gone beyond illuminating certain aspects of the thought.[253] Perhaps most significant in this regard is the Melchizedek speculation now known from Qumran.[254] This shows how another figure of the Old Testament became a focus of Jewish speculations in the first century and could provide a category with which Christians could inter-

250. J. H. Charlesworth, ed., *Jesus and the Dead Sea Scrolls* (New York, 1992).

251. E. F. Sutcliffe, "Hatred at Qumran," *RQ* 2 (1960):345-56, points out that Qumran said to hate wicked men, not "enemies," and argues that Jesus' words have no reference to Qumran.

252. Lucretta Mowry, "The Dead Sea Scrolls and the Gospel of John," *BA* 17 (1954):78-97; J. H. Charlesworth, ed., *John and Qumran* (London, 1972).

253. F. F. Bruce, "'To the Hebrews' or 'To the Essenes'?" *NTS* 9 (1962/63):217-32.

254. Joseph A. Fitzmyer, "Further Light on Melchizedek from Qumran Cave 11," *JBL* 86 (1967):25-41; Fred L. Horton, Jr., *The Melchizedek Tradition* (Cambridge, 1976).

pret the significance of Jesus, who for them was the fulfillment of all the varied expectations arising from the Jewish heritage.

There may have been connections between Christianity and Qumran through other persons unknown to us (e.g., Acts 6:7); and the Ebionites of the second and third centuries may have been influenced by Essenes.

Several features of the early church may parallel Qumran, but each has significant differences. Christian baptism is a step further removed from the Qumran baths than John's baptism. The Lord's Supper has in common with Qumran the blessing of bread and wine, but this was a common feature of Jewish meals. Nothing in the Qumran meals is comparable to the new significance given the bread and wine in Christianity — a memorial of the death of the Savior.[255] The organization at Qumran offers some parallels: a single overseer has been compared to the bishop in the second-century church (but the Greek sources speak of the Essene overseer as *epimelētēs* and not *episkopos,* so any direct dependence is unlikely). The council at Qumran has been likened to the twelve apostles or to the college of elders, and the assembly of the "Many" to exercise discipline (1QS vi.1-2) may be compared to Christian assemblies (cf. 2 Cor. 2:6). Early Christianity shows nothing of the dominance of priests at Qumran.

Various doctrines also show similarities. The Qumran people saw themselves as the redeemed, elect community of which one must be a member to be saved. They were the people of a new covenant, and they gave an eschatological interpretation to history. But Christianity and Qumran, although formally parallel in these respects, were yet different. They looked forward to two different kinds of new age: Qumran wanted a revival of the best ideals of the old age, whereas Christianity saw the new age as having already dawned in the coming of the Messiah.

The calendar at Qumran may offer an explanation of some anomalies in the New Testament — for example, the recognition that different groups followed different calendars may be the explanation for the apparent contradiction between the Synoptics and John on the date of the crucifixion (although other explanations are possible).[256]

There are more significant values to the student of early Christianity from the study of the Qumran documents than these efforts to establish direct connections. Qumran introduces us to an eschatological interpretation of the Old Testament in which prophecy was read as fulfilled in the events affecting the community.[257] This is the same approach as in early Christianity. More-

255. J. van der Ploeg, "The Meals of the Essenes," *JSJ* 2 (1957):163-75; John Pryke, "The Sacraments of Holy Baptism and Holy Communion in the Light of the Ritual Washings and Sacred Meals at Qumran," *RQ* 5 (1966):543-52.

256. A. Jaubert, *La date de la Cène* (Paris, 1957).

257. F. F. Bruce, *Biblical Exegesis in the Qumran Texts* (Grand Rapids, 1959); Joseph A. Fitzmyer, "The Use of the Explicit Old Testament Quotations in Qumran Literature and the New Testament," *NTS* 7 (1960–61):297-333; Krister Stendahl, *The School of St. Matthew and its Use of the*

over, the prophets were interpreted in their own right and not just as supplements to or commentary on the law. The three best-represented books at Qumran — Psalms (36 manuscripts), Deuteronomy (29), and Isaiah (21) — are also the three most quoted books in the New Testament. (Rabbinic Judaism quoted most the Torah and the Psalms.) Certain Old Testament readings documented from the biblical manuscripts at Qumran seem to represent the form of Old Testament text known by New Testament writers.[258] Qumran therefore helps us to understand some features of the use of the Old Testament by New Testament writers as in keeping with the practices of the time. The question remained: Who had the right key to the understanding? For Christians Jesus and the events surrounding him provided that key; history refuted the Qumran alternative.

The Qumran documents provide a better understanding of some terms and ideas in the New Testament. The list is extensive, but we will cite only a few. The correct reading and translation of Luke 2:14 as "Peace among men of God's good pleasure," that is, his chosen ones, is strongly supported by similar language at Qumran.[259] The use of "poor" as a religious term for the voluntarily poor and humble (Matt. 5:3) may be illuminated by the similar use at Qumran (1QpHab xii.3, 6, 10 and 1QH ii.32).[260] The terminology of flesh and Spirit referring to spheres of life and not to metaphysical dualism is illuminated by the Qumran documents.[261]

The Qumran community leads us into the atmosphere of piety and intense religious hope in first-century Palestine. The scrolls permit us to see the structure and life of a sectarian Jewish religious community. Qumran shows there is no contradiction between holding to a strong eschatological viewpoint and adhering to a strict observance of a carefully regulated community life. One cannot help but understand Christianity better as it is seen, both positively and negatively, against this new background.

The decisive difference for Christianity was provided by the person of Je-

---

Old Testament (Philadelphia, 1968); E. Slomovic, "Toward an Understanding of the Exegesis in the Dead Sea Scrolls," *RQ* 7 (1969):3-16, emphasizes connections with rabbinic principles; Isaac Rabinowitz, "Pēsher/Pittʾrōn: Its Biblical Meaning and its Significance in the Qumran Literature," *RQ* 8 (1973):219-32; M. P. Hogan, *Pesharim: Qumran Interpretations of Biblical Books* (Washington, 1979); G. Brooke, *Exegesis at Qumran: 4QFlorilegium in Its Jewish Context* (Sheffield, 1985).

258. J. de Waard, *A Comparative Study of the Old Testament Text in the Dead Sea Scrolls and in the New Testament* (Leiden, 1965).

259. Ernest Vogt, S.J., "'Peace among Men of God's Good Pleasure' Lk. 2:14," in *The Scrolls and the New Testament,* ed. Krister Stendahl (New York, 1957), 114-17.

260. Leander Keck, "The Poor among the Saints in Jewish Christianity and Qumran," *Zeitschrift für die neutestamentliche Wissenschaft* 57 (1966):54-78.

261. K. G. Kuhn, "New Light on Temptation, Sin and Flesh in the New Testament," and W. D. Davies, "Paul and the Dead Sea Scrolls: Flesh and Spirit," in *The Scrolls and the New Testament,* ed. Krister Stendahl (New York, 1957), 94-113, 157-82; John Pryke, "'Spirit' and 'Flesh' in the Qumran Documents and Some New Testament Texts," *RQ* 5 (1965):345-60.

sus. That difference was between seeking and finding. Jesus united in himself the various messianic concepts. He rather than the community was the suffering servant. His mission of salvation could not succeed by withdrawal from sinners. The resurrection in particular changed things: the Holy Spirit was given, the age of redemption had begun, and Gentiles were brought in. Christians were living in a later moment of eschatological time.

> There are numerous similarities between Essene and the authentic early Christian doctrine. . . . In early Christianity, however, all these features . . . are taken up into a new doctrinal structure and the integration of these elements with the central beliefs of the new faith transforms each one of them. Sometimes the transformation is merely qualitative, certain elements being more stressed and assuming a greater importance in the new system. . . . But in other cases the adoption of Essene beliefs into an organic unity with the new doctrines completely transforms them. So, for instance, the period of the End has for the Christian already been inaugurated with the coming of the Messiah. Further, the sense of the sinfulness of human nature is so radicalized that a merely human mediation of the New Covenant and a merely human Messiah would no longer seem effective. . . .
>
> Accordingly, although Essenism bore in itself more than one element that one way or another fertilized the soil from which Christianity was to spring, it is nevertheless evident that the latter religion represents something completely new which can only be adequately explained by the person of Jesus himself.[262]

Therapeutae [263]

Philo's *Contemplative Life* describes a Jewish community living near Lake Mareotis in lower Egypt. He calls them *Therapeutae,* meaning either "healers," "worshipers," or "miracle workers." Philo presents them as representing the contemplative life in parallel with the Essenes representing the active life. They may have been a dispersion branch or imitation of the Essenes.

The *Therapeutae* renounced private property in their quest for the vision of God. The community consisted of men and women, but they had renounced all family life. They prayed at sunrise and sunset and spent the intervening time studying the Scriptures ("law, prophets, and psalms") and writings, giving an allegorical interpretation of the Scriptures. They also composed

---

262. J. T. Milik, *Ten Years of Discovery in the Wilderness of Judaea* (London, 1958), 143.

263. F. C. Conybeare, *Philo about the Contemplative Life* (Oxford, 1895); G. Vermes, "Essenes and Therapeutai," *RQ* 3 (1962):495-504; David M. Hay, "Things Philo Said and Did Not Say about the Therapeutae," *Society of Biblical Literature Seminar Papers* (Atlanta, 1992) 673-83; Joan E. Taylor and Philip R. Davies, "The So-Called Therapeutae of *De Vita Contemplativa,*" *HTR* 91 (1998):3-24.

hymns and psalms. They fasted until sunset and even then took little food. The Sabbath was spent in a common assembly, seated by age with the men and women separated by a partition, listening to sacred discourses. Every fiftieth day (or Pentecost) there was a festal assembly with prayers, a discourse by the president, responsorial singing, a simple meal, and an all-night vigil of song concluded at sunrise with prayer.

Their community life, asceticism, and worship practices seemed so similar to the Christian monastic communities in Egypt with which he was familiar that Eusebius considered them to have been Christians (*Church History* 2.17), but if the treatise is genuinely by Philo this is chronologically impossible.

BIBLIOGRAPHY

Philo. *That Every Good Man Is Free* 12–13.75-91. *Hypothetica* (or *Apology for the Jews*), quoted in Eusebius. *Preparation for the Gospel* 8.11.
Pliny the Elder. *Natural History* 5.15.73.
Josephus. *War* 2.8.2-13 [119-61]. *Ant.* 18.1.5 [18-22].
(For the writings of the Qumran community itself see the Dead Sea Scrolls.)

Nötscher, F. *Zur theologischen Terminologie der Qumrân Texte.* Bonn, 1956.
Milik, J. T. *Ten Years of Discovery in the Wilderness of Judaea.* London, 1959.
Vermes, G. "The Etymology of 'Essenes.'" *RQ* 2:3 (1960):427-43.
Black, M. *The Scrolls and the Christian Origins.* London, 1961.
Black, M. *The Essene Problem.* Friends of Dr. Williams's Library. London, 1961.
Ringgren, H. *The Faith of Qumran.* Philadelphia, 1963.
Rengstorf, K. H. *Hirbet Qumrân and the Problem of the Library of the Dead Sea Caves.* Leiden, 1963.
Vaux, R. de. *Archaeology and the Dead Sea Scrolls.* London, 1973.
Davies, Philip R. *Qumran.* Guilford, Surrey, 1982.
Beall, T. S. *Josephus' Description of the Essenes Illustrated by the Dead Sea Scrolls.* Cambridge, 1988.
Callaway, Philip R. *The History of the Qumran Community.* Sheffield, 1988.
Talmon, S. *The World of Qumran from Within: Collected Studies.* Leiden, 1989.
Flusser, D. *The Spiritual History of the Dead Sea Sect.* Tel Aviv, 1989.
Ulrich, Eugene, and James VanderKam, eds. *The Community of the Renewed Covenant: The Notre Dame Symposium on the Dead Sea Scrolls.* Notre Dame, 1994.
Cross, Frank M. *The Ancient Library of Qumran and Modern Biblical Studies.* Rev. ed. Minneapolis, 1995.
García Martínez, F., and J. Trebolle Barrera. *The People of the Dead Sea Scrolls: Their Writings, Beliefs, and Practices.* Leiden, 1995.
Collins, John J., and Robert A. Kugler, eds. *Religion in the Dead Sea Scrolls.* Grand Rapids, 2000.
Fitzmyer, Joseph A. *The Dead Sea Scrolls and Christian Origins.* Grand Rapids, 2000.

Zealots

Josephus attributes to Judas of Galilee, who led a revolt in A.D. 6 against the Roman census undertaken when Judea became a Roman province, the ideology of the revolutionary "Fourth Philosophy" (after Pharisees, Sadducees, and Essenes) among the Jews: it was unlawful to pay taxes to Rome (cf. Matt. 22:17), for God alone was Lord; God would help the Jews throw off foreign rule if they undertook armed rebellion against Roman rule. In other respects they agreed with the Pharisees, differing only in their passion for liberty and willingness to die for their convictions.

The choice of the name *Zealot* harks back to Phinehas (Num. 25:1-11). The term appears primarily in the context of the revolt in A.D. 66. The Zealots were the extremists among the revolutionaries and took the lead in the revolt; consequently, they receive harsh treatment in Josephus's account. The position has been taken that as a technical term for a party, *Zealot* came into use only at this time. As a consequence, the designation of Simon, one of the Twelve, by this title (Luke 6:15; Acts 1:13), if not an anachronism, must mean a general characterization rather than a member of the Zealot party. Indeed, it may be that the Zealot party transformed the religious zeal of the biblical tradition into a political anti-Roman doctrine in the 50s, so the description of one of the Twelve as a Zealot is to be understood in the earlier religious sense.[264] Matthew 10:4 and Mark 3:18 use the term *Kananaios,* a transliteration into Greek of the Hebrew word Luke translates as "Zealot." The presence of revolutionary activity against Rome from the time of the census in A.D. 6, apparently motivated by a similar ideology, leaves open the possibility that *Zealot* was already in use earlier in the century, if not as a technical party name, at least as a semitechnical description. Indeed, on the other hand, it has been advocated that Jesus himself had very close connections with revolutionary sentiment and that it was not accidental that the authorities were suspicious and had him tried on a charge of sedition. This interpretation, however, has to ignore or deny such a large body of evidence in the New Testament about the teaching of Jesus that it has not won much scholarly support.

One branch of the revolutionaries were known as the Sicarii (Acts 21:38), the "knife-men," mentioned in connection with the events of the 50s (*War* 2.13.3 [254-57]; 4.7.2 [400-405]; *Ant.* 20.8.10 [186-87]). They mingled among the crowds on festival occasions with daggers hidden in their garments. After striking down prominent collaborators with Roman officials, they disappeared in the crowd. These terrorists contributed to the atmosphere of tension in first-century Palestine. They were the group that seized and held Masada, preferring suicide to capture by the Romans.

---

264. C. Mezange, "Simon le Zelote etait-il un revolutionnaire?" *Biblica* 81 (2000):489-506.

BIBLIOGRAPHY

Josephus. *War* 2.8.1 [118]; 4.3.1ff. [121ff.]. *Ant.* 18.1.1 [4-10]; 1.6 [23-25].

Farmer, W. R. *Maccabees, Zealots, and Josephus.* New York, 1956.

Brandon, S. G. F. *Jesus and the Zealots.* Manchester, 1967.

Cullmann, O. *Jesus and the Revolutionaries.* New York, 1970.

Smith, Morton. "Zealots and Sicarii, Their Origins and Relations." *HTR* 64 (1971):1-19.

Borg, M. "The Currency of the Term 'Zealot.'" *JTS* 22 (1971):504-12.

Applebaum, S. "The Zealots: The Case for Revaluation." *Journal of Roman Studies* 61 (1971):156-70.

Stern, M. "Zealots." In *Encyclopedia Judaica,* Supplement. Jerusalem, 1971.

Rhoads, David. *Israel in Revolution 6-74* C.E. Philadelphia, 1976.

Horsley, Richard A., and John S. Hanson. *Bandits, Prophets, and Messiahs: Popular Movements at the Time of Jesus.* Harrisburg, 1985; repr. 1999.

Horsley, R. A. "The Zealots: Their Origin, Relationships, and Importance in the Jewish Revolt." *Novum Testamentum* 28 (1986):159-92.

Hengel, M. *The Zealots: Investigation into the Jewish Freedom Movement in the Period from Herod I until 70* A.D. Edinburgh, 1989.

Mendels, Doron. *The Rise and Fall of Jewish Nationalism.* Grand Rapids, 1997.

Herodians

The Herodians are not mentioned outside the Gospels, and the Gospels tell us nothing about them. The formation of the word means the party or adherents of Herod. They evidently were supporters of the Herodian dynasty, specifically Herod Antipas. There is nothing in the name to indicate that they were other than political partisans.

The new study of the Essenes sparked by the Qumran scrolls has brought forward the theory that the Herodians were Essenes. It is known that Herod was favorable to the Essenes, and nothing in the Qumran discoveries can be said to speak disparagingly of the Herods. This or any other identification of the Herodians must remain hypothetical in the absence of further sources.

BIBLIOGRAPHY

Rowley, H. H. "Herodians in the Gospels." *JTS* 41 (1940):14-27.

Daniel, C. "Les 'Hérodiens' du Nouveau Testament: Sont-Ils des Esséniens?" *RQ* 6 (1967):31-53, 261-77.

Daniel, C. "Nouveaux arguments en faveur de l'identification des Hérodiens et des Esséniens." *RQ* 7 (1970):397-402.

Meier, John P. "The Historical Jesus and the Historical Herodians." *JBL* 119 (2000):740-746.

Samaritans

The origins of the Samaritans have traditionally been traced to the situation described in 2 Kings 17 (so Josephus, *Ant.* 9.14.3 [288-91] and Rabbinic literature), but this interpretation of the chapter seems to be a piece of later Jewish slander against the rival religious community that chose Shechem and Mount Gerizim rather than Jerusalem and Mount Zion as its holy place (pp. 378-79). The religious community of the Samaritans encountered in the New Testament (Luke 10:33; 17:16; John 4:9, 39-40; 8:48) and continuing until today appears to have been religiously very conservative and not inclined toward syncretism with paganism. They preferred to refer to themselves as *samerim,* "keepers" (of Torah), and to distinguish themselves from *someronim,* "inhabitants of Samaria." There seems to be no Old Testament text unambiguously referring to them.

By New Testament times the Jews looked upon the Samaritans as foreigners (Luke 17:18; cf. Matt. 10:5). Josephus was ambivalent toward them, sometimes treating them as a Jewish sect but at other times regarding them as non-Jews, a separate nation, and representing the anti-Samaritan hostility that is the basis for the traditional picture of them.[265] The earliest certain references to a rival religious community based on Mount Gerizim near Shechem are from the second century B.C. (Sirach 50:25-26; 2 Macc. 5-6; cf. Testament of Levi 5-7; Jubilees 30). The Samaritans shared with Jews who looked to Jerusalem many characteristic beliefs: an uncompromising belief in and worship of the one God; avoidance of images; loyalty to the law given by Moses, as shown in rigid observance of the Sabbath, circumcision, and festivals; a sense of being the chosen people with attachment to the land given to the fathers (associated in their case with the Joseph tribes); and expectations of a glorious destiny. Samaritanism evidently emerged in the postexilic period out of the common matrix that produced various other sectarian movements in Judaism. The sources do not permit us to pinpoint one event that constituted a definitive break and accounted for the intensity of mutual hostility. There was apparently a period of gradual drifting apart during which a number of antagonisms, economic and political advantages, as well as religious differences intensified feelings (see p. 402). The separation of Samaritans and Jews was more a process than an event.

Samaritan religious texts are from the fourth century and later. Substantial Christian and Jewish references are equally late, so the study of Samaritan history and beliefs in the New Testament era is extremely difficult. Moreover, the Samaritans did not form a uniform community. The Dositheans were a lay movement deriving their name from a first-century leader who was accepted as the Mosaic eschatological prophet. They were branded as heretical by the dom-

---

265. Louis H. Feldman, "Josephus' Attitude toward the Samaritans: A Study in Ambivalence," *Studies in Hellenistic Judaism* (Leiden, 1996), 114-136.

inant priestly party; nevertheless they survived into the Middle Ages and contributed to the ultimate synthesis of Samaritan theology.

The most obvious point of difference between the Samaritans and the Jews, and one that went right to the heart of religious unity, was the adherence to a rival sanctuary on Mount Gerizim. Josephus (*Ant.* 2.7.1–8.7 [297-347]) places the building of the Samaritan temple (from their standpoint a rebuilding) in the days of Alexander the Great, and archaeology offers some confirmation of this.[266] At the beginning of the Greek period, the noble families in Samaria, deprived of political leadership by the new Macedonian rulers, moved to the ancient site of Shechem, rebuilt it, and also built a sanctuary on the adjoining holy mountain of Gerizim. John Hyrcanus destroyed this sanctuary two centuries later, but the site was still considered sacred and worship was continued there (cf. John 4:20). Accompanying this rival sanctuary was the Samaritans' own priesthood, which they traced to the true Aaronite line through Eleazar (the *Samaritan Chronicle* places the schism in Israel in the time of Eli and Samuel, when a high priesthood descended from Ithamar was established at Shiloh instead of at the proper sanctuary at Shechem). The Qumran covenanters too, one should remember, rejected the Jerusalem priesthood.

In addition to the opposition to the Jerusalem cultus, the Samaritans had other points of difference from emerging Judaism. They preserved their own text of the Pentateuch, the Samaritan Pentateuch, deriving from a Hebrew text at least as old as the second century B.C. It preserves some north Israelite dialectical peculiarities and alterations in the interests of the Samaritan cultus, but in some passages preserves original readings. Only the five books of Moses were accepted by the Samaritans as authoritative, a view shared with the Sadducees. Other items of belief and practice also reflect the variety within Judaism of the pre-Christian centuries: the rejection of the resurrection was not unusual (cf. the Sadducees again); distinctive was the expectation of a prophetic figure, the *ta'eb* ("the one who restores" or "the one who returns"), in fulfillment of Deuteronomy 18:18, but again, messianic expectations took a variety of forms in early Judaism (see pp. 551-53).

The Samaritans were open to the same influences as Jews in the early Christian centuries (cf. Simon in Acts 8). Their position of religious proximity to but alienation from Jews who looked to Jerusalem meant that Christian preaching to them was a significant step toward the universalism of the gospel (Acts 8). The effort to find traces of Samaritan influence on the New Testament has concentrated on the Fourth Gospel and Stephen's speech in Acts,[267] but the results are inconclusive.

266. R. T. Anderson, "The Elusive Samaritan Temple," *BA* 54 (1991):104-7, raises doubts that there ever was a Samaritan temple.

267. C. H. H. Scobie, "The Origins and Development of Samaritan Christianity," *NTS* 19 (1972/73):390-414; J. D. Purvis, "The Fourth Gospel and the Samaritans," *Novum Testamentum* 17 (1975):161-98; O. Cullmann, *The Johannine Circle* (London, 1976); R. Plummer, "The Samaritan

BIBLIOGRAPHY

Josephus. *Ant.* 9.14.3 [277-91]; 11.2.1 [19-25]; 4.3-6, 9 [84-103, 114-19]; 7.1-7 [297-347]; 12.1.1 [10]; 5.5 [257-64]; 13.3.4 [74-79].

Macdonald, John. *The Samaritan Chronicle.* Berlin, 1969.

Bowman, John. *Samaritan Documents Relating to their History, Religion, and Life.* Pittsburgh, 1977.

Plummer, Richard. *Early Christian Authors on Samaritans and Samaritanism: Texts, Translations, and Commentary.* Tübingen, 2003.

Macdonald, John. *The Theology of the Samaritans.* Philadelphia, 1964.

Cross, F. M. "Aspects of Samaritan and Jewish History in Late Persian and Hellenistic Times." *HTR* 59 (1966):201ff.

Purvis, James D. *The Samaritan Pentateuch and the Origin of the Samaritan Sect.* Harvard Semitic Monographs, vol. 2. Cambridge, Mass., 1968.

Macdonald, J., and A. J. B. Higgins. "The Beginnings of Christianity According to the Samaritans." *NTS* 18 (1971):54-80.

Bowman, John. *The Samaritan Problem: Studies in the Relationship of Samaritanism, Judaism, and Early Christianity.* Pittsburgh, 1975.

Coggins, R. J. *Samaritans and Jews: The Origins of Samaritanism Reconsidered.* Atlanta, 1975.

Plummer, R. "The Present State of Samaritan Studies." *JSS* 21 (1976):39-61; 22 (1977):27-47.

Isser, S. J. *The Dositheans: A Samaritan Sect in Late Antiquity.* Leiden, 1976.

Lowry, S. *The Principles of Samaritan Bible Exegesis.* Studia Post-Biblica, vol. 28. Leiden, 1977.

Hall, B. W. *Samaritan Religion from John Hyrcanus to Baba Rabba: A Critical Examination of the Relevant Material in Contemporary Christian Literature, the Writings of Josephus, and the Mishnah.* Sydney, 1987.

Plummer, Reinhard. *The Samaritans.* IGB, Section 23.5. Leiden, 1987.

Crown, A. D., ed. *The Samaritans.* Tübingen, 1989.

Schur, N. *History of the Samaritans.* Frankfurt and New York, 1989.

Van der Horst, P. W. "The Samaritan Diaspora in Antiquity." In *Essays on the Jewish World of Early Christianity.* Freiburg, 1990. Pp. 136-47.

Grabbe, L. L. "Betwixt and Between: The Samaritans in the Hasmonean Period." *Society of Biblical Literature 1993 Seminar Papers.* Atlanta, 1993. Pp. 334-347.

Manns, F., ed. *Early Christianity in Context: Monuments and Documents.* Jerusalem, 1993. (Articles by Y. Magen and L. Di Segni.)

Hjelm, Ingrid. *The Samaritans and Early Judaism: A Literary Analysis.* Sheffield, 2000.

Anderson, Robert T. and Terry Giles. *The Keepers: An Introduction to the History and Culture of the Samaritans.* Peabody, Mass., 2002.

Crown, A. D. *A Bibliography of the Samaritans.* 2d ed. Metuchen, N.J., 1993.

Pentateuch and the New Testament," *NTS* 23 (1975/76):441-43; E. Richard, "Acts 7: An Investigation of the Samaritan Evidence," *CBQ* 39 (1977):190-208.

BELIEFS AND PRACTICES

At any given time it would be possible to find Jews believing almost anything and everything, and this is especially true at the beginning of the Christian era. To list the elements of Jewish "orthodoxy" is an all but impossible task. It could even be argued that Judaism was more a matter of "orthopraxy" than of "orthodoxy." Jews were not different from their Greek and Roman neighbors in defining religion in terms of action, not belief. One of the quotations of the scribes was attributed to Simeon the Just: "By three things the world is sustained: by the [study of] law, by worship, and by deeds of charity" (Aboth 1.2). All three were necessary to make the religious life complete. Judaism has traditionally emphasized ethical principles more than beliefs. Moreover, one identified a Jew (religiously) in the ancient world by his observance of male circumcision as the seal of belonging to the people, the Sabbath rest and the other religious holy days, and the keeping of food and purity laws. Nevertheless, certain fundamental convictions and attitudes were quite general among the Jews (even among many who were not practicing Jews). Most common were belief in the one God (the God of Israel), the special status of Israel (the chosen and separate people), and the Torah (the law given by the one God to his chosen people and read regularly in the synagogue assemblies).[268] The general characterizations of belief below may be considered the underlying Jewish attitude, but the specific illustrations will often be drawn from rabbinic literature, for that is the most extensive surviving source and represents the development of the belief into its authoritative expression.

BIBLIOGRAPHY

Moore, George Foot. *Judaism.* 3 vols. Cambridge, Mass., 1927–1930. Reprint in 2 vols., Peabody, 1997.

Stewart, R. A. *Rabbinic Theology.* Edinburgh, 1961.

Bonsirven, J. *Palestinian Judaism in the Time of Jesus Christ.* New York, 1964.

Kadushin, Max. *Worship and Ethics: A Study in Rabbinic Judaism.* Evanston, Ill., 1964.

Urbach, E. E. *The Sages: Their Concepts and Beliefs.* 2 vols. Jerusalem, 1975.

Avi-Yonah, M., and Z. Baras. *Society and Religion in the Second Temple Period.* Jerusalem, 1977.

Boccaccini, G. *Middle Judaism: Jewish Thought, 300 BCE–200 CE.* Minneapolis, 1991.

268. See pp. 427-29. Note the charges against Paul in Acts 21:28 that he taught against the people, law, and temple (cf. Acts 6:13-14). N. J. McEleney, "Orthodoxy in Judaism of the First Christian Century," *JSJ* 4 (1973):19-42. Harry Wolfson, *Philo* (Cambridge, 1947), 1:164ff., combines Philo's passages in *On the Making of Man* 61, 170-72, *Special Laws* 1.60.327–63.344, *Decalog* 4.15, and *Life of Moses* 2.3.4 to come up with eight principles that Philo thought constituted the essentials of biblical religion: the existence of God, the unity of God, divine providence, the creation of the world, the unity of the world, the existence of incorporeal ideas, the revelation of the law, and the eternity of the law.

Neusner, Jacob. *Rabbinic Judaism: Structure and System.* Minneapolis, 1995.
Harrington, Hannah. *Holiness: Rabbinic Judaism in the Greco-Roman World.* London, 2001.
Neusner, J. *Handbook of Rabbinic Theology.* Leiden, 2002.

One God

The chastisement of the exile largely cured the Jews of the problem of idolatry. Although difficulties with syncretism (identification of the God of Israel with the Most High God of Hellenism) continued, the emphasis upon monotheism was one of the characteristics of Jewish belief.[269] This was underscored in the daily recitation of the *Shema* (p. 561). Along with their emphasis on his oneness, the Jews also emphasized God's holiness and transcendence. They put equal stress on the personal nature of God and his nearness to his people. In contrast to Greek and Roman thought, for Jews God is the measure of all things.[270]

The effort to preserve proper reverence toward God led the Septuagint translators, the rabbis, and the Targumists to modify some of the anthropomorphisms of the Bible. Instead of making God the subject, they employed the passive voice: "it was seen before God," "there was happiness before God." (This practice may account for some of the passives in the Gospels.) The divine name *Yahweh* was not pronounced except in connection with the temple service. For instance, when the Scriptures were read, the word *Adonai* (Lord) was read instead of *Yahweh.* A number of substitutes for the divine name came into common use. The Targums regularly use *Memra* (Word) instead of the personal name of God. Other favorite substitutes were "the Name," "Power" (cf. Mark 14:62), "Heaven" (cf. the preference in Matthew for kingdom of heaven instead of kingdom of God), "Glory." Sanctification of the name entered into every reference to God: one meets repeatedly in rabbinic literature the phrase "the Holy One, blessed be he." Such may be seen as "putting a fence around the law" to avoid transgressing the command, "You shall not take the name of the LORD your God in vain" (Exod. 20:7).

Israel, the Chosen People

The conviction of being the chosen people was not weakened — if anything, it was enhanced — by the experience of the exile. Ezra's program called for a stringent separation from other peoples. The separatism of the holy nation

269. Larry Hurtado, "What Do We Mean by 'First-Century Jewish Monotheism'?" *Society of Biblical Literature 1993 Seminar Papers* (Atlanta, 1993) 348-368, answers: the sovereign and unique high God had a large retinue of heavenly beings.

270. The thought is expressed in the Greek context by Plato, *Laws* 4.716C.

found expression in a number of the practices discussed below — circumcision, observance of the Sabbath, etc. Exclusivism when practiced by others has not been a popular human characteristic, and this feature did not help the pagan estimate of the Jews. The Jews held a strong conviction of the necessity of being a member of the chosen race by pure descent in order to share the future blessings; thus a great deal of attention was given to racial purity. Associated with the belief in being the chosen people was the high regard for the land of Israel:[271] some Jews believed that burial in Israel guaranteed resurrection and that those buried there would be revived first when the Messiah came (*Genesis Rabbah* 74.1). A corollary of being the chosen people was the expectation of a glorious destiny; aspects of this will be discussed below under the headings "Messiah" and "Afterlife."

The basis of God's choice was sometimes stated as the merits of the fathers; at other times it was stated that Israel alone of all nations chose to be God's people. The mercy of God in choosing Israel was balanced by the picture of Abraham (and others) as the model of the righteous person so that Israel's election was the reward of his merit. The reverse of this was a conviction that all "Israel shall never see the inside of Gehenna" (*Fathers according to Rabbi Nathan* 16) and so a pride in being children of Abraham. Jewish confidence that they would not be rejected because of the promise to the fathers is combatted in the New Testament (Luke 3:8; John 8:33-39; Rom. 2:28-29; 9:7-8). Nonetheless, there was recognition in the New Testament that Israel was God's possession out of all the nations of the earth: Paul speaks authentically from his Jewish heritage in reciting Israel's blessings (Rom. 9:4-5). Closely associated with the idea of election was the gift of the law, which only Israel was worthy to receive.

Torah, Tradition, and Scripture[272]

The Jews understood the national tragedy of 586 B.C. as due to the failure to keep the law of Moses. Following the exile the study of the law became a duty of supreme importance (cf. 2 Baruch 85:3) and brought the class of professional scribes (*soferim;* cf. Ezra 7:6) to prominence as the interpreters of the law. The law was identified with Wisdom (Sirach 24) and so was assigned preexistence and a share in the world's creation. The law was to have an eternal validity. The relation of the law to the cosmic structure of things was such that

271. W. D. Davies, *The Gospel and the Land: Early Christianity and Jewish Territorial Doctrine* (Berkeley, 1974).

272. R. Marcus, *Law in the Apocrypha* (New York, 1927); G. Vermes, *Scripture and Tradition in Judaism* (Leiden, 1961); Z. W. Falk, *Introduction to the Jewish Law of the Second Commonwealth* (Leiden, 1972); E. P. Sanders, *Jewish Law from Jesus to the Mishnah: Five Studies* (Philadelphia, 1990).

each commandment, indeed each letter, had absolute importance. In copying the law, "if you leave out a single letter or write a single letter too much, you will be found as one who destroys the whole world" (Erub. 13a Baraita). It is notable that Christ is presented in the New Testament as law and wisdom. Many of the scriptural symbols (e.g., manna and living water) and the functions assigned to the law in Judaism are assigned to Christ in Christianity.[273]

The contrast between the Greek emphasis on seeing (and thus visual imagery) and the Hebrew emphasis on hearing (and thus on the written and preached word) finds support in the Jewish emphasis on Torah. The Hebrew word *torah* has been universally translated into other languages as "law," but Jewish scholars insist that it means "instruction" or "teaching." *Mizwoth* is the word for specific "commandments." Torah was at first the five books of Moses, but just as it was extended to include all Scripture, so it encompassed the oral law as well.

The Hebrew Bible is divided into three parts — Pentateuch, Prophets, and Hagiographa or Writings.[274] The modern Hebrew name for the complete Jewish Bible is Tanak, a word made up from the first letter of the name in Hebrew for each of the three parts (T = Torah [Law]; N = Nebiim [Prophets]; K = Kethubim [Writings]). All parts are viewed as divinely inspired but as unequal in authority. The five books of Moses were the law in the primary sense. It was binding; the rest was supplementary. The Former Prophets were the historical books (Joshua through Kings), and the Latter Prophets were Isaiah, Jeremiah, Ezekiel, and the twelve minor prophets. The Writings were Psalms, Job, Proverbs, the Five Scrolls (Ruth, Canticles, Ecclesiastes, Lamentations, Esther), Daniel, Ezra, Nehemiah, and Chronicles.[275] Also in use is the term *miqrā'* (or *mikra*), which primarily means the correct reading of the sacred texts, including the reciting and understanding of the words. The Hebrew order of the books seems to be reflected in Matthew 23:35. The terminology for the third part of the Hebrew Scriptures varied. Luke's statement, "the Law of Moses, the

273. W. D. Davies, *Torah in the Messianic Age and/or the Age to Come*, JBL Monograph Series 7 (Philadelphia, 1952).

274. Sid Leiman, *The Canonization of Hebrew Scripture: The Talmudic and Midrashic Evidence* (Hamden, Conn., 1976); Roger Beckwith, *The Old Testament Canon of the New Testament Church* (Grand Rapids, 1986), who traces the threefold division to Judas Maccabee (pp. 152-66); E. E. Ellis, *The Old Testament in Early Christianity: Canon and Interpretation in the Light of Modern Research* (Grand Rapids, 1991); David Noel Freedman, *The Unity of the Hebrew Bible* (Ann Arbor, Mich., 1991), and "The Symmetry of the Hebrew Bible," *Studia Theologica* 46 (1992):83-108, who argues that except for the book of Daniel the Hebrew biblical canon was essentially closed by the Persian period with final editing by Ezra and Nehemiah; Stephen B. Chapman, *The Law and the Prophets: A Study in Old Testament Canon Formation* (Tübingen, 2000). See pp. 423, 438.

275. This is the order in modern Hebrew Bibles. The Talmudic order (Baba Bathra 14b) for the Prophets is Joshua, Judges, Samuel, Kings, Jeremiah, Ezekiel, Isaiah, and the Twelve; for the Writings it is Ruth, Psalms, Job, Proverbs, Ecclesiastes, Canticles, Lamentations, Daniel, Esther, Ezra-Nehemiah, and Chronicles.

books of the Prophets, and the Psalms" (24:44), may be compared with statements from Jewish sources around or in the first century: Prologue to Sirach — "Law, Prophets, and the other Books of the fathers"; Halakhic Letter from Qumran — "the Book of Moses, the Prophets, and David and the history of the generations" (4QMMT); Philo — "the Laws and the Oracles given by inspiration through the Prophets, and the Psalms and the other books" (*Contemplative Life* 25); Josephus — "Books of Moses, . . . the Prophets after Moses, . . . Hymns and Precepts for the conduct of life" (*Against Apion* 1.7–8.37-43); early rabbis — "[Law], Prophets . . . , Sacred Writings" (Baba Bathra 14b Baraita). Whereas Jeremiah 18:18 referred to persons — priest, wise man, and prophet — as sources of divine instruction, Sirach 39:1 identifies the same three with the books of law, wisdom, and prophecy. His grandson in the Prologue to the Greek translation of his book refers to persons — "law, prophets, and others that followed them," but he expected to find their teachings in books (as quoted above).

Two foundational principles of rabbinic Judaism (taken over from the Pharisees) were the conceptions of written law and of unwritten law. The Bible was the source of religious knowledge and conduct. The description of the Bible as "holy books" (1 Macc. 12:9) and bestowing signs of reverence on biblical scrolls, especially of the Torah (*Aristeas* 177, 317), as themselves holy preceded the rabbinic development. As the constitution of Judaism, the written law gave the principle of continuity. The idea that the Bible should not always be taken literally and that the constitution could be amended by the oral law gave the principle of development and progress.

God's greatest gift to his people was the revealed Torah. The law was both a grace and a duty: it was to be kept, of course, but it was above all a gift, a privilege, and not a burden. The law was offered to all nations, but only Israel accepted it. Rabbinic literature often expresses the joy of keeping the commandments.[276] Josephus indicates a considerable part of the people observed the law (*Against Apion* 1.38-46). The Torah governed all aspects of life — the social and legal system as well as religion. Its study was an act of worship. The effort was made to instruct the whole nation in the Torah.

Among the Pharisees was the conviction that the law had to legislate on every problem of life. It was inconceivable that any problem could arise for which the law did not have an answer. "Turn it and turn it again for everything is in it; and contemplate it and grow gray and old over it and stir not from it for than it you can have no better rule" (Aboth 5.22). The rabbis found 613 commands in the law (*Mekilta* 67a is probably the earliest statement; cf. b. Makkoth 23b). As is characteristic of law codes, there were more negative than positive commands: 365 negative (the days in the solar year) and 248 positive (the members in the body, according to *Targum Yerushalmi* on Gen. 1:27). The nu-

---

276. *Sifre Deuteronomy* 90b; b. Sabbath 30b.

merical symbolism noted that the Decalogue in Hebrew has 620 letters, representing the whole Torah plus 7 rabbinical commands. To violate one was to reject the whole law (*Sifre on Numbers* 15:22; cf. Jas. 2:10).

For the Pharisees and rabbinical Judaism, alongside the written law existed the oral law. Aboth begins with the declaration: "Moses received the [oral] law from Sinai and committed it to Joshua, and Joshua to the elders, and the elders to the prophets; and the prophets committed it to the men of the Great Synagogue" (Aboth 1.1). The tractate continues with the succession through named teachers — Simeon the Just, Antigonus of Soko, the "Pairs" concluding with Hillel and Shammai and rabbis in the school of Hillel. A later story said that three thousand rules were forgotten in the days of mourning for Moses, and Joshua forgot another three hundred; but these were restored by clever rabbis (b. Temurah 16a). To the Great Synagogue is attributed the saying, which became the program of the rabbis: "Be deliberate in judgment, raise up many disciples, and make a fence around the law" (Aboth 1.1). Much of the oral law developed in the Jewish law-courts as they interpreted and applied the law. Rabbis served as judges and trained and ordained disciples to carry on their interpretations. The interpretations placed a hedge or fence around the law, on the principle that if one does not break through the fence then he will not be able to break the law itself. The definitive statement of the dual Torah is found in b. Shabbath 31a. The oral law itself was finally reduced to writing in the Mishnah and Talmud. In practice the unwritten law was the operative authority: "If a man . . . discloses meanings in the Law which are not according to the *Halakah*, even though a knowledge of the Law and good works are his, he has no share in the world to come" (Aboth 3.12; see further pp. 515-16).

The oral law had other purposes in addition to putting a fence around the written law. Some of its contents arose in the process of interpretation; some represented a deepening of ethical insights; and some of its prescriptions were designed to circumvent the letter of the law (for various motives). An example of the last, with a worthy intention, was the *prosbul* (or *prozbol*, a name for which there is no satisfactory explanation) of Hillel.[277] The law had prescribed the release of all debts in the seventh year (Deut. 15:1-3), quite suitably in an agricultural economy where the land was to lie fallow every seventh year. In the urban commercial setting of the first century this law meant that loans were not being extended as a sabbatical year approached and so a hardship was being worked on borrowers. The *prosbul* was a declaration made in court that the loan might be collected whenever the lender desired it; as a consequence the law requiring the release of debts in the seventh year did not apply to such a loan (Shebiith 10.3-4).

---

277. S. R. Llewelyn, "The Procedure of Execution and the προσβολή," *New Documents Illustrating Early Christianity,* Vol. 7 (Macquarie, 1994), 197-232.

Some Pharisees based the oral law simply on tradition: it along with the written law had been delivered to Moses and was transmitted through the succession given at the beginning of Aboth and referred to above. Hillel, on the contrary, sought to ground all *halakoth* in the exegesis of the Scriptures. The rabbinic literature preserves competing interpretations, for although the legal decision was according to the majority of the sages, freedom of interpretation was allowed. Opinions of the minority were preserved and studied as part of the tradition, because majority rule was an expedient for practical purposes and not a determination of final truth. Yet respect for the views of the majority of scholars was deeply rooted in the development of Judaism. It was a principle adhered to in the face of miracles and even a voice from heaven *(bath qol)*. After a series of miracles failed to convince the Sages of Rabbi Eliezer's *halakah*, he exclaimed,

"If the halakah agrees with me, let it be proved from Heaven!" Whereupon a Heavenly Voice cried out: "Why do you dispute with R. Eliezer, seeing that in all matters the halakah agrees with him!" But R. Joshua arose and exclaimed: "It is not in heaven." What did he mean by this? Said R. Jeremiah: That the Torah had already been given at Mount Sinai; we pay no attention to a Heavenly Voice, because Thou hast long since written in the Torah at Mount Sinai, "After the majority must one incline." (b. Baba Metzia 59b)

Three constant reminders of the law to Jews of Pharisaic persuasion were the *zizith, mezuzah,* and *tefillin.* The *zizith* were the fringes or tassels worn on ends of garments[278] and prescribed in Numbers 15:37ff. and Deuteronomy 22:12. The *mezuzah* was a small container for selected passages of Scripture attached to the door facing (in literal fulfillment of Deut. 6:9; 11:20). The practice dates at least from the first century B.C.[279] The *tefillin* (Gk. phylactery) were prayer straps containing passages of Scripture worn on one's arm and head in fulfillment of Exodus 13:9, 16 (cf. Matt. 23:5).[280] These symbols represented the commandments and life lived in obedience to them.

Although Christianity did not follow Judaism in its adulation of the law, it did take over Judaism's Scriptures in which the written law was contained. Christianity shared the Jewish conviction that the Scriptures were divinely inspired, but it attached itself more to the prophets than to the law. This may be seen in the way in which "law" was the designation among Jews for the entire Bible (cf. John 10:34), whereas for Christians "prophets" became the inclusive designation for the Old Testament (Justin, *Apology* 1.67).

278. Matt. 9:20; 23:5; Aristeas 158; the extracanonical small tractate *Zizith.*

279. Aristeas 158-60; Josephus, *Ant.* 4.8.13 (213); *Sifre Deuteronomy* 36 (65-68).

280. See n.279; J. Bowman, "Phylacteries," *Studia Evangelica* 1 in *Texte und Untersuchungen* 73 (Berlin, 1959):523-38.

The early church inherited from its parent religion not only a Bible, but also an interpreted Bible. The different methods of interpreting the Bible in the first century influenced New Testament writers in their handling of the Scriptures.[281] We may classify Jewish exegesis in the apostolic period under the following headings: (1) Literalist — the plain, straightforward meaning, though this was often applied in a hyperliteral way by the rabbis.[282] An example of the literalist approach in the New Testament is Paul's argument from "seed" in Galatians 3:16. (2) Targumic — interpretation by paraphrase (see discussion of the Targums, pp. 499-500). (3) Typological — a correspondence between people and events of the past and those of the future. The application by the prophets of events from Israel's history to their own day and for the future (e.g., the Exodus motif) may be seen as a kind of typological exegesis. Paul does the same in 1 Corinthians 10:1-11. (4) Allegorical — an eternal spiritual meaning (usually cosmological or ethical as practiced by Philo) divorced from its historical setting. Paul develops an allegory but not of the Philonic type in Galatians 4:21-31; a more Philonic-type allegory is Hebrews 7:1-3. (5) *Pesher* — the hidden mystery in a text clarified by its fulfillment. A *pesher* explained the meaning of the text by a one-to-one correspondence to its fulfillment. The Qumran commentaries employed this type of exegesis, as did Matthew. (6) Midrashic — a combining of Scriptures so as to give a new interpretation with an application to new situations according to personal experience or some event. Midrash expands the relevance of the text (see pp. 497-99). Found in much of the rabbinic literature, this type of interpretation can also be seen in much of Paul's handling of the Old Testament. The paraphrase of one Scripture by another often brings Midrash and Targum close together.

Since the issue between Jews and the earliest Christians was not the authority of the Torah but how to interpret it, how to live, the functional authority for Jews was the oral law and for Christians the teachings of Christ. Christian interpretation of Scripture employed the methods used by Jews but differed in its christological focus, interpreting according to Jesus rather than according to the law.

Rabbinic interpretation often seems strange to modern readers, but it

281. J. Bonsirven, *Exégèse rabbinique et exégèse paulinienne* (Paris, 1939); K. Stendahl, *The School of St. Matthew* (Uppsala, 1954); J. W. Doeve, *Jewish Hermeneutics in the Synoptic Gospels and Acts* (Assen, 1954); Earle Ellis, *Paul's Use of the Old Testament* (Edinburgh, 1957); Merrill P. Miller, "Targum, Midrash, and the Use of the Old Testament in the New Testament," *JSJ* 2 (1971):29-82; Daniel Patte, *Early Jewish Hermeneutic in Palestine* (Missoula, Mont., 1975); D. I. Brewer, *Techniques and Assumptions in Jewish Exegesis before 70 CE* (Tübingen, 1992); Richard E. Longenecker, *Biblical Exegesis in the Apostolic Period*, 2d ed. (Grand Rapids, 1999); Craig A. Evans, ed., *The Interpretation of Scripture in Early Judaism and Christianity: Studies in Language and Tradition* (Sheffield, 2000); A. J. Hauser and D. F. Watson, eds., *A History of Biblical Interpretation*, vol. 1: *The Ancient Period* (Grand Rapids, 2001).

282. D. W. Halivni, *Peshat and Derash: Plain and Applied Meaning in Rabbinic Exegesis* (Oxford, 1991).

proceeded according to formal rules. Hillel is credited with seven rules *(middoth)* of interpretation:[283] (1) *Qal wahomer* — inference from the less important to a more important case (lit., light to heavy), and vice versa. (2) *Gezerah shawah* — inference by verbal analogy from one verse to another; where the same words are applied to two separate laws it follows that the same regulations and applications pertain to both. (3) *Binyan 'ab mikathub 'ehad* — building up a family from a single text; when the same phrase is found in a number of passages, then a regulation found in one of them applies to all of them. (4) *Binyan 'ab mishene kethubim* — building up a family from two texts; a principle is deduced by relating two texts together, and the principle can then be applied to other passages. (5) *Kelal upherat* — the general and the particular; a general principle may be restricted by a particularization of it in another verse, or conversely a particular rule may be extended into a general principle. (6) *Kayoze bo bemaqom 'aher* — something similar in another passage; a difficulty in one text may be solved by comparing it with another that has points of general (though not necessarily verbal) similarity. (7) *Dabar halamed me'inyano* — a meaning established by its context.

Ishmael in the early second century expanded the list to thirteen logical principles.[284] Later in the second century lived Eliezer ben Jose Ha-gelili, to whom were ascribed thirty-two *middoth*.[285]

---

283. *Tos. Sanhedrin* 7.11; *Aboth de R. Nathan* 37; *Sifra* 3a.

284. These are still printed and translated in the *Authorized Daily Prayer Book;* the following are from the edition by Joseph H. Hertz (New York, 1963), 43. (1) Inference from minor to major, or from major to minor. (2) Inference from similarity of phrases in texts. (3) A comprehensive principle derived from one text or from two related texts. (4) A general proposition followed by a specifying particular. (5) A particular term followed by a general proposition. (6) A general law limited by a specific application, and then treated again in general terms, must be interpreted according to the tenor of the specific limitation. (7) A general proposition requiring a particular or specific term to explain it, and conversely, a particular term requiring a general one to complement it. (8) When a subject included in a general proposition is afterward particularly excepted to give information concerning it, the exception is made not for that one instance alone, but to apply to the general proposition as a whole. (9) Whenever anything is first included in a general proposition and is then excepted to prove another similar proposition, this specifying alleviates and does not aggravate the law's restriction. (10) But when anything is first included in a general proposition and is then excepted to state a case that is not a similar proposition, such specifying alleviates in some respects, and in others aggravates, the law's restriction. (11) Anything included in a general proposition and afterward excepted to determine a new matter, cannot be applied to the general proposition unless this be expressly done in the text. [Numbers 4–11 are elaborations of number 5 in Hillel's list.] (12) An interpretation deduced from the text or from subsequent terms of the text. (13) In like manner when two texts contradict each other, the meaning can be determined only when a third text is found which harmonizes them.

285. Listed in H. L. Strack and G. Stemberger, *Introduction to the Talmud and Midrash* (Minneapolis, 1992), 25-34.

Proselytes and Godfearers

The Greek word *proselytos* in the Septuagint and Philo are the *gerim* of the Old Testament — resident aliens friendly to or allied with Jews but not converts to Israel. This may be its meaning in the book of Acts, but in Matthew 23:15 it means a full convert to Judaism, the technical sense that *gerim* acquired in rabbinic literature. The Septuagint also spoke of "fearers of the Lord" (Ps. 115:9-11; 135:19-20; Mal. 3:16), and Luke in Acts may have adapted this phrase to give a description of Gentile sympathizers with Jews.

There was much interest in proselytes around the beginning of the Christian era. The Jews produced a considerable propaganda literature, and Jews scattered throughout the world attracted attention to their religion. Several features of Judaism appealed to many Gentiles: the pure monotheism, the high ethical standards, the philosophical (rational and nonsacrificial) worship of the synagogue, an ancient and inspired written revelation, and the social cohesiveness of the Jewish community. There is evidence of a considerable number of Gentiles drawn to Judaism, either as full proselytes or with a lesser degree of attachment to the Jewish community (see below on Godfearers). To become a proselyte meant to join the Jewish community.

There is a difference between proselytism and missionary activity. The principal source cited for the latter is from the New Testament itself (Matt. 23:15). It has been easy for Christians to interpret that verse in terms of the vigorous missionary enterprise associated with Paul but by no means limited to him. The practice in Judaism was different. A representative story is that of Izates, the young king of Adiabene (c. A.D. 40), recorded by Josephus (*Ant.* 20.2.1-5 [34-53]; 5.2 [101]; cf. Eusebius, *Church History* 2.12.1). The royal family was attracted to the Jewish way of life through the teaching of a merchant.[286] The requirements imposed were minimal, not even including circumcision. Then strict Jews appeared on the scene insisting on more complete compliance with the law, but they themselves did not undertake to make converts. This is the situation reflected in Matthew 23:15 (and also Gal. 2:11; Acts 15:1). Strict Jews went out from Judea endeavoring to maintain a higher standard of conformity to the law (by Jews and proselytes alike).

Not only was there not a vigorous missionary enterprise (as distinct from propaganda on behalf of Judaism and from the above described corrective movement), but not all Jews looked favorably upon proselytes. In theory the proselyte had every advantage that a Jew by birth enjoyed, but in practice not all Jews welcomed converts so completely. For instance, a priest could not marry a proselyte. Tannaitic literature records the differing attitudes of the

---

286. Laurence H. Schiffman, "The Conversion of the Royal House of Adiabene in Josephus and Rabbinic Sources," in *Josephus, Judaism, and Christianity,* ed. L. H. Feldman and G. Hata (Detroit, 1987), 293-312.

schools of Shammai and Hillel toward proselytes. Hillel was more receptive to proselytes and welcomed them even though their knowledge and performance were faulty, whereas Shammai required full assent to the written and oral law before accepting them.

In the first century there seems to have been diversity of practice, but according to later documentation three steps were required of the Gentile in order to be initiated into Judaism: circumcision, baptism, and an offering at the temple.[287]

Circumcision. This was the only requirement based on the written law. It was the most distinctive rite of the Jews in maintaining their separation from the surrounding world.

The male child born into a Jewish family or born to parents who had already become proselytes received circumcision on the eighth day after birth (Shabbath 18.3–19.6; 9.3). This was the covenant seal, the sign that the boy was within the elect people. He did not become responsible for keeping the commandments until thirteen years of age. The ceremony of *bar mitzwah* ("son of the commandment"), at which the boy began to wear phylacteries and assumed an active place in the community, originated at a later period. On a family's conversion to Judaism, all males received circumcision, regardless of their age.

Efforts to eliminate the sign of circumcision or to restrict its practice led to revolts against Antiochus Epiphanes and Hadrian. In view of the central significance of circumcision to Jews, Paul's teaching that Gentile converts did not have to receive it understandably caused a serious crisis for Jewish believers (Epistle to the Galatians).

Proselyte Baptism.[288] More controversial, as far as the secondary literature is concerned, has been the practice of baptism. Both men and women were required to bathe themselves on becoming Jews. This led to a controversy among the rabbis as to which was more important, circumcision (commanded in the written law) or baptism (applicable to females as well as to males). The debate in Judaism may indeed be reflected in the controversy in the early church over the relative importance of circumcision and baptism (Acts 15; Gal. 2). Controversy between the schools of Shammai and Hillel (c. A.D. 80) over the degree of impurity of a convert from paganism (Pesahim 8.8; Eduyoth 5.2) is the earliest secure evidence for the practice of proselyte baptism; therefore there is disagreement about the age of the practice, a matter of importance for determining whether proselyte baptism is part of the background for John's baptism and for Christian baptism. In spite of the lack of earlier attestation, it

---

287. S. J. D. Cohen, "The Rabbinic Conversion Ceremony," *JJS* 41 (1990):177-203.

288. I. Abrahams, "'How Did the Jews Baptize?'" *JTS* 12 (1911):609-12; L. Finkelstein, "The Institution of Baptism for Proselytes," *JBL* 52 (1933):203-11; T. M. Taylor, "The Beginnings of Jewish Proselyte Baptism," *NTS* 2 (1955/56):193-98; Karen Pusey, "Jewish Proselyte Baptism," *The Expository Times* 95 (1984):141-45.

is widely assumed that proselyte baptism was earlier than the Christian era. It would seem unlikely that Jews copied a Christian practice, and debate over its significance in A.D. 80 would seem to presuppose a practice already well established. On the other hand, the meaning given to the act and the details of procedure found in later rabbinic sources may not be so old. The origin of an immersion bath for proselytes is probably to be found in the washings for ceremonial cleansing prescribed in the Old Testament. A deeper religious significance and an emphasis on the moral meaning of becoming a Jew could very well have become more pronounced in Judaism as part of the competition with Christianity. Religious groups more readily borrow ideas and meanings than they copy basic rites.

Proselyte baptism, like other baths of purification, was self-administered. Unlike them, it required the presence of witnesses who gave instructions in the commandments of Judaism.

There is no doubt that proselyte baptism was an immersion. The tractate

MIKWEH, Masada
The *mikweh* ("immersion pool") on Masada was constructed according to prescriptions recorded in the Mishnah. On the left is the actual immersion pool, which had a small basin in front of it to wash feet before entering. The pool on the right collected pure water, a small amount of which would purify the water in the other pool when allowed to flow into it.

JEWISH INSCRIPTION, theatre, Miletus
Inscribed on the seats of the theatre are the words,
"Place of the Jews and the Godfearers" or "Jews who are Godfearers."

Mikwaoth ("Immersion Pools") in the Mishnah lays down requirements in regard to the size of the pool and the quantity of water in order to assure that a total immersion was possible. It maintains a clear distinction between those rites requiring sprinkling, pouring, and immersion. The preference for running water and natural sources accords with the preference expressed in the *Didache* 7. Several first-century baths *(mikwaoth)* for ritual immersion have been discovered at excavations in Israel (purifications were necessary on many occasions, and proselyte baptism would have been a minor use).[289]

Proselyte baptism also was administered to any children in the family. Those born after the family's conversion did not have to be immersed, for they were born "in holiness" (Yebamoth 11.2; cf. 1 Cor. 7:14) and the males needed only to receive circumcision. Children who received baptism and circumcision before being of age at the time of their parents' conversion, however, occupied an anomalous position. They were allowed to renounce Judaism, on coming of age, without being considered apostates. This curious position makes problematic any argument based on proselyte baptism for infant baptism in early Christianity.

Offering at the Temple. This requirement, if ever actually practiced, must have originated in the pre-70 period. Even then it could not have been kept by

---

289. E. P. Sanders, *Jewish Law from Jesus to the Mishnah* (Philadelphia, 1990), 214-27, surveys the types of immersion pools that have been found and cites the relevant secondary literature.

proselytes in the dispersion. The sacrifice was the same as required of Jews for purification. It, like the immersion bath, therefore, was not so much in origin a condition of becoming a proselyte as a condition of acquiring the necessary purification for the exercise of certain privileges in the Jewish community. But if Judaism is defined primarily in terms of practice, then this was an important aspect of what becoming a proselyte was all about.

Godfearers. Circumcision was not only painful but also disgusting to Greeks and Romans, hence many more women than men became proselytes (note the frequent mention of Greek women associated with the Jewish synagogues in Acts 13:50; 16:15; 17:4, 12). Often the men, husbands or kinsmen of the women converts, accepted the moral teachings and religious practices of Judaism without accepting the stigma of circumcision and so full identification with the Jewish community. Gentile sympathizers could show attraction to Judaism in varying degrees: admiring some aspect of Judaism, acknowledging the power of the God of the Jews or including him in the pagan pantheon, benefiting the Jews and being especially friendly toward them, practicing some of the rituals of the Jews, worshiping the God of the Jews and denying or ignoring the pagan gods, identifying with the Jewish community, or converting to Judaism and becoming a Jew.[290] The term "Godfearers" or "worshipers of God" *(theosebeis)* could be applied to any of these. Luke uses *phoboumenoi* ("fearers [of God]") in the early part of Acts (10:2, 22, 35; 13:6, 26) and *sebomenoi* ("worshipers [of God]") in the latter part (13:43, 50; 16:14; 17:4, 17; 18:7) — perhaps reflecting a difference between a terminology influenced by the Old Testament and that which was more Hellenized but without difference in meaning.[291] The discovery of a Jewish inscription at Aphrodisias, dated about A.D. 210 and containing a list of 126 donors to the Jewish community, of whom 54 are identified as "Godfearers" *(theosebeis),* gives indisputable evidence of the large number of Gentiles who could be attracted to the synagogue.[292] Wives and children of Godfearers often became full proselytes. Christianity had a great appeal in the circles of Gentile adherents of the synagogue, for it preserved the attractions of Judaism without the disagreeable features and racial identification.

Gentiles were not bound by the law of Moses, which was given to the covenant people alone. However, provision was made for Gentiles to come into the covenant and assume the yoke of the Torah. The rest of humankind lived under

---

290. S. J. D. Cohen, "Crossing the Boundary and Becoming a Jew," *HTR* 82 (1989):13-33.

291. A. T. Kraabel, "The Disappearance of the Godfearers," *Numen* 28 (1981):113-26, argued from the absence of archaeological evidence that the Godfearers in Acts are a Lukan theological construct. Although initially receiving sympathetic attention the thesis now does not receive much support. The evidence pro and con is discussed in *Biblical Archaeology Review* 12 (Sept./ Oct. 1986):44-69.

292. J. Reynolds and R. F. Tannenbaum, *Jews and God-fearers at Aphrodisias: Greek Inscriptions with Commentary* (Cambridge, 1987); L. H. Feldman, "Proselytes and 'Sympathizers' in the Light of the New Inscription from Aphrodisias," *Revue des études juives* 148 (1989):265-305.

the commandments given to Noah. The principle of the Noachian commandments, given to the descendants of Noah, is attested already in Jubilees 7:20.
Righteous Gentiles, who lived according to these commandments, could still
have a share in the world to come. This was considered the minimum requirement for Godfearers (cf. Acts 15:19-20, 28-29). Rabbi Johanan systematized the
Noachian commandments as follows: "Seven laws are binding on the descendants of Noah: establishment of courts of justice; prohibition of blasphemy;
prohibition of the worship of other gods, of murder, of incest and adultery, of
theft and robbery, and of eating the flesh of a living animal before it dies"
(b. Sanhedrin 56a).

BIBLIOGRAPHY

Goodman, Martin. "Jewish Proselytizing in the First Century." In *The Jews among
the Pagans and Christians in the Roman Empire*, ed. Judith Lieu, et al. London,
1992. Pp. 53-78.
Figueras, Pau. "Epigraphic Evidence for Proselytism in Ancient Judaism." *New Testament and Christian-Jewish Dialogue: Studies in Honor of David Flusser*, ed.
Malcolm Lowe. *Immanuel* 24/25 (1990):194-206.
McKnight, Scot. *A Light Among the Nations: Jewish Missionary Activity in the Sec-
ond Temple Period*. Minneapolis, 1991.
Goodman, Martin. *Mission and Conversion: Proselytizing in the Religious History of
the Roman Empire*. Oxford, 1994.
Porton, Gary G. *The Stranger Within Your Gates: Converts and Conversion in Rab-
binic Judaism*. Chicago, 1994.
Winter, Bruce W., ed. *The Book of Acts in Its First Century Setting*. Vol. 5. Irina
Levinskaya. *The Book of Acts in Its Diaspora Setting*. Grand Rapids, 1996.
Overman, J. Andrew. "The God-Fearers: Some Neglected Features." In Craig A. Ev-
ans and Stanley E. Porter, eds. *New Testament Backgrounds: A Sheffield
Reader*. Sheffield, 1997. Pp. 253-262.
Cohen, Shaye J. D. *The Beginnings of Jewishness: Boundaries, Varieties, Uncer-
tainties*. Berkeley, 1999.
Matthews, Shelly. *First Converts: Rich Pagan Women and the Rhetoric of Mission in
Early Judaism and Christianity*. Stanford, 2001.

Messianism and the Glorious Destiny

The Jewish national hope anticipated a glorious destiny for Israel, the "good
times coming" when God's blessings would reveal to all his favor toward his
people. This hope might or might not entail a personal Messiah as the agent for
bringing about these good times. The Jewish expectation centered on the nation and the age to come rather than on the Messiah, who forms the center of
Christian faith. Christian scholars, looking back from the perspective of the

early Christian interpretation of Jesus, have been responsible for the idea of "*the* Messianic hope" of the Jews. They have imposed a great deal more specificity upon this expectation than the sources will bear out. In fact, it can be said that "Messiah" was only one of the "handles" appropriated from Judaism by the early Christians to take hold of the person of Jesus and to interpret his meaning to their contemporaries. And that "label" itself covered several possible conceptions.

Messiah, or *anointed*, was used in the Old Testament for kings, priests, and metaphorically for prophets. Anointing with olive oil marked a person as a special object of God's favor chosen by him for some special task. The postbiblical literature, in looking forward to God's future blessings upon his people, continued to employ Old Testament categories to express how these blessings would be brought about and so gave a future reference to what was largely a historical category in the Old Testament (i.e., *Messiah* refers in the Old Testament to specific individuals at a given point in time). The Old Testament itself does not link the word with its expectations of future deliverance, and *Messiah* is not a particularly prominent concept in the intertestamental literature.[293] Sometimes God himself was seen as acting directly, without express reference to any human mediator or agent (e.g., Jubilees 1:19-28). Some works speak of a supernatural "Son of man" comparable to Daniel 7; unfortunately these sources are chronologically suspect (Similitudes of Enoch [*1 Enoch* 37–71]) or later than Jesus (2 Esdras 13). The Samaritans spoke of the *ta'eb* (reformer, restorer, a prophet like Moses; cf. John 4:25). The Psalms of Solomon 17–18 refers to the coming king who will be son of David and "the anointed of the Lord." The Qumran *Rule of the Community* 9.11 anticipates an eschatological "prophet and the messiahs of Aaron and Israel." The *Rule of the Congregation* speaks of the "priest," who has precedence, and the "messiah of Israel," presumably reflecting leadership in the postexilic community of the high priest from the tribe of Levi (through Aaron) and the governor (and hoped for king) from the tribe of Judah (through David).[294] A more recently available text from Qumran, 4Q521, has a Messiah very like the Christian Messiah.[295] Christians saw in Jesus the fulfillment of all these expectations — he was God acting among human beings, the Son of man who arises at the end of the age, the Son of David, and the anointed prophet, priest, and king.

---

293. James H. Charlesworth, "The Concept of the Messiah in the Pseudepigrapha," *ANRW* II, *Principat,* 19.1 (Berlin and New York, 1979), 188-218; M. de Jonge, "The Use of the Word 'Anointed' in the Time of Jesus," *Novum Testamentum* 8 (1966):132-48.

294. Raymond Brown, "The Messianism of Qumran," *CBQ* 19 (1957):53-82. Test. Sim. 7.2; Test. Judah 24.1-6; Test. Dan 5.10-13 also speak of deliverers from Levi and Judah without using the word *Messiah*.

295. James Tabor and Michael Wise, "4Q521 'On Resurrection' and the Synoptic Gospel Tradition: A Preliminary Study," *Journal for the Study of the Pseudepigrapha* 10 (1994):149-162; a popular study, idem, "The Messiah at Qumran," *Biblical Archaeology Review* 18 (Nov./Dec. 1992):60-65.

Rabbinic materials seem to indicate that in the first century the Davidic king became an essential part of Jewish eschatology, to be preceded by the coming of Elijah. It may have been only after 70 that this received special emphasis. Josephus tells of several revolutionary leaders who gathered followers, but does not use the word *Messiah* for them (see above, pp. 420-21). They would have fit the Christian category of "false messiahs" (Matt. 24:24; Mark 13:22). In some writings the concept of the "days of the Messiah" (Berakoth 1.5) was applied to a period of his righteous rule and its attendant blessings preceding the end of the world. The length of this period varied according to different sources: forty years (b. Sanhedrin 99a), four hundred years (2 Esdras 7:28-29; *Pesikta Rabbati* 4a), one thousand years (*Midrash on Psalms* 90:17). Jubilees 23:27 has a golden age of one thousand years without a Messiah. The kingdom of God (the rule or reign of God) could be applied to the messianic kingdom or to the heavenly kingdom.

First-century Judaism, therefore, presented a variety of expectations about an age to come. Where a particular agent figured in this expectation, there was no carefully defined view of him, and *Messiah* was not a particularly common designation. Where he appeared, the Jews thought more in terms of "days of the Messiah" rather than giving centrality to his functions or person. He was part of the "furniture" rather than the decisive factor. From a Christian perspective the Jews had expectations that might be called "messianic," but Messiah was not the central category it was for Christians. When Jesus was recognized as the Messiah, the person of Jesus himself filled the term with the content it has come to have.

BIBLIOGRAPHY

Ellison, H. L. *The Centrality of the Messianic Idea for the Old Testament.* London, 1953.

Mowinckel, S. *He That Cometh.* Nashville, 1954.

Klausner, J. *The Messianic Idea in Israel.* New York, 1955.

Ringgren, H. *The Messiah in the Old Testament.* Chicago, 1956.

Liver, J. "The Doctrine of the Two Messiahs in Sectarian Literature in the Time of the Second Commonwealth." *HTR* 52 (1959):149-85.

Scholem, Gershom. *The Messianic Idea in Judaism.* London, 1971.

Klein, R. W. "Aspects of Intertestamental Messianism." *Concordia Theological Monthly* 43 (1972):507-17.

Levey, Samson H. *The Messiah: An Aramaic Interpretation: The Messianic Exegesis of the Targum.* New York, 1974.

Patia, Raphael. *The Messiah Texts.* Detroit, 1979. (Includes also medieval and later Jewish texts.)

Neusner, J. *Messiah in Context.* Philadelphia, 1984.

Neusner, J., W. S. Green, and J. Z. Smith, eds., *Judaisms and Their Messiahs at the Turn of the Christian Era.* Cambridge, 1987.

Charlesworth, J. H. *The Messiah: Developments in Earliest Judaism and Christianity.* Minneapolis, 1992.

Horbury, William. *Jewish Messianism and the Cult of Christ.* Harrisburg, 1998.

Oegema, G. S. *The Anointed and His People: Messianic Expectations from the Maccabees to Bar Kokhba.* Sheffield, 1998.

Afterlife

There was no uniform Jewish doctrine in the New Testament period concerning the afterlife. A variety of viewpoints were expressed in the postbiblical literature. In general the Diaspora showed more interest in individual afterlife than in cosmological or nationalistic eschatology.

Sirach repeats the view found in most of the Old Testament that at death the person, whether good or bad, enters the underworld (Sheol; cf. the Greek Hades) and has a shadowy existence without reward or punishment (14:16-19; 17:25-32; 38:16-23; 41:4; 48:4-5; 51:5-6). The Wisdom of Solomon, by contrast, although not fully consistent, alludes to the Greek philosophical teaching of immortality, with death as the penalty for the wicked (2:23–3:10; 5:15; 8:13, 17; 15:2-3).[296] Fourth Maccabees speaks more explicitly of the "immortality of the soul" (14:6; 18:23). Neither describes immortality as a natural quality of the soul (as in Platonism) but rather as the reward for righteousness. The notion of resurrection, found occasionally in the Old Testament (Isa. 26:19; Dan. 12:2), finds expression in 2 Maccabees 7:9, 11, 14, 23; 12:43-45 (reserved for the godly only). Resurrection is denied to the wicked in Psalms of Solomon 2:31; 3:9-12; 14:9-10; 1 Enoch 22:13; 2 Baruch 30; Sanhedrin 10.3. Second Esdras 7:75ff. contains an extended description of the torments of the spirits of the ungodly and the blessings of the godly in the period between death and the day of judgment that brings the world to an end.

The doctrine of the resurrection became one of the essential dogmas of rabbinic orthodoxy, denial of which excluded one from a share in the world to come (Sanhedrin 10.1). Even so there remained varying ideas about the nature of the resurrection body. Some saw a repetition of activities in this life, only in a world of remarkable fertility and pleasure (Sibylline Oracles 4:181-91; b. Sanhedrin 91b; *Midrash Rabbah Genesis* 14:5; 95:1; *Midrash Rabbah Ecclesiastes* 1:4, 2). This view made the Sadducees' question in Luke 20 (and par.) so cogent and contrasts with the view of the resurrection body set forth in Jesus' reply. Others denied that there would be eating, drinking, sexual enjoyment, and the like (b. Berakoth 17a). Some statements seem not to allow the intermediate time described in 2 Esdras but place the judgment immediately at death (*Sifre on*

---

296. John J. Collins, "The Root of Immortality: Death in the Context of Jewish Wisdom," *HTR* 71 (1978):177-92.

Numbers 13:8; *Mekilta on Exodus* 15:1; b. Sanhedrin 91a). A great variety characterizes the descriptions of the abode of the righteous: with Abraham (4 Macc. 13:17; 18:23), in the Garden of Eden or Paradise (b. Berakoth 28b), the third heaven (Apocalypse of Moses 40), the seventh heaven under the Throne of Glory (b. Shabbath 152b).

There was an increasing tendency to use Sheol or Hades for the place of punishment for the wicked (cf. the English word *Hell* used for Hades). Sometimes, as in the New Testament, Gehenna was the name for the place of punishment (b. Hagigah 15a). Fire was the usual form of the punishment in Gehenna (e.g., b. Pesahim 54a). Normally the punishment was considered eternal, but occasionally one comes across the idea of extermination of the wicked at the judgment (*Midrash Rabbah on Genesis* 26 on 6:3) or even of a temporary Gehenna, somewhat like a purgatory, for lesser sinners after which they join the righteous (Tos. Sanhedrin 13.3ff.). The favorite phrase in rabbinic literature for the afterlife is simply "the world to come."

The Christian hope for the afterlife is often expressed as the "immortality of the soul" — a phrase that never occurs in the New Testament. Actually the biblical doctrine is of a resurrection of the body. The "immortality of the soul" is more a result of the philosophical (Platonic) tradition and its combination with the idea of resurrection in the church fathers.

BIBLIOGRAPHY

Stendahl, K., ed. *Immortality and Resurrection.* New York, 1965.

Nickelsburg, G. W. E. *Resurrection, Immortality, and Eternal Life in Intertestamental Judaism.* Cambridge, Mass., 1972.

Stemberger, G. *Der Leib der Auferstehung.* Rome, 1972.

Cavallin, H. C. C. *Life after Death.* Lund, 1974.

Fischer, U. *Eschatologie und Jenseitserwartung in hellenistischen Diasporajudentum.* Berlin and New York, 1978.

Bauckham, R. J. *The Fate of the Dead: Studies in Jewish and Christian Apocalypses.* Leiden, 1998.

Avery-Peck, Alan J. and Jacob Neusner, eds. *Judaism in Late Antiquity:* Part 4, *Death, Life-after-Death, Resurrection and the World-to-Come in the Judaisms of Antiquity.* Leiden, 2000.

Festivals and Holy Days

The Jewish religious calendar included observance of the weekly Sabbath, the monthly New Moon, and the annual festivals (Col. 2:16; 1QM ii.4; 1 Chron. 23:31; 2 Chron. 2:4). The three great pilgrim festivals — Passover, Weeks (Pentecost), and Tabernacles — brought large numbers to Jerusalem from Palestine (Luke 2:41ff.) and the Diaspora (Acts 2:5ff.). The biblical command of Exodus

23:17 and Deuteronomy 16:16 was not interpreted, however, as requiring every person to go three times each year to the temple. Those who lived at a distance sought to go at least once in a lifetime.

Sabbath

The observance of the seventh day of each week as a holy rest day was an important element in Jewish separatism.[297] Before New Testament times the day had become not only a day of rest but also a day of assembly when the principal synagogue service was conducted. As long as the temple stood, additional sacrifices were performed on the Sabbath. It was also the day for family and friends to share a common meal. The Sabbath and the wine with which the Sabbath evening meal began were sanctified by a benediction (the *Kiddush*).

Admittedly, "the rules for the sabbath are like mountains hanging by air, for Scripture is scanty and the rules many" (Hagigah 1.8). The Mishnah tractate Shabbath 7.2 lists thirty-nine classes of work, deduced from the Scriptures, that were forbidden on the Sabbath. These thirty-nine principal activities were defined to cover their cognate operations; for example, grinding included rubbing grain in the hands (Mark 2:2-3). Exodus 16:29 was understood as prohibiting travel on the Sabbath. The effort to define what was a person's "own place" and what constituted "going out" led to the limitation of two thousand cubits on a Sabbath day's journey.[298] It was possible, however, to extend this distance by depositing some of one's possessions within the two-thousand-cubit distance from home so as to make that too part of the domicile and thereby extend by another two thousand cubits from that spot the distance that could be traveled (see Erubin 3–4).

Certain activities took precedence over the Sabbath command — circumcision (John 7:22-23; Shabbath 18.3; 19.2) and sacrifice in the temple (Matt. 12:5; Shabbath 19.1; Pesahim 6). When human life was in danger, the Sabbath laws could be set aside, but since Isaiah 58:13 had rebuked "pursuing business on my holy day," the ordinary practice of medicine was considered a violation (Luke 13:14; Yoma 8.6; Shabbath 22.6). The Pharisees allowed rescuing an animal (b. Shabbath 128b) but the Essenes did not (*Damascus Document* xi.13).

The casuistry involved in the Sabbath laws was motivated by the noble intent of clarifying the law but involved the inconsistencies that accompany any legal system. These regulations come from literature representing only one

297. Exod. 20:8-11. Robert Goldenberg, "The Jewish Sabbath in the Roman World up to the Time of Constantine the Great," *ANRW* II, *Principat,* 19.1 (Berlin and New York, 1979), 414-47, argues that although the Sabbath was important to nearly all Jews, there was variety as to the manner in which it was observed; Heather A. McKay, *Sabbath and Synagogue: The Question of Sabbath Worship in Ancient Judaism* (Leiden, 1994).

298. Sotah 5.3; Josephus, *Ant.* 13.8.4 [252]; *Damascus Document* x.14–xi.18; Targum on Exod. 16:29; based on Josh. 3:4 and Num. 35:5.

segment of Judaism. Although religious Jews tried to keep the Sabbath in some way, the majority of ordinary Jews were probably unconcerned about minute restrictions.

Outsiders, seeing only the negative aspects of Sabbath regulations, considered it a dismal or gloomy observance or a sign of Jewish laziness. Not so, devout Jews. The best meal of the week was prepared in advance to eat on Sabbath evening. Fasting was forbidden (Jubilees 50:12; Judith 8:6; *Damascus Document* xiii.13). Things that might dampen the joy of the occasion, such as mourning and visiting the sick, were limited.

New Moon

The New Moon was observed like the Sabbath by rest and additional sacrifices at the temple. In the postexilic period it acquired eschatological connotations. Little note is taken of the New Moon in the sources pertinent for New Testament studies.

Passover (Pesach; Gk. Pascha)[299]

Passover and the week of Unleavened Bread *(Mazzoth)* that followed it were so combined as often to be treated as one festival with the two names almost interchangeable. Passover was celebrated in commemoration of the exodus from Egypt and was a festival of redemption. Since huge crowds have a potential for disturbances, the Roman governors left Caesarea for Jerusalem at the time of the festival in order to keep a closer watch on things. Eschatological expectations of future deliverance also ran high at Passover time.

Lambs, although killed by individual Israelites, could be slain only at the temple, for the blood was sprinkled on the altar, so this feature of the festival dropped out in the post-70 period except among the Samaritans, who continued a ritual slaughter of lambs without a temple. The waving of a sheaf of barley, the firstfruits of the grain harvest, on Sunday after Passover (Lev. 23:9-11) provides the background to Paul's language of firstfruits for the resurrection of Jesus (1 Cor. 15:20-23; Rom. 8:23; 11:16).

The Passover meal was eaten after nightfall in a family group of at least ten persons (Pesahim 7.13ff.), so individuals and small families combined for the celebration. They could not leave Jerusalem during the night of the meal. In addition to roast lamb the meal included unleavened bread and bitter herbs as a reminder of the bitterness in Egypt. It was eaten reclining, a symbol of be-

---

299. Exod. 12:1–13:10; Lev. 23:4-14. G. J. Bahr, "The Seder of Passover and the Eucharistic Words," *Novum Testamentum* 12 (1970):181-202, collects the Rabbinic texts; see more fully Baruch M. Bokser, *The Origins of the Seder: The Passover Rite and Early Rabbinic Judaism* (Berkeley, 1984). Cf. Jubilees 49; Philo, *Special Laws* 2.27.145–29.175; Josephus, *Ant.* 3.10.5 [248-51]; 17.10.3 [213].

ing free persons. Four cups of wine mixed with water were passed around during the meal. The order of events given in the Mishnah tractate Pesahim ("Passover") 10 is as follows. The occasion began with a benediction over the *Kiddush* cup and a benediction for the day. Green herbs, bitter herbs, and a fruit puree *(haroseth)* seasoned with spices and vinegar were eaten. Then in the dining room proper the second cup was mixed but not yet drunk. The son asked his father, "Why is this night different from all other nights?" and the father gave instructions about the people's history, "beginning with the disgrace and ending with the glory" (Pesahim 10.4). The first part of the Passover Hallel (Psalms 113–114) was sung responsorially, and the *haggadah* cup was drunk. The meal proper began with the blessing of unleavened bread, to which the guests said "Amen." Each person used bread to scoop food from the dish and tasted at least some of the lamb. The third cup was called the "cup of blessing." With the fourth cup (*hallel* cup) the remaining Hallel Psalms (115–118) were sung and the gathering concluded. Which of the last three cups was the "cup of blessing" (1 Cor. 10:16) of the Last Supper is disputed, but presumably it was the third of the four.

Passover came in the spring. The lambs were slain on the 13th of Nisan (the month corresponded to March 27 to April 25), and the meal was eaten on the evening of Nisan 14, since the Jewish day began at sunset. The knottiest problem in New Testament chronology is the date of Jesus' Last Supper in relation to the Passover; the Synoptics apparently put the meal on Nisan 14 as a Passover supper, but John apparently has Jesus die at the time the lambs were being sacrificed on the 13th. The alternatives are that one of these sources is wrong, one source is being read incorrectly (either Jesus wanted to eat the Passover with his disciples but was not actually able to do so, or John is referring to Unleavened Bread and not Passover by his word "Feast"), or Jesus and his disciples were following a different calendar from the official calendar of the Jerusalem priesthood (made more plausible by the discovery of the different calendar observed by the Qumran sect).[300] The identification of Christ as "our Passover lamb" (1 Cor. 5:7; cf. John 19:36) is independent of the problem of dating.

Pentecost or Weeks (Shabuoth)[301]

The name *Pentecost* ("the fiftieth day") was common in Greek sources for the Old Testament Feast of Weeks or Feast of Harvest. It fell fifty days "from the morrow after the Sabbath" (Lev. 23:15-16). The Pharisees contended that the Sabbath intended was Passover itself, so Pentecost might fall on any day of the week. The

---

300. J. Jeremias, *The Eucharistic Words of Jesus* (3d ed.; New York, 1966), defends the Passover character of the Last Supper and illuminates the event from Jewish customs.

301. Exod. 23:15-17; 34:22; Lev. 23:15-21; Philo, *Special Laws* 2.30.176-87; Josephus, *Ant.* 3.10.6 [252ff.]; Acts 2:1; 20:6; 1 Cor. 16:8; Tobit 2:1; 2 Macc. 12:32; *Megilla Ta'anith* 1; b. Menahoth 65a.

Sadducees understood the Sabbath to be the weekly Sabbath of Passover week. The calendar followed at Qumran (Jubilees 15:1; 44:1-4) counted from the Sabbath following Passover week. Both of the latter methods of reckoning had the effect of putting Pentecost always on Sunday. Josephus and Philo[302] calculated Pentecost according to the Pharisaic method, hence it has been widely concluded that their method prevailed in the first century. On the other hand, it seems more likely that the practice at Jerusalem and the temple prior to 70 would have followed the interpretation of the Sadducees, who had control of the temple.

Pentecost was originally a harvest festival, celebrating the conclusion of the spring grain harvest. Grain was planted in Palestine, as in other Mediterranean countries, in the fall, allowed to grow during the winter, and harvested in the spring. The festival eventually received a historical and redemptive significance as commemorating the giving of the law at Sinai. The evidence for this interpretation in the first century is unsatisfactory,[303] but it would be quite fitting for Luke's account of the promulgation of the new law of pardon on Pentecost in Acts 2.

Tabernacles (Sukkoth)[304]

The Feast of Booths or Tabernacles was the most popular festival with the people and is called in Tannaitic literature "the Feast." It began on 15 Tishri (the month from Sept. 20 to Oct. 19) and lasted for eight days, coming after the grape harvest. It too was given a redemptive significance, commemorating the living in tents during the time of the wilderness wandering. The practice of building individual booths for the week of the festival is referred to in connection with the transfiguration of Jesus (Mark 9:5).

The observance of Tabernacles included a procession of the people carrying palm branches (*lulav* or *lulab*, palm shoots bound together with three myrtle twigs and two willow branches) and citrons (*ethrog*), which were waved aloft during the daily singing of the Hallel (Pss. 113–118) as an expression of joy. (This practice led to the suggestion that Jesus' triumphal entry occurred at the time of Tabernacles and not a week before Passover as the traditional dating had it.) Each morning of the period of the feast priests brought water from the fountain of Siloam and poured it out as a libation on the altar. On the last day the priests marched around the altar seven times, praying for rain during the ensuing rainy season. Four large menorahs were set up around the temple courts and kept

---

302. Philo, *Special Laws* 2.30.176; *Decalog* 160; Josephus, *Ant.* 3.10.5-6 [250ff.]; cf. Lev. 23:15-16 in the LXX.

303. First mentioned in b. Pesahim 68b (c. A.D. 270); already in Jubilees 6:15-22, however, the Feast of Weeks was interpreted as a renewal of the covenant.

304. Exod. 23:14-17; Lev. 23:33-36, 39-44; Deut. 16:13-15. See the Mishnah tractate Sukkoth; cf. Philo, *Special Laws* 2.32–33.204-13; Josephus, *Ant.* 3.10.4 [244-47]; Jeffrey L. Rubenstein, *The History of Sukkot in the Second Temple and Rabbinic Periods* (Atlanta, 1995).

burning each night. Dancing and pipe-playing lasted most of the night. The Levites chanted the Psalms of Ascent (120–134), one for each of the steps between the court of Israel and the court of women. These customs at Tabernacles (John 7:2, 14) provide the background for Jesus' statements "If anyone thirst, let him come to me and drink" and "I am the light of the world" (John 7:32; 8:12). The cycle of Torah readings in the synagogue began at Tabernacles.

New Year's Day (Rosh Hashanah)[305]

The "head of the year" came on Tishri 1, following the ancient calendar, which began the year in the autumn. It was marked by the blowing of the ram's horn (shofar). Not a prominent day in its own right, it marked the beginning of a period of important religious days, including Tabernacles and the Day of Atonement.

Day of Atonement (Yom Kippur)[306]

The Day of Atonement fell on Tishri 10. It was not a feast day but a solemn fast day (cf. Acts 27:9, "the fast") — a day of repentance (Yoma 8.8-9) and prayer for forgiveness. The ritual of Leviticus 16 and 23:26-32 was carried out while the temple existed. The high priest made his annual appearance in the Holy of Holies with blood for the atonement of the nation's sins and called upon Yahweh in prayer. The ritual provided the background of Hebrews 5:5; 10:4; etc. Philo indicates the fast was observed even by those not careful of other religious observances (Special Laws 1.186-88). Jewish people today continue to observe Yom Kippur as a holy fast day.

Feast of Dedication (Ḥanukkah) or Lights [307]

This has been the most popular of the postbiblical feasts in Judaism. It was instituted by Judas Maccabeus to commemorate the rededication of the temple after its profanation by Antiochus Epiphanes (1 Macc. 4:42-59; 2 Macc. 10:1-8; Josephus, Ant. 12.7.6 [316-22]). The name Feast of Dedication (Heb. Ḥanukkah) appears in John 10:22. The name Feast of Lights appears in Josephus (Ant. 12.7.7 [325]) and is associated with the ceremonial lighting of eight lamps, an additional one on each day of the feast. This practice derives from the legend that only one cruse of oil was found when the Jews reoccupied the temple, but it miraculously lasted for seven days so the lamp in the temple was kept burning

---

305. Lev. 23:24-25. See the Mishnah tractate Rosh ha-Shanah.

306. Lev. 16; 23:26-32; Num. 29:7-11. See the Mishnah tractate Yoma and Philo, Special Laws 2.193-203; Daniel Stökl Ben Ezra, The Impact of Yom Kippur on Early Christianity (Tübingen, 2003).

307. O. S. Rankin, The Origins of the Festival of Hanukkah (Edinburgh, 1930); S. Zeitlin, "Hanukkah, Origin and its Significance," JQR 29 (1938/39):1-31.

until a new supply of oil could be consecrated (b. Shabbat 21b). Hanukkah begins on the 25th of Kislev (Nov. 29–Dec. 27) and lasts for eight days. Its proximity to the Christian Christmas has meant that it has acquired for some Jews a comparable social significance including the custom of exchanging gifts and greeting cards.

Purim

The institution of Purim is told in the Book of Esther (cf. Josephus, *Ant.* 11.6.13 [292-95]). It has been more of a joyous holiday, with no religious rites connected with it other than the reading of Esther in the synagogue (see Megillah).

BIBLIOGRAPHY

Philo. *Special Laws* 2.56-70; 140-214.
Josephus. *Ant.* 3.239-54.

Schauss, Hayyim. *The Jewish Festivals: From Their Beginnings to our Own Day.* New York, 1938.
Gaster, T. H. *Festivals of the Jewish Year: A Modern Interpretation and Guide.* New York, 1953.

Daily Devotions[308]

The faithful Jew recited the Shema not only in the synagogue but daily. *Shema* ("hear") is the opening word of Deuteronomy 6:4, the basic confession of Judaism. The recitation included Deuteronomy 6:4-9; 11:3-21; and Numbers 15:36-41. During the time of the temple it was accompanied by reciting the Decalogue, preceded by benedictions, and followed by an attestation of faith and praises of God as redeemer of Israel. The Shema was recited each morning and evening.

Prayer *(tefillah)* was said twice a day also, in the morning and at the time of the afternoon whole-offering in the temple (Berakoth 4.1; 1QS x:11; Josephus, *War* 2.8.5 [128-31], concerning the Essenes; cf. Acts 3:1). Some sources indicate prayer three times a day (Dan. 6:11; 2 Enoch 51:4). The *tefillah* consisted of a series of benedictions, finally fixed at eighteen (hence called *Shemone Esre*), about which more will be said in connection with the synagogue service (pp. 576-78).

Meals were set in a religious context of purification and blessing of the Creator. Hands were washed, bread was blessed and broken, and the meal was eaten, followed by a thanksgiving at the close. If wine was served, it received a separate blessing.

---

308. See the Mishnah tractate Berakoth.

ORGANIZATION AND INSTITUTIONS

Temple and Priesthood

Temple

As the goal of the pilgrim festivals, the seat of the Sanhedrin, and the site of the sacrificial cultus, the temple was the focal point of world Jewry. It was located near the site now known as the Dome of the Rock in Jerusalem. Herod the Great in 20/19 B.C.[309] had undertaken the rebuilding of the temple, which was largely completed in his lifetime but was still in progress during Jesus' ministry (John 2:20) and was not completed until about A.D. 63 — shortly before the revolt that brought its final destruction in 70. Josephus said that to approaching visitors the temple appeared as a "mountain of snow" as it glittered in the sunlight (*War* 5.11.6 [223]). Although Jews in Egypt built temples at Elephantine (sixth century B.C.) and Leontopolis (second century B.C.) and the Samaritans had their temple on Mount Gerizim, the overwhelming Jewish attitude was that expressed by Josephus, "We have but one temple for the one God" (*Against Apion* 2.23.193).

The temple proper *(naos)* was located in the northwestern part of an esplanade approximately 1,590 feet north-south and 1,030 feet east-west (the whole area was called the *hieron*). The esplanade was enclosed by colonnaded porches or porticoes (e.g., Solomon's Porch, John 10:23 and Acts 3:11, on the east) through which gates gave access from the city. The Western Wall, the only part that survives, was part of the retaining wall for the esplanade or terrace on the southern end of the west side. Just outside the sacred enclosure on the northwest was the Tower of Antonia (probably the "barracks" in Acts 21:34-40; 22:24; 23:10). The open area of the sacred enclosure, mainly to the south of the temple proper, was known as the Court of the Gentiles. It was a principal thoroughfare providing a shortcut across the temple mount and also a place for commercial activity (Mark 11:15-17). A low balustrade separated the Court of the Gentiles from the temple proper. Placed in the wall were stones bearing the inscription, "No man of another nation is to enter within the barrier and enclosure around the temple. Whoever is caught will have himself to blame for his death which follows."[310]

The Court of Women lay directly east of the temple, and any Israelite in a state of purity could gather in this area. Steps on the western end of the court gave access to the platform on which the temple was erected. On these

---

309. This is the date given by Josephus, *Antiquities* 15.11.1 [380ff.]; *War* 1.21.1 [401] gives the date 23/22 B.C.

310. J.-B. Frey, *Corpus Inscriptionum Iudaicarum* 1400 (OGIS 598); cf. Josephus, *War* 6.2.4 [125-26]; 5.5.2 [194]; *Ant.* 15.11.5 [417]; Mishnah Kelim 1.8; Acts 21:28-29; E. Bickerman, "The Warning Inscription of Herod's Temple," *JQR* 37 (1946/47):387-405.

MODEL OF JERUSALEM, Holy Land Hotel, Jerusalem
The temple, the outer Court of the Gentiles (separated from the other courts by
a barrier wall), and the Tower of Antonia (the barracks for the Roman garrison)
in the upper right have been reconstructed to scale as nearly as possible
to their appearance in the 1st century.

steps the Levites stood to sing the "Psalms of Ascents." At the head of the stairs
stood the Nicanor Gates, huge bronze gates extraordinary for their beauty
(perhaps the "Beautiful Gate" in Acts 3:2).[311] The Court of Israel surrounded
the temple proper; only Jewish men could come so far. A low wall separated
the Court of Priests from the Court of Israel. Within this area east of the entrance to the temple was the great altar of burnt offerings, reached by a ramp.
It was fifty feet square.

The temple proper kept the proportions and furniture (incense altar, table of showbread, seven-branched lampstand [menorah], and veil separating
the Holy of Holies) prescribed in the Old Testament, except that the long-lost
ark of the covenant had not been replaced. Golden spikes on the roof prevented birds from defiling it. Josephus gives the dimensions of the facade as
one hundred cubits broad and one hundred cubits high (*War* 5.5.4 [207]; cf. 5.5
[215-21] and *Ant.* 15.11.3 [391]).

Writers of the second temple period interpreted the temple as a symbol
of the cosmos. They understood it as holding the cosmos together and its cult

311. Middoth 2.3; Josephus, *War* 5.5.3 (201).

WARNING INSCRIPTION, temple in Jerusalem
Non-Jews were warned against passing from the Court of the Gentiles
to the Court of the Women on threat of death (cf. Eph. 2:14).
(Israel Department of Antiquities and Museums)

as providing stability and order. The temple, moreover, was a representation of heavenly reality. Its services were considered to unite with angelic worship in invocation of the Lord on behalf of Israel and the world.

During the first century A.D. the wealth of the temple probably reached its greatest amount. A major source of income was the half-shekel tax (Mishnah Shekalim) that was supposed to be paid by every male Jew over twenty (Matt. 17:24-27; cf. p. 93).[312] It was a sign of the attachment of Jews everywhere to their homeland that delegations from cities in the Diaspora made up these contributions and traveled with special governmental protection to deliver the large sums collected (see p. 429; Philo, *Special Laws* 1.14.76-78; cf. Paul's collection among Gentile churches). Free-will offerings were left in thirteen trumpet-shaped boxes in the temple precincts (Mark 14:41-44). Sources of revenue available to the priests included perquisites from sacrificial animals, firstfruits of the grain and fruit harvests, and tithes (Josephus, *Ant.* 20.7.8 [181]; 9.2 [206]).

312. J. Liver, "The Half-Shekel Offering in Biblical and Post-Biblical Literature," *HTR* 56 (1963):173-98.

The temple, as other Near Eastern sanctuaries, served as a depository for keeping valuables. Hence, Jesus' action in cleansing the temple looked revolutionary. It was an assault on the economic system and a challenge to the position of the temple authorities.[313]

Priests

The priests were divided into twenty-four courses,[314] each of which was responsible for conducting the temple ritual for one week at a time, twice a year, and all were to be available at the great pilgrim festivals. Most of the priests, therefore, lived outside Jerusalem and were there only when their course was on duty. There was a considerable social gulf between the priestly aristocracy centered on the temple and the ordinary priests scattered throughout the country. Specific duties at the temple were assigned by lot.

The installation of a high priest in Herodian and Roman times was accomplished by investiture with the garments of office (Horayoth 3.4; Josephus, *Ant.* 15.11.4 [403-8]; 18.4.3 [93]; 20.1.1 [16]). The office of high priest was inherited according to the Old Testament, but Hellenistic kings were accustomed to removing and appointing priests as political favors or in response to bribes (as the Seleucids did in Jerusalem on the eve of the Maccabean revolt). Herod the Great and his Roman successors changed high priests with some frequency — there were twenty-eight from Herod to A.D. 70. The family of Annas (who was high priest A.D. 6–15), however, furnished eight of the high priests in the first century. The expression *chief priests* in the New Testament and Josephus has been thought to refer to the ex–high priests and perhaps members of their family. An alternative explanation includes any distinguished priest of socially prominent families. Another possibility is that the high priests or chief priests were the permanent staff of officials at the temple who also had seats in the Sanhedrin.[315] This well-defined group would have included the anointed high priest, the invested high priest (if different), the captain (or prefect) of the temple (Acts 4:1, 5-6; 5:24, 26; Josephus, *Ant.* 20.6.2 [131]; *War* 6.5.3 [294]; Tamid 7.3; Yoma 4.1; 7.1), who had oversight of the cultus and was chief of the temple police, a temple overseer (there were at least seven of these in all, who held the keys to the gates and supervised the physical or external arrangements in the temple area; Luke 22:4, 52; Josephus passim), and three treasurers (who as agents of a seven-man council of supervisors administered the temple income and looked after its landed property and treasury; Josephus, *Ant.* 20.8.11 [194]). Serving under the captain of the temple were the directors of the weekly

313. Neill Q. Hamilton, "Temple Cleansing and Temple Bank," *JBL* 83 (1964):365-72.

314. 1 Chron. 24. M. Avi-Yonah, "The Caesarea Inscription of the Twenty-Four Priestly Courses," in *The Teacher's Yoke*, ed. E. J. Vardaman (Waco, Tex., 1964), 42-57.

315. J. Jeremias, *Jerusalem in the Time of Jesus* (London, 1969), 160-81.

courses and then the directors of the daily courses. These overseers and the retired high priests and other treasurers also held positions in the Sanhedrin.

The Levites too were divided into twenty-four courses. There were two main groups of Levites — singers and gatekeepers (1 Chron. 9:14-44; Ezra 2:40-42). Four chief Levites were on the permanent staff of the temple: two overseers of the musicians (one of instrumentalists and one of singers) and two overseers of the Levitical servants (a doorkeeper and a supervisor of those who did the menial work). The Levites provided the music for the different services, certain physical and custodial duties, and police functions (Josephus, *Ant.* 20.9.6 [216-17]; Philo, *Special Laws* 1.32.156).

Cultus

We have already noted something of the activity in connection with the annual festivals (pp. 557-61); it remains to say something about the daily routine and common features of temple procedure.

The *Tamid*, the whole burnt offering, was sacrificed twice daily, according to the prescriptions in Exodus 29:38-42 and Numbers 28:1-8. The times of the morning (sunrise) and "evening" (afternoon — 3:00 P.M.) sacrifice at the temple became hours of prayer for the people (cf. Acts 3:1). (The Mishnah records that the laity of the community from which the priests and Levites came for their tour of duty at the temple met at the times of prayer to fast, recite Scripture, and perhaps to pray on certain of the days of their service.) The priests who were to serve that day began by immersing themselves so that they would be in a state of purity. The various functions were assigned by lot: cleaning the altar of coals from the preceding day's sacrifice, preparing the cereal offering, burning incense, and trimming the lampstand. The lamb was completely burned on the altar, a drink offering was poured out, and the choir of Levites sang. At intervals in the singing, two trumpets were sounded, each time as a signal for the people to prostrate themselves. The priests themselves recited together benedictions, the Ten Commandments, and the Shema (p. 561). The incense offering on the altar in the Holy Place was the climax of the service. It was arranged that a priest ordinarily burned the incense only once in his lifetime (Tamid 5.2; Luke 1:5, 8-10). After this five priests stood on the steps to pronounce the priestly benediction (Num. 6:24-26) over those who came to pray. In Jerusalem the priests used the sacred name *Yahweh* in the benediction, but in the synagogue services in the provinces they used a substitute.

The high priest did not himself have to preside at the daily ritual and probably did so only on the major festivals or other special occasions. Sirach 50 gives a graphic description of the ceremony under the high priest Simon.[316]

---

316. F. O'Fearghail, "Sir 50:5-21: Yom Kippur or the Daily Whole Offering?" *Biblica* 59 (1978):301-16.

The number of sacrificial animals was increased on the Sabbath and festival days. Moreover, the priests had to be available to assist when individuals came to make guilt, votive, or thank offerings.

Also twice daily was a sacrifice "for Caesar and the Roman nation." This consisted of two lambs and an ox, and was accepted by the Roman authorities as a sufficient expression of loyalty. According to Philo, Augustus provided for the sacrifice out of his own funds.[317] The discontinuance of this sacrifice, on the orders of the captain of the temple, was the signal for revolt in A.D. 66 (Josephus, War 2.17.2-3 [409-16]).

Some statements have been taken as an indication that sacrificial worship continued even after 70 without benefit of the physical structure of the temple.[318] The evidence is tenuous, but even if there was some continuance, the destruction of the temple profoundly altered Jewish religious life and made irreversible the trend away from the temple to the synagogue as the focus of faith.

BIBLIOGRAPHY

Sirach 50:1-21.

Josephus. *Ant.* 15.11.1-7 [380-425]. *War* 5.5.1-6 [184-227].

Mishnah tractates Middoth and Tamid.

Hollis, F. J. *The Archaeology of Herod's Temple with a Commentary on the Tractate Middoth.* London, 1934.

Hayward, Robert. *The Jewish Temple: A Non-Biblical Sourcebook.* London, 1996.

Edersheim, A. *The Temple, its Ministry and Services as They Were in the Time of Christ.* London, 1874.

Smallwood, E. M. "High Priests and Politics in Roman Palestine." *JTS* n.s. 13 (1962):14-34.

Cody, A. A. *A History of Old Testament Priesthood.* Rome, 1969.

Sabourin, L. *Priesthood: A Comparative Study.* Leiden, 1973.

Mazar, B. *The Mountain of the Lord.* Garden City, N.Y., 1975.

Businck, T. A. *Der Tempel von Jerusalem von Salomo bis Herodes.* Leiden, 1980.

Sanhedrin

The word *Sanhedrin* represents the Hebrew transliteration of the Greek word *synedrion* ("council," "meeting"). In various sources at different periods we hear of the *gerousia,* council *(boulē),* Sanhedrin, and *Beth Din.* The immediate

---

317. *Embassy to Gaius* 23.157; but does this refer to the regular daily burnt-offering? Cf. Josephus, *War* 2.10.4 [197]. *Against Apion* 2.77 says the expense was borne by the nation; but that may be after Augustus's time.

318. Kenneth W. Clark, "Worship in the Jerusalem Temple after A.D. 70," *NTS* 6 (1959/60):269-80.

antecedent of the Sanhedrin in New Testament times was the council of elders or senate *(gerousia)* of Hasmonean times (1 Macc. 12:6; 2 Macc. 4:49; 11:27).

The greater Sanhedrin in Jerusalem during New Testament times was composed of the chief priests, elders of the people (lay aristocracy around Jerusalem), and scribes (sages learned in the law).[319] According to rabbinic literature it tried cases dealing with a whole tribe, a false prophet, and the high priest (Sanhedrin 1.5). In Tos. Sanhedrin 7.1 it also had appellate jurisdiction over a court of twenty-three in interpreting the law.

The rabbis replaced the Jerusalem Sanhedrin after 70 with the *Beth Din.* Executive, judicial, and academic functions were combined in the scholars. The high priest had presided over the Sanhedrin; since that office disappeared with the temple, the post-70 *Beth Din* was presided over by the president (*Nasi,* or prince) and vice-president, called the *'ab beth din* (father of the house of judgment or court, a title also used for the president of a local court). Rabbinic tradition assigned these titles also to the senior and junior members of the *zugoth* (the pairs in the rabbinic chain of tradition). The *Beth Din* was a council of scholars to provide interpretations of the law. Rome came to recognize the position of the *Nasi* and his council as the body through which local government in Palestine could be administered.

Doubt has been cast on the historical value for the New Testament period of the Mishnah's regulations concerning the Sanhedrin. They may have referred primarily to the *Beth Din* (so that the tractate Sanhedrin would be better entitled *Beth Din*), or may have been only hypothetical interpretations projected back on the pre-70 situation but not actually in force then, or may reflect a composite picture. The basis for the doubt is that the Greek sources (1 and 2 Maccabees, New Testament, Josephus) present a political council presided over by the head of state (king or high priest), whereas the rabbinic sources present a legislative-judicial body of scholars headed by the two leading Pharisaic scholars. The alternatives are that the Sanhedrin of the New Testament and Josephus and the *Beth Din* of rabbinic literature were the same (differently described), existed in different periods (as implied above), or were different institutions both existing in the first century (one of which survived). In support of the last interpretation it has been argued that there were two principal councils in Jerusalem in the first century: the political Sanhedrin mentioned in the New Testament and Josephus, which was convened by the political ruler and had authority only as authorized by the appropriate official; and the *Beth Din* described in the Mishnah, also called *boulē,* which was established in the Hasmonean period to promulgate laws not found in the Torah.[320] The Mish-

---

319. E.g., Matt. 16:21; Mark 8:31; 11:27; 14:43; 15:1; Luke 9:22; 20:1; cf. Josephus, *War* 2.14.8 [301]; 2.15.2 [316]; 2.15.3 [318]; 2.17.3 [411].

320. E. Rivkin, "Beth Din, Boulé, Sanhedrin: A Tragedy of Errors," *Hebrew Union College Annual* 46 (1975):181-99.

nah in fact mentions three courts in Jerusalem: one that sat at the gate of the temple mount, one that sat at the gate of the temple court, and one that sat in the chamber of hewn stone (Sanhedrin 11.2). Their identification and functions are disputed. It has been suggested that these three (of twenty-three members each) were subdivisions of the Great Sanhedrin. Since Judaism did not in general distinguish political, judicial, and religious functions, likely there was only one supreme council that in different periods had different powers and composition. At various times we find legislative, judicial, and advisory functions performed by this council.

The trial of Jesus becomes involved in this dispute. Were the judicial procedures described in the tractate Sanhedrin in force in the first century? The proceedings recounted in the Gospels are in flagrant violation of the regulations in the Mishnah. However, those regulations may not have obtained in Jesus' time or may have applied to a different court. On the other hand, the Sanhedrin may have been functioning only as a grand jury and not a trial body (see pp. 64-65).[321] The competence of the Sanhedrin to impose the death penalty has also come under discussion. John 18:31 agrees with what is known of Roman law in the provinces where capital punishment was reserved for the governor.[322] Rome, however, gave considerable scope to local bodies to administer justice according to local laws, and in the case of violators of the temple, for instance, seems to have delegated execution to the local authorities. Moreover, there are instances of the Jewish leaders executing those they found troublesome (e.g., Stephen [Acts 7]; James [Josephus, *Ant.* 20.9.1 (200)]).[323] These may be cases of taking the law into their own hands, particularly during the absence of a Roman governor.

According to the Mishnah, a court of three judges is required for judicial decisions in cases involving property (Sanhedrin 1.1-3; 3.1). Several sources refer to the "Seven of a City" who ruled a city, functioned as judges, and had charge of financial affairs (Josephus, *Ant.* 4.7.14 [214] and 38 [287]; *War* 2.20.5 [571]; j. Megillah 3.74a; b. Megillah 26a and b; cf. Acts 6:1-6). Capital cases required a court of twenty-three (Sanhedrin 1.4); these were called a lesser Sanhedrin, and were located in the larger towns throughout Palestine (cf. Matt. 5:22). A city was required to have 120 men in order for it to have a Lesser San-

---

321. G. D. Kilpatrick, *The Trial of Jesus,* Friends of Dr. Williams's Library Lectures, vol. 6 (London, 1953); Ernst Bammel, ed., *The Trial of Jesus* (London, 1970); Robert Gordis, ed., "The Trial of Jesus in the Light of History: A Symposium," *Judaism* 20 (1971):6-74; Paul Winter, *On the Trial of Jesus* (Berlin, 1974); Roy A. Stewart, "Judicial Procedure in New Testament Times," *Evangelical Quarterly* 47 (1975):94-109.

322. According to j. Sanhedrin 18a and 24b the power to impose the death sentence was taken away forty years before the destruction of the temple. John 18:31, however, may not be an absolute statement but might refer to the unlawfulness of executions at the Passover season (cf. Sanhedrin 4.1).

323. The apostle James was killed while Agrippa was king (Acts 12), so a different legal situation obtained.

hedrin (Sanhedrin 1.6; is this relevant to Acts 1:15?). The Greater Sanhedrin in Jerusalem had seventy-one members. Different interpretations as to whether or not this included the high priest gave rise to variant traditions whether the actual number was seventy or seventy-two.[324] The background was the group of seventy elders in Israel's earlier history (Exod. 24:9; Num. 11:10-24; 2 Chron. 19:8?). It was characteristic of Judaism that through much of its later history the judiciary held the leading place in the government as a whole.

The Mishnah explains how one was appointed to the Sanhedrin:

> The Sanhedrin was arranged like the half of a round threshing floor so that they all might see one another. Before them stood the two scribes of the judges. . . .
>
> Before them sat three rows of disciples of the Sages, and each knew his proper place. If they needed to appoint [another as judge], they appointed him from the first row, and one from the second row came into the first row, and one from the third row came into the second; and they chose yet another from the congregation and set him in the third row. (Sanhedrin 4.3, 4)

This seating in the chair constituted the "ordination." Rabbinic ordination by laying on of hands did not become the official method of instituting a judge and successor until after 70.[325] The significance of ordination in Judaism was judicial — the right to interpret and teach the law.

BIBLIOGRAPHY

Mishnah tractate Sanhedrin.

Hoenig, S. B. *The Great Sanhedrin*. Philadelphia, 1953.
Mantel, H. *Studies in the History of the Sanhedrin*. Cambridge, Mass., 1965.
McLaren, James S. *Power and Politics in Palestine: The Jews and the Governing of their Land 100 B.C.–A.D. 70*. Sheffield, 1991.

Community Organization[326]

Jewish community organization shows oligarchic, democratic, and monarchic expressions, and not infrequently all three aspects functioning together. Authority belonged to the community and "the assembly of men of the city." Not

---

324. This variation is reflected also in manuscripts of Luke 10:1. See Bruce M. Metzger, *Historical and Literary Studies: Pagan, Jewish, and Christian* (Grand Rapids, 1968), 67-76.

325. E. Ferguson, "Jewish and Christian Ordination," *HTR* 56 (1963):13-19.

326. J. T. Burchaell, *From Synagogue to Church: Public Services and Offices in the Earliest Christian Communities* (Cambridge, 1992), 209-71.

all, however, carried equal influence (in the sense of "one person, one vote"). Normally a council of older men provided the leadership. Sometimes a learned scholar, the rabbi, or in special circumstances some other influential person was the effective leader.[327]

At the legal head of Palestinian Jewish communities, according to the later rabbinic sources, were local Sanhedrins whose members were "ordained" and wore the title "elder." Their method of appointment was the same as that for the Great Sanhedrin at Jerusalem, described in the preceding section (b. Sanhedrin 17b). They had general oversight of community affairs, especially judicial and disciplinary. They interpreted and applied the law of Moses according to the precedents established by the scholars. The institutions or services that every city ought to provide were listed as "marketplace, bathhouse, synagogue, ark of the law, and Torah scroll" (m. Nedarim 5.5) or more extensively as "a law court competent to scourge, a prison, a charity fund, a synagogue, a public bath, a public latrine, a doctor and artisan, a scribe, a slaughterer, and a teacher of children" (b. Sanhedrin 17b).

The Diaspora communities are best known from the inscriptions at Rome (see p. 504n.210). The terms *presbyteroi* (elders) and *gerousia* (council of elders) do not appear (as they do elsewhere), but *gerousiarch* (ruler of the council) does several times. Since it always occurs with reference to a particular community and since there is no evidence of a central governing body for the Jews in Rome, we may conclude that each synagogue at Rome had its own council of elders and that there was no central organization of Roman Jewry.

The term most used for the leaders of Jewish communities in the Diaspora was *archons* (rulers), derived from Greek civic life. Individual members of the *gerousia* may have been called archon rather than elder, but it has been advocated that the archons were distinct from elders and formed an executive committee of the *gerousia*.[328] The *archisynagogos*, who presided at the assembly (p. 581), was not of necessity an archon but he could be. The archons in the inscriptions figure mainly in the business dealings of the synagogue, but this may be due to the nature of the contents of inscriptions. The title "archon" was not always a technical term but could be honorary, even applied to children.

The inscriptions employ a host of other titles for various functionaries in the Jewish communities. Most of these appear to have been borrowed from the private associations so much a part of Greek life. Quite frequent is the *grammateus*, clerk or secretary; it is not clear whether this was meant to translate *soferim* ("the wise men," i.e., scholars or scribes), was a Greek-style secretary or town clerk, or represents a distinctive Hellenistic Jewish office. The

---

327. For the combination of these three elements at Qumran and in early Christianity see Bo Reicke, "The Constitution of the Primitive Church in the Light of Jewish Documents," in *The Scrolls and the New Testament*, ed. Krister Stendahl (New York, 1957), 143-56.

328. Three archons in Judith 6:15-16 included elders but apparently not all the elders; 8:10; 10:6; 13:12.

"father" and "mother of the synagogue" appear to have been honorary designations for patrons or benefactors.

Some inscriptions identify women as priestess, elder, ruler of the synagogue, or other functionary. The older interpretation referred such designations to wives of priests, elders, rulers of the synagogue, or other community officials or as honorary titles. It is now considered likely that in some cases women actually filled these positions,[329] but many titles were honorary, even those that in some other contexts were functional.

The sizable Jewish community at Alexandria did have a central governing body. The emperor Augustus in A.D. 10–12 abolished the post of Jewish ethnarch in Alexandria and put the administration of the Jewish population into the hands of a supreme Jewish *gerousia*. Very little is known of their selection and functions. Tannaitic sources give their number as seventy or seventy-one (Tos. Sukkah 4.6; b. Sukkah 51b). Philo (*Flaccus* 74 and 117) mentions the *gerousia* and archons, the latter presumably an executive committee. The Jewish population of Alexandria and perhaps other cities formed a *politeuma*, a self-governing association within the framework of the city (pp. 42-43).

The plurality of elders, perhaps with an executive in larger centers, in the Jewish community organization, and not the synagogue organization, appears to account for the presence of elders in the early Christian communities, particularly those with close Jewish ties (Acts 11:30; 14:23; 20:17).

Rabbis[330]

The use of *Rabbi* as a technical term for an ordained scholar apparently belongs to the post-70 situation. In the period before 70 the term was used in a looser and more general way — note its use in the Gospels for addressing Jesus.[331] Professional, salaried rabbis do not begin until the Middle Ages.

Ordination as a rabbi was an appointment to an office. It gave one judicial authority in interpreting the Jewish law. This responsibility carried with it related functions of leadership, teaching, and preserving the tradition.[332] In the

329. B. J. Brooten, *Women Leaders in the Ancient Synagogue* (Chico, Calif., 1982); but the contrary view is still maintained by Burtchaell, *From Synagogue to Church* (n. 326), 244-45.

330. L. I. Levine, *The Rabbinic Class of Roman Palestine in Late Antiquity* (New York, 1989); Richard Kalmin, *The Sage in Jewish Society of Late Antiquity* (London, 1999).

331. "Rabbi" continued in use in a nontechnical sense even in Talmudic times — S. J. D. Cohen, "Epigraphic Rabbis," *JQR* 72 (1981/82):1-17.

332. J. Newman, *Semikhah* (Manchester, 1950); Eduard Lohse, *Die Ordination im Spätjudentum und im Neuen Testament* (Göttingen, 1951); Arnold Ehrhardt, "Jewish and Christian Ordination," *Journal of Ecclesiastical History* 5 (1954):125-38; David Daube, *New Testament and Rabbinic Judaism* (London, 1956), 224-46. *Sifre Numbers* 27:18, 20; j. Sanhedrin 1, 19a, 43; b. Sanhedrin 13b–14a.

period immediately after 70 when there was no central organization in Palestinian Jewry individual teachers ordained one or two of their own students to continue their work, but this was later replaced by a communal act when ordination was centralized under the Patriarch in the second century. Individual ordination was by the imposition of hands, but this was replaced by a ceremony giving the name or title of Rabbi.

Qualifications included such qualities as "wisdom, understanding, fame" and being men who are "able, fear God, men of truth hating unjust gain."[333] In addition, a married man who had raised children and reached the age of about forty was preferred.

Although the Judaism that took shape in the period after the revolts against Rome is often described as rabbinic Judaism, the rabbis did not represent or speak for all Jews. In drawing on, modifying, and reshaping the earlier tradition, the rabbis produced significant changes in Judaism: making the study of Torah a central act of piety incumbent on all male Jews, and developing prayer into a communal act of service to God. In the process, the rabbis elevated a new type of holy man — the scholar replaced the priest as the religious leader. Although the result in the circumstances of the post-70 period was something new, the rabbis were drawing on elements in the earlier Jewish tradition in fashioning "rabbinic Judaism."

Synagogue

History

The word *synagogue* (here parallel to the word *church*) referred to the assembly of people and came to be applied to the building where the assembly occurred and then to the related institutional life. The word *proseuchē*, "(place of) prayer," was also in common use, especially in Egypt. After the destruction of the temple the name in inscriptions for synagogues in Palestine was "holy place." We have already looked at the physical features of synagogue buildings (pp. 505-7); here our attention will be on the organization and activities associated with synagogues.

The origin of the synagogue is unknown. More plausible theories refer to the time of the exile or the postexilic period in gatherings for the reading and study of the law (Neh. 8:1 would reflect the situation out of which the synagogue emerged if not describing the actual precedent). Archaeological evidence indicates synagogues in Egypt from the third century B.C.[334] Synagogues were cer-

---

333. *Midrash Rabbah Deuteronomy* 1.

334. J. Gwyn Griffiths, "Egypt and the Rise of the Synagogue," *JTS* n.s. 38 (1987):1-15, argues for the Egyptian origin of the synagogue.

SYNAGOGUE, Masada
One of the few pre-70 synagogues to be identified was used by
the defenders of Masada. The congregation gathered on the steps or
benches on the walls around the room.

tainly a well-developed reality by the first century, when they were located throughout Palestine and the Diaspora. Philo, for instance, has numerous references to synagogues (clearly referring to meeting places).[335] The synagogue would not seem to have been created as a replacement or substitute for the temple, since the two coexisted for some time, although after 70, synagogues increasingly incorporated such of the furniture, terminology, and ritual of the temple as could be adapted to them. "Holy place" became a common designation for synagogues in the third/fourth centuries and after. The application of temple motifs to the synagogue was a factor in the use of this name, but a more important source of synagogue sanctity was the presence of biblical scrolls, considered not only as containing the word of God but to be themselves holy.

The synagogue was the most important institutional development within Judaism insofar as Christian origins are concerned: it provided the locus for the teaching of Jesus and later his apostles and so the place of recruitment of

335. Some of these are *Life of Moses* 2.216; *Hypothetica* 8.7.12-13; *Special Laws* 2.62; *Every Good Man Is Free* 81. The *Embassy to Gaius* contains many references to synagogues, called *proseuchai* (but *synagogē* in 311 with reference to a letter by Augustus), not only in Alexandria but also in Rome (156). *Proseuchai* are buildings in *Against Flaccus* 41-49, 53, 122.

the earliest Christian converts, and many aspects of the worship and organization of the early church were derived from the synagogue. Although a new institution, the synagogue represented an organized way of carrying out activities commanded in the law.[336]

Activities

The synagogue was the center of community, religious, and social life for the Jewish people. It served as the schoolhouse *(beth midrash)*, house of prayer *(beth tefillah)*, meeting house *(beth kenesseth)*, and house of judgment *(beth din)* for administering community discipline. The combination of religious, instructional, and social-benevolent functions in the synagogue is seen in an inscription found in Jerusalem and sometimes dated to the mid-first century but perhaps later:

> Theodotus, son of Vettenus, priest and archisynagogue, son of an archisynagogue, built the synagogue for the reading of the law and the teaching of the commandments, and the guest-house and the rooms and the water supplies as an inn for those who have need when they come from abroad; which synagogue his fathers founded and the elders and Simonides. (*Corpus Inscriptionum Judaicarum* 1404)[337]

Organized charity, as well as hospitality, was characteristic of Judaism. In Palestine there were community agencies for feeding the poor, clothing the needy, caring for the sick, burying the dead, ransoming captives, educating orphans,

---

336. H. C. Kee, "The Transformation of the Synagogue after 70 C.E.: Its Import for Early Christianity," *NTS* 36 (1990):1-24, appropriately calls attention to the important institutional developments after 70 and the circumstance that the earliest meeting places were often domestic quarters indistinguishable architecturally and used for many purposes; but these facts should not be equated with a lack of organization and of structured forms of worship, something inconceivable for community life and contradicted by other first-century sources outside the New Testament. Richard Oster, "Supposed Anachronism in Luke-Acts' Use of ΣΥΝΑΓΩΓΗ: A Rejoinder to H. C. Kee," *NTS* 39 (1993):178-208 corrects Kee on several points and notes the evidence for "synagogue" as referring to a building in the pre-70 period, even if these buildings were not distinguished architecturally. Kee responded in "The Changing Meaning of Synagogue: A Response to Richard Oster," *NTS* 40 (1994):281-83 and elaborated his views in "Defining the First-Century C.E. Synagogue," *NTS* 41 (1995):481-500. See n.337. Rachel Hachlili, "The Origin of the Synagogue: A Re-assessment," *JSJ* 28 (1997):34-47, sees the synagogue as originating earlier but becoming a center of worship only after the destruction of the temple; although some of the appropriation of temple elements to the synagogue likely belongs after 70, the fact that the first name for the synagogue was "house of prayer" would argue that worship was central from the beginning.

337. John S. Kloppenborg Verbin, "Dating Theodotos (CIJ II 1404)," *JJS* 51 (2000):243-80, after a thorough review of Kee (preceding note) and study of the inscription concludes in favor of a pre-70 date. Some have identified this synagogue with the "Synagogue of the Freedmen" mentioned in Acts 6:9, but this remains an unsupported conjecture.

and providing poor girls with dowries. Jewish education (pp. 112-13) was essentially religious education, designed to further the study of the written and oral law. Knowledge of the law was important to the performance of the law. The importance of education in Jewish life was indicated by the later dictum that a synagogue could be replaced by a schoolhouse, but a schoolhouse could not be replaced by a synagogue. Very often the synagogue building itself was the place of instruction.

Synagogue Service [338]

The synagogue service had two foci: prayer and the study of Scripture. Several sources describe the service itself primarily in terms of reading and study of the Scriptures.[339] This was the heart of the Sabbath service, but meetings were also held on market days (Monday and Thursday) for reading from the Scriptures. As indicated by its name "place of prayer," the second focus of the synagogue service was prayer. Prayer and confession of faith were also daily duties.

The basic structure of the synagogue service has remained the same to the present.[340] The meeting opened with a call to "Bless the Lord," followed by the Shema (see p. 561) with its two preliminary blessings and concluding profession of faith and praise. The passages of the Shema were chanted by the leader and congregation in unison (b. Sotah 30b).

The prayer *(tefillah)* of the public meeting was the Eighteen Benedictions *(Shemoneh Esre)*, also called *Amidah* ("standing," because it was said while standing). Rabbinic tradition assigns to Rabban Gamaliel II about A.D. 80 the requirement to recite them daily (Berakoth 4.3). The date of origin of the benedictions is disputed. Most may go back to pre-Christian times, but all in their present form are post-70, at least in basic structure, although exact wording varied. Different versions were in use in Palestine and Babylon, for example. Although originating at different periods, all are pre-Christian except twelve and thirteen (which fall between 90 and 117) and three, four, five, seven, and eighteen (which are first century but before 70). The basic structure as developed was three opening blessings or praises, twelve (now thirteen) petitions,

---

338. J. J. Petuchowski, ed., *Contributions to the Scientific Study of Jewish Liturgy* (New York, 1970); Joseph Heinemann, *Prayer in the Talmud: Forms and Patterns* (Berlin, 1977); R. S. Sarason, "On the Use of Method in the Study of the Jewish Liturgy," *Approaches to Ancient Judaism: Theory and Practice*, ed. W. S. Green (Missoula, Mont., 1978), 97-172; Lawrence Hoffman, *The Canonization of the Synagogue Service* (Notre Dame, 1979); Carmine DiSante, *Jewish Prayer: The Origins of the Christian Liturgy* (New York, 1991); Ismar Elbogen, *Jewish Liturgy: A Comprehensive History* (Philadelphia, 1993; German original, 1931); S. C. Reif, *Judaism and Hebrew Prayer: New Perspectives on Jewish Liturgical History* (Cambridge, 1993).

339. Philo, *Life of Moses* 2.39.215-16; Josephus, *Against Apion* 2.175; cf. the Theodotus inscription below, p. 577; Megillah 3.6.

340. Cf. Megillah 4.1-7 with the *Authorized Daily Prayer Book*.

SYNAGOGUE INSCRIPTION, Jerusalem
Theodotus, "a priest and ruler of the synagogue," set up this inscription to
commemorate his building of a synagogue for those who came to Jerusalem from
abroad (cf. Acts 6:9). *(Courtesy Israel Department of Antiquities and Museums)*

SYNAGOGUE, Capernaum
The 3d- or even 4th-c. synagogue at Capernaum occupied the site
of the 1st-c. synagogue. *(Werner Braun)*

and three thanksgivings. On Sabbaths and festivals the central section of twelve blessings was replaced by a single prayer suitable for the day. The order of the prayers became the basis of the Jewish prayer book of today. The set forms secured uniformity and participation by all, and the place for extemporaneous prayer gave room for individual needs. The Eighteen Benedictions in the Palestinian recension are as follows:

1. Blessed art Thou, O Lord, Our God and God of our fathers, God of Abraham, God of Isaac, and God of Jacob, the great, mighty, and revered God, God Most High, who art the Creator of heaven and earth, our Shield and the Shield of our fathers, our confidence from generation to generation. Blessed art Thou, O Lord, the Shield of Abraham!

2. Thou art mighty, who bringest low the proud, strong, and He that judgeth the ruthless, that liveth for ever, that raiseth the dead, that maketh the wind to blow, that sendeth down the dew; that sustaineth the living, that quickeneth the dead; in the twinkling of an eye Thou makest salvation to spring forth for us. Blessed art Thou, O Lord, who quickenest the dead!

3. Holy art Thou and Thy Name is to be feared, and there is no God beside Thee. Blessed art Thou, O Lord, the holy God!

4. O favor us, our Father, with knowledge from Thyself and understanding and discernment from Thy Torah. Blessed art Thou, O Lord, who vouchsafest knowledge!

5. Cause us to return, O Lord, unto Thee, and let us return anew [in repentance] in our days as in the former time. Blessed art Thou, O Lord, who delightest in repentance.

6. Forgive us, our Father, for we have sinned against Thee; blot out and cause our transgressions to pass from before Thine eyes, for great is Thy mercy. Blessed art Thou, O Lord, who dost abundantly forgive!

7. Look upon our affliction and plead our cause, and redeem us for the sake of Thy Name. Blessed art Thou, O Lord, the Redeemer of Israel!

8. Heal us, O Lord our God, from the pain of our heart; and weariness and sighing do Thou cause to pass away from us; and cause Thou to rise up healing for our wounds. Blessed art Thou, O Lord, who healest the sick of Thy people Israel!

9. Bless for us, O Lord our God, this year for our welfare, with every kind of the produce thereof, and bring near speedily the year of the end of our redemption; and give dew and rain upon the face of the earth and satisfy the world from the treasuries of Thy goodness, and do Thou give a blessing upon the work of our hands. Blessed art Thou, O Lord, who blessest the years!

10. Blow the great horn for our liberation, and lift a banner to gather our exiles. Blessed art Thou, O Lord, who gatherest the dispersed of Thy people Israel!

11. Restore our judges as at the first, and our counsellors as at the beginning; and reign Thou over us, Thou alone. Blessed art Thou, O Lord, who lovest judgment!

12. For apostates let there be no hope, and the dominion of arrogance [Rome] do Thou speedily root out in our days; and let the Nazarenes [Christians][341] and the heretics perish as in a moment, let them be blotted out of the book of the living and let them not be written with the righteous. Blessed art Thou, O Lord, who humblest the arrogant!

13. Towards the righteous proselytes may Thy tender mercies be stirred; and bestow a good reward upon us together with those that do Thy will. Blessed art Thou, O Lord, the trust of the righteous!

14. Be merciful, O Lord our God, in Thy great mercy towards Israel Thy people, and towards Jerusalem Thy City, and towards Zion the abiding place of Thy glory, and towards Thy glory, and towards Thy temple and Thy habitation, and towards the kingdom of the house of David, Thy righteous anointed one. Blessed art Thou, O God, God of David, the Builder of Jerusalem!

15. Hear, O Lord our God, the sound of our prayer and have mercy upon us, for a God gracious and merciful art Thou. Blessed art Thou, O Lord, who hearest prayer!

16. Accept us, O Lord our God, and dwell in Zion; and may Thy servants serve Thee in Jerusalem. Blessed art Thou, O Lord, whom in reverent fear we serve!

17. We give thanks to Thee, who art the Lord our God and the God of our fathers, for all the good things, the lovingkindness, and the mercy which Thou hast wrought and done with us and with our fathers before us: and if we said, Our feet slip, Thy lovingkindness, O Lord, upheld us. Blessed art Thou, O Lord, unto whom it is good to give thanks!

18. Bestow Thy peace upon Israel Thy people and upon Thy city and upon Thine inheritance and bless us, all of us together. Blessed art Thou, O Lord, who makest peace![342]

In the later synagogue service the Shema and *Tefillah* are followed by the priestly blessing (Num. 6:24-26) before the Scripture readings. The benediction was pronounced by the priests present with their hands raised (Sotah 7.6). If no priest was present, the benediction took the form, "Our God . . . bless us

---

341. See p. 491n.172 for reservations concerning this being original to the prayer.

342. According to the text reconstructed by G. Dalman, *Die Worte Jesu* (Leipzig, 1898). Translation based on C. W. Dugmore, *The Influence of the Synagogue upon the Divine Office* (Oxford, 1944), 115-24. Different translations may be found in F. C. Grant, *Ancient Judaism and the New Testament* (New York, 1959), 46-48, and Emil Schürer, *The History of the Jewish People in the Age of Jesus Christ*, ed. G. Vermes, et al. (Edinburgh, 1979), 2:460-61; ibid., 456-58 and Dugmore also give the Babylonian recension.

with the threefold blessing . . . which was spoken by Aaron and his sons, the priests. . . ."

There were two readings, one from the Torah *(parashah* or *seder)* and one from the Prophets *(haftarah),* in the first-century service; there is a lack of evidence for a separate reading from the Writings. The cycle of readings apparently was not yet fixed in the first century, but soon there was established a cycle whereby the Torah was read through in three years in Palestine and in one year in Babylon. This calls into question efforts to analyze New Testament books in terms of the Jewish cycle of readings.[343] After the readings from the Torah were set, the passage from the Prophets was chosen on the basis of linguistic affinity (less often by a common topic) with the opening verses of the Torah passage, with the purpose of bringing a message of comfort. On feast days and other special Sabbaths there were special readings related to the day.

The Scriptures were read in Hebrew, which in many places was imperfectly (if at all) understood by the majority of the people. Hence, a running translation was provided in the vernacular. These paraphrases, the Targums, were in Aramaic in Palestine and lands to the east. The reading was from the Septuagint in Greek-speaking communities. Although the Targums were eventually reduced to writing (see pp. 499-500), the original requirements were that they remain oral so as not to be put on the same level with the written law. Certain restrictions were placed on the targumist: the translation was not to be prepared beforehand; he could have no notes before him; the translation was not to be literal but was to give the people the sense of the passage (b. Kiddushin 49a). Certain common interpretations became an established feature of the Targums.

A sermon regularly accompanied the readings, unless no one present was qualified. The sermon might be topical, drawing its text from something in the reading, or expository, developing the meaning of the text and applying it to the contemporary situation. It was characteristic to associate by key words passages from the Law, Prophets, and Writings. The style of preaching as known from the Midrash (pp. 498-99) has been found to underlie the structure of some parts of the New Testament,[344] but the rabbinic examples are later.

Other prayers and exhortations were added on certain occasions. Sometimes alms were collected.

The present synagogue service begins with the chanting of the Psalms and other hymns, the use of which seems to be as early as the beginning of the

343. R. G. Finch, *The Synagogue Lectionary and the New Testament* (London, 1939); Leon Morris, *The New Testament and the Jewish Lectionaries* (London, 1964), is perhaps too skeptical; J. Mann and I. Sonne, *The Bible as Read and Preached in the Old Synagogue,* 2 vols. (Cincinnati, 1966); J. Heinemann, "The Triennial Lectionary Cycle," *JJS* 19 (1968):41-48.

344. P. Borgen, *Bread from Heaven* (Leiden, 1965); J. W. Bowker, "Speeches in Acts; a Study in Proem and Yelammedenu Form," *NTS* 14 (1967):96-111; Wilhelm Wuellner, "Haggadic Homily Genre in 1 Corinthians 1–3," *JBL* 89 (1970):199-204.

Christian era. The Hallel Psalms (113–118) are best attested from rabbinic literature for this period, and b. Sotah 30b (cf. Sotah 5.4) describes different forms of
responsorial recitation. Philo (*Contemplative Life* 80, 83-87) gives a detailed description of the singing of Psalms and other hymns by the Therapeutae, presumably a more developed expression of synagogue practice. The *Thanksgiving
Hymns* from Qumran may have been written for the community's use.

Organization

A synagogue could be formed wherever ten men wanted to organize one. Any
male could read the Scriptures, translate, preach, or lead the prayers and
Shema. No special class had a monopoly on the conduct of the service.

The "ruler of the synagogue" *(archisynagogos)* in Greek sources or "head
of the assembly" *(rosh hakeneseth)* in Hebrew sources may refer to the head of
the community as well as to the one who presides over and made arrangements
for the services of the synagogue, designating the persons to perform each
function (cf. Acts 13:15). In addition, he might also assume responsibility for
maintaining the traditional Jewish life and teaching (Luke 13:15; Acts 18:17).
Sometimes the term appears in the plural (as Acts 13:15), and sometimes it appears as more an honorary title for benefactors of the synagogue.[345]

The "servant" of the synagogue (Heb. *ḥazzan;* Gk. *hyperetēs*) was a salaried person who appears in many varied roles in different sources: the attendant with charge of the scrolls of Scripture (Luke 4:17, 20; cf. Sotah 7.7 and
Yoma 7.1) and so with functions in the service (Sukkah 4.6); a sexton with care
of the building and its furniture; a learned man who was the targumist and
schoolteacher; an officer of the community who administered the stripes on
those punished by the court (Makkoth 3.12).[346] One man was probably not all
of these things, but the functions varied at different times and at different
places according to the size and needs of the community.

The *archisynagogos* and *ḥazzan* have been seen as the precedents for the
offices of bishop and deacon in the church. There are points of similarity,
mostly arising from comparable needs, but the Christian functionaries certainly soon developed in their own distinctive ways.

The relation of the "ruler of the synagogue" to the community organization of the Jews is not clear. His position seems not to have given him a voice in
the administration of the community's affairs unless he was otherwise a member of the *gerousia*, but in some inscriptions the head of the synagogue was also
a member of the ruling council. Practice probably varied (with the influence of

---

345. T. Rajak and D. Noy, "Archisynagogoi: Office, Title, and Social Status in the Greco-
Jewish Synagogue," *JRS* 83 (1993):75-93.

346. H. I. Sky, *Development of the Office of Hazzan Through the Talmudic Period* (San
Fransicso, 1992).

a person as well as at different places) whether the ruler was a figurehead or the dominant personality.

BIBLIOGRAPHY

Tos. Sukkah 2.10 (Translations of Early Documents, Series III).

Krauss, S. *Synagogale Altertümer*. Berlin, 1922.

Gutmann, J., ed. *The Synagogue: Studies in Origins, Archaeology, and Architecture.* New York, 1975.

Gutmann, J., ed. *Ancient Synagogues: The State of Research.* Chico, Calif., 1981.

Levine, Lee I., ed. *The Synagogue in Late Antiquity.* Philadelphia, 1987.

Fine, Steven, ed. *Sacred Realm: The Emergence of the Synagogue in the Ancient World.* Oxford, 1996.

Fine, Steven. *This Holy Place: On the Sanctity of the Synagogue during the Greco-Roman Period.* Notre Dame, 1998.

Binder Donald D. *Into the Temple Courts: The Place of Synagogues in the Second-Temple Period.* Atlanta, 1999.

Fine, Steven, ed. *Jews, Christians, and Polytheists in the Ancient Synagogue.* London, 1999.

Kee, Howard Clark, ed. *Evolution of the Synagogue: Problems and Progress.* Harrisburg, 1999.

Levine, Lee I. *The Ancient Synagogue: The First Thousand Years.* New Haven, 2000.

Runeson, Anders. *The Origins of the Synagogue: A Social-Historical Study.* Stockholm, 2001.

6. CHRISTIANITY IN THE ANCIENT WORLD

BIBLIOGRAPHY

MacMullen, Ramsay, and E. N. Lane, eds. *Paganism and Christianity, 100-425 c.e.: A Sourcebook*. Minneapolis, 1992.

Lee, A. D. *Pagans and Christians in Late Antiquity: A Sourcebook*. London, 2000.

Harnack, A. *Mission and Expansion of Christianity*. London, 1908.

Nock, A. D. *Conversion*. Oxford, 1933.

Klauser, T., ed. *Reallexikon für Antike und Christentum*. Stuttgart, 1950–.

Cadbury, H. J. *The Book of Acts in History*. New York, 1955.

Nock, A. D. *Early Gentile Christianity and its Hellenistic Background*. New York, 1964.

Simon, M. *La civilisation de l'antiquité et le Christianisme*. Paris, 1972.

Markus, R. A. *Christianity in the Roman World*. London, 1974.

Kim, Seyoon. *The Origin of Paul's Gospel*. Grand Rapids, 1982.

Benko, Stephen. *Pagan Rome and the Early Christians*. Bloomington, Ind., 1984.

Nash, Ronald. *Christianity and the Hellenistic World*. Grand Rapids, 1984.

Sardi, M. *The Christians and the Roman Empire*. Norman, Okla., 1986.

Ferguson, E., ed. *Christianity in Relation to Jews, Greeks, and Romans*. Recent Studies in Early Christianity, Vol. 2. New York, 1999.

Esler, Philip R., ed. *The Early Christian World*. 2 vols. London, 2000.

Chadwick, Henry. *The Church in Ancient Society: From Galilee to Gregory the Great*. Oxford, 2001.

IT is possible in this chapter to address only a few specific topics and to provide a general orientation, although we will also highlight some information from the other chapters. I have deliberately excluded an introduction of the

New Testament writings and other early Christian literature. Rather, I intend to introduce additional sources not elsewhere covered, to point to the complexities of the historical setting of early Christianity, to summarize the varieties of early Christian expressions and the different accommodations by and responses to Christian preaching, and then to review what the background means for the study of early Christianity and to indicate its special place in its milieu.

LITERARY REFERENCES TO CHRISTIANITY
IN NON-CHRISTIAN SOURCES

This section merely lists references, since many of these passages are quoted or discussed elsewhere in this book. The page number accompanying the reference locates this quotation or discussion.

Latin Authors

Suetonius, *Claudius* 25.4 (p. 32); *Nero* 16.2 (pp. 593-94).
Tacitus, *Annals* 15.44 (pp. 593, 602).
Pliny the Younger, *Epistles* 10.96, 97 (pp. 594-95, 604-5).

Greek Authors

Lucian, *On the Death of Peregrinus* 11-14, 16 (pp. 596-98); *Alexander the False Prophet* 25, 38 (pp. 218-19).
Celsus, *True Doctrine* (preserved in quotations by Origen, *Against Celsus*) (pp. 598-99).
Epictetus, *Discourses* 4.7.6 (p. 600); 2.9.19-122 (?).
Marcus Aurelius, *Meditations* 11.3 (p. 600).
Galen. See R. Walzer, *Galen on Jews and Christians* (London, 1949) (p. 601).

Jewish Sources in Greek

Josephus, *Ant.* 18.5.2 [117-19] (p. 487); 18.3.3 [63-64] (p. 488); 20.9.1 [200] (p. 488).

Jewish Sources in Hebrew and Aramaic

Benediction 12 [11] (p. 579).
See the bibliography below.

BIBLIOGRAPHY

Den Boer, W., ed. *Scriptorum paganorum I–IV saec. de Christianis testimonia.* Leiden, 1965.

Herrmann, L. *Chrestos. Témoignages Païens et juifs sur le Christianisme au 1er siècle.* Brussels, 1970.

Bruce, F. F. *Jesus and Christian Origins Outside the New Testament.* Grand Rapids, 1974.

Stroker, W. D. *Extracanonical Sayings of Jesus.* Atlanta, 1989.

Morrice, William. *Hidden Sayings of Jesus: Words Attributed to Jesus Outside the Four Gospels.* Peabody, 1997.

Van Voorst, Robert E. *Jesus Outside the New Testament: An Introduction to the Ancient Evidence.* Grand Rapids, 2000.

Herford, R. T. *Christianity in Talmud and Midrash.* London, 1903. Reprint. Clifton, N.J., 1966.

Lauterbach, J. "Jesus in the Talmud." In *Rabbinic Essays.* Cincinnati, 1951.

Bammel, E. "Christian Origins in Jewish Tradition." *NTS* 13 (1966/67):317-35.

ARCHAEOLOGICAL REMAINS BEARING ON EARLY CHRISTIAN HISTORY

Inscriptions

The Delphi Inscription of Gallio.[1] Seven fragments of an inscription containing a rescript of the emperor Claudius were found at Delphi, Greece. The crucial dating formula (with probable restorations in brackets) may be translated as follows:

> Tiberius [Claudius] Caesar Augustus Germanicus . . . [in his tribunician] power [year 12, acclaimed emperor] the 26th time, father of the country. . . . [Lucius] Junius Gallio my friend and [pro]consul [of Achaia wrote]. . . .

From other sources it is known that Claudius's twenty-sixth acclamation as *imperator* must have occurred between the end of A.D. 51 and August 1, 52. At that time Gallio was governor of Achaia. Since governors of senatorial provinces entered upon their office in the summer, about July 1, and normally served for one year, Gallio's governorship must have occurred between the summer of 51 and the summer of 52. The probable meaning of Acts 18:12 is that it was shortly after the assumption of his office that the Jews brought charges against Paul,

---

1. Adolf Deissmann, *Paul* (1927; repr. New York, 1957), 261-86; Jack Finegan, *Handbook of Biblical Chronology* (Princeton, 1964), 316-19; J. Murphy-O'Connor, *St. Paul's Corinth* (Wilmington, Del., 1983), 141-52, 173-76.

GALLIO INSCRIPTION, from Delphi
A rescript of the emperor Claudius mentioning Gallio, the proconsul of Achaia,
by its dating formula permits the dating of Paul's stay in Corinth to the early 50s.
(Courtesy École Française d'archéologie, Athens)

that is, the summer or fall of 51. Since Paul's ministry in Corinth lasted eighteen
months (Acts 18:11) and his departure was some time after the Gallio episode,
we can place his arrival in Corinth early in 50. The importance of this information is that it gives the one fixed date for an absolute chronology of Paul's life
and one of the few relatively certain dates in New Testament history.

    The Nazareth Inscription Against Grave Robbing.[2]

      Ordinance of Caesar. It is my pleasure that graves and tombs remain un-
disturbed in perpetuity for those who have made them for the cult of their

2. F. deZulueta, "Violation of Sepulture in Palestine at the Beginning of the Christian Era,"
JRS 22 (1932):184-97, whose translation is quoted, finds an Augustan date more probable and con-
sequently a different provenance from Nazareth; M. P. Charlesworth, *Documents Illustrating the
Reigns of Claudius and Nero* (Cambridge, 1939), 15; Bruce M. Metzger, "The Nazareth Inscription
Once Again," in *Jesus und Paulus*, ed. E. E. Ellis and E. Grasser (Göttingen, 1975), 221-38, repr. in
New Testament Studies: Philological, Versional, and Patristic (Leiden, 1980), 75-92; H. F. Stander,
"The Nazareth Inscription Revisited," *Acta Patristica et Byzantina* 15 (2004):254-66.

ancestors or children or members of their house. If, however, any man lay information that another has either demolished them, or has in any other way extracted the buried, or has maliciously transferred them to other places in order to wrong them, or has displaced the sealing or other stones, against such a one I order that a trial be instituted, as in respect of the gods, so in regard to the cult of mortals. For it shall be much more obligatory to honor the buried. Let it be absolutely forbidden for any one to disturb them. In case of contravention I desire that the offender be sentenced to capital punishment on charge of violation of sepulture.

The ordinance (probably a rescript) says nothing about Christianity, and it represents the normal attitude of the ancient world against grave-robbing (which was nonetheless often enough done to be a subject for concern) and the normal pagan terminology. On the other hand, the story reported in Matthew 28:11-15 and the place where the inscription was reportedly found have provoked conjectures. Was the story of the missing body and its significance for the origins of the Christian movement, which was so disturbing Jews throughout the empire by Claudius's time, behind this reaffirmation of traditional attitudes and the setting up of this inscription in Nazareth? We will probably never know, and any relevance of this ordinance to Christian origins is at best conjectural. We do not need official Roman testimony to know the centrality of the resurrection in Christian preaching. If we had it, it would only indicate how early this came to governmental attention as a matter of concern.

Papyri

Letter of Claudius to the Alexandrians, A.D. 41.[3] Claudius's disposition of the controversy between Greeks and Jews over political rights in Alexandria (which occasioned the embassy headed by Philo to Rome under Caligula [p. 479]) has great importance for first-century Jewish history and implications for the legal status of Diaspora communities in general.[4] The following passage from the letter is noted here because of the claim that it contains an allusion to Christian missionary activity:

> I explicitly order the Jews not to agitate for more privileges than they formerly possessed, and not in the future to send out a separate embassy as if they lived in a separate city, a thing unprecedented, and not to force their way into gymnasiarchic or cosmetic games, while enjoying their own privi-

3. P. Lond., 1912 (A. S. Hunt and C. C. Edgar, *Select Papyri* [Cambridge, Mass., 1934], vol. 2, no. 212); see H. I. Bell, *Jews and Christians in Egypt* (London, 1924), 23-29.

4. V. Tcherikover, *Hellenistic Civilization and the Jews* (Philadelphia, 1961), 296-332. See p. 429 above.

leges and sharing a great abundance of advantages in a city not their own, and not to bring in or admit Jews who come down the river from Syria or Egypt, a proceeding which will compel me to conceive serious suspicions; otherwise I will by all means take vengeance on them as fomenters of what is a general plague infecting the whole world.

Claudius seems often to have had to deal with "the Jewish problem," frequently acerbated by the disturbances in the Jewish communities caused by Christian preaching (cf. Suetonius, *Claudius* 25). Christian preachers likely reached Alexandria from Palestine and Syria, and that as early as Claudius (Acts 18:24, D text), but it is doubtful that there is a reference to such in this passage, in spite of the language about fomenting "a . . . plague infecting the whole world" (cf. Acts 24:5).

Christian Papyri.[5] The papyri have furnished our earliest written remains of Christianity. There are now several papyri dated as early as the third century containing parts of the New Testament. Quite famous is the oldest known fragment of a New Testament book, the John Rylands fragment of John (P52), dated before A.D. 150, which has given a *terminus ante quem* for the writing of the Fourth Gospel. Many of the Christian papyri represent noncanonical documents, only some of which were previously known. Their addition to the knowledge of Christian origins will be variously assessed. The number is subject to constant increase with new finds, so the bibliographical note gives reference works where information about these papyri may be found.

Coins

The extensive coinage of the early Roman empire affords numerous points of contact with the New Testament and its historical background. Recent studies show the possibilities.[6]

---

5. C. H. Roberts, "P. Yale 1 and the Early Christian Book," *American Studies in Papyrology* 1 (New Haven, 1966):25-28; Mario Naldini, *Il Christianesimo in Egitto: Lettere private nei papiri dei secoli* II–IV (Florence, 1968); J. Finegan, *Hidden Records of the Life of Jesus* (Philadelphia, 1969); K. Treu, "Christliche Papyri, 1940–1967," *Archiv für Papyrusforschung* 19 (1969):169-206 and following volumes; K. Aland, *Repertorium der griechischen christlichen Papyri* (Berlin, 1976); J. van Haelst, *Catalogue des papyrus littéraires juifs et chrétiens* (Paris, 1976); E. A. Judge and S. R. Pickering, "Papyrus Documentation of Church and Community in Egypt to the Mid-Fourth Century," *Jahrbuch für Antike und Christentum* 20 (1977):47-71.

6. An older work is J. Y. Akerman, *Numismatic Illustrations of the New Testament* (repr.; Chicago, 1966); more recent is Larry J. Kreitzer, *Striking New Images: Roman Imperial Coinage and the New Testament World* (Sheffield, 1996); for resources see bibliography, pp. 94-95.

BIBLIOGRAPHY

Finegan, Jack *The Archaeology of the New Testament: The Life of Jesus and the Beginnings of the Early Church.* Rev. ed. Princeton, 1992.

McRay, John. *Archaeology and the New Testament.* Grand Rapids, 1991.

SOME CLAIMED ARCHAEOLOGICAL REMAINS OF EARLY CHRISTIANITY

It is now generally accepted that there are no securely datable Christian archaeological remains before about A.D. 200. This applies to the catacomb paintings[7] and the identifiable Christian inscriptions.[8] There are some remains for which a first-century date is certain but the Christian character of which is dubious.

The *Rotas-Sator* Word Square

This Latin word square is as follows:

```
R  O  T  A  S
O  P  E  R  A
T  E  N  E  T
A  R  E  P  O
S  A  T  O  R
```

Examples have been found as far apart as Cirencester in Britain and Dura Europus in Mesopotamia; two at Pompeii must date before A.D. 79. The

---

7. J. Wilpert, *Die Malereien der Katakomben Roms* (Freiburg, 1903) claimed a second century date for some of the paintings, but recent study has disproved this. For current statements on the origins of Christian art and on the catacombs, see Paul Corby Finney, *The Invisible God: The Earliest Christians on Art* (Oxford, 1994); idem, "Art," and "Catacombs," in E. Ferguson, et al., eds., *Encyclopedia of Early Christianity,* 2d ed. (New York, 1997), 1.120-26, 220-223; V. F. Nicolai, F. Bisconti, and D. Massoleni, *Les Catacombes Chrétiennes de Rome* (Turnhout, 2000); L. V. Rutgers, *Subterranean Rome: In Search of the Roots of Christianity in the Catacombs of the Eternal City* (Leuven, 2000).

8. E. Diehl, *Inscriptiones Latinae Christianae Veteres,* 4 vols. (Berlin, 1961); H. Lietzmann, N. A. Bees, and G. Sotiriu, eds., *Corpus der Griechisch-Christlichen Inschriften von Hellas* (*Christianikai Epigraphai tes Hellados* [Gk.]), vol. 1 (Athens, 1978); W. M. Calder, ed., *Monumenta Asiae Minoris Antiqua,* 8 vols. (Manchester, 1928–1962); Elsa Gibson, *The "Christians for Christians" Inscriptions of Phrygia* (Missoula, Mont., 1978). For further bibliography, see Michael P. McHugh, "Inscriptions," in E. Ferguson, *et al.,* eds., *Encyclopedia of Early Christianity,* 2d ed. (New York, 1997), 1.574-76.

meaning is not clear and scholars have offered many different interpretations. Its connection with Christianity rests on the rearrangement of the letters to spell Pater Noster ("Our Father" in Latin of the Lord's Prayer) twice in the form of a cross, with the N of Noster forming the point of intersection and with an A and an O left over for each cross bar. This rearrangement, although striking, appears to be coincidental. It demands assumptions of a liturgical use of the Lord's Prayer in Latin in the first century, the existence of a Christian community at Pompeii before its destruction, the use of the cross this early in Christianity, and the representation of the Greek letters *alpha* and *omega* by an *A* and *O*. Even if the Pater Noster interpretation is correct, a better case can be made for a Jewish origin.[9] A good case also can be made for the Mithraic origin of the word square.[10] The nature of the Latin language is ideal for producing word squares from which other words and phrases can be constructed, so it is not remarkable that apparently Christian formulae can be abstracted.[11]

The "Cross" at Herculaneum[12]

A second-floor apartment in Herculaneum (destroyed by Vesuvius in 79) contained a chamber in which on one wall was a rectangle covered with white plaster. In the plaster was engraved a sign in the shape of a Latin cross, 0.43 meter high and 0.365 meter wide. A chest on the floor underneath and slightly to one side of the "cross" was interpreted as an altar and the room therefore as a Christian cult place. Further consideration, however, has given a more utilitarian purpose: the imprint in the plaster was left by wooden brackets for a wall cabinet or perhaps a shelf or mantel with a supporting upright piece.

Other supposed "evidence" for Christianity at Pompeii and Herculaneum before A.D. 79 seems similarly capable of alternative, more likely interpretations.

9. Duncan Fishwick, "On the Origin of the Rotas-Sator Square," *HTR* 57 (1964):39-53.

10. Walter O. Moeller, *The Mithraic Origin and Meanings of the Rotas-Sator Square* (Leiden, 1973).

11. W. Baines, "The Rotas-Sator Square: A New Investigation," *NTS* 33 (1987):469-76. The Christian interpretation is reaffirmed by K. Aland, "Noch ein-mal: der ROTAS/SATOR-rebus," in *Text and Testimony*, ed. T. Baarda et al. (Kampen, 1988), 9-23.

12. L. de Bruyne, "La 'crux interpretum' di Ercolano," *Rivista di Archeologia Cristiana* 21 (1945):281ff.; P. de Jerphanion, "La Croix d'Herculaneum?" *Orientalia Christiana Periodica* 7 (1941):5ff. The Christian meaning is defended by L. W. Barnard, "The 'Cross of Herculaneum' Reconsidered," *The New Testament Age: Essays in Honor of Bo Reicke*, ed. W. C. Weinrich (Macon, Ga., 1984).

Ossuaries[13]

Ossuaries from a tomb complex in the vicinity of the Talpioth suburb of Jerusalem have been thought to provide the earliest evidence of Christianity in the land of its birth. Since these ossuaries come from the middle of the first century, their evidence would be sensational indeed. One of the ossuaries was marked with a charcoal plus-shaped symbol on each of its four sides; the same sign has appeared on other ossuaries found on the Mount of Olives. They are inscribed with Hebrew names familiar from the New Testament: "Simeon Barsaba," "Miriam, daughter of Simeon," an abbreviation of Mattathias. Most striking are two Greek inscriptions: one in charcoal, *Iēsous iou* ("Jesus woe"), and one incised, *Iēsous alōth*. The latter is difficult to interpret: it may be a lamentation, and it has even been interpreted as a transliteration from Hebrew, "Jesus, (let him who rests here) arise."[14] The *iou* and *alōth* may have been variants of Yahweh and Sabaoth; at least the former occurred with this meaning in the magical papyri. Actually, it seems both should be read as personal names, "Jesus, son of Judas," and "Jesus, son of Aloth." Most of the names on the ossuaries were common enough Jewish names that their identity with any New Testament figures is problematic. Even the name Jesus itself (Gk. of the Heb. Joshua) was quite common.

The plus- and X-shaped crosses have been interpreted as the Hebrew letter *taw*, the sign of Yahweh in Ezekiel 9:4ff., and thus perhaps of apotropaic significance to protect the bones of the deceased against demonic malevolence or a general expression of faith in deliverance through the use of the sign of God's protection in Ezekiel's vision (cf. Rev. 7:3). The mark occurs in Jewish funerary settings (including a Jewish catacomb in Rome) with some frequency. On the Jerusalem ossuaries it may have had the utilitarian purpose of marking correspondence of lid and body of the ossuary.

Although the earlier claim to have found "the earliest records of Christianity" lacked proof, it was not out of the question that some of the ossuaries found in the vicinity of Jerusalem contained the bones of believers in Jesus. Greater probability attaches to a plain and now empty ossuary, whose authenticity seems assured, inscribed, "James, son of Joseph, brother of Jesus."[15] Unfortunately the location of the find is unknown. This plus the fact that the names were common makes impossible a certain identification with the family of Jesus of Nazareth, but this particular combination of relationships is striking.

13. E. L. Sukenik, "The Earliest Records of Christianity," *AJA* 51 (1947):3-30; D. Fishwick, "The Talpioth Ossuaries Again," *NTS* 10 (1963):49-61; Erich Dinkler, "Comments on the History of the Symbol of the Cross," *Journal for Theology and the Church*, ed. Robert W. Funk (1965), 1:124-46; R. H. Smith, "The Cross Marks on Jewish Ossuaries," *Palestine Exploration Quarterly* 106 (1974):53-66; J. P. Kane, "The Ossuary Inscriptions of Jerusalem," *JSS* 23 (1978):268-82.

14. B. Gustafsson, "The Oldest Graffiti in the History of the Church?" *NTS* (1956/57):65-69.

15. Andre Lemaire, "Burial Box of James the Brother of Jesus," *Biblical Archaeology Review* 28 (2002):24-33, 70.

The Tomb of Peter[16]

The excavations under St. Peter's basilica in the Vatican and the discovery of bones claimed to be those of Peter have created an enormous bibliography. From the latter half of the second century there was a memorial *(tropaion)* on Vatican hill commemorating Peter's martyrdom, but not definitely the site of his grave (Caius of Rome, cited by Eusebius, *Church History* 2.25.6-7). This appears now to have been certainly located by the excavations under St. Peter's and has been restored. The identification of the bones as Peter's is a more difficult and seemingly insoluble matter, further clouded by confessional loyalties. The bones could be but are not necessarily his. Literary and archaeological evidence do confirm a ministry in Rome by both Paul and Peter and their separate deaths there under Nero.[17]

BIBLIOGRAPHY

Schneider, A. M. "Die ältesten Denkmäler der Römischen Kirche." *Festschrift zur Feier des Zweihundertjahrigen Bestehens der Akademie der Wissenschaften in Göttingen* 2 (1951):166-98.

Dinkler, E. "Älteste Christliche Denkmäler." *Signum Crucis.* Tübingen, 1967. Pp. 134-78.

Andresen, C. *Einführung in die Christliche Archäologie.* Göttingen, 1971.

Snyder, Graydon F. *Ante Pacem: Archaeological Evidence of Church Life Before Constantine.* Macon, Ga., 1985; new ed. 2003. (Collects the genuine archaeological evidence.)

Frend, W. H. C. *The Archaeology of Early Christianity: A History.* London, 1995.

ATTITUDES OF PAGANS TOWARD CHRISTIANS

Pagan comments on and criticism of Christianity are significant for several reasons: what they tell us about the viewpoints and values of the society into which Christianity came; what they tell us about how Christianity and Christians were perceived by others and so what was viewed as distinctive and what was considered commendable or disturbing (perception by others, as well as

---

16. J. M. C. Toynbee and J. B. Ward-Perkins, *The Shrine of St. Peter and the Vatican Excavations* (London, 1956); Angelus A. DeMarco, *The Tomb of Saint Peter: A Representative and Annotated Bibliography of the Excavations* (Leiden, 1964); Graydon F. Snyder, "Survey and 'New' Thesis on the Bones of Peter," *BA* 32 (1969):2-24.

17. H. Chadwick, "St. Peter and St. Paul in Rome: the Problem of the Memoria Apostolorum ad Catacumbas," *JTS* 8 (1957):30-52; E. Kirschbaum, *The Tombs of St. Peter and St. Paul* (New York, 1959); O. Cullmann, *Peter* (2d ed.; London, 1962); D. W. O'Conner, *Peter in Rome: The Literary, Liturgical, and Archaeological Evidence* (New York, 1969).

self-perception, is part of a historical understanding of persons and movements); and what they tell us about the significant issues of the time.

When Christianity was first mentioned in the literature of the Roman upper classes in the early second century, it was described as a superstition (*superstitio;* cf. Acts 25:19). The word had connotations of "credulity," but it especially denoted the emotional personal religions from the east in contrast to *religio,* which was the due respect for the traditional public religion. Seneca contrasted proper versus unacceptable practices, "*Religio* honors the gods, *superstitio* dishonors them" (*On Mercy* 2.5.1).

Tacitus described the great fire of Rome in A.D. 64 and the subsequent persecution of Christians by Nero:

> But all human efforts, all the lavish gifts of the emperor, and the propitiations of the gods, did not banish the sinister belief that the conflagration was the result of an order. Consequently, to get rid of the report, Nero fastened the guilt and inflicted the most exquisite tortures on a class hated for their abominations *[flagitia],* called Christians by the populace. Christus, from whom the name had its origin, suffered the extreme penalty during the reign of Tiberius at the hands of one of our procurators, Pontius Pilatus, and a deadly superstition, thus checked for the moment, again broke out not only in Judaea, the source of the evil, but also in Rome, where all things hideous and shameful from every part of the world meet and become popular. Accordingly, an arrest was first made of all who confessed; then, upon their information, an immense multitude was convicted, not so much of the crime of arson, as of hatred of the human race. Mockery of every sort was added to their deaths. Covered with the skins of beasts, they were torn by dogs and perished, or were nailed to crosses, or were doomed to the flames. These served to illuminate the night when daylight failed. Nero had thrown open his gardens for the spectacle, and was exhibiting a show in the circus, while he mingled with the people in the dress of a charioteer or drove about in a chariot. Hence, even for criminals who deserved extreme and exemplary punishment, there arose a feeling of compassion; for it was not, as it seemed, for the public good, but to glut one man's cruelty, that they were being destroyed. (*Annals* 15.44.2-8)[18]

Tacitus did not believe the charge of arson, but he had no regard for Christianity: it was "hideous and shameful," a "deadly superstition" from his aristocratic standpoint. He had the basic facts of its origin straight. The charge of being enemies of all other peoples had been made against Jews (Diodorus Siculus 34.1.1-2; Tacitus, *Histories* 5.5; Josephus, *Against Apion* 2.121, 258-59) and was extended to Christians as sharing with them the same characteristic of withdrawal from the activities of pagan society. Suetonius's reference to Chris-

---

18. J. Stevenson, *A New Eusebius* (London, 1957), 2-3.

tianity was a capsule report of the same event: "Punishment was inflicted on the Christians, a class of men given to a new and wicked superstition" (*Life of Nero* 16.2). Christians continued to be a convenient scapegoat to blame for political problems and natural disasters for a long time thereafter (cf. Tertullian, *Apology* 40).

Pliny, the Roman governor of Bithynia, in his correspondence with Trajan (c. A.D. 112), also labeled Christianity a "superstition," but while learning that much of what was said about the Christians was not true, he learned something else about them for which he did not care. Their obstinacy (*contumacia*) was no less a threat to Roman order and rule than their beliefs were to traditional religion.

It is my custom, lord emperor, to refer to you all questions whereof I am in doubt. Who can better guide me when I am at a stand, or enlighten me if I am in ignorance? In investigations of Christians I have never taken part; hence I do not know what is the crime usually punished or investigated, or what allowances are made. So I have had no little uncertainty whether there is any distinction of age, or whether the very weakest offenders are treated exactly like the stronger; whether pardon is given to those who repent, or whether a man who has once been a Christian gains nothing by having ceased to be such; whether punishment attaches to the mere name apart from secret crimes [*flagitia*], or to the secret crimes connected with the name. Meantime this is the course I have taken with those who were accused before me as Christians. I asked them whether they were Christians, and if they confessed, I asked them a second and third time with threats of punishment. If they kept to it, I ordered them for execution; for I held no question that whatever it was that they admitted, in any case obstinacy and unbending perversity deserve to be punished. There were others of the like insanity; but as these were Roman citizens, I noted them down to be sent to Rome.

Before long, as is often the case, the mere fact that the charge was taken notice of made it commoner, and several distinct cases arose. An unsigned paper was presented, which gave the names of many. As for those who said that they neither were nor ever had been Christians, I thought it right to let them go, since they recited a prayer to the gods at my dictation, made supplication with incense and wine to your statue, which I had ordered to be brought into court for the purpose together with the images of the gods, and moreover cursed Christ — things which (so it is said) those who are really Christians cannot be made to do. Others who were named by the informer said that they were Christians and then denied it, explaining that they had been, but had ceased to be such, some three years ago, some a good many years, and a few even twenty. All these too both worshipped your statue and the images of the gods, and cursed Christ.

They maintained, however, that the amount of their fault or error had been this, that it was their habit on a fixed day to assemble before daylight and recite by turns a form of words to Christ as a god; and that they bound themselves with an oath, not for any crime, but not to commit theft or robbery or adultery, not to break their word, and not to deny a deposit when demanded. After this was done, their custom was to depart, and to meet again to take food, but ordinary and harmless food; and even this (they said) they had given up doing after the issue of my edict, by which in accordance with your commands I had forbidden the existence of clubs. On this I considered it the more necessary to find out from two maid-servants who were called deaconesses, and that by torments, how far this was true; but I discovered nothing else than a perverse and extravagant superstition. I therefore adjourned the case and hastened to consult you. The matter seemed to me worth deliberation, especially on account of the number of those in danger; for many of all ages and every rank, and also of both sexes are brought into present or future danger. The contagion of that superstition has penetrated not the cities only, but the villages and country; yet it seems possible to stop it and set it right. At any rate it is certain enough that the almost deserted temples begin to be resorted to, that long disused ceremonies of religion are restored, and that fodder for victims finds a market, whereas buyers till now were very few. From this it may easily be supposed, what a multitude of men can be reclaimed, if there be a place for repentance. (*Ep.* 10.96)[19]

This letter, along with Trajan's reply (which will be quoted in the next section), is of fundamental importance for determining the legal status of Christianity and will be more fully discussed in that connection. At this point we should note that Pliny found Christianity to be only a "perverse and extravagant superstition," but he was disturbed that, as with other private associations, it might be a center of sedition. His main interest was a policy that might encourage apostasy, since his examination had not revealed any of the "secret crimes" supposedly associated with being a Christian.

These "secret crimes" are known from the writings of the Christian apologists. Athenagoras stated the charges against Christians succinctly: "Three things are alleged against us: atheism, Thyestean feasts, Oedipodean intercourse" (*Plea* 3). The charge of atheism, surprising to modern ears, is a special form of the charge of being a superstition and not a religion. It meant that Christians did not worship the state gods and the popular gods of paganism. The same charge was made against the Epicureans, who did not deny the existence of the gods (pp. 373-75). The Thyestean banquets (cannibalism) and Oedipodean intercourse (incest) are no less shocking. These charges have their broader background in the suspicions held of a foreign, aloof, and despised people. They had their immediate basis in a misunderstanding of Christian

19. J. Stevenson, *A New Eusebius* (London, 1957), 13-14.

terminology and practice and perhaps a confusion of Christians with certain libertine Gnostic groups.[20] Minucius Felix gives the version in which the story of Christian initiation circulated:

> An infant covered over with meal, that it may deceive the unwary, is placed before him who is to be stained with their rites: this infant is slain by the young pupil who has been urged on as if to harmless blows on the surface of the meal, with dark and secret wounds. Thirstily — O horror! — they lick up its blood; eagerly they divide its limbs. . . . On a solemn day they assemble at the feast, with all their children, sisters, mothers, people of every sex and of every age. There, after much feasting, when the fellowship has grown warm, and the fervor of incestuous lust has grown hot with drunkenness, a dog that has been tied to the chandelier is provoked, by throwing a small piece of offal beyond the length of a line by which he is bound, to rush and spring; and thus the conscious light being overturned and extinguished in the shameless darkness, the connections of abominable lust involve them in the uncertainty of fate. (*Octavius* 9)[21]

Pagans had heard just enough of "eating the body" and "drinking the blood" and of Christian talk about "love" and "love feasts" and being "brothers and sisters" (terminology for husband and wife in Egypt) to get the wrong ideas. These stories circulated among the lower classes, but even the cultured orator from North Africa, Fronto, repeated them — whether as rhetorical appeal to prejudice or as a convinced acceptance of the popular charges we do not know (Minucius Felix, *Octavius* 31).

The popular ridicule of Christianity also is seen in the graffito scratched on a stone in a guardroom on Palatine Hill near the Circus Maximus in Rome.[22] The figure of a man with the head of an ass is shown hanging on a cross. Nearby another man raises his hand in a gesture of adoration, and the inscription reads, "Alexamenos worships his god." Jews had been charged with worshiping an ass; this calumny was here transferred to Jesus.[23] As repulsive as the picture is to Christians now, it conveys strongly how contemptible the idea of a crucified Lord was to pagan thinking.

Generally by the mid–second century educated pagans knew the popular slanders were not true and were above the kind of crude ridicule of the Alexamenos graffito. Nevertheless, Christians could still be considered objects of humor. The satirist Lucian, who found nearly everything laughable, was the

---

20. Justin, *Apology* 1.26; Clement of Alexandria, *Miscellanies* 3.2.10.

21. Trans. R. E. Wallis in *Ante-Nicene Fathers*, vol. 4 (repr. Peabody, 1994).

22. Stored at the Palatine Antiquarium: H. Solin and M. Iktonen, *Graffiti del Palatino, I Paedagogium* (Helsinki, 1966), 209-12.

23. Tacitus, *Histories* 5.3-4; Josephus, *Against Apion* 2.80; Tertullian, *To the Nations* 1.14; *Apology* 16.2; Minucius Felix, *Octavius* 9.3.

ALEXAMENOS GRAFFITO
Ridicule and slander of the Christian faith is expressed in this graffito from the
vicinity of the Palatine Hill. *(Courtesy Palatine Antiquarium, Rome)*

mocking rationalist as he talked about how the imposter Peregrinus (or Proteus) "took in" the gullible Christians:

> It was then that Proteus learned the wondrous lore of the Christians, by as-
> sociating with their priests and scribes in Palestine. And — how else could

it be? — in a trice he made them all look like children; for he was prophet, cult-leader, head of the synagogue, and everything, all by himself. He interpreted and explained some of their books and even composed many, and they revered him as a god, made use of him as a lawgiver, and adopted him as their patron, next after that other, to be sure, whom they still worship, the man who was crucified in Palestine because he introduced this new cult into the world.

Then at length Proteus was apprehended for this and thrown into prison, which itself gave him no little reputation to help him in later life and gratify his passion for imposture and notoriety. Well, when he had been imprisoned, the Christians, regarding the incident as a calamity, left nothing undone in the effort to rescue him. Then, as this was impossible, every other form of attention was shown him, not in any casual way but with assiduity; and from the very break of day you could see aged women lingering about the prison, widows and orphans, while their officials even slept inside with him after bribing the guards. Then elaborate meals were brought in, and sacred books of theirs were read aloud, and excellent Peregrinus — for he still went by that name — was called by them "a new Socrates."

Indeed, people came even from the cities in Asia, sent by the Christians at their common expense, to succor and defend and encourage the hero. They show incredible speed whenever any such public action is taken; for in no time they lavish their all. So it was then in the case of Peregrinus; much money came to him from them by reason of his imprisonment, and he procured not a little revenue from it. The poor wretches have convinced themselves, first and foremost, that they are going to be immortal and live for all time, in consequence of which they despise death and even willingly give themselves into custody, most of them. Furthermore, their first lawgiver persuaded them that they are all brothers of one another after they have transgressed once for all by denying the Greek gods and by worshipping that crucified sophist himself and living under his laws. Therefore they despise all things indiscriminately and consider them common property, receiving such doctrines traditionally without any definite evidence. So if any charlatan and trickster, able to profit by occasions, comes among them, he quickly acquires sudden wealth by imposing upon simple folk.

However, Peregrinus was freed by the then governor of Syria. . . .

He left home, then, for the second time, to roam about, possessing an ample source of funds in the Christians, through whose ministrations he lived in unalloyed prosperity. For a time he transgressed in some way even against them — he was seen, I think, eating some of the food that is forbidden them [meat sacrificed to idols, or has Lucian confused Jewish food laws?] — they no longer accepted him. (*On the Death of Peregrinus* 11-14, 16)[24]

24. Translation by A. M. Harmon in Loeb Classical Library (Cambridge, 1936).

The confusions with Judaism, which are recurrent in these texts, suggest that sometimes Christians are meant in passages which speak of Jews.[25] This passage, besides its testimony to Christian attitudes and practices, reveals the pagan despising of Christians for worshiping a crucified man, abandoning Greek religion, believing in the resurrection ("immortality"), and accepting doctrines by faith rather than by demonstration.

It has been suggested that the baker's wife in Apuleius, *Metamorphoses* (or *Golden Ass*) 9.14 is a caricature of a Christian woman. On this reading, Apuleius is presenting the cult of Isis as an alternative on those points on which pagans directed criticism against Christians: the one God, non-observance of pagan ceremonies, and desire for death (martyrdom).[26]

A more serious attack was launched on Christians by the philosopher Celsus in his book *True Doctrine*.[27] Although he too confused Christians, Jews, and Gnostics, he had made an effort to be informed. Much of his work is known from the quotations by Origen, who answered him in the large apologetic work *Against Celsus*. Celsus as a philosopher shared Lucian's intellectual scorn and objected to the Christian doctrines of the incarnation, crucifixion, and resurrection. He was critical of their emphasis on faith at the expense of reason (as he understood reason).

> Celsus urges us to "follow reason and a rational guide in accepting doctrines" on the ground that "anyone who believes people without so doing is certain to be deceived." And he compares those who believe without rational thought to the "begging priests of Cybele and soothsayers, and to worshippers of Mithras and Sabazius and whatever else one might meet, apparitions of Hecate or of some other demon or demons. For just as among them scoundrels frequently take advantage of the lack of education of gullible people and lead them wherever they wish, so also," he says, "this happens among the Christians." He says that "some do not even want to give or to receive a reason for what they believe, and use such expressions as 'Do not ask questions; just believe,' and 'Thy faith will save thee.'" (Origen, *Against Celsus* 1.9)[28]

Christians, Celsus further charged, were unprofitable members of society — weaklings, women, and slaves:

---

25. Is this the case in Dio Cassius, *Epitome* 67.14 (p. 603)?

26. Victor Schmidt, "Reaktionen auf das Christentum in den *Metamorphosen* des Apuleius," *Vigiliae Christianae* 51 (1997):51-71.

27. Text reconstructed by R. Bader, *Der Alēthēs Logos des Kelsos*, in *Tübinger Beiträge zur Altertumswissenschaft* 23 (1940); Eng. trans. by R. Joseph Hoffmann, *Celsus on the True Doctrine: A Discourse against the Christians* (New York, 1986); see Eugene V. Gallagher, *Divine Man or Magician? Celsus and Origen on Jesus* (Chico, Calif., 1982).

28. Trans. Henry Chadwick, *Contra Celsum* (Cambridge, 1953), 9.

"Their injunctions are like this. 'Let no one educated, no one wise, no one sensible draw near. For these abilities are thought by us to be evils. But as for anyone ignorant, anyone stupid, anyone uneducated, anyone who is a child, let him come boldly.' By the fact that they themselves admit that these people are worthy of their God, they show that they want and are able to convince only the foolish, dishonorable and stupid, and only slaves, women, and little children."

"Those who summon people to the other mysteries make this preliminary proclamation: 'Whosoever has pure hands and a wise tongue.' And again, others say: 'Whosoever is pure from all defilement, and whose soul knows nothing of evil, and who has lived well and righteously.' Such are the preliminary exhortations of those who promise purification from sins. But let us hear what folk these Christians call. 'Whosoever is a sinner,' they say, 'whosoever is unwise, whosoever is a child, and, in a word, whosoever is a wretch, the kingdom of God will receive him.'"

He asks, "Why on earth this preference for sinners?" (*Against Celsus* 3.44, 59, 64; Chadwick, pp. 158, 168, 171)

Especially upsetting to Celsus was the way in which Christians broke the order of society, abandoned the traditional religion, and did not help the emperor fight against Rome's enemies (e.g., *Against Celsus* 3.5; 5.25, 34; 8.65ff.).

The obstinacy with which Christians chose martyrdom over conformity provoked the emperor Marcus Aurelius:

> What a soul that is which is ready, if at any moment it must be separated from the body, and ready either to be extinguished or dispersed or continue to exist; but so that this readiness comes from a man's own judgment, not from mere obstinacy [as with the Christians], but considerately and with dignity and in a way to persuade another, without tragic show. (*Meditations* 11.3)[29]

Marcus Aurelius refers to Epicurean, Stoic, and Platonic views, respectively, of what happens to the soul at death. His own Stoic creed permitted suicide, but he contrasted it to the disadvantage of the Christian's readiness for martyrdom. Epictetus also notes this characteristic of Christians. In commenting on freedom from fear of death and not caring for the things of life, he says:

> Therefore, if madness can produce this attitude of mind toward the things which have been mentioned, and also habit [*ēthos*], as with the Galilaeans, cannot reason and demonstration teach a man? (4.7.6)

---

29. P. A. Brunt, "Marcus Aurelius and the Christians," *Studies in Latin Literature and Roman History* I, ed. C. Deroux, Coll. Latomus 164 (Brussels, 1979), 483-520.

Once more Christian conduct was not attributed to reason, but this time to a habit — or a way of life, an ethical principle.

Galen gave the most favorable report on the Christians. Going further than Epictetus, he saw Christians teaching and practicing a morality and way of life corresponding to that of philosophers.

> "Most people are unable to follow any demonstrative argument consecutively; hence they need parables, and benefit from them" — and he [Galen] understands by parables tales of rewards and punishments in a future life — "just as now we see the people called Christians drawing their faith from parables [and miracles], and yet sometimes acting in the same way [as those who philosophize]. For their contempt of death [and its sequel] is patent to us every day, and likewise their restraint in cohabitation. For they include not only men but also women who refrain from cohabiting all through their lives; and they also number individuals who, in self-discipline and self-control in matters of food and drink, and in their keen pursuit of justice, have attained a pitch not inferior to that of genuine philosophers."[30]

Thus at least one pagan intellectual accepted the claim of the Christian apologists that their Master attained what philosophers did not in reforming the common people.

BIBLIOGRAPHY

Wilken, R. L. "Pagan Criticism of Christianity: Greek Religion and Christian Faith." In *Early Christian Literature and the Classical Tradition: In Honorem Robert M. Grant*, edited by W. R. Schoedel and R. L. Wilken. Paris, 1979.

Wilken, R. L. "The Christians as the Romans (and Greeks) Saw Them." In *Jewish and Christian Self-Definition*. Vol. I. Edited by E. P. Sanders. Philadelphia, 1980.

Benko, Stephen. "Pagan Criticism of Christianity During the First Two Centuries A.D." *ANRW* II, *Principat*, 23.2. Berlin and New York, 1980. Pp. 1055-1115.

Benko, Stephen. *Pagan Rome and the Early Christians*. Bloomington, Ind., 1984.

Wilken, R. L. *The Christians as the Romans Saw Them*. New Haven, 1984.

Whitaker, Molly. *Jews and Christians: Graeco-Roman Views*. Cambridge, 1984.

Hargis, J. W. *Against the Christians: The Rise of Early Anti-Christian Polemic*. New York, 2001.

THE LEGAL STATUS OF CHRISTIANITY

The Romans allowed the Jews, since they had an ancient religion and had formerly been independent allies of Rome, the free exercise of their religion (pp.

---

30. R. Walzer, *Galen on Jews and Christians* (London, 1949), 15.

428-29). Initially, the Roman authorities did not distinguish Christianity from Judaism, and Christians shared the legal protection (and often social opprobrium, see below) of Jews. The Book of Acts reflects this situation, where Rome treated Jewish complaints against Christians as an internal problem (see esp. 18:12-17). The author may have had apologetic reasons for emphasizing favorable treatment of Christians by the authorities, but the nonantagonistic attitude was correct to the legal situation (13:4-12; 19:23-41; 25:13-19, 25; 26:30-31). Paul, of course, had the added protection Roman citizenship afforded (16:35-39; 22:25-29; 23:26-30; 25:9-12). On the other hand, Acts also reflects the background to the later treatment of Christians: accusations by Jews eager to make a distinction between Christians and themselves (13:50; 14:2, 19; 17:5-6, 13; 18:12; 24:1-2; 25:1-3),[31] popular turmoil (14:5; 19:23ff.; cf. Suetonius, *Claudius* 25.4), and the recognition that Christianity involved a way of life threatening to traditional pagan society (16:20-21). Everything depended on the attitude of the magistrates, which was at first friendly or at least indifferent. But Christianity started with several legal liabilities. It took its name from and was founded on a man who had been executed by Roman authority on a charge that amounted to treason. This was sure to provoke suspicion if not hostility in official circles. And then everywhere the teaching went it seemed to provoke disturbances and riots, something neither Rome nor the local establishments could view kindly.

The first indication that the Jews had succeeded in convincing the Roman authorities that Christians were a distinct group to be treated differently comes in Nero's reign. Tacitus's account of Nero's action against the Christians in Rome (p. 593) is the first recorded official persecution of Christians by the empire. The charge of arson might have had a certain plausibility against a group that claimed that the world would be destroyed by fire. Whether one accepts Tacitus's explanation that Christians were scapegoats (were Jews responsible for shifting the blame from themselves?), the underlying problem was one of hostility: Tacitus reflects an aristocratic outlook, but it may have been shared on the popular level. Christians were now clearly regarded as distinct from Jews. Nero apparently acted against the group, which would mean that "the name" itself placed one in jeopardy. First Peter 4:16 indicates "the name" as sufficient evidence for punishment. (However, the date of 1 Peter is in dispute, and it is not clear whether the background of this reference was local disturbances in Asia or the circumstances in Rome.) At any rate, although Nero's persecution applied only to Rome and even if any general proscription he might have issued against Christianity would have expired with him (the issue is debated), the action set a precedent.

From primarily Christian sources Domitian is remembered as a persecu-

---

31. W. H. C. Frend, "The Persecutions: Some Links Between Judaism and the Early Church," *Journal of Ecclesiastical History* 9 (1958):141-58.

tor. He took action against selected individuals in Rome, killing among others his cousin, the consul Flavius Clemens, and the latter's two sons, while banishing his wife Domitilla (Dio Cassius, *Epitome* 67.14; Suetonius, *Domitian* 15). The charge was "atheism" and reference was made to "Jewish customs,"[32] but the primary reasons were probably political. Although the author of 1 Clement was presumably a member of the household of Flavius Clemens and a Christian cemetery was later located on Domitilla's property, the evidence is inconclusive that they were themselves Christians instead of adherents of Judaism. Domitian also had relatives of Jesus called in for questioning: again this was politically motivated by concern about revolutionary movements among the Jews. Eusebius quotes Hegesippus on the incident:

> There still survived of the family of the Lord the grandsons of Jude, his brother after the flesh, as he was called. These they informed against, as being of the family of David; and the officer brought them before Domitian Caesar. For he feared the coming of the Christ, as did also Herod. And he asked them if they were of David's line, and they acknowledged it. Then he asked them what possessions they had or what fortune they owned. And they said that between the two of them they had only nine thousand denarii, half belonging to each of them; and this they asserted they had not in money, but only in thirty-nine plethra of land, so valued, from which by their own labors they both paid the taxes and supported themselves. They then showed him their hands, adducing as testimony of their labor the hardness of their bodies and the tough skin which had been calloused on their hands from their incessant work. They were asked concerning the Christ and his kingdom, its nature, origin, and time of appearance, and explained that it was neither of the world nor earthly, but heavenly and angelic, and it would be at the end of the world, when he would come in glory to judge the living and the dead and to reward every man according to his deeds. At this Domitian did not condemn them at all, but despised them as simple folk, released them, and decreed an end to the persecution against the church. (*Church History* 3.20)[33]

These events were distinct from the troubles in Asia that provide the background to the Book of Revelation. Christian tradition placed John's banishment to Patmos under Domitian and thus his reign as the date of the publication of Revelation (Irenaeus, *Against Heresies* 5.30.3). Asia had been the strongest center of the imperial cult since Augustus, and it seems that the religio-political issue came to the fore in that area.

The reign of the emperor Trajan provides a fixed point in the knowledge

---

32. Suetonius also says that Clemens was "a man of most contemptible laziness" (from Sabbath observance or from nonparticipation in pagan activities?).

33. Trans. by Kirsopp Lake in Loeb Classical Library (Cambridge, 1926).

of the legal status of Christianity.[34] It is noteworthy that Pliny, a well-educated member of the Roman aristocracy who had risen to the governorship of Bithynia, had never been present at the trial of a Christian and had only the vaguest notions about Christianity. When informers brought the names of suspected Christians to his attention, his examinations raised problems about which he sought guidance from the emperor (see pp. 594-95). Pliny found the accused to fall into three classes — about the first two of these he had no serious doubts concerning his treatment: (1) Those who confessed to being Christians and persisted in the confession were executed (except for Roman citizens, who were sent to Rome for judgment). Pliny knew that Christianity was not officially recognized, although he did not know why. At any rate he concluded that if for no other reason Christians deserved to be punished for obstinacy *(pertinaciam)* and unbending perversity *(inflexibilem obstinationem)*, that is, refusing to do what a Roman governor told them to do. (2) Those who denied ever being Christians were released when they performed religious acts before the images of the emperor and the gods and cursed Christ. He had learned that genuine Christians would not do these things. Since no one was under normal obligation to burn incense or pour out a libation before the emperor's statue, the requirement appears to have been an improvised test as a means of determining who was a Christian and a reasonable way of establishing loyalty in view of the Neronian charge. Refusal to perform these acts when commanded by a magistrate could be viewed very seriously by the authorities. Performance of them satisfied Pliny that these persons were not Christians and were loyal. (3) Those who had once been Christians but had become apostates (and confirmed this by worshiping the images and cursing Christ) posed the most difficult problem. From examining them Pliny acquired the sketchy information he had about the nature of Christianity, and this made him doubt that Christians were necessarily involved in serious crimes. But he had a more important reason for referring the matter to the emperor: he wanted to encourage apostates, and he felt that many could be reclaimed from Christianity if the way was made easy to renounce it. Hence, he began his inquiry with three questions: (1) Is any distinction in treatment to be made for age and physical condition? Trajan ignored this question in his reply, for that was within a governor's discretion. (2) Are apostates to be pardoned? (3) Is it the name *(nomen)* or the crimes *(flagitia)* supposedly associated with the name that is to be punished? The latter two questions are interrelated. If the punishment was for the name (i.e., being a member of the group), the apostates could be pardoned. If the punishment was for the crimes, the inquiries and trials must proceed and the guilty be punished no matter how long ago the crimes were committed. Deniers and apostates would prefer the former policy, for this would release them

---

34. I follow here G. E. M. de St. Croix, "The Persecutions," in *Crucible of Christianity*, ed. A. Toynbee (London, 1969), 345-47.

immediately. Faithful Christians preferred the latter, because they were loyal to the name and insisted that they were not guilty of any crimes. Pliny's very uncertainty whether guilt attached to the name (membership in the group) or to crimes associated with the name presupposes that the name (Christian) was already suspect (since Nero?) and was not a new situation originating in his own time.

Christian apologists of the second century argued that Christians should not be judged for the name but examined for specific crimes. This, however, was not government policy. Trajan answered according to Pliny's preference:

> You have adopted the proper course, my dear Secundus, in your examination of the cases of those who were accused to you as Christians, for indeed nothing can be laid down as a general ruling involving something like a set form of procedure. They are not to be sought out; but if they are accused and convicted, they must be punished — yet on this condition, that whoever denies being a Christian, and makes the fact plain by his action, that is, by worshipping our gods, shall obtain pardon on his repentance, however suspicious his past conduct may be. Papers, however, which are presented unsigned ought not to be admitted in any charge, for they are a very bad example and unworthy of our time. (Pliny, *Ep.* 10.97)

Christians did receive two concessions: they were not to be sought out, and anonymous accusations were not to be heeded. They lost on the crucial issue: the government remained opposed to Christianity and encouraged those who rejected it.

Hadrian reaffirmed this legal policy. His rescript to Caius Minucius Fundanus, proconsul of Asia, about 125 was quoted by Justin and Eusebius; its genuineness has been doubted but is now generally accepted.[35]

> I received the letter written to me by your predecessor, the most illustrious Serenius Granianus, and it is not my pleasure to pass by without inquiry the matter referred to me, lest both the innocent should be disturbed, and an opportunity for plunder afforded to slanderous informers. Now, if our subjects of the provinces are able to sustain by evidence this their petition against the Christians, so as to accuse them before a tribunal, I have no objection to their prosecuting this matter. But I do not allow them to use mere clamorous demands and outcries for this purpose. For it is much more equitable, if any one wishes to accuse them, for you to take cognizance of the matters laid to their charge. If therefore any one accuses and proves that the aforesaid men do anything contrary to the laws, you will also determine their punishments in accordance with their offences. You will on the other hand, by Hercules, take particular care that if any one de-

---

35. P. R. Coleman-Norton, *Roman State and Christian Church* (London, 1966), 1:5-8.

mand a writ of accusation against any of these Christians, merely for the sake of libelling them, you proceed against that man with heavier penalties, in accordance with his heinous guilt. (Justin, *Apology* 1.68; Eusebius, *Church History* 4.9)[36]

Justin understood this rescript to mean that Christians were to be punished only for specific crimes and so in effect to secure them from persecution (cf. his argument in *Apology* 1.2-4). It seems, rather, that Hadrian was mainly concerned with protecting non-Christians from slander and preventing the kind of popular tumult that so often forced the hand of magistrates against Christians (as in the case of Polycarp; see *Martyrdom of Polycarp* 8-12). Hadrian's rescript was designed to regularize proceedings to the law courts where proper legal safeguards could be observed.

This remained the official legal position of Christianity until the mid-third century. Persecutions, therefore, were local and sporadic, depending on charges being brought and magistrates following through. The threat of persecution was ever present, but persecution was not a constant experience. Everything depended on the general circumstances of the empire, the attitude of the populace, and the policy of individual governors. Often the pressure from the crowds provoked persecution, while the authorities tried to get Christians to conform outwardly so as to avoid the death penalty. Thus times of economic or political disaster when someone was needed on whom to place the blame were particularly bad times for Christians.[37]

This situation changed in 250 when Decius declared a *supplicatio* in which he called upon all the residents of the empire to sacrifice to the gods. Machinery was set up to enforce the decree whereby each person who complied received a *libellus* or certificate from the official before whom he performed the sacrifice.[38] Christianity was now legally proscribed: those who failed to comply were imprisoned and tortured, some killed. Fortunately, Decius did not live long enough for his threat to be fatal in the church. Later efforts to revive his policy did not obtain their objectives, for the church had grown too large and powerful to be crushed by force.

The Roman government's treatment of Christianity may be profitably compared with its treatment of certain other religious groups.[39] Rome was tolerant except for religions associated with debauchery, disorder, or disloyalty. Druidism and the Bacchanalia were proscribed when they gave rise to anti-

---

36. J. Stevenson, *A New Eusebius* (London, 1957), 16-17.

37. Tertullian, *Apology* 40; Paul Keresztes, "Marcus Aurelius a Persecutor?" *HTR* 61 (1968):321-41.

38. J. R. Knipfing, "The Libelli of the Decian Persecution," *HTR* 16 (1923):345-90.

39. A. N. Sherwin-White, "The Early Persecutions and Roman Law Again," *JTS* B.C. 3 (1952):199-213; cf. A. D. Nock, "The Roman Army and the Roman Religious Year," *HTR* 45 (1952):211-23 (*Essays*, 757-66).

social acts. Because of the shameful things *(flagitia)* and crimes, the *nomen* (membership in the group) was constituted a capital charge by direct magisterial action. When the worshipers of Isis and the Jews were banished from Rome under Tiberius, no question arose whether this or that individual had committed any offense save that of being what he or she was, a member of the religious group determined to be unacceptable and therefore to be excluded. Similarly, when the Druids were suppressed, all their practices were put down, not simply the human sacrifice or magic, which was the official reason (it may well be suspected that political loyalty was the more basic concern). The *nomen* acted as a pointer to a man proper to examine if accused. One was presumed guilty by confession of the name.

Ulpian's discussion of the Magi and Chaldeans illustrates the course of development in regard to Christians. A law was passed against the practice of magic because of the political unrest occasioned by the prophecies of astrologers; there was at first no objection to beliefs of the magicians. But *contumacia* in the open practice of the forbidden acts produced a reaction and the basis of the objection was widened to include the name. The law first pertained only to Italy, but was then extended to the provinces by a series of imperial rescripts and imitative *coercitio* (governors acting on their own authority to enforce order by following the precedent set in Rome). Finally there was a universal suppression of magicians, but it was enforced by the normal system of private accusation *(delatio)*.

The action against the Christians followed a similar process. Under Nero there may have been a suppression of Christianity on account of the *flagitia* — arson, magic, and perhaps the other charges known from the second century — by a magisterial edict. Christians had been the occasion of disturbances in Rome since the days of Claudius (cf. Suetonius *Claudius* 25.4), and popular animosity had been aroused by their aloofness and secretiveness (Tacitus's "hatred of the human race"). The action by Nero's magistrate established a precedent, which might or might not be followed in the provinces. Local enemies of Christians could try the precedent out, and Pliny provides evidence of such in Bithynia. When Pliny started investigating, he found so many Christians that he became worried.

Bibliography

Coleman-Norton, P. R. *Roman State and the Christian Church.* Vol. I. London, 1966.

Guido, Marco. *Fonti per i rapporti tra l'Impero Romano e il Cristianesimo.* Bologna, 1970.

Novak, Ralph. *Christianity and the Roman Empire: Background Texts.* Harrisburg, 2001.

Sherwin-White, A. N. "The Early Persecutions and Roman Law Again." *JTS* B.C. 3 (1952):199-213.

Grant, R. M. *The Sword and the Cross.* New York, 1955.

Stauffer, E. *Christ and the Caesars.* London, 1955.

De Ste. Croix, G. E. M. "Why Were the Early Christians Persecuted?" *Past and Present* 26 (1963):6-38; 27 (1964):23-33.

Frend, W. H. C. *Martyrdom and Persecution in the Early Church.* Oxford, 1965.

Ferguson, E., ed. *Church and State in the Early Church.* Studies in Early Christianity, Vol. 7. New York, 1993. (Reprints articles by Sherwin-White and De Ste. Croix above, among others)

HINDRANCES TO THE ACCEPTANCE OF CHRISTIANITY

The pagan attitudes toward Christianity presented above — both sophisticated disdain and popular prejudice — formed a major obstacle to Christian preaching. The legal status of Christianity, at least after the time of Nero, constituted another hindrance. Such were the ambiguities and complexities in the situation, however, that the hindrance could become a means of promoting Christianity. Martyrdom was often a public spectacle that drew attention to Christianity and advertised it. Second-century Christian apologists testified that the way in which Christians faced death convinced them of Christianity's truthfulness.[40] Tertullian's bold declaration has become an axiom: "The blood of Christians [the martyrs] is seed" (*Apology* 50). Nevertheless, we must remember that the spread of Christianity was not an uninterrupted success story. Not everyone eagerly awaited the gospel message and was prepared to accept it immediately, nor was everything in the environment conducive to the spread of Christian teaching.

A major barrier to a pagan becoming a Christian was the whole force of tradition and the structure of society. Christianity's legal status was only the outward symptom of the situation. Social, economic, and cultural life, as well as political, was interwoven with the polytheistic tradition. Even today missionaries in many countries and cultures face the power of family custom, and they can understand the pressures to conformity that must be overcome by one who would break with the past to accept a new religion. The most conservative elements in pagan society — the aristocracy and the rural peoples — proved most resistant to Christianity. Its initial success came among city dwellers, those always most open to new ideas and to change.

Some of the central articles in the Christian faith would have been initially unacceptable to outsiders. To worship as Son of God a man crucified was, as Paul said, "a stumbling block to Jews and folly to Gentiles" (1 Cor. 1:23). The idea of a suffering and dying son of God was not foreign to pagan thought, but

---

40. Justin, *Apology* 2.12; cf. Eusebius, *Church History* 2.9.

a crucifixion as a criminal by official authority was hardly the sort of teaching to find an immediately favorable response.[41]

Although paganism had its stories of divine births, particularly of a deity fathering a hero through a human mother,[42] and its stories of heroes such as Heracles who attained entrance into the circle of the immortal gods, it had no genuine doctrine of an incarnation. In fact such was repugnant, contrary to all notions about the divine.

The doctrine of a bodily resurrection ran counter to hopes about the afterlife. Those who advocated most strongly and vividly an afterlife thought in terms of the immortality of the soul. The body was commonly thought of as a hindrance from whose weaknesses the soul must escape. To define hope in terms of a return to "bodily" existence was not what the educated pagan would have wanted.[43]

One circumstance about the origins of Christianity was particularly ambiguous in its consequences — its Jewish beginnings. As noted above, the Jewish identity gave the church an initial protection from Roman authorities; and as we will develop below, the Jewish connections provided the initial point of contact for missionary activity. Nevertheless, as reflected in some of the pagan attitudes toward Christians, the church had to share the opprobrium in which Jews were held by many in the ancient world (p. 513). Gentile distaste for Jewish exclusivism, resentment of Jewish privileges, hostility to Jewish ambition, and later suspicion of Jewish loyalty — all these affected attitudes toward Christians and were transferred to them to some degree at one point or another.

The mention of Jews is a reminder of the religious environment into which Christianity came: an environment that was both an obstacle and an opportunity.

RELIGIOUS RIVALS

Judaism

Despite negative pagan attitudes toward Jews — their exclusivism and intolerance of other religions, strange customs (Sabbath), repulsive practices (circumcision) — and despite a tendency among the Jews toward withdrawal from contact with Gentiles after the Bar Kokhba revolt, Judaism remained a powerful

---

41. See M. Hengel, *Crucifixion* (Philadelphia, 1977), for the ancient testimonies about crucifixion.

42. Justin Martyr used these to explain the virgin birth while warning against a physical interpretation of the begetting; see *Apology* 1.21-22.

43. O. Cullmann, *Immortality of the Soul or Resurrection of the Dead?* (New York, 1958); K. Stendahl, ed., *Immortality and Resurrection* (New York, 1965).

rival to Christianity for pagan converts. The appeal of Judaism (see p. 540) was still there. The Godfearers were a fruitful recruiting ground for Christianity, but their presence also testified to the appeal Judaism had for pagans, an appeal that did not end with the coming of Christianity, so Christianity was in a struggle with Judaism for their allegiance. Much of the tension between Jews and Christians and the Christian polemical literature against the Jews (even when academic and not reflecting real contact) resulted from this sense of competition. Even in the late fourth century there were Christians who were attracted to Jewish customs and had to be warned not to frequent the synagogues. Christianity eventually won the field as far as proselytes were concerned, but was frustrated in its expectations of converting Jews themselves to Jesus. Although Christianity proved to have advantages over Judaism in the competition for the Gentile mind, it did not have overwhelming appeal to Jews after the first century.

BIBLIOGRAPHY

Parkes, J. *Conflict of the Church and the Synagogue: A Study in the Origins of Anti-Semitism*. London, 1934.

Williams, A. L. *Adversus Iudaeos*. Cambridge, 1935.

Wilde, Robert. *The Treatment of the Jews in the Greek Christian Writers of the First Three Centuries*. Washington, 1949.

Simon, M. *Verus Israel: A Study of the Relations Between Christians and Jews in the Roman Empire (135-425)*. Oxford, 1986; French orig. 1948.

Simon, M., and A. Benoit. *Le judaisme et le christianisme antique d'Antiochus Epiphane à Constantin*. Paris, 1968.

Judant, K. *Judaïsme et Christianisme. Dossier Patristique*. Paris, 1969.

Hruby, K. *Juden und Judentum bei den Kirchenvatern*. Zurich, 1971.

Wilken, R. L. *John Chrysostom and the Jews: Rhetoric and Reality in the Late Fourth Century*. Berkeley, 1983.

Wilson, S., ed. *Anti-Judaism in Early Christianity 2: Separation and Polemic*. Waterloo, Ont., 1986.

Shanks, Hershel, ed. *Christianity and Rabbinic Judaism: A Parallel History of their Origins and Early Development*. Washington, 1992.

Borgen, Peder. *Early Christianity and Hellenistic Judaism*. Edinburgh, 1996.

Ferguson, E., ed. *Early Christianity and Judaism*. Studies in Early Christianity, Vol. 6. New York, 1993. (Contains several articles also on Jewish Christianity)

Skarsaune, Oskar. *In the Shadow of the Temple: Jewish Influences on Early Christianity*. Downers Grove, Ill., 2002.

Pagan Religion and Philosophy

As the chapters on Greco-Roman religion and philosophies have shown, Christianity did not enter a vacuum. The presence of so many rivals for the intellectual, moral, and emotional loyalties of the populace gave Christianity ample competition. Many different factors have been suggested as important in Christianity's eventual triumph. For those which pertain to the internal nature of Christianity itself, in comparison with its pagan rivals, see below on "Factors Favorable to Christianity" (pp. 616-19). A detailed comparison of Christianity with some of its principal rivals has already been given in connection with their descriptions, for example, Stoicism, Mithraism, and mystery religions in general. Here we will attempt only a summary generalization about the weaknesses of its rivals.

Although Stoicism allied itself with the traditional religion, not even Stoicism, nor any other pagan philosophy or religion, effectively integrated philosophy and religion into a single entity. A few Neoplatonists, as Julian, in the last stages of paganism accomplished this as a personal synthesis, but no ancient religion other than Christianity created its own philosophy out of the materials furnished by Greek thought.[44] Not even Judaism did this to the extent of Christianity, in spite of the promising beginnings by Philo, to whom Christian philosophical theology owed so much. Nor did any Hellenistic philosophical school fully achieve the motivation and devotion of a religious faith. Thus none of the Gentile religions completely freed themselves from the anthropomorphism, naturalism, bloody sacrifices, and crude mythologies with which they were associated. The extent to which the philosophies accommodated themselves to these weakened their appeal, and the extent to which they distinguished themselves from these features of paganism separated them from the emotional and psychological appeal of religious faith and ceremony. None of Christianity's pagan rivals rose above the limitations of nature religions and mythological origins.[45]

Determinism and fate, magic, and superstition had their appeal, as they still do. Such, however, could not provide complete explanations of reality (moral freedom, in particular) and were unable to provide an explanation for conscience or a basis for moral conduct.

Popular religion was unable to hold the conviction of the educated, and philosophy was unable to reach the masses. Christianity successfully integrated a religious faith with a worldview and pattern of life that were philosophically defensible, if not "philosophical" in the strict sense.

Nevertheless, the situation was not clear-cut. The pagan beliefs in demons, astrology, and magic were so resistant that they did not really die but were absorbed into the triumphant Christianity of a later age. Similarly, much of the traditional ritual survived in Christian ceremonies.

44. H. A. Wolfson, *The Philosophy of the Church Fathers* (Cambridge, Mass., 1956).

45. For the different view by the pagans after Christianity became the state religion, see Pierre Chuvin, *A Chronicle of the Last Pagans* (Cambridge, Mass., 1990).

BIBLIOGRAPHY

Dodds, E. R. *Pagan and Christian in an Age of Anxiety.* Cambridge, 1965.
Ferguson, E., ed. *The Early Church and Greco-Roman Thought.* Studies in Early Christianity, Vol. 8. New York, 1993.

Gnosticism and Other Rival Versions of Christianity

The religious vitality released by the Christian faith was accompanied by numerous accommodations of its teachings to other current beliefs. The variety of responses to the Christian message is indicated in the New Testament Epistles by the corrections made to incorrect responses (note esp. 1 Corinthians, Galatians, Colossians, 1 John). The canon itself reflects differing emphases between Paul, James, John, and Luke — to mention the more obvious. Walter Bauer advanced the thesis that heresy preceded orthodoxy, that is, that variety came first, that responses later judged heretical initially represented the majority of Christians at most places, and that "orthodox Christianity" only secured the upper hand at the end of the second century, primarily through the influence of the church at Rome and its allies. Bauer weighted the case in his favor by a narrow definition of "orthodoxy" in institutional terms to the neglect of normative elements of belief in the early preaching. He also minimized the evidences for "orthodoxy" in the apostolic fathers of the early second century.[46] He and later scholars (e.g., Robinson and Koester) have performed a useful service in reminding us of the considerable diversity in early Christianity and that the early history of the church was not a straight line development, doctrinally or organizationally. On the other hand, the variety can be emphasized to the neglect of the extent of the central core of faith, and the diversity can be taken as normative in such a way as to make unintelligible the sense of an apostolic norm, the history of the canon, and the development toward "orthodoxy."[47]

The principal variant forms of Christianity fall under the general heading of Gnosticism (see pp. 300ff.). The second century also saw other powerful movements from within the church. Marcionism[48] rejected the Old Testament

46. Frederick W. Norris, "Ignatius, Polycarp, and I Clement: Walter Bauer Reconsidered," *Vigiliae Christianae* 30 (1976):23-44. Bauer was simply wrong on some points, according to J. F. McCue, "Orthodoxy and Heresy: Walter Bauer and the Valentinians," *Vigiliae Christianae* 33 (1979):118-30; Gary Burke, "Walter Bauer and Celsus: The Shape of Late Second-Century Christianity," *The Second Century* 4 (1984):1ff.

47. Leander E. Keck, "Is the New Testament a Field of Study? or From Outler to Overbeck and Back," and Robert L. Wilken, "Diversity and Unity in Early Christianity," *The Second Century* 1 (1981):19-35, 101-10.

48. A. von Harnack, *Marcion: The Gospel of the Alien God* (Durham, 1989; German orig. 1921); John Knox, *Marcion and the New Testament* (Chicago, 1942); E. C. Blackman, *Marcion and*

and the Jewish roots of the church and postulated two gods, the just Creator of the world and the merciful Father of Jesus Christ. It accepted as Scripture a revised version of Luke and ten edited Letters of Paul. Montanism[49] was orthodox in doctrine but disturbed the harmony of the churches by its attempted revival of prophecy, its ascetic morality of marriage, fasting, and martyrdom, and its eschatological speculations. Doctrinal controversies disturbed the "mainstream" of the church. All of this disunity adversely affected the spread of Christianity. This occurred not only because outsiders confused unrepresentative elements with Christianity at large (e.g., pagan charges of immorality against Christians had some basis in fact in the practices of libertine Gnostics), but also because of the energy absorbed in controversy and clarification. Disunity blunted the Christian witness.

Variant forms of Christianity resulted not only from the mixture of Gentile religion and philosophy with the gospel but also from efforts to domesticate it within its Jewish matrix.

BIBLIOGRAPHY

Turner, H. E. W. *The Pattern of Truth*. London, 1954.

Bauer, Walter. *Orthodoxy and Heresy in Earliest Christianity*. Edited by Robert Kraft and Gerhard Krodel. Philadelphia, 1971.

Robinson, James M., and Helmut Koester. *Trajectories through Early Christianity*. Philadelphia, 1971.

Vallée, Gérard. *A Study in Anti-Gnostic Polemic: Irenaeus, Hippolytus and Epiphanius*. Waterloo, Ont., 1981.

Jewish Christianity

Some Christian converts from Judaism never broke out of the Jewish mold, and even a survey of Christianity in the ancient world must take some note of this variant form of Christianity.

Paul met virulent opposition to his ministry from Jewish believers loyal to the law of Moses who insisted that Gentile converts keep certain requirements of the law (Gal. 2:1-16; 2 Cor. 3:11; 11:15; Acts 15:1-2; 21:17-36). Their leader was James, but they often acted in ways he did not support.[50] According to

---

his Influence (London, 1948); R. Joseph Hoffmann, *Marcion: On the Restitution of Christianity* (Chico, Calif., 1984); special issue of *The Second Century* 6 (1987-88):129-191.

49. R. E. Heine, *The Montanist Oracles and Testimonia* (Macon, Ga., 1989); C. Trevett, *Montanism: Gender, Authority, and the New Prophecy* (Cambridge, 1996); W. Tabbernee, *Montanist Inscriptions and Testimonia: Epigraphic Sources Illustrating the History of Montanism* (Macon, Ga., 1997).

50. J. Munck, *Paul and the Salvation of Mankind* (Atlanta, 1959), 112-19, 231-42; W. Schmithals, *Paul and James* (Naperville, Ill., 1965).

Eusebius (*Church History* 3.5.3) the Jewish Christian community in Jerusalem fled before the Roman siege and settled in the Transjordan (p. 421).

It is certain that Jewish Christian believers continued after New Testament times, although their history is vague and the sources are limited.[51] As the church became predominantly Gentile, some Jews gave up the Jewish way of life and became absorbed into the larger Gentile Christianity. Other Jewish believers remained Jewish, increasingly a minority and increasingly alienated from Gentile Christianity, which came to regard them as heretical. These were subject to various influences, and although there is likely a genealogical continuity with the Jewish Christians of New Testament times, we cannot assume that there was an identity of belief. Distinct tendencies (if not clearly defined sects) emerged and may be characterized in general terms.

(1) Gnostic tendencies. Gnostic ideas affected some Christian Jews. This could produce some curious combinations, as with Cerinthus, a contemporary of the apostle John.[52] If the sources are to be believed,[53] he advocated some very Jewish ideas (millennialism) but also held to Docetic ideas (the divine Christ came upon the man Jesus at his baptism and departed before the crucifixion) and made the Gnostic separation between the primary God and the Creator.

A Jewish Christian sect from the beginning of the second century is known to us as the Elkesaites, from the prophet Elkesai, who flourished during the reign of Trajan. Some of his utterances have been preserved by church writers.[54] The Elkesaites practiced frequent immersions for purification and ate only food that had been carefully cleaned. They have assumed new importance in the history of religions from the discovery of the Mani Cologne Codex, which reveals that Mani, the third-century founder of Manichaeism, grew up in an Elkesaite community.[55]

(2) Mediating tendencies. Some Christian Jews continued to live by the law but accepted Gentile Christians, and did not require them to do so. Justin Martyr knew some of these in the second century (*Dialogue* 47). Jerome made frequent references to Christian Jews under the name Nazareans (cf. Acts

---

51. For archaeological remains identified with Jewish Christians, see B. Bagatti, *The Church from the Circumcision, History and Archaeology of the Judaeo Christians* (Jerusalem, 1971). For a negative evaluation of the claims, J. E. Taylor, *Christians and the Holy Places: The Myth of Jewish-Christian Origins* (Oxford, 1993).

52. Eusebius, *Church History* 3.28.6.

53. Irenaeus, *Against Heresy* 1.26; Eusebius, *Church History* 3.28.2. A reconciliation of the reports is provided by Charles E. Hill, "Cerinthus, Gnostic or Chiliast? A New Solution to an Old Problem," *Journal of Early Christian Studies* 8 (2000):135-172.

54. Hippolytus, *Refutation of All Heresies* 19.8-12; 10.25; Epiphanius, *Heresies* 30.17.7; 19.1.8-9; 3.5-7; 4.3.

55. A. F. J. Klijn and G. J. Reinink, "Elchasai and Mani," *Vigiliae Christianae* 28 (1974):277-89; R. Cameron and A. Dewey, eds. and trans., *The Cologne Mani Codex: "Concerning the Origin of His Body"* (Missoula, Mont., 1979).

24:5).[56] Epiphanius distinguished Nazareans (*Heresies* 29) and Ebionites (ibid., 30), but his classification and descriptions reflect some confusion.

(3) Sectarian tendencies. Best known to us are the Ebionites, who developed exclusive, sectarian characteristics. Their name continued the religious use of the term "the poor" (Heb. *ebion*) with reference to the humble oppressed who trusted in the Lord, a use known from the Psalms (10; 25; 34; 37) and Qumran (4QpPs 37; 1QpHab xii.2; 1QM xi.13) and perhaps reflected in the New Testament (Matt. 5:3; Luke 6:20; Jas. 2:5).[57]

The Ebionites appear to represent a considerable segment of the Christian Jews who found refuge in the Transjordan. The Pseudo-Clementine literature incorporated some of their writings and thus furnishes some original source material. Unfortunately, its usefulness is mitigated by the very complicated problem of source analysis.[58] The fourth-century Clementine *Homilies* (Gk.) and *Recognitions* (Lat. version of Rufinus) rest on a common third-century source *(Grundschrift)* that incorporated several Ebionite works from the second century, among others, and sought to "catholicize" them. The recovery of these Ebionite sources from a work that itself must be reconstructed from later documents obviously has led to considerable disagreement among scholars as to their exact limits and contents.

Comparison of the antiheretical writings of the orthodox church with the Pseudo-Clementines permits a general outline of their beliefs. The Ebionites, as Jews, believed in the one God, the law, and the hope of Israel. They continued certain Jewish practices — circumcision, observance of the Sabbath, and the dietary laws (extended to a prohibition of meat). They were antagonistic to Paul and said Gentiles must submit to the law. As Christians, they accepted Jesus as the Messiah, but regarded him as a man, the true prophet like Moses (Deut. 18:15), who became the Messiah by reason of his righteous life. Thus, they rejected the virgin birth. Jesus taught the resurrection from the dead and himself arose from the dead. He came to destroy the temple and its cultus and instituted water baptism in place of sacrifice as the means of forgiveness of sins. They used the Gospel of Matthew but also produced their own Gospel of the Ebionites. They removed many passages from the Old Testament

56. *Lives of Illustrious Men* 3; *In Matthew* 13.53-54; *In Galatians* 3.13-14; 5.3; *In Isaiah* 1.3, 12; 8.14, 19–9.3; 29.20-21; 31.6-9; 66.20.

57. Contrary to patristic interpretations: a man — Tertullian, *Prescription of Heretics* 33; *Flesh of Christ* 14; the poverty of their theology — Origen, *First Principles* 4.3.8; *Against Celsus* 2.1.

58. H. Waitz, *Die Pseudoklementinen*, Texte und Untersuchungen 25.4 (Berlin, 1904); Carl Schmidt, *Studien zu den Pseudo-Clementinen* (Leipzig, 1929); O. Cullmann, *Le problème littéraire et historique du roman pseudoclementin* (Paris, 1930); Georg Strecker, *Das Judenchristentum in den Pseudoklementinen*, Texte und Untersuchungen 70 (Berlin, 1958); F. Stanley Jones, "The Pseudo-Clementines: A History of Research, Part 1," and "Part 2," *The Second Century* 2 (1982):1-33, 63-96; repr. in E. Ferguson, *Literature of the Early Church*, Studies in Early Christianity, Vol. 2 (New York, 1993), 195-262.

as "false pericopes," claiming that passages about animal sacrifice and the monarchy and offensive stories about the patriarchs were interpolations.

BIBLIOGRAPHY

Hegesippus in Eusebius. *Church History* 2.23; 3.11, 19, 20, 32; 4.22.

Irenaeus. *Against Heresies* 1.26.2; 3.2.7, 15.1, 21.1; 4.33.4; 5.1.3.

Hippolytus. *Refutation of All Heresies* 7.22.

Origen. *Against Celsus* 5.61, 65; 2.1. *On First Principles* 4.22. *Homily in Genesis* 3.5. *In Jeremiah* 17.12. *Commentary in Matthew* 17.13. *Homily in Romans* 3.11. *In Luke* 7.

Eusebius. *Church History* 3.27; 6.17.

Epiphanius. *Heresies* 29–30.

Klijn, A. F. J., and G. J. Reinink. *Patristic Evidence for Jewish-Christian Sects*. Leiden, 1973.

Schoeps, H.-J. *Theologie und Geschichte des Judenchristentums*. Tübingen, 1949.

Simon, M. *Recherches d'histoire judéo-chrétienne*. Paris, 1962.

Aspects du Judéo-Christianisme. Colloque de Strasbourg, 1964. Paris, 1965.

Pines, S. *The Jewish Christians of the Early Centuries of Christianity according to a New Source*. Jerusalem, 1966.

Schoeps, H.-J. *Jewish Christianity*. Philadelphia, 1969.

Longenecker, R. N. *The Christology of Early Jewish Christianity*. London, 1970.

Mancini, I. *Archaeological Discoveries Relative to the Judaeo-Christians: Historical Survey*. Jerusalem, 1970.

Klijn, A. F. J. "The Study of Jewish Christianity." *NTS* 20 (1973/74):419-31.

Malina, B. J. "Jewish Christianity: A Select Bibliography." *Australian Journal of Biblical Archaeology* 2/2 (1973):60-65.

Malina, B. J. "Jewish Christianity or Christian Judaism: Toward a Hypothetical Definition." *JSJ* 7 (1976):46-57.

FACTORS FAVORABLE TO CHRISTIANITY

External Circumstances

After all has been said that can be said about the hindrances to Christianity — the power of tradition, prejudice, governmental authority, religious rivals on the outside, and Christianity's own unpalatable teachings and disunity — the historical fact remains that Christianity succeeded. We have seen that most of the negative factors were not entirely one-sided; the same was true for the positive factors.

Background contributions to the spread of Christianity have often been summed up as "the fullness of time" (Gal. 4:4).

The Roman empire brought a unified rule to the Mediterranean world — and with it an end to the almost constant warfare there since the death of Alexander the Great. Even on the frontiers of the empire there were extended periods of peace. The blessings of a single, stable government were an important external factor in the growth and spread of Christianity. Not least of these blessings was the resultant ease of travel. Along with maintaining external peace Rome attempted to suppress piracy and brigandage; this too contributed to the safety of travel routes. Further, Rome's practice of building and maintaining roads greatly facilitated land travel. The Roman peace encouraged commerce; and travelers as well as merchants, missionaries as well as government officials benefited.

Another important background contribution to Christianity was the spread of the Greek language. Greek was a sufficiently universal language in the Roman empire that it provided a means of communication nearly everywhere. A common language provided more than direct intelligibility: with it went certain common ideas and ways of thinking, a certain level of education, and a manner of perception — that is, Greek philosophy, literature, and religion. This common frame of reference assisted vastly the task of preaching the gospel of Jesus.

These external factors were available to everyone, so we must turn more specifically to the religious environment. One aspect here helped Christianity in a special way: Hellenistic Judaism.

Hellenistic Judaism

By the first century the Jews were numerous, spread widely over the Roman empire and even outside it, especially in the Parthian empire (see pp. 399-400). The synagogues of the Diaspora had already made the important adjustment of the Semitic faith to the Hellenized world. Here language provided the important contact. The Hebrew Scriptures had been translated into Greek (the Septuagint), making the Old Testament faith available to Greek-speakers and beginning the conceptual translation of biblical thought into the Greek view of reality. Jews who lived in the Greek world had begun the process of defending biblical religion, propagating its virtues, and making intelligible its central affirmations (in the process modifying some of those features in order to make them more acceptable). The synagogues in the Diaspora provided a base of operations for Christian preachers in the early years of the church. Moreover, they attracted many Gentiles who proved to be prime prospects for the Christian gospel and the beachhead into the wider Gentile world. The Hellenistic synagogue provided an outlook congenial to Christianity: some Jews who had moved away from a rigid adherence to details of their ancestral faith but were still loyal to its central affirmations, and Gentiles who were attracted to elements of the biblical faith. As there had been a variety of responses by Jews to Hellenistic culture (pp. 428-29), so Paul and other Christian preachers met all kinds of response among Diaspora Jews: an even more intense opposition than he faced in Jerusalem (note Acts 21:27); those ready to reject Judaism altogether; Gentiles wanting to copy Jewish rites (Galatians); and religious Jews ready to hear the Christian gospel.

Christianity offered all of the advantages that made Judaism appealing to serious-minded pagans: monotheism, high ethical standards, a close-knit social community, the authority of an ancient sacred Scripture, a rational worship. It did not carry the liabilities that Judaism did: the association with a single nationality, the rite of circumcision, restrictions that seemed meaningless (Sabbath, food laws). Christianity offered a contact with antiquity through its claim to the fulfillment of biblical prophecy, but it also offered a satisfaction of the newer religious aspirations: salvation and deliverance through a personal redeemer.

Religious Quest

Part of the environment of early Christianity that prepared for its coming was the religious quest of the Gentile world. We have already noted the competing religions of the Roman empire, whose very presence testified to the religious interest of the time. Their presence thus was not altogether a negative factor. They were both symptomatic of and contributed to the spiritual longing. Many people, dissatisfied with their moral condition and with the available religions, were receptive to Christian preaching. This situation varied greatly with different people, in different localities, and in different economic and social situations. Nonetheless, there was a vital religious interest in the early centuries of the Christian era. Christianity was not perceived as satisfying all of these yearnings; the very diversity that developed within Christianity itself, however, testifies to the enormous appeal that some of its aspects had and to the spiritual energy it brought.

The strengths of Christianity in the religious competition of the early Roman empire included several features.[59] Its founder was a historical personage with a real life story. The person of Christ himself was an important factor in the success of Christianity.[60] It offered a sure triumph over death and a happy afterlife. It made exclusive claims and demanded an exclusive loyalty. It combined high moral standards with religious faith. It developed a worldview

59. Ramsay MacMullen, *Christianizing the Roman Empire (A.D. 100-400)* (New Haven, 1984), has called attention to the importance of miracle in the conversion of the masses.

60. Jan N. Bremmer, "'Christianus sum': The Early Christian Martyrs and Christ," in G. J. M. Bartelink, et al., eds., *Eulogia: Mélanges offerts à Antoon A. R. Bastiaensen* (Steenbrugis, 1991), 11-20 collects the evidence for a close affective relationship of his followers with Jesus.

with a philosophical explanation and defense of its teachings. It had a social cohesiveness that provided material security and psychological support. It promised deliverance from the power of demons, fate, and magic as well as redemption from sin and guilt. It offered salvation to all classes and conditions of persons. It released a powerful zeal and determination to propagate and conquer. A. D. Nock sums up the advantages of Christianity this way:

> The success of Christianity is the success of an institution which united the sacramentalism and the philosophy of the time. It satisfied the inquiring turn of mind, the desire for escape from Fate, the desire for security in the hereafter; like Stoicism, it gave a way of life and made man at home in the universe, but unlike Stoicism it did this for the ignorant as well as for the lettered. It satisfied also social needs and it secured men against loneliness.[61]

Nilsson, after noting that the imperial cult was strong on organization but weak on religious content and that the mysteries were too tied to national origin to form a truly universal religion, lists the fundamental causes for Christianity's advance as these: a firm belief in the truth of the Christian religion, universalism, brotherly love, charity, vitalizing force of self-government in a bureaucratic world, and ability to organize.[62]

WHAT WAS UNIQUE IN CHRISTIANITY?

Christianity presented itself as the result of a new act by God in human affairs, as a divine revelation. Its authority is not dependent on absolute originality in its teachings and practices. Many Christian believers in fact have minimized the originality in order to emphasize the divine preparation for Christianity. Christian claims rest on whether it is a revelation from God, not on its originality, and this is a claim not directly verifiable by historical examination. The decision for or against Christianity is a matter of faith, however much historical inquiry might support or discourage the decision.

Neither the truth nor the value of Christianity depends on its uniqueness. The contents of this volume point to a number of areas where Christianity was not exactly paralleled in its contemporary setting. But if none of these points should stand further examination or future discoveries, nothing essential to Christianity is lost.

That which is truly unique to Christianity is Jesus Christ. He was what was essential to its beginning and remains central to what it is. This is so in a historical sense. However much of his life and teachings might be paralleled

61. *Conversion* (Oxford, 1933), 210-11.
62. *Greek Piety* (Oxford, 1948), 183.

from one part of the ancient world or another, Jesus — his person and work —
are what was unique to Christianity. The point is well made by Frank Cross in a
more limited context:

> It is not the idea of redemption through suffering but the "event" of the
> crucifixion understood as the atoning work of God that distinguishes
> Christianity. It is not the doctrine of resurrection but faith in the resurrec-
> tion of Jesus as an eschatological event which forms the basis of the Chris-
> tian decision of faith. It is not faith that a Messiah will come that gives
> Christianity its special character, but the assurance that Jesus rules as the
> Messiah who has come and will come. It is not the hope of a New Creation
> that lends uniqueness to Christianity, but the faith that Jesus is the New
> Adam, the first of the New Creation. Finally, it is not a "love ethic" that dis-
> tinguished Christianity from Judaism — far from it. The Christian faith is
> distinguished from the ancient faith which brought it to birth in its knowl-
> edge of a new act of God's love, the revelation of His love in Jesus' particu-
> lar life and death and resurrection.[63]

These historical statements are true regardless of the truth claims of Christianity. Yet the truth claims of Christianity are bound up with the "person and
work" of Jesus, who he was and what he did. What would make Christianity
unique in an absolute sense, with no possible historical rival, would be for Jesus
to be what is claimed for him — the one and only Son of God, God who has
come in the flesh; and to have done what is affirmed for him — to have
brought a salvation and relationship with God that no one else than the Son of
God could have brought. There we pass from history to faith.

63. Frank Moore Cross, *The Ancient Library of Qumran* (London, 1958), 184.

INDEX OF SUBJECTS

Boldface numbers indicate pages on which subjects are discussed in detail.

INDEX OF SCRIPTURE REFERENCES

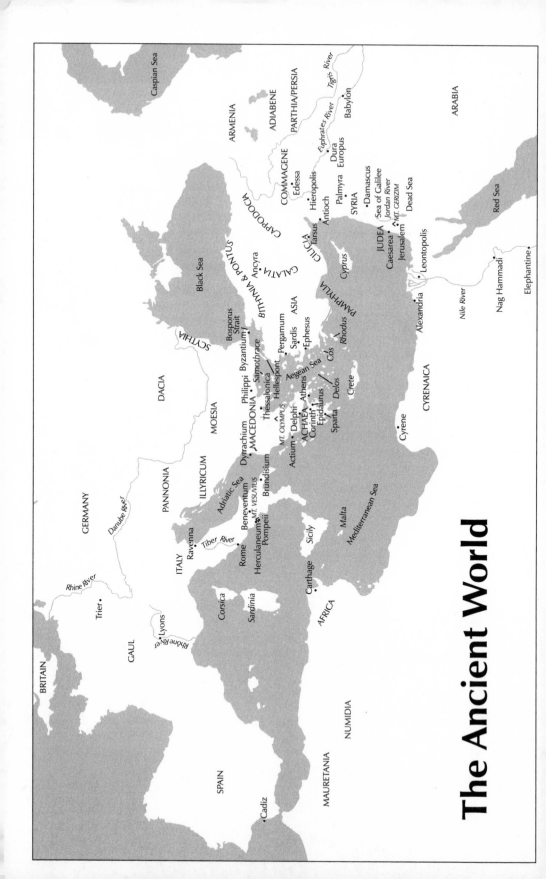

The Ancient World